NEW INTERNATIONAL
BIBLICAL COMMENTARY

Old Testament Editors,
Robert L. Hubbard Jr.
Robert K. Johnston

PSALM

NEW INTERNATIONAL BIBLICAL COMMENTARY

PSALMS

CRAIG C. BROYLES

Based on the New International Version

© 1999 by Hendrickson Publishers, Inc.
P. O. Box 3473
Peabody, Massachusetts 01961–3473

First published jointly, November 1999, in the United States by
Hendrickson Publishers and in the United Kingdom by the
Paternoster Press, P. O. Box 300, Carlisle, Cumbria CA3 0QS.
All rights reserved.

Printed in the United States of America

First printing — December 1999

Library of Congress Cataloging-in-Publication Data

Broyles, Craig C.
    Psalms / Craig C. Broyles.
        (New International biblical commentary. Old Testament
Series; 11)
        "Based on the New International Version."
        Includes bibliographical references and indexes.
        1. Bible. O.T. Psalms—Commentaries. I. Title.
II. Series.
        BS1430.3.B75   1999
        223'.2077—dc21   99–40849
                                                                CIP
    ISBN 1–56563–220–6 (U.S. softcover)
    ISBN 1–56563–535–3 (U.S. hardcover)

British Library Cataloguing in Publication Data
A catalogue record for this book is available
from the British Library.

ISBN 0–85364–732–1 (U.K. softcover)

Table of Contents

Foreword xi

Preface xiii

Abbreviations xv

Introduction 1

§1 Blessed Are Those Who Meditate on the Lord's
    Instruction (Ps. 1) 41
§2 The Lord's King and Rebellious Peoples (Ps. 2) 44
§3 Security in the Midst of Attack (Ps. 3) 49
§4 The True God of Agricultural Blessing (Ps. 4) 52
§5 Entering the Lord's House (Ps. 5) 56
§6 Mercy for the Languishing (Ps. 6) 62
§7 Acquittal for the Falsely Accused (Ps. 7) 66
§8 The Lord's Majesty and the Crowning of Humanity (Ps. 8) 71
§9 Delivering the Helpless from Social Oppression: Part I
    (Ps. 9) 74
§10 Delivering the Helpless from Social Oppression: Part II
    (Ps. 10) 77
§11 The Lord on His Heavenly Throne (Ps. 11) 79
§12 The Lord's Refined Words and Humans with Double
    Tongues (Ps. 12) 82
§13 How Long, O Lord? (Ps. 13) 85
§14 There Is No One Who Does Good: Version 1 (Ps. 14) 88
§15 Instruction for Temple Entry (Ps. 15) 91
§16 Confessing Loyalty to the Lord of the Land and His
    Benefits (Ps. 16) 96
§17 Holding to the Lord's Paths Amidst Threatening Stalkers
    (Ps. 17) 98
§18 The King's Thanksgiving for Military Victories (Ps. 18) 102
§19 God's Revelation in the Skies and the Scriptures (Ps. 19) . . 108
§20 Intercession for the King Before Battle (Ps. 20) 110

§21 Thanksgiving for the King's Victories in Battle (Ps. 21) 113
§22 My God, My God, Why Have You Forsaken Me? (Ps. 22) .. 115
§23 My Shepherd and My Host (Ps. 23) 123
§24 A Victory Procession and Instruction for Temple Entry
 (Ps. 24)... 127
§25 A Wisdom Prayer for Those Who Fear the Lord (Ps. 25) ... 133
§26 Walking in Integrity and Loving the Lord's House (Ps. 26) ... 136
§27 Seeking Security in the House of the Lord (Ps. 27) 141
§28 To Be Spared from the Lord's Judgment on the Wicked
 (Ps. 28)... 145
§29 The Voice of the Lord in the Thunderstorm (Ps. 29) 151
§30 Living Praise Versus Deathly Silence (Ps. 30) 154
§31 My God as Refuge from Social Alienation (Ps. 31)......... 156
§32 Blessed Are Those Whose Transgressions Are Forgiven
 (Ps. 32)... 161
§33 The Trustworthy Lord Over Nature, Nations, and Armies
 (Ps. 33)... 164
§34 Taste and See that the Lord Hears and Delivers (Ps. 34).... 168
§35 Images of War, the Hunt, False Accusation, and Wild
 Beasts (Ps. 35).. 170
§36 Deceived Deceivers, and the Feasting Followers of the
 Lord (Ps. 36).. 173
§37 Cultivating Faithfulness Until the Flourishing Wicked
 Wither (Ps. 37) 178
§38 A Prayer for the Sick (Ps. 38)............................ 185
§39 Turn Your Gaze from Me before I Am No More (Ps. 39).... 187
§40 Past and Future Deliverances and Present Trust and
 Obedience (Ps. 40) 190
§41 Vindication for the Sick Person (Ps. 41) 193
§42 The Would-Be Pilgrim Who Thirsts for God: Part I
 (Ps. 42)... 195
§43 The Would-Be Pilgrim Who Thirsts for God: Part II
 (Ps. 43)... 199
§44 Betrayed by God in Battle? (Ps. 44)...................... 201
§45 In Praise of the King at His Wedding (Ps. 45) 206
§46 Our Mighty Fortress (Ps. 46)............................ 208
§47 Applause for the Ascending King of All the Earth (Ps. 47).. 213
§48 Zion's Divine Defender (Ps. 48)......................... 217
§49 God Will Redeem My Soul from the Grave (Ps. 49)........ 221
§50 A Misunderstanding of Sacrifice and the Presumption of
 Hypocrites (Ps. 50) 223
§51 The Penitential Psalm (Ps. 51)........................... 226

§52 The Wicked Uprooted and the Righteous Flourishing in
God's House (Ps. 52)................................... 231

§53 There Is No One Who Does Good: Version 2 (Ps. 53) 235

§54 Deliverance from Godless Opponents (Ps. 54)............ 236

§55 Betrayed by a Friend (Ps. 55) 239

§56 When I Am Afraid, I Trust in God (Ps. 56) 241

§57 God's Salvation for the Individual and the International
Manifestation of His Glory (Ps. 57) 243

§58 A God Who Judges Unjust Judges (Ps. 58) 247

§59 Threats from Personal Attackers, Urban Unrest, and
Foreign Nations (Ps. 59)............................... 249

§60 Defeat in Battle with Edom (Ps. 60)..................... 252

§61 A Pilgrim's Prayer to Fulfill Vows at God's House (Ps. 61). . 255

§62 Rest in God (Ps. 62).................................. 258

§63 The Pilgrim's Thirst for God in a Dry and Weary Land
(Ps. 63)... 260

§64 The Wicked with Tongues like Arrows and the Divine
Archer (Ps. 64) 264

§65 Praise to the God of Zion as Creator and God of
Agricultural Fertility (Ps. 65).......................... 266

§66 Corporate and Individual Thanksgiving to the God Who
Acts (Ps. 66).. 272

§67 The God Who Blesses Israel's Harvests and His
International Praise (Ps. 67) 277

§68 In Celebration of the Ritual Procession of the
Cherubim-Ark (Ps. 68) 281

§69 From the Miry Depths (Ps. 69) 285

§70 Shame for My Persecutors and Joy for God's Worshipers
(Ps. 70)... 289

§71 When I Am Old and Gray (Ps. 71)...................... 290

§72 Intercession for the King to Bring Prosperity to the Land
and Justice to the Needy (Ps. 72) 295

§73 God's Goodness Redefined: The Nearness of God (Ps. 73) . . 299

§74 The Destruction of the Temple and the Eruption of Chaos
(Ps. 74)... 306

§75 It Is God Who Brings Down and Exalts (Ps. 75) 310

§76 The God of Zion Breaks the Weapons of War (Ps. 76)...... 312

§77 Has God Forgotten to Be Merciful? (Ps. 77).............. 314

§78 A History Lesson: From Ephraim to Judah, from the
Exodus to Zion (Ps. 78) 319

§79 God's Reputation and the Destruction of Jerusalem
(Ps. 79)... 327

§80   The Vinedresser and the Plundered Vine of Israel (Ps. 80). . . . 330
§81   Listening to the Liberator (Ps. 81) 333
§82   God Judges the Gods (Ps. 82) 335
§83   The Conspiracy of the Nations (Ps. 83) 339
§84   The Pilgrim's Longing to "See" the God of Zion (Ps. 84) . . . 341
§85   A Forgiven People Seeking Forgiveness and God's
       Promise of *Shalom* (Ps. 85) 344
§86   A Servant Appeals to His Lord for Protection (Ps. 86) 347
§87   The Nations "Reborn" in Zion (Ps. 87) 350
§88   From the Darkness of the Grave (Ps. 88) 352
§89   A Hymn of Yahweh's Kingship, an Oracle of David's
       Kingship, and a Lament over David's Defeat (Ps. 89) 355
§90   Human Frailty and Sin, Divine Eternality and Anger, and
       a Prayer for Mercy (Ps. 90) 359
§91   The Protection of My God in the Midst of Threat (Ps. 91) . . 361
§92   The Withering of the Wicked and the Flourishing of the
       Righteous (Ps. 92) 364
§93   The Divine King Is Mightier than the Chaotic Waters
       (Ps. 93) 367
§94   Impending Judgment on the Oppressive Wicked and
       Interim Promises for the Righteous (Ps. 94) 370
§95   Today, If You Hear His Voice (Ps. 95) 373
§96   The Divine King Comes to Judge the Earth (Ps. 96) 375
§97   The God of the Thunderstorm and the Proclamation of
       His Righteousness (Ps. 97). 378
§98   The Saving Righteousness of the Divine King and the
       Cheers of Nature and the Nations (Ps. 98) 381
§99   Holy, Holy, Holy Is the Responsive Divine King (Ps. 99) . . . 383
§100   An Invitatory to Enter the Temple's Gates with Praise
       (Ps. 100). 386
§101   Vows About Acceptable and Unacceptable Associates
       (Ps. 101). 388
§102   A Prayer for the Afflicted and for the Ruins of Zion
       (Ps. 102). 390
§103   The Lord Compassionate and Slow to Anger (Ps. 103) 394
§104   The Creator and His Providential Ordering of Creation
       (Ps. 104). 398
§105   In Praise of the Lord of History: From Abraham to the
       Settlement in the Land (Ps. 105) 402
§106   A Confession of Sin from Israel's History: Mercy for the
       Generations of the Exodus and the Exile (Ps. 106). 405

§107 The Lord of Reversals: Thanksgiving of Desert
      Wanderers, Prisoners, the Sick, and Sailors (Ps. 107) 408
§108 Prayer for God's Exaltation and for His Victory over
      "Edom" (Ps. 108) 411
§109 A Prayer Against Those Who Curse and Accuse (Ps. 109) . . 412
§110 The Davidic King Promised Dominion over Enemies
      (Ps. 110) 414
§111 Pondering the Lord's Great Works of the Exodus and
      Conquest (Ps. 111) 417
§112 Blessings of Those Who Fear the Lord (Ps. 112) 421
§113 The Incomparable God of Condescension and Exaltation
      (Ps. 113) 424
§114 Trembling at the Appearance of the God of the Exodus
      (Ps. 114) 426
§115 The Maker of Heaven and Earth Praised and Invoked to
      Bless Israel (Ps. 115) 429
§116 A Thank Offering for Deliverance from Death (Ps. 116) . . . 434
§117 Nations to Praise the Lord for His Faithfulness (Ps. 117) . . . 436
§118 A Festival Procession for Giving Thanks (Ps. 118) 438
§119 Meditating on the Lord's Instruction: From A to Z
      (Ps. 119) 442
§120 Sojourning in a Foreign Land Among the Deceitful and
      Warlike (Ps. 120) 445
§121 The Maker of Heaven and Earth Watching Over His
      Pilgrims (Ps. 121) 448
§122 Peace for Jerusalem, the City of Pilgrims (Ps. 122) 450
§123 Seeking Mercy with Eyes Lifted Heavenward (Ps. 123) 452
§124 Providing Escape from the Malevolent (Ps. 124) 453
§125 Wicked Rule to be Removed from the Land of Zion
      (Ps. 125) 455
§126 The Restored Exiles Sowing in Tears and Reaping with
      Joy (Ps. 126) 457
§127 The Lord, the Builder of the House(hold) (Ps. 127) 460
§128 A Blessing on the Family Who Fears the Lord (Ps. 128) 463
§129 Oppressed But Not Crushed (Ps. 129) 466
§130 Out of the Depths (Ps. 130) 468
§131 The Quieted Soul (Ps. 131) 470
§132 A Tale of Two Oaths: David's for the Lord's Dwelling
      and the Lord's for David's Dynasty in Zion (Ps. 132) 471
§133 The Heavenly Blessing of Harmonious Fellowship
      (Ps. 133) 474
§134 Nocturnal Praise (Ps. 134) 475

§135   Dumb Idols and the Living God of the Exodus (Ps. 135) . . . 476
§136   The Enduring Love of the Creator and Saving God of
        the Exodus (Ps. 136) 478
§137   Remembering Jerusalem by the Rivers of Babylon
        (Ps. 137) 479
§138   The Lord on High Preserves the Lowly in the Midst of
        Trouble (Ps. 138) 481
§139   Surrendering to God's Inescapable, All-Searching
        Presence (Ps. 139) 483
§140   Just Justice for the Violent and for the Needy (Ps. 140) 489
§141   A Prayer for the Heart in the Midst of Threat and
        Temptation (Ps. 141) 492
§142   Alone and Persecuted (Ps. 142) 494
§143   No One Is Righteous before God (Ps. 143) 497
§144   The Davidic Mercies and Deliverance from Foreigners
        (Ps. 144) 501
§145   The Divine King and His Universal Kingdom (Ps. 145) 504
§146   The Helper of Those Who Cannot Help Themselves
        (Ps. 146) 509
§147   God of Creation and Restorer of Jerusalem (Ps. 147) 512
§148   Praise from the Heavenly Hosts and Creatures Here
        Below (Ps. 148) 515
§149   Praise in the Mouth and a Sword in the Hand (Ps. 149) 517
§150   Doxology to the Book of Psalms (Ps. 150) 519

For Further Reading 521

Subject Index 525

Scripture Index 529

Foreword
New International Biblical Commentary

As an ancient document, the Old Testament often seems something quite foreign to modern men and women. Opening its pages may feel, to the modern reader, like traversing a kind of literary time warp into a whole other world. In that world sisters and brothers marry, long hair mysteriously makes men super-human, and temple altars daily smell of savory burning flesh and sweet incense. There, desert bushes burn but leave no ashes, water gushes from rocks, and cities fall because people march around them. A different world, indeed!

Even God, the Old Testament's main character, seems a stranger compared to his more familiar New Testament counter-part. Sometimes the divine is portrayed as a loving father and faithful friend, someone who rescues people from their greatest dangers or generously rewards them for heroic deeds. At other times, however, God resembles more a cruel despot, one furious at human failures, raving against enemies, and bloodthirsty for revenge. Thus, skittish about the Old Testament's diverse portrayal of God, some readers carefully select which portions of the text to study, or they avoid the Old Testament altogether.

The purpose of this commentary series is to help readers navigate this strange and sometimes forbidding literary and spiritual terrain. Its goal is to break down the barriers between the ancient and modern worlds so that the power and meaning of these biblical texts become transparent to contemporary readers. How is this to be done? And what sets this series apart from others currently on the market?

This commentary series will bypass several popular approaches to biblical interpretation. It will not follow a *precritical* approach that interprets the text without reference to recent scholarly conversations. Such a commentary contents itself with offering little more than a paraphrase of the text with occasional supplements from archaeology, word studies, and classical theology. It mistakenly believes that there have been few insights into the Bible since Calvin or Luther. Nor will this series pursue an *anticritical* approach whose preoccupation is to defend the Bible against its detractors, especially scholarly ones. Such a commentary has little space left to move beyond showing why the Bible's critics are wrong to explaining what the biblical text means. The result is a paucity of vibrant biblical theology. Again, this series finds inadequate a *critical* approach that seeks to understand the text apart from belief in the meaning it conveys. Though modern readers have been taught to be discerning, they do not want to live in the "desert of criticism" either.

Instead, as its editors, we have sought to align this series with what has been labeled *believing criticism*. This approach marries probing, reflective interpretation of the text to loyal biblical devotion and warm Christian affection. Our contributors tackle the task of interpretation using the full range of critical methodologies and practices. Yet they do so as people of faith who hold the text in the highest regard. The commentators in this series use criticism to bring the message of the biblical texts vividly to life so the minds of modern readers may be illumined and their faith deepened.

The authors in this series combine a firm commitment to modern scholarship with a similar commitment to the Bible's full authority for Christians. They bring to the task the highest technical skills, warm theological commitment, and rich insight from their various communities. In so doing, they hope to enrich the life of the academy as well as the life of the church.

Part of the richness of this commentary series derives from its authors' breadth of experience and ecclesial background. As editors, we have consciously brought together a diverse group of scholars in terms of age, gender, denominational affiliation, and race. We make no claim that they represent the full expression of the people of God, but they do bring fresh, broad perspectives to the interpretive task. But though this series has sought out diversity among its contributors, they also reflect a commitment to a common center. These commentators write as "believing critics"—scholars who desire to speak for church and academy, for academy and church. As editors, we offer this series in devotion to God and for the enrichment of God's people.

ROBERT L. HUBBARD JR.
ROBERT K. JOHNSTON
Editors

Preface

"If you want to know how to pray, read the Psalms"—this advice from one of my early Bible teachers has generated and nurtured my interest in the Psalms over the years. To encounter God, speak with him, and listen to him are the deepest longings of the human soul, though often ignored in the busyness and distractions of day-to-day life (as I can attest). Writing this commentary has been one of my greatest joys and greatest challenges. Even the most significant biblical commentaries can only shed light and send us back to the scriptures. It is in praying the Psalms that encounter with God takes place.

At the beginning of this project my mother came down with bacterial meningitis and fell into an eighteen-day coma. She miraculously survived but it has left her disabled. We thank the Lord she is still with us; her steadfast joy and courage are a sign of strength beyond ourselves, as is my father's watchful devotion. At the end of this project my father-in-law died suddenly from a heart attack. Amidst these tragedies my wife and I also gained a new appreciation of the gift that life is with the births of our sons, Nathan and Stephen. These events have brought home to me that the psalms were carved out of the lives and deaths of real people. They are not mere words dispassionately plucked from a dictionary or composed from a poet's quiet retreat, nor should any comment on them be made from the detached world of an academic's library. It is one thing to comment on the literary artistry of well-crafted imagery or to comment on a theological critique of a cultural tradition; it is quite another to recognize that these cries and exultations are real human voices, and can give voice to our own pain and joy.

In the preface to my first book, my revised Ph.D. dissertation, I thanked "my dear wife, Karelle, who has helped this specialist in lament to see new horizons of praise." I am grateful to God that this has continued to be true. She has urged me to climb the next ridge and also to see what has been right under my nose—with no little help from our sons, Nathan and Stephen. She has helped me perceive the gifts of God in the smallest details of nature and in the many relationships we enjoy, especially our own. I dedicate this book to Karelle and to the loving memory of her father, Rev. Dr. Bernard L. M. Embree.

I gratefully acknowledge the many helpful suggestions of Robert Johnston and Robert Hubbard, the general editors of the NIBC series. I want to thank Nathan Bauman, Suzanne Staryk, Victor Cornish, Andrea Alvarez, and especially Chris Young for compiling the Scripture Index. I also want to thank my diligent editor, Shirley Decker-Lucke. The book is better because of her work.

Abbreviations

//	parallel
=	is the same as
AB	Anchor Bible
ANET	J. B. Pritchard, ed., *Ancient Near Eastern Texts Relating to the Old Testament*
BDB	F. Brown, S. R. Driver, and C. A. Briggs, *Hebrew and English Lexicon of the Old Testament*
BHS	*Biblia Hebraica Stuttgartensia* (the critical edition of the Hb. Bible, based on the MT and used by most scholars; it notes select textual variants from the Hb. MSS and ancient translations, esp. the LXX, and recommends what was probably the "original" reading)
Bib	*Biblica*
DSS	Dead Sea Scrolls
esp.	especially
FOTL	Forms of the Old Testament Literature
FRLANT	Forschungen zur Religion und Literatur des Alten und Neuen Testaments
Gk.	Greek
GKC	*Gesenius' Hebrew Grammar*, ed. E. Kautzsch, trans. A. E. Cowley
Hb.	Hebrew
ICC	International Critical Commentary
Int	*Interpretation*
JBL	*Journal of Biblical Literature*
JETS	*Journal of the Evangelical Theological Society*
JSOTSup	Journal for the Study of the Old Testament, Supplement Series
JSS	*Journal of Semitic Studies*
Kethib	what is "written" in the main text of the MT
lit.	literally

LXX	Septuagint (the ancient Greek translation of the Hb. Bible)
MS(SS)	manuscript(s)
MT	Masoretic Text (the "received text" of the Hb. Bible)
NCB	New Century Bible
NIV	New International Version
NRSV	New Revised Standard Version
NT	New Testament
OT	Old Testament
OTL	Old Testament Library
pl.	plural
prob.	probably
Qere	what is to be "read," noted in the margin of the MT
SBLDS	Society of Biblical Literature Dissertation Series
SBS	Stuttgarter Bibel-Studien
SBT	Studies in Biblical Theology
sing.	singular
SJT	*Scottish Journal of Theology*
Syriac Peshitta	the Bible of the ancient Syriac church
Targum	ancient Aramaic paraphrases of the Hb. Bible
TB	*Tyndale Bulletin*
TDOT	G. J. Botterweck and H. Ringgren, eds., *Theological Dictionary of the Old Testament*
TOTC	Tyndale Old Testament Commentaries
VT	*Vetus Testamentum*
VTSup	Vetus Testamentum Supplements
Vulgate	the ancient Latin Bible traceable to Jerome
WBC	Word Biblical Commentary

Introduction

In California's Yosemite National Park a visitor once asked a ranger, "What would you do if you had only one day to see Yosemite?" The ranger replied, "I'd weep." A tour of the Psalms in a single volume is even more daunting. In these models of prayer and praise, Israel—with God's superintendence—shaped appropriate and effective ways of speaking to God. Through them, Israel expressed painful experiences of loss and turmoil, and jubilant experiences of rescue and blessing.

What Is a Psalm?

Is each psalm a liturgy written by professional Levites for temple services? Is it sacred scripture written by the pious for meditation? Is it a prayer David composed in response to his historical experiences? Is it a prophecy anticipating Jesus and the age to come? The nature of a psalm will determine how we study it, what questions are appropriate to ask of it, and ultimately how we use it. We shall discover that each of these applications has a place in defining a biblical "psalm."

To do justice to the biblical book of Psalms, we must respect the diversity represented in this collection. It contains some of the oldest literature in the OT and some of its most recent, thus spanning several centuries. The psalms stem from a variety of social circles and traditions: the royal court, priests, Levites, prophets, wise sages, and the poor. And psalms reflect a variety of purposes: to praise, pray, testify, teach, crown a king, etc. With a collection so vast and varied, we must always be careful not to oversimplify, but several *general* observations may help show how psalms are different from other literary genres in the Bible.

First, psalms are poetic compositions, usually presented in a tightly woven, balanced structure (e.g., where the petitions echo the respective laments, the dovetailing of imagery, and poetic devices such as refrains and word plays). Even when describing the direst of distresses, such as apparent execution, desiccation, and being utterly surrounded by vicious enemies (Ps. 22:12–18), a psalm may possess carefully placed poetic devices (see the comments on Ps. 22). Psalms are different from the spontaneous prose prayers that are often contained in OT narrative, where they respond to particular circumstances.

Second, the language of the psalms is largely open-ended. Rarely are the people involved named within the psalm itself. The identities of the "I," "we," and "they" are seldom specified. By contrast, David's historical lament over the deaths of Saul and Jonathan (2 Sam. 1:17–27), though it employs similar poetic parallelism, names particular people and so is appropriate for only that occasion. This lament was not incorporated into the Psalter but into "the Book of Jashar" (2 Sam. 1:18). Moreover, the poetic descriptions of distresses are replete with images, sometimes multiple and mutually exclusive if taken literally (e.g., see the commentary on Pss. 31; 35; 69). It is therefore difficult, if not impossible, to discern whether we are looking at a literal reference or a graphic image portraying the notion of (objective) threat or the feeling of (psychological) dread.

Third, all the 150 psalms, though each is unique in its own right, follow established literary patterns. Each psalm generally follows one of the patterns or genres described below, each of which has its own characteristic motifs: temple entry liturgies, hymns, individual prayers, corporate prayers, thanksgivings, royal psalms, and wisdom psalms.

Fourth, the psalms are replete with liturgical and ritual allusions. The frequent plural imperatives, such as "Praise the LORD" (or "hallelujah"), presuppose that a congregation or choir is being addressed. Their poetic form and many references to musical accompaniment imply a performance of song and music. The recurrent shifts from addressing God directly in prayer to referring to him in testimony (from "you" to "he") and the changes of speaker (e.g., from "I" to "we") suggest a liturgical development. The many allusions to the Jerusalem temple, Mount Zion, sacrifices, and processions point to particular locations where psalms were performed and to particular rituals that accompanied them. The movement and development of some psalms, we shall discover, can be explained only in connection with liturgical and ritual developments (e.g., Ps. 68).

In view of these observations, first, it appears that psalms were composed not ad hoc but with careful craftsmanship. Second, they were written not for single occasions but for recurring occasions. Third, they were not free verse but followed established patterns and conventions. And, fourth, they were not merely read; they were performed—publicly within some kind of group. We may thus define a "psalm"—according to its original function—as a liturgy recited (probably sung) within some kind of formal worship service.

Within this broad definition, we should note two general kinds of formal service. There are psalms that reflect usage in regular worship services (i.e., applicable to all worshipers at any time) and those that reflect usage in special services. The former are exemplified by the hymns sung at the great pilgrimage festivals, such as Passover, and the latter are exemplified by the prayer psalms of the individual, where a particular emergency has arisen. These may have been performed on an individual's behalf with a liturgist presiding (e.g., for a sick person at the bedside). As in the *Book of Common Prayer* in the Episcopal/Anglican Church, there are liturgies for regular use, such as Morning Prayer and Evening Prayer, and there are special prayers and thanksgivings for special occasions.

It should be no surprise that psalms have to do with worship and even with formal services. But these observations on the psalms themselves and the conclusion that they function as liturgies have profound implications for how psalms relate to their authors and to the experiences they depict. We should not imagine that a psalm was composed when an individual encountered distress or deliverance and then wrote a psalm as a direct reflection of that experience and resulting personal feelings. Psalms, as distinct from spontaneous prose prayers, were written for worshipers to use. They are thus models of prayer for a wide variety of circumstances. They do not report on particular, actual circumstances; they use images that befit typical situations of distress or deliverance. Psalms are not descriptive poems; they are prescriptive liturgies. In other words, they are not private reflections of poets on a recent, private experience; they are composed as models to guide the expressions of Yahweh's worshipers in prayer and praise. Psalms are more concerned with leading the worshipers' experience than with following the composer's. In other words, instead of supposing, "The psalmist now feels like praising God," we should rephrase our comments, "The psalm leads the worshipers to praise God." Similarly, the self-descriptions of the speaker as "righteous" or as a "servant" do not reflect the boasting of the composer; rather they are to be adopted by worshipers if they wish the psalm to have its desired effect. Though it is not explicit, psalms do have this educative and behavior-modifying function. In other words, if worshipers want the Lord to answer a given prayer psalm, they had better act according to its claims. This is not to say that psalms were not informed by a personal experience of God. They certainly were, so long as we understand an experience that is characteristic of the people of God. The psalms were hammered out over generations of living with God. We moderns should not impose upon the Psalms our assumptions that individual, private experience is to be valued more highly than the experience of God reflected in a corporate identity.

These general observations of the psalms themselves lead to the conclusion that the authorship and historical setting of psalms are not decisive factors in their interpretation. The historical narratives of the OT refer to David's love of and talent for music (esp. 1 Sam. 16:14–23; 18:10), and the historical David probably did write psalms. But, even if there are psalms actually composed by David among the select 150, the reason for their preservation lies not in their autobiographical information about David, but in their helpfulness in guiding believers in their worship of God. They are model prayers and praises. Hence, the key question is not, "Where does this psalm fit into David's life?" but "Where does this psalm fit into Israel's worship?"

With this understanding of "psalm" we should now consider the term "psalmist." This term has traditionally been used to refer mostly to the original composer of a psalm and occasionally to the worshiper using a psalm. Because of this ambiguity and because the use of "psalmist" often suggests in the minds of modern readers that a psalm is the personal expression of that individual, we will try to avoid the term in this commentary. Instead, we will refer to the speaker, liturgist, or worshiper using the psalm. Just as today we sing hymns and recite set prayers without any reference to or interest in their actual authors and their personal experiences, so we should read and appreciate the psalms as vehicles for expressing our own voice to God, not as records of a historical individual. As we use the psalms ourselves, the "I/We" of the psalms is not to be conceived as a particular historical figure but as we who use the psalm. In other words, the "I" is not meant for reference but for identification.

We cannot stop here and rest with our first definition of a psalm because the history of the psalms' transmission did not end with Solomon's temple. With the Babylonian exile of 587 B.C., their use in the liturgical worship at the temple came to end for a time. But their preservation beyond this crisis is evidence that the words of these *liturgies* were rescued as sacred *literature* on scrolls. While they were, no doubt, recited in exilic gatherings— especially the laments (see Zech. 7:3; 8:19)—they were also read as Scripture. They became regarded not simply as discrete liturgies for various worship services; they could now be read as chapters of a book, where each chapter may have some connections to and may build on the preceding ones. The psalm introducing this literary anthology commends them as part of "the law of the LORD" and worthy of daily meditation (1:2). Thus, a "psalm" may be defined secondly as sacred literature for meditation.

The gradual growth of the entire "book" of Psalms can be seen in its five smaller "books" and "collections." The former are marked by doxologies ("Praise be to the Lord . . ."), which close each book. In the enumeration of the psalms and their verses, each doxology is counted with the last psalm of each book, though it is not a constituent part of that psalm: 41:13 marks off Psalms 1–41 as Book I; 72:18–19 marks off Psalms 42–72 as Book II; 89:52 marks off Psalms 73–89 as Book III; 106:48 marks off Psalms 90–106 as Book IV; and Psalm 150 marks off Psalms 107–150 as Book V and the book of Psalms as a whole. There remains a "loose end" in 72:20 ("This concludes the prayers of David son of Jesse"), which had apparently marked off an earlier grouping of the psalms that had concluded at Psalm 72. Later, other Davidic prayers or psalms were appended (see esp. the superscription to Ps. 86). The "collections" are noted by superscriptions (i.e., the headings that precede v. 1 of most psalms). There are the "Davidic" psalms (Pss. 3–41, except Ps. 33; 51–65; 68–71; 86; 101; 103; 108–110; 138–145), the psalms of "the sons of Korah" (Pss. 42–49; 84–85; 87–88), the psalms of Asaph (Pss. 50; 73; 83), and the Psalms of Ascent (Pss. 120–134). In the Hebrew Bible (which we have in the Masoretic Text, i.e., the "received text") most of these superscriptions count as verse 1. Thus, the verse numbering in the Hebrew book of Psalms is generally one off from the verse numbering in the NIV and most English translations.[1] Finally, we should also note a collection that overlaps some of those just noted, namely the Elohistic Psalter, those psalms in which the generic name "Elohim" or "God" is preferred over the personal name "Yahweh" (Pss. 42–83; cf. esp. Pss. 14 and 53).

Once in the postexilic period the temple was rebuilt (515 B.C.), the psalms were again used as liturgies, but also continued as sacred literature. In fact, during and after the exilic period the whole focus of Israel's religion began to shift. In the preexilic period, the temple was the primary locus of Yahweh's revelation, but from the crisis of the exile a second locus developed in Yahweh's written "torah." This term is usually translated "law" but more accurately rendered by the broader term, "instruction." This shift is evidenced by Ezra's public readings of "the book of the law of Moses" (Ezra 7:10; Neh. 8:1–3; 10:29) and the subsequent emergence of Judaism. A new kind of psalmody developed, namely literary psalms—those that were not used in a liturgical service but were simply read for public or private meditation. Psalm 119, a torah psalm whose verses begin with the successive letters of the Hebrew alphabet (an "acrostic"), clearly exemplifies this use. Thus, postexilic Yahwism had two foci, the temple and torah. The temple symbolized encounter with God, that is, "seeing his face" (see the Additional Note on 42:2). The torah symbolized "hearing" God's words. The former has the implicit danger of ritualism, the latter of legalism. For both to be helpful sacraments, worshipers and readers must remember the greater reality to which these symbols point.

Once the psalms became sacred literature and were incorporated with other scriptures, a third way of reading them emerged. The "psalms 'of' David" were correlated with the "David" of 1–2 Samuel. Some of the psalm superscriptions thus invite us to read them as psalms "by" David. Since he was "a man after God's own heart" (1 Sam. 13:14; Acts 13:22), his prayers became exemplary prayers for the people of God. Thus, a third way of defining "psalm" emerged: it is a model prayer of David. (See further below, the section on "David and the Psalms.")

Another historical development encouraged a fourth way of reading of the Psalms. With the appearance of Jesus Christ, the Psalms were seen in a new light. For example, he was the supreme "lamenter" (Ps. 22:1 and Matt. 27:46), "son of man" (Ps. 8:4 and Heb. 2:6–10), and "son of David" (Matt. 1:1; 21:9, 15; 22:41–45). In sum, he became the new David of the Psalms, as one who was both human and the anointed king or "messiah." In this sense, the psalms became prophecies. While they had always contained prophecies or oracles of divine, first-person speech (e.g., Pss. 50; 60; 81; 95), now even psalms where human beings addressed God could be read as prophetic because Jesus was *the* representative human. Passages referring to psalms as prophetic "Scripture" are Luke 24:44–47; Matthew 21:42 and Psalms 118:22; John 19:24, 28, 36 and Psalms 22:15, 18; 34:20 (cf. Acts 1:16, 20 and Pss. 69:25; 109:8). By extension, the Psalms may also refer to the experience of the Church (e.g., Ps. 44:22 and Rom. 8:36).

A "psalm" cannot therefore be reduced to a single definition or reading. Its varying uses through the history of psalms transmission invite us to read it as liturgy, literature, Davidic prayer, and prophecy. The psalms are generally words of human beings addressed to God. And yet they have been incorporated into the canon of Scripture that is regarded as "the word of God" (Luke 24:44–45; and the passages listed immediately above). And so we believe not only that generations of the people of God forged appropriate ways of addressing God, but also that God guided the whole process. Here we see the mystery of divine "inspiration" (2 Tim. 3:16), that a psalm has both human authors and a divine one. It is thus no surprise that psalms should have such a richness of meanings and readings. They can simultaneously be read as liturgies, literature, and prophecies.

To appreciate the historical process by which God revealed himself to his people and educated them, we must distinguish between OT literature and Israelite religion. We now have the whole OT, but what did the Israelites of the preexilic period have for their understanding of Yahweh? We should not assume Yahweh began with Genesis and then proceeded with the rest of the Pentateuch, the historical books, and all the prophets. For Israel's religion, we must not think anachronistically of printing presses and "pocket Pentateuchs." Public readings of the written scriptures were rare, as noted in the OT itself (e.g., 2 Kgs. 23:2; Neh. 8:1–8). The legal material of the Pentateuch would have been known primarily to judges and priests. Much of the historical books derived from records found in the royal palace. Much of the prophetic material would have originally been announced orally, but we cannot be certain how widely these oracles were circulated among common Israelites. Much of the Wisdom literature, especially Proverbs, came from a class of "wise sages," probably associated with the royal court. The Psalms, however, were heard and sung whenever the Israelites worshiped, whether in clan meetings or in pilgrimage festivals at the temple. They were the vehicles of the people's worship and a primary means of how they learned about their faith. In the preexilic period at least, they were thus the most widely known portion of the OT. It was not until the Second Temple period that written "torah" was regularly read in public (cf. Neh. 8:1–8). The Psalms are thus our best window into this earlier period of Israel's ancient, yet ever relevant faith.

The Approach of This Commentary

This commentary will focus on the psalms' original use as liturgies. The reasons for this choice are several. First, if we want to make sense of a psalm as we move from one verse to the next, we must recognize that it was shaped primarily by liturgical factors, and not simply by literary considerations. Because a psalm was originally designed as a liturgy and not as a chapter in a book, we must first consider its use in a liturgical service.

Second, we must respect the psalms' original function: the first reason they came into existence was to help the people of God in their worship. This realization should draw our attention to the importance of worship within the whole of biblical revelation. Indeed, the Psalms contain many theological propositions, spiritual and devotional insights, literary artistries, and prophetic predictions, but this entire content is presented as prayers and praises to God. The hymns, for example, are not mere confessions of faith; they are doxologies. The psalms have their context in an encounter with God himself. If we remove the psalms from this encounter, we deny the purpose for which they originally came to be.

A third reason for this commentary's focusing on the psalms as liturgies is that this reading is the most remote from modern readers. That many of the psalms were sung with choirs at temple festivals is plain to today's readers (e.g., "O house of Levi, praise the LORD; you who fear him, praise the LORD," 135:20). Yet this feature is often considered to be merely historical and is thus dismissed as irrelevant. But in view of the growing interest in developing new songs and styles for worship today, the ways the people of God in Bible times were directed to worship become eminently relevant. In addition, in many Christian circles so much emphasis is given to proper beliefs and evangelical activism that the personal encounter that should take place between believers and God is inadequately nurtured (i.e., what is often called "spirituality"). In the Psalms we see that Israel's faith was "sung" as prayer and praise, not "signed" as a statement of orthodoxy.[2] Because this commentary attempts to respect each psalm as unique, no single interpretive model or outline is followed. Different psalms speak to different issues. In addition, because many, if not most, of the psalms were composed for preexilic liturgies, and the book of Psalms in its final form is a postexilic literary anthology, we should not assume any *original* connections between consecutive psalms. Thus, the first question posed to any given psalm is, What place did this psalm have in Israel's worship? The primary way to answer this question is to look for a psalm's affinities to other psalms in order to see what light psalms can shed on one another (i.e., comparing scripture with scripture). Psalms research is like trying to piece together an enormous jigsaw puzzle by looking for common edges, colors, and patterns. What complicates the process is that many of the pieces are missing. The 150 psalms that we have are only a selection of the many that were used through a millennium of Israel's worship. The evidence for this conclusion comes in part from the psalmic fragments scattered throughout the prophets. The psalms themselves invite this kind of research, despite its being speculative at times.

Two other questions are also emphasized in this commentary. First, how does each psalm form and develop as an integrated—liturgical and literary—whole? While we can often understand isolated verses, only when we examine the connections from one verse to the next and the connections of each to the whole do we realize that the whole is greater than the sum of the parts. Second, what spiritual and theological significance does a particular psalm contribute to our lives? The interaction between the Bible and ourselves, especially our theological and ideological assumptions, must be addressed deliberately and methodically as we live before God. Otherwise, we deny the Psalms' ultimate purpose. Looking at ourselves in the mirror of the Psalms (James 1:23–25) can be simultaneously the most encouraging and disturbing engagement of our lives.

Genres and Life Settings

If our method of studying psalms is going to follow from the nature of what psalms are, then our groupings of the psalms must stem from their function in Israel's worship. We should not study them merely by their topics or contents but also by their roles in liturgical services. Psalms 105 and 106, for example, are both historical psalms covering roughly the same period. Their accounts of this period, however, might be regarded as contradictory if we failed to regard their distinct purposes in drawing from these traditions.

The Psalter is a diverse collection, reflecting various centuries, literary patterns, life settings, and social circles. We should not speak of the psalms as branches from a single tree because it is doubtful they came from a single seed. "Rather, the Psalter is a garden, fenced in on various terrains (some on the hilltop, some in the valley, and some on the flats) and containing a variety of species (some native and some imported, some wild and some domesticated, some flowering and some shade-bearing, and some thorny!)."[3]

The *main* roots of psalmody, however, are to be found in worship services, especially those centered at the Jerusalem temple. As part of the regular liturgies, the book of Psalms contains liturgies related to temple entry, hymns, and royal coronations. As part of the special public liturgies, we find the corporate prayers for crises such as a battle defeat or social unrest.

The Psalter also testifies to special liturgies on behalf of individuals, both prayers and thanksgivings occasioned by some kind of need or emergency. While these prayers employ roughly the same literary motifs as those found in the corporate prayers, they do not employ the same traditions. They appear to reflect a simpler, more popular piety and may thus have stemmed from outside the circles of the Jerusalem temple (a kind of folk psalmody).[4]

Finally, we should note that some psalms appear to be meant for teaching and reading, not for singing. Here we find the wisdom psalms, which share literary motifs and themes with the Wisdom literature as found in the book of Proverbs.

Temple Entry Liturgies. Psalms 15 and 24 have long been recognized as liturgies for worshipers entering the temple.[5] They, along with Isaiah 33:14b–16, follow a set pattern: (a) a double question of who may sojourn on Yahweh's holy hill, (b) a reply consisting of the qualifications for worshipers, and (c) a promise. The commentary on these psalms argues they are temple instruction (i.e., "torah") recited by the priests to the worshiping congregation.

Entry into God's holy temple was obviously a momentous rite of passage for worshipers, and it would be surprising if only two of the 150 psalms echoed this critical procedure. In this commentary I will present evidence that this ritual makes better sense of several psalms that other interpreters have seen as "individual laments" or as "psalms of the falsely accused."[6] Psalms 5, 26, 28, 36, and 52 share several features with Psalms 15 and 24. Although these features may not be unique to these psalms, this particular constellation of features does point to a special grouping. (a) Each psalm makes explicit mention of the temple and implies the speaker is present there. (b) None of these psalms contains an "I" lament regarding the speaker's affliction, a "thou" or "God" lament offering complaint, or a "they" or "foe" lament decrying what opponents do to the speaker and his group. (c) Each of these psalms merely has a description of the wicked that contains no explicit mention of threat directed to the speaker and no lament on behalf of victims. These character descriptions contain common terminology of "the wicked," focusing especially on their deceitful speech. (d) All of these psalms contain hints that the speaking "I" is not a lone individual in a special need (such as false accusation), rather he is one who speaks on behalf of the general class of worshipers in the regular liturgy. (e) These psalms contain indications of judgment where there is a parting of the ways: the "righteous" who may enter and the "wicked" who may not and who are to be punished.

The commentary on Psalms 5, 26, 28, 36, and 52 (also note Ps. 73) details why these psalms should be read as part of the liturgies of temple entry and how they fit into this larger liturgy. In brief, they give voice to a liturgist who represents the congregation and who responds to the priestly temple instruction as found in Psalms 15 and 24. In other words, they were composed not for lone individuals in special circumstances of need (e.g., false accusation) but for a congregation in the regular liturgies of the temple. The speaking "I" is thus a liturgist speaking on behalf of the individual worshipers.

This reconstruction of the temple entry liturgies has some far-reaching implications for our understanding of "the righteous" and "the wicked"—groups that are frequently mentioned in the Psalms. As part of the temple instruction, they are presented as character profiles. They do not function as descriptive designations of actual social parties in ancient Israel. Their stereotypical terminology reflects this. In other words, they are not comparable to a "letter of reference" reporting biographical facts about an actual individual. Respect for their literary form shows they are oracular "torah," teaching God's will about the kind of person he desires and the kind of person he rejects. They are not descriptive reports; they are prescriptive models. As a rule, the OT does not speak in abstract or purely spiritual terms but in terms that are concrete and tangible. "Righteousness" and "wickedness" were presented as concepts embodied as "the righteous one" and "the wicked one." For the sake of clarity, the temple liturgies present the congregation with two alternatives—the two "ways." Each individual worshiper is presented with a clear choice: What kind of company do you identify with? Either one identifies with "the righteous" and so becomes "righteous," or one identifies with "the wicked" and so becomes "wicked."

This means that claims of righteousness in the Psalms, often abhorrent to Christians as being "pharisaic," are not claims to moral blamelessness but simply claims of identifying with and aspiring to the model of the righteous, as distinct from that of the wicked—there are only two choices. We find that, in fact, righteousness (24:5, NIV "vindication") is received by the pilgrim "from God his savior." The righteous are so called, not because they claim moral perfection but because Yahweh grants his righteousness to all genuine "seekers of his face" at the temple. This observation may help to explain both the relative absence of confessions of sin in the Psalms and the presence of claims of righteousness. Thus, while admissions of sin are infrequent in the Psalms, temple religion was nonetheless based on God's mercy, exhibited by his saving bestowal of righteousness.

This also means that "the wicked" must not always be construed as personal enemies in the Psalms. Corresponding to the profile of the "doer of righteousness" (Hb. *pōʿēl ṣedeq*, 15:2) is the profile of the "doers of iniquity" (Hb. *pōʿᵃlê ʾāwen*) or "the wicked" (Hb. *rᵉšāʿîm*). It derives not from historical circumstances but from temple instruction. As Psalm 15 is an oracle profiling the "doer of righteousness," so Psalm 36:1–4 is an oracle (see the commentary) profiling the wicked. Both are stylized, idealized portraits. The wicked are given mention not because they single the speaker out for attack but because loyalty to Yahweh is to be exhibited in part by one's disassociation from those whose character is contrary to Yahweh's (15:4). Their mention serves as an illustrative contrast. In this connection we should also consider "the enemies" (Hb. *'ōyᵉbîm*) in the Psalms. In some psalms this designation is also applied to "the wicked" (Hb. *rᵉšā'îm*), and so the comments above may apply here as well. In other psalms, however, the enemies are portrayed as personal enemies, that is, "my enemies." Here we should observe that their portrayal also uses stereotypical terms. In other words, these laments are not biographical reports but images that individual worshipers may apply to those who oppose them.

These images are often painted in the extremes. For example, the designation, "those who seek my life," sounds as if it points to attempted murder. Such opponents seek not merely a person's property but his life. This speaking in extremes is, in fact, characteristic of the descriptions of distresses in general. If the use of these psalms was actually to be limited to such extreme circumstances, it would be difficult to account for their preservation in the OT period and their widespread usage as models for prayer and praise beyond the biblical period. Rather, it appears that psalms speak in the extremes so as to include every possible distress. Thus, if God can intervene in near-death distresses, he can surely help in moderate circumstances. In some cases, these extreme portrayals of the opponents are actually mitigated by other contextual hints. In 38:12, for example, "those who seek my life" simply attempt to ruin the sick person's reputation by spreading rumors and so jeopardize his social position as a legitimate member of God's society. It is not physical homicide as such. In 127:5, the weapons or "arrows" that one may use when contending "with their enemies in the gate" are identified as the number of children one has! These are not mortal enemies but simply "those who do not respect me." Thus, conflict in the Psalms, even if military language is used, need not point to physical confrontation. A final example outside the Psalter should help because it provides a specific narrative context for this language. In the psalmic "Song of Hannah" (1 Sam. 2:1–10), "my enemies" (2:1) are simply her rival wife (1:6–7), not life-threatening militants.

Hymns. The hymnic praises[7] praise God's attributes and deeds in a general or summary fashion.[8] Psalm 145, for example, speaks in general terms of his "mighty acts"; Psalm 136 speaks specifically of God's acts in creation and the exodus deliverance.

(1) *Imperative Call to Praise* ("Give thanks to the LORD," 136:1–3)
(2) *Introductory Summary* ("for he is good," 136:1)
(3) *Body*
   a. *God's greatness* ("who spread out the earth upon the waters," 136:4–20)
   b. *God's goodness* ("to the one who remembered us in our low estate," 136:21–25)
(4) *Conclusion* ("Give thanks to the God of heaven," 136:26)

(1) The *imperative call to praise* commands the congregation to participate in praise. This contrasts with the proclamation of praise in thanksgiving psalms, where the congregation initially acts simply as the audience. (2) The *introductory summary* is similar to the one found in thanksgivings except that the reason for the praise is general, not specific. (3) The *body* celebrates God's greatness and his goodness, which are not always clearly distinguishable (e.g., Is God's gift of the land to Israel in vv. 21–22 an expression of his greatness or goodness?). (4) The *conclusion* may be a renewed call to praise, a blessing, or a wish.

Originally, the hymns were sung primarily at the national festivals, such as Passover or the Feast of Tabernacles. The pilgrims journeyed to Jerusalem "to seek" and "to see his face" (see the note on 42:2) at the temple. We should not think anachronistically of the temple as a building where the congregation gathered to worship. Rather, it was God's dwelling. The Hebrew term usually translated "temple" *(hêkāl)* also means "palace," thus portraying Yahweh as the divine king and the worshipers as his subjects.

The throne of "Yahweh of hosts" (rendered "LORD Almighty" in the NIV) was symbolized by his cherubim, whose inner wings formed the seat (80:1; 99:1; and 47:8; 89:15; 97:2), and his footstool by the ark (132:7–8; 99:5). Yahweh was thus depicted as both king and judge (hence the frequent petition, "Arise!"). The cherubim also signified mobility, so Yahweh's throne was also a chariot, thus depicting "Yahweh of hosts" also as a warrior or as the "rider of the clouds" (see 68:1, 4, 33–35; 97:2–6; cf. 18:9–10). Some of these psalms reflect a ritual procession led by the cherubim-ark, sometimes in its "ascent" into Yahweh's "palace" (Pss. 24; 47; 68; 89; and perhaps 132). The expression, "seeking refuge under his wings," probably derived from this symbol (17:8; 36:7; 57:1; 61:4; 63:2, 7). Other psalms that presuppose its symbolism are Psalms 78; 96; 105.

(a) Songs of Zion. Zion, or Mount Zion, is the hill on which the Jerusalem temple was built. Its significance is thus tied to Yahweh's dwelling in the temple. Most hymns enjoin the congregation to join in the singing of Yahweh's character and deeds. The Zion psalms differ from most hymns in that they generally describe Yahweh's special relationship to Zion and the benefits that follow, especially that of protection.[9] For further discussion see below, "Zion Tradition."

(b) Psalms of Yahweh's Kingship. These psalms share several distinguishing characteristics.[10] They all contain the acclamation "Yahweh/God reigns" (except Ps. 98, which uses the title, "the King"). They are also more international and cosmic in scope. They speak of God's revelation extending to all nations with all the cosmos reverberating with praise, rather than simply concerning Israel's welfare.

Phrases from these psalms are echoed in Isaiah 40–55 (e.g., Ps. 97:6 and Isa. 40:5; Ps. 98:3 and Isa. 52:10; Ps. 98:8 and Isa. 55:12), which predicts Judah's restoration from exile and anticipates that this event will capture the attention of the nations. The phrases, therefore, had some clear relevance to the late exilic or early postexilic periods. But because they seem to presuppose that Zion/Jerusalem (97:8; 99:2) and the cherubim-ark (see comments on 47:5, 8–9; 96:6; 99:1; and 97:2, 9) are intact, they probably originated in the preexilic period. Here they were probably used at one of the major festivals (perhaps Tabernacles in the fall; note Zech. 14:16–17 associates it closely with worship of Yahweh as "the King"). In particular they may have accompanied the ritual procession and ascent of Yahweh's cherubim-ark into the sanctuary.

The Chronicler's account of David's bringing the cherubim-ark into Jerusalem (16:23–33) illustrates the use of Psalm 96 in connection with the ark's "ascent" (Hb. ʿlh, used five times in 1 Chron. 15). Although the Chronicler may not claim that Psalm 96 was actually used on this particular historical occasion, he does faithfully reflect some of the liturgies and rituals of preexilic worship (on the Chronicler's postexilic rewriting of preexilic history and esp. of this event, see below, "David and the Psalms"). Thus, in the preexilic period these psalms probably enacted in festival liturgy (i.e., dramatized) the reality of Yahweh's kingship. The events reflected in these psalms demonstrate his existing kingship, not his becoming king. They speak of public revelation (e.g., "the LORD has made his salvation known," 98:2), not of attainment.

Isaiah 40–55 thus appears to allude to these psalms to say that what God's people have celebrated in their worship will become manifest in their history, namely, in their restoration back to their homeland. This application probably gave further impetus to the expectation that these psalms would be realized or fulfilled on the broadest historical stage. Once the restoration took place and it became clear that it fell far short of fulfilling these psalms, they were given a decidedly future or prophetic orientation. In fact, they appear to underlie the frequent image of God "seated on his throne" in Revelation (e.g., Rev. 19:4; cf. Ps. 47:8) and the acclamation, "Our Lord God Almighty reigns" (Rev. 19:6; cf. esp. Ps. 97:1–6; note also Rev. 11:17; 19:11 and Pss. 96:13; 98:9.)

Prayer Psalms of the Individual. For this genre this commentary will use the category of "prayer,"[11] which, in fact, is the designation used by the psalms themselves.[12] Many psalms scholars, however, designate such psalms as "laments." This label, however, gives undue prominence to one motif over others. It can also be misleading because these psalms do not merely lament, as one might do at a funeral; they also seek to change the lamentable circumstances through petition. Similarly, it would be misleading to label these psalms as "petitions" because they consist of more than a mere list of requests. Their elements are:

(1) *Address* and *Introductory Petition* ("O LORD," 13:1a)
(2) *Lament*
   a. *I/we* ("How long must I wrestle with my thoughts?" 13:2a)
   b. *Thou/God* ("How long . . . ? Will you forget me forever?" 13:1)
   c. *they/foe* ("How long will my enemy triumph over me?" 13:2b)

(3) *Confession of Trust* ("But I trust in your unfailing love,"
13:5a)
(4) *Petition(s)*
 a. *for favor* ("Look on me and answer," 13:3a)
 b. *for intervention* ("Give light to my eyes," 13:3b)
 c. *motive* ("lest my enemy say, 'I have overcome him,' "
 13:4)
(5) *Vow of Praise* ("I will sing to the LORD," 13:6a)
(6) *Thanksgiving in Anticipation* ("for he has been good to
me," 13:6b)

(1) Most often the *address* is simply God's name ("LORD" or
"God") or title ("my God"). The *introductory petition* is of a very
general nature. (2) The *lament* may be expressed with three possible subjects: the speaker who laments his suffering, God who is
charged with negligence or hostile action, and the enemies who
either cause or exacerbate the affliction. The distress is usually described in such a way as to evoke a response from Yahweh. Generally the I-lament should evoke his pity, the God-lament his
sense of obligation to help, and the foe-lament his anger. (3) The
confession of trust may claim something directly about God ("God
is/will . . . "), or it may simply declare the speaker's own trust in
God ("I trust/hope . . . "). A few psalms consist solely of this motif
in an expanded form, and so are called "psalms of trust."[13] (4) The
petitions usually seek God's attention and favor first of all and then
directly implore his intervention, whether to save the speaker
and/or punish the enemies. The motives, or "motifs to motivate
God to intervene," supplement the petitions with reasons and arguments as to why God should act on the speaker's behalf. (5) In
the *vow of praise* the speaker promises to praise God, presumably
at a public offering of a *todah*, or thanksgiving sacrifice, once he
has been delivered. (6) A prayer psalm may close with *thanksgiving*, which is sung *in anticipation* of deliverance.

The individual prayer psalms echo a much simper piety,
which may be summarized in the expression "my God." Yahweh
is hailed as the personal, guardian God, who answers when
called upon (see below, "My God"). Most of them do not appear
to be suited for use in the regular liturgical services of the temple.
They reflect the special emergencies of individuals and generally
lack allusions to a sacred place and to ritual actions. They were
probably used in less official and more private ceremonies, overseen by a liturgist within a smaller group of intimates. On the

other hand, this commentary argues that while some psalms contain the motifs shared by prayer psalms of the individual, they also contain hints that they are suited for a more congregational setting where the speaker serves as a representative for each individual worshiper. Thus, their speaker was probably a liturgist singing on behalf of believers within the regular liturgy, not a lone individual in prayer services specially called for him or her. Their laments reflect the typical, recurring opposition that the people of God face, not special crises.

As is typical of psalms, the prayer psalms lack references to particular people, places, and distresses; they are open-ended and so fit any such recurring need. Typically the ancient biblical poets employ concrete images rather than using general, abstract language. To convey the notion of threat, these psalms employ a variety of images—often in the same psalm—such as military attack, legal accusation, and the oppression of the poor, widows, and orphans. Thus, looking at these psalms together provides a wider context for interpreting each psalm individually. It becomes clear they often do not report particular social circumstances (in the manner of a newspaper article), but rather they paint in familiar strokes scenes that evoke the general psychological and spiritual predicaments that worshipers may face (in the manner of a poem). Because the psalms are highly allusive, any original circumstances that occasioned them or original situations for which they were composed are highly elusive.

Corporate Prayer Psalms. The corporate prayers contain roughly the same motifs as the individual prayers.[14] (1) Their *address* of God is sometimes more elaborate, containing a variety of divine titles. (2) Their *lament* against God is more frequent and developed. (3) Instead of a simple confession of trust, they contain a *reference to past saving deeds* (e.g., "You brought a vine out of Egypt," 80:8–11). Thus, they draw from the great historical traditions of Israel's ancestors, the exodus, Yahweh war (where Yahweh acts as a divine warrior, especially as evidenced in the conquest of Canaan), Zion, and the temple. While these are phrased in ways similar to hymnic praise, they do not function as such in these prayers. Rather, they serve as historical precedents, arguing that God should now deliver as in past generations. (4) The corporate prayers generally draw from the same stock of *petitions* as those of individual prayers. (5) The *vow of praise* does not stand out as an independent motif as clearly as in the individual prayers. (6) As a result, the corporate prayers lack the expression of *thanksgiving in anticipation*. It is interesting to note that virtually all the thanksgiving psalms contained in the Psalter are for individuals. It is possible that corporate thanksgiving was expressed through the regular hymns. It is also possible that for some unknown reason corporate thanksgivings were not included in the collection of 150 preserved psalms. Like the individual prayers, the corporate prayers reflect special emergencies, and were most probably performed at the central sanctuary (e.g., 1 Kgs. 8:33–40; 2 Chron. 20:3–5).

Thanksgivings. While the hymnic psalms praise God's attributes and deeds in a general or summary fashion, the thanksgivings (Hb. *tôdâ*) praise him for a single, recent deliverance (called "declarative praise" by Westermann).[15] Thanksgiving psalms generally contain the following motifs:

(1) *Proclamation of Praise* ("I exalt you, O LORD," 30:1a)
(2) *Introductory Summary* ("for you lifted me out of the depths," 30:1)
(3) *Report of Deliverance*
   a. *recounting the lament* ("when you hid your face, I was dismayed," 30:6–7)
   b. *recounting the petition* ("To you O LORD, I called," 30:8–10, also v. 2)
   c. *recounting God's response and deliverance* ("You turned my wailing into dancing," 30:11, also v. 3)
(4) *Renewed Vow of Praise* ("I will give you thanks forever," 30:12)
(5) *Hymnic Praise* ("Sing to the LORD . . . for his anger lasts only a moment," 30:4–5)

A comparison with the motifs of the prayer psalms shows that thanksgivings are the other side of these prayers. They form the praise vowed at the close of the prayer psalms. (1) In the *proclamation of praise* the speaker announces his intention to praise God. (2) The *introductory summary* begins with "for" or "because" and briefly states in general terms the reason for the intention to praise God. (3) The *report of deliverance* forms a kind of testimony to the congregation. It rehearses elements of the

individual prayer, which had been recited in the midst of distress, by recounting the lament and the petition. Recounting
God's response and deliverance is the distinctively new element
in this report. (4) The *renewed vow of praise* announces that the
worshiper has not completed his duty by this performance of
praise—he will now engage in a lifetime of praise. (5) The inclusion of *hymnic praise* shows that the specific deliverance exemplifies in particular what is hymned of Yahweh in general.

These psalms presuppose that a congregation is present
during their performance (30:4; 116:14, 18–19; cf. 22:22, 25).
Thanksgiving was considered a public affair and all the people of
God benefited from an individual's deliverance. A thanksgiving
sacrifice was probably a regular part of the performance of a
thanksgiving psalm (see commentary on 116:17–19).

Royal Psalms. In these psalms the Davidic king is a central
figure.[16] Strictly speaking, this category does not form a single
genre because these psalms contain a variety of literary motifs
and reflect a variety of social functions, such as coronations (Pss.
2; 110; and possibly Ps. 72), a wedding (Ps. 45), and prayers before and after battles (Pss. 18; 20; 21; 89).

A number of Psalms scholars have argued that the king
played a major role in the worship services at the temple and
that there are many more royal psalms than those traditionally
so labeled.[17] S. Mowinckel, for example, has argued that the "I"
speaking is the king in the prayer psalms of the individual especially.[18] But even in those psalms that are clearly royal, the king
is not the primary speaker. Among them, there are intercessions
for the king (Pss. 20; 72; 89:38–51; cf. Ps. 132), a thanksgiving
sung on his behalf (Ps. 21), prophetic oracles addressed to him
(Ps. 110; cf. 89:18–37; 132:11–12), and the wedding song sung in
his honor (Ps. 45). In these, he is given no lines to speak. There is
also a liturgy (Ps. 2), wherein the king is simply one of the speakers. And there is a composite psalm (Ps. 18), which draws on
other psalmic genres and motifs such as a thanksgiving of the individual, a theophany, an echo of a temple entry liturgy, and a
victory song of the warrior. Finally, the prayer psalms of the individual generally appeal simply to "my God," a tradition that
appears to reflect the piety of the common people. They do not
have the same appeals to traditions and prerogatives that are
seen in the standard royal psalms.

The portrayal of the monarchy in the royal psalms is decidedly positive because it reflects the *prescribed* ideal to which the kings should aspire. This is in stark contrast to the *described* realities found in the historical books of 1–2 Kings. The psalmic portrayal is so different and so elevated that some readers believe these psalms were originally composed as prophecies, pointing not to the historical kings of the Davidic dynasty but to a future "messiah," or "anointed one" (Hb. *māšîaḥ*). But we should observe that Psalm 89, for example, uses such elevated terminology (esp. vv. 26–27) specifically of "David" (vv. 3, 20, 35) and of "his sons" (v. 30). And the final third of the psalm laments the king's miserable failure in battle (esp. v. 49). We as Christians must therefore conclude that these psalms were written originally for the Davidic kings and later found a greater fulfillment in *the* son of David, namely Jesus Christ (Matt. 1:1). It is probable these psalms were seen to promise a new David even before the appearance of Jesus. This is the best explanation for why they were retained in the book of Psalms. Its final collection and editing was done in the postexilic period when there was no Davidic monarchy under the Persian empire. This reinterpretation and the hope of a new David was probably engendered by the prophets, who had taken up the language of the royal psalms and of the Davidic court and had promised a new David who would not repeat the failures of David's sons (Isa. 9:6–7; 11:1–5; Mic. 5:2–5a; Jer. 23:5–6; Ezek. 34:23–24; 37:24–28; Zech. 9:9–10).

Wisdom and Torah Psalms. Some psalms reflect the same wisdom tradition evident from Proverbs, Job, and Ecclesiastes.[19] A psalm may be considered a "wisdom psalm" if it contains three characteristics. First, its emphasis is on teaching skillful living, not on addressing God directly in worship. Second, it employs formulaic expressions of wisdom literature (e.g., "Blessed is . . . ," Hb. *ʾašrê* as distinct from *bārûk;* proverbs, exhortations, numerical sayings, and acrostics, i.e., alphabetical structures). Third, it contains wisdom themes (e.g., instruction for daily living, the problem of the prosperity of the wicked, written torah). The contrast of the two ways of the righteous and the wicked is another wisdom theme, though it is also characteristic of the temple entry liturgies. In this grouping, we may thus include, for example, Psalms 34, 37, and 49.

This combination of psalmody, which has its roots in public worship, and wisdom instruction, which betrays more of a teaching setting, creates an intriguing problem, especially for us moderns who generally think of church and school as two distinct areas of life. We should not, however, assume that the wisdom psalms form a distinct category separate from other psalms, or that wisdom psalms are to be lumped together as a foreign import. Murphy, for example, observes that several prayer and thanksgiving psalms contain wisdom elements. The key link between the two traditions and settings of wisdom and worship, probably lies in the kinship between the teaching explicit in wisdom psalms and the teaching implicit in the testimony of thanksgiving psalms. Thus, both psalmists and sages (if the distinction is to be maintained here) reflect a keen interest in learning from experience of God and his world, whether it be taught at temple or at school. Perhaps the closest we can get to identifying the social setting that combines worship and wisdom surfaces in Psalm 111, which reflects both hymnody (vv. 2a, 3–9) and wisdom instruction (vv. 2b, 10): "I will give thanks (or 'make confession') . . . in the council of the upright and in the congregation" (lit.).[20]

Key Traditions of the Psalms

We may define a tradition as a complex of sacred beliefs associated with particular persons, events, places, institutions, symbols, or rituals. We should first observe the enormous diversity contained in this one collection called the Psalms. These traditions depict Yahweh in a variety of roles. He is "my God" (i.e., one's personal, guardian deity), deliverer, (rock of) refuge, warrior, shepherd, judge, the Holy One, the rider of the clouds, the cosmic King, "God of the fathers," covenant partner, etc. If we consider the relative frequency of these roles and traditions in the Psalms, it is striking to observe that the traditions so prominent in the rest of the OT are given relatively little space in the Psalms. The historical traditions of the ancestors (e.g., Abraham, Isaac, Jacob, Joseph), the exodus, the wilderness, Yahweh war, and the judges surface primarily in the so-called historical psalms (e.g., Pss. 78; 105; 106; 135; 136) and occasionally in the corporate prayer psalms (e.g., Ps. 44 reflects a battle defeat and so calls on the Yahweh war tradition). When Yahweh is portrayed as King, it is usually not as Israel's (political) king but as (cosmic) King of creation. When he is depicted as the God who comes in the storm (i.e., a theophany), he is not associated directly with Sinai, which receives little mention. Even the great covenant traditions of Abraham, Sinai, and David are given infrequent mention. We might naturally assume that the covenant was the central and defining feature of the OT or covenant. But this is certainly not the case in the liturgies of Israel's worship. In the preexilic period of Israel's religion particularly, the temple and the simple loyalty to "my God," not the covenant per se, defined their relationship with Yahweh. Among the psalms of the individual, Yahweh is depicted as "my God," who answers when called upon. Among the corporate psalms, he is the resident of the temple whom they have come to worship. More attention is devoted to the exclusive worship of Yahweh and the fair treatment of one's neighbor than to the particulars of sacrifice, festivals, and the priesthood.

"My God." The traditions of the individual prayer psalms and their corresponding thanksgivings are much simpler than the variety of traditions informing the corporate psalms, whether prayers or hymns. In brief, they reflect the conviction that Yahweh answers when called upon.[21] Their common divine title is "my God," in which the worshiper is making a claim to a special relationship with this deity (see esp. the comments on 22:9–10). In these psalms of the individual, the worshiper's obligations are to trust (e.g., 31:14), to call upon God when in distress, and to praise God once delivered (e.g., 30:11–12). The divine obligation that surfaces repeatedly is to answer with deliverance (e.g., 13:3; 22:2; 30:2; 38:15). In the ancient Near East "my God" (i.e., my personal, guardian deity) was simply one deity among many and was certainly not the highest god.[22] In this light we see that the claim to Yahweh (rendered "the LORD" in the NIV) as "my God" is remarkable. The personal guardian God of the worshiper is none other than Yahweh, the God of Israel, the Most High, the one incomparable to all other spiritual beings.

Zion Tradition. A cursory study of the use of "Zion" in the OT reveals that it occurs predominantly in the Psalms and Isaiah. Zion first became significant with David's conquering of the Jebusite city of Jerusalem, also called "the fortress of Zion" (2 Sam. 5:7). After making it his political capital, David made it the religious capital of Israel by bringing into it "the ark of God, over which is called the name, the name Yahweh of hosts" (2 Sam. 6:2, NIV reads "the LORD Almighty," a divine title conspicuous in the psalms of Zion, 46:7, 11; 48:8; 84:1, 3, 8, 12). The prominence of "Zion" in the royal psalms (see 132:13 and also 2:6; 20:2; 110:2; cf. 78:68–72) confirms that its significance emerged with the Davidic dynasty. The term is also used frequently in the book of Isaiah, especially in its first half. The prophet uses the Zion tradition in much the same way as do these psalms, especially as a rallying point that Yahweh will protect Zion when Hezekiah is faced with the question of military alliances against the Assyrians (e.g., Isa. 14:32 [which may be an allusion to Pss. 87:1; 76:9]; Isa. 18:7; 29:8; 31:4–9). A climax is reached in Isaiah's prophecy that Jerusalem/Zion will be miraculously delivered from the Assyrians in 701 B.C. (Isa. 37:22–35). Three of the psalms of Zion (Pss. 46; 48; and 76) appear to report on a particular event where Yahweh miraculously defended the city from foreign invasion. It seems very possible, therefore, that Zion theology received a great impetus at the turn of the eighth century, since the uses of "Zion" in Jeremiah and Lamentations are largely negative.

Although some of the psalms of Zion may have originated as a witness to a particular historical event, it is likely they were used regularly to commemorate Yahweh's choice and vindication of Zion. Several themes of the psalms of Zion converge in Zechariah 14:9–21, which alludes to foreigners attacking Jerusalem, Yahweh destroying them, and the survivors making a pilgrimage "to worship the King, Yahweh of hosts, and to celebrate the Feast of Tabernacles" (v. 16). Some of the psalms of Zion may thus have had a special place in this festival, even in the postexilic period.

To define the psalms of Zion as a group is helpful, but it would be wrong to assume that Zion theology was preoccupied with military defense. Rather, Yahweh's miraculous deliverance of Zion simply vindicated the tradition that Jerusalem was Yahweh's chosen place for his self-revelation. In Psalms 9:7–12 and 50:1–6, 16–21, for example, the God of Zion is depicted not as a divine warrior but as the just judge who rages against social abuses.

In this tradition we encounter a firm belief in sacred space (cf. 46:4; 48:1; 87:1), that is, that God's presence specially inhabits a particular locale. From the perspective of Christian theology, this may be viewed as primitive or at least as an earlier stage of progressive revelation. But two observations must be made. First, Christian emphasis on God's omnipresence can all too easily lead to taking that presence for granted. If we assume that God is everywhere equally present, we lose the sense of encounter with God. We fail to seek face-to-face meetings because of our vague sense that God is always around us. But if we imagine ourselves as Israelite pilgrims entering God's holy dwelling during a festival, we may begin to appreciate how momentous it is to appear before God. Second, NT theology does, in fact, teach an idea of sacred space. Paul clearly understood that the church is God's temple and that God's Spirit lives in this corporate body (1 Cor. 3:16; cf. Eph. 2:20–22). While it is correct to say that God is everywhere present, it is also true that something special should be expected when believers gather to worship. As Zion was sacred space for the Israelites, so the gathered church is sacred space for Christians.

Tradition of Divine Kingship. In the psalms of Yahweh's kingship and a number of other psalms, there are three recurring motifs: Yahweh proves himself superior to the seas and establishes the world (24:1–2; 29:3; 65:5–8; 74:13–17; 89:9–12; 93:1–4; 104:3–16); he is acclaimed as king (24:7–10; 29:10; 74:12; 89:14; 93:1–2; 104:1–2a); and reference is made to his temple or palace (24:3; 29:9; 65:1–4; 74:2–11; 93:5; 104:3, 13).

This same threefold pattern is prominent in ancient Near Eastern literature. In Mesopotamia, exhibited especially in the creation myth "Enuma Elish,"[23] Marduk, the storm god, defeats in battle Tiamat, the goddess of the sea. The gods then acclaim him king of the gods and build a palace/temple for him in Babylon. In Syria-Palestine, exhibited in the Baal epic,[24] Baal, the storm god, overcomes Yam, the god of the sea. The gods then acclaim him king, and efforts are undertaken to build a palace for him in the skies. Both of these stories were recited at major festivals. The prominence of this motif in the ancient world is probably due to the ancients' perception of the fundamental needs of creation and human existence, namely, the establishment of order and the balance of the agricultural year. Nowhere was this struggle more dramatically evident than in a thunderstorm over the sea. Here it appeared that the sky, with its wind and arrow of lightning, was in conflict with the waters, as shown by its chaotic, threatening waves. Once the storm subsided, it appeared the waters had been laid to rest and would not flood the life-supporting land. There were many gods in the ancient world, but the god of the skies was thus the most popular. He defended the land and provided the life-giving rains that supported the year's agriculture.

Within this cultural context, the psalms frequently acclaim Yahweh as the true God of the skies (18:7–15 [= 144:5–7]; 29:1–11; 68:4, 7–10, 33–35; 77:16–19; 93:1–5; 97:2–6; 104:1–4, 32; cf. 50:1–6; 74:12–17; 89:5–13; 114:3–7). Is this a case of the Bible "borrowing" from pagan literature? We must recall that as the Bible adopts languages held in common with other peoples (for example, Aramaic and Greek; even Hebrew is a derivative of Canaanite), so it appropriates imagery and figures of speech. In fact, we should not conceive of this practice as "borrowing," as though biblical writers were somehow deficient, but simply as good communication. They could not speak out of an inspired vacuum or no one would understand them. Rather, they spoke of new things in terms common with and understandable to other peoples. Thus, by means of this language and imagery of divine kingship, the biblical poets proclaimed Yahweh to be the true divine King.

The writers of the psalms, however, were careful in their use of ancient Near Eastern literary motifs. These ancient Near Eastern stories were indeed myths—by which we do not mean "falsehoods" but prescientific attempts to explain natural phenomena by reference to gods and their stories. And they reflect myth-making (mythopoeic) thinking; that is, the recital of the myth was actually believed to create the reality of which it spoke. Thus, "Enuma Elish" and the Baal epic had to be recited at the beginning of each agricultural year to ensure world order.[25] While the OT uses the imagery of these myths, it does not do so as a magical way to promote world order, for world order was established "of old" (Pss. 74:12–17; 93:1–2; 104:5–9), or "in the beginning" (Gen. 1:1).

David and the Psalms

The traditional understanding is that David was the primary author of the Psalms. Indeed, the most natural interpretation of the phrase prefacing many psalms, "a psalm *of* David," is to read "a psalm *by* David." For many believers, this issue is of more than historic or academic interest, because the psalms have been personalized by their association with this beloved figure of the Bible. David's life of highs and lows is familiar to many, and he has long been a testimony of God's grace. This is especially true if one believes one has access to both the objective events of his life as reported in 1–2 Samuel and the subjective feelings of his life as reflected in the Psalms. But is Davidic authorship actually a historical claim of the Bible? And if not, how—according to the Bible—should believers find personal value in and appreciation of the Psalms? We shall begin by surveying the general notion of authorship within the Bible itself. The Bible has functioned as authoritative Scripture for believers not because it was written by extraordinary people of God, but because it is believed to be inspired or, more literally, "God-breathed" by Yahweh himself (2 Tim. 3:16). Many of the "books" in the OT are anonymous (e.g., Josh., Judg., Ruth, 1–2 Sam., 1–2 Kgs., 1–2 Chron., Esth., and Job), yet they are no less authoritative than those associated with historical figures.

Many of the references within the Bible to other parts of the Bible are references to where one may find a passage, not claims to historical authorship. For example, the Greek phrase behind the NIV's rendering, "in the passage about Elijah" (Rom 11:2), is simply "in Elijah." The NIV rightly understands the phrase to be a place reference, not a claim to Elijah's authorship of 1 Kings. Similarly, Hebrews 4:7 uses the Greek phrase, "in David," to introduce a quotation from Psalm 95, which in the Hebrew OT is not prefaced with "a psalm of David." The writer of Hebrews was simply using a form of shorthand for "in (the book of) David," that is, the Psalms. The names of biblical books, which we take for granted, were not used in biblical times, nor were chapter and verse numbers. So texts were often identified by prominent historical figures. The Pentateuch or Torah was associated with Moses, Proverbs with Solomon, and the Psalms with David. (Note also Mark 1:2–3, which says, "It is written in Isaiah the prophet," and then proceeds to quote Malachi first and then Isaiah.)

What does the phrase, "a psalm of David," mean? By itself, it is ambiguous. "David" can mean either the historical individual or the Davidic king (Jer. 30:9; Ezek. 34:23–24; 37:24–25; Hos. 3:5 do not promise the resurrection of David himself but a restoration of the Davidic dynasty). The preposition "of " (Hb. l^e) is even more ambiguous in Hebrew than it is in English. It could mean:

(1) "of " or "(belonging) to" David in the sense of possession, because he authored the psalm;

(2) "(belonging) to" the Davidic collection of psalms (similar phrases are so used in other ancient Near Eastern poetry)—in

other words, a royal collection of psalms (as distinct from Levitical collections, such as those of Asaph and Korah), reflecting the royal patronage of the temple;

(3) "(dedicated) to" David or to the Davidic king (like a book dedication);

(4) "for (the use of)" David or the Davidic king, that is, for the king to use either personally or as the leading liturgist in public worship;

(5) "concerning/about" David.

The traditional arguments against Davidic authorship have been based on the fact that these psalms do not fit perfectly with David's historical circumstances. This problem is significant, though not necessarily insurmountable. First, several Davidic psalms refer to the "temple" (e.g., 5:7; 27:4; 65:4; 68:29), which does not really befit the structure of David's time described in 2 Samuel 6–7 ("tent" in 6:17 and "tent-curtains" in 7:2). Such a designation is not impossible, however, if the term was transferred from the Shiloh sanctuary (1 Sam. 1:9; 3:3, though this structure does have "doorposts") or if these Davidic psalms were updated once the Solomonic temple had been constructed.

Second, at times the situation reflected in Davidic psalms does not match David's situation described in 1–2 Samuel. (We shall limit our observations to those twelve or fourteen psalms whose superscriptions mention a particular historical moment in David's life.) For example, the scope of Psalm 59 is international: God is to "punish all the nations" (v. 5) and the demise of the speaker's foes will make "known to the ends of the earth that God rules over Jacob" (v. 13). But the citation of 1 Samuel 19:11 contained in the psalm's superscription merely points to internal political intrigue. The superscription to Psalm 63 points to the period when David was "in the desert of Judah" fleeing from Saul (1 Sam. 23–26). But the speaker's claim or petition in verse 11 of the psalm that "the king will rejoice in God" seems inappropriate to King Saul. David's adultery with Bathsheba and murder of Uriah, her husband (2 Sam. 11–12), find echo in the "bloodguilt" confessed in Psalm 51, but in 2 Samuel David's acts of mourning and pleading with God are concerned solely with the welfare of Bathsheba's baby, not with his own sin against God (2 Sam. 12:15–24).

Observations such as these are not conclusive that such psalms could not have been written by David. However, this observation that we cannot say conclusively that such psalms are inappropriate for situations in David's life indicates the inclusive nature of these psalms. They are appropriate for almost any human dilemma or victory. In other words, psalms, as distinct from prose prayers or poems in narrative contexts (e.g., David's lament over Saul and Jonathan in 2 Sam 1:17–27), appear to have been written for recurring use by any believer. Even if a psalm had been composed by David for a particular historical moment, it was preserved not to give us information about David's biography but to give us verbal models for prayer and worship. Therefore, as model prayers and hymns, their authorship is not a key concern. As church worshipers recite liturgies and sing hymns without reference to their authors, so we recite and sing the psalms of the OT.

Because the phrase, "a psalm of David," is itself so ambiguous, the primary reason for supposing David wrote the Davidic psalms lies in the twelve or fourteen psalm superscriptions containing historical notes (Pss. 3, 7?, 18, 30?, 34, 51, 52, 54, 56, 57, 59, 60, 63, 142). We should first note that the musical and liturgical terminology contained in the superscriptions (e.g., "the director of music" and its verb "to supervise") is paralleled only in Habakkuk 3:19 and especially 1–2 Chronicles and Ezra, both of which were postexilic works. It thus appears likely that the superscriptions were added in the early postexilic period. This historical distance, of course, does not imply their historical unreliability. But it does mean we must pay proper regard to the kind of history the Chronicler (as the author/compiler of 1–2 Chronicles is often called) wrote.

In the account of David's bringing the ark into Jerusalem (1 Chron. 13–16), the Chronicler adds a considerable amount of material not found in 2 Samuel 6. The three chief Levites appointed as singers (1 Chron. 15:16–17) are also names found in psalm superscriptions: Heman (Ps. 88), Asaph (Pss. 50, 73–83), and Ethan (Ps. 89). The technical musical terms "alamoth" (1 Chron. 15:20; Ps. 46) and "sheminith" (1 Chron. 15:21; Pss. 6; 12) are found only here and in psalm headings.

The Chronicler also included a psalm (1 Chron. 16:8–36) which David "committed" (Hb. *ntn*, 1 Chron. 16:7) to Asaph. In the Psalter, this psalm from 1 Chronicles 16 is found among three psalms, each of a different genre: 105:1–15; 96:1–13; and 106:1, 47–48. There are several features in the 1 Chronicles 16 psalm

that indicate it comes from exilic or postexilic times, thus implying the Chronicler has drawn from these three psalms in the
book of Psalms, not vice versa. First Chronicles 16:35 adds "deliver us" to the petition of Psalm 106:47: "gather us . . . from the
nations." This may have been done to suit David's victories over
neighboring nations in 1 Chronicles 18, and would be appropriate to the exilic and early postexilic times of the Chronicler. Instead of "glory" in Psalm 96:6, 1 Chronicles 16:27 reads "joy"
(Hb. *ḥedwâ*), a term that is found elsewhere only in postexilic
passages (Neh. 8:10 and Ezra 6:16, which is in Aramaic). With
this evidence, the most likely explanation for the variations between "his dwelling place" (1 Chron. 16:27) and "his sanctuary"
(Ps. 96:6) and between "before him" (1 Chron. 16:29) and "into
his courts" (Ps. 96:8) is that the Chronicler has edited selections
from the book of Psalms to remove anachronisms referring to
the temple structure.

Another illustration will help us to see how the Chronicler
uses his historical sources to make theological and liturgical
points to his postexilic audience. In 2 Samuel 5–6 David defeats
the Philistines and then recovers the ark of the covenant. In
1 Chronicles 13–14, the order is reversed. In so doing, the Chronicler implies that David's two inquiries of the Lord (1 Chron.
14:10, 14–15) about his engagements with the Philistines were
performed in connection with the ark, which was the designated place from which God spoke (Exod. 25:22; Num. 7:89).
The reader of Samuel must suppose David does so in connection with the ephod (see 1 Sam. 23:1–12; 30:7–8), which was
associated with the Urim and Thummim (Exod. 28:28–30; Lev.
8:7–8; Num. 27:21). Neither the priestly ephod nor Urim and
Thummim, however, find a place in 1–2 Chronicles.

These examples bring to light that the Chronicler's chief
interest was to instruct the postexilic generation how to restore
their worshiping relationship with God. He does so through key
historical figures and events. In the case of 1 Chronicles 13–16,
he uses the momentous event of David's bringing the ark into
Jerusalem to illustrate later preexilic and postexilic liturgical
worship.[26] Thus, as the Chronicler teaches theology and temple
practices through key historical figures and here attributes a
later psalm (or rather a composite of three psalms) to David in
1 Chronicles 16, so we find the same practice in the psalm headings. Psalms are associated with key moments in the life of the
chief patron of Israel's worship in Jerusalem.

We must see the psalm superscriptions as part of a wider phenomenon of the Bible. The entire Pentateuch, as we know it, was not formally called "the book of Moses" until the exilic or early postexilic literature (2 Chron. 25:4; 35:12; Ezra 6:18; Neh. 13:1).[27] Not surprisingly, therefore, the terminology found in the superscriptions is paralleled in 1–2 Chronicles. With the destruction of the temple, the liturgies of the psalms were rescued from destruction by being taken as literature with the people into exile. Then, as literature, they became collected with the other sacred writings. The scribes naturally searched this new, sacred anthology for connections with other parts of the sacred canon, and the Hebrew superscription, *ledāwid*, naturally led them to 1–2 Samuel. The historical superscriptions thus invite readers to engage in a new way of reading the Psalms, that is, to read "the psalms of David" as the psalms authored "by" David. We may thus read psalms as both as liturgical texts for public worship and as model prayers of David for private use.

The Psalms and Spirituality

If we wish to investigate the spirituality of the psalms, it is best that we respect not only their contents but also their literary form and function—in other words, their genres. Here we shall consider some theological implications of the temple entry liturgies, the prayers of the individual and the community, and the praises expressed in the hymns and thanksgivings. We may first observe a key feature shared by these liturgies, prayers, and praises: they are addressed primarily to God himself. It is an obvious point but also one that makes all the difference, namely that we must consciously fix in our minds the one to whom we address our prayers and praises. Readers of the psalms often overlook their opening address, such as "O LORD," and their petitions, such as "Hear, O LORD." They seem so conventional, but the mere fact that they are repeated so often implies they are not to be overlooked. This is precisely the key event of prayer and praise: a human requests an audience with the Most High! It is an encounter infinitely greater than any meeting with president, king, or judge. We need this conscious reminder that worship is an encounter with the living God.

The Spirituality of the Temple Entry Liturgies. The temple entry liturgies highlight for us the momentous event of appearing before God at the temple. Modern believers, who sometimes take God's omnipresence for granted, can miss the significance of seeking an audience with the holy God. It is an encounter that can either take life or give it.

When believers first approach "his holy place" (24:3), we might be surprised to discover that the primary issue God puts before us concerns treatment of one's neighbor. These liturgies demonstrate Yahweh's keen interest in social relationships (the parallels with prophetic religion become obvious). Dissolved are the partitions we make between our religious and social lives. The litmus paper he employs to determine our true color is dipped into our daily public lives, not the private corners of our "spirituality" (as, e.g., our attendance at a place of worship, our prayer life, our "personal" relationship with God). Yahweh considers how we treat our neighbor as symptomatic of our inner life. In the NT, Jesus endorses the same values and priorities (Matt. 5:23–24).

The Spirituality of the Prayer Psalms. Perhaps the most striking feature of the prayer psalms for the modern reader is their laments, the longest motif of these psalms. Prayer psalms do not consist solely of petitions. They were not mere business agenda or "shopping lists" telling God what to do. The laments testify of the value of simply telling our story to God. This is no mere fix-it relationship but a personal one. These laments serve as a reflection on God himself, that he is interested not only in healing but also in pain. Remarkably, they testify that God can be moved. These laments are also strikingly frank, especially noteworthy when a complaint is addressed to God himself. The laments are unabashedly told from the speaker's perspective. They are a reflection of his perceptions and feelings, not necessarily of the bald facts of reality. They do not attempt to allow for qualifications, mitigating circumstances, other possible explanations, etc. Thus, for example, the classic lament, "My God, my God, why have you forsaken me?" (22:1), reflects a feeling of God-forsakenness, but later claims in the psalm show that this lament may not be an accurate report and evaluation of the circumstances when viewed in retrospect (note v. 24 and the mere fact the psalm appeals to God in the first place). These observations have obvious pastoral benefit. The psalms allow for a free vent to one's feelings. Remarkably, believers are not required first to screen their feelings with a reality check or to censor "theologically incorrect" expressions before voicing their prayer to God. In effect, God allows our feelings to be validated, even if in the final analysis they miss the mark. Reflected in these lament expressions is a deity who is not easily shaken or offended and who does not need to be pacified. In other words, he is a God whom we can trust. The openness and frankness of the laments presuppose a relationship that is direct and personal. Even the complaint "Why do you hide your face?" (44:24) exhibits the high expectation of a face-to-face relationship with God. This invites forthrightness and candor, not averted eyes and politeness for its own sake.

These laments also exhibit a realistic faith, one that is bluntly honest with the realities of life and also takes the promises of God seriously. The faith reflected here does not try to deny reality (mind over matter) or to rationalize the dilemma away, nor does it reject God's word as a falsehood. It recognizes the gap between God's promises and human experience, and believes this dissonance should be presented to God for him to resolve. Accordingly, we must also be struck that these laments were not regarded as aberrations from the faith; they were part of the set prayers for the people of God. Questions and claims of betrayal were not relegated to the counseling session but remained a part of prayer services.

The presence of petitions in prayer psalms shows that lament was not lamentation over unchangeable circumstances (as at a funeral). Prayer psalms do invite worshipers to vent their frustrations and pour out their feelings, but there comes a time to seek a way out. The petitions indicate that these psalms seek change and that they are based ultimately on promise, not doubt. They acknowledge something is wrong and believe God can put it right. Some readers of the Psalms characterize the praises as psalms of faith and the laments as psalms of doubt. On the contrary, the prayer psalms exhibit faith under the most contrary circumstances.

A feature apparent from the motives and the overall aim of these prayer psalms is that they argue with God. They offer reasons why God should intervene on the speaker's behalf. This is most evident in those psalms that set God's promises (or a reference to God's earlier saving deeds) side-by-side with a description of the disaster (e.g., Pss. 44; 89). In this sense, the composers were theological lawyers arguing the people's case before the Most High. We do not see here a passive faith that simply accepts circumstances as God's will. Rather, the psalmists take the promises of God seriously and believe they should be manifest. Assumed here is that God can be moved not only emotionally, as expressed in the laments, but also by reason and by argument.

Apparent from the confessions of trust and the vows of praise is that the ultimate goal of the prayer psalms is the praise of God. As readers of the psalms, we may vent our feelings and seek to get something from God, but we must also seek to give something back to him.

Ultimately, we observe that lament and prayer are part of what makes our faith grow. This may not be self-evident within the Psalter alone because all we have are the prayers themselves. We do not know their final outcome (an exceptional case is Ps. 73). But the phenomenon of lament is prevalent elsewhere in the OT. Moses (Exod 3:1–4:17; 5:22–6:8; 32:1–34:35), Habakkuk, and Job (note Job 42:7–8) engaged in lament. And remarkably, these passages represent some of the most profound breakthroughs in OT faith and some of the most profound revelations in OT theology.[28]

The Spirituality of the Hymns and Thanksgivings. Grammar is generally not a subject that arouses a great deal of interest, but a study of the grammar of praise yields some striking insights into the spirituality of the Psalms. First, in psalmic praise, God is the grammatical subject of the sentence: "you are . . ." or "you have done . . ." This contrasts sharply with our own common expressions of thanks, where we say, "I thank you that you . . . ," or "I feel so grateful that you . . ." The difference is profound. In the latter, we express *our* thanks and how we feel, and we thus make ourselves the starting point. In the former, the psalms express *God's* praise, who God is, and what he has done, so he is the starting point and basis of praise.

A second grammatical observation is that there are two forms of praise. There is the "you" form, where God is addressed directly in the second person, and there is the "he" form, where God is referred to in the third person. The former is clearly for God's greater glory and pleasure. This reveals a striking contrast with many of our contemporary worship services. God is to be the primary audience in worship, not the congregation. The worship service is called primarily for his sake, not for the entertainment of the congregation. The "he" form of praise serves as a testimony to the congregation. What is striking here is that its focus is not on the obligations of the worshipers but on God's character ("God is . . .") and deeds ("God has done . . ."). Worship builds faith, not by exhortation ("Let us . . .") but by proclamation.

A third grammatical observation is that praise is commanded. Even the familiar Hebrew phrase "hallelujah" means "Praise (a plural imperative) Yahweh!" This command to praise regardless of whether we feel like it may seem to be a command to be insincere. But the very awkwardness of this command should remind us that praise is not about *our* feelings; it is about *God's* character and deeds. As a command, praise is addressed to our wills, not to our feelings. The Psalms are not so naïve to think that God's worshipers should be governed by how they happen to feel. But, by this act of obedience, we are invited to participate in the joy-evoking act of praising God's wonders.

Limits of Psalmic Spirituality. Few books of the Bible are cherished more deeply than the Psalms, especially for how they give voice to our feelings about God and the experiences we face. Yet, we must admit that the Psalms have their own limitations, especially when we consider God's progressive revelation that extends beyond this OT book. The main roots of psalmody lie in the preexilic period of Israel's or Judah's monarchy, where evil was identified primarily in the enemies and the solution was encapsulated in petitions such as, "deliver me," "crush them," and "may they be ashamed." Militaristic images dominate, not only for the worshipers and their situations, but they are also applied to God as warrior. In addition, the temple liturgies instructed the worshipers about Yahweh's way by means of two clearly distinct character profiles, the righteous and the wicked. It is in the judgment of the exilic period and thereafter, however, that Israel came to realize more fully that evil lies also *among* the people of God. The human dilemma lies largely within, that is, the problems and tragedies they experience are, in part, consequences of their own attitudes and behaviors. It is here that Israel squarely encounters sin and the need for inner transformation (see esp. the comments on Pss. 51; 106; 143; cf. 79:9; 103:10; 130:3–4; Isa. 63:7–64:12; Jer. 24:7; 31:31–34; Ezek. 36:24–32). Passages like these also raise expectations about a more immediate encounter with God, particularly through the agency of his Holy Spirit (Pss. 51:11; 143:10; Isa. 63:10–11, 14; Ezek. 36:27). Such revelations about the Holy Spirit, the universal reality of human sin (among both "the righteous" and "the wicked"), and the possibility of inner transformation are, of course, consummated in the New

Testament. Personal transformation thus becomes a possibility not only for the people of God but also for the "enemies."

In view of this later unfolding of biblical revelation, the preexilic understanding of good and evil and its solution is not the whole picture. But by no means does this development make these psalms archaic relics. First, they serve as a clear reminder that if justice and fairness are to have a place in this world, force may be necessary. If, for example, the widow and the orphan are to be spared from abuse, their abusers must be forcibly restrained and punished. The psalms that call for punishment on enemies reflect not irrational, emotional vengeance but just retribution. They seek an end of violence and the beginning of a liberated and just society defined by *shalom*. And they are a distinct reminder that, through prayers, retaliation is to be committed to God. As E. Zenger comments in his insightful critique, *A God of Vengeance?*, "The irritating and provocative talk about a 'God of punishments' and the 'wrath of God' says something, at the outset, about the violent and wretched state of society and the world—and that this situation is not created by God, nor can it be legitimated or tolerated as something God-given—not by us as human beings, and certainly not by God. The 'psalms of enmity' intend to, and must, remind us of that."[29]

Second, later psalmody itself invites us to reinterpret the earlier psalmody. For example, the closing psalms, Psalms 144–150, appear to offer a reinterpretation of the seat of power and the use of force. The militaristic imagery of Psalm 18, which in its original, preexilic context of the Davidic monarchy must be interpreted literally, is reinterpreted and reapplied in Psalm 144, in which context the postexilic community lived without king and army under the Persian empire. Thus, the militaristic language is used figuratively to point to the aggressive resolve God's people must maintain against the forces that threaten their security (see the commentary). Psalm 145 refers to a "kingdom" but instead of speaking about Israel's kingdom or those of other nations, we hear of "your kingdom" (vv. 11–13). (In the Psalms, reference is made to Yahweh's kingdom only here and in 22:29; 103:19.[30]) Psalm 146 enjoins God's people not to "trust in princes" but in "the God of Jacob," who liberates "the oppressed"—it is he who "reigns." In Psalm 147, it is Yahweh who gathers the helpless and rules all creation, and his interest is not in power but in faith (vv. 10–11). Israel is special not because they have the superior army or culture but because they have been entrusted with Yahweh's revealed word (vv. 19–20). In Psalm 148, Israel's horn of strength is identified with their praise of God (esp. v. 14), as, in Psalm 149, their sword is associated with the praise of God (v. 6). Thus, in view of these closing psalms, powerless Israel is to entrust the use of force to Yahweh.

Similarly in the postexilic Psalm 141 (esp. vv. 2–5), as the temple symbols of incense and the evening sacrifice may be substituted with the worshiper's simple prayer and "the lifting up of my hands," so there is the keen awareness that the evil that is practiced by evildoers may also find a place in "my mouth" and in "my heart." Indeed, the worshipers themselves may be in need of rebuke. Likewise, in the neighboring Psalm 139, while the worshiper separates himself from the wicked, he also petitions Yahweh regarding his anxious thoughts and the offensive way within him (vv. 23–24). And Psalm 143 confesses, "no one living is righteous before you" (v. 2). (Also note that both these psalms make a rare mention of God's "Spirit" in 139:7 and 143:10.) Thus, the late psalms that close the book of Psalms invite the reader to see that Yahweh's religion transcends the temple, that his kingdom transcends human institutions, that evil resides not simply in evildoers, and that God's own people are in need of transformation. In sum, more and more is entrusted to divine agency, including the use of force against evil. And the problem is perceived to be not only from without but also from within.

Another feature of the Psalms is clearly in need of revision in light of later revelation, namely the issue of life and death. Several psalms are explicit that the dead do not praise God (6:5; 30:9; 88:10–12); this is the sole prerogative of the living (115:17–18; 118:17; 119:175; cf. Isa. 38:18–19). It is not until the emergence of the apocalyptic tradition in OT times that we begin to hear clear references to life beyond death (Isa. 25:7–8; Dan. 12:2). But, again, these psalmic passages do not thereby become obsolete. On the contrary, they reveal to us the insightful connection between praising and living on the one hand and between not praising and not living on the other. Our primary symptom of being truly alive is the extent to which we praise. According to the Psalms, praising God is our reason for living.

Notes

---

1. Because the superscription alone may count as verse one in the Hebrew Bible, the remaining verses in each of the following psalms are numbered one higher than they are in the NIV (thus v. 1 in the NIV equals v. 2 in the Hebrew Bible): Pss. 3–9; 12–13; 18–22; 30–31; 34; 36; 38–42; 44–49; 53; 55–59; 61–65; 67–70; 75–77; 80–81; 83–85; 88–89; 92; 102; 108; 140; 142. Psalms 51–52; 54; 60 have longer superscriptions that each count as two verses (thus v. 1 in the NIV equals v. 3 in the Hebrew Bible).

2. G. W. Anderson, "Israel's Creed: Sung, Not Signed," *SJT* 16 (1963), pp. 277–85.

3. See my review of James L. Mays, *Psalms*, in *JETS* 42 (1999), p. 113.

4. E. S. Gerstenberger, *Psalms, Part 1: With an Introduction to Cultic Poetry* (FOTL 14; Grand Rapids: Eerdmans, 1988), 30–34.

5. The temple entry liturgies are Pss. 5; 15; 24; 26; 28; 36; 52. Also related are Pss. 73; 100; 101; 118; 139.

6. The theory of the "psalms of the falsely accused" is particularly evident in the leading commentary of H.-J. Kraus and argued at length in W. Beyerlin's *Die Rettung der Bedrängten in den Feindpsalmen der Einzelnen auf institutionelle Zusammenhänge untersucht* (FRLANT 99; Göttingen: Vandenhoeck & Ruprecht, 1970). Certain psalms, esp. Pss. 7 and 17, contain images of one who is falsely accused and who seeks refuge or asylum. Elsewhere in the OT one thinks of the "cities of refuge" (Exod. 21:12–14; Num. 35:9–34; Deut. 4:41–43; 19:1–13; Josh. 20:1–9). Deut. 17:8–13 speaks of legal cases too difficult for the local judges (cf. Deut. 16:18). They are to be brought to the temple and the priests, and the judge in office will render the verdict. According to 1 Kgs. 8:31–32, if a person sins against his neighbor, he is to take up an oath (cf. Ps. 7:3–5) and put himself under it before the temple altar. Yahweh is then implored to pronounce judgment. He is "to declare wicked/guilty the wicked/guilty" and "bring his way upon his head," and he is "to declare righteous/innocent the righteous/innocent" and "render to him according to his righteousness." While this theory may account for some verses in some psalms, it has its limitations. First, although the texts above may imply there were "psalms of the accused," the ones we have in the Psalter are decidedly psalms of the *falsely* accused. The innocence of the speaker and the guilt of his accusers are presumed. First Kgs. 8:31–32 refers to an oath. The only psalmic verses that come close to this description are 7:3–5. But the rest of the psalm is hardly an objective formulary for ritual interrogation; it clearly presupposes the innocence of the speaker and in effect grants him acquittal. Second, the proposed setting of a ritual of divine judgment for the accused hardly accounts for the

content and development of Pss. 5; 26; 28; 36; 52 (see the commentary). Third, is it reasonable to think that texts written for accused criminals became meditative poetry foundational to Israel's worship and piety? It seems strange that these texts would have migrated from the experiences of an unfortunate few to the experiences of all God's people, and from the juridical sphere to the religious.

7. Hb. *tᵉhillâ*, called "descriptive praise" by Westermann, *Praise and Lament*, pp. 31, 34, 116–35.

8. The hymns are Pss. 8; 29; 33; 65; 66; 68; 75 (also combining elements of thanksgiving and prophecy); 78 (though explicitly "teaching"); 81; 92 (with elements of individual thanksgiving); 95; 100; 103; 104; 105; 107 (though a form of corporate thanksgiving); 111 (with elements of thanksgiving and wisdom psalms); 113; 114; 115 (with elements of corporate prayer); 117; 118 (with elements of individual thanksgiving); 135; 136; 145; 146; 147; 148; 149; 150. Some hymns also contain prophetic oracles (75:2–5; 81:6–16; 95:8–11). Psalm 50 uniquely consists entirely of prophecy, a judgment oracle in particular. Psalm 82, whose last verse is a corporate prayer, also consists almost entirely of Yahweh's words.

9. The Songs of Zion are Pss. 46; 48; 76; 84; 87 (note also 132:13–18).

10. The psalms of Yahweh's kingship are Pss. 47; 93; 96; 97; 98; 99.

11. Hb. *tᵉpillâ*, e.g., Pss. 17:1; 86:6; 102:1, and their respective superscriptions.

12. The individual prayers are Pss. 3; 4; 6; 7; 13; 17; 22; 25; 27; 31; 35; 38; 39; 40; 41; 42–43; 51; 54; 55; 56; 57; 59; 61; 64; 69; 70; 71; 77; 86; 88; 102; 109; 139; 140; 141; 142; 143. In some individual prayers the speaking "I" appears to be a representative liturgist leading a regular service, not a lone individual in special crisis: see esp. the comments on Pss. 4; 25; 40; 57; 61; 64; 139. Some individual prayers reflect corporate concerns, such as social unrest (Pss. 59; 64; 140) and the exile (Pss. 77; 102), and thus perhaps corporate usage. Some individual prayers are particularly suited for pilgrims: Pss. 23 (a psalm of trust); 27 (possibly); 42–43; 61; 63 (a psalm of trust); 84. The Psalms of Ascent, Pss. 120–134, appear to be a collection designed especially for pilgrims visiting the second temple.

13. The psalms of trust are Pss. 11; 16; 23; 62; 63; 91 (all possibly used in regular services led by a representative liturgist).

14. The corporate prayers are Pss. 9–10; 12; 14; 44; 53; 58; 60; 67; 74; 79; 80; 82; 83; 85; 89 (also a royal psalm); 90; 94; 106; 108; 137; 144 (with royal adaptations).

15. *Praise and Lament in the Psalms,* (Edinburgh: T&T Clark, 1981), pp. 31, 34, 102–16. The thanksgiving psalms are Pss. 30; 32; 34; 116; 138 (note also 40:1–10; 66:13–20; 118: 5–18, 21, 28).

16. The royal psalms are Pss. 2; 18; 20; 21; 45; 72; 89 (also a corporate prayer); 101 (though perhaps related to temple entry); 110; 144

(though probably a composite applied to the postexilic community). Note also 132:1–12.

17. Most notably J. Eaton, *Kingship and the Psalms* (SBT; London: SCM, 1976).

18. *The Psalms in Israel's Worship* (vol. 1; Oxford: Blackwell, 1962), pp. 225–46.

19. The wisdom and torah psalms are Pss. 1; 19; 37; 49; 73; 112; 119. Note also Ps. 111.

20. See further R. E. Murphy, "A Consideration of the Classification, 'Wisdom Psalms,' " in *Congress Volume [Bonn] 1962*, VTSup 9 (Leiden: Brill, 1963), pp. 156–67.

21. For further evidence and discussion see Broyles, *The Conflict of Faith and Experience: A Form-Critical and Theological Study of Selected Lament Psalms* (JSOTSup 52; Sheffield: JSOT Press, 1989), pp. 121–22.

22. See, e.g., "Prayer of Kantuzilis," *ANET*, pp. 400–401, and "Man and his God," *ANET*, pp. 589–91.

23. See *ANET*, pp. 60–72, 501–503.

24. See *ANET*, pp. 129–42.

25. See, e.g., A. Heidel, *The Babylonian Genesis* (Chicago: University of Chicago, 1951), p. 16; *ANET*, p. 72, VII:132–34.

26. See further H. G. M. Williamson, *1 and 2 Chronicles* (NCB; Grand Rapids: Eerdmans, 1982), pp. 21–23, 113–32.

27. For further discussion of the growth of tradition connecting "Moses" and the Pentateuch see the helpful summary in W. S. La Sor, D. A. Hubbard, and F. W. Bush, *Old Testament Survey* (Grand Rapids: Eerdmans, 1982), pp. 61–62. The designation, "(the book of) the law of Moses," in Josh. 8:31–32; 23:6; 1 Kgs. 2:3; 2 Kgs. 14:6; 23:25 refers only to the book of Deuteronomy. The appearance of this phrase is traceable to the editing of Joshua and 1–2 Kings (i.e., the "Deuteronomistic History") that was instigated by the rediscovery of Deuteronomy during Josiah's reform in 622 B.C.

28. See further C. Westermann, "The Role of Lament in the Theology of the Old Testament," *Int* 28 (1974), pp. 20–39.

29. *A God of Vengeance? Understanding the Psalms of Divine Wrath* (Louisville: Westminster, 1996), p. 73.

30. The only OT occurrences of the phrase "the kingdom of Yahweh" are 1 Chron. 28:5 and 2 Chron. 13:8. These uses appear to stem from the Chronicler's reinterpretation of 2 Sam. 7:16 found in 1 Chron. 17:14, where he changes "your (i.e., David's) house and your kingdom" to "my house and my kingdom." Thus, in the postexilic Persian period, the Chronicler reinterprets David's kingdom to be traced ultimately as God's. Under the Persians, of course, there was no Davidic monarchy, so God's kingdom was seen to transcend these political realities. Thus, it appears that in the postexilic period there emerged this talk of "the kingdom of Yahweh."

§1 Blessed Are Those Who Meditate on the Lord's Instruction (Ps. 1)

Psalm 1 may appear simplistic and naïve to modern readers. It seems to divide humanity into two distinct classes whose fates can be easily distinguished. But we are unfair to psalms if we presume they provide a full, accurate report of current circumstances. A psalm is not a newspaper article. A psalm of instruction, for example, seeks to correct improper attitudes and so offers an alternative perspective, referring to aspects of reality that are not so obvious (e.g., that the wicked will ultimately be judged). It does not *describe* mere observable reality; instead, it teaches God's *prescribed* ordering of life. And it does so by presenting us with two character profiles: the righteous and the wicked (see further the Introduction on temple entry psalms). We are thus challenged to ask ourselves which model we follow. Closer examination of the psalm, in fact, reveals that it contains a temporal tension. In verse 1 it is possible to "stand in the way of sinners," but verse 5 notes "the wicked will not stand in the judgment." Sinners do have a "way" in verse 1, but in verse 6 "the way of the wicked will perish." The psalm does not necessarily describe a present, visible reality; it describes what will transpire at some unspecified time in the future.

Elsewhere in the Psalms the expression, "the law of the LORD," is found in 19:7 and 119:1. Our psalm shares with them a keen interest in the way of wisdom revealed in "the law of the LORD." "Law" is an unfortunate translation of the Hebrew term *tôrâ*, which is more literally "instruction" (cf. the Hb. verbal form, *hôrâ*, "to instruct"). Psalms 19 and 119 use parallel expressions such as "statutes" and "commands." The phrase may thus have special reference to Yahweh's written instruction, particularly as embodied in the Pentateuch. We also need to observe the placement of our psalm as the introduction to the book of Psalms. Virtually all of the psalms in Book I (Pss. 1–41) of the Psalter have superscriptions, except the first two. Thus, it appears likely that Psalms 3–41 had earlier formed a Davidic collection. Once the Psalter, perhaps with all of its five "books," had been compiled, Psalms 1 and 2 were added to introduce the collection. Thus, in its present location, Psalm 1 introduces the book of Psalms and so enjoins meditation in this book as "the law of the LORD." The psalm pronounces who is to be counted blessed and describes that person's character and fate (vv. 1–3). It then pronounces the fate of the antitype, "the wicked" (vv. 4–5), and concludes with a summary statement that reveals Yahweh's role in determining their fates.

1:1–3 / The character and behavior of the blessing's recipient is first described negatively: this one avoids **the wicked.** The opening verse contains three triads: **walk, stand, sit; counsel, way, seat; wicked, sinners, mockers.** We should not read a progression into this verse, as some do. Rather, the poetic parallelism sets up a mirror image, where the second line is more specific than the first. Paralleling the general category of "wicked" are the more particular categories of "sinners," the same group but viewed religiously, and of "mockers," the same group but focusing on their speech. Paralleling the activity of "walking" are the polar postures of "standing" and "sitting." Paralleling the "counsel" or beliefs of the wicked are their "way" or behavior and their "seat" or company.

The positive portrayal of the **blessed** defines that person by what "turns him on" **(his delight)** and by what preoccupies him **(he meditates day and night)**—in other words, by what he truly values. The blessed one is thus identified not by social status or by mere behavior but by attitude and by what draws one's attention. While the psalm certainly encourages meditation, the emphasis here lies on its object, as the word order makes clear: **on his law** he meditates. Biblical texts such as this one certainly endorse "meditation" as a biblical activity. In contrast to other kinds, however, biblical meditation is focused on a specific content. The Hebrew verb means literally "to mutter." It is somewhat analogous to "reading" (Remember that silent reading is a relatively recent invention), but it also connotes the notion of "mulling" something over and over. It thus comes to have the derived mental notion of "pondering."

The form that the blessing of verse one will take is now portrayed in verse 3. The respective destinies of "the righteous" and "the wicked" are described by agricultural similes. The righteous person is like a well-watered tree; the wicked are like wind-blown chaff. That its **leaf does not wither** implies this tree is able to sustain its greenness and shade even through the dry season of the Middle East because it is **planted** (lit. "transplanted") **by streams** (lit. "[irrigation] channels") **of water.** This word choice implies that the tree is able to transcend natural circumstances, but not because of its natural or inherent abilities. The phrase, **which yields its fruit in season** (lit. "in its time"), is a simple image illustrating a profound truth: while believers may be able to sustain spiritual life through times of adversity, they may be productive only at certain times, whose determination is beyond their control. Continual blossoming is not in view here. The claim **whatever he does prospers** breaks the agricultural imagery and echoes Joshua 1:8.

1:4–5 / By contrast, the image of **chaff** illustrates the absence of blessing for **the wicked,** who lack both life and substance. To what judgment does **the wicked will not stand in the judgment** refer? Christian readers tend to think of the *final* judgment, but that is not a prominent feature within the Psalms. We are best advised to begin with the clue offered by the psalm's own parallel line: **nor sinners in the assembly of the righteous.** The judgment relates to the righteous assembly, that is, the worshiping congregation (cf. 74:2; 111:1). Other psalms allude to a judgment taking place when one seeks entry into the temple (e.g., "Who may stand in his holy place?" 24:3; see further on the temple entry psalms in the Introduction). Thus, the wicked are forbidden access to the life and drink made available only to Yahweh's worshiping congregation, and so they are "not able to stand" (36:8–12).

1:6 / The only mention of a divine action in this psalm is withheld until the last verse: **the LORD watches over the way of the righteous.** On the surface, the fates of the righteous and the wicked have appeared to be determined by natural law: the former go the way of a tree planted by streams of water, and the latter go the way of chaff. But the process is not automatic. The enigmatic word choice in verse 3 ("planted" and "streams," noted above), may hint that the mysterious "transplanter" and "irrigator" is revealed now in verse 6. No divine action is explicitly predicated for **the way of the wicked;** it simply **will perish.** The implication is that without divine intervention life will degenerate into death; it is only with divine aid that it is possible to sustain life.

§2 The Lord's King and Rebellious Peoples (Ps. 2)

Like Psalm 1, but unlike almost every other psalm of Book I (Pss. 1–41), this one has no superscription. Psalm 1 opens with a blessing and Psalm 2 closes with a blessing, which may indicate that this pair is meant to be read together as an introduction to the final collection of the Psalter. If so, they appear to establish twin guides for reading it: we are to meditate on this "torah" ("instruction") of the Psalms collection and so discover the enduring "blessing" of "the righteous," and we are to take refuge under Yahweh's rule and in his Anointed One (Hb. "messiah" or Gk. "Christ") in particular.

The importance of Psalm 2 for the Christian is underscored by its frequent citation in the NT as a prooftext of Jesus' claim to being Israel's messiah (v. 7 is echoed some ten times and the rest of the psalm some eight times). Yet the psalm in itself is not one that endears itself to most modern readers as either a "delightful" passage for meditation (1:2) or as an indication of the kind of kingdom for which we pray, "Thy kingdom come." Its militarism and references to "chains" and "rule . . . with an iron scepter" hardly seem appropriate to the Jesus of the Gospels. We must recognize at the outset, therefore, that the psalm is occasioned by rebellion instigated by "the nations" (Hb. *gôyim* "Gentiles") and that the psalm as a whole is a rebuke (v. 5) and a warning (v. 10) and ultimately promises a blessing (v. 12).

Before Psalm 2 was placed near the beginning of the Psalms collection in postexilic times, it was probably used as a liturgy at the enthronement of the Davidic king in preexilic times (esp. vv. 6–7). The poetic and theological nature of the psalm works against a more precise dating. This psalm may reflect the fact that in the ancient Near East subjected territories often rebelled against their ruling empires when the king's inexperienced successor took over (cf. esp. vv. 1–3). This psalm may also have been recited annually "in the spring, at the time when kings go off to war" (2 Sam. 11:1). Like Psalm 110, it refers to

Yahweh's installation of the king on **Zion** and to his promise of military dominion over enemies. The changing voices of the psalm indicate original liturgical performance: a narrator describes and quotes the subjected but conspiring nations (vv. 1–3), a prophet or a priest quotes and describes "the Lord . . . enthroned in heaven" (as in a heavenly vision, vv. 4–6), the king quotes Yahweh's decree (vv. 7–9), and the narrator then addresses the **kings** described in the opening verses with a warning and a promise (vv. 10–12).

2:1–3 / The nations' conspiracy of rebellion is not merely described; the logical sense of it is questioned rhetorically: **Why . . . in vain?** Its senselessness is simple: it cannot succeed. The enforcer of the Israelite empire is none other than "the LORD, the One enthroned in heaven" (v. 4), who has given **his Anointed One** a decree promising him, "I will make the nations your inheritance" (v. 8). We must keep in mind that **chains** and **fetters** are part of a quotation from **the kings of the earth**. This is how *they* characterize Yahweh's rule over them; we cannot infer that bondage is, in fact, characteristic of his rule. (In this regard, Ps. 2 is merely introductory. It says nothing of the nature of Yahweh's kingdom. It will take the rest of the psalms to spell this out.) How their conspiracy is to be characterized, however, is clear—it is one of defiance (they **take their stand . . . against** and vow to **break** and **throw off**).

2:4–6 / Verse 4 transports us immediately in a heavenly vision and leads to a divine oracle (v. 6). The voice speaking here is a prophetic one. A key tension in this psalm lies in what is seen and what is unseen. The nations plot rebellion simply against Jerusalem's king, but in actuality they do so "against the LORD and against his Anointed One" (v. 2). Moreover, this **LORD** is, in fact, **enthroned in heaven.** He is not only a king—he is the cosmic king. And we are given insight not only into his position but also into his emotions. In response to their defiance, Yahweh experiences the extremes of emotions: laughter (of a scoffing nature) and **anger.** Again, we must note that these are not presented as his characteristic emotions—he has been provoked. **His wrath** is only toward unruly rulers. His sole action to this point, though "terrifying," is to speak: **I have installed my King on Zion, my holy hill.** What is "terrifying" in these words is not the enthronement of Jerusalem's king but "I have installed" him (the Hb. text makes this emphasis clear). The intimidation that Zion's king possesses stems not from an earthly military but from a heavenly King.

This divine oracle from a prophet or priest on "my holy hill," however, cuts two ways. It serves as a warning to the nations' kings but also as a reminder to Jerusalem's king. His authority is not autonomous or absolute; it is a derived authority (cf. 20:6–7, 9; 21:1, 13). The king now enthroned in Jerusalem sits under **the One** "enthroned in heaven" and on *his* "holy hill."

2:7–9 / To make plain that Jerusalem's king is (merely) Yahweh's agent, the king himself now speaks, publishing **the decree of the LORD.** By themselves the phrases, **you are my son** and "today I have begotten you" (Hb. *ʾaṇî hayyôm yᵉlidtîkā*, NIV **I have become your Father**), might imply a kind of genetic relationship between the Israelite king and God, especially in the ancient Near East. Within the horizon of the OT, however, this language points to legal adoption. First, these phrases issue from a legal decree. Second, they have become a reality only **today,** that is, the day of the king's enthronement. Third, this decree echoes the Davidic covenant: "I will become to him a father and he will become to me a son" (2 Sam. 7:14; more clearly than the NIV, this literal translation shows the language is metaphoric). The point of this metaphor is to show that Yahweh would punish disobedient Davidic kings, not disown them as he had removed Saul. The king certainly enjoys a privileged position with Yahweh (though note Exod. 4:22; Deut. 14:1) but he is not deified. The remarkable revelation in the NT, however, is that the fulfillment of 2:7 exceeds the original expectation. What was originally a figure of speech has become a literal historical reality.

Yahweh offers the king upon his enthronement not merely a kingdom or empire—but worldwide dominion (v. 8). This astounding verse, in the face of Israel's never impressive military might, is not an unconditional promise forecasting automatic results; it is an offer: **Ask of me.** The Hebrew verbs in verses 8–9 do not contain the same ring of certainty as the NIV's **I will** and **you will.** It is better to read, "so I may make" and "you may break." Many an OT passage goes misinterpreted because it is read in isolation, as though we should expect each passage to spell out all the conditions under which certain claims apply. We have already observed, for example, that Psalm 2 says nothing of the character of Yahweh's kingship, nor that of Davidic kingship. Likewise, Psalm 2 says nothing of the conditions of this offer, nor should we expect each liturgy of enthronement to spell out all the legal provisos. Psalm 72 similarly promises worldwide dominion (among the royal psalms, "the ends of the earth" is found only in 2:8 and 72:8), but makes it clearly contingent on the king's governing with justice and righteousness, exemplified especially in his care for the poor (vv. 2, 4, 12–14). Thus, a king may ask, but unless he is the just king of Psalm 72, he will not experience the rest of 2:8–9. In addition, we must note that in this psalm the possibility of worldwide dominion stems not from the king's political or military might but solely from the cosmic King. As we shall see in Psalm 89, the possibilities of the Davidic kingship for dominion (vv. 25, 27) are predicated on the realities of Yahweh's kingship (vv. 9, 11).

2:10–12 / The verses closing this liturgy show that the psalm as a whole is a warning, containing both threats and promises that would be forfeited should the nations' kings carry out their rebellion. If the kings do not **serve** (*ʿbd*), they will **be destroyed** (*ʾbd*). To survive and to obtain God's blessing, these kings must change their social status to that of refugees under his appointed messiah. This is a stumbling block for all human beings, to surrender position and power voluntarily.

There is no avoiding the fact that Psalm 2 threatens the use of force, which may not be a popular notion today. But we must be clear that Yahweh uses force only when provoked in the face of defiance. And we must be clear what is at stake: not merely the status of one ethnic nation but the rule of "the One enthroned in heaven" expressed through his appointed earthly agent. Now with the advantage of retrospect and the knowledge that Jesus will have two advents, we can understand how Psalm 2 befits him. The Gospels' use of Psalm 2 is limited to verse 7. Verses 1–2 and 8–9, however, are frequently cited in Revelation (1:5; 2:26–27; 11:18; 12:5; 19:15, 19). Here he will appear not simply as God's Son but also as God's warrior-king.

Additional Notes §2

2:8–9 / **I will** and **you will**: for reading this "so I may make" and "you may break," see B. K. Waltke and M. O'Connor, *An Introduction* *to Biblical Hebrew Syntax* (Winona Lake: Eisenbrauns, 1990), p. 563, example 3.

Verse 9 deserves special comment because it is easily subject to much misuse and abuse. As already noted, it is not a **you will** prediction but a "you may" threat contingent on the nations' carrying out their plot of defiance (vv. 1–3). The NIV's "you will" **rule them** also implies the king's rule may be characterized by **an iron scepter.** A more literal translation is, "you may break them" (Hb. *t*e*rōʿēm*). The closing verses confirm that v. 9 describes the king's provoked behavior, not his characteristic behavior.

2:11–12 / Rejoice with trembling. Kiss the son: The MT, as rendered accurately in the NIV, is possibly the psalm's original text, but it contains at least two awkward features: the combination of "rejoicing" and "trembling," and the use of the Aramaic *bar* for "son," when the normal Hebrew *bēn* is used earlier in the same psalm (v. 7). Most commentators, thus, see the text as corrupt and reconstruct it to read, "with trembling kiss his feet," thus forming a likely parallel to v. 11a. P. C. Craigie, however, offers a persuasive defense of the MT (*Psalms 1–50* [WBC 19; Waco: Word, 1983], p. 64). We should note that Hebrew *rgš* (v. 1) and *rʿʿ* (v. 9) are also Aramaic loanwords.

§3 Security in the Midst of Attack (Ps. 3)

Psalm 3 is a prayer psalm of the individual and reflects a situation of personal attack (e.g., "rise up against me" and "many are saying of me," vv. 1, 2). Even so, we must note the closing verse is almost hymnic in nature, with a general statement of praise and a benediction on behalf of "your people." The alternation between direct address to Yahweh (vv. 1–3, 7, 8b) and third-person reference to him (vv. 4–6, 8a) may imply liturgical shifts between prayer to God and testimonies of trust addressed to a group of supporters, perhaps a congregation. Thus, even in the midst of personal attack, the psalm maintains connections between the individual and the corporate community by its use of a closing benediction and a probable liturgical setting. The psalm develops by first alerting Yahweh to the threat (vv. 1–2) and then confessing that one's security lies in God (vv. 3–6). The sole petition is very brief (v. 7a) and is followed by thanksgiving given in anticipation (v. 7b). The psalm then closes on a hymnic note (v. 8). (On interpreting the superscription, "when he fled from his son Absalom," see pp. 4, 26–31 in the Introduction.)

3:1–2 / The psalm opens with a lament emphasizing the **many** (three times) who **rise up against me.** Like several other psalms it quotes these **foes** (e.g., 22:8; 42:10; 64:5; 71:11), especially what they have to say about God, as a way of motivating him to intervene. Because they claim, **"God will not deliver him,"** he should now prove them wrong.

3:3–6 / These verses are a confession of trust, testifying of Yahweh's protection through several images. Characteristic of the psalms of the individual, which call upon "my God" (v. 7), is the belief that Yahweh is a responsive deity: **he answers** when **I cry aloud** (see the Introduction). His protection of the defenseless is portrayed by the expression, **I lie down and sleep . . . , because the LORD sustains me.** God lifts **up my head,** in an intimate gesture that reflects restoration and exaltation over shame or depression. The opening and closing images in this section are clearly military: **you are a shield** and **I will not fear the tens of thousands.** Possibly all the images derive from this sphere. Yahweh's answering **from his holy hill** is found elsewhere in royal psalms where the king is away in battle (18:6; 20:2, 6). Even the lifting of the head could be a gesture of military victory or of an enemy's taunt (27:3, 6; 83:2; 110:7; Judg. 8:28).

3:7–8 / The psalm's petitions are very brief. One calls for God to **arise,** as from his throne or judgment seat (cf. Num. 10:35, where the same petition is addressed to Yahweh symbolically seated on the throne of the cherubim-ark and leads to the scattering of enemies). The petition is appropriate to the threat: arise against the many who "rise up against me" (v. 1). Another imperative calls for God to **deliver me** (Hb. *hôšîʿēnî*), which if the imagery of the psalm is primarily militaristic, should be translated, "Give me victory!" Similarly, **from the LORD comes deliverance** (Hb. *lyhwh hayyᵉšûʿâ*) should then read, "from Yahweh comes victory." The parallelism of the divine titles associated with these petitions makes plain that **my God** (i.e., my personal God/protector) is none other than the **LORD** himself. Although we may take this claim for granted, other ancient Near Easterners sometimes prayed to their personal deity for him/her to intercede with higher gods. In Yahwism, however, the believer's guardian deity and the Most High are one.

The past tense of the Hebrew "for you have struck" **all my enemies on the jaw** might seem odd (the NIV has present tense), unless we observe that prayer psalms sometimes give thanks in anticipation of Yahweh's deliverance. Most often these expressions occur after a vow of praise (e.g., "I will give thanks," 13:6; 54:6–7). The anticipated celebration centers on my enemies' getting either a knockout blow or becoming harmless (God will **break the teeth**), not necessarily on their extermination. Following this thanksgiving for a particular rescue comes hymnic praise that generalizes on this theme—"From the LORD comes deliverance"—and a benediction or **blessing** on **your people.** The psalm thus reminds worshipers that an individual's experience should be connected with that of the larger community. (Psalm 28, where a speaker also struggles with "the wicked," similarly closes with an affirmation of Yahweh's salvation of and blessing on his people.)

What is perhaps most remarkable about this psalm is the security (esp. vv. 3–6) and assurance (esp. v. 7b) believers can enjoy in the midst of dire threat. We should not hear the statement, "I will not fear" (v. 6), as a speaker's boast with which we cannot identify. Rather, the psalm is meant to lead us into such experiences that are possible with God (see the Introduction).

§4 The True God of Agricultural Blessing (Ps. 4)

Psalm 4 is a prayer psalm of an individual in distress (v. 1), which is either caused or exacerbated by men who "turn my glory into shame" (v. 2). But like the preceding psalm, its concerns are not merely individual: "Many are asking, 'Who can show us any good?' Let the light of your face shine upon us, O LORD." In fact, aside from the general, introductory petitions, this is the only other petition. It is possible the speaking "I" is a liturgist (perhaps a priest; see below) speaking on behalf of a group. The opening and closing verses (vv. 1, 6–8) are clearly a prayer to God, but after the opening "hear my prayer" (v. 1) we should expect to hear one. Instead, the middle section (vv. 2–5) contains instruction addressed to these troublesome men. They may have been physically present to hear it, or they may be imagined to be present and the section said for the benefit and encouragement of fellow believers (cf. 6:8; 62:3; 114:5–6). Thus, the psalm is not a private prayer but was probably a liturgy performed for the benefit of others as well.

For what kind of conflict might Psalm 4 have been written? Three possibilities are most likely. (a) The opponents are false accusers. The expressions "you turn my glory into shame" and "seek lies" (see the NIV marginal note, v. 2) may imply they seek to tarnish the speaker's reputation. "My righteous God" could also be translated, "God of my right." But this scenario does not account for the full contents of the psalm, (e.g., its corporate petition and vv. 6–7). (b) The opponents are the wealthy class. Verse 7 may imply "their grain and new wine abound"—in contrast to me/us whose heart God has "filled . . . with greater joy." The Hebrew terminology for "men" (Hb. $b^e n\hat{e}$ $\hat{i}\check{s}$) elsewhere in the Psalms points to the wealthy (49:2; 62:9). (c) The opponents are worshipers of other gods. This interpretation appears to make best sense of the entire psalm. The "who?" of "many are asking, 'Who can show us any good?' " is probably a deity, as implied by the parallel petition to the Lord. The prophet Hosea refers to "the grain, the new wine . . . , which they used for Baal" (Hos. 2:8; cf. 7:14), presumably at harvest festivals celebrating the bestowal of fertility. "My glory" (v. 2) may not refer to the speaker's reputation but to God himself (the same Hb. expression is rendered "my Glorious One" in 3:3). The parallel line may point to the worship of other gods, which is the obvious interpretation of the NIV translators ("false gods"). Verse 5 may imply that the troublesome men do offer sacrifices but not right ones, and that they do trust but not in the Lord. (The particular expression used in the Hb. text, *bṭḥ ʾel* instead of the more frequent *bṭḥ bᵉ*, places special emphasis on the *object* of the trusting. See 31:6; Jer. 7:4; Zeph. 3:2.) It makes sense that the book of Psalms should reflect this conflict between Yahwists and worshipers of other gods, so prevalent in the prophets. In several places, the OT is reticent to acknowledge explicitly other so-called gods and instead employs wordplays (see, e.g., Amos 5:26 and 2 Sam. 2:8, which uses Ish-Bosheth, "man of shame," instead of Esh-Baal as in 1 Chron. 8:33) or euphemisms (as perhaps here in v. 2b and in 24:4b; cf. esp. Ps. 16, with which Ps. 4 shares a number of terms and motifs in common). Thus, the fundamental issue of the psalm is probably not the private issue of false accusation but the corporate issue, to what deity should people appeal for agricultural produce?

4:1 / The opening petitions are mostly typical of prayer psalms. The request, **Give me relief from my distress** (for the NIV's rendering see the textual note in *BHS*) contains a wordplay: "in a narrow place make for me a wide place" (lit.). The psalm's opening address brings the divine attribute of "righteousness" center stage, that is, the God who acts "rightly" in his relationships (see G. von Rad, *Old Testament Theology* [vol. 1; New York: Harper, 1962], pp. 370–83). We must be clear that the OT uses the term "righteousness" in a sense very different from what most modern readers assume. In this psalm, for example, it is used primarily not in a moral or legal sense but in a relational one. What the **righteous God** does for the speaker and his people is to "set apart the godly for himself," to "hear when I call to him" (v. 3), to "show us . . . good," to "let the light of your face shine upon us," to "fill my heart with greater joy," and to "make me dwell in safety" (vv. 6–7).

4:2–5 / Most prayer psalms contain a lament regarding the foes, but this one is unusual in that it is not addressed to God. Here the rhetorical question, **How long?**, is posed to the opponents themselves. The next three verses are also unusual in that they consist of exhortations to these **men**. The first thing in need of correction is their ignorance: **Know!**—in particular the special privileges Yahweh has for his own. The psalm reflects a bold confidence that he will do what has just been petitioned of him in the opening verse: **the LORD will hear when I call to him.** In verse 4a, the NIV paraphrases the LXX (cf. Eph. 4:26), not the Hebrew text, which reads, "Tremble (in dread) and do not sin." Thus, verse 4 appears to admonish the opponents to fear what Yahweh may do when defending his own. The reference to **your beds** seems strange until we note that some prophetic passages draw a connection between the "bed" and pagan rituals (Isa. 57:7–8; Hos. 7:14, which also mentions "grain and new wine"). Hence, these exhortations prescribe what they are to know, the (probably pagan) behaviors they are to cease, and now the new behaviors they are to practice. They are concretely to affirm allegiance to **the LORD** by "trusting" and "offering" **right sacrifices** (or "sacrifices of righteousness"). Right sacrifices must be given to the righteous God (v. 1). While the latter phrase could be taken in a "spiritualized" sense of worship exhibited through a righteous lifestyle (on such "spiritualization" cf. 141:2), it probably refers to ritual sacrifice (the same phrase is used in 51:19). If we are correct in surmising these opponents are idolaters (or at the very least those who grossly misunderstand Yahweh), then the command, **offer** "right sacrifices," is meant to counter the kinds of sacrifice these opponents offered "when their grain and new wine abound," that is, at fertility celebrations (esp. for Baal). (On the fundamental connections between agriculture, ritual sacrifice, and Yahweh's righteousness, see Ps. 65.) Psalm 50 may reflect a similar situation: here the people have been infected with the pagan notion that sacrifice is meant to feed God (vv. 8–13) and their primary sins have to do with their speech (vv. 19–20; cf. 4:4). As a result, this psalm similarly gives them reason to fear God (vv. 21–22) and advises them on the proper understanding of sacrifice as a means of honoring God (vv. 14–15, 23), that is, by offering him gifts of tribute.

4:6–8 / This final section raises the issue of **grain and new wine**. In this connection the question **Who can show us any good?** probably has particular reference to agricultural "goods" (cf. 34:10, 12; 104:28; 107:9; and esp. 85:11–13, which also connects Yahweh's gift of "good" with his "righteousness"). The psalm's answer to this question is clear: **Let the light of your face shine upon us, O LORD.** This request echoes the Aaronic benediction (Num. 6:22–27) and may imply the speaker is a priest (also note the concern for right sacrifices). The Aaronic benediction also closes with the bestowal of "peace," which is precisely the note on which Psalm 4 closes: **I will lie down and sleep in peace.** This is in direct contrast to the opponents who are to tremble "when you are on your beds." Thus, Yahweh's people may enjoy security *in the midst of* distress. Verse 7 does make an implicit contrast between **their** enjoyment of material goods and the **greater joy** with which Yahweh has **filled my heart.** Priority is given to what Yahweh grants within, as opposed to what people enjoy outwardly. But the bestowal of agricultural prosperity is also part of Yahweh's promises, as the psalms (e.g., Pss. 65; 85) and the prophets (esp. Hos.) make clear.

Additional Note §4

4:3 / **The LORD has set apart the godly for himself:** We should perhaps instead read, "Yahweh has made wonderful his love to me" (see *BHS;* cf. 31:21), which forms a more fitting parallel line.

§5 Entering the Lord's House (Ps. 5)

Most commentators have read this psalm as a lament of an individual. But in verses 4–6, 9–12 attention is devoted to general classes of people, the wicked and the righteous. Strictly speaking, this is not a psalm of the individual merely. The speaking "I" may, in fact, be a liturgist representing "the righteous."

Some commentators who regard this psalm as an individual lament have specified it further as a psalm of the falsely accused, where the speaker seeks acquittal at Yahweh's sacral court. This interpretation looks plausible because the chief fault of the wicked lies in their speech, which is deceitful and cannot be trusted. They tell lies and are intent on destruction. But a literal translation of verse 9b reveals that their words are deceitful and destructive for reasons other than false accusation: "their throat is an open grave; their tongues they make smooth" (an OT idiom for flattery, as the NIV translators show not here but in 12:2–3; 36:2). Here is painted the graphic picture of someone being enticed by their flattering speech and slipping on their smooth tongue into their grave-like throat. In light of this image, their words are enticing and tempting, not accusatory.

Now what is the relationship between "the wicked" (vv. 4–6) and "my enemies" (v. 8) and the speaker? Verses 4–6, while describing the wicked, cannot be considered a lament. As phrased, they are a confession about God. The wicked are given mention simply as a foil to describe God in terms of the kind of company he cannot tolerate. God's character is described as the antithesis of the wicked. Similarly in verses 9–10, no mention is made of their victimizing the speaker or anyone else. The supporting reason for God to banish them is "for they have rebelled against you." The wicked are presented primarily as opponents of God.

The wicked also serve as a foil for the speaker. In contrast to the arrogant who would dare take their "stand in your presence," the speaker would enter this presence "by your great

mercy" and "in reverence . . . bow down." Now reference is made
to "my enemies" (v. 8), but a more literal rendering is, "my
lurkers" (see Additional Notes). The next verse, as explained above,
helps to fill out the picture: "my lurkers" are smooth-talkers
lurking with enticing words to lure one away from following
Yahweh's way and into an open grave. The psalm does not present the speaker as one singled out by threat, because the closing
verses seek protection for the righteous group (vv. 11–12).

In light of the above, the wicked do pose a threat, not by
overt attack but by tempting the righteous. And the psalm nowhere contains a lament concerning how they victimize others.
They are given mention as those who contrast with God, and
thus cannot "stand in your presence," and as those who contrast
with the speaker in terms of the posture they assume before that
presence. Thus, the psalm hinges on this issue: given God's character, who is permitted to "come into your house"?

This psalm's connection to the liturgy of temple entry is
supported by the following parallels with Psalms 15 and 24. If we
regard Psalms 15 and 24 as typical of such "entrance torahs" and
so combine them to gain a fuller picture of the possibilities of expressions typical of the entry liturgy, we may note some clear
correspondence between these psalms and the confession of
Psalm 5:4–6.

Psalms 15 and 24	*Psalm 5*
Setting: "your holy hill/taber-nacle" and "his holy place" (15:1; 24:3).	"Your holy temple" (v. 7).
"Who may sojourn in your tent?" (15:1).	"Evil may not sojourn with you" (v. 4).
"And who may stand in your holy place?" (24:3).	"Boasters may not take their stand before your sight" (v. 5).
"A doer of righteousness" (15:2).	"Doers of iniquity" (v. 5).
"He who speaks the truth with his heart" (15:2).	"You destroy those who speak a lie" (v. 6).
"He does not swear deceit-fully" (24:4).	"A man of blood and deceit" (v. 6)
"A doer of righteousness" (15:2) "will receive blessing from Yahweh" (24:5).	"You bless the righteous, Yahweh" (v. 12).

In Psalm 5, the descriptions of the wicked, who may not sojourn with Yahweh, mirror in reverse the descriptions of the
righteous, who may sojourn in his tent, in Psalms 15 and 24.
Thus, Psalm 5 probably belongs to the same "rite of passage" as
Psalms 15 and 24. They are the voice of the priests, and Psalm 5
contains the confessional response of pilgrims. As the description of the "doer of righteousness" in Psalms 15 and 24 does not
refer to a particular person or group but portrays a character profile, so the description of the wicked in Psalm 5 is probably also a
character profile. Thus, the mention of the wicked in Psalm 5
may stem not from the actual circumstances of the speaker but
from the entry liturgy itself. Psalm 5 was probably not a special
psalm designed for individuals who fell into the particular circumstances of false accusation; rather it was a regular liturgy for
all entrants into Yahweh's presence.

We may now summarize the development of Psalm 5 as
follows. In the opening section a speaker expresses the desire
that Yahweh "give ear to my words" (vv. 1–3). In verses 4–6
we hear confessed Yahweh's abhorrence and judgment of the
wicked, who thus may not have an audience with him. The
speaker then petitions to be granted entry into "your holy
temple" (vv. 7–8). To ensure that one would not enter this sacred
space under false pretenses, we next hear the wicked indicted
and a petition that Yahweh pass the guilty verdict and banish
them as their punishment (vv. 9–10). Then we hear petitioned
that "those who love your name" may have access to and enjoy
the privileges of the temple, namely refuge, blessing, and praise
(vv. 11–12).

Because the subjects of the psalm appear in such distinct
sections ("I" in vv. 1–3 and 7–8, God vs. the wicked in vv. 4–6 and
9–10, and the "righteous" in vv. 11–12), it is possible that different
speakers performed this liturgy. The "I" sections may be in the
mouth of a liturgist speaking on behalf of pilgrims. The sections
referring to corporate groups, the wicked and the righteous, may
be in the mouth of a priest. This scenario seems to suit the alternation of topics treated in the psalm, as described above.

5:1–3 / In the language common to the individual
prayer psalm, this one begins with petitions for Yahweh to **give
ear** to the speaker's **cry for help**. Perhaps in response to the performance of an entry liturgy such as Psalm 24, the opening address
is particularly mindful of **my God** (an address frequent in in-

dividual laments) as **my King** (only here among the individual laments, though note 84:3). **Morning,** perhaps because of the appearance of first light, symbolized salvation, newness, and hope (30:5; 46:5; 90:14; 130:6) and was thus considered the most opportune time for God to **hear** the petitioner's **voice.** The confession, **I . . . wait,** shows that worshipers cannot presume on God's favorable hearing (cf. 130:5; Mic. 7:7; Hab. 2:1). No ritual conveys the notions of respect for and dependence on God more strongly than that of waiting.

5:4–6 / Next we hear described the addressee of these opening cries for a hearing. Yahweh is characterized, even praised, through a description of the kind of company he does not tolerate. Emphasis is given to face-to-face encounter (**with you** and **in your presence,** lit. "before your eyes") and to Yahweh's emotional reaction to such company (whom he hates and abhors). It is clear that (contrary to the expectations of many ancient Near Easterners and even some modern Christians) entering before this Yahweh is a deeply personal experience. The characteristics most abhorrent to and unlike Yahweh are arrogance, violence, and deceit. He is characterized by truth and peace.

5:7–8 / The speaker contrasts himself with the wicked by both attitude and means of entry (**in reverence** and **by your great mercy,** cf. "boasting") This contrast is emphasized even by posture ("bowing down"). The Hebrew verbs of verse 7 should probably be translated in the present tense ("I come," "I bow down") instead of the NIV's future tense, because they point to rituals that attend the singing of the psalm, not to a vow of future action. In light of the explicit reference to the rituals of entering into God's house and of prostration, it is likely that the petitions, **Lead me . . . in your righteousness** and **make straight your way before me,** are not general petitions for guidance but are requests for direct admittance into Yahweh's holy court. As Psalms 24:5 and 65:1–5 (see the commentary) make clear, entry into the temple is achieved not by claims of moral rectitude but "by your great mercy." As righteousness is a blessing bestowed on Yahweh's seekers who enter the temple in 24:5, so here "your righteousness" is not a threat to the speaker's entry into the temple, as though it indicated retributive righteousness. On the contrary, it is a *saving* righteousness and the basis by which the speaker is "led" into the temple.

5:9–10 / As a lament preceding the petition, **Declare them guilty,** verse 9 functions as an indictment. The picture painted here is a graphic one: "their tongues they make smooth" (lit.), **their throat is an open grave,** and "their inner part" (Hb. *qirbām*) is **destruction.** They are likened to a slippery chasm leading to Sheol itself. The liturgist requests a speedy verdict from God, "Declare them guilty," but the punishment is to come from two parties: from God **(Banish them)** and from the wicked **(Let their intrigues be their downfall).** Here the psalm holds in the balance the dual aspect of retribution: it is both divinely instigated and self-inflicted. Evil recoils on its perpetrators (cf. Pss. 7:9–16; 9:15–16), but the process is not necessarily automatic, so divine oversight sees to its execution. The petitions also emphasize just justice: the wicked are to become their own victims, and thus their punishment will be in like measure to their crimes. A final reason for this judgment is added, one that makes explicit what was implicit in the indictment of verse 9: **for they have rebelled against you.** Their actions impinge not only on the human sphere but also on God directly.

The Hebrew text draws our attention to a contrast that is very telling. The speaker would enter Yahweh's house in "the abundance (Hb. *bᵉrōb*) of (his) mercy" (v. 7), but the wicked are to be banished, presumably from the temple, in "the abundance (Hb. *bᵉrōb*) of their transgressions" (v. 10).

5:11–12 / While the wicked are to be excluded, **all who take refuge in** God are to find that refuge; God will **spread** his **protection over them.** "Your protection" is supplied by the translators because the Hebrew text has no direct object for "spread." It is odd for this verb to lack an object. It may be that the reference to the symbolism of temple worship was readily apparent to the original worshipers. The Hebrew verb *skk* is frequently used in connection with the cherubim, whose wings "cover" the ark of the covenant (Exod. 25:20; 37:9; 1 Kgs. 8:7; 1 Chron. 28:18; cf. Ezek. 28:14, 16). Psalm 91:4 illustrates how the symbol of the protective cherubim became a metaphor for Yahweh himself: his feathers "cover" the one who "takes refuge" (the same words as in 5:11) under his wings. Also like 91:4, Psalm 5 shifts to a military metaphor for God: **you surround them with your favor as with a shield.** The symbol of the cherubim-chariot is in part a military image where "Yahweh of (the military) hosts" presides as warrior (see the Introduction).

The ultimate goal sought in this psalm is not entry into the temple or protection but **joy,** mentioned three times in the space of a single verse. And it is to be a joy enjoyed by both the worshipers themselves (**let** them **be glad** and **sing** for joy) and by God **(rejoice in you).** Joy is to have a central place in the pilgrimage with God.

It is interesting to note that the psalm distinguishes the two parties by different criteria. The enemies are described morally: they "do wrong, tell lies," and are "bloodthirsty and deceitful." The **righteous,** however, are described religiously: they "by your great mercy . . . come into your house, take refuge in you," and "love your name." The key feature that separates the righteous from the wicked is not their moral conduct but their affinity to Yahweh's house. In addition, if we are correct in seeing Psalm 5 as the pilgrim's confessional response to priestly entry liturgies like Psalms 15 and 24, it is striking to observe that it does not explicitly lay claim to the righteous behaviors prescribed in those psalms. Rather, it disclaims the company of the wicked and seeks entry into Yahweh's holy temple by his great mercy and by self-descriptions such as "refugees" and "lovers of his name" (v. 11).

Additional Notes §5

5:3 / **Morning** by **morning:** The Hb. text reads lit., "by/at morning," and so does not indicate repeated prayers.

I lay my requests before you: "My requests" is absent in the Hb. text and is supplied by the translators. This supplementation can be supported from the use of this Hb. verb ʿrk elsewhere. On the other hand, the verb's frequent use in connection with ritual sacrifice (Lev. 1:8–9, 12; 1 Kgs. 18:33) could indicate that a sacrifice was to be offered with the singing of the psalm.

5:6 / **The LORD abhors:** Instead of Hb. ytʿb, "he abhors," we should perhaps read, ttʿb, "you abhor," since the duplicate Hb. t could easily have been omitted.

5:8 / **My enemies** is lit. "my lurkers" or "watchers" (Hb. šôrēr), a Polel participle derived from šwr. The verb's negative connotation, "to watch stealthily, lie in ambush," is evidenced in Jer. 5:26; Hos. 13:7 (see BDB, pp. 1003–4).

§6 Mercy for the Languishing (Ps. 6)

Psalms generally are written not *out of* the particular experiences of their composers but *for* the various experiences Yahweh's worshipers may face. Therefore, we should ask not, "Out of what circumstances was this psalm written?" but rather, "For what kind of circumstances is it appropriate?"

This prayer psalm of the individual uses language pointing to physical illness: "I am faint; O LORD, heal me, for my bones are in agony" (v. 2). It speaks of being near death (v. 5) and of possibly being bedridden (v. 6). Other features surface that are often associated with sickness in the OT: God's anger and discipline (v. 1, which is identical to 38:1; see also 32:1–5; 39:8–13), and enemies and friends-turned-enemies who thus believe the sick person suffers under God's judgment (38:1–22; 41:3–10). Social alienation results. This background may explain why foes are mentioned so late (vv. 7–10); they are not the cause of the distress but simply the aggravators.

Is this language of sickness literal or figurative? In other words, is this psalm suitable only for those suffering physically? As is characteristic of psalms, Psalm 6 leaves the question open. Just as mention of Yahweh as one's "shield" need not imply a military context for a psalm, so mention of the physical weakness that is the obvious origin of this imagery need not restrict this psalm's utility to those with a medical condition.

The liturgical connections of the individual prayer psalms are less explicit. They were probably written for recurring needs of individual worshipers on particular occasions. Their use was not limited to the Jerusalem temple; psalms of sickness, in particular, were probably recited right at the sickbed and overseen by a liturgist or elder. This psalm's abrupt shift from despair (vv. 6–7) to confidence (vv. 8–10), inspired by the certainty that "the LORD has heard my cry," may be the response to a "salvation oracle" delivered by a priest between verses 7 and 8. The reference to a sleepless night (v. 6) may suggest our psalm was to be recited in the morning. This would be consistent with the previous psalms, which appear to be either morning (3:5; 5:3) or evening psalms (4:8).

6:1–3 / This psalm's appeal is structured around two sets of petitions (vv. 1–3 and 4–7), each with its own supporting reasons. The word order in the original Hebrew reveals the emphasis of the opening petition: "don't *in your anger* rebuke me!" The psalm may not shun divine discipline as such, only its being done with hostility. Is this mention of rebuke a tacit admission of sin and guilt, an awareness that one suffers illness as a punishment? Because this identical petition opens Psalm 38, which explicitly refers to sickness (vv. 2–10, 17) and to sin and divine punishment (vv. 2–5, 18), some interpreters believe Psalm 6 must bear the same assumptions. But the similarity of their opening petitions makes the absence of any confession of sin in Psalm 6 all the more striking. It does not draw an inevitable connection between sin and sickness; it simply prays, **Be merciful to me, LORD.** If we take the psalm as it stands, we cannot impose on it a belief that all human conditions—whether for good or ill—have a moral cause. Some passages in the OT, in fact, indicate that God's discipline of his people stems not from specific human sins but from divine love, and should thus be welcomed (Hb. *ysr*, "discipline, chastise," in Pss. 16:7; 94:12; Deut. 8:5; cf. Jer. 10:24; Hb. *ykḥ*, "correct, rebuke, reprove," in Prov. 3:11–12; Job 5:17). The motives supporting these opening petitions for mercy and healing draw God's attention to the speaker's pitiful condition and to God's implicit allowance for its prolonged duration: "My soul is very distressed—but you, Yahweh, how long?"

6:4–5 / The second set of petitions focus on rescue—there is a hope that God will **turn, deliver,** and **save** (v. 4) presumably from that final enemy, death (v. 5). Two motives support these petitions: **because of your unfailing love** and *"for* (Hb. *kî*, omitted in the NIV) . . . in Sheol who will give you thanks?" Yahweh is called to intervene for the sake of the bond of his covenantal love. The second motive is related to this (as the Hb. connective *kî* makes clear), in that it refers to the "memorializing" (Hb. *zkr*) of that love through public praise (30:4; 135:13; 145:7). Were Yahweh not to intervene, he would lose a worshiper and the speaker would lose God.

6:6–7 / The following verses testify that this reality already encroaches upon the speaker's life. Together verses 5–7 imply, "while no one praises you from the grave, I can only groan and weep." Already he shares with the dead the inability to praise God. (To express the depth of despair the psalm does not shy away from poetic hyperbole: literally, "I make my bed swim; with my tears I dissolve my couch.") Such feelings surface especially at **night,** when darkness, silence, and the cold forebode the loneliness of the grave.

6:8–10 / At this point the psalm makes two dramatic shifts: one is from despair to confidence, the other is from addressing God directly to referring to him in the third person. It is difficult to account for these shifts merely on literary or psychological grounds. The most satisfactory explanations are liturgical. First, we could understand them as liturgical directions. In other words, the liturgy of Psalm 6 *leads* worshipers to claim the certainty that Yahweh hears when called upon, especially as articulated by this psalm (note the frequency of this tradition: 3:4; 4:3; 17:6; 31:22; 50:15; 55:16–17; 56:9; 57:2–3; 86:7; 138:3). And it does so by having the worshiper face the opponents head on, so to speak, with a testimony of God's impending intervention. (We need not suppose that **all you who do evil** are actually present to hear the speaker's words. As dramatic poetry, the Psalms sometimes address an imaginary audience. Cf. 4:2; 62:3; 114:5.) Second, we could understand these shifts as a response to a "salvation oracle," pronounced by a priest or liturgist between verses 7 and 8. Thus, we need not suppose that a psychological shift in the composer prompted these changes; rather, the liturgical text itself directs worshipers to make them.

In sum, this psalm's appeal is threefold. First, it pits Yahweh's love against his wrath. Second, it seeks to move him to pity and to heal by focusing on the intensity (e.g., "my bones are in agony") and duration ("How long?") of the distress. Third, it seeks rescue from death so that God's worship and praise may continue. Once the appeal has been sung (and perhaps a salvation oracle has been heard), the psalm directs the worshiper to testify to any who would oppose him that God has heard and will make a difference.

How can Christians make use of a psalm that claims that death silences God's praise? It is clear that within the wider scheme of God's progressive revelation we must regard Psalm 6 as pre-Christian, but it is not sub-Christian. We would be remiss if we treasured only the final stage and the final form of God's revelation. There is still a valuable lesson to be learned from this earlier stage, namely that the inability to praise God leaves his people feeling near death. Life without worship, in the liturgists' view, is no life at all. Not to praise is a form of death. The primary indicator of our being truly alive is our praise of God. This psalm is correct in that sickness, or at least symptoms similar to physical illness, should remind us of our mortality and prompt us to think of God and our relationship with God. Does our "life" share more in common with the "dead" or with the "living" who praise God? (For further thoughts on the theological value of this psalm see Craigie, *Psalms 1–50*, p. 96.)

The church has traditonally regarded this psalm as one of the seven penitential Psalms (Pss. 6, 32, 38, 51, 102, 130, 143). Although this psalm, as argued above, does not explicitly express penitence, it reflects emotions that make it applicable to the act of penitence.

Additional Note §6

6:8–10 / Even if there were an intervening oracle between vv. 7 and 8, these closing verses are no mere addition. They are integral to the unity of the psalm as evidenced by shared terminology: "be merciful to me" in v. 2 and **my cry for mercy** in v. 9, Hb. *nbhl* in vv. 2–3 ("in agony, in anguish") and 10 **(dismayed),** and **turn** in vv. 4 and 10. Note that the foes are to experience the same "dismay" (Hb. *nbhl*) that the speaker has experienced.

§7 Acquittal for the Falsely Accused (Ps. 7)

Psalm 7 is a prayer psalm of the individual. It uses a variety of images (God as refuge and judge, enemies as lions and hunters; legal, militaristic, and birth imagery), and it is difficult to discern which features might indicate the speaker's personal circumstances and which might derive from the general symbolism of the temple and its regular liturgies. There is also a combination of individual ("me" in vv. 1–6, 8, 10, 17), corporate ("peoples" and the "righteous" and "wicked" in vv. 7–10), and generalized experiences (vv. 11–16). Rather than being frustrated by this ambiguity, we should accept that this very feature is what has allowed the psalm to be used for numerous occasions for readers throughout the centuries.

If we try to probe for the original occasion for which Psalm 7 was composed, we should first note its probable liturgical origins, as implied by the ritual oath (vv. 3–5; cf. 1 Kgs. 8:31–32), the shift from prayer addressed to God (vv. 1–9) to testimony about God (vv. 10–17), and the interplay among individual, corporate, and general experiences. Viewing the psalm simply as a private prayer does not account for all these features. Second, the psalm portrays the conflict as not merely between classes of people (e.g., the righteous and the wicked, v. 9) but also between the individual speaker and "all who pursue me." Third, the ritual oath seems to imply an actual occasion of personal accusation, especially in view of 1 Kings 8:31–32. Our psalm should probably be read in light of this passage, which also refers to a possible wrong done to a neighbor, an oath sworn at the temple altar, Yahweh's "judging," (cf. Ps. 7:8), "condemning the guilty" (the same Hb. word rendered "the wicked" in Ps. 7:9), "bringing down on his own head what he has done" (cf. Ps. 7:16), and acquitting "the innocent" (the same Hb. word rendered as "the righteous" in Ps. 7:9).

7:1–2 / The opening address is a simple one but still a significant confession: the **LORD**, Yahweh, is **my God**. From the outset the accused person who would use this psalm must confess his loyalty to Yahweh who is also confessed to be "a righteous judge" (vv. 9, 11). Thus, anyone who prays for him to judge **all who pursue me** must also expose oneself to the same judgment, hence the petition, "Judge me," in verse 8. Although the **refuge** sought may have been originally symbolized by the temple sanctuary, the language of the psalm also clearly allows for this image to function as a metaphor of God himself. The introductory petition is simple and to the point (to be developed in vv. 6–9)—**save and deliver me**—to underscore the dire urgency: **or they will tear me like a lion.**

7:3–5 / The oath (cf. 1 Kgs. 8:31) is a hypothetical self-curse: **if I have done evil . . . , then let my enemy pursue and overtake me. . . .** The hypothetical actions mentioned in the "if" clauses echo somewhat those mentioned in the liturgies of temple entry (on the cleanness of one's "hands" and the doing of evil/wrong to the neighbor, cf. 24:4 and 15:3). In this oath, the acts are clearly unjust and **without cause.** By affirming that each action should have its just consequence the confessor acknowledges the way of the righteous God (v. 9) and the righteous judge (v. 11), for whom right order must be maintained. From the human perspective the punishment would be executed by the enemy, but we must be clear on the ultimate agent of judgment. This oath is addressed to the **LORD my God,** and so its execution is entrusted to his discretion: "let my enemy . . . overtake me."

7:6–9 / This petition section apparently presupposes the preceding self-curse is hypothetical, as it immediately specifies the guilty party and calls for Yahweh to confront them: **rise up against the rage of my enemies.** The imperative, **Arise,** evokes the image of Yahweh seated on his judgment throne (cf. 3:7; 9:7–8, 19; 10:12; 82:1, 8). At the temple, this image was symbolized by the cherubim-ark. This same imperative introduces the song of the ark in Numbers 10:35 (cf. Ps. 132:8). If the cherubim-ark tradition is echoed here, it can help us make sense of several features in the psalm that otherwise appear to be incongruous. One concerns the puzzling references in verse 7 (see the Additional Notes below). Another is the combination of both legal (vv. 6–9) and military (vv.10–13) language applied to God. In the OT, the cherubim symbolized both Yahweh's throne of judgment and his war-chariot (see the Introduction). A third feature is the surprising reference to Yahweh's international judgment **(the as-sembled peoples** and **let the LORD judge the peoples)** in a psalm that appears to concern a lone individual. But recurring elements in the psalmic liturgies that were ritually performed with the cherubim-ark (esp. the psalms of Yahweh's kingship; see the Introduction) are the assembly of the nations (47:9; 99:1) and his judgment of the nations (96:13; 98:9; and esp. 96:10, which uses the same phrase found in 7:8a). Thus, Psalm 7 is not simply an ad hoc private prayer for one falsely accused; it must be heard in light of the wider tradition of Yahweh's judgment as celebrated in the corporate, festival liturgies. Once again, the Psalms connect the experience of the individual with the wider framework of God's judging all peoples.

We would be unfair to the psalm if we supposed the petition, **judge me . . . according to my righteousness, according to my integrity,** smacked of pharisaic presumption. What probably occasioned this petition is a charge brought against the speaker (v. 3) by those who pursued him (v. 1). This claim of righteousness must be heard relative to this charge; it is not an absolute claim of moral purity (see further the comments on Pss. 15; 24; 26). This is a civil case between human parties. If we are correct in reading this psalm in light of 1 Kings 8:31–32, then we need to recognize there are only two alternatives in this court: either one is "guilty/wicked" (Hb. *rš*ᶜ) or one is "innocent/righteous" (Hb. *ṣdq*). Yet we must also recognize that Yahweh does not distinguish **the wicked** and **the righteous** solely on behavioral grounds, because he is confessed to be the one **who searches minds and hearts.** He probes not merely the act but also the person.

7:10–16 / Now that the petitions for Yahweh to "judge me" and to "rise up against the rage of my enemies" have been expressed, the psalm turns to a confession about the nature of his justice, perhaps addressed to a congregation or a group supporting the accused. Yahweh is no longer addressed but referred to in the third person. The psalm leads the speaker to confess **God . . . , who saves the upright in heart,** as his **shield.** In effect, the speaker must identify himself as "upright in heart," remembering that one cannot be upright merely in conduct because God "searches minds and hearts."

While the identity of the **he** in verses 12–13 is unclear, whether **God** or the wicked (see further below), the main point of verses 11–16 is clear: the wicked will receive their just retribution. The military images of verses 10–13 imply that the Defender of the righteous ("my shield") is also the Aggressor against the wicked **(his sword** and **bow).** Verses 14–16 then view retribution from another perspective: it is self-retribution. The birth and hunting images illustrate that the wicked will become their own victims. This standpoint emphasizes that justice is just—the punishment is in like measure to the crime. Together these two perspectives give us insight not only into retribution but also into the mystery of divine intervention. Reading verses 15–16 in isolation might lead us to believe retribution is automatic, but in the larger context it is an expression of **a God who expresses his wrath every day.** Divine intervention need not be cataclysmic to be divine—in fact, a divine act may appear to have happened by the normal course of events. Divine judgment takes place every day, not merely in historic judgments.

7:17 / The liturgy now turns from confessing God as "a righteous judge" to vowing to **give thanks to the LORD,** once the petitions of verses 6–9 have been answered. The promise to **sing praise** (Hb. *zmr*) is the promise to sing another "psalm" (Hb. *mzmr*). Consistent with the preceding confession (vv. 10–16), its subject is **his righteousness** (not "my," as in v. 8).

Additional Notes §7

7:1 / **I take refuge . . . from all who pursue me:** The images of "refuge" (Hb. *ḥsh*) and "pursuers" evoke echoes of the cities of refuge to which one may flee from a pursuer (see esp. Deut. 19:6; Josh. 20:5). It is doubtful, however, that Ps. 7 derives from this institution because these passages apply to cases of murder (note esp. "the avenger of blood") and because their Hb. term used for "refuge" is *miqlāṭ,* not *maḥsê.*

7:7 / **Let the assembled peoples gather around you. Rule over them from on high:** The NIV's translation, "rule," is based on the Hb. conjecture, *šēbâ* (see *BHS* note), which means lit., "sit (enthroned)," perhaps because the MT's *šûbâ* ("return") seems to make little sense. We should note, however, that the song of the ark (Num. 10:35–36) also contains the imperatives, "Arise" (Hb. *qûmâ*) and "Return" (Hb. *šûbâ*), as found here in Ps. 7:6–7. In the context of Num., they refer to the daily cycle of the wilderness journeys; in the context of Ps. 7, they may refer to the cycle of Yahweh's judgment as he arises from his judgment throne to act and returns to this position of authority once he has completed it. Another alternative appears from a possible parallel with Ps. 68:1, 18, a psalm that was performed with the procession and "ascent" of the ark. It opens with the song of the ark, "Let God arise" (Hb. *yāqûm*), and later sings of Yahweh "on high" (v. 18), as in 7:7 (only here in the Pss.). In fact, the Hb. consonants of 68:18, "you ascended to the height; you took captivity captive" (Hb. *ᶜlyt lmmrwm šbyt šby*), are very similar to 7:7 (Hb. *ᶜlyh lmmrwm šwbh*). Thus, it is possible 7:7 originally read, "you ascended to the height; you took (them) captive." (Cf. also Judg. 5:12.)

7:11 / A God who expresses his wrath every day: Instead of the MT's *ʾēl zōᶜēm* ("a God being indignant"), the LXX appears to have the Hb. reading *ʾal zōᶜēm* ("*not* indignant"). Several factors make the MT the more likely original. (a) The parallel line has **God** followed by a Hb. participle. (b) The context refers to God's protecting "the righteous" and judging "the wicked" justly. A note of God's mitigating his anger would seem out of context. (c) Verses 9–11 describe defining attributes of God by Hb. participles ("who searches," "who saves," "who judges," "who is indignant"), which are characteristic of "doxologies of judgment" (Amos 4:13; 5:8–9; 9:5–6). They give praise to God who judges decisively. Among them Zeph. 3:5 bears a close resemblance to Ps. 7:11: "Morning by morning he dispenses his justice."

7:12–13 / If he does not relent, he will sharpen his sword: The Hb. text is as ambiguous as the English. There are several options. (a) "If *God* does not turn, *God* will . . ." (so apparently the NIV text). (b) "If *the wicked* does not turn, *God* will . . ." (so the NIV margin). (c) "If *the wicked* does not turn, *the wicked* will . . ." Each of these options involves an unannounced change of subject (i.e., a pronoun with no immediate antecedent). Even if the "he" of vv. 12–13 is the "God" of v. 11 (option [a]), the wicked "he" of v. 14 has no near antecedent. And each option retains the awkward shift to referring to a singular, wicked person (whether at v. 12 or v. 14), even though "the wicked" and "my enemies" have to this point been mentioned in the plural. (Note, however, the shift in the MT of vv. 1–2: "all my pursuers . . . , lest *he* tear.") These grammatical shifts probably can be explained by the shift in the psalmic motifs: the liturgy has moved from a lament and petition on behalf of the petitioner (vv. 1–9) to a generic confession of God's justice (vv. 10–16). The option that seems to fit best with the context, as described above on 7:11, is (b). The issue is not whether God turns (option [a]) or what the wicked person would do if he did not turn (option [c]); the confession has to do with how God responds decisively in the face of wickedness. Moreover, the military image of a "shield" applied to God in v. 10 implies that the military images of vv. 12–13 also apply to him. The "he" of v. 12 is probably best translated with an impersonal pronoun: "If *one* does not turn . . ."

§8 The Lord's Majesty and the Crowning of Humanity (Ps. 8)

When we think of Psalm 8, we usually think of humanity's exalted position, but the frame in which this image is set makes plain that this is but one expression of a greater reality: "How majestic is your name in all the earth!" From beginning to end this is a psalm about the Lord and his majestic condescension. This little hymn is unusual in that it speaks in the "I" form (v. 3), but we should note this individual speaks on behalf of others (our Lord) and is thus probably a liturgist. We should perhaps imagine its being sung under a night sky.

8:1 / In the opening and closing refrain (v. 9) **your name** points particularly to Yahweh's self-revelation. The psalm sings of it in universal and cosmic terms by referring to the twin spheres of **all the earth** and **the heavens**. This does not imply his name is recognized universally. Rather, those who know his name and so confess him as **our Lord** can perceive that heavenly and earthly phenomena reflect his handiwork. The horizon of this psalm is all creation, not Israel's history or the experience of the individual, as in most psalms.

8:2 / This verse is puzzling. The NIV follows the LXX, which reads **praise**. The MT reads, **From the lips of children and infants you have ordained** "strength." What either of these versions means and what either has to do with "silencing the foe" is not self-evident. The rest of the psalm may provide the clue. In verses 3–8 we shall see celebrated that although humans initially appear insignificant, they have a position of power—not by virtue of their innate abilities but by virtue of God's ordaining it. How then are the lips of mere infants connected with strength? Their cries are heard by their parents. So, strength resides in the cry of one who has privileged access to one who embodies strength. The same word pair, **the foe and the avenger,** appears in 44:16 (though not clear from the NIV). Earlier this psalm confesses that Israel's victories in battle came not by "their arm" but by "your arm." God has so ordered creation that the innately powerless have access to power.

8:3–8 / In the body of the psalm, eyes are cast first towards **your heavens**, "above" (or probably "on") which "you have set your glory" (as noted in the introductory verse). They are awe inspiring to ancients and moderns alike, yet to God they are simply **the work of** his **fingers**. This image conveys God's immense power as builder and artistry as craftsman. No sooner does this psalm open for us this towering vision that it brings us to look at ourselves: **what is man that you are mindful of him?** The question is not merely, "what is man"? It is not primarily anthropological but theological: "that you are mindful of him." In other words, in view of God's glory that has been set on the heavens, why does God preoccupy himself with mere mortals? The question is rhetorical and cannot be answered. This psalm expands our perspective to the heavens to see that God has other alternatives for his attention and delight, namely the vast and well-ordered heavens (as implied by "the work of your fingers . . ." **which you have set in place**). And yet it is humankind that he is mindful of, and **care[s] for**. In the midst of innumerable possibilities—as many as the stars of the heavens—God's interest in us remains undistracted. Egocentric humans need not be reminded that we are the center of the universe, but we do need to be reminded that our place at the center is a surprise: "what is man that you are mindful of him?"

What is so helpful about this psalm is that it gives us reason to celebrate what we take for granted. Since day to day we humans normally need not struggle for our position in the natural world, we tend to accept it as a given. But the key revelation of this psalm is not that humanity can dominate the animal world but that **you made him a little lower than the heavenly beings and crowned him**, and **you made him ruler**, and **you put everything under his feet**. This psalm reminds us that our supremacy in the natural world did not result from our own efforts or from something inherent in nature but from God's deliberate choice. The psalm takes a radical departure from ancient Near Eastern ideology by its declaration that Yahweh has made every human a king (cf. the terminology used in 21:5, a royal psalm).

The "everything" that God has put under his feet is spelled out in verses 7–8, which list creatures **of the field, of the air,** and **of the sea.** Thus, Psalm 8 echoes the horizons of Genesis 1, where humanity is given rule over the creatures. Later in Hebrews 2:6–8, verses 4–6 are quoted. But here in view of God's new act in Christ the horizons of "everything" expand to unqualified proportions (significantly, the writer of Hebrews stops before this listing of creatures). Because Jesus "has tasted death" and thus overcome it, the writer of Hebrews can recognize in retrospect that "at present we do *not* see everything subject to him," that is, "man." But now because Jesus "has tasted death for everyone," he "brings many sons to glory" (Heb. 2:8–10). Thus, in view of the greater dominion of Jesus, one that includes death, Psalm 8 also becomes a prophecy of a greater fulfillment of the "everything" of verse 6.

8:9 / On this closing refrain see the comments on verse 1.

Additional Note §8

8:5 / **Than the heavenly beings:** The MT reads *mē ᵉlōhîm,* which in most contexts should be translated, "from/than God," as noted in the NIV margin. The LXX reads *par' aggelous*, "than angels." This is the version quoted in Heb. 2:7. The LXX need not reflect a paraphrase because an expression denoting angels in the Hb. Bible is "sons of ᵉlōhîm" (Gen. 6:2, 4; Job 1:6; 2:1; 38:7). In Ps. 82:1, 6, ᵉlōhîm by itself appears to denote such spiritual beings.

§9 Delivering the Helpless from Social Oppression: Part I (Ps. 9)

Originally Psalms 9 and 10 were one psalm. Psalm 10 has no superscription, which is unusual in Book I of the Psalter. Together these psalms form an acrostic, that is, an alphabetical psalm, and Psalm 10 picks up right where Psalm 9 leaves off (Ps. 9 closes with Hb. *k*, and Ps. 10 opens with Hb. *l*, the Hebrew letters *kāp* and *lāmed* respectively). As noted below, the psalms contain numerous linguistic and thematic links. The LXX, in fact, preserves them as one psalm. But what a contrast these psalms form! Psalm 10 is a lament and appears to contradict the praises of Psalm 9 almost point by point. In Psalm 9, the conflict is largely past and was staged between the speaker (I) and the "wicked nations" (implying international battles). In Psalm 10, the conflict is very present and is staged between "the wicked" and "the helpless" (implying social oppression within the nation). How can these psalms be seen to work together? After closer examination we shall discover the "I" of the psalm speaks as a representative on behalf of the helpless. When viewed as a whole, Psalm 9 appears to appeal to Yahweh's past, praiseworthy judgments (esp. regarding the nations) as precedents for how he should intervene in the current social unrest within Israel/Judah, as described in Psalm 10 (note the sole reference to "nations" in Ps. 10 speaks of them perishing "from his land," v. 16).

Psalm 9–10 contains no hints about how it was used and about its date. Because it contains many phrases found elsewhere in the Psalms (formulaic language) and because it is an acrostic (a feature self-evident to a reader of the Hebrew but not necessarily to a listener), it has the style of an anthology. This may point to its function as literature to be read, not as a liturgy to be performed orally. If so, a postexilic date is likely because it would have been during the exile that the once-liturgical psalms became literature.

9:1–12 / This section consists of thanksgiving (vv. 1–6) and hymnic praise (7–12). The thanksgiving opens with the usual proclamation of praise (**I will tell of all your wonders,** vv. 1–2) with one significant alteration: thanksgivings characteristically praise God for a specific, recent deliverance of an individual (e.g., Pss. 30; 116), but this praise appears to be summative in nature. The reference to the utter destruction of **the nations** and **their cities** in the body of the thanksgiving is reminiscent of the conquest of the land (v. 6b implies their destruction was long past). In this light, **my enemies** may refer to any who have—in the recent or distant past—opposed the people of Zion, not to a particular group personally attacking the speaker. Similarly, the nations and the wicked mentioned in verses 15–16 may simply illustrate the premise, "the LORD is known by his justice," and have no direct connection to the speaker's immediate distress. (Cf. the confession of Deut. 26:5–10, where later generations identify themselves with earlier generations in God's mighty acts: "the LORD brought us out of Egypt.") Yahweh is depicted in the role of judge, not warrior, in both this thanksgiving (v. 4) and the hymnic praise that follows (vv. 7–8). These hymnic praises celebrate Yahweh's international judgment in the same terms as the psalms of Yahweh's kingship (cf. 93:2; 96:10, 13; 98:9). Why this judgment is something to look forward to (not the inclination of most Christians when thinking of divine judgment!) is explained in verses 9–10: **the LORD is a refuge for the oppressed.** The case before the divine judge is a "civil suit" between the wicked and the oppressed, not a "criminal case" between Yahweh and the sinner. This is not a situation where God prosecutes sinners on the basis of his absolute righteousness (where God measures the heart), but a case where the speaker, as the advocate for the oppressed, prosecutes the wicked on the basis of relative social justice (where actions are measured). Yahweh is **he who avenges blood** and thus acts in response to **the cry of the afflicted.** Closing off this section of praise is the command, **Sing** (pl.) **praises to the LORD.** Such an imperative call to praise is normally addressed to a congregation, but it may be that it simply suits the psalm's alphabetical form (this verse needs to begin with Hb. z, the Hebrew letter zayin, with which the Hb. imperative form, *zammᵉrû,* begins). While verses 7–8 draw from the traditions of the psalms of Yahweh's kingship, verse 11 draws from the traditions of the Songs of Zion (the Lord, **enthroned in Zion,** cf. 132:14–15).

9:13–20 / This section consists of motifs belonging to the prayer psalm: there are opening and closing petitions. There is also a vow of praise with its attached thanksgiving said in anticipation of deliverance (expressed by the Hb. perfect in v. 15; cf. 13:6; 54:6–7; 56:12–13; 71:22–24; 86:12–13). The opening petition concerns **my enemies** and the closing petition **the nations,** which together form the same dual designation used for the opponents in the earlier thanksgiving. The image of "gates" links this section's opening petition with its vow of praise: the speaker anticipates being transported from **the gates of death** to **the gates of the Daughter of Zion.** Verses 15–18 offer a foretaste of the thanksgiving that will follow the deliverance. In these verses, we hear the same twin themes found in the hymnic praises of verses 7–10, namely Yahweh's international judgment on **the wicked** and his protection of **the afflicted.** The fairness of **his justice** is exhibited by the wicked becoming their own victims (self-retribution). The closing petitions appeal to creation order, implying the opponents seek to overstep their creaturely status: **let not man triumph** and **let** the nations **know they are but men.**

§10 Delivering the Helpless from Social Oppression: Part II (Ps. 10)

For an introduction to Psalm 10 see the introductory comments on Psalm 9.

10:1–11 / At this point the psalm makes a sudden turn to lament: **Why, O LORD, do you stand far off?** So dramatic is the shift we might think this was a separate psalm, except that it contains so many echoes from Psalm 9 (where the Hb. text uses the same word I have modified the NIV's translation accordingly):

Psalm 9	Psalm 10
The LORD is . . . a stronghold *in times of trouble* (v. 9).	Why do you hide yourself *in times of trouble* (v. 1)?
He does not *forget* the cry of the afflicted (v. 12).	He says to himself, "God has *forgotten*" (v. 11).
Their feet are caught in the *net* they have hidden (v. 15).	He catches the helpless and drags them off in his *net* (v. 9).

(Contrast also 9:16 and 10:2; 9:9–10 and 10:8; 9:5 and 10:5.) Far from denying reality (as reflected by the lament) or from rationalizing God's promises (as reflected by the praises), the psalm sets them side by side and forcibly shows how present realities fly in the face of God's praises. Not only do **the wicked** freely abuse **the helpless,** they are also persuaded of their autonomy (10:6) and of God's apathy (10:11), and—apparently—there is nothing in their experience to suggest the contrary.

10:12–15 / Consistent with the genre of prayer psalms, this one now turns to petition. These petitions and their supporting motivations also echo the praises of Psalm 9:

Psalm 9	Psalm 10
He does not *forget* the cry of the *afflicted* (v. 12).	Do not *forget* the *afflicted* (v. 12).

He who *avenges* blood remembers (v. 12).	Why does the wicked man . . . say to himself, "He won't *avenge*" (v. 13)?
	May you *avenge* his wickedness (v. 15).
The LORD is a refuge for the oppressed . . .	The victim *abandons* himself to you; you are the helper of the fatherless (v. 14).
Those who know your name will trust in you, for you, LORD, have never *abandoned* those who seek you (vv. 9–10).	

Thus, these petitions solicit Yahweh to re-enact his deeds that had earlier elicited praise. And these requests are supported by statements and questions that remind and thus motivate Yahweh to intervene. As he has earlier been depicted as sitting on "his throne for judgment" (9:7), so he is now implored to **arise** (10:12).

10:16–18 / The psalm's closing verses return to hymnic forms, which do offer praise to God but also serve to remind him of the actions he must now reenact. Again, the verbal echoes tie the psalm into an integrated unit:

Psalm 9	*Psalm 10*
The LORD reigns *forever* (v. 7).	The LORD is king *forever* and ever (v. 16).
You have rebuked the *nations* . . .	The *nations* will *perish* from his land.
The memory of them has *perished* (vv. 5–6).	
Nor the hope of the *afflicted* ever *perish* (v. 18).	You hear, O LORD, the desire of the *afflicted* (vv. 16–17).
He will *judge* the world in righteousness . . .	. . . *judging* the fatherless and the *oppressed* (v. 18).
The LORD is a refuge for the *oppressed* (vv. 8–9).	

Psalm 9–10 presents a powerful appeal to God. It neither retreats from reality, using God's promises as a security blanket, nor rejects God's promises in view of the lamentable reality. Rather, it sets the contradictions side by side and leaves their resolution to God.

§11 The Lord on His Heavenly Throne (Ps. 11)

Psalm 11 contains lament (vv. 2–3) but no petition. It is largely a confession of trust (vv. 1, 4–7). The speaking "I" appears only in the opening verse. Otherwise, the situation portrayed concerns groups: the wicked (vv. 2, 5, 6) threatening the righteous/upright (vv. 2, 3, 5, 7). We should perhaps imagine a liturgist dramatically instructing a congregation to be patient under social threats.

11:1–3 / The threat is depicted by three images: an endangered **bird**, hunted humans, and shaky **foundations.** The intimidation is spurned (**How then can you say to me: "Flee like a** bird") as groundless, not because of the speaker's prowess but because of his position: **in the LORD I take refuge.** The image of a bird is particularly suited here because refuge in Yahweh is often under his "wings" (36:7; 57:1; 61:4; 91:4). The notion of hunting continues into the second image, but here the prey are humans. Other psalms also depict social conditions where the wicked stalk the innocent (e.g., 10:2, 8–10). The third image of shaky foundations also appears in 82:5, a psalm similarly concerned with rampant injustice where the wicked are shown partiality in the courts over against the poor and oppressed.

11:4–7 / The question closing the psalm's first half, "What can the righteous do?," is answered, not by an act they should perform but by **the LORD,** who is the grammatical subject throughout. The statement, the LORD **is in his holy temple,** may initially not seem particularly relevant, but here our attention is drawn to a building whose foundations will never be destroyed. It is the supreme image of stability and order. Habakkuk 2:20 and Zechariah 2:13 help us to see that this statement does not merely locate God's presence; rather, it affirms that he has assumed his role as universal Judge and is about to exercise that role. There is the sense that all the world stands before him in his court: **he**

observes the sons of men. Thus, even though **the wicked . . . love violence**, from Yahweh's heavenly perspective **his eyes examine them.** We should not try to distinguish too sharply between **his holy temple**, associated with Jerusalem, and **his heavenly throne.** In the minds of the ancients the earthly temple was the immanent symbol participating in the transcendent reality. The Jerusalem temple was a window, as it were, into the heavenly temple (cf. 20:2, 6; 150:1). The speaker can claim without contradiction that he takes direct refuge in Yahweh and that Yahweh **is on** "his heavenly throne."

The word order of verse 5 is somewhat uncertain. The Greek LXX and the Syriac Peshitta read, "The LORD examines the righteous and the wicked. . . ." The NIV follows the Hebrew Masoretic Text. If this reading was the original, it contains a surprise. In contrast to "the wicked," whom **his soul hates,** we might expect to read, "the LORD *loves* the righteous." Instead, the opposite of God's "hating" someone is his "examining" someone. We usually consider examination as something to be avoided, but this psalm presents it as a privilege. The point is this: the righteous matter to God. The person he loves is the one he cares to examine and know. (The same point and the same contrast are found in 1:6.) The images of divine judgment in verse 6 (**he will rain fiery coals,** etc.) are directly related to Yahweh's position **on** "his heavenly throne" (the Hb. for "heaven," *šāmayim*, equally denotes "skies"). Yahweh is depicted as Lord of the skies thundering judgment on his enemies (see 18:7–15, where he descends from the heavens/skies on a cherub and hurls hailstones). At the temple, his throne-chariot was symbolized by the cherubim wings (see the Introduction).

The basis for distinguishing the righteous from the wicked lies not in a moral code or law but in the character of God himself and in his personal preferences: **for the LORD is righteous, he loves justice** (lit. "righteous acts," v. 7), and **the wicked . . . his soul hates** (v. 5). Yahweh is fundamentally a God of order and fairness (cf. Jer. 9:23–24). What evokes the extremes of divine emotion, whether love or hate, is not how "the sons of men" treat God but how they treat other people, whether with **violence** or justice. The NIV's **upright men will see his face** is the likely reading (see Additional Note) and, if correct, shows that the result of upright behavior is spelled out, not in terms of tangible rewards, but in terms of personal encounter with God's presence at the temple.

Additional Note §11

11:7 / Upright men will see his face: Two Hb. words cause difficulty here. Hb. *pānêmô* should usually be construed as "their face," but who is the antecedent to "their"? GKC (p. 302) notes, however, that there appear to be other OT instances where this Hb. suffix should be rendered, "*his* face." The ancient versions support this reading. Hb. *yāšār* is a singular adjective ("upright"), though according to BDB it can function as a noun ("the right," "the upright one"), even a collective noun ("the upright ones"). We should observe, however, that Hb. *yōšer* is the normal form for the singular noun and Hb. *yᵉšārîm* for the collective noun (as in v. 2). In addition, it is unclear which of these two Hb. words is the subject of the pl. verb and which is the object (sing., collective nouns can be combined with pl. verbs, as in 74:18). There are thus three possibilities: "His face will see the right" (a claim consistent with the rest of the v., so LXX), "His face will see the upright one" (a claim consistent with vv. 4–5), and "The upright ones will see his face" (cf. 17:15).

§12 The Lord's Refined Words and Humans with Double Tongues (Ps. 12)

Believers today often feel the pressures of taking a minority and unpopular position in society. Psalm 12 assures us this is no new problem and that God's people have survived nonetheless. The variations in references to Yahweh—who is addressed directly ("you"), referred to ("the LORD"), and speaks himself ("I")—make best sense in a liturgical setting. The opening petitions address Yahweh directly with the psalm's chief concern (vv. 1–2). This is expanded in the form of a wish that refers to him in the third person (vv. 3–4). In response, Yahweh speaks and promises to intervene (v. 5, perhaps through a prophetic voice, cf. Hab. 1). A liturgist then responds to Yahweh's words with a confession of their purity to the congregation (v. 6). In closing, he addresses Yahweh directly regarding the security "we" can now have in the midst of a wicked culture (vv. 7–8).

Psalm 12 may have been specially occasioned by social disintegration within Israel, so evident from the prophets (cf. Mic. 7:2, 5; Jer. 5:1–2; and esp. Hab.). On the other hand, it may have had a place in the regular liturgy. As drastic as the situation appears in the opening verses, it is evidently described hyperbolically. First, although the godly are described as "no more" and having "vanished," the liturgist himself later mentions a faithful group, "us" (v. 7) and Yahweh identifies the recipients of his salvation as "the needy" (v. 5). Second, while verse 2 appears to point to behavior nearby in Israelite society, the phrase "the sons of men" in the opening and closing verses (NIV "men") points to humanity in general. Third, the psalm exhibits some connections to the regular practice of the temple entry liturgy. Isaiah 33 uses an identical oracle, " 'Now will I arise,' says the LORD" (v. 10), which is followed by an echo of the temple entry "torah" (vv. 14b–16) found in Psalms 15 and 24. Moreover, in Psalm 12:2–4 the characterization of the wicked, especially with its focus on deceptive speech, is very similar to the behaviors that disqualify one from entering the temple (cf. esp. 15:2–3; 24:4). The echoes of the temple entry liturgies, in effect, strengthen the psalm's appeal by making clear to Yahweh that those fit to worship him are few and in dire need of protection.

In general terms, the liturgy moves from a prayer (vv. 1–4) to God's promising response (v. 5). It concludes with the liturgist's response of praise, addressed to both the congregation (v. 6) and to God (vv. 7–8).

12:1–4 / The opening petition is general in nature: it is simply "Save!" (Hb. *hôšîʿâ*, NIV **Help**). A more literal translation of the description of the opponents in verses 1–4 gives insight into why **the faithful have vanished:** "Each speaks vanity with his neighbor; with smooth lips they speak with a double mind" (i.e., deceitfully), and they "speak of great things" (vv. 2, 3b). Verse 4 cites their arrogant speech, which asserts their self-proclaimed independence and ability to determine their own destiny. Their grand advertisements and promises may thus have drawn some of the faithful to defect from Yahweh. Another reason surfaces in the following oracle, which points to the oppression of the weak, no doubt resulting from the assertion of the wicked, **"we will triumph,"** presumably over the weak.

12:5 / In contrast to what the arrogant tongue says (v. 4), is what Yahweh **says** (v. 5). The oracle responds to their rhetorical question, "Who is our master?" with Yahweh's answer, **"I will now arise," says the LORD.** We are also presented with a contrast of promises: the enemies' "we will triumph" versus Yahweh's "I will now arise" and **"protect them."** The oracle also responds in part to the liturgist's opening petition, "Save, Yahweh" (v. 1), and so promises, "I will set him in salvation" (Hb. *ʾāšît bᵉyēšaʿ*, NIV **I will** "protect them"). But it also diverges from the opening petitions in two respects. First, while verse 3 requests Yahweh to "cut off all flattering (lit. 'smooth') lips," his promise specifies no more than protection for the oppressed. Second, while the petitions designate God's people by moral categories, "the godly" and "the faithful," Yahweh uses social categories, **the weak** and **the needy.** He thus clarifies that they become objects of his salvation not by virtue of their moral behavior but because of their helplessness and need of a savior.

The oracle may also contain another promise. Instead of the difficult phrase rendered in the NIV as **from those who malign**

them, we should probably read, "I will shine forth for him," as in a theophanic appearance (see the Additional Notes and the commentary on 50:2; 80:1).

12:6–8 / These verses respond to the vouchsafed oracle with praise. We might expect Yahweh's words to be described as saving, gracious, or powerful, but they are described as "clean" or "pure" (Hb. *ṭhr*, NIV **flawless**) and **refined.** (This may reflect a priestly background to the oracle.) In the context of the psalm, we can see the implicit contrast between Yahweh's speech, which is pure, and the speech of the wicked, which is "vain" or "empty" (Hb. *šāwʾ*), deceitfully flattering (v. 2), and arrogant (vv. 3–4). Verse 7 does not merely repeat Yahweh's promise; it moves the congregation to address him directly with an act of praise and to express the assurance that he has heard their petitions. Verse 8 sounds like a disappointing anticlimax. It is a lament that echoes the opening verses (the term **men** in vv. 1 and 8 is lit. "sons of men," which forms an inclusio for the psalm), but its placement here also highlights the nature of Yahweh's protection. **You will keep us safe** even when **the wicked** have gained the upper hand.

In this psalm, we see that in spite of the fact that the wicked dominate culture, what they say is "empty" (v. 2), and what Yahweh says is "pure" (v. 6). The psalm may also perform an educative function for the congregation by clarifying how Yahweh intervenes. While the opening petitions express their wish for help and the destruction of "every boastful tongue," Yahweh's oracle simply promises protection. As a result, the liturgist concludes with praise for deliverance in the midst of, not from, wickedness.

Additional Note §12

12:5 / **From those who malign them:** The MT's wording, *yāpîaḥ lô*, is awkward, meaning either, "he blows against him" (i.e., the wicked malign the needy, so NIV, cf. 10:5) or "he pants for it" (i.e., the needy longs for Yahweh's salvation, so NRSV). The Syriac, Symmachus, and the LXX (cf. its rendering of 94:1) probably read Hb. *ʾôpîaʿ lô*, "I will shine forth for him."

§13 How Long, O Lord? (Ps. 13)

In the words of H. Gunkel, the pioneer of form-critical study of the Psalms, Psalm 13 is "the model of a 'lament of the individual' . . . , in which the individual components of the genre step forth most clearly" (*Einleitung in die Psalmen* [Göttingen: Vandenhoeck & Ruprecht, 1933], p. 46). It exhibits a compact, tightly woven structure.

13:1–2 / The opening lament names all the parties involved in the distress: Yahweh, the speaker, and the speaker's opponents. The psalm gives worshipers occasion to lament their foes' having the upper hand (v. 2b) and their personal grief (v. 2a). Hardship often causes introspection that amounts to "spinning one's wheels": **How long must I wrestle with my thoughts?** Questions of guilt and longing to change the past plague the mind. But the psalm also goes a step further—a complaint against Yahweh himself and his adverse disposition. Whether or not Yahweh is to be considered the cause of distress is not stated, but he is held responsible for its perpetuation. Since all of these **How long?** questions are addressed to Yahweh, he is believed to have the power to determine their answer and thus is held ultimately responsible. As "hiding the face" implies a deliberate act, so **Will you forget me forever** may imply the same—in other words, these problems may not have merely slipped God's mind, God may be deliberately ignoring them.

Were we to hear someone praying in this fashion today, most of us would take offense at such irreverence against the holy and faultless God. Since Christian theology, and indeed postexilic OT theology (see the commentary on Ps. 106), contain a deeper awareness of human sin, we may not immediately appreciate the face-to-face relationship implicit in this psalm. Even the complaint **How long will you hide your face from me?** contains the assumption of a direct relationship, which Yahweh is charged with breaching. As we readers interpret such a harsh

accusation, we should be struck by the speaker's high expectations. The petitions for God himself to "Look" and to "Give light
to my eyes" divulge the face-to-face relationship as well. This
context allows for direct, candid confrontation. Certainly the
partners are not assumed to be equals, but the assumed strength
of the divine-human bond encourages frankness.

13:3–4 / To resolve these dilemmas, petitions next seek
God's attention: **Look on me and answer,** and his intervention:
Give light to my eyes. Supporting these requests are motivational clauses that try to influence God to act on the speaker's behalf. These motivational clauses respond to the "How long?"
phrases in verses 1, 2. They describe the consequences of God's
forgetting, "Lest I sleep in death," and "lest my enemy say, 'I
have overcome him,' " as well as the speaker's struggle and the
enemy's triumph. These motives add a note of urgency to the request for intervention. They suggest that anything but speedy
action will be too late. Responding to the opening God-lament,
"How long, O LORD," is the affirmation, **O LORD my God,** which
supports the petitions for God's favorable attention. Here the
psalm reminds "the LORD" that he bears an obligation to those
who call him "my God."

13:5–6 / Verse 5 is a confession of trust, but it also argues that God should intervene on the worshiper's behalf. The
opening **but** connects it to the preceding motif by way of contrast. In other words, "unlike those who would rejoice over
the downfall of one who trusts in your love, I am of the sort
who would rejoice **in your salvation.**" This confession of trust
thus also exemplifies the contrasting character of the worshiper.
While the Hebrew text indicates the trust is a present reality ("I
have trusted," Hb. perfect), the rejoicing is probably future.
Verse 5b could be rendered either as a simple future, "my heart
will rejoice," or more likely as a wish, "May my heart rejoice"
(Hb. *yāgēl libbî*; note this is a variation on the preceding, "my foes
will rejoice," Hb. *ṣāray yāgîlû*).

The closing vow of praise spells out what will be the content of that rejoicing. It should probably be translated: "I will
sing to Yahweh, 'He has been good to me.' " (The Hb. *kî,* translated in NIV as **for,** probably has a recitative function. See R. J.
Williams, *Hebrew Syntax: An Outline* [Toronto: University of
Toronto Press, 1976], p. 73.) This is praise in anticipation of the
deliverance.

Some interpreters who try to pinpoint the distress that occasioned the psalm (i.e., is it a psalm of sickness?) are frustrated by its general language. Does "Give light to my eyes" point to a physical or psychological weakness? But this open-ended language helps explain the long-standing popularity of psalms, which can be used for a variety of personal needs. This image may, in fact, derive not from the speaker's circumstances but from the poetic imagery of a face-to-face relationship evident elsewhere in the psalm. It may be an echo of the Aaronic Benediction, "May Yahweh cause *his face* to *give light* to you" (Num. 6:25, lit.).

The change of mood reflected in this psalm is remarkable. One may be tempted to think its composer was manic-depressive or perhaps a nervous pietist who thought he should tack on some positive praise to soften his harsh complaint. Some commentators seem to suggest that the speaker abandons his feelings of lament by the time he reaches the praise a few verses later (see, e.g., A. Weiser, *The Psalms* [OTL; Philadelphia: Westminster, 1962], p. 163). But as argued in the Introduction, a psalm is not an autobiographical poem reflecting on a poet's recent personal experience. It is written for other worshipers to guide their responses to their own experiences. As we have just seen, this psalm reveals an intricate, tightly knit structure that moves logically from one verse to the next. When we try to pick out one poetic line, we find it attached to every other line in the psalm. It guides us to express heartfelt emotions, to seek a release from our pitiful state, and to express praise in a way distinct from our opponents. In so doing, the psalm allows believers to voice the mixed emotions often felt toward God while in the midst of hardship, namely complaint (v. 1) and trust (v. 5). We must also note that the praise mentioned in the closing verses is promised, not necessarily actual. The psalm may thus also reflect worshipers' emotional turmoil and their determination to praise God nonetheless. For the faith reflected in the Psalms, complaint need not indicate a lack of trust, nor does trust make complaint unnecessary. In fact, it is this trust in God that allows for the expression of such protests in the relationship.

§14 There Is No One Who Does Good: Version 1 (Ps. 14)

Psalm 14 is almost identical to Psalm 53. They appear to have been transmitted separately, the former finding a place in Book I of the Psalter and the latter in Book II. The most obvious difference between them lies in the divine name. Psalm 14 uses the personal name "Yahweh" (rendered "the LORD" in the NIV), and Psalm 53 uses "God" (Hb. ʾelōhîm), as is customary in the Elohistic Psalter (Pss. 42–83).

These psalms stand apart from the rest for their universal perspective, their universal condemnation of humanity, and their reference to atheism. Their literary form is also unique, a fact that makes it difficult to determine their social setting and date. Scholars have variously characterized them as a prophetic liturgy (H.-J. Kraus, *Psalms 1–59*, vol. 1 of *Psalms, A Commentary* [trans. H. C. Oswald; Minneapolis: Augsburg, 1988], pp. 220–21), a wisdom poem (Craigie, *Psalms 1–50*, pp. 145–47), and postexilic synagogal instruction (Gerstenberger, *Psalms,* pp. 219–20). Mention of "those who devour my people" and the anticipation of a time "when the LORD restores the fortunes (or 'turns the captivity') of his people" fit Judah's situation in the exilic and even early postexilic periods (see commentary on Ps. 85).

14:1–3 / The term **fool** in the Hebrew Bible denotes not a silly person but one who ignores realities. The prime reality a fool denies is God. Following from these fools' assertion, **There is no God,** is their moral corruption: **They are corrupt, their deeds are vile.** Their morality stems from their theology, or lack of one. Verse 2 hinges on the motif of seeking: **the LORD looks down . . . to see if there are . . . any who seek God.** The choice of the generic designation "God" (Hb. ʾelōhîm) in a verse that begins with "the LORD" (i.e., God's personal name) underscores the psalm's universal scope. His search is not restricted to those who have been informed of Israel's God. Yahweh's perspective is **from heaven** and his field of view is **the sons of men.** The result of this polling is unanimous: **all have turned aside, they have together become corrupt; there is no one who does good, not even one.**

14:4–7 / Curiously, however, the psalm's second half refers to a class of people who receive Yahweh's special care (**my people,** i.e. the speaker's, v. 4; **the company of the righteous,** v. 5; **the poor,** v. 6; **Israel . . . his people,** i.e. Yahweh's, v. 7). The designation of "the righteous" seems irreconcilable with the judgment, "there is no one who does good." (Ps. 53:5 deviates from its parallel in 14:5–6 by omitting "the righteous" and any mention of God's protection in the meantime, and by expanding on God's judgment of the **evildoers.**) In addition, a particular class of evildoers is singled out, namely **those who devour** "my people." Could it be that "the sons of men" described as so godless in verses 1–3 merely denote "them" and not "us," that is, "my people"?

Fortunately, our interpretation of Psalm 14 may be helped by neighboring psalms. The phrase, "the LORD looks down from heaven on the sons of men," is closely paralleled in 11:4. But in this psalm Yahweh discovers two classes of people: "the righteous" and "the wicked." Hence, it seems unlikely we should explain the tension between the two halves of the psalm simply by assuming "the sons of men" refers to "them" only. Rather, Psalm 14 probably includes "Israel" among those who "have turned aside" because of its peculiar exilic perspective (see on Ps. 85). Like our psalm, Psalm 12 also begins with what initially sounds like a universal condemnation of humanity (vv. 1–2), but we then learn that Yahweh offers special protection for the poor (Hb. *ʿānî*, v. 5, the same term used in 14:6) and for "us" who pray the psalm (v. 7). And Psalm 15 opens with the question "Who may live on your holy hill?" and answers it with "he . . . who does what is righteous" (15:1–2). Although this may sound like a claim of moral perfection, the other psalm of temple entry (Ps. 24) makes clear that such a person still needs to "receive righteousness from his saving God" (24:5; see the commentary). In fact, 14:5 uses the same designation for "the company of the righteous" (Hb. *dôr ṣaddîq*) as found in 24:5–6 (where the NIV translates *dôr* as "generation"). Thus, "the righteous" are so-called not by their own merits but by the grace of their saving God. With knowledge of such parallels we can better reconstruct the thinking reflected in these verses. We now see that God's finding "all have turned aside" need not imply that he has condemned everyone. In fact, there are those whom God simply calls "his people" (v. 7), apparently for no other reason than his grace.

§15 Instruction for Temple Entry (Ps. 15)

Psalm 15 is part of a liturgy of temple entrance (see the Introduction for a fuller discussion of this momentous rite of passage). It shares with Psalm 24:3–6 and Isaiah 33:14b–16 the threefold pattern of a question of who may sojourn on Yahweh's holy hill (v. 1), a reply consisting of the qualifications for worshipers (vv. 2–5a) and a promise (v. 5b).

15:1 / A literal translation of verse 1, "Who may sojourn (Hb. *gwr*) in your tent (Hb. *'ohel*); who may camp (Hb. *škn*) on your holy hill?" makes plain that the liturgist is inquiring not about taking up permanent residence as a priest or Levite but about making a pilgrimage (see on Ps. 61, esp. v. 4). The reference to Yahweh's "tent" need not imply pre-temple origins for the psalm. This term continued to be used well after Solomon (see on 27:4–6). Its use here suits the notion of sojourning and echoes the ancient custom of the traveler who comes under the protection of the (divine) host, whose "tent" he has entered (note again 61:4 and its parallel line where refuge is sought; cf. also Ps. 23).

15:2–5a / As a question directed to Yahweh himself, verse 1 seeks an oracle of instruction or "torah." The answer contained in the rest of the psalm should thus be regarded as a divine speech delivered by a priest or temple prophet. (Although v. 4 does refer to Yahweh in the third person, it is part of a phrase that identifies a certain class of persons, namely "Yahwehfearers.") The psalm is thus a kind of catechism.

This torah is presented as ten "commandments." Three positive character descriptions (all Hb. participles, v. 2) are matched by three negative actions related primarily to speech (all Hb. perfects, v. 3). The positive descriptions focus on integrity and the negative statements on not abusing people verbally. There follow two qualifications (each with a Niphal verb and an imperfect verb, v. 4) which refer to the company one keeps and to keeping promises (oaths). The final two are negative statements (both Hb. perfects, v. 5a) referring to not abusing one's resources and position.

The number ten invites comparison with the Ten Commandments (actually not so labeled by the OT, which refers to them as the "Ten Words," see Exod. 20:1; 24:3; Deut. 5:22, where the NIV wrongly translates "commandments"). Among the "words," four center on relationship with God and six center on human relationships. In Psalm 15, however, all ten concern human relationships. The only "word" with which Psalm 15 specifically overlaps is the ninth, which concerns "false testimony against your neighbor" (Exod. 20:16). We should, therefore, consider the list in Psalm 15 as partial.

This observation invites us to examine the selectivity used for the description of candidates qualified for entry into the temple. First, these qualifications are ethical, not sacral, in nature. Nothing is mentioned regarding one's attendance at festivals, correct offering of sacrifice, prayer life, daily meditations (cf. Ps. 1:2), etc. Would-be worshipers are here called to examine how they have lived with their neighbors since their last pilgrimage festival. Second, these qualifications focus on social or civil, not criminal, behavior. Worshipers may not casually assume that they pass the requirements simply because they are not part of society's criminal element; these verses condemn sins that any citizen might commit. They do not point to unusual, heinous crimes but to matters of daily conversation. Third, these qualifications point to inner attitudes, not merely to what is observable and legally enforceable (only usury and bribery would qualify). They transcend what comes under the jurisdiction of the legal system and go to matters of the heart: **who speaks the truth from** (lit. "in" or "with") **his heart** (cf. Deut. 6:5). **Slander** could be understood in its legal sense as libelous slander, but one must also ask whether one has always "walked with integrity," "spoken truth in one's heart," and never "done harm to one's neighbor." Thus, one's judgment could not be conceded to another; self-examination under the scrutiny of conscience was required (cf. one's approach to the rite of the Lord's Supper in 1 Cor. 11: 28, 31). Rather than attempting to be comprehensive, these qualifications use one's social relationships and especially one's speech as the "litmus test" to indicate one's true "color." (Jesus foresees the same standard for "the day of judgment," Matt. 12:33–37.) They do not allow one to hide behind a cloak of religiosity.

These qualifications also make it clear that any people who wish to enter the temple must be capable of judging themselves. We may be troubled that judgment is left to conscience, thus allowing deceivers, the self-deceived, and hypocrites into the sanctuary. Shouldn't the Bible seek "objective" standards for membership in the people of God? Yet this query misunderstands the initial double question. In both entry liturgies of the Psalms (Isa. 33:14 is even more explicit: "Who of us can dwell with the consuming fire?") the question focuses on who may approach Yahweh's holy place. This question is not raised out of mere doctrinal interest or out of concern for church membership; it is raised out of deep respect for consuming Holiness. Implicit here is mortal danger. After Aaron's sons had been consumed by fire that came out from the presence of the LORD, Yahweh explained, "Among those who approach me I will show myself holy; in the sight of all the people I will be honored" (Lev. 10:3). Rather than being legalistic prerequisites for coming to God, these qualifications are safeguards against premature divine judgment. Entrants are thus given the opportunity to judge themselves and depart, before God's holiness judges and consumes them (again the view of the Lord's Supper in 1 Cor. 11:27–32 is no less solemn). At issue here is not merely entry into a building but survival. The sentiment of the initial double question is not "Whom should we allow in?" but "Who dares enter in?" The purpose is not to safeguard God, the temple, or the sacred community; it is to safeguard the individual and his or her survival. These qualifications are not a checklist but a warning.

But the question may still remain for many Christians, Isn't this a legalistic approach to God's holiness? We may ask, "How could anyone claim to meet the standards of verses 2–5a and have the nerve to face the holy God? And isn't this law before grace, where one must make oneself right before approaching God? What of the NT's emphasis that we have access to God solely on the basis of his gracious atonement that he initiated himself?" Such questions are not answered by Psalm 15 alone, and in isolation the psalm could be very misleading. But other psalms that refer to temple entry do give some clear answers and they are thoroughly consistent with the NT. (See the Introduction and the commentary on Pss. 5:7; 24:3–6; 65:1–5.) This profile of the "doer of righteousness" contained in verses 2–5a is not to be used as a checklist of qualifications; rather, it is to be endorsed as Yahweh's "torah" and embraced as the seeker's ambition. Psalm

24 makes plain that once the seekers enter they receive Yahweh's saving righteousness.

Unfortunately, the NIV translation contributes to the impression of legalistic righteousness in Psalm 15. Instead of reading, **he whose walk is blameless,** we should read, "he who walks with integrity" (Hb. *tāmîm*). He is an "integrated" person. This word denotes wholeness or soundness, not blamelessness with respect to a legal standard. The notion of wholeness is echoed in the three bodily parts mentioned in verses 2, 3, and 4. He **speaks . . . truth from his heart and has no** slander **on his tongue,** and, literally, "despised in his *eyes* is a rejected one." Through a minor modification, the translation, "who does what is right" (instead of **righteous**), conveys more accurately the meaning of the Hebrew term *ṣedeq* (see esp. von Rad, *Old Testament Theology,*vol. 1, p. 370–83). In the OT it is used in the context of relationships, not of moral codes. Thus, one should do what is right or fair or appropriate to the relationship. (We should also note that "righteousness" in the Psalms is not a static concept or entity. One *is* not righteous unless one *does* righteousness.) The same should be said for the term "truth" (Hb. *ᵓemet*). It does not mean "*the* truth" as though it were an abstract entity (the Hb. text has no "the," as in the NIV); rather it means being "true to the relationship." In many respects, the translation "fidelity" is closer to the sense of the Hebrew.

According to the contrast in verse 4a, one demonstrates loyalty to Yahweh by the company one keeps: he **honors** "fearers of Yahweh" (lit.) but "a rejected one . . . is despised" (lit.). It will become evident in other psalms connected with temple entry that Yahweh's worshipers must endorse any judgment pronounced on those who are not fearers of Yahweh.

Verse 5a gives special attention to requirements for people of means and position, in terms of what they "give" (Hb. *ntn*, NIV **lends**) and "take" (*lqḥ*, NIV **accept**). Those who have **money** must not give it with **usury;** those who hold the power of judgment must not take **a bribe.** Yet we should not suppose this verse may be ignored by those without means or position. Speaking after the fashion of Hebrew legal literature, this verse presents a concrete example of how all God's people should live.

15:5b / In light of the above, we should not misunderstand the closing declaration of verse 5b to affirm that one's own behavior will in itself guarantee security or stability. The opening rhetorical question makes clear that **he who does these things** is the one "who may dwell in your sanctuary" and who thereby **will never be shaken.** One's behavior enables one to be mercifully admitted to Yahweh's sanctuary, and it is the sanctuary on the firm "holy hill" (or "mountain") that provides security. This promise was not one randomly chosen by the speaker; it is derived from the tradition of "the holy mountain," which symbolizes stability in both nature (e.g., the pillars of the earth) and the imagery of the ancient Near East. On the cosmic mountain lies the temple of the divine king who has vanquished all chaotic forces. (This background is made more explicit in Ps. 24, another entrance liturgy.)

Additional Notes §15

15:4 / **Who keeps his oath even when it hurts:** The NIV translation is difficult to support. Instead of the MT's "he swears to do evil" (Hb. *lᵉhāraᶜ*), we should probably follow the LXX and Syriac and read, "he swears to the/his neighbor and does not change" (Hb. *lᵉhārēaᶜ/lᵉrēᶜēhû*).

15:5 / **Usury:** OT law forbade lending with interest to Israelites because the only reason in view for loans was to help one "who is needy" (Exod. 22:25; Lev. 25:35–37; Deut. 23:19–20). Thus, lending in the OT should be understood as a means of extending help to the needy, not as a means of investing for the lender. These laws curbed the interest rates current elsewhere in the ancient Near East (Kraus, *Psalms 1–59*, p. 230, mentions rates of 33–50 percent).

§16 Confessing Loyalty to the Lord of the Land and His Benefits (Ps. 16)

The overall function of Psalm 16 is hard to determine, in part because the Hebrew text of verses 2–4 is difficult, but it appears to be a psalm of trust or more particularly a confession of faith in and loyalty to Yahweh.

16:1–4 / It opens with a general petition for protection in the image of **refuge**. Verses 2–4 probably act as a report **(I said)** of the worshiper's confession declaring, **"You are my Lord,"** as distinct from **other gods**. He resolves that Yahweh will be his sole source for **good**. This loyalty is further spelled out by a refusal to participate in pagan rituals **(libations of blood** and taking up **their names on my lips)**. Hosea 2:17 may provide a parallel here: "I will remove the names of the Baals from her lips." Baal was considered by many to be the god of the land of Canaan, so in the verses immediately following Yahweh promises to settle his people in the land, provide them with agricultural produce, and they in turn will confess, "You are my God" (vv. 18–23).

16:5–6 / These verses elucidate the good that "my Lord" has provided the worshiper, namely **my portion**, which is a **delightful inheritance**. The terminology here is drawn from the apportioning of the promised land: "According to the *lot* shall each *inheritance* be *apportioned*" (the Hb. verb form of the noun "portion," Hb. *ḥlq*; lit. Num. 26:56; cf. 33:54; Josh. 13:7; 14:2). **The boundary lines have fallen,** as an expression of Yahweh's allotting Israel's "inheritance," is paralleled in Psalm 78:55, which literally reads, "and he caused to fall for them an inheritance with a boundary line" (cf. Josh. 17:5). A more literal translation of verse 5a of our psalm is, "the LORD is the part of my portion" (not **you have assigned me**). Here the psalm makes a claim that is elsewhere exclusive to the Levites. They are said to have no portion or inheritance in the land; rather Yahweh is to be "your portion and your inheritance" (Deut. 10:9; Num. 18:20). In material terms, "they shall live on the offering made to the LORD" (Deut. 18:1–2). Our psalm therefore uniquely combines claims and privileges that belong to both the Levites and to the other tribes that receive land. Thus, either one or both of these claims are metaphoric. Either a Levite here "spiritualizes" his "inheritance" amidst "the boundary lines" as a spiritual inheritance from Yahweh, or the psalm directs any worshiper irrespective of tribe to claim Yahweh as "my portion." The latter is possible especially if we are to view the claim of Yahweh as "my portion" as a parallel claim to Yahweh as "my Lord" (v. 2). In effect, the worshiper would be affirming his choice of Yahweh, as opposed to other gods of the land.

16:7–11 / Once the worshiper (whether Levite or otherwise) has confessed allegiance to Yahweh and acknowledged the gift of Yahweh, the worshiper now vows to praise (lit. "bless") him and provides further reasons for this praise (vv. 7–11). The worshiper also reaffirms loyalty to Yahweh, **I have set the LORD always before me** (cf. Exod. 20:3). As a result, **I will not be shaken.** Fundamental to the psalms of the individual, both prayers and thanksgivings, is the issue of life and death and the belief that "my God" will preserve his worshiper from premature death (see Broyles, *Conflict of Faith and Experience,* pp. 117–22). Thus, **my tongue rejoices . . . because you will not abandon me to the grave** and **you have made known to me the path of life.** (The NIV's marginal reading, "your faithful one" [Hb. *ḥaṣîdekā*], is a more literal rendering than the one in the main text, **your Holy One.**) "The path of life" may allude to the pilgrim way since its goal is **your presence** (lit. "your face"; cf. 11:7; 63:2) and **eternal pleasures** (Hb. *neʿîmôt*) **at your right hand** (cf. 27:4, where "beauty" translates Hb. *nōʿam*), both of which are found at the temple.

§17 Holding to the Lord's Paths Amidst Threatening Stalkers (Ps. 17)

This prayer psalm of the individual concerns Yahweh's judgment and enemies like a pride of lions who threaten the speaker. It opens with a prayer to have a hearing with God and for him to pass his final judgment or verdict (vv. 1–2). It then declares the speaker's innocence by confessing that Yahweh *has* already "examined" him (contra NIV; vv. 3–5). The next section prays for refuge (vv. 6–8), and the following lament makes the reason plain: the wicked hunt him down (vv. 9–12). The final section prays for rescue (vv. 13–14) and closes with a confession of trust that the speaker will have the right to face God (v. 15).

Psalm 17 shares some similarities with Psalm 7 and so could reflect a similar situation of personal accusation. But, unlike Psalm 7, it contains no clear suggestion the speaker has done anything against his pursuers. Their speech is depicted not as accusatory but as arrogant (v. 10). In fact, the wicked are described in ways very similar to those in Psalm 73 ("violent" in 17:4 and 73:6; "callous" in 17:10 and 73:7; characterized by "arrogance," Hb. *gē'ût* in 17:10 and *ga'ᵃwâ* in 73:6). Moreover, both psalms refer to the speaker's feet not slipping (17:5 and 73:2), to his keeping himself from evil (17:4 and 73:13), to Yahweh's right hand (17:7 and 73:23), to taking refuge in Yahweh (17:7 and 73:28), and to Yahweh's personal reception of the speaker (17:15 and 73:23–25, 28). Although Psalm 73 does not refer to the wicked attacking the speaker directly, they are described as oppressive and devouring (vv. 8–9). It is therefore possible that Psalm 17 reflects a similar social situation where the wealthy wicked, who enjoy their portion (NIV "reward") in this life (v. 14), oppress the righteous.

Again, Psalm 17 may reflect a situation of seeking Yahweh's acquittal from accusations brought by personal enemies. But this interpretation assumes a direct connection between Yahweh's

judgment of the speaker and the enemies' attack. These two issues, however, are treated in discrete sections of the psalm (vv. 1–5
and 6–14). Psalm 17 may depict the wealthy wicked people op-
pressing the righteous, and Yahweh's judgment of the speaker is
similar to that in the psalms related to temple entry (see the Introduction). Psalm 26:1–5 particularly has several parallels to 17:2–5
(Yahweh's vindication/judgment; his acts of examining and testing, Hb. *bḥn* and *ṣrp;* not slipping; walking in Yahweh's ways and
avoiding the wicked). These psalms show that a judgment that
separates the righteous and the wicked is presupposed in the process of entering the temple and finding refuge (e.g., 5:11; 36:7;
73:28). Seekers of refuge must therefore establish that they are
"righteous" and not "wicked." A key piece of evidence is the avoidance of deceitful speech (17:1 and 5:6; 24:4; 36:3; 52:4). The declaration of innocence in 17:3–5 is not an oath said in the face of
specific accusation, as in 7:3–5 ("if I have done this"). Rather it confesses a general lifestyle of an avoidance of the ways of the violent
and of an allegiance to God's paths.

17:1–2 / As is typical of many prayer psalms, this one
opens with a petition for God to **hear.** In particular he is to hear
"my right" or "my righteous cause" (following the LXX reading, as
the NIV has paraphrased; cf. 35:27 and possibly 4:1). The point
sought in verse 2 is that "my judgment" (lit., NIV **vindication**)
would come **from you** and **your eyes** (as emphasized by the Hb.
word order). The speaker is thus to seek *God's* valuation of his life.

17:3–5 / The Hebrew verbs of verse 3 imply completed
action, thus "you have probed, examined, and tested" (not the
hypothetical action of the NIV). Yahweh has already "assayed"
(lit., NIV **test**) the speaker, who now awaits Yahweh's public
verdict (v. 2). In contrast to human judges, Yahweh probes
not mere behavior but the **heart.** In view of the full extent of
Yahweh's examination, we may be surprised, even appalled, at
the psalm's apparent claims of sinlessness **(you will find nothing,** and **my mouth will not sin).** But these must be read in the
context of similar claims, found especially in psalms related to
temple entry. We do violence to the liturgical genres of the
psalms if we read them as absolute claims reporting on one's
moral status. Rather they are confessions given to worshipers
to affirm (and thus encourage) their loyalty to Yahweh's way
of righteousness. For the sake of educative clarity the liturgy

presents only two choices: either one is righteous/innocent or
one is wicked/guilty.

The time of Yahweh's probing is specified as **at night.** Later
the speaker confesses to "seeing your likeness—when I awake"
(v. 15). Some scholars have suggested this may allude to a ritual
whereby an accused individual would sleep in the precincts of the
temple, and if he survived the night before Yahweh's holy "face,"
he would be judged innocent. On the other hand, other psalms
speak of the night while one lies in bed as the time when in privacy one's true heart surfaces (esp. 4:4; 16:7; 77:6; and also 6:6;
36:4; 119:55). And other psalms speak of the morning, the moment
when light dispels darkness, as symbolic of salvation, newness,
and hope (30:5; 46:5; 90:14; 130:6; cf. also 3:5; 4:8; Lam. 3:23).

17:6–12 / This next section echoes the psalm's opening:
give ear to me and hear my prayer. Why does the liturgy repeat
what has already been asked? This repetition may mark a distinct stage in the liturgy, perhaps even introducing a separate
concern. Once the speaker has established his loyalty to Yahweh,
he now confesses, **I call on you, O God, for you will answer me,**
and turns to seek the privilege of **refuge** in Yahweh. It is only in
the psalm's second half that we learn he is under attack **from the
wicked who assail me.** This appeal for refuge is based on a close
personal bond between Yahweh and the worshiper. The mighty
act of Yahweh's "saving" by his **right hand** is an expression of **the
wonder of your great love** and is depicted in images that speak
of the worshiper as dear to God: **as the apple of your eye** and **in
the shadow of your wings.** The subsequent lament uses vivid
images to add motivation and urgency to these petitions: these
**enemies . . . have tracked me down . . . like a lion hungry for
prey** (cf. 7:1–2).

17:13–15 / The first petition section had sought a hearing with and a judgment from Yahweh (vv. 1–2). The second
sought protection with Yahweh (vv. 6–8). The third now seeks
his punishment on **the wicked.** He is implored to **rise up** as a
judge from his judgment seat, to **confront them,** and to **bring
them down** (lit. "cause them to bow down"). The Hebrew text of
verse 14 is extremely problematic, and the NIV's interpretation is
strained. A more likely explanation is to read it as a continuation
of the petition in the preceding verse.

The psalm concludes with a startling claim: **And I—in
righteousness** (or perhaps, "in the right"; cf. discussion of v. 1

above) **I will see your face.** How does this square with other biblical claims that "you cannot see my face, for no one may see me and live" (Exod. 33:20)? Included in Psalm 42–43, a prayer to make a pilgrimage to the temple, is the phrase, "When may I enter so I may see the face of God?" (See the commentary there; cf. also 11:7; 84:7.) In Isaiah 1:12 Yahweh similarly says to those who offer sacrifice at the temple, "when you enter to see my face . . ." It thus appears that this expression is a metaphor for meeting with God at his temple dwelling. The claim of our psalm is thus that the speaker will be admitted to meet directly with Yahweh within his temple.

Additional Notes §17

17:7 / You who save by your right hand those who take refuge in you from their foes: The NIV has added words not present in the Hb. text ("in you," "their") and has altered the word order. We should probably read "O savior of those who take refuge from those who rebel *against* your right hand." On Hb. *qwm b* as "arise against," see 27:12; Mic. 7:6; Job 16:8.

17:14 / The MT is probably corrupt. It seems best to render the verse in light of the preceding verse. The MT has no verb in v. 14a, so the NASB translates it as a clause dependent on the imperative, "rescue," in v. 13. To make v. 14 an independent clause the NIV translators apparently inserted the synonym, **Save me.** Instead of **from such men** (Hb. *mimtîm*), we should perhaps read, "putting them to death" *(memîtām).* Instead of the MT's "from a world" *(meheled,* NIV **of this world**), we should probably read "make an end" *(hadal).* Instead of **whose reward is in this life,** a more literal rendering is, "their portion in life." **You still the hunger of those you cherish** is a loose paraphrase. This phrase is more literally, "may you fill their belly with what you have stored up." The *Kethib* reading (lit. what is "written" in the main text of the MT), *sepûneka,* could be understood positively as "what you have treasured up" (hence the NIV's "those you cherish") or simply as "what you have stored up" (Hos. 13:12 uses this verb with Israel's sin). Instead of **their sons have plenty, and they store up wealth for their children,** we should translate, "may their sons be sated and deposit the remainder to their children," rendering the Hb. imperfect/jussive verb as a wish in keeping with the petition of the preceding verse. Thus, we may translate this verse: "putting them to death by your hand, Yahweh, putting them to death; make an end of their portion in life; may you fill their belly with what you have stored up, may their sons be sated and deposit the remainder to their children." (Cf. Job 21:19; Exod 20:5.)

§18 The King's Thanksgiving for Military Victories (Ps. 18)

Psalm 18, which is also recorded with some variations in 2 Samuel 22, is a royal psalm, but relatively little of its language is the distinct prerogative of the king (only vv. 43–44 and 50). Many of its phrases are shared by Psalm 144, another royal psalm, and both psalms reveal a composite structure. Psalm 18 is an unusually long psalm, even among the royal psalms (see the comments on Ps. 89), probably because of its composite nature. Verses 1–6 and 16–19 read like a thanksgiving (Hb. *tôdâ*) of an individual. Interrupting the normal sequence of thanksgiving is a "theophany" (where the God of the skies appears to save) in verses 7–15. The testimony of integrity in verses 20–26 echoes the declaration of integrity that pilgrims presented to gain entry into the sanctuary (e.g., 26:2–8). Verses 29–42 are a warrior's victory hymn (the first clear indication this psalm has to do with battle is here in v. 29). The psalm is thus not an authored composition but an edited one.

The total effect and genius of this compilation is to bring together spheres of life often kept separate: warfare and morality, human and divine agency, and the responsibilities and privileges of the king and ordinary people. Success in Yahweh's battles, we will find, depends on the moral stature of Yahweh's army and the justice of their cause. On one hand, a person's success can be traced back to that person's integrity and skills, but on the other, the same success may be explained by divine intervention. Although the king may enjoy a privileged position (both with respect to humans, v. 43, and to God, v. 50), his character and experience are judged by the same standards as those of everyone else.

This royal thanksgiving for battle victory may have been performed after actual battles, or it may have served as a regular testimony at an annual festival. While there are no explicit ritual connections, each of the distinct literary forms identified above is rooted in liturgical settings. Although it may have later editorial additions, much of its language appears to be early preexilic (see F. M. Cross and D. N. Freedman, "A Royal Song of Thanksgiving: II Samuel 22 = Psalm 18," *JBL* 72 [1953], pp. 15–34).

18:1–3 / The opening verses follow the standard pattern of individual thanksgiving: a proclamation of praise, divine address, and an introductory summary. But instead of the normal "I will exalt/bless/give thanks" (30:1; 34:1; 138:1), we hear, **I love you** (Hb. *rḥm,* cf. 116:1, *ʾhb*), thus injecting a notable tone of intimacy. In addition, the normally simple address, "O/the LORD," is supplemented with several epithets of a distinctly military tone (though many individual prayers having nothing to do with warfare also use such epithets). Some of these titles are echoed later in the psalm, thus tying the composite together: **rock** (vv. 31, 46), **shield** (vv. 30, 35), and the notion of **refuge** (v. 30). The rest of this psalm's thanksgiving (vv. 4–6, 16–19) sticks to the general motif of deliverance from death, which is typical of thanksgiving psalms (e.g., Pss. 30; 116) and says nothing directly of battle.

18:4–6 / The thanksgiving continues by narrating the distress, the speaker's cry to **my God** (an expression at home in the psalms of the individual, also v. 2) and the claim that he has heard. As is typical, the description of the distress does not detail any particulars, so as to limit the psalm's application, rather it paints with images of the hunt **(cords . . . entangled, cords . . . coiled around,** and **snares)** and of drowning **(torrents;** on such imagery see further O. Keel, *The Symbolism of the Biblical World: Ancient Near Eastern Iconography and the Book of Psalms* [New York: Seabury, 1978], pp. 62ff., 89ff.). Although he cried from the brink of **the grave** (lit., **Sheol,** as in NIV's margin) or the underworld, the repetition, **my cry came before him, into his ears,** emphasizes that distance in prayer is no problem and that the cry comes to Yahweh's personal attention. The place from which Yahweh **heard my voice** (not a silent prayer) is **his temple,** by which we would be inclined to think first of the Jerusalem temple, but the following theophany also points in another direction.

18:7–15 / Suddenly, with the insertion of a theophany, the perspective of the psalm shifts: there is no mention of the speaker (no "I" is here) and nothing but a passing reference to Yahweh's opponents (in v. 14 the Hb. text does not have **the enemies;** it only mentions "them"). Instead, all we see is the appearance of

God, who is depicted as God of the skies and of the thunderstorm. At this point, we do not look down to the underworld but up to the skies. The language is highly figurative (esp. v. 15) and by itself this theophany shares much in common with the imagery of Baal in the Ugaritic tablets (see Craigie, *Psalms 1–50*, p. 173). The psalmists sometimes drew on this popular imagery to assert that Yahweh, not Baal, was God of the skies. In striking departure from the Ugaritic texts, however, Yahweh's appearing has a clear salvific purpose, as the surrounding thanksgiving evidences. The Sinai theophany (Exod. 19) no doubt also had a key influence here.

The theophany begins with the earth's "quaking" response to his appearing. **He parted the heavens** (Hb. *šāmayim* also denotes "the skies") **and came down** in the midst of **dark clouds** (vv. 9, 11). Yet the poem also makes reference to **the brightness of his presence**—a seeming contradiction until we reckon with the mix of cloud and sun often seen in thunderstorms. The **bolts of lightning** (other sky phenomena related to heat and light are mentioned in vv. 8, 12), as the parallel line shows, are **his arrows,** thus presenting the God of the storm as a divine warrior. The wind is also felt in **the blast of breath from your nostrils,** also seen as a form of **rebuke. The voice of the Most High** is heard in the "thunder" **from heaven.** Thus, what we might regard as a mere thunderstorm, the ancient poets regarded as symbolic of Yahweh's dramatic intervention.

There is a striking tension in this poem where God is revealed yet also concealed, especially evident in the frequent mention of darkness. In fact, the closest we get to a description of Yahweh himself is verse 10, but even here only his vehicle is described: **He mounted the cherubim and flew; he soared on the wings of the wind.** While the latter phrase has an obvious counterpart in the skies, the former does not. This is the one image of the theophany that derives not from nature but from the Jerusalem temple. The cherubim figures above the ark served as both throne and chariot (see T. N. D. Mettinger, *In Search of God* [Philadelphia: Fortress, 1988], pp. 126–31), the latter function being prominent here. To make sense of this union of heavenly and temple imagery we need to recognize that the Jerusalem temple was a symbol both of Yahweh's dwelling in the midst of his people and of his palace in the skies/heavens (Hb. *šāmayim,* much as the church's worship symbolizes the worship of God in heaven). It is interesting to note that "dark clouds" (Hb. *ʿarāpel*) also have their counterpart in the temple (1 Kgs. 8:12). Thus, "his temple" in verse 6 is intentionally ambiguous. The same dual reference to Yahweh's dwelling may be found in another royal psalm, Psalm 20:2, 6.

18:16–19 / The thanksgiving now continues, picking up where verse 6 left off. Having heard the cry for help (v. 6), Yahweh now comes with saving action. So in contrast to the "narrow place" of **my** "distress" (the basic meaning of *ṣar* is "narrow[ness]," which comes to mean "distress"), **he brought me out into a spacious place.** Had verses 7–15 never appeared in the psalm, they would not have been missed. The reason for their insertion probably lies in the linking images of Yahweh's reaching **down from on high** and the threat of **deep waters** (also "the torrents" of v. 4). The mysterious "them" of verse 14 is thus explained by "my enemies" and **my foes** of verses 3 and 17. The effect of this insertion is to add drama to the thanksgiving. The God of the heavens can expose "the valleys of the sea" (v. 15), that is, the underworld (vv. 4–5). We have here not just another deliverance from death but a cosmic one. It will become plain once we get to verse 29 that the scene is one of a monumental battle.

18:20–27 / The traditional thanksgiving is now complete, and the psalm moves into a testimony of integrity, which is a motif drawn from another genre entirely. It is probably here to develop the meaning of "because he delighted in me" (v. 19). These verses thus have to do with character. To modern Christian ears, they smack of Pharisaic self-righteousness. But in their psalmic context, the terms used in this testimony of integrity are those found in the confessions of integrity, which were part of the temple entry liturgies (see the Introduction): **righteousness, cleanness of my hands, not done evil, blameless** (a regrettable translation of Hb. *tāmîm,* which points to "having integrity"), and **pure** (see esp. 15:2; 24:4; 26:1, 6, 11). (The chief difference between the two forms is that here Yahweh has already acknowledged the speaker's integrity. It is part of a thanksgiving and is thus a testimony.) These are not claims of moral perfection but affirmations that one embraces **the ways of the LORD** and that one is a "seeker" and "fearer" of Yahweh (see on Pss. 15; 24). They simply profess that one is a loyal adherent, as opposed one who rejects or disregards Yahweh and his ways. We cannot read this testimony as an expression of pride, for God saves **the humble but** brings **low those whose eyes are haughty.** In stark contrast to most leaders, the Davidic king must count himself alongside, literally, "a humble people" (Hb. ʿam-ʿānî, v. 27).

Although we notice first the speaker's claim to righteousness, the primary point of this section is to say something about God: **The LORD has** . . . (vv. 20, 24) and **to the faithful you** . . . (vv. 25–26). In other words, Yahweh has proven himself consistently faithful. It is also striking that here the king judges his own experience (vv. 20–24) by the experience of others (vv. 25–27). He has invoked no special privilege either here or in the preceding thanksgiving.

18:28–45 / Now the psalm shifts from a testimony of one's character to a military victory song. Implicit here is the moral responsibility of those who bear the sword. Key terms in verses 30–31 link this section to others (Yahweh's "way" is first mentioned in v. 21; **perfect** [Hb. *tāmîm*] is the same term as "blameless" in v. 23; **shield, refuge,** and **rock** are epithets first heard in v. 2 and are mentioned later in vv. 35, 46). Particularly enlightening is the observation that in verse 32 the psalm traces the earlier claim of "having integrity" (Hb. *tāmîm*, NIV "blameless," v. 23) to Yahweh's "giving integrity" (Hb. *wayyittēn tāmîm*) to **my way,** because **as for God, his way** has integrity (Hb. *tāmîm*, v. 30).

In this section we have the first clear reference to the psalm's military context: **With your help I can advance against a troop; with my God I can scale a wall.** In contrast to the theophany, which refers only to Yahweh in the third person (v. 15 addresses Yahweh directly, though its parallel in 2 Sam. 22:16 refers to him in the third person), this song is dominated by first and second persons (**he** is used, however, in vv. 30–34). While the theophany gives focus to divine intervention, and a dramatic one at that, this section gives attention to Yahweh's equipping (**you give me your shield of victory,** v. 35, and **you armed me with strength,** vv. 39 and 32) and training (**he trains my hands for battle,** v. 34) of his agent of victory. In addition, Yahweh influences his agent's circumstances and opponents so his victory would be complete: **You broaden the path beneath me, so that my ankles do not turn** and so **I pursued my enemies and crushed them** (vv. 36–38). **You made my enemies turn their backs in flight, and I destroyed my foes** (v. 40). The victory

Yahweh has effected through his agent is so complete that he claims, **you have made me the head of nations** (v. 43).

18:46–50 / Climaxing the psalm is hymnic praise and a vow to praise yet more widely. The essence of this praise is, **Exalted be God my Savior,** because he in turn **exalted me above my foes.** Yahweh's intervention far exceeds expectations: he provides not only deliverance (vv. 4–6, 16–19) but also victory and exaltation.

Psalm 18, a royal psalm of military victory, invites comparison with Psalm 89, a royal psalm of military defeat. It is interesting that in the face of defeat appeal is made to the special privileges Yahweh promised in the Davidic covenant, but in the face of victory attention is given to Yahweh's majestic appearing and the faithfulness he shows to every true worshiper. The fact that the king here speaks through literary motifs that express the faith of every worshiper shows that his relationship to Yahweh was like theirs. His experience of victory is presented as an example of hope for every worshiper.

Additional Notes §18

The antiquity of the psalm may well vouch for this psalm's actually being Davidic. The superscription itself implies the psalm does not reflect a single military victory but is summative in nature. In contrast to the 2 Sam. 22 version, this heading adds, "for the director of music," implying the psalm became the property of Israel's public liturgy, and was not just a personal poem of David.

18:22 / The only terms of the confession of vv. 20–24 (note the inclusio here) not echoed in the entry liturgies are found in the middle verse. "His judgments" (Hb. *mišpāṭāyw*, NIV **his laws**) and **his decrees** (Hb. *ḥuqqōtāyw*) find their closest parallel in 89:30–31, a royal psalm reciting the Davidic covenant. Although the version of the Davidic covenant in 2 Sam. 7 makes no such reference, these terms may point to "this law and these decrees" (Hb. *ḥuqqîm*) of Deut. 17:19. Verse 20 echoes the same notion observed here in Ps. 18, namely, that the king is to see himself no differently than he does his fellow citizens.

18:30 / **The word of the LORD** probably refers not to Scripture as we think of it but, in the context here of military engagement, to Yahweh's oracular word (cf. 1 Sam. 23:2, 4, 9–12; 30:8; 2 Sam. 5:23–24).

§19 God's Revelation in the Skies and the Scriptures (Ps. 19)

Perhaps more profoundly than any other OT passage, this psalm holds together two spheres of God's revelation that believers hold dear, namely creation and scripture. Natural and special revelation complement one another, "declaring" different facets of the one Revealer. Yet in this psalm it would appear the Revealer did not make this complementarity known to an author but to an editor, who joined together two or perhaps three compositions that were originally independent.

19:1–9 / Even in English translation verses 1–6 and 7–14 read like two separate compositions. Their poetic styles (esp. their metrical patterns), genres, and traditions (and perhaps time periods) are markedly different. Verses 1–6 appear to be a hymn about creation (cf. Pss. 8; 104), but they are unlike other psalmic hymns, which regularly contain a call to praise and address Yahweh directly. In fact, these verses reflect a background of the wider ancient Near East (e.g., the personification of **the sun;** the term for **God** in v. 1 is "El," a Semitic name for God held in common with other ancient Near Eastern peoples; see further Gerstenberger, *Psalms,* p. 101). Like Psalm 29, these verses may have been adopted from preexilic, non-Israelite poetry. Verses 7–10 are akin to the torah psalms (Pss. 1; 119), which reflect on the wonders of Yahweh's written instruction and stem from the wisdom tradition, probably in the postexilic period (on **the law of the LORD** cf. Ezra 7:10; Neh. 9:3). Unlike other psalms, **the fear of the LORD** here refers not to the attitude of faith in God but, in keeping with its parallel expressions, to the codified faith of written torah. Verses 11–14 alone address God directly and are most like the prayer psalms of the individual. Although these three sections bear some thematic links, they use different terms (noted below), thus implying the psalm is an edited unit, not an authored one (i.e., one where the poet would be free to choose his own echoing terms).

The psalm makes a remarkable journey from the general to
the particular in three stages: from the vastness of God's skies
(vv. 1–6) to Yahweh's law (vv. 7–10), and finally to the worshiper
himself (vv. 11–14). This threefold movement is also reflected in
the divine names: "God" (or "El"), **the LORD** (Yahweh), and **my
Rock and my Redeemer.** When we observe the thematic links
among these sections, we appreciate the complementarity of
God's natural and special revelation. As **the heavens . . . pour
forth speech** (Hb. *ʾōmer*, vv. 2–3), so God has spoken in "the law
of the LORD" (v. 7). In response, the speaker requests that his own
words (Hb. *ʾēmer*, v. 14) **be pleasing** to his Redeemer. As **the skies
. . . display knowledge** (v. 2), so **the statutes of** the LORD are described as **making wise the simple** (v. 7). **In the heavens he** has
provided the sun (v. 4), and **the commands of the LORD** give
light to the eyes (v. 8). As the sun is depicted as **rejoicing** (Hb.
śwś, v. 5), so **the precepts of the LORD** are described as **giving joy
to the heart** (Hb. *śmh*, v. 8), thus implying that when God's creatures follow his laws, whether natural or revealed, there is joy. As
nothing is hidden from the sun's **heat** (v. 6), so the speaker prays,
Forgive my hidden faults (v. 12).

The differences between these two spheres of revelation
should also be noted. The heavens, in particular, **declare . . . glory**
and knowledge. Although this creation section makes no mention of human respondents, the torah section repeatedly notes
the immediate effects of Yahweh's written revelation on the individual (**reviving the soul,** etc.). While God's creation in the skies
may move one to awe, it is **the ordinances of the LORD** that are
more valuable **than gold** and that warn Yahweh's **servant.** They
lead him finally to petition Yahweh's forgiveness and to own
Yahweh as his Redeemer. Yahweh's revelation leads not merely
to awe and fear of natural powers, nor to legalistic religion, but to
a relationship so personal and cherished that one's desire is
simply to be pleasing **in** Yahweh's **sight.**

§20 Intercession for the King Before Battle (Ps. 20)

Both Psalms 20 and 21 are royal liturgies (as implied by the changing speakers and addressees observed below). Psalm 20 appears to be an intercession for the king before battle (esp. vv. 5, 7–8), and Psalm 21 is a thanksgiving on the king's behalf either after battle victory or in anticipation of it. Psalm 20 may have been intoned at the temple, not only before particular battles as they arose, but as part of the regular liturgy "in the spring, at the time when kings go off to war" (2 Sam. 11:1).

Both psalms make abundantly clear that the king's power is not absolute but derived—from Yahweh (esp. 20:1–2, 7; 21:1, 5, 7, 9, 13). While some Psalms scholars have made much of the king's role in the temple's liturgies and rituals (even making him *the* central figure at festivals), we must observe that although the king is the primary subject in these two psalms, he is at no point a speaker in either liturgy. Prayer for victory and thanksgiving for victory are both made on his behalf by someone else. (See further discussion in the Introduction.)

20:1–5 / These verses are an intercession throughout (to be consistent with the other Hb. jussives, the cohortative of v. 5a should also be rendered as a wish, "May we shout for joy"), where the king is addressed directly **(you)** in the form of a wish where Yahweh is the subject of the action **(May the LORD answer you . . .)**. Special significance is attached to **the name of God** (vv. 1, 5, 7), probably because Yahweh's name was a key rallying point for Israel's army (e.g., 1 Sam. 17:45; Pss. 44:5; 118:10–12). Explicit references to **the sanctuary** on **Zion** and to the king's **sacrifices** and **burnt offerings** exhibit the psalm's attachment to temple rituals and testify to their importance. Ritual sacrifice may have been part of the psalm's liturgical performance. (On sacrifices offered before battle see 1 Sam. 7:9–10; 13:9–12.) Yet the psalm also makes clear that ritual sacrifice in no way manipulates or binds the God of Israel to act favorably on the worshiper's behalf, even if that worshiper is a king. Yahweh's freedom is affirmed by the fact that his acceptance of these offerings is petitioned, not presumed. Given Yahweh's acceptance of the king's sacrifices, however, the psalm also reflects a give-and-take relationship: as the king gives his offerings, so **may he** (Yahweh) **give you** (the king) **the desire of your heart.**

The psalm is careful to circumscribe the king's exalted position not only with respect to God (as noted above) but also with respect to his subjects. His desire (v. 4) and **requests** (v. 5) have special significance only because they have bearing on the welfare of his people: "May *we* shout for joy in *your* victories" (lit., NIV **we will shout for joy when you are victorious,** v. 5). He is the object of their intercession because their well-being is bound up with his. The parallelism of the psalm's closing petition underscores this (v. 9): petition for the king is also a petition for **us.** In other words, our calling and the king's requests (vv. 4–5) are to be one and the same. The king in Israel has significance, not in his own right, but because he is empowered by God and because he represents the people.

20:6–8 / In these verses, we hear a liturgist (**I**, v. 6) speaking on the people's behalf (**we**, vv. 7–9). Neither Yahweh (**the LORD**) nor the king (**his anointed,** Hb. *mᵉšîḥô*) are addressed directly, so these verses appear to function as a confession of trust or a testimony addressed to and on behalf of the congregation. The opening **Now** implies a decisive moment in the liturgy, and the affirmation, "I" **know that the LORD saves** his anointed, may imply the liturgist is a temple prophet, announcing the intercession has been heard.

In response to the earlier petition, "May the LORD answer you . . . . May he send you help from the sanctuary (lit. 'holy place') and grant you support from Zion" (vv. 1–2), is the assurance, **he answers him from his holy heaven** (v. 6). In these parallel expressions we gain insight into the function of Zion's temple: it is both Yahweh's dwelling in the midst of his people and symbolic of Yahweh's dwelling in heaven. We should not imagine Yahweh dwelling in two different places at the same time; rather the temple was the gate of heaven, so to speak.

Verse 7 contains what may be the most profound biblical revelation concerning power: **Some trust in chariots and some in horses, but we trust** (better to read "will prevail") **in the name of** the LORD **our God.** This confession is both disarming and empowering. It recognizes the reality of military might but also implicitly takes hold of a superior power. This belief is fundamental to Deuteronomy (20:1–4), which presents itself as Moses' speeches to Israel prior to the conquest of Canaan. Here the king was explicitly forbidden to "acquire great numbers of horses" (17:16). Insofar as the state of Israel exercised military force, it did so not by virtue of its military armaments but by virtue of its faith in Yahweh.

The ultimate consequences of this choice could not be more opposed: **They . . . fall, but we rise up.** We should not infer, however, that the psalm presumes the victory will be straightforward and without cost. We need to recognize that the Hebrew verb (Hithpolel of ʿwd) behind the NIV's "we . . . **stand firm**" really denotes "we restore ourselves" or "we help each other up" (see W. L. Holladay, *A Concise Hebrew and Aramaic Lexicon of the Old Testament* [Grand Rapids: Eerdmans, 1971], p. 267).

20:9 / The liturgy closes by turning to Yahweh, for the first time, in a summarizing petition. It is interesting to note that it requests what was earlier affirmed as true ("the LORD saves his anointed; he answers him," v. 6): **O LORD, save the king! Answer** "**us.**" This repetition should alert us to something fundamental about Israel's faith and liturgy. The affirmation of a belief does not mean that the belief thereby becomes a reality and that God will automatically ensure its realization. Its becoming a reality remains dependent on the relationship between believer and God, wherein the believer must turn to God and address him with a request. (In contrast to conceptions that are more Greek or Western, where truth and reality are considered as states of being in their own right, the conception of the Hb. Bible views truth and reality in a predominantly relational context, that is, between God and humans. The Hb. term closest to what we tend to mean by "truth" is ʾᵉmet, which is more accurately translated "constancy, reliability, fidelity" [see Holladay, *Hebrew Lexicon*, p. 22; *TDOT*, vol. 1, pp. 309–16, 322–23].)

§21 Thanksgiving for the King's Victories in Battle (Ps. 21)

Psalm 21 contains praise in response to God's answering the intercession for the king in Psalm 20. While it may be a thanksgiving after battle victory, it is more probably a thanksgiving in anticipation of it, inspired by a prophetic oracle claiming that the intercession of Psalm 20 has been heard. This psalm also testifies that the king's power derives from Yahweh (21:1, 5, 7, 9, 13).

21:1–6 / The liturgy begins by addressing Yahweh directly with a thanksgiving that appears to respond to Yahweh's answering the intercession of Psalm 20. **You have granted him the desire of his heart,** as requested earlier, "May he give you the desire of your heart" (20:4, cf. also 21:2b and 20:5b). At the forefront is the celebration of *Yahweh's* strength, as a literal translation of verse 1 shows, "Yahweh, in your strength the king rejoices." The **blessings** here bestowed upon the king are not automatic, nor are they the king's divine right. Rather, Yahweh has "granted him" (Hb. *nātattâ lô* in both vv. 2 and 4) these blessings in response to specific requests from the king (**the request of his lips** in v. 2 and **he asked you** in v. 4). (The interplay of the king's "asking" [Hb. *šʾl*] and Yahweh's "giving" [Hb. *ntn*] is prominent in 20:4–5; 21:4; 2:8.) In other words, these qualities derive directly from the king's personal relationship with Yahweh. The confession, **you . . . made him glad with the joy of your presence** (lit. "your face," v. 6) highlights this intimacy.

21:7 / This verse appears to address neither **the LORD** nor **the king;** both are referred to in the third person. It therefore appears to serve as a transitional testimony to the congregation (cf. the function of vv. 6–8 in Ps. 20), as the liturgy moves from thanksgiving addressed to Yahweh to an oracle addressed to the king. The parallelism of the verse moves from cause (v. 7a) to effect (v. 7b). The divine title, **Most High,** serves as a reminder to the king of the hierarchy of power. The term **unfailing love** (Hb. *ḥesed*) may echo the Davidic covenant (89:24, 28, 33, 49; 2 Sam. 7:15; note also "for ever" in v. 4 and 2 Sam. 7:13, 16).

21:8–12 / In what appears to be a divine oracle the king is told of the power he may wield against his **enemies** and **foes** (lit. "haters"). In the middle of this promise Yahweh is made the subject: **in his wrath the LORD will swallow them up.** Thus, the king does what he does because he is enabled by God. The enemies' character is made plain by expressions like **they plot evil against you and devise wicked schemes.** Verse 10, with its reference to destroying **their posterity,** makes modern readers uncomfortable. But we must recall here the underlying assumption that generations often reproduce after their own kind. Evil begetting evil becomes particularly ruthless when the family is a royal family in power over others (see on 137:8–9).

21:13 / As in Psalm 20, this psalm closes with a petition addressed to Yahweh, except here it rings with praise: **Be exalted, O LORD.** In a psalm celebrating the king's successes, this desire that Yahweh be the one ultimately exalted stands out in bold relief. Similarly, as the liturgy opened with attention to **your strength,** so it closes. Yahweh's power, not the king's, is to be the focus of the congregation's interest.

Additional Note §21

21:4, 6 / We should not presume that preexilic Israel was here praying that the king receive eternal life. Within the horizons of OT, the terms themselves, **for ever and ever,** generally denote for a "long time" (Holladay, *Hebrew Lexicon,* p. 267; see, e.g., 1 Sam. 27:12), not necessarily beyond one's lifespan. We must also keep in mind, however, that the Davidic king represents not just himself but also the Davidic dynasty. To this extent, such prayers go beyond an individual lifespan (2 Sam. 7:29). In addition, we can see—with the advantage of our post-Easter retrospect—that this language can, in fact, be stretched to extend to eternity. Israel's king messiah will, in fact, live "for ever and ever!"

§22 My God, My God, Why Have You Forsaken Me? (Ps. 22)

This is an extraordinary psalm that takes us to the extremes. Its haunting words, "My God, my God, why have you forsaken me?" were quoted by Jesus on the cross. It develops from an individual in the dust of death (v. 15) to universal acknowledgment of the kingdom of God. In the lament we read "all who see me mock me" (v. 7) and "all my bones are out of joint" (v. 14), but in the praise sections we hear, "All you descendants of Jacob, honor him!" (v. 23), "All the ends of the earth will . . . turn to the LORD" (v. 27), and it even appears that all the dead will worship (v. 29, see below). This psalm is particularly powerful for Christians, and it is virtually impossible to hear it without overtones of Christ's passion and resurrection. Yet we would be the poorer if we did not also try to hear it within its earlier OT contexts. God's word is often multidimensional and multilevel. Even if the final application of a scripture is as sublime as this one, it does not exclude the significance of earlier applications. In addition, it is not only the final product of scripture that is revelational; the process is as well.

It is this psalm's extraordinary and unique character that creates both problems and possibilities for interpreters. The conclusion argued in the Additional Notes below is that verses 1–21 formed an originally independent prayer psalm of the individual. In the exilic period, it was also used as a vehicle for the personified people of Israel to express their grief. In the late exilic or early postexilic periods, the praises of verses 22–31 were attached to express Judah's thanksgiving for their restoration from exile and the promise of the nations' praising Yahweh.

The prayer (vv. 1–21) shows no clear ritual or liturgical connections. As with most, its presupposed situation is open-ended. It makes great use of imagery, some of which is suited to sickness (note esp. the desiccation, or total dryness, in vv. 14–15, 17).

Enemies are prominent but the actions clearly attributed to them
are not of direct attack but of scorn (vv. 6–8). With this scorn, they
surround the speaker and await his death (vv. 12–13, 16–18). In the
three psalms most explicitly connected with sickness (38, 41, 88),
there is social alienation (38:11; 88:8, 18) and enemies who talk of
harm (38:12) and slander while awaiting the speaker's death
(41:5–9). On the other hand, the possible mention of their "pierc-
ing his hands and feet," and the references to the sword and the
dividing of garments (vv. 16–20), may depict an execution. One
may speculate on their interrelationships (e.g., his illness led to
the inference of divine punishment and of his guilt, or his desiccation was caused by an imprisonment in turn caused by false accusations) but the evidence does not allow one to be conclusive.

22:1–2 / **My God, my God, why have you forsaken me?**
are familiar words that both haunt us and remind us of the costly
salvation Christ achieved through the cross. Unlike most prayer
psalms this one contains and opens with a lament pointed at God
himself. These opening verses introduce the two chief problems
faced in the psalm, both having to do with God. First, there is
his remoteness, **Why are you so far** "from my cry for help?" (see
Additional Notes), a theme that is developed in verses 11–21
(marked off by the repeated "do not be far"). Second and related,
there is his silence at the speaker's cries, **I cry out . . . but you do
not answer;** this theme is developed in verses 3–10 (also marked
off by the repeated confession of **my God**).

22:3–5 / These verses sound like hymnic praise and a
reference to God's earlier saving deeds in their own right. In the
context of this psalm, as we shall see, they serve to heighten the
anomaly of God's silence. Yahweh is **the praise of Israel,** whose
praise consists of how **in you our fathers put their trust, cried to
you, and you delivered them.**

22:6–8 / The contrast with the preceding story of "our
fathers" is striking: **But I am a worm and not a man.** People
scorn the speaker, saying: **"He trusts in the Lord; let the
Lord deliver him"** (the same word used for Yahweh's "delivering" of "our fathers" in v. 4). It is not unusual for enemies to be
quoted in prayer psalms, but in this case the speaker agrees with
their logic! The history of the fathers has established a precedent, that if one trusts in Yahweh, Yahweh should deliver him.
In contrast to other citations of opponents, this one does not

misrepresent either God or the speaker; rather it is a "dare" that they wage.

22:9–10 / By themselves, these verses sound like a confession of trust again or a reference to earlier saving deeds (cf. vv. 4–5), though on the level of personal, not corporate, experience. But again they actually heighten the anomaly developed in the preceding verses. They serve as evidence that Yahweh has, in fact, "delighted in him," as the taunters have said, and that he has trusted in Yahweh, as his fathers had. And thus, Yahweh should "answer" when "I cry out" (v. 2), just as he had for the forefathers and just as the mockers have dared. Thus, verses 3–5 and 9–10 are not attempts to console the speaker but are arguments presented to God.

This psalm illustrates well for us the assumptions that underlie the relationship between Yahweh and the speaker in the individual prayer psalms. The theology of this relationship may be encapsulated in the title **my God** (vv. 1, 2, 10; see further the section on "My God" in the Introduction). The obligations implicit upon the speaker are to **trust** (v. 4 [2x], vv. 5, 9), to cry out for help (vv. 1, 2, 5), and to praise God once delivered (vv. 3, 22). The obligations implicit upon Yahweh are to delight in the individual (v. 8 and implied in vv. 9–10; note the antonyms in the post-deliverance reflections of v. 24, "not despised or disdained"), to hear his cries for help (implied in vv. 1–2, and again note v. 24, "has listened," Hb. *šmᶜ*), and to deliver him (vv. 4–5, 8, 19–21). The intimacy of this relationship is most poignantly illustrated in the speaker's birth story (cf. 71:5–6; 139:13–16), where Yahweh is depicted as midwife: **you brought me out of the womb.** There is even a parallel drawn between the speaker's mother and Yahweh: as the speaker was at (Hb. *ᶜal*) **my mother's breast** after being "brought . . . out of the womb," so **from birth** (lit. "womb") **I was cast upon** (Hb. *ᶜal*) **you.** Paradoxically the trust that the individual is to place in "my God"—even this is traced back to Yahweh: **you made me trust in you.**

22:11–18 / In this section, petitions addressing the problem of God's remoteness (cf. v. 1) surround a lament of the deepest order: **do not be far from me, for trouble is near** (vv. 11, 19). In the lament concerning the foes, wild animals **(strong bulls, roaring lions,** and **dogs),** possibly with mythic or demonic overtones (see Keel, *Symbolism,* pp. 86–88), surround the speaker. In verse 16b, the imagery shifts to humans encircling the speaker, either at his deathbed or execution (possibly suggested by the phrase, **they have pierced my hands and my feet,** and by "the sword" in v. 20). They apparently count him as good as dead: **They divide my garments among them and cast lots for my clothing.** The I-lament describes extreme desiccation, without water and without life (vv. 14–15, 17). The lament concerning God is the briefest of the three (v. 15c), but it is at the very heart of this literary section (vv. 11–18) and at the very heart of the theological problem. The one who has sapped him of life and made him vulnerable to ferocious attack is God himself: **you lay me in the dust of death.**

22:19–21 / The petitions of the psalm are familiar ones. **Deliver my life** echoes the taunt or dare of the enemies in verse 8. The same images of the opponents are employed as in the preceding section, first as humans **(the sword),** then as wild beasts, here listed in reverse order **(dogs, lions,** and **wild oxen).**

22:22–26 / As a typical vow of praise, verse 22 rounds off the prayer, but as a proclamation of praise it also introduces the thanksgiving (see the Introduction). In prayer psalms, the vow normally has attached to it a single verse of thanksgiving given in anticipation of the deliverance (as perhaps in v. 24). But here the actual thanksgiving is developed at length. The praise is to be performed formally **in the congregation.** (As noted below in the Additional Notes, it is possible we should understand vv. 23–24, 26 to be in quotation marks and are thus promised praise, not actual praise.) Verse 23 is an imperative call to praise, normally part of corporate hymnic praise but it can also found in a thanksgiving of an individual (30:4). It is striking, however, that the command is issued to **all . . . Israel.** The actual report of the distress and deliverance is brief and a stunning about-face from the opening lament (v. 24). By claiming God **has listened to his cry for help,** this retrospective report, in effect, withdraws the insinuation that God had been "far from my cry for help" (see Additional Note on 22:1). Yet we must note that this psalm allows for the expressing and venting of such feelings of forsakenness while in the midst of distress. Though perhaps not "theologically correct," they are not censored. Verse 25 may be a second vow of future praise **(will I fulfill my vows)** or simply part of the thanksgiving where the speaker announces his intention now to perform his vows (i.e., "I [now] fulfill my vows"). (See further on 116:12–19. The Hb. imperfect verb can denote present or future action.)

The reference to eating may seem strange (v. 26) until we recognize that thanksgiving in the OT often included a thanksgiving sacrifice, which was to be shared, as it were, as a communal meal with Yahweh, the priests, and the worshiper's family (Lev. 7:15–16; Deut. 12:5–7; 1 Sam. 1:3–4, 9). Deuteronomy 16:10–17 implies that society's **poor** may also share in the offerings of those especially blessed. The exclamation, **may your hearts live forever,** appears to be addressed to the worshiper's guests at the thanksgiving meal. Because of this direct address, it is probably best to read the verbs of verses 25–26 in the present tense.

22:27–31 / These verses have an affinity to the psalms of Yahweh's kingship, where **all the families of the nations** (cf. 96:7) **bow down** (cf. 96:9, where "worship" translates the same Hb. verb, also 99:5, 9) before Yahweh and **all the ends of the earth** (cf. 98:3) acknowledge that he **rules over the nations** (cf. 47:8). (Cf. also 22:31 and 97:6.) They differ, however, in that 22:27–31 promises future actions of worship that the nations will undertake, whereas the Yahweh kingship psalms issue commands to the nations to undertake these actions of worship. But in both cases their worship appears to be in response to both past acts of God (suggested by **remember** in 22:27) and present and future realities (regarding Yahweh's kingship in 22:28 and his righteousness in v. 31). (In 96:10, the acclamation, "The LORD reigns," is evidenced in past and future acts of God. In 98:1–4 and 7–9, the world responds to both past and future revelations of Yahweh's righteous acts.)

Here in Psalm 22, Yahweh's worship takes on vast, universal proportions, with respect to both geography and time. It will extend across the entire globe (note the repeated **all** in v. 27). Further, it will extend into future generations (vv. 30–31) and most remarkably—here Psalm 22 goes beyond any other psalm—into past generations. Even the dead, **all who go down to the dust, will kneel before him.** In verse 29, we should probably read, "all who sleep in the earth will bow down" (see the Additional Notes; in the OT only Dan. 12:2; Isa. 26:19 come close to this). This is a striking revelation, especially in light of earlier psalms that claim, "It is not the dead who praise the LORD" (115:17; cf. 6:5; 30:9; 88:10–12).

Our exploration of Psalm 22 in its OT contexts has uncovered its singular character and perhaps reasons why it is heard on the very lips of Jesus. By taking up the words, "My God, my God, why have you forsaken me?" (Matt. 27:46, see also vv. 35, 39, 43), he becomes the lamenter par excellence. No other individual prayer psalm is as dark as this one (aside from Ps. 88, which complains of lifelong suffering and would be inappropriate to Jesus). Our exploration has also uncovered the developments in the psalm's usage. It was used to express not only an individual's lament and prayer but also a nation's lament and praise for restoration from captivity. Now with our post–Easter vision, we can see that it foreshadows both the resurrection of an individual, that is, the Christ and the resurrection of his people, that is, the church. Its original composers obviously said more than they knew. Our exploration has also uncovered the psalm's remarkable development of key OT themes, particularly because God's saving act celebrated in the psalm reverberates not only to "all the ends of the earth" and to **future generations** but also to the dead. Finally, a question heard throughout the prayer psalms, "Do you show your wonders to the dead? Do those who are dead rise up and praise you?" (88:10), can be answered in the affirmative.

Additional Notes §22

22:1–31 / When read in light of other psalms, vv. 1–21 sound like a prayer psalm, and vv. 22–26 sound like a thanksgiving psalm. The closest analogies to vv. 27–31 are the psalms of Yahweh's kingship (Pss. 47; 93; 96–99). As separate psalms we could more readily understand these verses, but how are we to make sense of their combination? Did these sections originally belong together as a single psalm, or were they added in stages? Whether they originally formed a unit or not, they are now part of a single psalm, so how do these distinct genres and their functions work together?

Verses 27–31 show no direct verbal or thematic connections with the rest of the psalm (Hb. *zera^c*, **descendants** or **posterity,** in vv. 23, 30 is the only exception), so there is nothing in their contents to suggest the nations are responding directly to the speaker's deliverance. If the prayer (vv. 1–21) and the thanksgiving (vv. 22–26) were originally together and we give priority to the prayer, they would form a prayer with an extended vow of praise. This, however, is largely unparalleled in the Psalms. In support of this possibility, we should note that in the thanksgiving only vv. 22 and 25, both of which appear to be vows of praise, are addressed directly to Yahweh, which has been the pattern throughout the prayer. They thus may introduce quotations of the kind of praise vowed to be performed. If so, vv. 23–24, 26 should be put in quotation marks and regarded as praise said in anticipation. On the other hand, if we give priority to the thanksgiving, the prayer would function as a "recollection of the distress." But there are no clear examples of this elsewhere in the Psalms. It is conceivable the prayer had a dual function: during the actual distress it could be performed as a prayer and after the deliverance as a recollection. Yet another possibility comes from observing that v. 24 does not go so far as to claim actual deliverance has taken place; it simply asserts that God **has listened to** (lit. "heard") **his cry for help.** Thus, given the liturgical setting of many psalms, it is possible that an intervening oracle of salvation was delivered by a temple prophet between vv. 21 and 22. Verses 22–24 would then be a thanksgiving for the oracle and vv. 25–26 would vow thanksgiving once the actual deliverance had come. (This could well be the reason the Hb. verb, *ʿᵃnîtānî,* "you have heard," as noted in the NIV margin, is in the perfect. On the other hand, this verb could be explained as a "precative perfect." See I. W. Provan, "Past, Present and Future in Lamentations iii 52–66: The Case for a Precative Perfect Re-examined," *VT* 41 [1991], pp. 164–75.)

Each of these theories is possible, but they cannot be proven. It would be best to seek any comparable psalms to see if they can shed any additional light. Psalm 69 is another lengthy prayer that also laments near-death distress, and social alienation and mockery. To this prayer are attached praises and promises that contain some striking parallels to those in Ps. 22. In both there are vows (22:22; 69:30), the claim that Yahweh does not "despise" (Hb. *bzh*) the afflicted but "hears" (Hb. *šmʿ*) them (22:24; 69:33), allusions to a thanksgiving ceremony where "the poor" (Hb. *ʿᵃnāwîm*) and the "seeker" (Hb. *dōrᵉšîm*) of God are enjoined "may your hearts live" (22:26; 69:32), references to universal praise (22:27–31; 69:34) that parallel the psalms of Yahweh's kingship (cf. 69:34 and 96:11; 98:7), and descriptions of future worship (22:27–31) and future praiseworthy (69:35–36) actions of God. This commentary notes that 69:33, 35–36 make clear reference to Judah's restoration after the Babylonian exile. Another lengthy combination of prayer, praise, and promise that also refers to the restoration from exile is Ps. 102. Like Ps. 22, it laments near-death desiccation as well as social alienation and mockery, all of which are traced back to God (vv. 3–11, 23). Like Ps. 22, its praises and promises refer to Yahweh as king (22:28; 102:12), his consequent worship by both Israel and the nations (22:23, 27; 102:15, 21–22), and the transmission of his praise to the next "generation" (Hb. *dôr,* 22:30; 102:18). Like both Pss. 22 and 69, it claims that Yahweh does not "despise" (Hb. *bzh*) the afflicted but "hears" (Hb. *šmʿ*) them (vv. 17, 20). We should also note Ps. 51, which is another individual prayer to which is attached concern for Judah's restoration after exile and the attending thanksgiving offerings (vv. 18–19). Finally, we should also observe that Lamentations combines features of the individual prayer psalm (Lam. 3) with corporate prayers (esp.

Lam. 5) in a lengthy lament over Jerusalem's destruction and a prayer for its restoration.

In light of the analogies of Pss. 51, 69, and 102, it seems most likely that Ps. 22 consists of an individual prayer psalm to which were later attached praises and promises concerning the restoration of the nation (see further J. Becker, *Israel deutet seine Psalmen: Urform und Neuinterpretation in den Psalmen* [SBS 18; Stuttgart: Katholisches Bibelwerk, 1966], pp. 49–53). If so, vv. 1–21 (or thereabouts) originally functioned like any other prayer psalm of the individual. Then, in the exile the individual prayer was used as a vehicle for the personified nation to express its grief. Zech. 7:5 indicates that lament rituals, including fasting (note vv. 14–15, 17 in our psalm), were observed during the exile. In the late exilic or early postexilic periods, the praises of vv. 23–31 were attached to express Israel's thanksgiving and anticipations. This may have been done in two distinct stages: first there was added the thanksgiving psalm to express Israel's praise (vv. 23–26) and then the promises of the nations' praise, which are akin to the psalms of Yahweh's kingship (vv. 27–31).

22:1 / **From saving me:** The NIV follows the MT's *mîšû'ātî,* but we should probably read, *miššaw'ātî,* "from my cry for help," which suits the parallelism and train of thought better.

22:16 / **They have pierced:** It is difficult to make sense of the MT's "like a lion (Hb. *kā'ărî*) my hands and feet." Two MT MSS read *kārû,* "they have dug," perhaps figuratively for "pierced." This is supported by the LXX's *ōruxan* (Gk. 21:17).

22:29 / **All the rich of the earth will feast and worship:** The MT has "all the fat (Hb. *dišnê*) of the earth." The NIV paraphrases this expression to refer to "the rich," but there are no instances in the OT where it is used as a designation for the rich (though it is tempting to provide a complement to "the poor" in v. 26). Instead we should probably read "sleepers" (Hb. *y'šēnê,* cf. Dan. 12:2) because it suits the parallelism of the verse. The MT also has "they have eaten and bowed down" (Hb. *'āk'lû wayyištaḥªwû,* see BHS), a Hb. perfect that the NIV simply transposes into the future. Instead we should probably read, "Surely to him will they bow down" (Hb. *'ak lô yištaḥªwû*).

§23 My Shepherd and My Host (Ps. 23)

23:1–6 / Psalm 23 is a favorite for many, largely because it unveils an intensely intimate relationship with the Lord wherein he provides protection and providence. Yet, as familiar as this psalm is, there is more than first appears. It is not a tranquil psalm, as many assume. We must observe its intent: it affirms what the Lord provides; it does not pretend to report on worshipers' circumstances (note **the LORD** is the grammatical subject). What he provides is peaceable, but the echoes we get of what life may bring our way may be quite disturbing. We may **walk through the valley of the shadow of death** and we must affirm, **I will fear no evil,** because we are tempted to fear. We confess, **I shall not be in want,** because we fear we shall. The confession, **he leads me beside quiet waters,** has meaning because many dangers—including **my enemies**—threaten to sap us of life. **He restores my soul,** indicates that there are times when it becomes weary. Our shepherd provides for and protects "the sheep" but he does not fabricate a world free from hardship.

Psalm 23 is a psalm of journey and of nourishment, both along the way and at the final destination. When we think of believers on a journey, we think of pilgrimage, and that is probably the situation portrayed here. Several psalms link the temple with the motif of shepherd and sheep (28:2, 9; 74:1; 79:13; 95:7; 100:3–4). Perhaps in the pilgrimage festivals there was the conception of Yahweh as shepherd gathering his people as sheep into his temple, which acts as a sheepfold. Elsewhere the temple is designated an "abode," a term associated with the abode of the shepherd and sheep (Hb. *nwh,* related to the same term for **pastures** in 23:2; see 83:12; 93:5; Exod. 15:13; 2 Sam. 15:25; Isa. 33:20; Jer. 31:23; see BDB, p. 627). It is perhaps no accident that Psalm 23 shares several terms and motifs with Psalm 65: flocks of sheep in their pastures (Hb. *neʾôt,* 23:1–2; "grasslands" in 65:12–13), Yahweh's waters (23:2; 65:9) and **paths** (Hb. *maʿgāl,* 23:3; paraphrased as "carts" in 65:11), the notion of abundance depicted by images of fat (Hb. *dšn,* **anoint** in 23:5; "abundance" in 65:11) and saturation (Hb. *rwh,* **overflows** in 23:5; "drench" in 65:10), and dwelling at Yahweh's **house,** where one is satisfied with his **goodness** (23:5–6; 65:4). Psalm 65 was probably sung at one of the major agricultural festivals when God's people offered their thanksgiving sacrifices. The **cup** and **table** of Psalm 23 may not be merely metaphoric. They depict a meal, and being at **the** house **of the LORD** they probably allude to the thanksgiving offering, which was to be shared as a communal meal with Yahweh, the priests, and the worshiper's family (Lev. 7:15–16; Deut. 12:5–7; 1 Sam. 1:3–4, 9; cf. Pss. 22:26; 36:8; 63:2–5). Psalm 116, sung in connection with a thanksgiving sacrifice, similarly confesses, "I lift up the cup of salvation" (see vv. 13, 17–18), probably referring to a drink offering. Psalm 23 was thus a pilgrim psalm anticipating the worship rituals at the Jerusalem temple.

Most commentators perceive two images in this psalm: Yahweh as shepherd (vv. 1–4) and as host at the temple (vv. 5–6). In both roles, Yahweh provides nourishment (vv. 1–3a, 5) and safe passage (vv. 3b–4, 6). The former provision is implicit in the absence of want for the sheep, to whom the shepherd gives pasture, water, and restored vigor, and it is implicit in the second section in the table prepared by the divine host. The provision of safe passage is clear from God's **rod** and **staff** that **comfort** "through the valley of the shadow of death" (cf. Mic. 7:14) and it is implicit in the phrase, **Surely** goodness **and love** (i.e., not "my enemies") **will** "pursue" (lit.) **me.** The opening (vv. 1–3) and closing (v. 6) verses refer to Yahweh in the third person while the middle verses (vv. 4–5), which overlap the images of him as shepherd and host, are praise addressed to him. Thus, the psalm opens and closes with testimony about God, and the praise to God in the middle ties together the two roles Yahweh plays.

While Psalm 23 is an intensely personal psalm, it may also echo Israel's corporate experience of God (adapted from Craigie, *Psalms 1–50,* pp. 206–7, who also refers to articles by D. N. Freedman and P. Milne):

Ps. 23: "The LORD is my *shepherd*" (v. 1).	Ps. 80: God is addressed as "*Shepherd* of Israel" (v. 1) in a psalm alluding to the exodus-wilderness-conquest (esp. vv. 8–11).
"You are *with* me" (v. 4).	Deut. 2:7: During the wilderness years . . .

"I shall *lack nothing*" (v. 1).	"The LORD your God has been *with* you, and you have *lacked nothing*."
"... green *pastures* (Hb. *n*^{e}*'ôt*), he *leads* me" (v. 2).	Exod. 15:13: Israel sang at the Reed Sea.
"He *guides* me" (v. 3).	"You will *lead* ... You will *guide* them to your holy *dwelling* (Hb. *n*^{e}*wê*)."
"He leads me beside *quiet* (Hb. *m*^{e}*nûḥôt*) waters" (v. 2).	Num. 10:33: During the wilderness journeys "the ark of the covenant of the LORD went before them ... to find them *a place to rest* (Hb. *m*^{e}*nûḥâ*)."
"He guides me ... *for his name's sake*" (v. 3).	Ps. 106:8: At the Reed Sea Yahweh "saved them *for his name's sake.*"
"Even though I walk through the valley of *the shadow of death*" (v. 4).	Jer. 2:6: The "wilderness" through which Yahweh led Israel after Egypt is described as "a land of ... *the shadow of death.*"
"You *prepare a table* before me in the presence of my enemies" (v. 5).	Ps. 78:19: After leaving Egypt Israel "spoke against God, saying, 'Can God *prepare a table* in the desert?'"

The psalm may thus draw a parallel between the historical experience of Yahweh's shepherding Israel through the wilderness to his future house on Zion and the ritual experience of Yahweh's shepherding pilgrims to his house on Zion. If so, the richness of the psalm is enhanced because we now see the individual's experience of Yahweh as part of a larger whole. We should also probably understand "my enemies" as any who have and would oppose the people of God as they seek to worship Yahweh at his temple.

Additional Notes §23

23:1 / **The LORD is my shepherd:** This famous psalm is sometimes called "the shepherd psalm," but it is not the only passage to characterize Yahweh as shepherd (see Pss. 28:9; 80:1; Gen. 49:24; Isa. 40:11; Hos. 4:16; Mic. 7:14) and his people as his sheep (Pss. 74:1; 77:20; 78:52; 79:13; 95:7; 100:3; Jer. 23:3; Ezek. 34:11–16; Zech. 9:16). The distinctive word of this psalm is not "shepherd" but "my." Elsewhere Yahweh is the shepherd of his people, but here he is the shepherd of the individual (cf. Gen. 48:15).

23:6 / **I will dwell:** The NIV here follows the LXX and the parallel in 27:4 (Hb. *šibtî*). But in keeping with the dominant theme of journey and pilgrimage the MT's "I will return" (Hb. *šabtî*) is probably the correct reading.

§24 A Victory Procession and Instruction for Temple Entry (Ps. 24)

It is difficult to make sense of what is going on in Psalm 24 without acquaintance with ancient Near Eastern traditions and Israelite ritual worship. Who is involved in the dialogue concerning Yahweh's entry in verses 7–10? Why is there such interest in his militaristic qualities? And what does this have to do with his establishing the earth on water (an odd conception!) in verses 1–2, and what does any of this have to do with prerequisites for worship that sound so legalistic?

The occasion of the psalm is Yahweh's victory procession entering his temple-palace. A liturgist opens with a shout of victory over the forces of chaos, whereby all creatures are liberated under his kingship (vv. 1–2). But before the victory procession can begin, would-be celebrators ask who may join (v. 3). A liturgist replies: those who have aligned themselves toward this ordering God are those whose actions and motives are pure and who do not ally themselves to falsehood (v. 4). A promise is also given: these pilgrims will receive Yahweh's righteousness (vv. 5–6). Only then does the actual procession through the temple gates begin, wherein a new title for Yahweh is proclaimed. First, the procession commands the gates to open for the King of glory (vv. 7, 9). Then the gatekeepers inquire about his identity (vv. 8a, 10a). Once he is identified as "Yahweh of hosts, the warrior" (lit., vv. 8b, 10b), the procession proceeds.

24:1–2 / Modern readers are bound to look at verse 2 as prescientific naïveté. But this reaction, in fact, reflects on our own naïveté regarding ancient imagery. This poem employs the ancient Near Eastern motif of the divine warrior who becomes king by virtue of his victory over chaotic waters (see the Introduction). This background helps us to make sense of the strange claim, **he founded it upon the seas** (Hb. *yammîm*) **and established it upon the waters** (lit. "rivers," Hb. *nehārôt*). In the

Canaanite epic the storm god, Baal, becomes king once he van-
quishes Prince Sea *(Yam)*–Judge River *(Nahar)*. His dual name
contains the same word pair we see here. Thus, in language familiar to the ancients, Psalm 24 sings of Yahweh's right to divine
kingship.

We can now also understand the point of verse one. What
may sound to modern readers like a confession of Yahweh's pos-
sessiveness is, in fact, a proclamation of victory and of liberty for
the world, and all who live in it. The point is not that "the earth
belongs to Yahweh" but that "*to Yahweh* the earth belongs," not to
chaos (this is the word order in the Hb. text). The issue is not possession but *who* possesses it. These verses are no mere doctrinal
confession; they are a victory shout. (This is similar to the point
of the confession, "*Jesus* is lord." He is lord, not death, human ty-
rants, principalities and powers, etc.)

Also contrary to the expectations of most modern readers,
Yahweh's kingship is not described as a static state but is portrayed as a dynamic victory. The ancient Near Eastern motif of divine kingship also helps us to make sense of the divine roles in
verses 7–10. Because he had vanquished the seas (v. 2), "Yahweh of
(the military) hosts" (NIV "the LORD Almighty," v. 10), "a warrior
(Hb. *gibbôr*) mighty in battle" (v. 8), is now the King of glory
(vv. 7–10) over all the world (v. 1). These verses alert us to the fact
that creation order is not a given, rather Yahweh must continue to
exert his heroic strength to maintain it. This is a message that we in
the nuclear and environmentally critical age must take to heart.

24:3–6 / Now why is this victory celebration that consistently runs through verses 1–2 and 7–10 interrupted by verses
3–6 with their moral conditions for worshiping Yahweh? If
verses 7–10 had immediately followed verses 1–2, it is doubtful
we would notice anything was missing. The answer is twofold:
these verses describe Yahweh's worshipers, and his worshipers
are also presented as a reflection of Yahweh himself. (A god may
be known by the kind of worshipers he/she desires.) Yahweh
has proved himself the victor, but is this good news and if so,
for whom? These verses thus explain the character of the conqueror: he is the kind who would be king over a society based on
truth. As in all victory celebrations, this one is selective. Only for
those on the conqueror's side is it a victory celebration. These
verses thus spell out those who are truly aligned with Yahweh.
They answer the question, "Who may participate in this victory

procession?" Yahweh's temple or royal palace symbolized the achievement of world order (see the Introduction). Thus, only those who conform to Yahweh's right order may enter his royal palace. We can also see verses 3–6 linked to the rest by the motif of entry into the temple area. Yahweh is about to enter his temple-palace, so who now may join him? These verses reflect a temple entrance liturgy (see the Introduction). The threefold pattern of inquiry (v. 3), conditions (v. 4), and a promise (vv. 5–6) is echoed in Psalm 15 and Isaiah 33:14b–16. Our psalm shows us that this liturgy has its place in corporate worship and in a ritual procession in particular. Corresponding to Yahweh's "ascent" (Hb. *ʿlh;* see the comments on 47:5; 68:18) in the procession, symbolized by the cherubim-ark, was the worshipers' "ascent" (Hb. *ʿlh*). A liturgist on behalf of the worshipers in procession thus asks, **Who may ascend the hill of the LORD?** The following priestly instruction or "torah" contains two positive descriptions of character, the first related to behavior **(he who has clean hands)** and the second to thoughts and motives **(and a pure heart).** These are matched by two negative descriptions of action: "who does not lift up his soul to what is empty (Hb. *šāwʾ*) and does not swear to falsehood" (lit.). These phrases are ambiguous, perhaps intentionally so, whether they forbid vain pursuits and lying/perjury in general or forbid appealing to idols (so NIV) and false gods in particular. The former phrase is used in the opening of the next psalm, which endorses lifting one's soul *to Yahweh* (25:1, also 86:4; 143:8). These qualifications for entering the temple are obviously not meant to be an exhaustive checklist, but they are a teaching that makes clear what is essential by a contrast: one is to be "clean" (lit. "innocent") and "pure" and not characterized by "vanity" or "falsehood." Yahweh's adherents are people of integrity, that is, they are loyal to truth and integrate themselves around it. They are loyal to God and have no intention of harming or misleading their neighbor.

We Christians may be uncomfortable with any such prerequisites for coming before God. But Jesus was unequivocal on this point: "the kind of worshipers the Father seeks" are "the true worshipers" who "worship the Father in spirit and truth" (John 4:23). And we should not be misled into thinking Psalm 24 allows into God's house only "the righteous" who live with utter blamelessness. It is unfortunate the NIV translates the promise of verse 5 as **He will receive . . . vindication from God his Savior,** because it is better to translate as "he will receive righteousness" (Hb. $\bar{s}^e d\bar{a}q\hat{a}$). The psalm is clear that the person so described in verse 4 is in need of a Savior and in need of righteousness. (The doctrine of imputed righteousness was not invented by Paul!) Thus, if one is in need of Yahweh's "saving righteousness," then it follows that the standards of verse 4 are not absolute and ultimate. In other words, one must not claim moral perfection before one can consider entering. On the contrary, to receive this righteousness from "God his Savior" one must enter into worship. Upon entry worshipers were granted righteousness and became one of "the righteous."

After the inquiry (v. 3), the description of Yahweh's worshiper (v. 4), and the consequent promise (v. 5), verse 6 follows either as a conclusion to the preceding description (as suggested by the NIV's **Such is . . .**) or as a declaration about the particular group of worshipers now assembled in the festal procession. A literal translation, "This is the generation of those who seek him," reveals that "this" could refer either to the description in verses 4–5 or to the participating congregation. Thus, verse 6 may be the pronouncement (by either a priest or a spokesman on behalf of the procession) that this group qualifies to proceed in the procession. But whether it refers to the description or to the worshipers, the terms used to define such people are very telling: they are those **who seek** God. The bottom line an entrant must profess is, "I am a seeker of Yahweh." This is a claim of willingness, not perfection. Thus, "the righteous" are so called, not because they claim inner moral perfection but because Yahweh grants his "righteousness" to all genuine seekers of his face at the temple. To be sure, seekers must exhibit some conformity to the prescriptions of verse 4, but not absolute conformity.

The use of the terms "to seek" (Hb. *drš* and *bqš*) Yahweh in this context of a processional at the temple also implies that they indicate not merely seeking God in a general spiritual sense (as in prayer) but more specifically making a pilgrimage to participate in the worship at Yahweh's temple. But as is typical of the Psalms, the temple with all its symbols, rituals, and sacred words is never allowed to overshadow the spiritual reality to which these symbols point, namely God himself. The object of seeking is clear: the **face** of the **God of Jacob.** Personal encounter is essential to worship (cf. Amos 5:4–6). It is striking that the OT insists on continuing to use this phrase in light of other assertions that no one can "see" God's face and live (Exod. 33:20) and especially in light of its possible ambiguity regarding worshiping with an image of the deity. Its survival can probably be traced to its powerful presentation of this notion of personal encounter with God.

24:7–10 / Verses 7–10 make sense only in light of a procession. The picture of gates' being required to open so Yahweh may enter requires some physical symbol of his presence. The most likely possibility is the cherubim-ark. The particular name of God used as a "password" through the gates, "Yahweh of hosts" (NIV **the LORD Almighty**), confirms this theory (see esp. 1 Sam. 4:4; 2 Sam. 6:2). The depiction of Yahweh as **mighty in battle** (lit. "a warrior of war") also suits both the cherubim-ark symbol (see esp. Num. 10:35; Josh. 6:4–13) and the name "Yahweh of (military) hosts."

In these verses we hear different voices: those in procession behind the cherubim-ark and the gatekeepers. The procession issues the command for the gates to open **that the King of glory may come in.** The questioning reply of the gatekeepers implies this title is unknown to them. The first answer from the procession is "Yahweh, a warrior (or hero) of war." This dialogue is repeated, perhaps for dramatic effect and certainly to highlight the climactic name, "Yahweh of hosts." We may presume that once this identification was made the gates opened. Now Yahweh may be known by a new title: he is not only a military hero ("Yahweh of hosts") but also a royal sovereign **(the King of glory).**

Precise dating of psalms is notoriously tenuous, but this one shows some strong affinities to the time of David. David's "bringing up" (Hb. ʿlh in 2 Sam. 6:2, 12, 15, the same verb used for "ascend" in Ps. 24:3) the ark into Jerusalem for the first time is an obvious parallel to our psalm. Whether it was sung on this occasion or later sung regularly to commemorate this occasion, we cannot be certain. On the other hand, verses 7–10 do make it sound as though this was the first occasion on which the titles "Yahweh of hosts" (one prominent at the Shiloh sanctuary; see 1 Sam. 4:4; again 2 Sam. 6:2) and **King of glory** ("King" was a prominent title in the Jerusalem sanctuary) were linked.

Psalm 24 has much to contribute theologically, as already noted. One of the most striking ideas is that worship of Yahweh does not take place just in a religious realm. It is integrally connected with our day-to-day social behavior (vv. 3–6) and with the entire cosmic order (vv. 1–2, 7–10). "Yahweh of hosts" (v. 10), "the hero in war" (v. 8), and the King of glory (vv. 7–10) over the world is also the "God of Jacob" (i.e., of the nation, v. 6) and "God his Savior" (i.e., savior of each individual, v. 5). In other ancient Near Eastern religions each individual has his personal God, alongside the patron god of the state and other gods of nature. But Yahweh is all of these. Psalm 24 calls for worship that is ecologically aware, that is, which sees the cosmos fitted together under Yahweh's kingship—not "naturally" but only by the exertion of his heroic strength. And we also see that Yahweh's created order is to be reflected in his people (see esp. v. 4)—a realization that is vital in our age of disintegration, where nuclear, environmental, and social crises face us daily.

Additional Notes §24

24:4 / **Swear by what is false:** In the OT the Hb. phrase *nišbaʿl* is used of both swearing to a deity and of swearing falsely. Yahweh can be the object of the preposition, meaning that one is swearing (allegiance) to God (e.g., Isa. 45:23; 19:18). But "falsehood" (Hb. *šeqer,* a synonym of *mirmâ*) can also be the object of the preposition in the context of swearing by Yahweh: "Although they say, 'As surely as the LORD lives,' still they are swearing falsely" (Jer. 5:2).

Who does not lift up his soul to an idol: The MT reads "who does not lift up *my* soul in vain," which sounds odd to our ears until we look at a literal translation of the Third Commandment: "You shall not lift up the name of Yahweh your God in vain" (Exod. 20:7). The MT may therefore have the correct reading.

24:5 / **He will receive blessing from the LORD:** A more literal translation reveals the possibility that this verse refers to the offering of sacrifice: "he will lift up a blessing (received) from Yahweh, and righteousness (received) from his saving God" (perhaps a pregnant use of the Hb. preposition *min*). Cf. the command, *"lift up* an offering" (96:8).

24:6 / **Your face, O God of Jacob:** With the LXX we should probably read, "the face of the God of Jacob." Hb. *ʾlhy* may have been omitted by haplography either with *pny* or with *mʾlhy* in the verse immediately above.

§25 A Wisdom Prayer for Those Who Fear the Lord (Ps. 25)

Psalm 25 is like the prayer psalms of the individual, but several features make it unusual. It is an acrostic, that is, its verses begin with the successive letters of the Hebrew alphabet. Many of them concern instruction and guidance in God's ways (vv. 4–5, 8–10, 12). Both of these features are prominent in psalms reflecting wisdom influence (Pss. 34; 37; 112; 119). "Fearing" the Lord (vv. 25:12, 14) is also a recurring motif in wisdom psalms (19:9; 34:7, 9, 11; 112:1; Ps. 119, five times; cf. 145:19), though not exclusive to them. The concern for inheriting the land is an important motif in Psalm 37 (vv. 9, 11, 22, 29, 34). Psalm 25 also reflects a keen awareness of personal sin (vv. 7, 11, 18). Generally among the psalms, those that speak of sin as part of the general human condition (i.e., its mention is not connected with a current sickness or affliction) stem from the time of the exile or shortly thereafter (Ps. 51; and 79:9; 103:10).

The rhetorical question, "Who, then, is the man that fears the LORD?" (v. 12), may imply an audience is present during the psalm's performance. Because it combines both petition on behalf of the individual speaker and instruction to a group, he may function as a representative or liturgist. "My enemies" (v. 2) may not refer to a particular party but simply to any who would distract "the man that fears the LORD" from following his way.

25:1–7 / As the word order makes plain, the emphasis of the opening verses lies on the object of the speaker's trust: **To you, O LORD, I lift up my soul.** What the first three verses clearly seek to avoid is **shame** (three times). Yahweh is thus being implored to vindicate—publicly—the trust placed in him. The phrase, **whose hope is in you,** is more literally, "who wait for you" (so also in vv. 5, 21). This posture thus emphasizes dependence on God for any change in the speaker's circumstances. In the midst of **my enemies** who would **triumph over me** are petitions for direction and instruction: **Show me your ways, O LORD, teach me your paths.** These are not requests seeking God's will, as though it were an itinerary for daily decision-making. The psalm spells out these general terms of "ways" and "paths" with more specific references to **your truth** and, as unfolded in verses 8–10, to "what is right," to "ways" that "are loving and faithful," and to "his covenant." The psalm seeks general guidance for proper conduct in relationships with God and people. This need for divine direction in the midst of **enemies** who **are treacherous** is particularly acute because of **my rebellious ways.** If the speaker wants to have a relationship with the LORD, who is characteristically good and upright (v. 8), then the LORD must **remember** his **great mercy . . . from of old** and so **remember not . . .** the speaker's rebellious ways.

25:8–11 / These verses hymn the very attributes and characteristic behaviors of Yahweh that the speaker has just petitioned for himself, referring to the LORD as **good** (vv. 7, 8), to his **ways** (vv. 4, 8) and paths (v. 4), to his guiding (vv. 5, 9) and teaching (vv. 4, 5, 9), and to his truth or **faithful**ness (Hb. *ʾemet* in both vv. 5, 10). Thus, the petitions of verses 4–7 seek to ensure that the speaker, though having "rebellious ways," may be counted among those Yahweh instructs, who—fortunately for the speaker (and us!)—are designated as both **the humble** *and* **sinners.** Yahweh's character determines the content of his teaching: being **good and upright, he instructs . . . in what is right.** Verse 11 rounds off this half of the psalm with another reference to Yahweh's forgiving **my iniquity.** The Hebrew text may be rendered either as a continuation of the praise ("you will forgive") or as a petition (as in the NIV). Remarkably, Yahweh is the kind of deity for whom forgiveness actually upholds his **name** or reputation (**for the sake of your** "name"); it is not a denial of it. For Yahweh to maintain his reputation he need not disassociate himself from those who shame it.

25:12–15 / The psalm again turns from the speaker's personal concerns to general claims of what Yahweh does for **the man that fears the LORD.** Again, attention is given to Yahweh's instructing, not sinners (v. 8) this time, but "the man that fears the LORD." The rewards of this homage are now promised: **He will spend his days in** "goodness" (Hb. *tôb*, a term that can include material goods but need not connote **prosperity,** as the NIV puts it). The most remarkable reward, however, is, that **the LORD**

confides in (Hb. *sôd*, lit. "Yahweh's confidential counsel/intimacy is for") **those who fear him.** Verse 14 makes clear that **his covenant** is not a mere document to be read, but one with which Yahweh himself acts as tutor. Yahweh, in effect, takes the believer into his confidence. Closing this section of praise is the speaker's affirmation of loyalty: **my eyes are ever on the LORD.** Its supporting reason, namely that Yahweh is rescuer, also acts as a bridge to the following petitions.

25:16–21 / These verses are typical of prayer psalms, petitioning Yahweh to **be gracious, look** (or probably "attend to," if one reads *qᵉšōb* in v. 18 to restore the acrostic, instead of Hb. *rᵉʾê,* which is probably a scribal dittograph from the following v.), and **rescue,** etc., and again to **take away all my sins.** Further, they lament "loneliness," **troubles,** and increasing **enemies,** who **fiercely** (lit. "violently") **hate.** The closing verses round off the psalm by echoing its opening, as they petition, **let me not be put to shame** (cf. v. 2), and by affirming that **my hope is in you** (cf. v. 5) and that Yahweh's **uprightness** exhibits itself in watching over God's people (cf. v. 8).

25:22 / The final verse lies outside the acrostic (which ended in v. 21 with the Hb. letter *tāw,* "*t*") and, unlike the others, is a petition for the corporate body: **redeem Israel, O God, from all their troubles** (cf. v. 17).

§26 Walking in Integrity and Loving the Lord's House (Ps. 26)

It seems remarkable, if not strange, that one should invite God to judge and examine him (vv. 1–2). The reason given with this invitation, "for I have led a blameless life," hardly encourages us to identify with the speaker or even endorse such claims to righteousness. But we must allow him more than one verse to explain himself. We must first note that at some points the NIV translation is misleading. "Blameless life" (v. 1) is a questionable translation for the Hebrew term *tummî* in verses 1 and 11, for it connotes absolute moral purity. A more literal rendering in each verse is "I *in my integrity* (have) walk(ed)." The Hebrew term denotes integrated wholeness. This assertion is not intended as grounds for boasting because it is followed immediately with "redeem me and be merciful to me" (v. 11). "Without wavering" (v. 1) is also misleading for it implies the speaker points solely to his own abilities. A more literal translation, "in the LORD have I trusted; *I do not slip*," helps us to see the ambiguity, perhaps intentional, that his steadfastness is as much attributable to Yahweh as to his own trust. The word order also shows that emphasis is not given to the speaker's action of trusting but to the object of trust (this explains why reference is made to the name of the Lord, even though he is the addressee). We should also note he asserts his stability most forcibly, "my feet stand on level ground" (v. 12), only after his petition, "redeem me and be merciful to me" (v. 11). Finally, truth (v. 3) connotes for us an absolute standard, but *ʾemet* for the ancient Hebrew, especially when it was specified as Yahweh's and used in connection with his love, denotes "faithfulness" and "reliability." Thus, this second reason for the invitation for Yahweh's judgment (note "for" in vv. 1a, 3a) points primarily to merciful and protective attributes of God, not to the speaker himself.

What is this psalm about? Most commentators read it as an individual lament, and others more specifically as a psalm of the

falsely accused. But it contains no lament of enemies who single
out the speaker for attack (similarly Pss. 5; 28; 36; 52). The wicked
are given mention in two places in the psalm. Verses 4–5 confess
a rejection of evil company and more specifically, "I do not
enter" (Hb. *bw*ʾ, NIV "consort") or "sit" in "the assembly of evildoers." This contrasts with the great assembly in which the praise of
Yahweh is heard (v. 12). The ritual actions confessed in verses 6–8
appear to have been performed at the entrance of Yahweh's
house. The washing of hands was probably done at a font of holy
water at the entry to the shrine (see Keel, *Symbolism*, pp. 123, 127,
395). The altar was also at its entrance (so Lev. 1:3, 5). The
psalm thus uses these wicked as a foil to confess one's loyalty to
Yahweh's worship. Thus the sense is, "in contrast to entering
their assemblies I choose to enter Yahweh's."

The second mention of the wicked appears in verses 9–10,
where the speaker requests, "Do not take away my soul along
with sinners." The place from which he does not want to be removed is apparent from the preceding verse ("I love the" house
"where you live") and from the closing verse (in the great assembly "I will praise the LORD"). The psalm does not ask for judgment
on them—which appears to be a given—but only that Yahweh
redeems the speaker from that impending doom (v. 11). In both instances the wicked are given mention simply as a contrast to the
speaker's desire to participate in the praise of God at the temple.

That Psalm 26 has to do with entering Yahweh's temple is
confirmed by some striking parallels with Psalms 15 and 24, both
liturgies of temple entrance (see the Introduction). Psalm 26 appears to endorse what these psalms prescribe as qualifications
for temple entry. In this light we begin to grasp the importance of
walking in integrity (NIV "led a blameless life," 26:1, 11 // 15:2), of
"truth" and the "heart" (26:2–3 // 15:2; 24:4), of avoiding "vanity"
(NIV "deceitful," 26:4 // 24:4, NIV "an idol"), of "innocent hands"
(26:6 // 24:4, NIV "clean hands"), and of the "place of the tent of
your glory" (26:8 // 24:3, 7–10; 15:1, "Who may 'tent' on your holy
hill?"). We may also understand why bribes are specially mentioned here (in the Psalms, Hb. *šōḥad* appears only in 26:10 and
15:5). These parallels may also explain why attention is given to
the motif of stability at the psalm's close (26:12 // 15:5). Also to be
noted are several other parallels with the liturgies of temple
entry (see the Introduction), especially Psalm 5: the importance
of hating evil (26:5 // 5:5) and of confessing one's affinity to
Yahweh's house (26:8 // 5:7), the image of bloodthirsty men

(26:9 // 5:6) and of what one puts "before one's eyes" (NIV "before me," 26:3 // 15:4, lit. "despised in his eyes"; 36:1–2; cf. 5:5), and a judgment that distinguishes the fates of the speaker and the wicked (26:1, 9 // 5:8, 10). These psalms of temple entry emphasize the reverse of Psalms 15 and 24, that is, the exclusion of the wicked from Yahweh's holy place (5:4–6, 10; see also 36:1–4, 7–12; 52:1–6, 8). The petition, "Do not take away my soul along with sinners," is very similar to the one found in 28:3. Thus, the concern for the wicked evident in Psalm 26 stems not from the supposed circumstances of the liturgist but from the entry liturgy itself. In light of the above, it seems to have been composed not for lone individuals who happen to be accused falsely but for any pilgrim as a response to the entry instruction ("torah") found in Psalms 15 and 24.

Psalm 26 opens with a petition that Yahweh judge the pilgrim—a judgment that is prerequisite for entering the sanctuary (vv. 1–2). He declares his loyalty to Yahweh's assembly, in part by disclaiming any association with "the assembly of evildoers" (vv. 3–8). He then petitions Yahweh to recognize his integrity and so distinguish him from such people, and to "be merciful" to him in his judgment (vv. 9–11). In closing, he vows praise to God (v. 12), thus implying that other psalms followed this one in the larger liturgy. Key terms help to interlock these sections. The claim of "walking in integrity" (NIV "a blameless life") underlies the two petition sections related to judgment (vv. 1–2 and vv. 9–11). And references to assemblies and to Yahweh's praise tie together verses 3–8 with verse 12.

26:1–2 / Vindicate me (v. 1) is a fitting translation for the Hebrew word, *šopṭēnî*, if one reads the psalm as a psalm of the falsely accused. But "judge me" is more appropriate, because the purpose of the psalm is not to acquit the speaker before personal accusers but to establish before Yahweh that he meets the qualifications to "stand in his holy place" (24:3; cf. 15:1). As noted in the Introduction, a judgment is presupposed in these liturgies. The pilgrim's confessed love for "the place where your glory dwells" (v. 8) compels him to undergo the prescribed examination, without which he may not enter the holy place. Verse 9 confirms that a judgment is presupposed: God will judge sinners, whether invited to do so or not. Hence, the speaker requests that his trial may proceed now to distinguish his fate from theirs. That Yahweh alone is qualified to be the judge is evident from the data to be examined: **my heart and my mind** (lit. "my kidneys and my heart"), that is, the innermost and secret parts of human personality. The issue is not mere behavior (i.e., one's walk and speech) but "what makes one tick." (This invitation contrasts with the character of "hypocrites," lit. "the hidden ones," from whom the speaker dissociates himself.)

26:3–8 / In verses 3–8 the speaker presents his case. Verse 3 begins with the divine attributes that define his guiding goal **(your love is ever before me)** and the process he follows **(I walk continually in your truth)**. Verses 4–8 unpack this general claim in specific terms of ritual actions. The speaker disclaims entering and sitting in **the assembly of evildoers** (note that only the human participants are named, not the supposed deities they worship) and confesses his desire to participate in the rites of entering Yahweh's house. As **I abhor** (lit. "hate") "the assembly of evildoers" (v. 5), so **I love the house where you live, O LORD** (v. 8). In verse 8 there surfaces the attitude motivating the pilgrim, and in verse 7 his ultimate intention: **proclaiming aloud your praise and telling of all your wonderful deeds.**

26:9–11 / The petitions of verses 9 and 11 seek to distinguish the speaker from **sinners** by Yahweh's "redeeming" and "being merciful," so he may "stand on level ground" and "praise the LORD in the great assembly." The request, **Do not take away my soul along with** sinners, reflects the fear of the holy, noted in 15:1 and 24:3. Supporting these petitions is a contrast of behaviors. While those described in verses 3–8 are primarily religious (i.e., concerning rituals and assemblies of worship), those mentioned in verses 9–10 are social, focusing especially on one's treatment of innocent people. But we must note that claims to a distinct lifestyle do not entitle one by right to enter Yahweh's worshiping assembly. The psalm's ultimate appeal is to Yahweh's merciful redemption.

If we assumed verses 9–10 merely referred to a particular group of opponents in ancient Israelite society, the psalm's use would be limited to those circumstances. But the description probably derives from the character profile of the wicked developed within the temple entry liturgies, which instruct worshipers about Yahweh's way. This profile was constructed as the opposite to the character profile of the righteous: contrasting with the speaker's hands washed "in innocence" (v. 6, note also the "innocent hands" of 24:4) are the hands of sinners, which are full of **wicked schemes** and **bribes.** The entry liturgy of Psalm 15 prescribes that would-be entrants despise vile company and honor fearers of Yahweh (v. 4). Thus, Psalm 26 should not be restricted to individuals who are actually persecuted by **bloodthirsty men.** On the contrary, through this psalm, all pilgrims are asked to confess their loyalty to Yahweh by disassociating themselves from evildoers.

26:12 / Between the petitions of verse 11 and the affirmation of standing **on level ground** and **in the great assembly,** there may have been a pause as the speaker or liturgist actually entered the sacred precincts. The psalm's closing echoes its opening. As "I have walked in my integrity" (v. 1), so "I do/will walk in my integrity" (v. 11). As "I do not slip" because "I have trusted in the LORD" (v. 1), so **my feet stand** on level ground because I **praise the LORD** (v. 12). The speaker thus repeats (cf. v. 7) his ultimate intention of praising (lit. "blessing") Yahweh. It is probable that the larger liturgy of which Psalm 26 was a part was followed by the performance of praise psalms.

The key factor in this case of judgment is not absolute moral purity—it is a question of allegiance: is one loyal to the assembly of the wicked or to the assembly of Yahweh's worshipers? It is about loyalty, not legalism. We must not read verses 4–5 as a reflection of "holier-than-thou" attitudes because verses 9–11 echo with "There but for the grace of God go I."

In sum, Psalm 26 petitions Yahweh to verify the pilgrim's loyalty to Yahweh's worship and mercifully to redeem him from the judgment of the wicked made plain in the liturgies of temple entrance. In them there was dramatized the separation of the two ways, for those who may enter and those who may not. Psalm 26 shares similarities with Psalm 139, where Yahweh is petitioned to judge the speaker and where the wicked do not pose a direct, personal threat but by contrast demonstrate his loyalty to Yahweh.

§27 Seeking Security in the House of the Lord (Ps. 27)

When compared with others, Psalm 27 reads like two distinct psalms: one of testimony or confidence, perhaps occasioned by military threat (vv. 1–6), and one of prayer, perhaps occasioned by false accusation (vv. 7–14). A testimony or confession of trust is usually part of a prayer psalm, but some psalms of testimony stand on their own without expressing any petition (Pss. 11; 16; 23; 62; 63; 91). It seems odd the psalm should first make confident assertions about Yahweh's protection but then petition him repeatedly, "Do not reject me or forsake me" and "do not turn me over to . . . my foes."

Several observations, however, should incline us to read this psalm as a unit. First, key terms and phrases appear in both sections, thus linking them together: Yahweh as "(the God of) my salvation" (Hb. $yi\check{s}^{\epsilon}\hat{\imath}$, vv. 1, 9), "my foes" (vv. 2, 12), "heart" (vv. 3, 8, 14), hostilities "rise up against me" (Hb. $qwm\ ^{\epsilon}ly/by$, vv. 3, 12), "I seek" Yahweh's presence (vv. 4, 8), and the term "life/living" (Hb. $\d{h}yym$, vv. 4, 13). Second, there are other psalms that make confessions of trust and also petition Yahweh to ensure their realization (20:6 and 9; 28:8 and 9; 31:2 and 3; 33:5, 18, and 22; 71:3a and 3b; 128:1–4 and 5–6; 139:1, 10, 16, and 23–24). These psalms do not presume that Yahweh's promises will automatically become reality. Third, both sections of Psalm 27 contain hints of a pilgrimage: to "seek your face" and to "dwell in the house of the LORD" and there to "sacrifice with shouts of joy" (vv. 4–6, 8). Like verse 12 of our psalm, Psalm 43, which clearly is a pilgrim psalm, uses language normally associated with a legal court, petitioning God to judge and "plead my cause against . . . deceitful and wicked men" (43:1). It similarly prays for God to "lead" or "guide" (both Hb. $n\d{h}h$ in 27:11 and 43:3) "to your holy mountain." This petition for guidance in Psalm 27 is very similar to the one in Psalm 5:8; both use a comparatively rare term for the opponents (Hb. $\check{s}\hat{o}r^{e}ray$,

"oppressors" in 27:11 and "enemies" in 5:8). In both cases the
petition, lead "me in a straight path," appears to have particular
reference to the pilgrims entering the temple. Fourth, closer examination of the first half will reveal that it confesses the faith
that one resolves to attain, not that one has attained. In this light,
petitions to ensure one's relationship with God, as found in the
second half, are an appropriate complement.

So it is entirely possible that Psalm 27 reflects the regular
concerns of making a pilgrimage to enter the temple to meet
with God. We should, however, be wary of trying to pin down
such a psalm too precisely and too definitely, because it consists
largely of formulaic (i.e., common) phrases found scattered
among many other prayer psalms (see Craigie, *Psalms 1–50*, 233;
R. C. Culley, *Oral Formulaic Language in the Biblical Psalms* [To-
ronto: University of Toronto Press, 1967], p. 103). Since these
psalms reflect a variety of recurring distresses, it is likely this
psalm was composed for a wide spectrum of circumstances.

The closing testimony and exhortation (vv. 13–14) imply
some kind of audience is present during the psalm's performance. It may thus be a liturgy, first confessing Yahweh as the
petitioner's security from attack (vv. 1–3), then expressing his intent to seek for that security (vv. 4–6), and then petitioning
Yahweh for that security (vv. 7–12). Only the psalm's petitions
are addressed to Yahweh (vv. 7–9, 11–12); the rest of the psalm—
the confessions of trust and the closing exhortation—refers to
him in the third person, and is thus probably addressed to the
audience. As we shall see, there unfolds a clear logic in the development of the psalm.

27:1–6 / The rhetorical questions of the opening verse
raise the issue of fear: **whom shall I fear?** The cause of fear is represented by the image of a besieging army (vv. 2–3). The NIV's
phrase, **even then will I be confident,** is literally, "in *this* I trust."
The "this" is not the **war** of verse 3 (as implied by the NIV) but the
object of trust, which is spelled out in the following verses. Verses
4–6 unpack the opening confession of Yahweh as **the stronghold
of my life.** Here we learn that the referent behind the image of
military defense is **the house of the LORD. There he will keep me
safe. A rock** can be both an image of a secure military position (cf.
18:2; 31:2; 94:22) and an allusion to the rock on which Yahweh's
temple is founded, as the parallelism of verse 5 suggests (**his
dwelling, his tabernacle;** see further on 28:1; 61:2–4). The loca-

tion at which **my head will be exalted above the enemies who surround me** is specified as **at his tabernacle.** There the speaker will not be engaged in activities of military defense but of worship **(I sacrifice).** Thus, the military language of the opening verses does not report on the speaker's actual circumstances; rather the verses are an image depicting severe threat, from which the secure height of the temple mount provides refuge.

Modern readers often imagine sacrifice to be an onerous duty or to be mere ritual. But here it is accompanied by **shouts of joy.** Sacrifice was clearly not a silent ritual but was accompanied by psalm-singing **(I will sing and make music to the LORD).**

Verse 4 is one of the most profound and intimate of the Psalter: **One thing I ask of the LORD, this is what I seek: that I may dwell in** the house of the LORD . . . **to gaze upon the beauty of the LORD** (cf. 16:11, where "pleasures" translates the same Hb. root as "beauty"). It is this verse that ties the two halves of the psalm together. Verse 8 in the second half uses the same verb to describe the speaker's intent: "Your face, LORD, I will seek." Though phrased as statements of resolve, these verses also describe a request, one that is explicitly expressed in the petitions of verses 7–12. Thus, we read too much into verses 1–6 if we assume they are meant to report a composer's actual feelings of confidence. Rather, they express a trust that a worshiper should resolve to adopt. To paraphrase the closing line of verse 3: "in the security of Yahweh's temple I am determined to trust." Because the point of verses 1–6 is to lead the worshiper to resolve to trust in Yahweh's provision of sanctuary (not to publish that one possesses a bold faith), we can see that the petitions of verses 7–12 follow as a logical sequence.

27:7–12 / The psalm's formulaic language, noted above, is particularly concentrated here. These verses stack together common petitions to ensure the bond between Yahweh and worshiper is maintained, especially in the midst of dire threat. Psalm 71 uses similar negative petitions (vv. 9, 12, 18) in connection with extended confessions of trust (vv. 5–8, 14–17, 19). In the middle of these petitions stands a testimony that Yahweh has a stronger bond to the worshiper than one's own parents (v. 10). Other prayers of the individual refer to the bond the worshiper has with his personal God as existing from birth (22:9–10; 71:5–6, both of which are followed by negative petitions; 139:13–16).

We should not read the statement, **for false witnesses** (Hb. ʿēdê-šeqer) **rise up against me,** as a report identifying the particular threat against the speaker. The language of the psalm is formulaic and so collects together various phrases and images from recurring occasions of distress. Verse 4 uses the same verbal expression but a different image: "though war *arise against* me" (lit.). The psalms when describing the wicked opponents characteristically point to their speech (all using Hb. *šeqer:* 31:18; 52:3; 63:11, also a pilgrim psalm; 101:7; 120:2; 144:8, 11). Among the Ten Commandments, the one that addresses evil speech prohibits "false witness" (Hb. ʿēd šeqer, Exod. 20:16).

27:13–14 / After making petition to Yahweh, the psalm closes with a testimony about Yahweh. As the speaker has expressed his intent "to gaze upon the beauty of the LORD . . . in his temple" (v. 4), so he **will see the goodness of the LORD in the land of the living** (i.e., beyond the confines of the temple). The psalm closes with an exhortation, one very similar to that closing Psalm 31 (cf. also 55:22), to **wait for the LORD.** Such advice can be the most frustrating for eager, anxious, or impatient believers until they themselves feel, and actually are, desperately powerless; then it becomes the deepest source of hope. While the exhortation implies believers are powerless in themselves to make a difference, it also implies the powerless are not helpless: Yahweh will act on their behalf.

§28 To Be Spared from the Lord's Judgment on the Wicked (Ps. 28)

If we attempt to explain this psalm's development on purely literary grounds, we will be frustrated because psalms were also governed by liturgical and ritual considerations. Otherwise, how do we explain the following features? (a) The psalm shifts between addressing Yahweh directly (vv. 1–4, 9) and referring to him in the third person (vv. 5–8). (b) Without explanation, the speaker shifts from praying, "Hear my cry for mercy" (v. 2), to asserting, "he has heard my cry for mercy" (v. 6). (c) In verses 1–4, the psalm petitions Yahweh to hear, to exclude the speaker from the fate of the wicked, and to give the wicked their just reward. But once the speaker announces that Yahweh has heard this cry for mercy, he expresses the realization that now Yahweh is his strength and shield and that he is helped. How do the negative petitions result in these positive benefits for the speaker? (d) In a psalm devoted to the speaking "I" through verse 8, the closing verses shift to God's people. As we shall see, reading the psalm as a liturgy performed before God's Most Holy Place (v. 2, i.e., the Holy of Holies) makes the best sense. It may reflect more than one speaker: a liturgist representing worshipers recites the opening prayer (vv. 1–4); a priest or prophet, the declaration or oracle (v. 5); a liturgist, the personal praise (vv. 6–7); and a priest, the corporate praise and intercession (vv. 8–9).

Now what is the occasion for this liturgy? The opening verse may be suggestive of sickness, but this hypothesis does not account for the contents of the psalm, whose central section (vv. 3–5) concerns the destiny of the wicked. And the closing interest in the salvation of God's anointed one and his people would seem out of place in a psalm focused on an individual's restoration. Is the psalm to be used on those special occasions when an individual is under personal attack from enemies (perhaps false accusation)? That the wicked pose a threat to the

speaker is suggested by the metaphors of protection ascribed to
Yahweh after the assurance of being heard; God is "my strength
and my shield" (v. 7) and "a fortress of salvation" (v. 8). But there
is no lament suggesting that they single him out for attack and, in
the verse describing their activities (v. 3), they threaten society in
general. Verses 3–5 imply there is more to the psalm's occasion
than the speaker's seeking relief from the wicked. Verse 3, like
26:9, reckons that judgment on the wicked is a given, and verse 4
seeks to ensure that their punishment be in like measure to their
crime. The issue is not whether or not there will be a judgment
but the degree of the judgment. Moreover, the reason given for
their judgment in verse 5 is not their abuse of the speaker or even
of God's people in general but their disregard of the works of the
Lord. This implies the context of the judgment is larger than the
circumstances facing the speaker.

Psalm 28 echoes the psalms of temple entry (see the Introduction). Verse 3's description of the "doers of evil" (Hb. *pōᶜᵃlê
ʾāwen*, NIV "those who do evil") provides a clear contrast to the
description of the "doer of righteousness" (Hb. *pōᶜēl ṣedeq*) in
15:2–3, in terms of how they speak with neighbors and whether
or not they intend "malice" or "wrong" (both Hb. *rāᶜâ*) in their
hearts. Both psalms give attention to deeds (Hb. *pᶜl*, 28:4; 15:2,
"who does") and what they have done (Hb. *ᶜśh*, 15:5, "he who
does"), and both appear to have been performed directly before
the holy place (28:2; 15:1). Psalm 28:3–4 in its assessment of one's
character refers to the same bodily parts as 24:4: hearts and
hands (Hb. *yad* in 28:4, *kap* in 24:4). Other psalms that probably
belonged to these entry liturgies emphasize the other side of
Psalms 15 and 24, namely the exclusion of the wicked from
Yahweh's holy place: "the wicked . . . cannot stand in your presence" (5:4–6, 10; see also 26:8–9; 36:1–4, 7–12; 52:1–6, 8). Seen in
the light of these liturgies, the issue behind Psalm 28 may be,
"Who may live (or 'camp') on your holy hill?" Since the "doers of
evil" cannot, the speaker petitions, "Do not drag me away . . ." with
those who do evil (a petition very similar to 26:9). Thus, the reason the psalm shows such interest in the wicked is not because of
the supposed circumstances of the speaker but because of the
key issue of the entry liturgies. Reading Psalm 28 in this context
also explains how the negative petitions result in positive benefits for the speaker and why attention is turned from the speaking "I" to God's people. The speaking "I" was probably not a lone
individual but a liturgist praying on behalf of fellow worshipers.

In light of this liturgical setting, the psalm appears to develop as follows. It opens with petitions before the Most Holy Place that the worshiper be spared the impending judgment on the wicked. The worshiper endorses this judgment by asking that the wicked be punished in like measure to their crime (vv. 1–4). A liturgist or temple prophet responds by announcing Yahweh "will tear them down" because they disregard his works (v. 5). In return, the worshiper blesses Yahweh for hearing these petitions and vows to sing further praise (vv. 6–7). In closing, it is perhaps a priest who widens the horizons to Yahweh's people, praises Yahweh for his salvation, and petitions that it continue forever (vv. 8–9). Repeated phrases link the psalm's parts. The petitioned cry for mercy (v. 2) is heard in verse 6. From "my hands" uplifted toward the sanctuary (v. 2) attention shifts to what "their" hands have done (v. 4) and then to what Yahweh's hands have done (v. 5). As the speaker "blesses" (Hb. *bārûk*, NIV "Praise be," v. 6) Yahweh, he in turn is invoked to "bless your inheritance" (v. 9). As Yahweh is "my strength" (v. 7), so he is the strength of his people (v. 8).

28:1–2 / Faced with the issue of entering or not entering the temple, we can now make sense of the opening petition. The issue of life and death may be explained not with reference to the supposed circumstances of a particular liturgist (e.g., sickness) but with reference to the imagery of the temple itself. To have access to it is to have access to "light" and "life" itself; to be denied is to become like the "fallen" who are "not able to rise" (36:8–9, 12).

My Rock may not sound to us like an endearing title, especially in light of the following petition that Yahweh **not turn a deaf ear.** It could be a general metaphor for a high rock of refuge or protection, but this image may have been chosen here because of the symbolism of the "holy rock" associated with the temple and the **Most Holy Place,** mentioned in the following verse. (For further discussion see Keel, *Symbolism,* pp. 118–19, and R. de Vaux, *Ancient Israel* [New York: McGraw-Hill, 1965], pp. 318–19. Beneath this rock at the temple site is a cave, and Keel offers the intriguing suggestion that it may have symbolized "the pit" or underworld. If so, we can better understand the juxtaposition of "my Rock" and **the pit** in 28:1.)

The opening petitions help promote an expectation of immediate encounter with God. The negative verbs of verse 1 relate to his face: God is to hear with his ear and speak with his mouth.

Verse 2 also directs the worshiper's voice and body to look beyond himself. "Hear the *sound* of my supplications" (NIV **my cry
for mercy**) points to a prayer said aloud. The posture to be assumed by the worshiper (**I lift up my hands toward your** Most
Holy Place) provides spatial focus for expecting some transcendent response from the divine side. While we today may not believe in "sacred space," our prayers with closed eyes and vague
thoughts of omnipresence can diminish our anticipation of personal encounter with God. At the very least, our inward eyes
must be focused without, not within. *The* essential issue of life
and death is determined by one thing: whether or not God hears
and speaks (not whether or not he hears and heals). If relationship with God is not alive, there is no life.

28:3–4 / In verses 3–4 the worshiper seeks to distinguish himself from **the wicked** and their impending judgment
(as in 26:9–11). As in the temple entry instruction ("torah") found
in Psalms 15 and 24, the decisive measure is what lies in one's
heart and what one says to one's neighbor. In particular, the behavior that identifies the wicked most clearly is their hypocrisy
and manipulation of others. The petition thus follows that their
punishment be in equal measure to the crime (the three Hb.
prepositions, all *kᵉ* or "according to," are clearer on this point
than the NIV's threefold **for** in v. 4).

28:5 / If verse 5 had continued in direct address to Yahweh, we might consider it to be a supporting motivation for the
preceding petitions (instead of **will** the verbs of v. 5b could be
translated as "should") or as a petition itself (these verbs could
also be translated, "may he tear . . . and never build"). But the
change in address may be a signal that the liturgist now turns to
assure the congregation. It is also possible this verse is an oracle
from a temple prophet. This would explain the sudden shift from
the urgent petition "Hear my cry for mercy" (v. 2) to the confident assertion "he has heard my cry for mercy" (v. 6). The meter
in verse 5 is distinct and the word pair, "to build" and "to tear
down," is a favorite in the book of Jeremiah (Jer. 24:6; 42:10; 45:4).
Verse 1, we should recall, raises the worshiper's expectation that
God will hear and speak. Verse 5, in fact, affirms that the petition
of verse 4 will be answered.

In any case, the explicit reason for their judgment here has
to do with their attitude toward God, not toward the speaker or
God's people. "Their deeds" (Hb. *poᶜŏlām*) and "what their hands

have done" (v. 4) are what they are because **they show no regard for the works** (Hb. *pᵉ ʿullōt*) **of the LORD and what his hands have done** (v. 5).

28:6–7 / With the assurance the petitions will be answered, the speaker now knows he will not be "dragged away with the wicked" (v. 3), that is, with those who cannot enter Yahweh's holy place. He thus makes a confession of praise to the congregation (Yahweh here is mentioned in the third person). The epithet, **my strength,** is elsewhere associated with the symbolism of the cherubim-ark (78:61), which resided in the Most Holy Place (v. 2; cf. 1 Kgs. 6:19; 8:6–8). (The closing image of Yahweh as shepherd is also associated with the cherubim-ark in 80:1.) Because **my heart,** in contrast to their hearts (v. 3), **trusts in him, I am helped** and **my heart leaps for joy** (the heart being one of the measures for one's fitness for temple entry, 15:2; 24:4; 26:1–2; 36:1, 10). Thus, once the speaker is assured he is not counted among the wicked, he is able to enter the temple and claim the benefits symbolized there. He also promises to **give thanks to him in song,** perhaps referring to praise psalms that follow in the liturgy.

28:8–9 / Since the liturgy of entrance, though addressed to worshipers as individuals (Pss. 15 and 24) is performed within the congregation, the shift in verses 8–9 to corporate concerns is no surprise. As **the LORD is** the **strength** (Hb. ʿōz) of the representative liturgist (v. 7), so the Lord is **the** strength **of his people.** Moreover, perhaps by the association of wordplay, he is also **a fortress** (Hb. *māʿōz*) **of salvation for his anointed one,** referring probably to the king but possibly to the priest (Exod. 29:7; Lev. 4:3).

The liturgy returns to addressing Yahweh directly in prayer in the closing verse. As we have seen several times in this psalm, it is linked to the preceding by key words. As Yahweh is hymned as "a fortress of salvation," so he is petitioned, **save your people.** There is a lesson here that even though Yahweh possesses certain attributes and has exercised them in the past, his people should not rest complacently in the assumption they will continue automatically.

As the speaker has "blessed" (Hb. *bārûk,* NIV "Praise be to," v. 6) Yahweh, so Yahweh is petitioned, **bless your inheritance.** Here the imagery of Yahweh turns from the military sphere (strength, shield, fortress) to the pastoral sphere (shepherd).

Elsewhere in the Psalms, Yahweh's inheritance refers to his people
(e.g., 33:12; 74:2) but also to his land (e.g., 68:9; 79:1). The closing
petitions are thus comprehensive, including both protection and
providence. Overall, the liturgy of Psalm 28 reflects a respect for
Yahweh and his house as holy, not accessible to the wicked. But
once entry is granted, it also reflects a desire that all God's people
enjoy his beneficent care.

§29 The Voice of the Lord in the Thunderstorm (Ps. 29)

Thunderstorms are impressive to us moderns, but they were especially so to the ancients. For them, they spoke not only of earth-shaking natural phenomena, but also of the gods. A recurring theme in ancient Near Eastern literature is that of the god of the storm vanquishing the mighty waters (v. 3). In the thunderstorm over the sea, they saw the god of the skies, who provided life-giving rains, at battle with the god of the sea, whose waters were chaotic and life-threatening. This story line was thus considered fundamental to orderly creation, including human existence and survival. The defeat of the chaotic seas also established who was to be acclaimed as king among the gods (v. 10). And since a king needs a palace, it also gave legitimacy to that deity's palace or temple (the Hb. word *hêkāl*, translated "temple" in v. 9 and elsewhere in the Psalms, also means "palace").

Psalm 29 names geographical locations, all of which lie outside the borders of Israel. Lebanon is to the north, as is Sirion or Mount Hermon. The Desert of Kadesh is not to be confused with Kadesh-barnea in the Negev to the south, known from the Hebrews' wilderness wanderings (Num. 13:26; 20:1). It is located in Syria, to the east of the Lebanon Mountains. These locations may seem strange until we recognize the similarity the psalm has with the Baal texts from Ugarit on the Syrian coast (e.g., J. C. L. Gibson, *Canaanite Myths and Legends* [Edinburgh: T&T Clark, 1977], pp. 63, 65). It appears that the Hebrew liturgists sang of Yahweh's kingship in a way immediately understandable to all ancients, especially their Canaanite neighbors. It is very possible that they had taken a hymn to Baal and substituted the name Yahweh. In fact, if we were to read Baal where the Hebrew text has Yahweh ("the LORD"), a number of poetic alliterations (re-)appear. The particular type of parallelism found in verses 1–2 is characteristic of Canaanite poetry.

29:1–2 / If Psalm 29 is a plundered Canaanite hymn, it would also explain the expressions, **O mighty ones** and **the splendor of his holiness.** The Hebrew phrase for "mighty ones" is literally "sons of gods" (Hb. *bᵉnê ʾēlîm*). In the OT, comparable expressions designate the angelic host in Yahweh's heavenly council (1 Kgs. 22:19; Isa. 6:2–4; Pss. 8:6; 82:1–7; 89:6–9; 97:7; 103:20; 148:1–2; Job 1:6; 2:1; 38:7; cf. Gen. 6:2, 4). The usage of "sons of gods," an expression seemingly foreign to Israelite monotheism, is probably to be explained as Israel's "demythologizing" of pagan theology. What their neighbors regarded as gods serving their divine king, Israel regarded as heavenly beings who do Yahweh's bidding. It is difficult to be certain about the meaning of "the splendor of his holiness" because it is found only here and in 96:9 (cited in 1 Chron. 16:29; 2 Chron. 20:21). It is possible the term for splendor (Hb. *hᵃdārâ*) has Canaanite roots, where it means "divine visitation, appearance" (Gibson, *Canaanite Myths*, p. 86).

Thus, Psalm 29 opens with the congregation at the Jerusalem temple commanding Yahweh's heavenly congregation to **ascribe** due praise to him. This hymnic imperative, **ascribe,** is elsewhere found only in 96:7–8, a psalm of Yahweh's kingship. There, it is addressed to "families of nations." What they are to ascribe is **strength** and **glory** (repeated for emphasis). The basic meaning of "glory" (Hb. *kābôd*) is "weight" (cf. Isa. 22:24). Therefore, this imperative implies giving Yahweh his due "weight"— because he is, in fact, the God of glory (v. 3).

29:3–9 / What we today regard as a mere thunderstorm the congregation in Jerusalem heard as an expression of **the voice of the LORD.** It would not be consistent with the rest of the OT to assume Hebrews actually identified Yahweh's voice with the thunder, any more than 84:10 identifies Yahweh as "a sun and shield." These are poetic illustrations or symbols (i.e., implicit comparisons) helping us to gain a sense of what Yahweh's majesty is like. **The voice of the LORD** proves superior to all that is vast, high, and seemingly unshakable. **The LORD thunders over the mighty waters; the LORD breaks in pieces the cedars of Lebanon; the voice of the LORD . . . strips the forests bare** (here we may think of **lightning** sparking a forest fire); **the LORD makes** Mount Hermon **skip . . . like a young wild ox; the LORD shakes the Desert of Kadesh.** Appropriately, this **powerful** and **majestic** display elicits a response: **and in his temple all cry,**

"**Glory!**" This cry is also a response to the opening twofold imperative to ascribe to the LORD the glory due his name, which name is **the God of glory** (v. 3). This title is reminiscent of the "King of glory" in 24:7–10, another liturgy celebrating Yahweh's kingship (note the same three elements of his superiority, to "the seas" in 24:2, his "holy place" in 24:3, and his acclamation as king in 24:7–10). "His temple" points first of all to his temple above—it is the mighty ones who are commanded to "ascribe . . . glory." But also in the mere singing of this psalm, the earthly choir at the Jerusalem temple echoes this cry of praise.

29:10–11 / The closing fourfold praise of **the LORD** (Yahweh) describes his status (v. 10) and how he exercises that status (v. 11). He is acclaimed as **King, enthroned over the flood.** We should thus imagine him seated on his throne in his palace surrounded by his royal court. The closing verse comes as a surprise. All we have heard thus far is of royal glory, a thunderous voice that is powerful and majestic. But now we hear of what this monarch grants his subjects. The **strength** that is to be appropriately ascribed to him in the opening verse he in turn bestows **to his people.** It is also remarkable that the strength dramatically exhibited in the thunderstorm, seemingly violent and out of control, is here channeled to God's people (cf. 68:33–35). Throughout the psalm, we have heard Yahweh's thunderous voice, but in closing **the LORD blesses his people with peace.**

§30 Living Praise Versus Deathly Silence (Ps. 30)

Psalm 30 is among the thanksgiving psalms, which form the flip side to the prayer psalms of the individual. The prayer psalms generally close with a vow of praise that once Yahweh has delivered the supplicant, the supplicant will sing a thanksgiving psalm to Yahweh. The issue of Psalm 30 in particular is death and silence versus life and praise. It begins with a proclamation of praise and an introductory summary of Yahweh's deliverance (v. 1) and of the worshiper's calling and Yahweh's responding (vv. 2–3). A congregation is then summoned to hymnic praise (vv. 4–5). The report of the deliverance is repeated, this time narrating briefly the distress (vv. 6–7). Then the report spells out further the substance of the worshiper's cry for help (vv. 8–10), which climaxes in Yahweh's transforming intervention (v. 11). Rounding off the thanksgiving is a renewed vow of praise (v. 12).

30:1–3 / The opening line, **I exalt you . . . for you lifted me out of the depths,** directs the worshiper to repay Yahweh "in kind." As Yahweh has raised him up, so the speaker wishes to do toward Yahweh. **My enemies** are not presented as a direct cause of the distress; rather they would **gloat** after the fact. The belief that **God** answers when **called** upon (v. 2) is the fundamental tradition of the prayer psalms of the individual (see the Introduction). This psalm celebrates its vindication.

30:4–5 / "Thanksgiving," according to the Psalms, is clearly not to be a private affair between the believer and God, but is to be sung before all **saints of his.** This call to hymnic praise offers the congregation a general lesson that is exemplified by the worshiper's own distress and deliverance. This lesson describes first God's initiative, **for his anger lasts only a moment, but his favor lasts a lifetime,** and then the human responses, **weeping may remain for a night, but rejoicing comes in the morning.** The celebratory nature of Yahwistic faith is evident here, as is the prevailing nature of God's grace, but implicit here is also a lesson many modern believers overlook. Yahweh is a God who delivers, not a God who preserves his people from ever experiencing hardship in general and his anger in particular. We may hope that life would be a consistent, upward progression, but the Psalms clearly show it will have its ups and downs. After all, we should note that much of this thanksgiving psalm consists of repeating elements from an earlier prayer psalm. Obviously there would be no thanksgiving in this formal sense without prior distress and lament. Also implicit in this confession is the personhood of God: God is not a detached, dispassionate deity, but one who is personally and emotionally involved in his people's lives.

30:6–12 / The speaker's feeling of security (v. 6) need not be construed as self-assured arrogance, for the psalm attributes his security to Yahweh's favor (v. 7a). But while Yahweh's favor provides the speaker with security, it is the apparent withdrawal of his **face** that leads the worshiper to draw near to Yahweh in prayer (vv. 7–8). And as a result of his prayer's being answered, he obtains a singing **heart** (v. 12) and **dancing** feet (v. 11). Thus, healing does not mean mere restoration to one's former estate— it provides benefits that will be celebrated **forever** (v. 12). It brings to the heart the awareness that life is God's gift, which is best enjoyed through praise. While this psalm should not be construed as a treatise on the meaning and value of suffering, it does imply that a benefit of suffering is a heightened appreciation of life as it comes from God's favoring face (v. 7).

The appeal to God which is expressed in the rhetorical questions cited in verse 9 may sound like spiritual blackmail. But the issue is not, "Will the praise of God continue?" but "Who may continue the praise of God?" (Note **my destruction** and **my going down into the pit.**) Immediately following this recollection of the cry **for mercy,** the speaker expresses joy that he may participate in continuing the praise of God. He affirms in the last two verses that **my wailing** has turned to dancing, **my sackcloth** into a garment of **joy, that my** heart **may sing to you and not be silent.** The closing verses build on the image of one's mourning death in sackcloth to show the divine transformation that has taken place. Instead of the unheard-of proposition that **the dust** should **praise** God, we see that God **removed** the speaker's sackcloth **and clothed** him **with** joy. "That my heart may . . . not be silent" has a dual reference. Silence refers to both the negation of praise and life itself. The ultimate purpose of one's deliverance is thus the praise of God.

§31 My God as Refuge from Social Alienation (Ps. 31)

Psalm 31 reads like two self-contained prayers (vv. 1–8 and 9–18), with additions of praise (vv. 19–22) and an exhortation (vv. 23–24). Its process of composition is difficult to determine. It could be an authored piece or an edited piece, where separate prayers and a subsequent thanksgiving were spliced together. These segments do complement one another somewhat, as noted below. Another factor, however, needs to be considered. The terms and phrases of the psalm are highly formulaic (i.e., consisting of stock phrases). And the imagery jumps from one sphere to another: refuge and asylum (vv. 1, 20), military conflict (vv. 2–3 and possibly v. 21), hunting (v. 4), economic recovery ("redeem" or "buy back," v. 5), sickness (vv. 9–10), social alienation (vv. 11–13), and the underworld for the enemies (the Hb. for "grave" denotes Sheol, vv. 17–18). As with psalms in general, this one does not report on particular, actual circumstances; it uses images that befit any situation of distress and conflict (see "What is a Psalm?" in the Introduction).

Psalm 31 in its final form reflects a public setting. Thanksgiving (vv. 21–22) is customarily given as public testimony (note v. 21 is addressed not to Yahweh, but probably to a congregation), and the closing exhortation clearly presupposes an audience of Yahweh's saints. It is possible that "the shelter of your presence" (v. 20, cf. 61:4) and "your dwelling" (Hb. *sukkâ*, cf. *sukkô* in 76:2) denote the temple (see esp. 27:5).

31:1–8 / These verses contain the elements necessary for a self-contained prayer: petitions, confessions of trust, and a vow of praise with its anticipatory thanksgiving. The petitions and confessions of trust use formulaic language and are mixed together, rather than in discrete sections. The petitions for God's favor **(Turn your ear)** and for his intervention **(let me never be put to shame, deliver, rescue, lead, guide, free, redeem)** are generally common among the prayer psalms. (The Hb. text of vv. 3–5 could also be rendered as statements or confessions of trust.) In one petition, the psalm requests Yahweh to be—in experience— what he is confessed to be, namely, **my rock and my fortress** (vv. 2b–3a). These confessions of trust (or motivations to move God to intervene) draw attention to the relational obligations between Yahweh and the speaker. **In you . . . I have taken refuge** (vv. 1, 4) and **into your hands I commit my spirit** (note Luke 23:46) focus on actions the speaker has taken that in turn oblige Yahweh to protect him. As the word order indicates, the emphasis of these claims lies on the object he has chosen for refuge. His choice in Yahweh is made more explicit in verse 6, where the alternatives to Yahweh are obliquely mentioned (**worthless idols** is lit., "the nothings of emptiness"). Underscored here is the notion of loyalty. To strengthen his appeal, the speaker appeals to Yahweh's attributes of fidelity: **your righteousness, your name,** and **the God of truth.** The vow of praise is characterized by joy: **I will be glad and rejoice in your love.** From this, thanksgiving follows that is given in anticipation of Yahweh's hearing the prayer and is stated as accomplished facts: **for you saw . . . and knew . . . . You have.**

These motifs round off the prayer, and were it to conclude here, we would not suspect a portion of the psalm had dropped off. It does, however, lack any explicit lament (though not all prayer psalms have formal laments). Curiously, the first mention of **the enemy** comes in the concluding thanksgiving (v. 8). The Hebrew text of verse 4 reads, **the trap that** "they have set for me," but "they" has no antecedent until verse 8. (These features may be signs of editing or formulaic composition.) Thus, we see how the second prayer of verses 9–18 supplements the first.

31:9–18 / While in the first prayer confessions of trust were dominant, in this one laments and petitions are dominant. The transition from the first to the second prayer reflects a tension in time (see further below). In anticipation of Yahweh's hearing the prayer, the speaker has just claimed, "you . . . knew the anguish (lit. 'narrow places') of my soul. You . . . have set my feet in a spacious place." But he now laments, **I am in distress** (lit. "narrowness"). The I-lament (vv. 9–10) continues and speaks of his **strength** languishing **with grief.** Whether this refers to physical illness or psychological distress is left open-ended. The lament regarding opponents (vv. 11–13), stated largely in the "I"

form, complains of **my enemies,** who **conspire against me** and
have thus triggered social alienation (which frequently accompanied sickness in the ancient Near East) from **my neighbors** and
friends as well.

Midway through Psalm 31 there is a shift in the depiction
of the opponents and the conflict. In verses 4, 8, 11–15, the conflict is between **me** and **my enemies** (esp. Hb. *'ôyēb*), but in verses
17–20, 23–24, two distinct groups emerge, both defined in moral
terms: **the righteous** (and their various designations) and **the
wicked** (Hb. *rešā'îm*). This shift may imply that the psalm was
written in stages, perhaps at the hand of different liturgists
(though the shift does not occur at v. 9), or it may imply a thematic development, namely that "my" suffering is simply part of
the larger suffering of "the righteous."

As a transition from the laments (vv. 9–13) to the petitions
(vv. 15b–18), there is a confession of trust that lays claim to the
central tradition of the individual prayer psalms: **I say, "You are
my God."** The speaker's obligation is that of trust **(I trust in you)**
and entrusting **(My times are in your hands).** The expectations
laid on Yahweh are expressed in the petitions. In verses 15–16 the
petitions are phrased as imperatives on behalf of the speaker **(deliver, save,** and "make your face shine") and the opponents are
described as "my enemies." In verses 17b–18, the petitions are expressed as wishes (Hb. jussives) against the opponents **(let the
wicked be put to shame and lie silent in the grave. Let their
lying lips be silenced)** and the opponents are described as "the
wicked." Bridging these developments is, **Let me not be put to
shame,** which echoes the petition opening the psalm. (These
kinds of literary links at key literary seams evidence the artistry
of the Hebrew poets, whether they be authors or editors.) Supporting these petitions are motivations contrasting what each
party has said: **I have cried out to you** but **they speak arrogantly
against the** righteous.

31:19–20 / The psalm now turns to hymnic praise, expressed in terms of **you** and **them** (vv. 19–20). It centers on the
image of **refuge,** which echoes the psalm's opening line. The
threat from which "they" are protected is primarily verbal **(ac-
cusing tongues).** The contrast with the speaker's own experience in verse 13 is striking. Key to understanding this praise is
the recognition that Yahweh's help has dimensions that are both
hidden **(stored up,** refuge, **in the shelter of your presence you**

hide them, **in your dwelling)** and public **(in the sight of men).** In addition, although these verses serve as praise in their own right, they also serve as a motivation to the preceding petitions, namely that Yahweh would make real in *my* experience what he does for *them*.

31:21–22 / Verses 21–22 are thanksgiving on behalf of **me.** As is characteristic of psalmic thanksgivings (Pss. 30; 116), Yahweh is both addressed directly (**you,** v. 22) and referred to in the third person (**he,** v. 21), implying a congregation is addressed. (The NIV's **Praise be to the LORD** is lit., "Blessed be . . . ," in which exclamation Yahweh is virtually always in the third person.) What is the nature of this thanksgiving: is it given in anticipation of future deliverance or does it presuppose the deliverance has already taken place? It makes best sense as interim thanksgiving, where the speaker is assured Yahweh has heard the prayer but where actual liberation is yet to be made public. The confession is careful to say that God has revealed himself to the speaker (he **showed . . . to** me and you **heard my cry**) but makes no claim of a change in circumstances (on the contrary, note **in a besieged city**). It is interesting to observe that here, and not in the lament, admission is made of earlier despair (v. 22), which the speaker now rejects.

31:23–24 / The public performance of this psalm is also evidenced in the closing exhortation to **all his saints** (cf. 27:14; 55:22). Similar imperatives (esp. 30:4–5) and hymnic praise (116:5–6, 15) are found in other thanksgivings. (Such imperatives make little sense if a congregation is not actually present. Otherwise, a confession of trust would do.) The commands to **love the LORD** and **be strong and take heart** imply that **the faithful** are to maintain patience and not reject Yahweh because of immediate trials from **the proud.** In view of the earlier lament of contempt from neighbors and friends, we may wonder how this exhortation in the company of Yahweh's devout fits in. First, it helps to understand the nature of psalmic laments. While they may sound utter and complete, they do not describe all the circumstances. Second, we may gain some insight into ancient Israelite society, which may not be too different from our own. Yahweh's faithful were in a minority position (as reflected in the historical books and preexilic prophets). While one may feel alienated in the neighborhood, one still belongs to a believing community.

The closing exhortation is very telling about the nature of psalmic faith. It is understood that Yahweh does not automatically and instantaneously solve problems. This faith calls for courageous hope in the midst of circumstances that give little evidence of relief or divine intervention. We should also note that admitting the absence of these things does not lie outside the bounds of that faith. In addition, these verses admit that sometimes encouragement is needed and makes a difference. Finally, we see here that this faith is a quest for justice: **The LORD preserves** the faithful, **but** the proud **he pays back in full.**

Central to this psalm is the tension between what is known privately and theologically, namely, God as refuge, and what is known publicly and socially, namely, slander and alienation. Resolution is experienced in two stages: first in terms of protection, then as public vindication (esp. v. 19). The key motif that makes this psalm work is Yahweh's love (Hb. *ḥesed*), which surfaces in each of its four major sections (vv. 7, 16, 21; in v. 23 "his saints" is *ḥªsîdāyw*, or "his loved ones").

Additional Notes §31

31:6 / **I trust in the LORD:** Although Yahweh is here referred to in the third person, this verse is probably still addressed to him. It is the only verse of the prayer (vv. 1–18) that is not in the "you" form. In view of the alternatives of **idols,** there may have been the need to name the Lord specifically.

31:10 / **My affliction:** This reading (Hb. *ᶜonî*), adopted by the NIV, follows that of the LXX and Syriac. The MT has "my iniquity" (Hb. *ᶜªwōnî*).

§32 Blessed Are Those Whose Transgressions Are Forgiven (Ps. 32)

Psalm 32 is most akin to the thanksgiving psalms of the individual (cf. Pss. 30; 116), but it forms a combination of features unlike any other psalm. Most notably, it incorporates a confession of sin (surprisingly rare among the psalms) and a divine oracle, along with an overall didactic (i.e., teaching) emphasis. Its liturgical setting is implied by its closing, plural imperative call to praise addressed to the righteous, and by its changes of address. It opens with a "blessing" that refers to the Lord (vv. 1–2; cf. Ps. 41, a psalm of sickness) and moves to thanksgiving addressed to him ("your hand," etc., vv. 3–7). Then, without introduction, Yahweh himself speaks ("I will"). While the absence of a transition is awkward when the psalm is read as literature, it would not have been so when another voice, a prophet, stepped forward. Other psalms containing prophetic oracles proceed to them without giving notice of a change of speaker (50:7; 81:6, where the Hb. text lacks "he says"; 75:2, where the Hb. text lacks "you say"). In closing, Psalm 32 addresses the audience/congregation and refers to the Lord (vv. 10–11).

32:1–2 / The liturgist begins by pronouncing a blessing on him **whose transgressions are forgiven** and thus brings center stage the psalm's chief topic. Yahweh's forgiveness is depicted by three images. "Forgiven" is literally "lifted up" (cf. 25:18; 85:2), as in the removal of a burden. The **sins** are also **covered** and are "not counted," as in an accounting ledger (Lev. 25:27, 52; 1 Kgs. 10:21; 2 Kgs. 12:15; 22:7). For most readers, however, what the blessing offers by way of forgiveness it takes away by the condition of applying it to a person **in whose spirit is no deceit**—a quality with which few of us can identify. There are three possible explanations. First, this line appears to lie outside the normal metrical structure of the poetry (though the metrics of this psalm are generally uneven). It may be a later scribal gloss.

Second, it parallels somewhat the character profiles of those who may or may not enter Yahweh's temple (5:6; 24:4; 36:3; 52:2, 4). In this light it should not be read as a claim to absolute moral purity but as an affirmation that one aspires to be true to Yahweh's way (see on Ps. 24). The third and most likely explanation is that the meaning of this phrase is exemplified by the confession that follows. This absence of "deceit" is spelled out as acknowledging "my sin to you" and by not covering up "my iniquity." Because "I . . . confess, you forgave." Verse 5 thus links confession and forgiveness, just as this opening blessing links the absence of deceit and forgiveness. (Instead of "spirit," the LXX reads "mouth," and if correct provides further support for the second and third explanations.)

32:3–7 / Like the pattern found in thanksgiving psalms, these verses contain a recollection of the distress (vv. 3–4), but instead of the normal call for help and report of deliverance there are a confession of **sin** and a report of God's forgiveness (v. 5). The cause of the distress is traced not so much to the speaker's sin as to his "silence" about his sin and to his "covering it up." This cover-up is described as having its psychological and perhaps even physiological effects (cf. 31:9–10; 38:2–8; 102:3–5). In the highly figurative language of the Psalms, emotional distress can be depicted by bodily images. The act of testifying is characteristic of thanksgiving psalms, and verse 6 does so in the form of an invitation: **therefore let everyone who is godly pray to you.** The qualifier, **while you may be found,** warns against any presumption that one may confess sins simply at one's own convenience (cf. 69:13; 101:2). Supporting this invitation are incentives expressed in the form of praise addressed to God and portrayed by the images of protection from **mighty waters** (which denote personal distress in 18:16; 144:7; and echo primeval chaos in 29:3; 77:19; 93:4), of a **hiding place,** and of **songs of deliverance.**

32:8–9 / Integral to this thanksgiving ceremony are Yahweh's own words. While they may have been delivered by an official ritual prophet, they could also be a quotation of an earlier oracle and delivered by a liturgist. Yahweh promises to **teach** (the verb form of the noun, "torah," which can be rendered "instruction" or "law") the individual (**you** is sing.). What is striking here is Yahweh's personal engagement: he offers his personal **counsel** "with my eye upon you" (lit., NIV **and watch over you**). But this promise carries with it a warning that is made explicit in the following verse. Its relevance is clear to the worshiper's situation: Yahweh has been "instructing" him, but he has acted like **the mule,** who does not go "in the way he should go" or "come to" his master/driver without force. In other words, the worshiper has learned a lesson he should not repeat.

32:10–11 / Closing this thanksgiving liturgy is hymnic praise that contrasts **the woes of the wicked** (explained perhaps by their willful lack of "understanding" mentioned in the preceding oracle) and **the LORD's unfailing love** that **surrounds the man who trusts in him,** just as Yahweh "surrounds" him "with songs of deliverance" (v. 7). Climaxing this ceremony is a call for joy **(rejoice in the LORD)** addressed to the **righteous.** We must recall, however, that these righteous ones are those whose transgressions are forgiven (v. 1).

§33 The Trustworthy Lord Over Nature, Nations, and Armies (Ps. 33)

Psalm 33 is a hymn wherein a liturgist summons the congregation (v. 1) and the musicians (vv. 2–3) to perform their praise of God. The congregation is designated as the "righteous" and "upright," that is, those admitted through the temple entry liturgy (see on Pss. 15 and 24). The chief quality sought in this liturgy is not moral blamelessness but loyalty to Yahweh (in 24:3–6 "righteousness" is received, not presupposed). The promise of deliverance from death and famine (v. 19), along with the mention of military forces (vv. 16–17), may imply that a situation of military siege underlies this psalm. The casual way 2 Samuel 11:1 mentions the regularity of war in the spring shows that the Israelites could not presume on their national security as we might today. But even if this psalm originated out of such circumstances, its application extends beyond them. The psalms frequently use imagery, especially military imagery, to convey the notion that the most foreboding powers that humans can wield pale before Yahweh. They often speak of the extremes of the human condition, such as death, to show that Yahweh's providence embraces all of life.

This psalm concerns various topics that initially do not appear to share a common thread: righteousness and uprightness, Yahweh's creative word, his sovereignty over the nations, and the superior value of hoping in him rather than in militaristic power. But the repetition of key words, as noted below, helps to knit these topics together into a coherent pattern. The psalm moves from general theological claims about Yahweh to specific qualities that he seeks from humans. The significance of these general statements and the psalm's specific purpose do not become apparent until the final section.

33:1–5 / The opening section focuses on Yahweh's character. The qualities given special emphasis by their repetition are "uprightness" (**the word of the** LORD **is** "upright" [NIV **right and true**]) and **righteousness, which the** LORD **loves**. His worshipers who bear those same traits—**you righteous** and **the upright**—are called to join in this praise.

33:6–19 / This section focuses on Yahweh's sovereign power with respect to nature (vv. 6–9), the nations (vv. 10–12), and their armies (vv. 13–19). Yahweh has made the awesome **heavens** and he has contained the fearsome **deep**. To appreciate the full impact of these claims we must recognize that many of the ancients considered both the starry heavens and the watery deep to contain fearsome powers or to be those powers themselves. Verses 6–7, in effect, eliminate these causes for fear. History shows that **the plans of the** LORD succeed, even when **the nations** plan otherwise. Next we discover there is a rival to trusting in Yahweh, namely trusting in **the size of** an **army** and the **great strength** of the **warrior** and the **horse** (cf. David's enrollment of Israel's fighting men in 2 Sam. 24). This is the issue facing the congregation: will they choose to grasp for power or to hope in Yahweh? Now the purpose of the general theological claims becomes plain. They give the rationale for choosing Yahweh by describing his character and power. He alone has the all-seeing perspective **from heaven** and is the maker of all (vv. 13–15).

33:20–22 / The clearest clues about the psalm's specific purpose lie in these last three verses, where we first hear the congregation speaking **(we)** and in the last verse where Yahweh is first addressed directly. Here the congregation claims, we **wait in hope for the** LORD and **we put our hope in you**, and then prays, **may your unfailing love rest upon us**. In effect, they seek to appropriate the promise of providential protection contained in verses 18–19: "those who fear him" and "whose hope is in his unfailing love" Yahweh will "deliver . . . from death."

In all, therefore, this psalm celebrates Yahweh as the only one who—by virtue of his trustworthy character and his unassailable power—deserves our trust. Its purpose is to elicit from the congregation a steady hope in Yahweh. Put another way, this psalm simplifies our fears. We need fear Yahweh alone, no other heavenly or underworldly power, and no other nation.

Once we recognize the "pastoral need" this psalm addresses, it is striking to observe (a) the content, (b) order, and (c) literary form that it employs. (a) Its content does not focus on human obligations but on pure theology: a declaration of who

Yahweh is. The psalm presents a revelation of God, not demands.
(b) Its ordering of this content is to move from general theological claims to specific human responses. The psalm is careful to
specify the responses that are appropriate. In verses 13–15 "from
heaven the LORD looks down" and "considers everything" people
do, but what he is looking for is not stated until verse 18. He
seeks not the "righteous" or the "upright" but those who fear him
and whose hope is in his unfailing love. (c) The psalm's literary
form is not wise instruction to the people or even a prayer to
God; it is hymnic praise. Faith here is not to be generated by self-
counsel, nor is it made the object of a prayer request. It is elicited
by the act of praise. We must observe that the command to sing
praise (vv. 1–3) precedes the confession of trust (vv. 20–21). We
often assume that we can worship God only when our faith is
right and sure. In other words, we tend to see praise as a product
of the current state of our faith. But according to the psychology
reflected in this psalm, it is faith that stems from praise. Faith is
not self-engineered but is a product of encounter with God.

This psalm's theology focuses on Yahweh's word by which
he created the cosmos (vv. 4–9, cf. Gen. 1), his plans (or "counsel")
by which he governs the nations (vv. 10–12, cf. Isa. 8:10; 14:24–26),
and his eyes by which he observes all humanity (vv. 13–19). The
one divine power oversees the realms of creation, history, and
providence. Verses 16–17 draw upon Israel's ancient songs of
Yahweh war: in view of Yahweh, the warrior, armies, and horses
fail (Exod. 15:1–4; Judg. 5:18–22).

Perhaps what is most remarkable is how the psalm moves
from universal to particular claims. Yahweh is celebrated as
Creator of the universe and Lord of history but also as he
who forms the hearts of each individual (v. 15; lit., "the fash-
ioner," cf. Gen 2:7). All the people of the world are to revere
him (v. 8), but there is one people he chose for his inheritance
(v. 12). We must observe that God's people are not here defined
by political or ethnic criteria ("Israel" is not named). Yahweh's
criteria surface in the following universal and particular claims:
although from heaven the LORD looks down and sees all mankind (v. 13), the eyes of the LORD are on those who fear him, in
particular, that is, he watches over them to deliver them from
death (vv. 18–19). He *looks upon* all, but he *watches over* only those
who fear him. The earth is full of his unfailing love (v. 5), but one
must put one's "hope . . . in his unfailing love" (v. 18) and pray
for it: "May your unfailing love rest upon us" (v. 22). This love is

everywhere present, but it is neither self-evident nor automatically effectual.

The grand theology sung in this psalm engenders grand expectations, and that is why verse 19, which contains the psalm's sole specific promise, must be one of the biggest let-downs of the Bible for believers of the prosperous West. The Creator of the universe and Lord of the nations will simply "deliver them from death and keep them alive in famine." They may survive the famine, but they are not necessarily spared from its presence. A high theology need not entail a comfortable lifestyle for God's people. This gap between what is possible under the sovereign and loving God and what is certain for God's people in the here and now may help explain the posture of the congregation at the psalm's close: "we wait in hope for the LORD" (v. 20). Even the ancient congregation of Israel sensed that there was more this God would grant. New Testament faith is no different in this respect (see Rom. 5:1–5; 8:23–25; Heb. 11). What is therefore striking about this psalm is not the "guarantees" it offers but the God that it portrays. It aims the focus of faith in the right direction, not at the promises of God—as though we should hold God to a legal contract—but in the person of God himself. The greatest promise God offers is himself. (See also Isa. 40, which is an echo of this psalm.) By entrusting themselves to his will, the people of God leave to his discretion how he wishes to reveal himself.

§34 Taste and See that the Lord Hears and Delivers (Ps. 34)

Psalm 34 is an acrostic (each verse begins with a successive letter of the Hb. alphabet), consisting of an individual's thanksgiving (vv. 1–7), exhortation (imperatives dominate vv. 8–14), and praise or instruction (vv. 15–22 are statements). It reflects motifs from the wisdom tradition (esp. in vv. 11–14). The opening thanksgiving and closing praises focus on deliverance from distress, and the exhortations in the middle focus on blessing, especially for provision and long life. A public setting is presupposed, whether the psalm be a testimony for a congregation or instruction for an assembly. Participation from the audience is invited (vv. 2–3), and the psalm's imperatives are plural (vv. 3, 8, 9, 11, with the exception of the wisdom, moral imperatives of vv. 13–14 (addressed to "whoever of you," lit. "who is the man?").

34:1–7 / Only in this section does an individual speaker refer to himself **(I, my soul, this poor man)**. As found in thanksgiving psalms of the individual (Pss. 30; 116), there is the opening proclamation of praise (vv. 1–2), the report of the speaker's call for help and Yahweh's deliverance (vv. 4, 6), and hymnic praise that calls the audience to join in praising and that offers general praises, which his deliverance exemplifies (vv. 3, 5, 7).

34:8–14 / This section exhorts the audience with imperatives to experience **(taste and see) the LORD** himself and to **fear him, so they may enjoy his "blessing" (v. 8)** of providence **(vv. 9–10) and a life** of **many good days** (v. 12). The image of **refuge** (v. 8) connects this section with the preceding thanksgiving for deliverance from troubles (v. 6) and with the third section, which also speaks of refuge for Yahweh's servants (v. 22). The recurring terms of **fear** and **good** highlight the proper human attitude toward God and the divine benefits for fearing him. We are to **do good** (v. 14) and to fear **the LORD** (vv. 7, 9, 11), who is good

(v. 8) and provides **good things** (vv. 10, 12). In fact, **fear**—not strength—is the key to survival (vv. 9–10; cf. 33:16–19). In addition to the attitude of fearing the Lord, several moral imperatives direct the audience's behavior: they are to avoid **speaking lies** (a key characteristic of the psalms of temple entry, e.g., 15:3; 24:4; 36:3; 52:2–4) and to **turn from evil** and **seek peace.** As in the wisdom literature of Proverbs, the teacher commands **children** (Prov. 1:8; 4:1; 5:7; 7:24; 8:32) about **the fear of the** LORD (Prov. 1:7; 2:5; 8:13; 9:10; 10:27), and uses the desire for long life and "many . . . days" (Prov. 3:2, 16; 4:10; 9:11) as a motivation for moral behavior (Prov. 2:12; 3:7; 11:27; 16:6; 12:13; 13:21).

34:15–22 / Like the first section, this one returns to the theme of deliverance. Its statements are similar to the praises of the Psalms that offer congregational testimony and to the instruction of Proverbs. Verses 15–18 focus on Yahweh's attentiveness, which acts on behalf of **the righteous** (referring to his **eyes** and **ears**) and **against those who do evil** (referring to his **face**). To the former, he is both responsive (v. 17) and **close** (v. 18). In verse 18, this group is designated not by their religious, moral standing (i.e., **the righteous**) but by their personal attitude (i.e., **the brokenhearted;** cf. "the afflicted" and "this poor man" in vv. 2, 6). As for the wicked, the psalm touches on the mystery of retribution and its divine-human causation. On the one hand, **evil will slay the wicked** (v. 21), and on the other, **the** LORD opposes them directly (v. 16). The final verse, which lies outside the acrostic pattern, highlights the theme of "redemption."

The teaching in this psalm contains enormous promises (esp. vv. 9–10, 20). Most striking are the repeated uses of seemingly absolute, universal terms: **all** (vv. 1, 4, 6, 17, 19), always (v. 1), never (v. 5), nothing (v. 9), no good thing (v. 10), **not one** and **no one** (vv. 20, 22). In this regard, verse 19 is key; it admits **a righteous man may have many troubles, but**—after some unspecified interval and in some unspecified manner—**the** LORD **delivers him from them all.** Believers are given every confidence to entrust themselves to Yahweh, but they are not given guarantees of avoiding troubles altogether. Yahweh is presented as Deliverer, not as one who preserves his own from ever experiencing hardship. Trouble is a given. Its mere appearance does not signal a failure on Yahweh's or the believer's part (see further on Ps. 37, which is also an acrostic and reflects wisdom influence and makes promises that appear to be overstated).

§35 Images of War, the Hunt, False Accusation, and Wild Beasts (Ps. 35)

Psalm 35 may not be one of our favorites, but we have all felt, at some point, attacked and accused. The "secret" of this psalm is to allow us to vent our frustrations and to commit those feelings of aggression and the need for vindication to God. It rises and falls in three cycles, each containing petition and lament and climaxing in a vow of praise. Linking these sections are images and key terms.

35:1–10 / The first cycle is dominated by petitions that heap one image of conflict and hostility upon another. In verses 1–3 the petitions are imperatives calling on Yahweh to engage himself as a warrior. He is asked to match the hostilities of the opponents **(Contend, O LORD, with those who contend with me)** and take up military weapons (to **fight** with **shield** and **spear**). The final imperative of this section is, **Say to my soul, "I am your salvation."** It certainly adds a personal note to this rescue, and it may be a formal request for a responding oracle of salvation.

The rest of the petitions of this section are wishes (Hb. jussives: **may . . .**). While the imperatives emphasize actions that Yahweh is to perform, the wishes emphasize the consequences the opponents should face: **those who plot my ruin** are to be **put to shame** (v. 4), **those who pursue me** (v. 3) are to have **their path be dark and slippery, with the angel of the LORD pursuing them** (v. 6), and the hunters are to become their own prey (vv. 7–8). In another image, the fate of the foe will be to become **like chaff before the wind,** scattered and without substance and life. In this cycle only one verse is a formal lament, and it simply sets up the request that the opponents become their own victims (vv. 7–8).

Rounding off this section is a vow of praise. In anticipation of deliverance, there is normally attached a thanksgiving, which will celebrate Yahweh's specific action on behalf of this individual. In this case, there is attached hymnic praise that celebrates

Yahweh's characteristic action on behalf of **the poor and needy.** Here he is depicted as the incomparable rescuer, and the opponents as strong robbers.

35:11–18 / The psalm's second cycle contains only one petition and is dominated by laments concerning the foes. They begin with legal imagery, where the opponents are depicted as **ruthless witnesses** guilty of betrayal **(they repay me evil for good).** Their treachery is illustrated by the contrasting responses to each party's time of need: **when they were ill, . . . I went about mourning,** but **when I stumbled, they gathered** and "tore" (lit.) **me without ceasing, and gnashed their teeth at me.** Here the imagery of the opponents begins to shift to that of **lions.** (This image may also be echoed in the third cycle: "We have swallowed him up" in v. 25 and "they have widened their mouth over me" [lit.] in v. 21a.) In turn, Yahweh is depicted as the rescuer: **Rescue my life from their ravages.** Attached to this petition and closing off this second cycle is a vow to **give you thanks in the great assembly.** Most prayer psalms do not lodge a formal complaint against God, but prefacing this petition is one that implicates him as a passive bystander: **O Lord, how long will you look on?** In context, it appears that the anticipated praise of verse 10 has raised expectations. Yahweh is characterized as "you" who "rescue the poor from those too strong for them," but the apparent lack of rescue gives grounds for complaint.

35:19–28 / The third cycle is again dominated by petitions. Like those in the first cycle, they consist of imperatives emphasizing actions God should perform and of wishes emphasizing consequences to those **who gloat over my distress** (v. 26) and to **those who delight in my vindication** (v. 27). The first wish stresses that they are **my enemies without cause** (cf. v. 7). The subsequent two-verse lament depicts them as "plotters" (NIV **devise,** cf. v. 4) and violators of peace in society **(false accusations** is a more specific translation than "deceitful words" warrants) and as gloaters. The transition to petitioning God is determined by a key verb: they **have seen it,** so surely, **O Lord, you have seen this** (vv. 21–22). This verb also ties the third cycle with the second, which complained, "O Lord, how long will you look on?" (lit. "see," v. 17). To stir God from his apparent passivity, he is now petitioned, **be not silent** and **awake!** The petitions of verses 22–24 are imperatives that call on God to take legal actions **(rise to my defense** and **vindicate**—lit. "judge"—**me).** Thus, while the first set of imperatives in the psalm (vv. 1–3) puts God in the role of warrior, this second set (vv. 22–24) puts him in the role of judge. Supporting the appeal that Yahweh become the advocate for "my defense" is the twofold reference to **my God.**

The petitions of verses 25–27 are wishes (jussives), which focus on consequences. Those "who rejoice (NIV 'gloat') over my distress" are to **be put to shame** (cf. v. 4), but "those who delight in my vindication" are to **shout for joy and gladness** (lit. "rejoice"). The issue of who "rejoices" is key to the psalm. This is the same verb behind the NIV's "glee" in verse 15 and **gloat** in verses 19, 24, 26. Another key word is the verb "to say" (Hb. ʾmr), in verses 3, 10, 21, 25, 27, though variously rendered in the NIV. As the speaker had "put on sackcloth" (lit. "my clothing was sackcloth") on behalf of his opponents (v. 13), so now they are to **be clothed with shame.** Although the enemies **exalt themselves over me,** ultimately my fellow rejoicers will **say, "The LORD be exalted."** As they "delight in my vindication," so Yahweh **delights in the well-being** (lit. "peace," contrast v. 20) **of his servant.** The third and final cycle closes with a vow of praise that draws attention to God's **righteousness,** a divine attribute that was upheld earlier in support of a petition (v. 24). This denotes no mere static quality but a dynamic character and ability that "puts things right."

§36 Deceived Deceivers, and the Feasting Followers of the Lord (Ps. 36)

Initially verses 1–4 and 5–9 appear to share little in common, and their abrupt change of subject matter may suggest they were artificially spliced together. What connection is there between describing the character of the wicked and praising Yahweh's love and righteousness, along with the riches of his house? Interpreters have struggled with this issue, particularly, because the psalm does not fit the standard form-critical categories. Kraus has thus described it as "didactic poetry" (*Psalms 1–59*, p. 397) and Craigie as "a literary and devotional composition" (*Psalms 1–50*, p. 291). The sections of the psalm (vv. 1–4, 5–9, 10–12), however, are interlocked by key terms. The issue of the heart and the wicked ties together the opening (v. 1) and closing sections (vv. 10–11), while Yahweh's righteousness and love tie together the second and third (vv. 5–6, 10). Most importantly, however, an awareness of the liturgy of temple entrance (as outlined in the Introduction) helps us to make sense of the psalm as an integrated unity.

When attempting to reconstruct the circumstances surrounding the psalm's use, most commentators begin with the apparent conflict between the speaker and the wicked. Kraus, for example, believes he "is persecuted by insolent enemies" and thus looks for "asylum" (*Psalms 1–59*, pp. 398–400). But the first and only mention of "I"/"me" in this psalm occurs in verse 11. The parallelism of these verses implies that the "me" of verse 11 is simply a representative speaking on behalf of the upright in heart of verse 10. The four opening verses provide a description of the wicked, but say nothing about threats against the speaker or anyone else—the wicked are simply described in their own right. Threat is implied in verse 11, but it is mentioned only as a possibility, not as an imminent reality.

To understand verses 1–4, we must ask "What is said?" and "Why is it said?" Why does the psalm bother to present a character description of the wicked? It does not lament any distress the wicked inflict on God's people, nor does it contain a verdict of judgment or a sentence of punishment. To answer this question, we must first note that verse 1 should probably read, "An oracle. Transgression belongs to the wicked; it is in the midst of his heart" (see below). Thus, "an oracle" (v. 1) probably belongs with the superscription. Verses 1–4 are an oracle describing the wicked. This is similar to the temple entry liturgy of Psalm 15, where verses 2–5 should be regarded as an oracle describing "the doer of righteousness." As the description of the righteous answers the question, "LORD, who may dwell in your sanctuary?" in Psalm 15, so the description of the wicked in Psalm 36 informs God's people who may not feast on the abundance of God's house (v. 8).

Several verbal parallels also connect Psalm 36 with the temple entry liturgies of Psalms 15 and 24. The character profiles found in Psalms 15 and 36 illustrate with the same three bodily parts: the heart (reading "his heart," 36:1; 15:2), the eyes (36:1, 2; 15:4, lit., "despised in his eyes is a rejected one"), and the mouth (36:3) or "tongue" (15:3). In each, attention is given to wicked speech which is described as "deceitful" (Hb. *mirmâ*, 3 and 24:4, NIV, "what is false"). In Psalm 36, the wicked do not reject (Hb. *mᵓs*, v. 4) what should be "rejected" according to 15:4 (NIV, "a vile man"). Also in each, Yahweh's righteousness is to be imputed to the upright in heart (36:10) or those with "a pure heart" (24:4). Psalm 36 also contains a number of parallels with other psalms of temple entry (see the Introduction), especially Psalm 5 (36:1–2 // 5:9–10; 36:2 // 5:5 and 26:5; 36:3 // 5:6; 36:7 // 5:11; 36:4, 12 // 5:5, 10 and 52:5; 36:10–11 // 26:9 and 28:3). Thus, Psalm 36 was probably written for all worshipers participating in the regular liturgy, not for lone individuals in a particular crisis.

In light of the temple entry liturgy, we can make sense of the development of Psalm 36. In an oracle, delivered by a temple prophet, Yahweh describes to the congregation the character of the wicked (vv. 1–4). In response to this oracle, the congregation next hears (perhaps through a choir) praise addressed to him describing his loving and righteous character. This provides a striking contrast (vv. 5–9). The closing petitions respond first positively to the hymnic praise of God and then negatively to the wicked described in the opening oracle (vv. 10–12).

36:1–4 / "Transgression" (NIV **sinfulness**) penetrates to the very **heart** of **the wicked** person. Displacing the **fear of God before his eyes, he flatters himself** (lit. "he makes smooth") **in his own eyes.** This amounts to self-idolatry. When primacy is given to one's self, God need not be feared. But to carry out this action, self-deception is necessary: "he hates to find his iniquity" (lit., v. 2b). Because transgression has penetrated his *heart* and self-flattery has displaced God in his *eyes,* now **the words of his mouth are wicked and deceitful.** He is both deceived and deceiving. Illustrating the comprehensive nature of his evil are contrasting bodily postures: **on his bed he plots evil** (cf. Mic. 2:2) and "he takes his stand on a way not good" (lit., cf. 1:1). Evil thus proceeds from one's thinking to one's speech and to one's actions.

36:5–9 / In this contrasting hymnic description of Yahweh, two pairs of attributes are celebrated in their vast cosmic dimensions—**love** and **faithfulness,** and **righteousness** and **justice.** We then hear how these attributes are demonstrated toward all God's creatures **(both man and beast)** and his worshipers in particular. He provides shelter, food, drink, and light, not only as needed but in **abundance.** The symbolism of the temple may underlie this praise of Yahweh. Psalm 89:14–15 celebrates the same two pairs of attributes in connection with a ritual procession of the cherubim-ark. Both psalms celebrate Yahweh's **light,** which may have had its symbolic counterpart in the ritual worship. In Psalm 36, the linking of the cosmos (vv. 5–6) and **your house** (vv. 7–9) may be explained by the cherubim-chariot, which symbolized Yahweh as "him who rides the ancient skies above" (see on Ps. 68, esp. vv. 33–34). "**They feast on the** abundance **of** your house" is not merely a metaphor for a rich banquet but points to the symbolism of the "thanksgiving" or "fellowship offerings," portions of which were to be eaten by the worshipers themselves (Lev. 3; 7:11–36).

36:10–12 / The closing petitions and confession of trust tie together the preceding, seemingly disparate sections. The first responds to the praise of Yahweh's **love** and **righteousness** (the first word of each of the word pairs) and so is positive. It requests that these attributes **continue** to God's people, who are described first by their relationship to him **(those who know you)** and then by their moral stature **(the upright in heart).** The second petition responds to the oracle about **the wicked** and so is negative. It picks up again the motif of bodily parts: **the foot of**

the proud and **the hand of** the wicked. Its verbs make plain the significance of Yahweh's oracle about the wicked: may they **not come against me, nor . . . drive me away.** Thus, after hearing Yahweh himself describe the character of those he rejects, the congregation is given greater motivation to say their "Amen" to these petitions. To be subject to the influence of the wicked is to be driven away from "the abundance of your house," because they are the ones not permitted to enter the temple. Thus, as the psalm progresses, the circle narrows from all God's creatures (v. 6) to his worshipers (vv. 7–10) and finally to the individual worshiper (v. 11).

The first thing heard by the congregation when this psalm is performed is the contrast of the character of the wicked with the character of Yahweh. They are thus faced with the question of whose company they wish to join. Only after the issue of relationship is presented does that of rewards and punishment surface. First, they hear of the benefits of entering Yahweh's house. Then, after the congregation hears their petition expressed and so declare their loyalty, they hear of the fate of **the evildoers.** Their judgment is consistent with their presumption: they who would "take their stand" (Hb. *yityaṣṣēb*, NIV "commits himself," v. 4) now **lie fallen—thrown down, not able to rise** (v. 12). Thus, the petition of the psalm, **may the** "foot of the proud not come against me" (v. 11) is seen to have its effect.

In the closing petitions, we hear echoed, "There but for the grace of God go I." They, in effect, acknowledge the temptation that the wicked present. Those who hear this psalm now realize their status as Yahweh's worshipers is not guaranteed unconditionally. While the in-group is called "the upright in heart," they are still in need of his love and righteousness to enter (v. 10, cf. 5:7). It is Yahweh's righteousness that is central here, not that of humans. This righteousness, celebrated in verse 6, is here imputed to his people (see Introduction and commentary on Ps. 24 for further discussion on imputed righteousness). Yahweh is depicted as magnanimous in the extreme, willing to help all his creatures. He is a rich host par excellence (cf. 23:5–6) and the source of life (cf. Garden of Eden, Hb. *ʿēden*, perhaps echoed in "river of," Hb. *ʿᵃdānêkā*). But those who find fascination in themselves, instead of him, find themselves excluded from his gifts.

Additional Notes §36

36:1 / An oracle is within my heart concerning the sinfulness of the wicked: The NIV's rendering of this verse is awkward, in part because the Hb. of the MT IS awkward. The expression "an oracle of transgression" is without parallel in the OT. We should probably read with a few MSS, the Syriac, and the LXX Hb. *libbô*, "in his heart," instead of Hb. *libbî*, "in my heart." Craigie's proposal is the most satisfactory: "an oracle" stands independently, probably as part of the superscription (*Psalms 1–50*, p. 290).

36:7 / Both high and low among men: With this translation, the NIV attempts to render the MT as it stands. But the Hb. phrase, *ᵉlōhîm ûbnê ᵓādām*, should normally be translated, "God and sons of man." It is possible *ᵉlōhîm* belongs with v. 7a, thus forming a parallel with "O LORD" in v. 6b ("O LORD, you preserve . . . your unfailing love, O God!"). *BHS* proposes reading *ᵓēlêkā yābōᵓû*, thus "to you the sons of man come" (cf., 65:2), which forms a suitable parallel to "they" **find refuge in the shadow of your wings.**

§37 Cultivating Faithfulness Until the Flourishing Wicked Wither (Ps. 37)

To make sense of this wisdom psalm we must first pay heed to hints of its social setting. The wicked have wealth, the righteous little (v. 16). A chief concern is that of "possessing (Hb. *yrš*, NIV 'inherit') the land" (vv. 9, 11, 22, 29, 34). Verse 3b literally reads, "Tent the land and shepherd faithfulness." This may suggest that the righteous live as pastoralists or semi-nomads, not as settlers. They live in the land but the wicked are its owners. The notions of righteousness and justice (esp. vv. 6, 28 [lit. "Yahweh loves justice"], 30, 33) are not general moral categories but point to particular legal issues of the day, namely that the families who are the rightful owners of land have lost it to the wealthy wicked.

This psalm offers wonderful promises, several of which have been favorites among believers (e.g., vv. 4–6). But readers who have claimed such promises for their own lives and have experienced deep disappointment may think it misleading. Other believers familiar with the harsh realities that many of God's people have suffered through the ages may think its claims go too far, perhaps to the point of naïveté (e.g., vv. 10, 19, 25–26, 32–33). Within the OT, one may think of Naboth's false accusation and execution (1 Kgs. 21:8–13), and of prophets imprisoned (1 Kgs. 22:26–27; Jer. 20:2; 37:15) and executed (1 Kgs. 19:10; 2 Chron. 24:20–21). And several psalms express deep concern that the result promised so assuredly in verses 6 and 33 is not so assured (e.g., Pss. 7; 17; 73). To assume, however, that these promises are blanket guarantees is to misjudge the genre (or kind of literature) and purpose of the psalm. In addition, if one expects the psalm to explain philosophically the problem of the wicked having wealth and the righteous having little (e.g., v. 16), one will leave it disappointed. But this too reflects a misjudgment of the psalm's genre.

The opening series of imperatives indicates the psalm is concerned with educational instruction, not philosophical argument. Unlike most psalms this one contains no hints of liturgical use (there are no ritual instructions, references to temple or altar, changes of liturgical speaker, mentions of prayer or praise, etc.). It is an acrostic, and each successive verse pair (roughly) begins with a letter of the Hebrew alphabet and contains a self-contained proverb. In fact, many of its verses closely parallel those in the book of Proverbs (37:1 // 24:19; 37:5 // 16:3; 37:16 // 15:16; 37:24 // 24:16; 37:28a // 2:8; 37:30 // 10:31; 37:37–38 // 23:18 and 24:14; 37:38 // 24:20). The autobiographical style of some observations (37:25–26, 35–36) is also echoed in Proverbs (24:30–34). Psalm 37 is thus more of a collection of proverbs than a traditional psalm. These features help to explain why it does not contain strophes or develop the way most psalms do (note the many repetitions: e.g., vv. 10 and 35–36, 1–11 and 34, 12–15 and 32–33).

The primary purpose of proverbs is to instruct "the simple" and "the young" to understand and practice wise attitudes and conduct (Prov. 1:1–7, 8; 2:1–11; 3:1, etc.). They offer observations on the *general* patterns of life (Prov. 24:30–34) and do not pretend to offer blanket guarantees. Footnotes concerning temporary setbacks or exceptions do not have a place in such pithy statements (usually a single v.). They teach primarily by contrasting the "way" (Hb. *derek* or *ʾôrâ*, meaning lifestyle or pattern of conduct) of "the righteous" and the "way" of "the wicked" (e.g., Prov. 2:12, 20; 4:11, 14, 18; 15:9–10, 19). The prime test in this contrast lies with the ultimate "end" or "outcome" (Hb. *ʾaḥᵃrît*, see Prov. 5:4, 11; 14:12–13; 19:20; 20:21; 23:18; 24:14, 20) of each "way."

This same concern and, in fact, the same Hebrew term (*ʾaḥᵃrît*, NIV "future"), appears in the conclusion of our psalm (vv. 37–38), which contrasts the righteous and the wicked throughout. Its aim is thus to instruct people to follow Yahweh's way (v. 34) to its ultimate outcome (v. 37) in spite of temptations en route. These temptations are most evident from the psalm's imperatives, and include selling out to the wicked (v. 27) because of envy (v. 1), loosing faith in Yahweh (vv. 3–5), and becoming enraged at life's inequities and at God himself (vv. 1, 7, 8; a more accurate translation than "do not fret" is "do not become enraged"). The starting point for the psalm is thus not the problem of the wicked prospering and Yahweh's righteous suffering; this issue is given mention simply because it calls into question the value of pursuing Yahweh's way. While Psalm 37 may not satisfy our curiosity about such enigmas, it may ultimately be more helpful than a treatise on suffering. The psalm's development may be traced as follows. The opening imperative section (vv. 1–11) concerns trusting in Yahweh and the eventual "withering" of the wicked. Verses 12–15 turn to the attack they mount against the righteous, and verses 16–20 return to their inevitable withering. Verses 21–31 focus on the prescribed behavior of the righteous: they are generous (vv. 21–26), and do good (vv. 27–29), and are motivated by the inner guide of God's law (vv. 30–31). The subsequent sections return to topics of attack (vv. 32–33), trust in God (v. 34), and the withering of the wicked (vv. 35–36). The psalm concludes with moral imperatives and points to the ultimate (vv. 37–38) and meantime (vv. 39–40) solutions of the problem.

Pastoral images dominate the psalm. Repeatedly the righteous are promised they will inherit the land (vv. 9, 11, 22, 29, 34). (The verb, however, is actually not "inherit" but "possess": Hb. *yrš*.) In the meantime, the wicked are apparently the landowners, but they are likened to grass or a tree that withers (vv. 2, 20, 35–36)—in contrast to the righteous, who do not wither (v. 19). So the righteous are now to live as pastoralists, who "tent" (Hb. *škn*, vv. 3, 27, 29, NIV "dwell"/live) in the land and "shepherd (Hb. *rʿh*) faithfulness" (v. 3, see above) and "uprightness" (v. 37, see Additional Notes). The strangeness of "shepherding faithfulness and uprightness," in effect, seeks to divert one's preoccupation with material property to relational qualities that please Yahweh.

37:1–11 / The opening section contains a concentrated series of imperatives. Its opening and closing imperative is "do not become enraged." This indignation is provoked not by the existence per se of **evil men** but by their material prosperity and success (see esp. v. 7). The second imperative in verse 1 concerns another temptation the righteous are to avoid: do not ... **be envious.** In the first temptation, one is repulsed by the wicked and, in the second, one is drawn to them. Though they go in opposite directions from their object, they share a fallacious assumption, namely, that the current prosperity of the wicked is indicative of lasting success and stability. This psalm has no illusions about "success": it is often obtained via **wicked schemes** (v. 7) and thus cannot serve as an unequivocal sign of God's blessing.

Anger and **wrath** are the natural reactions to unfair treatment, but they are to be curbed because they lead to means that
are no different from the "schemes" of the wicked. The psalm,
however, does not wish to encourage social indifference. The
reason that it seeks to curb emotions that motivate social revolu-
tion is that **evil men will be cut off,** and in **a little while, the
wicked will be no more** (vv. 9, 10) The end is assured. The only
question is the means one will pursue. It is **those who hope in the
LORD** and **the meek** that **will inherit the land** (vv. 9, 11), not
those who oust the wicked themselves. In the future, they will
"take great delight (Hb. *ʿng*) in the abundant well-being/peace"
(v. 11), but in the meantime they are commanded, **Delight yourself** (Hb. *ʿng*) **in the LORD** (v. 4). This Hebrew root in other contexts means to "pamper oneself" (Deut. 28:54, 56; Isa. 47:1; 55:2).
To divert one's preoccupation with material prosperity and success, the psalm instructs us to find our delight in relationship
with Yahweh himself.

37:12–15 / Here the posture of the wicked changes.
They are not mere objects of temptation for the righteous but are
active aggressors against them. These verses promise that for the
wicked **their day** (of judgment) **is coming** and that they will
become their own victims, but the verses do not pretend to
offer guarantees that the righteous are spared their hostility
altogether.

37:16–20 / This section, in fact, admits the wicked (also
called here **the LORD's enemies**) have **wealth** and **power** and can
be compared to **the beauty of the fields.** It also indicates the righteous have **little,** and there are **times of disaster** and **days of famine** of which they are a part. The well-being of the righteous is
not absolute but relative; it is **better . . . than** that of the wicked,
not in terms of quantity but in terms of lasting quality: **the days
of the blameless are known to the LORD, and their inheritance
will endure forever.**

37:21–24 / Aside from the general imperative to do
good (v. 3), verse 21 is the psalm's first comment on the behavior
of the righteous: they **give generously.** Implicit in verse 22 is that
Yahweh's blessing or cursing does not necessarily exhibit itself
in the current state of one's welfare. His blessing *will* result
in inheriting the land; his cursing *will* result in being cut off.
(The context of the psalm indicates that the Hb. imperfect should

be interpreted as a future action.) Verses 23–24 offer promise through the image of a child whose feet may slip out but whose hand is grasped by the parent (cf. 73:2, 23). Again, the righteous are not spared from stumbling but they are promised support.

37:25–26 / Readers may misunderstand verse 25 as an indication that the speaker has led a narrow or sheltered life. The next verse makes clear that focus is not given to mere individuals. It is the generosity of the righteous community (note also v. 21) that precludes righteous children from begging bread. These verses speak in the plural.

37:27–29 / This section continues an interest in children but here in negative terms: **the offspring of the wicked will be cut off.** The righteous, on the other hand, receive Yahweh's protection and assurance that they **will inherit the land.**

37:30–31 / Four bodily images now describe the character of the **righteous:** the **mouth** that speaks of **wisdom** and the **tongue** of justice (lit., because "the LORD loves justice," v. 28), the **heart** that receives God's law, and the **feet** that are secure. This may be contrasted with the "arms (NIV 'power') of the wicked" that will be broken (v. 17).

37:32–36 / These verses, for the most part, simply repeat earlier motifs. Verses 32–33 echo verses 12–15: the wicked are hostile toward the righteous but the Lord will ultimately preserve them. Verse 34 repeats the imperative advice of the opening section, verses 1–11: **Wait for the LORD** and **he will exalt you to inherit the land.** Likewise verses 35–36 restate the same notion and some of the same phrases as verse 10.

37:37–40 / The final four verses summarize the ultimate and immediate solutions to the problem. The ultimate end of the two ways is that **the man of peace** has **a future** (lit. "outcome"), but **the future of the wicked will be cut off.** In the meantime, believers are assured Yahweh **delivers them from the wicked . . . because they take refuge in him.**

Overall, therefore, the moral of this psalm is that one should pursue Yahweh's way because in the end the righteous will inherit the land and the wicked will be cut off from it. But what, then, specifically does it promise believers, and what is the time frame of the judgment? We cannot appeal to retribution beyond death. This psalm, along with the rest of the Psalter (with only a few possible exceptions), makes no hint of such. In fact, it claims the "cutting off" of the wicked will take place **soon** (v. 2) and in a little while (v. 10). "You [i.e., in your lifetime] will see when the wicked are cut off" (v. 34). And verse 10 appears to indicate this will be no isolated act of judgment but a comprehensive extermination.

Verses of the psalm also give the impression that believers may always expect to be "satisfied" (Hb. *śbᶜ*; the NIV's "will enjoy plenty" clearly overstates the Hb. text here) in days of famine (v. 19, also vv. 25–26). Believers may also expect never to be victims of injustice (vv. 6, 32–33) because the wicked will cut their own throats first (vv. 12–15).

But as we noted above, this psalm is a collection of proverbs, and no single proverb in isolation intends to be the final or comprehensive word. This is clearly not the point of such short sayings. In the context of the whole collection that Psalm 37 forms, certain tensions emerge, where one proverb clarifies or moderates another (cf. Prov. 26:4–5). A righteous person is promised that his feet do not slip (v. 31), but he may stumble (lit. "fall," v. 24). One is also promised the desires of his heart (v. 4), but one may also possess little (v. 16). And one is not promised to be spared entirely from experiencing times of disaster (v. 19) and of trouble (v. 39). Perhaps most significant is how this collection ends. It is the ultimate outcome that is clear (vv. 37–38). In the meantime, Yahweh promises his help (vv. 39–40). But there is no triumphalism here. The righteous must see themselves—for the present at least—as Yahweh's refugees (v. 40).

Additional Notes §37

37:26 / **Their children will be blessed:** A more literal translation is, "and his descendants become a blessing."

37:28 / **They will be protected forever:** In the MT the acrostic is complete except the *ayin*-strophe is disturbed by Hb. *lᵉᶜôlām*. Instead of the NIV's rendering of the MT (which may reflect haplography), we should probably read, "wrongdoers will be exterminated forever," as suggested by LXX (see *BHS*).

37:35 / **Flourishing like a green tree in its native soil:** The second colon makes little sense in the MT, a literal rendering of which is, "pouring himself out [or 'showing himself naked'!] like a luxuriant native." We should probably follow LXX: "raising himself up like the cedars of Lebanon."

37:36 / **He soon passed away:** The versions read, "And *I* passed by."

37:37 / **Consider the blameless, observe the upright:** Instead, we should probably read, "Keep integrity and shepherd uprightness." In place of the MT's adjectives, "a blameless one" and "an upright one," the versions suggest that nouns form the correct reading: "integrity" and "uprightness" (their consonants are identical). For the MT's *wrʾh* ("and see" or "observe") we should perhaps follow the Syriac and read *wrʿh* ("and shepherd"), which is used similarly in v. 3b: "and shepherd faithfulness" (NIV "and enjoy safe pasture").

§38 A Prayer for the Sick (Ps. 38)

This prayer psalm of the individual suits the special needs of sickness (cf. Ps. 41). It reflects the typical predicament in which the sick found themselves. It was common in ancient Israel (Job is the most notable OT case) and elsewhere in the ancient Near East to assume the sick person was suffering divine judgment for some sin against God or the gods (for a graphic portrayal of this world view in the ancient Near East, see Keel, *Symbolism*, pp. 79–81). As a result, acquaintances kept their distance from the "sinner." The sick suffered not only physical and emotional anguish ("My back is filled with searing pain," and "I groan in anguish of heart," vv. 7, 8) but also social alienation ("My friends and companions avoid me because of my wounds," v. 11), personal guilt ("My guilt has overwhelmed me," v. 4), and God's displeasure ("because of your wrath," v. 3). Moreover, in this psalm the belief in personal sin and God's punishing wrath is not merely presumed by cultural convention; the reciter must own his own failure before God. Yet it is to this God the psalmic liturgy directs the sick. While it is a liturgy in the sense that it is a set prayer to be overseen by a recognized liturgist (perhaps even an elder of the local clan), we should not expect the sick person to be transported to a sacred site. Rather, it was probably intoned at the bedside (see further Gerstenberger, *Psalms*, p. 164).

The psalm does not merely describe the speaker's anguish; the poem portrays it with several metaphors and images. God's hostility is depicted as a military assault: arrows and a striking hand (v. 2). Guilt is likened to a burden too heavy to bear (v. 4). The expressions of the speaker's emotional state are drawn from mourning rites for the dead (v. 6). His eyes are an extinguished lamp (v. 10). The opponents are portrayed as hunters (v. 12).

38:1–12 / The psalm unfolds with an introductory petition (v. 1, cf. 6:1) and a lament that concerns Yahweh's afflicting **wrath** (vv. 2–3), the speaker's personal anguish (vv. 4–10), and his rejection by **friends** and **neighbors** (vv. 11–12). This extended lament is aimed to move God to pity. Among these laments stands a confession of trust, laying claim to God's already intimate acquaintance with his condition: **all my longings lie open before you** (v. 9).

The expression, frequent in the Psalms, **those who seek my life** (v. 12) sounds to our ears like the enemies attempt murder. As a result, we find it difficult to identify with a psalm such as this. But before we assume we know what this expression means, we should note that it is elucidated further by its context. First, the primary circumstance reflected in the psalm is sickness. Second, the actions of the others in the psalm are presented as a reaction to this sickness—they are not the initial cause of distress (vv. 11–12, 19–20). The speaker's nearness to death is due to his physical illness, not to social enemies (e.g., v. 17). Third, the actions attributed to "those who seek my life" in particular are that they **talk of my ruin, plot deception,** and commit slander. In other words, the **traps** they **set** and the **harm** they "seek" (lit.) are to ruin the sick person by spreading rumors that destroy his reputation and his social position as a legitimate member of God's people. They are not attempting physical homicide as such.

38:13–22 / Another confession of trust (vv. 13–16) follows the lament, where the speaker disclaims any attempt to present his own defense to others. Rather, because the speaker has called on Yahweh, he asserts his vindication will come from Yahweh, not from his own lips. Here there surfaces the tradition fundamental to the psalms of the individual, namely that **my God . . . will answer** when I call (see further in the Introduction). Verses 17–20 largely repeat what was said in the earlier lament, though adding a measure of urgency. Verse 17 laments again his personal anguish but notes the imminence of his demise **(I am about to fall).** Verse 18 echoes the reference to his burdensome **sin** and adds an explicit confession. Verses 19–20 echoes the lament of his social alienation and notes how prevalent **(many** and **numerous)** and undeserving (they **repay my good with evil**) it is. Rounding off the psalm are general petitions for God's nearness and for a quick intervention (cf. 22:11, 19). These petitions also remind God of the bond that exists between them (**my God** and **my Savior,** vv. 21–22).

§39 Turn Your Gaze from Me before I Am No More (Ps. 39)

Psalm 39 is most akin to the prayer psalms of the individual but it is unlike any other, as its closing petition alone shows: "Look away from me, that I may rejoice again before I depart and am no more." It resonates with Job and Ecclesiastes more than with other psalms. The refrain, "each man's life is but a breath" (Hb. *hebel*, vv. 5, 11), echoes that of Ecclesiastes: "Everything is a breath" (Hb. *hebel*, NIV "meaningless," Eccl. 1:2; 12:8). Unlike most psalms, this one has a ring of autobiography (esp. vv. 1–3, 9). It also reflects a contrast between those who heap up wealth (vv. 6, 11) and the speaker who characterizes himself as a social alien and stranger (or "sojourner," v. 12; cf. the situation in Ps. 37). These two features are also prominent in Psalm 73 (vv. 3–5, 12), which similarly reflects personal anguish (39:1–3, 9; 73:13–14, 16, 21–22), restraint of speech (39:1; 73:15), and the realization that the Lord is one's sole hope (39:7; 73:25–26). It also uses the same Hebrew terminology to describe the speaker's scourge and rebuke (39:10, 11; in 73:14 the NIV renders these Hb. words as "plagued" and "punished"). Similarly, Psalm 90 echoes the brevity of our days (39:4–5; 90:9–12)—especially when viewed before God (39:5; 90:4–6)—and the conception of God's "consuming" anger enflamed by human "sin" (39:11; 90:7–9, 11, 15). These psalms may thus stem from the same social circles.

Psalm 39 uses terms of sickness ("anguish" or "pain" in v. 2, "scourge" or "plague" in v. 10), which is consistent with the reflections on the frailty of life (vv. 5, 11, 13). On the other hand, they may also be metaphoric for deep emotional distress. Both of these terms are used in connection with the speaker's bridle of silence before the wicked.

39:1–3 / The psalm opens with a confessed **(I said)** vow of silence, **as long as the wicked are in my presence.** The reason is to **keep my tongue from sin.** The form of sin is not spelled out—whether it reflects a temptation to join them (cf. 73:3), a denial of one's faith and friends (cf. 73:13–15), or a lashing out with hostile words. Nevertheless, the speaker's passion is aroused **(My heart grew hot within me)**, and he breaks his vow but only to voice a prayer to God. He "keeps" his "tongue from sin" before "the wicked" by "speaking" with his **tongue** before God. Although not said explicitly to God, these opening verses serve to show God the speaker's personal anguish.

39:4–6 / The resulting prayer is not what we expect. It is initially a prayer about knowledge or insight (Hb. *yd*ᶜ is used twice, rendered in the NIV by **show me** and **let me know**), not about a moral dilemma, but about **how fleeting is my life.** This is thus a prayer for perspective. The realization that he asks God to impress upon him (introduced in v. 5 with Hb. *hinnê* and emphasized in v. 6 with Hb. *ʾak*) is **the span of my years is as nothing before you,** and in fact, **each man's life is but a breath.** Verse 6 shows the relevance of this prayer for the speaker's moral dilemma: **Man . . . bustles about, but only in vain** (Hb. *hebel*, "as a breath"); **he heaps up wealth, not knowing who will get it.** One's life is too short of time and of guarantees to busy oneself with piling up things.

39:7–11 / **But now** signals a turning point. In view of this futility, **what do I look for?** There is only one prospect: **My hope is in you.** The prayer that follows this affirmation of loyalty to God is, **save me** (lit. "deliver me") **from all my transgressions.** Should God not do so, he would become **the scorn of fools,** that is, those wicked before whom he was silent and had muzzled his **mouth** at the psalm's beginning (cf. vv. 1–2 and 9). His profession of faith in God would prove to be nonsense. Yet this dilemma of being **silent** before the wicked is no personal accident, rather, God is **the one who has done this.** While it is possible that God's **scourge** could refer to an illness, it suits the context better to see it connected to the divine action just mentioned, namely, that of muzzling the speaker's mouth. (Rather than **the blow of your hand,** we should probably read, "the strength of your hand.") The parallelism of verse 8 and the progression developed in verses 9–10 seem to suggest that the speaker's dumbness before the fools or wicked is due to his acute awareness of his transgressions. Before the wicked, he is faced with the moral dilemma of being both a person of faith (or hope, v. 7) and a person of transgressions (v. 8). Similarly, believers today often shy from sharing their faith because they feel hypocrites themselves.

39:12–13 / The psalm's closing petitions begin with phrases typical of the prayer psalms **(Hear, listen)** but soon shift to those more in keeping with Job (see esp. 14:6) and Ecclesiastes. The psalm characterizes the speaker as **an alien** and **a stranger— with you** (cf. Lev. 25:23; 1 Chron. 29:15). He is without social connections and support. As confessed already, his only connection, his only hope (v. 7), is the God who hears the prayer. Yet ironically it is God's scrutinizing gaze that is his chief problem: **Look away from me, that I may rejoice again before I depart and am no more.** As noted in verse 11, "you"—characteristically— "rebuke and discipline men for their sin" (cf. Ps. 90:8–9). This psalm, perhaps like no other, recognizes the tension that God is our only hope and yet his gaze consumes us. The only relief in sight lies in the petition, "Deliver me from all my transgressions" (v. 8). For the ultimate deliverance we must await the pages of the New Testament.

§40 Past and Future Deliverances and Present Trust and Obedience (Ps. 40)

Psalm 40 looks like two psalms of the individual spliced together. Verses 1–10 sound like a thanksgiving psalm and verses 11–17 like a prayer psalm. In support of this division we should note that verses 13–17 elsewhere form an independent prayer psalm, namely Psalm 70. Closer examination, however, reveals the integrity of the whole psalm. The thanksgiving of verses 1–10 lacks the report of distress characteristic of thanksgiving psalms (see the Introduction). The prayer of Psalm 70 also lacks any formal lament, which is found only in verse 12 of Psalm 40. In addition, the verses closing the so-called thanksgiving (vv. 9–10) actually appear to set the stage for the subsequent petitionary section. Psalm 70 may therefore be a selection drawn from Psalm 40. As Psalm 53 in Book II of the Psalter is a variant of Psalm 14 in Book I, so Psalm 70 in Book II may have been transmitted in a collection separate from Psalm 40 that found its way into Book I.

The speaker is an individual, but the mention of "our" (v. 3) and "us" (v. 5) appears to assume the psalm is performed before and, thus at least to some extent, on behalf of a congregation. Verse 5 is particularly suggestive that the speaker serves as a spokesperson for the "us": "were I to speak and tell of . . . the things you planned for us . . . they would be too many to declare." The praise that the "I" recites includes not merely what concerns him but also what concerns the congregation. It is therefore possible that the entire psalm was performed on behalf of a congregation, not merely on the speaker's own behalf. In other words, the "I" of the psalm may be a representative.

What would be the primary function of this liturgy? Characteristic of Yahweh and his plans for his worshipers (see esp. v. 5) is salvation. Worshipers come to the sanctuary with experiences of deliverance (esp. vv. 1–3, 9–10) and then depart from it with prayers for future rescues (esp. vv. 11–17). Verse 5 makes especially plain that this psalm concerns not merely a single instance of thanksgiving but many wonders. Within this scheme of praise for salvation past and petition for salvation future lie the blessing on those who trust (v. 4), the hymnic praise for Yahweh's many wonders (v. 5), and the acknowledgment that Yahweh desires obedience above sacrifice (vv. 6–8). Thus, verses 4–8 present the attitude that Yahweh blesses (namely, trust) and, likewise, the behavior that he desires (namely, obedience).

40:1–10 / **The slimy pit** and **the mud and mire** present the image of a cistern (cf. 69:1–2, 14–15). By contrast, Yahweh's salvation is depicted in the image of **a rock** and **a firm place to stand.** As seen in Psalm 22, this speaker is confident that his experience of deliverance will have repercussions to others (v. 3b). As in 31:6, one's trust in Yahweh is contrasted not with trust in false gods but with "looking to" people **who turn aside to false gods.**

The psalm's disclaimer regarding **sacrifice and offering** and its preference for doing **your will** and **your law** (or more accurately, "your instruction," Hb. *tôrâ*) are striking. They may even sound more prophetic than psalmic (e.g., 1 Sam. 15:22–23; Isa. 1:11–17; Mic. 6:6–8). However, they are found elsewhere in the Psalms (51:16–17; 69:30–31; cf. 50:8–15, 23). Perhaps the meaning of this confession is that Yahweh's prerequisite for entrance into his temple is not sacrifice but willingness to obey Yahweh's "instruction" or "torah." This would be consistent with the entry or torah liturgies of Psalms 15 and 24. If verses 6–8 are to be related directly to those that follow, we should understand the doing of "your will" to be the proclaiming of **your righteousness** (vv. 9–10). In this light, these verses are not a polemic against sacrifice per se; they merely assert that sacrificial offerings are not the prerequisite for entrance into the temple. In that sense, one cannot buy oneself into the temple. Verses 6–8 may be thus paraphrased as follows: "You do not require sacrificial offerings as a prerequisite for temple entry, but ears to hear your 'instruction.' So now I enter your temple—as my name is recorded in the 'scroll of the righteous'—to do your 'instruction.' " (On **the scroll,** see commentary on 87:6.) We should also note the later claim, "I am poor and needy." Psalm 69:30–31 similarly appears to make a disclaimer regarding ritual sacrifice, but it does so in connection with the poor and the needy (vv. 32–33). In other words, these are not polemics against sacrifice per se but confessions that Yahweh cherishes the thanksgiving of the economically disadvantaged (cf. 22:24–26). It is characteristic of Hebrew literary style to state a preference of one thing over another in terms that sound like an absolute dichotomy to our Western ears (see G. B. Caird, *The Language and Imagery of the Bible* [Philadelphia: Westminster, 1980], pp. 110–17).

The main subject of the speaker's proclamation is Yahweh's **righteousness** (vv. 9–10). Other terms spell out its significance, namely his **faithfulness and salvation,** and his **love** and **truth.** They indicate that "righteousness" in this context is a relational term, not a moral one. It points to his "putting things right" in a saving way, not to his moral perfections, which may condemn the sinner (which is how the term is often understood in Christian theology).

40:11–17 / While verse 11 appears to turn the psalm toward prayer, as distinct from praise in verses 1–10; there is really no clear break between verses 10 and 11, as the following verbal links between verses 9, 10, and 11 make clear: "I proclaim righteousness in the great assembly; I do not *restrain*" (Hb. *kl'*, NIV 'seal') my lips . . . . I do not conceal your love and your truth from the great assembly." **Do not** *restrain* (Hb. *kl'*, NIV **withhold**) **your mercy from me, O LORD; may your love and your truth always protect me.**

The lament of verse 12 concerns the speaker's sins and his failing heart, but the subsequent petitions concern his enemies (vv. 14–15). (Psalm 70 omits this lament and consists solely of the petitions in vv. 13–17.) Most interpreters of verses 14–15 have supposed the psalm refers to actual enemies who threaten to take the speaker's life. But several features call this assumption into question. First, the language is highly formulaic. The poet is not describing matters autobiographically. Second, the phrase **all who seek you** (v. 16) appears to denote all worshipers of Yahweh, and it echoes the earlier phrase **all who seek to take my life** (v. 14). This may imply that the latter is simply an antitype to the former. These verses thus show that, in principle, the people of God will have enemies and that God may be petitioned for protection. The phrase "those who seek my life" is normally understood to mean "those who would murder me." But the judgment this psalm seeks is not condemnation or death but **shame, confusion,** and **disgrace.**

§41 Vindication for the Sick Person (Ps. 41)

This psalm of the individual is suitable as a prayer for the sick. In this context, it focuses on the petitioner's vindication before "my enemies" and, thus, may not form a self-contained prayer for healing like Psalm 38 (see also the comments below on vv. 4, 10).

41:1–3 / The opening blessing is unusual for a prayer psalm. Unlike the rest of the psalm, it is not addressed to Yahweh directly and was thus either spoken by a liturgist overseeing the sick person's prayer or was adopted into this prayer psalm because of the promises, **the LORD will . . . not surrender him to the desire of his foes** but will **restore him from his bed of illness.** (It is interesting to note the subsequent prayer makes no mention of the speaker's **regard for the weak.**)

41:4–9 / The petition of verse 4, because it is cited **(I said),** may refer to an earlier petition. Here is the explicit confession of sin and prayer for healing. The following lament (vv. 5–9) is connected to this petition because it provides the contrast of what **my enemies say,** namely **"When will he die and his name perish?"** It is possible the perishing of one's name refers to the absence of an heir to one's family property. This would explain the significance of the promise in the opening verses: "he will bless him in the land" (v. 2). If so, this sheds light on the enemies' motive, namely economic greed. They may have become **my enemies,** not merely because they spread **slander . . . abroad,** but also because they wish for his death (vv. 7–8) so his real estate can become theirs. What makes matters worse is that they pretend to make comforting visits **(whenever one comes to see me)** and one of them was **even my close friend, whom I trusted.** Not only is there duplicity, there is also betrayal.

41:10–12 / The petition of verse 10 echoes the quoted petition of verse 4 ("have mercy on me") but this one focuses on

restoration and retribution: **raise me up, that I may repay them.**
The speaker "knows" Yahweh is **pleased** with him because his
enemy does not triumph over him (v. 11). This circumstance evidences Yahweh's favor, as based on the opening benediction:
"the LORD will . . . preserve his life . . . and not surrender him to
the desire of his foes" (v. 2). The assurance that Yahweh will **set**
him **in** his **presence forever** (v. 12) may refer to Yahweh's en-
abling the speaker to go to the temple. (After Hezekiah's prayer
psalm for healing, he asks in Isa. 38:22, "What will be the sign
that I will go up to the temple of the LORD?")

41:13 / The last verse is not a constituent part of the
psalm but a doxology closing Book I of the Psalter.

§42 The Would-Be Pilgrim Who Thirsts for God: Part I (Ps. 42)

Psalms 42 and 43 were probably originally one. This is evidenced by the repeated refrain (42:6, 11; 43:5; also 42:3b, 10b; and 42:9; 43:2), by the absence of a superscription for Psalm 43 (unusual esp. in Book II of the Psalter), and by the structure of the psalm, which is incomplete without Psalm 43. Prayer psalms characteristically begin with lament, which comprises Psalm 42, and then move to petitions and a vow of praise, which comprise Psalm 43. Many Hebrew manuscripts, in fact, do join these two psalms. The threefold refrain breaks the psalm into clear sections, and the repetition found in 42:3b, 10b ties together sections one (42:1–5) and two (42:6–11); and the repetition found in 42:9; 43:2 ties together sections two and three (43:1–5).

The psalm appears to place us at some distance from the temple (42:6–7; 43:3). At issue is the speaker's desire to "enter" (Hb. *bwʾ*, rendered "go" or "bring" in 42:2; 43:3, 4) before God's presence "to offer thanksgiving" (or "praise," Hb. *tôdâ* and *hôdâ*, 42:4, 5, 11, 43:4, 5), but he is inhibited from making the pilgrimage. Whether "deceitful and wicked" people (43:1) actually cause the distress or simply use the occasion to taunt the speaker (42:10), we cannot be certain. Another possible circumstance is that of sickness, suggested by "my bones suffer mortal agony" (42:10) and perhaps by his going about mourning (42:9; 43:2; cf. 38:3, 5–8). On the other hand, psalms often use the image of physical trauma to reflect emotional distress. What is particularly unique about this psalm is that, unlike most psalms in which the speaker struggles with enemies and/or with God, here the speaker struggles with himself. Here he engages his soul in a dialogue (cf. 103:1, 22; 104:1).

42:1–5 / The psalm opens with a lament that expresses a longing for **the living** and life-giving **God** by using the image of thirst and more particularly of a **deer** panting **for streams**

of water (cf. 63:1–2; and 36:8; 46:4, where streams flow from the holy place, refreshing God's worshipers). Ironically, the speaker's only drink has been **tears**. They (i.e., his tears, not **men**, which is not in the MT) seem to **say** persistently, **"Where is your God?"** What the psalm envisages here is not merely a spiritual encounter through prayer but an encounter of worshiping God at the temple. The question, **When can I go and meet with God?**, points to a pilgrimage and a "face-to-face" encounter at **the house of God** (see the Additional Notes). This sense of longing is engendered by the memory **(I remember)** of **shouts of joy and thanksgiving** at the house of God. (The Hb. verb used for **go**, *ʿbr*, is a term used to denote making a pilgrimage. Cf. Amos 5:5.) Instead of the normal practice of pouring out one's heart *before God* (62:8; the title to Ps. 102; 142:2), this psalm reads, **I pour out my soul** "upon myself" (Hb. *ʿālay*), thus underscoring the sense of aloneness and alienation from God.

At this point the psalm uniquely interrupts the lament with an interrogation of **my soul: Why are you . . . so disturbed within me?** (lit., "upon me," the same Hb. phrase used in the preceding verse). Grammatical imperatives usually denote petitions in the Psalms, but this one is advice the speaker directs to himself: **Put your hope in God.** Assurance for the present is based on an event in the future, namely, that **I will yet praise him** (or "give thanks," Hb. *hôdâ*, i.e., offer a thanksgiving psalm and a thanksgiving sacrifice). The assurance of this future event is also based on the character of God himself as **my Savior and my God** (or "the deliverances/victories of his face," lit.).

42:6–11 / This second strophe of the psalm elicits a measure of honesty from the worshiper. In spite of this self-encouragement for "my soul" not to be downcast, the psalm leads the worshiper to admit the futility of a mere bootstrap operation: **My soul is downcast within me** (lit., "upon me"). Perhaps most significantly, this admission is addressed to God, as the psalm now returns to direct address (cf. 42:1). Because God is both the problem and the solution, the psalm continues, **therefore I will remember you.** With this separation from God's house, the worshiper is led again to exercise his memory (cf. 42:4). Whether the geographical references of verse 6 are literal (which would locate the speaker at the headwaters of **the Jordan** River near Mount **Hermon**, far to the north of Jerusalem) or figurative (for a region remote from the temple) is not clear either way, but the notion of alienation is clear. This region is especially appropriate for this psalm not only because of its remoteness but because it is the source of the headwaters of the Jordan. Hence, the psalm employs the image of **the roar of your waterfalls.** Now instead of the living God supplying streams of water for the speaker's thirsting soul (42:1–2), he drowns him: **all your waves and breakers have swept over me.** (On 42:8 see the Additional Notes.) In view of God's threatening flood the psalm appeals to **God** as **my rock** and complains, **Why have you forgotten me?** The irony of God's "forgetting" is heightened by the preceding confession, "I . . . remember you." Verse 9 is the first mention of **the enemy.** They do not, therefore, appear to be depicted as the primary cause of distress. Rather, they appear simply to exacerbate the speaker's existing **agony** with their taunt, **"Where is your God?"** This quote from his **foes** echoes his own tearful question about his **God** (42:3, and vv. 6, 11; 43:4, 5). The self-interrogation and advice is repeated (42:11) and closes off the psalm's lament before turning the worshiper to petition God for change.

Additional Notes §42

42:2 / **When can I go and meet with God?:** The Hb. word for "go" *(bwʾ)* is the usual term for "entering" the temple (5:7; 73:17). The MT is awkward: "and appear *the face of* (Hb. *pᵉnê*) God" (lit.). We should expect Hb. *lipnê:* "and appear *before* God." This same awkward phrase is used repeatedly in connection with the three annual pilgrimage festivals (Exod. 23:15, 17; 34:20, 23–24; Deut. 16:16; 31:11) and in Ps. 84:7; Isa. 1:12. Here in Ps. 42:2, instead of the MT's *ʾērāʾê* ("I appear"), a few MSS of the MT, the Syriac Peshitta, and the Targum read, *ʾerʾê,* ("I see"). Exodus 34:23–24 and Deut. 16:16 confirm that "face" was originally the direct object of the verb "to see" by the inclusion of the Hb. direct object marker, *ʾet-*, before "face." By reading, "When shall I enter so I may see the face of God?" the grammatical difficulty is removed, but this raises a theological one (see Exod. 33:20). To avoid it, later scribes appear to have added vowel points to this verb so it means "to appear" but, in deference to the sacred text, did not insert the normal Hb. consonant *lāmed,* "l," before *pᵉnê.* We should note, however, that the Psalms elsewhere do, in fact, use the image of "seeing God" as a metaphor for worshiping him at the temple (11:7; 17:15). In other words, this phrase when it was originally coined did not claim an actual, unveiled, face-to-face encounter with God.

42:8 / **By day the LORD directs his love:** It is not clear how we should render the tense of the Hb. imperfect verb here *(yᵉṣawwê;* NIV puts it in the present tense) nor how this verse fits into the context. Two possibilities seem most likely. First, the Lord's action described here appears to be part of the speaker's remembering him, introduced in 42:6. This is similar to his earlier remembering "how I used to go . . . to the house of God" (42:4). The NIV rightly translates this Hb. imperfect verb as a past action ("used to . . ."). Since 42:6–8 follows the same pattern, we should perhaps translate 42:8 as, "By day the LORD *used to* direct his love." This translation then leads logically to the complaint of 42:9. Another possibility, proposed by Gunkel (*Psalmen*, pp. 177, 182–83), is that a scribal error entered the MT and we should read, "By day I watch (Hb. *ᵃṣappê*) for the LORD and for his love at night; I will sing (Hb. *ʾāšîrâ*) by myself a prayer. . . ." This conjecture maintains the 3 + 2 meter dominant in the psalm and forms a smooth transition to the next verse.

§43 The Would-Be Pilgrim Who Thirsts for God: Part II (Ps. 43)

For an introduction to Psalm 43, see the introductory comments on Psalm 42.

43:1–5 / The psalm's first petitions, "judge me" (Hb. *šopṭēnî*, NIV **vindicate me**) and **plead my cause,** are legal in nature and might lead us to speculate about circumstances of false accusation (see Ps. 7). The petitions of 43:3, however, clearly pray for God's **light** and **truth** to escort the speaker to God's **holy mountain.** We should also observe that the psalms of temple entry (see the Introduction) use legal language for God to "judge me" (26:1) and spare the speaker from the impending fate of the wicked (26:9–10; 28:3; cf. 5:6; 24:4). Psalm 74:22 uses the same expression, "plead your cause" (both use Hb. *rîbâ rîb*), in connection with God's "dwelling place" (Hb. *miškān* in 43:3; 74:7). The particular cause these psalms share in common is the praise of God (43:4–5; 74:21). Hence, the petitions of 43:1 need not refer to legal circumstances of a court case but to circumstances that threaten God's worship at the temple and the speaker's participation in it. The prayer for **rescue** from **deceitful and wicked men** may imply that they somehow restrain the would-be pilgrim from journeying to the temple, a circumstance entirely possible through much of Israel's and Judah's troubled history. Between these petitions in 43:2 is a variant of the complaint of 42:9, except this time, in view of threatening enemies, appeal is made to **God** as **my stronghold.**

After the petitions have been voiced, the psalm draws to a close with a variant of the vow of praise. This one shows that it will be a fulfillment of his **hope** of going (Hb. *bw²,* cf. 42:2) to the temple, of praising God (cf. 42:5, 11), and of renewing his joy of worship (cf. 42:4) and his bond with **my God** (cf. 42:6, 11). Closing the psalm is the repeated refrain, which is not merely repeated but sung, as it were, in a higher key because now the matter has been entrusted to God through lament and petition. The psalm as a whole is a clear testimony that, while circumstances may put restraints on the people of God, they do not have ultimate control. Worshipers can exercise a measure of control over how they respond to hardship and over the state of their soul, especially when they commit their hopes to God through prayer.

§44 Betrayed by God in Battle? (Ps. 44)

Adversity is never easy to bear, but what makes it worse is feeling that God has brought it on (v. 4). What makes it unbearable is the utter disappointment of what were believed to be legitimate expectations from God. As one turns to prayer, God becomes both the problem and its solution.

Psalm 44 is a prayer psalm lamenting a battle defeat. The people have been killed, despoiled, and dispersed (esp. vv. 10–11, 19, 22). The survivors feel humiliated (vv. 13–16) and downcast (v. 25). The psalm contains no historical or geographical allusions that point to a particular defeat known from the historical books of the OT, but Sennacherib's invasion in 701 B.C. during Hezekiah's reign (2 Kgs. 18:13–19:37) or the death of Josiah in battle with Pharaoh Neco in 609 B.C. (2 Kgs. 23:29–30) are likely candidates. The latter is particularly suitable because of the explicit appeal to the people's loyalty to God's covenant (v. 17), the renewal of which was central to Josiah's reform (2 Kgs. 22–23). Yet, the lack of historical specifics is consistent with the genre of corporate prayers, which were written and preserved because they suited recurring occasions. They were not written to be used only once. Psalm 44 was probably used for many battle defeats, and may have been edited and adjusted as it was transmitted from generation to generation. For example, the complaint, "you . . . have scattered us among the nations," would have made the psalm very appropriate after the Babylonian deportations of 597 and 587 B.C.

The psalm is in the "we" form throughout, except in verses 4, 6, and 15, where "I" appears and a liturgist or the king (as the human commander-in-chief) speaks on behalf of the congregation. We might imagine the people gathered before Yahweh at the temple, perhaps fasting, as illustrated in 2 Chronicles 20. The psalm has a clear structure; the poetic sections match the motifs of corporate prayers, which in turn match the changing depictions of God. The first section is ten lines of Hebrew verse (5 + 5,

vv. 1–8), containing a reference to past saving deeds and a confession of trust, and it depicts God as the divine warrior fighting
for his people. The second section is a lament of eight lines (4 + 4,
vv. 9–16) and portrays him as the shepherd selling his sheep.
The third is a protest of loyalty of six lines (3 + 3, vv. 17–22),
where God betrays his covenant. The fourth is four lines (2 + 2,
vv. 23–26), containing petitions and laments, and implores God
to awake before his people die in the dust.

44:1–8 / In the first three verses (five lines of Hb. verse)
the people testify of what **our fathers have told us** of **what you
did . . . in days long ago.** This is not merely age-old tradition but
"what you did" **in their days**—in other words, eyewitness testimony. (Here we must recognize that "our fathers" denotes not
merely "our immediate fathers" but the chain of ancestors.) **You
drove out the nations and planted our fathers** points to the days
of the conquest. Verses 2–3 emphasize God's agency **(with your
hand, your right hand, your arm, and the light of your face)** to
the near exclusion of human effort **(not by their sword, nor did
their arm;** cf. 33:16–17).

Verses 4–8 (five Hb. lines) contain a confession of trust
made before the battle. The confession for this generation (note
my King) is modeled on the report **heard** from previous generations. The expectations it contains are thus held to be legitimate.
Especially notable is its emphasis on divine agency that overshadows human weapons **(not . . . my bow** or **my sword, but
you . . . , you . . .).** Verse 5, however, does show the blending of divine and human means **(through you we . . . ; through your
name we . . .).** God is portrayed as King, with his accompanying
role as ultimate commander-in-chief **(who decrees victories).**
Verse 8 testifies to a life of past praise (lit. "we have praised/
boasted) and vows a life of future praise. Considering the assem-
blage of deities in the ancient Near East, we can understand the
importance of **your name** in the act of praising. Prior to its inclusion in the Elohistic Psalter (Pss. 42–83, in which the name "God"
is preferred over "the Lord"), this verse probably read, **In** "Yahweh" (or "the Lord") **we make our boast.** The opening verses
thus establish that the people's expectations had a basis in history and that their motives were in order.

44:9–16 / The structure of the psalm itself reflects the
utter disappointment felt in the moments after the battle. Without transition we move from the expectation of praising God to

the reality of lamenting his rejection. The lament interpreting the battle defeat is written in light of the confession made before the battle. Thus, its main point is not to describe the defeat in journalistic fashion but to assert that Yahweh was its instigator. His actions are portrayed as those of cruelty and betrayal. Because the people had expected the battle to be waged between God and the enemy, not between "us" and "them," the defeat was one God brought on **us.** If "our fathers" enjoyed "victory . . . for you loved them" (v. 3), the speakers experience defeat for you **have rejected** them (v. 9). If victory comes by "the light of your face" (v. 3), defeat comes because "you hide your face" (v. 24). If, in victory, "you put our adversaries to shame" (v. 7), then, in defeat, **you have made us a reproach to our neighbors** (vv. 13–14, 9). The enemies play a surprisingly minor role in the psalm and are not even mentioned in the petition section.

But the lament is more than a mirror image of the pre-battle confession, which emphasized the divine warrior's warring against the foe ("you drove out the nations," v. 2) and achieving victory for Israel (vv. 5–7). The lament emphasizes that Yahweh deserted Israel and handed them over to their enemies **(you no longer go out with our armies, you gave us up, you sold your people).** It is not so much that Yahweh has worked for the enemy (contrast 89:42), as it is that he has worked against Israel, as illustrated in verse 10: **You made us retreat,** so **our adversaries** were at liberty to plunder us.

44:17–22 / Some psalms of the individual contain protests of innocence (7:3–5; 17:3–5; 26:1–8; 59:3–4), where the speaker avers he has not sinned against other people and against God's ways. The protest of loyalty in this psalm goes one step further. In addition to asserting, **we had not . . . been false to your covenant,** the speaker claims that God in turn **crushed us.** In other words, not only are the people innocent, God is guilty of cruel betrayal. "We had not" **forgotten you,** so "why do you . . . forget our misery" (v. 24)? Although the people had remained loyal in the midst of opposition **(all this happened to us),** God repays that loyalty with further affliction.

Verses 20–21 unexpectedly turn to referring to God in the third person. As in verse 8, reference is made to God's **name** (also v. 5), and the title **God** has probably replaced the name "Yahweh" (the Lord) in verse 21 (see above). Because verse 22, which is closely connected ("yet," Hb. *kî*), continues the direct address of

God, these verses appear to ask God a question about God. In effect, they ask him to judge his own conduct! Mention of his penetrating knowledge is often made when he acts as judge (7:9; 11:4; 17:3; 26:2; 139:1–24). Yet the question is somewhat rhetorical because the possibility of their "forgetting" (v. 20) has already been answered (v. 17) and because a conclusion is already reached in the next verse: **Yet for your sake** (lit. "on account of you," Hb. *ᶜālêkā*)—not on our account—**we face death** and **are considered as sheep to be slaughtered** (cf. v. 11; quoted in Rom. 8:36).

44:23–26 / The closing and the shortest section contains the only petitions. Perhaps because Yahweh seems unaware of the people's continued allegiance to him, the first petition is **Awake, O Lord! Why do you sleep?** This marks a curious twist in the psalm's depiction of God's activity. To this point Yahweh has actively opposed his people; here he is negligent. The reason for this can probably be traced to an implicit shift in the role attributed to God. In verses 1–16, he is the divine warrior on the battlefield and the selling shepherd in the marketplace, but from verse 17 onwards he is the divine judge overseeing the covenant relationship (see esp. 50:5–6). As judge, he is to **rouse** himself to the facts of their case, and so **rise up and help us.**

Supporting these petitions are laments. The first questions **why** Yahweh has done what a covenant judge should not do to a loyal partner, that is, estrange himself and disregard their plight (v. 24). The second emphasizes that the people's situation is desperate **(we are brought down to the dust)** and that only a divine judge can remedy it ("rise up and help us"). The final petition may echo the earlier image of the shepherd selling his sheep. **Redeem** means literally "buy back," that is, "your people" whom "you sold . . . for a pittance" (v. 12).

What is perhaps most remarkable about this psalm is that it is part of Scripture at all. Included within this sacred collection that reveals God is this public liturgy that expresses utter disappointment in God. And no editorial comments are appended to make clear that God eventually came through for his people. As it stands it is left unanswered. If we take this canonical shaping seriously, we have here a testimony that such disappointment in God may occur for believers; nonetheless, this does not invalidate other testimonies of the saving God. Both of these experiences have their legitimate place in the life of faith. If we encounter an inexplicable loss in our lives, we are not guaranteed an explanation from God. If one is not forthcoming, this should not catapult us into doubting all other testimonies of God's salvation that we have heard and made ourselves.

We may be offended at the direct way Psalm 44 accuses God, especially of betrayal. But in fact, this psalm shows us a response to disappointment with God that is better than what we tend to make. When we encounter tragedy, we sometimes in our heart of hearts blame God. We may not even admit this to ourselves, let alone to God, since our piety tells us that fault must lie elsewhere, especially with ourselves. So our response to disappointment with God is to withdraw. But this psalm presents the way of direct confrontation. It displays a higher view of God's integrity and does not fear embarrassing God. It acknowledges that he alone can solve the dilemma—especially since he may be its cause. It also displays a higher view of personal integrity. The whole, integrated person, even with one's embittered feelings, addresses God, not just the acceptable, pious parts of human personality.

§45 In Praise of the King at His Wedding (Ps. 45)

Psalm 45, a royal psalm, is unlike any other psalm. Most psalms praise God (with God as the sentences' grammatical subject), but this one praises the king. It opens with, "You (i.e., the king in v. 1) are the most excellent of men," and closes with, "the nations will praise you (i.e., the king) for ever and ever." This departure from the norm is explained by the superscription. This is not a hymn set in God's temple but "a wedding song" set in the king's court.

45:1–5 / The speaker opens with an explicit statement that these are **verses for the king,** and he raises our expectations for what is to follow by announcing it as a stirring **noble theme.** He addresses the king directly with verses that sound appropriate to a pre-battle liturgy anticipating victory and that highlight the military accoutrement of this supreme warrior (NIV **mighty one**).

45:6–9 / Moving from the battlefield to the royal court, the speaker continues his praise by describing the court's awe-inspiring furnishings. Yet the audience to whom these praises are addressed, including the king himself, hear of not only the symbols of power but also the moral qualities that are to characterize his rule. In his military garb, he is to "ride . . . in behalf of truth, humility and righteousness." In other words, his military exploits are to be governed by these attributes—no mention is made of the quest for more power or territories. His **scepter,** the symbol of his authority, is to embody **justice** (or "equity"). The king is reminded that his **anointing** and exaltation are predicated on his "loving" **righteousness** and his "hating" **wickedness.**

45:10–17 / Verse 10 turns the audience's attention to the bride by addressing her directly. She too is described by her **embroidered garments,** along with the procession that accompanies her (vv. 10–15). **Joy and gladness** are to characterize the ceremony. The closing verses address the king (made clear by

Hb. masculine, sing. suffixes, **you** and **your,** vv. 16–17), promising
him posterity and a legacy.

Additional Note §45

45:6 / The phrase **Your throne, O God,** is problematic because
it appears to address the human king as divine (Hb. *ʾelōhîm*). While
kings of Egypt and early Mesopotamia may have claimed divinity, the
OT is elsewhere most explicit that this was not the case for Yahweh's appointed king. The closest the OT gets is in the language of Yahweh's "begetting" the royal "son," but this is simply a metaphor (see on 2:7 and
110:3). One possible explanation emerges from the recognition that
psalms were originally performed as liturgies. As frequently noted in
this commentary, there is often a change of addressee during the course
of a liturgy, especially between the congregation (referring to God in
the "he" form) and God (addressing him in the "you" form). When we
read this psalm as literature, however, there appears to be no seam before or after v. 6. But if we were to hear it performed, it may have been
obvious these words were directed to God above, not to the king. As a
possible confirmation of this theory, we should note this change of address would establish a somewhat symmetrical structure for the psalm
with changes of address at v. 2 (the king), at v. 6 (God) with a return to
the king in the next verse, at v. 10 (the bride), and at v. 16 (the king
again). Verses 6–7 would thus make the same point as the one made in
the longer liturgy of Ps. 89, namely that Yahweh's kingship is the basis
for David's (vv. 1–2 and vv. 3–4, and vv. 5–18 and vv. 19–37). The human
king must "love righteousness and hate wickedness" because the **scepter of God's kingdom is a scepter of justice.** We should also recall that
Ps. 45 is part of the Elohistic Psalter (Pss. 42–83), where "the LORD"
("Yahweh") is sometimes substituted with *Elohim*. So, v. 6 may have
originally read, "Your throne, O LORD," thus making the change of address obvious.

If, however, the king is addressed as *ʾelōhîm*, we should note
that he is still reminded that it is "God, your God," who "has set you
above your companions." The Hb. term *ʾelōhîm* has a wider range of
meaning than our terms "God" and "gods." In Exod. 21:6 and 22:8–9, 28
(possibly 1 Sam. 2:25), it appears to be applied to human judges (see
also Exod. 4:16; 7:1). We should also note that the related Hb. term *ʾēl*,
usually translated "God," can also denote "power" (Prov. 3:27; Mic. 2:1),
"mighty" (Ps. 36:6; 80:10), and "mighty one" or "ruler" (Ezek. 31:11;
32:21). Thus, vv. 6–7 may use a pun to make the point that the
enthroned king, while "a mighty ruler," must acknowledge his God
above. Finally, we should realize that once this verse is applied to Jesus
Christ, *the* son of David (as in Heb. 1:8–9), the problem of a human and
divine identity disappears.

God as our fortress (vv. 7, 11)—as a "Mighty Fortress" (thanks to Martin Luther)—has been an image comforting believers living in turmoil through the centuries. Psalm 46 is one of the Songs of Zion (also Pss. 48, 76, 84, 87, 132). Psalms 46, 48, and 76 follow the same pattern: (a) a confession that "God is . . . in Zion," (b) a report that God has stilled Zion's attackers, and (c) imperatives to acknowledge God as sovereign protector—not the usual hymnic imperatives to join in verbal praise (46:8, 10; 48:12–13; 76:11). Like Psalm 48, it appears to be a liturgy punctuated by "we/our/us" confessions about God in the opening verses and in the refrain of verses 7 and 11. It is possible these may have been sung by a choir representing the congregation. In verses 4–6, a liturgist introduces and describes the city of God and the saving help he offers "her" (not "us"), to which the "we" refrain responds. Then a liturgist invites the congregation to make eyewitness testimony ("Come and see") of "the works of the LORD" (vv. 8–9). After the climax of a prophetic oracle, perhaps delivered by a temple prophet (v. 10), the choir/congregation once again make their personal confession (v. 11). Reference is made to several features often associated with the ark of the covenant (the divine name, "the Lord of hosts" or "the LORD Almighty" in the NIV, who is engaged in military conflict, and references to his strength and exaltation), though the psalm gives no explicit indications of its ritual use.

46:1–3 / This Song of Zion begins with a confession familiar from the individual prayer psalms that **God** is a **refuge**. At the outset attention is drawn to God, not the city of Zion itself. While the psalms of Zion speak of the city as a virtual sacrament (48:12–14), the symbol is never allowed to overshadow the reality to which it points. While the symbol is there before the worshipers' eyes, these psalms are phrased in such a way as to attribute to God, not to the symbol, the power to bestow blessing.

It is one thing to confess God **is our** "refuge"; it is another to resolve **therefore we will not fear.** Confessing what we should believe is easy; bringing our hearts to feel that confessed security is monumental. This is the case especially in view of the magnitude of the threat: **though . . . the mountains fall into the heart of the sea.** In the ancient world, the mountains symbolized the pillars of the earth that stabilize it over the chaotic waters (18:7; 104:5–6; Job 9:5–6). A fear that can withstand the collapse of creation is made possible solely by a faith in the Creator. As sublime as the faith represented here is, we must not romanticize it. The psalm dares us to believe in God when the ground falls out from underneath us. To this extent, this psalm of Zion goes beyond the psalms of Yahweh's kingship, which also allude to the chaotic **waters** (93:3–4) but assert, in light of his ordering kingship, "The world is firmly established; it cannot be moved" (93:1; 96:10; cf. 24:2; 89:11; 104:5). In these psalms, the stability of the earth is evidence of Yahweh's kingship, but Psalm 46 challenges worshipers not to fear even in spite of the collapse of this evidence.

46:4–7 / This section begins with a surprise. As we continue to hear of waters, we expect to hear of chaotic and destructive waters, but instead we hear of life-giving and joy-giving waters (contrast Ps. 42): **There is a river whose streams make glad the city of God.** Readers have often been puzzled as to what river in Jerusalem this might refer. Some have suggested the Gihon spring (1 Kgs. 1:33; 2 Chron. 32:30). But, instead of looking at Jerusalem's geography, we should probably look at the theology and imagery of the Jerusalem temple. Since the Hebrew term for "temple" (Hb. *hêkāl*) also denotes "palace," the temple symbolizes Yahweh's kingship. This was demonstrated, in part, when he subdued the chaotic waters at creation (see on Pss. 24; 29; 74; 93). Yahweh not only subdued the chaotic waters (104:6–9), he transformed them into life-giving waters (104:10–16). Psalm 65, which also sings of the Zion temple (vv. 1–4) and of Yahweh's "stilling the roaring of the seas" (vv. 5–7), refers to "the stream of God" (v. 9, Hb. *peleg,* the same term used in 46:4) that waters the land and similarly results in joy (v. 13). Thus, this river of Psalm 46 is probably an image depicting **the holy place** (i.e., the sanctuary) **where the Most High dwells** as the source of life for the city of God. This image is developed later in Ezekiel's vision of a new temple after the restoration from exile (47:1–12).

The security of the city of God is due not to its inherent or mythical strength but solely to its chief resident: **God is within her.** Similarly, the claim, **God will help her at break of day,** does not imply a belief in something magical about morning. Rather, the moment when light dispels darkness was symbolic of salvation, newness, and hope (30:5; 90:14; 130:6).

Verse 6 closely parallels verses 2–3. As "the earth give[s] way," so here **the earth melts.** As "the mountains fall," so here **kingdoms fall.** As "waters roar," so here **nations are in uproar** (cf. 65:7). The chaos of cosmic collapse and the chaos of political and military upheaval are thus presented as parallel forces. What is striking, however, is how the city of God stands contrary to these forces. By contrast, **she will not fall.** While waters roar, there is another body of water—"a river"—that gladdens this city.

In this second portrayal of apparent chaos there is also an intervening voice: **He lifts his voice** alludes to God's thunder (18:13; 68:33; 77:17; cf. 29:3; 104:7). "The earth melts" is, in part, the rains' erosion of the soil (cf. 97:2–5). In such contexts, the Most High (also in 18:13 and probably in 68:34; see the commentary) is depicted as the "rider of the clouds" (18:10–11; 68:33), the God of the storm, who rages against chaotic and earthly powers. Thus, in Psalm 46, God enters the storm not to still it but, as the next section spells out, to bring "desolations . . . on the earth." The tumult of the nations and God's thundering voice depict a terrifying scene, but within the city we hear the psalm's refrain, "the Lord of hosts is with us; the God of Jacob is our fortress" (lit. "our high refuge" from the underlying chaos).

46:8–11 / The psalm's final section opens with imperatives inviting the congregation (and perhaps the nations themselves) to witness how Yahweh has destroyed the weapons of war (cf. another Song of Zion, Isa. 2:2–5; Mic. 4:1–5). In this section, Yahweh's voice (v. 6) becomes articulate by means of a prophetic oracle, but no less thunderous: **"Be still, and know that I am God; I will be exalted among the nations."** In this explosive context, "be still" is not an invitation to tranquil meditation but a command to allow God to be God, to do his work of abolishing the weapons of war. This language of exaltation is the language of kingship (e.g., 99:1–2, 5, 9; 113:4–5; 145:1). Thus, although Psalm 46 does not use the terms "king" or "reign," it is still an assertion of Yahweh as King. (We must beware of drawing too sharp a line between psalms of Zion and psalms of Yahweh's kingship or assuming that they stem from different festivals or traditions.) This is confirmed by the earlier reference to God's ruling over chaotic waters, which is a constituent image relating to divine kingship both in Israel (29:3–10; 74:12–17; 89:9–14; 93:1–4) and in the ancient Near East.

What is the time frame of this psalm? To some extent it appears to report a past event (esp. **Come and see** what **he has brought**). Yet, we must be struck that while the first half speaks of God's protection of a city, the second half appears to announce prophetically, in the first person, God's public exaltation **in the earth,** even **to the ends of the earth.** The fact that this event is announced in a prophetic oracle may imply that it is not now self-evident. Perhaps God's deliverance of Jerusalem is simply a foretaste of something yet to come. Thus, the congregation may be summoned to recognize or "know" now a reality about God that will some day be self-evident publicly. Consequently there is also a present-tense dimension to the psalm. It is characteristic of OT liturgy that theological realities are presented to the congregation, not as concepts or propositions, but as dramatic—even dramatized—events (see, e.g., the psalms of Yahweh's kingship). The NIV has shown this dimension of the psalm well by putting these words in the dramatic present tense.

If we search the historical witnesses of the OT, we are hard pressed to find a moment that fits such a universal revelation of God. Even if, as suggested in the Introduction, Psalms 46, 48, and 76 reflect on Jerusalem's deliverance from Assyria in 701 B.C., the record is plain that the Assyrians had earlier succeeded in capturing "all the fortified cities of Judah" (Isa. 36:1) and only Jerusalem escaped. Further, it is obvious that only some time later (in 681 B.C. as it turns out) the king of Assyria was killed (37:38) and that the ancient Near Eastern nations and empires went on as usual. Perhaps most importantly, how can we explain the preservation of these psalms after the decimation of Jerusalem in 587 B.C.? It seems best to conclude they were retained in the exilic and postexilic period because they indicated that something more can be expected from God, namely, that war shall be abolished and Yahweh "will be exalted among the nations" (cf. Luke 21:25).

Additional Notes §46

46:4 / A river . . . , the holy place where the Most High dwells: We should perhaps read instead, "a river . . . , *from* the holy place, the dwelling of the Most High," assuming haplography (reading Hb. *ʾelōhîm miqqōdeš*, instead of the MT's *ʾelōhîm qᵉdōš*). In the Ugaritic texts, El's mountain palace is "at the source of the rivers" (Gibson, *Canaanite Myths*, p. 37).

46:8 / Come and see . . . the desolations: If Pss. 46, 48, and 76 are reporting about a particular military rout that Yahweh has performed for Jerusalem, as suggested in the Introduction, then it is possible this verse reenacts the moment "when the people got up the next morning" and "there were all the dead bodies" of Sennacherib's armies in 701 B.C. (Isa. 37:36).

§47 *Applause for the Ascending King of All the Earth (Ps. 47)*

Applause is something most of us associate with a football stadium, not a church, but in this psalm we are directed to applaud God. This is not a quiet psalm—it also includes "shouting" and trumpets (vv. 1, 5)—but for good reason: it celebrates the great King over all the earth (v. 2).

We cannot make sense of Psalm 47 in isolation; it is one of the psalms of Yahweh's kingship and must be interpreted in light of the others. Particularly puzzling is the expression, "God has ascended" (v. 5). To what could this refer? There are several hints that it alludes to Yahweh seated invisibly on his symbolic cherubim-throne and its "ascending" in a victory procession into the inner temple (see Additional Notes). Thus, a liturgist first commands an international congregation (v. 1; cf. v. 9) to applaud and shout as this symbol of Yahweh's throne (cf. v. 8) is marched in procession up into the inner temple. This opening call to worship is substantiated with historical reasons for praise (vv. 2–4). Because verse 5 appears to view this ritual event in retrospect, we may suppose the actual procession and a great deal of applause, shouting, and the sounding of trumpets took place between verses 4 and 5. Once the fanfare subsides, the liturgist enjoins the congregation to continue the sound of celebration but this time in articulate praises (or "psalms," vv. 6–7). This second call to worship is also substantiated with reasons for praise that are based in the symbolism of the cherubim-throne and the congregation itself (vv. 8–9).

47:1–4 / This hymn opens, as most do, with a call to praise. Unlike most hymns, however, this one bids **all you nations,** not merely God's special people. Substantiating (v. 2 should begin with "for," Hb. *kî*) the call for praising this *one* deity by *all* is the assertion that he is **LORD Most High, the great king over all the earth.** Two divine attributes are brought center stage: he is described as **awesome** (Hb. *nôrā'*, also "feared") and "great" (Hb. *gādôl*). This word pair is a unique characteristic of the psalms of Yahweh's kingship (also in 96:4; 99:3). Historical evidence is also adduced: **he subdued nations under us.** This could refer either to conquests under Joshua and the judges or to David's victories surrounding the ark's original ascent (2 Sam. 5; 8). **Our inheritance** (the LXX and the Peshitta read "his") and **the pride of Jacob** refer to the land of Israel. Thus, the reason for the conquest as stated in this psalm lies in Yahweh's "choice" **(he chose)** of which land should belong to **us.** One may wonder why nations would **clap** (v. 1) when nations are "subdued . . . under" Israel (v. 3). First, it is likely these groups are not one and the same. Verse 3 is a historical reference to the former residents of Canaan, and verse 1 addresses "all . . . nations" currently alive. Second, the primary cause for celebration is not Israel's conquest but Yahweh's rule. If we look ahead to verse 9, we discover the nations join as (or "with") the people of the God of Abraham. Implicit here is Yahweh's promise to Abraham: "all peoples on earth will be blessed through you" (Gen. 12:3; cf. Ps. 72:17).

47:5 / Verse 5 then describes in retrospect (the NIV's **has ascended** correctly renders the Hb. perfect as a past event) what verse 1 called for initially, namely **shouts of joy.** In the interlude between verses 4 and 5, we would see the Levites carrying Yahweh's symbolic throne up into the temple while the congregation made their applause and victory shouts heard. What then does this ascent signify? First, it simply describes the geographical passage the ark must take to get up Zion's hill and up the steps of the sanctuary (2 Sam. 6:2, 12, 15). Second, it appears to be associated with the king's victory procession, in which the vanquished (note vv. 3–4) offer tribute before his ascended throne and everyone acknowledges him victor (see 68:17–18, 24). Psalm 24 also sheds light on this ritual. Here Yahweh's cherubim-throne ascends in victory procession and enters through the gates. And a new name is announced for "Yahweh of hosts," "mighty in battle": he is also "the King of glory."

47:6–7 / After the ritual ascent of the ark, another summons to praise breaks forth, this time calling for praise articulated in psalms (**sing praises**, Hb. *zammerû*, related to the noun "psalm," Hb. *mizmôr*). This indicates that other psalms would be sung later in the liturgy. Once again, substantiating this command to praise is the claim, **for God is the King of all the earth** (cf. v. 2).

47:8–9 / This time the supporting evidence lies not in history but in the liturgical proceedings themselves. First, we hear the acclamation characteristic of the psalms of Yahweh's kingship, **God reigns.** The phrase **God is seated on his holy throne** may imply the symbolic cherubim-throne is still visible to the congregation (and has not yet entered the Most Holy Place). The second piece of evidence set forth is the makeup of the congregation: **the nobles of the nations assemble** with (probably not **as) the people of the God of Abraham.** This seems to indicate that international representatives attended some of Jerusalem's major festivals. Thus, a congregation crossing international and cultural barriers is in itself a testimony that Yahweh is "the King of all the earth." The conjunction of the two divine titles, "the God of Abraham" and "Most High" (v. 2), is not surprising in light of Genesis 14:18–22. The closing words underscore the central event of this liturgy: "he has greatly ascended" (the Hb. word rendered **exalted** in the NIV has the same verbal root as is used in v. 5 for God's ascent; cf. 97:9). It is no surprise that this psalm is a particular favorite for Christians on Ascension Day.

Additional Notes §47

47:2, 7, 9 / **The earth:** *hāʾāreṣ* can also mean "the land," that is, the land of Israel. This understanding means the psalm could readily be located within a historical context, in particular David's conquests of Israel's land and surrounding territories (2 Sam. 5; 8). Thus, "all you nations" (v. 1) and "the kings of the earth" (v. 9) would denote Israel's immediate neighbors. It is possible this is what the psalm meant originally, esp. if it was sung during the ark's original "ascent" in 2 Sam. 6 (see the similarity between Ps. 47:5 and 2 Sam. 6:15 noted below). In light of the other psalms of Yahweh's kingship, however, *hāʾāreṣ* in Ps. 47 must, at some point, come to mean "the earth." This development from local to global is a possible scenario esp. in light of the development of the Davidic promises from "a place for my people" and "rest from all your enemies" (2 Sam. 7:10–11) to a worldwide empire (Pss. 2:8; 72:8–11; 89:25).

47:5 / **God has ascended:** Several hints indicate this phrase points to a victory procession with the cherubim-ark's ascent into the inner temple. First, the description, "God is seated on his holy throne"

(v. 8), points to what the cherubim symbolize (see the Introduction). It is paralleled by the acclamation, "God reigns." Another psalm of Yahweh's kingship similarly praises Yahweh who "sits enthroned between the cherubim" (99:1). This is in parallel with the same acclamation. Second, God "ascends" (Hb. *ʿlh*) **amid shouts of joy** (Hb. *bitrûʿâ*) and **amid the sounding of trumpets** (Hb. *bᵉqôl šôpār*), which are the precise expressions used when David and "Israel brought up (Hb. *ʿlh*) the ark of the LORD with shouts (Hb. *bitrûʿâ*) and the sound of trumpets (Hb. *bᵉqôl šôpār*)" (2 Sam. 6:15). Third, Ps. 68:17–18, 24 also refers to God as "King" "ascending" (Hb. *ʿlh*). Here the place to which he ascends is identified: "into the sanctuary" (also described as "on high"). This event was most probably symbolized by the ark because the psalm opens with the song of the ark. This was intoned whenever the people moved camp in the wilderness (Num. 10:35). Another reason for suggesting that the ark is the intended symbol arises from Ps. 68:17–18, in which a narrative that begins with God's "going out before his people" in "the wasteland" (68:7) climaxes with his arrival "from Sinai into his sanctuary." In both Pss. 47 and 68, God "ascends" after defeating opponents (47:3–4; 68:18, also vv. 1–2, 11–14). Elsewhere shouting and trumpets are associated with the king in Num. 23:21; 1 Sam. 10:24 and with battle cries made before battle in Josh. 6:5, 10, 16, 20; 1 Sam. 4:5–6; 17:52; Amos 1:14; 2:2.

§48 Zion's Divine Defender (Ps. 48)

Like Psalm 46, Psalm 48 is a psalm of Zion. Both psalms begin with descriptions of Zion that are cosmic in nature and colored with familiar ancient Near Eastern imagery and then move to report political and historical events that demonstrate these claims. Here we see faith vindicated by history. This liturgy is performed "within your temple" (v. 9) and is punctuated by "we/our" confessions (vv. 1, 8, 14), perhaps sung by a choir on behalf of the congregation. The opening confession focuses on Yahweh himself. There follow two verses describing his city and mountain (note here it is "her fortress," not "our fortress" as in 46:7, 11). After a description of Yahweh's rout of invaders (vv. 4–7), the next we-confession responds with the people's personal testimony of the security God gives the city (v. 8). This is followed by praise addressing God directly (vv. 9–11). The liturgist then commands the congregation to join in procession around Zion and her defenses (vv. 12–13). The psalm closes with the third confession, a response to how these defenses symbolize the ultimate defense God offers (v. 14).

48:1–3 / Similar to the other psalms of Zion, Psalm 48 begins with the praise of God: **Great is the LORD.** Jerusalem obtains significance solely because it is **the city of our God** and particularly because in it resides **his holy mountain.** It is holy not because of moral qualities but because it is set apart (the concrete meaning of "holy") by God's choice (87:1–2; 132:13). The psalm describes it as **beautiful in its loftiness.** The temple mount is impressive when viewed from the Kidron Valley, but one would be hard pressed to establish it as **the joy of the whole earth** because of its inherent qualities. The mountains around it are, in fact, higher (cf. 125:1–2), and it would probably go unnoticed were it not for the temple and its resident, **the Great King.** This geographical observation yields an important theological point, namely that Yahweh's choice (including his choice of people) is not determined by the inherent qualities of what he is choosing.

The mountain and its city are to enjoy international acclaim solely because their patron deity (every major city in the ancient Near East had a patron god) is "the Great King." In the theologies and mythologies of the ancient Near East, there were many gods, but only one was regarded as king (e.g., Marduk in the Babylonian "Enuma Elish" and Baal in the Canaanite Baal epic). The description of Zion as "the joy of the whole earth" does not report a historical fact, as the description of the nations' aggression in verses 4–8 makes clear, but celebrates a theological truth. The city possesses this status because "the Great King" possesses "the earth . . . and everything in it" (24:1). The commentary on Psalm 24 unfolds the theology of divine kingship implicit here. Psalm 65:5 makes a similar claim describing Yahweh as "the hope of all the ends of the earth" and also bases it on his divine kingship, whereby he "formed the mountains" and "stilled the roaring of the seas" (vv. 6–8; note also the reference to joy). This background of divine kingship is also evident in the reference to the **heights of Zaphon**, which was Baal's sacred mountain north of Ugarit in modern-day Syria. Verse 2, in effect, claims that Zion is the true "Zaphon" or holy mountain (lit. "Mount Zion, the recesses of Zaphon, is the city of the great king"). Verse 3 continues the description of Zion but shifts to the military sphere and echoes 46:7, 11 by using the same term for **fortress**. It is this description in particular the next section exemplifies.

48:4–8 / God's presence "in her citadels" (v. 3) is demonstrated by a narration of the panic that **seized** invading armies, and is reminiscent of the panic that Yahweh inflicted on the Canaanites during the conquest (Deut. 7:23; Josh. 2:8–11; 5:1; note **her** is not in the Hb. text). Yahweh's destruction of the invading infantry is likened to the destruction of the mighty sailing **ships of Tarshish.** In the summary statement of verse 8, the congregation or choir testifies that the reports about God **we have heard** are now a reality **we have seen.** Visible evidence and eyewitness testimony are also important in 46:8 ("Come and see"), another Song of Zion. The divine title used in this confession is "Yahweh of hosts" (NIV **the LORD Almighty**), which is the name associated with the ark of the covenant (1 Sam. 4:4; 2 Sam. 6:2). This observation underscores the point that Zion obtains significance not because of its inherent qualities but because this symbol of Yahweh's throne (hence "the Great King," v. 2) has taken residence here.

48:9–11 / Now the liturgist directs the thoughts of the worshipers, saying, **Within your temple** (also royal "palace"), **O God, we meditate on your unfailing love.** This leads naturally to praise addressed to God directly. His defense of the city is seen as an expression of "unfailing love" (Hb. *ḥesed*, or "loving loyalty") and **righteousness,** which can denote both his "right dealings" within their relationship and his "putting things right" in a saving way. The praise expresses a certain tension within God's self-revelation, for which the OT uses the phrase, **your name.** On the one hand, this self-revelation results in **your praise** that **reaches to the ends of the earth.** On the other, it is **Mount Zion** and **the villages of Judah** in particular that **are glad because of your judgments** (a verse identical to 97:8, a psalm of Yahweh's kingship). As already noted, Psalm 65 also indicates that, while there is a sense that Yahweh "calls forth songs of joy" from "the ends of the earth" (vv. 5–8), it is at Yahweh's holy temple in Zion that articulate praise, in particular, is offered to him (vv. 1–4). This awareness reflects an aspect of God's sovereignty that we in the church often overlook, namely that—even apart from missionaries—God makes himself known and people respond with a measure of praise, however ill-defined it may be.

48:12–14 / The liturgist now commands the congregation to join in procession around **Zion** and **her citadels.** The reason for this procession is explained by the connective, **for,** which implies these defenses symbolize, but are clearly not to be identified with, **our God.** Verse 3 is clear that "her citadels" work because **God is** there—he is the fortress himself. (In the postexilic period there was a sense that even these symbolic defenses would be rendered unnecessary by Yahweh's immediate presence, as seen in Zech. 2:4–5.) In this context, the claim of Yahweh's being **our guide** does not point to his guidance in personal decision-making but to his guidance as our military commander-in-chief (cf. 1 Chron. 20:1; 2 Chron. 25:11).

Additional Note §48

48:2   /   **The utmost heights of Zaphon:** This expression (Hb. *yarkᵉtî ṣāpôn*) is remarkably similar, though not linguistically identical, to the Ugaritic expressions, "the recesses of Zaphon" (Ugaritic *bṣrrt ṣpn*, Gibson, *Canaanite Myths*, p. 46) and "the heights of Zaphon" (Ugaritic *mrym ṣpn*, p. 68).

§49 God Will Redeem My Soul from the Grave (Ps. 49)

49:1–4 / Unlike most psalms, this one explicitly labels its genre as a **proverb** and a **riddle**, though sung **with the harp.** The reason for the latter designation becomes evident in the question of verses 5–6. The psalm stems from Israel's wisdom tradition—comparable especially to Ecclesiastes—and its purpose is didactic. This proverb is not just for Israelites but for **all you peoples, all who live in this world**—irrespective of social station **(both low and high)** and economic status **(rich and poor alike).** For the rich and poor, however, this psalm bears different messages. For the former it conveys a warning, for the latter a hope. The reason the psalm commands such universal attention is because it contains **words of wisdom** and **understanding.** For some readers this claim smacks of arrogance. But this is because we tend to think of "wisdom" and "understanding" as subjective (i.e., *my* wisdom). The Bible, however, acknowledges a wisdom that is objective, one that is true whether or not humans recognize it. This is the wisdom represented here; it is presented not to showcase the speaker's insight but to reveal something that is true.

49:5–6 / After this introduction, the question opening the body of the psalm serves to capture the attention of this wide audience. It addresses an issue that all face, namely **fear,** and especially the fear of the wealthy—and therefore powerful—**wicked** who would swindle us of what is rightfully ours. The feature that especially characterizes this group is that they **trust in** and **boast of** (the same Hb. root meaning "praise") **wealth.** Throughout the Psalter, these are verbs that have God as their object. In this light, we learn that these are people whose ultimate security and values lie in their possessions—this is their god. The issue here is not wealth per se but trusting in that wealth.

49:7–12 / We know that the question is rhetorical because the reasons for the assumed negative answer follow immediately in the statements of verses 7–15. **Redeem** and **give . . . a ransom** are economic terms, meaning "to buy back" and "to pay a ransom price." But no one, not even these wealthy, can afford the price **that he should live on forever.**As wealth has no bearing on the inevitability of death (vv. 7–9), so wisdom and foolishness are likewise irrelevant (vv. 10–11). The first of the refrains (v. 12, cf. v. 20) concludes, **man, despite his riches, does not** understand (the NIV paraphrases this as **endure,** but it is better to read Hb. *ybyn* with the LXX, Peshitta, and v. 20, instead of *ylyn,* "to lodge").

49:13–15 / Verses 13–14 powerfully depict the helplessness of the rich by an image of **sheep** appointed for death, which will then "shepherd them" (lit., NIV **feed on them**). To this point the speaker's wisdom (v. 3) could derive from observational wisdom, but verse 15 clearly comes from the other side: **God will redeem my** "soul" (as noted in the NIV's margin) **from the grave; he will surely take me to himself** (further on this key claim, see Gen. 5:24 and the commentary on Ps. 73:24). Verse 15 thus responds to verse 7: only God can afford to redeem one's life from this inevitability.

49:16–20 / As a result of this testimony about himself, the speaker advises the audience, "Do not fear" (the same verb as in v. 5) **when a man grows rich.** Key to interpreting this psalm is recognizing that its dominant image lies in the economic sphere (wealth and redemption). The turning point of the psalm comes with the realization that life is determined not by what you possess but by what or who possesses you. In surprising fashion, this speaker finds freedom from fear through the fact of death. He, unlike these wealthy, will be bought out of it.

§50 A Misunderstanding of Sacrifice and the Presumption of Hypocrites (Ps. 50)

In contrast to most psalms, it is God who addresses his people in Psalm 50. As a psalm, it is set in Israel's liturgical worship at the temple on Zion (v. 2). As a prophecy, it shows us that temple worship was no mere monologue. Psalms 81 and 95 are also prophetic psalms and are explicitly set in the context of corporate, liturgical worship. Each of these psalms also alludes to Mosaic traditions (Sinai, exodus, and wilderness).

50:1–6 / This prophetic psalm introduces Yahweh in the language of a thunderstorm theophany, that is, an appearance of God **(our God comes)**. He reveals himself as God of the skies: he **shines forth** like the sun and **a fire** (lightning) **devours before him, and around him a tempest rages.** (Cf. the psalms of Yahweh's kingship, where he reveals himself as the God of the storm in 97:2–6, and where "he comes to judge"—"to judge the earth" in 96:13; 98:9. For an explanation of the peculiar statement, **the heavens proclaim his righteousness,** see the comments on 97:6. Other theophanic passages are listed there.) The thunderstorm theophany, which is associated with Mount Sinai in Exodus, is here applied to Mount **Zion.** As in the Songs of Zion, it is celebrated as a thing of **beauty** (48:2). (For similar theophanic introductions to prophetic judgment speeches, see Amos 1:2; Mic. 1:2–4.)

As the God of the skies, he is able to **summon the earth from the rising of the sun to the place where it sets.** Verse 4 adds that **he summons the heavens above, and the earth.** This universal summons seems strange, as does Yahweh's own command addressed to these realms, **Gather to me my consecrated ones** (Hb. *ḥᵃsîdāy,* lit. "my devout/faithful ones," i.e., those who are bound to Yahweh's *ḥesed,* which is the Hb. term the NIV translates as "[unfailing] love"), **who made a covenant with me by sacrifice.** This appeal to the heavens and the earth is clarified elsewhere by the wider covenant tradition, a key element of which are its "witnesses," who serve as a kind of notary public verifying the people's agreement to the covenant (Deut. 31:28; 32:1; also 31:19–22). Isaiah 1:2–3 and Micah 6:1–8 (cf. 1:2–7), though not making explicit reference to the term "covenant," are also prophetic lawsuits, in which Yahweh takes his people to court (as our psalm says, **that he may judge his people**) and calls on similar natural phenomena to serve as witnesses.

50:7–15 / Yahweh resumes his oracle (begun in v. 5) with a reminder of the covenant formula, **my people** and **your God.** He does not accuse them of failing to be religious enough. Rather, they have abundantly fulfilled their ritual obligations: **I do not rebuke you for your sacrifices . . . , which are ever before me.** The heart of his accusation concerns their fundamental misunderstanding of their God and of the purpose of ritual sacrifice. They regard sacrificial offerings as his food (**If I were hungry** and **do I eat . . . or drink?**; this view is reflected in the Babylonian "Enuma Elish" and the "Gilgamesh Epic"; see *ANET*, pp. 68–69 and 95 respectively). In the people's view, Yahweh is dependent on them (as echoed in the NIV's paraphrase, **need,** in v. 9). By feeding him, they believe they do him a favor. But in this prophetic lawsuit Yahweh forcibly asserts his independence: **for the world is mine, all that is in it** (cf. 24:1). The fundamental purpose of sacrifice is simply to honor the God who **will deliver you** (vv. 14–15, 23). Thus, the dependence works the other way around: it is the people who need Yahweh for **the day of trouble.** Isaiah 1:10–17 offers a similar prophetic indictment.

50:16–22 / At the heart of Yahweh's accusation of **the wicked** is their hypocrisy. At the root of this hypocrisy is another fundamental misperception of Yahweh himself: **you thought I was altogether like you.** They, in effect, create God after their own image. They misinterpreted his silence (**These things you have done and I kept silent**) as license. "If Yahweh tolerates our behavior, even our breach of his laws, then he must condone it," they conclude. The evidence Yahweh sets forth for their hypocrisy lies not in religious sins but in social injustices, spelled out in terms of his **covenant** instruction. The instructions reflected here echo both the "ten words" of the Decalogue (**thief, adulterers, tongue to deceit;** cf. Exod. 20:14–16) and the psalms of temple entry (**mouth for evil,** "tongue to deceit"; cf. 15:3; 24:4, among others). While Yahweh as heavenly judge may have every right to pronounce the sentence immediately, he offers a warning: **Consider this . . . or I will tear you to pieces.** Previously he kept silent, but now he says, **I will rebuke you . . . to your face.**

50:23 / Closing the psalm is a reminder of the fundamental purpose of sacrifice, which is to "honor" God, who pledges his **salvation.**

§51 The Penitential Psalm (Ps. 51)

Every psalm is special, but with this one we feel that we enter upon holy ground. While it is a confession of sin, it reflects an intimacy with God few psalms can rival. In most psalms, blame for a lamentable condition is attached to enemies or to sickness, but this psalm is uniquely introspective before God. In the traditions of the early church, there are the seven penitential psalms (Pss. 6, 32, 38, 51, 102, 130, and 143). Upon closer inspection, however, we discover that only Psalms 32, 51, and 130 give concerted attention to sin and forgiveness as their chief issue. (Psalms 6 and 102 make no explicit mention of sin. Most of the verses of Ps. 38 concern sickness and enemies and those of Ps. 143 concern being near death and under enemy attack.) Only Psalm 51 gives sin exclusive attention apart from other distresses such as sickness (implied in 32:3–4) and the judgment of the exile (see on Ps. 130). In other psalms, the awareness of sin appears to be prompted by circumstances, but in Psalm 51 it is prompted by the inner conscience instructed by God. It is also unrivaled among the psalms for its interest in inner transformation, rather than a transformation of circumstances (e.g., enemies, sickness).

How can we account for this unique psalm? It comes as no surprise that the editor who wrote the superscription thought of David. His adultery with Bathsheba and murder of Uriah, her husband (2 Sam. 11–12), echo the bloodguilt confessed in this psalm (cf. also 2 Sam. 12:13 and Ps. 51:4). But as noted in the Introduction, the historical superscriptions provide us with a secondary setting, one that helps readers (not worshipers) to see their use illustrated in other parts of biblical literature. We should also recall that Psalm 51 is unparalleled among the other Davidic psalms, most of which concern external enemies.

Although there is nothing in Psalm 51 that makes impossible its coming from David and his time period (aside perhaps from the closing references to the rebuilding of Jerusalem's walls), it does show remarkable affinity to several prophetic pas-

sages around the time of Judah's exile and shortly thereafter.
The designation Holy Spirit (v. 11) elsewhere occurs only in Isaiah 63:10, 11, and the mention of a broken/contrite heart/spirit
(v. 17), as an attribute pleasing to God, occurs only in Psalm
34:18; Isaiah 57:15; and 66:2. Isaiah 66:3 also reflects a similar
negative view of ritual sacrifice as found in Psalm 51:16. Similarly,
Isaiah 63:7–64:12 is a prayer of penitence and reflects an exceptional intimacy with God. It too confesses the dilemma of human sin, that no human effort can save one from its downward
spiral—only God can (Isa. 63:16–17; 64:5–9). Among the motifs
of the prayer psalms, the introductory petitions follow the standard vocabulary ("hear," "save," etc.). But the main petition section of this psalm (vv. 7–12) is, remarkably, unique in the Psalter
but strongly paralleled by the promises of a new covenant found
in exilic prophecies (Ezek. 36:24–32; Jer. 24:7; 31:31–34). Psalm 51
most likely originated within the same worshiping communities
of the exilic period.

51:1–2 / The opening petitions draw attention to the
immediate need, using several synonyms for sin: **transgressions**
(rebellion against a norm that defines a relationship), **iniquity**
(crookedness or perversion), and **sin** (missing a mark, illustrated
in Judg. 20:16). The attitude sought from God is **mercy,** and the
actions sought are that he should **blot out** (as in blotting out
a name from a book, see 9:5; 69:28; 109:13–14; Exod. 32:32–33;
Deut. 29:20; in reference to "transgressions" see Isa. 43:25; 44:22;
cf. Neh. 4:5), **wash** (the Hb. text adds "frequently" or "copi-
ously"), and **cleanse** (the same verb used for "pronouncing clean"
in priestly literature). Special appeal is made to the divine attributes of **love** (Hb. *ḥesed*) and **compassion.**

51:3–6 / The psalm now moves to a confession, first of
self-awareness **(I know)** that his **sin** is, as it were, always staring
him in the face **(always before me)**. It would be inappropriate to
infer from verse 4 **(against you, you only, have I sinned)** that the
speaker's action had no social effects, only religious ones (one
might think of idolatry). The confession must be understood
within the context of this immediate encounter with the God of
purity, truth, and holiness (vv. 2, 6, 7, 11). As the rest of the verse
makes plain, the point of this confession is to establish that the
speaker has **done what is evil in your sight, so that you are . . .
justified when you judge.** While verses 3–6 are the speaker's
confession of sin, they are also a "doxology of judgment" giving

praise to the just God who reveals his thoughts to humans. In Joshua 7:19–21 after Achan is commanded "give glory to the LORD" and "tell . . . what you have done," he confesses, "I have sinned against the LORD"—even though his action resulted in Israel's defeat and the death of thirty-six men (vv. 4–5). The book of Amos contains several "doxologies of judgment," one of which praises God "who reveals his thoughts to man" (4:13), which is a confession similar to Psalm 51:6. (Elsewhere in the Psalms, whenever the phrase "you only" [Hb. *lĕbaddĕkā*] is used, its primary function is to denote Yahweh to the exclusion of other deities and powers. See, e.g., 83:18; 136:4.) The evil becomes "sin" only because it is contrary to Yahweh's demands.

The confession of verse 5 has also often been misunderstood. It would be inappropriate to infer that the psalm is confessing something specific to its composer's circumstances, that is, that he was born out of wedlock (v. 5b reads lit., "in sin my mother conceived me"). It would also be putting too much on this single verse to read into it a doctrine of original sin. The Psalms and the OT in general speak less in terms of "being" (ontology) than in terms of experience and history (existence). Verse 5 must also be seen as part of this doxology of judgment. The point is to contrast God, the just judge (v. 4), and the speaker, who has lived in a world of sin since birth. Verse 6 continues this doxology of judgment. This remarkable self-understanding is not common knowledge, nor is it the result of scrutinizing introspection—it is the result of divine revelation: **you teach me wisdom in the inmost place** (cf. Jer. 17:9–10). Recognizing now that **you desire truth in the inner parts,** the speaker must realize how much he has missed the mark (which is the basic meaning of "sin," as noted previously).

51:7–12 / The opening verses of this petitionary section echo the petitions opening the psalm, though in reverse order (**I will be clean, wash me, blot out;** the NIV's **cleanse me** translates a different Hb. verb). Interjected among these petitions for cleansing (vv. 7, 9) is a request for **joy** (v. 8). The next three verses include petitions for **a steadfast spirit** and **a willing spirit** (vv. 10, 12), along with another request for **joy** inserted between them. The psalm thus emphasizes that penitence is to lead to full, joyful restoration. Between these twin references to the human spirit is the petition **Do not . . . take your Holy Spirit from me**. This juxtaposition of God's Spirit and the human spirit represents a striking breakthrough in the OT revelation, one that is also witnessed in the prophets.

The sequence of the petitions also matches the promises of a new covenant in Ezekiel 36:25–27. As they promise "you will be clean" (Ezek. 36:25), so verse 7 seeks the same claim, "I will be clean." As they promise "a new heart" and "a new spirit" (Ezek. 36:26), so verse 10 seeks **a pure heart** and "a steadfast spirit." As they promise God's "Spirit" (Ezek. 36:27), so verse 11 seeks to forestall the removal of "your Holy Spirit." The new covenant passages in Jeremiah also promise a new "heart" (24:7; 31:33) and add that Yahweh will forgive "their iniquity" (NIV "wickedness") and "their sin" (31:34)—the same word pair used in Psalm 51:9. We should not think of mere literary dependence on the part of either liturgist or prophet because each passage contains its own unique elements. Psalm 51, for example, boldly petitions, **Create in me,** an act reserved solely for God in the OT for unprecedented mighty acts of creation. It also distinctively petitions God to imbue with joy (vv. 8, 12a) his acts of cleansing (vv. 7, 9) and of creating a new inner spirit (vv. 10, 12b).

51:13–17 / This section is a distinctive variation of the vow of praise: **my tongue will sing of your righteousness** (vv. 14b and 15b). In this psalm attention has been devoted to cleansing from transgressions (v. 1) and sin (v. 2). Hence, the speaker's praise will be instructive for **transgressors** and **sinners.** Psalm 51 also uniquely adds the petition, **O Lord, open my lips,** to the vow, thus indicating that even the mere act of praising must be divinely initiated (though cf. 40:3, where praise is divinely given and results in "conversion"; Ps. 40 also shares a disclaimer of ritual sacrifice, vv. 6–8, a proclamation of Yahweh's "righteousness," vv. 9–10, and a confession of sin, v. 12).

Added to this vow of praise is a qualification of the kind of thanksgiving the speaker intends to offer. The OT term for "thanksgiving" (Hb. *tôdâ*) could include both verbal thanksgiving and a thanksgiving offering (see on 22:22–26; 116:17). In this case, however, **you do not delight in sacrifice** (Hb. *zebaḥ,* the so-called fellowship offering of Lev. 3 and 7:11–21) or **burnt offerings** (Hb. *ʿôlâ,* the so-called burnt offering of Lev. 1; 6:8–13). Rather, **the sacrifices of God are a broken spirit.** As noted above, this replacement of ritual sacrifice with a contrite spirit is also found in Isaiah 66:1–3. This sentiment reflects a long-standing abuse of ritual sacrifice by the people's presumption regarding the size and needs of their God (Mic. 6:6–7; Isa. 66:1–2; cf. Ps. 50:8–13) and their disregard for him (Isa. 66:3b–4).

51:18–19 / Normally the prayer psalm closes with a vow, but here another, seemingly unrelated petition is added, one that now extends to corporate concerns. Unlike most psalms, it appears to concern a particular historical event, namely the restoration of **Jerusalem** and its **walls** after the Babylonian exile (cf. 102:13, 16, 21). (It may be no coincidence that the transformation described in Ezekiel's promises is prerequisite for living in the land, as noted in Ezek. 36:28.) These verses may be a later addition to the psalm (see the Additional Notes on Ps. 22), especially if the view of sacrifice in verse 19 clarifies that in verses 16–17 (at least from the perspective of human authors). If so, verses 1–17 may have functioned originally as a prayer for an individual and then later as a prayer for the people of God personified as an individual.

The closing verse notes with a decisive and repeated **then** that after the restoration, **sacrifices** and **burnt offerings . . . will be offered.** But the shift from Yahweh's not delighting in sacrifice (v. 16) to his delighting in them may be due to more than the rebuilding of Jerusalem and the temple. Two qualifiers are added: the sacrifices will be **righteous** (cf. 4:5) and the burnt offerings will be **whole,** implying they will be accompanied by a repentant shift in the worshipers' attitudes. After all, according to Isaiah 57:14–21, the exile was to be characterized by the contrite spirit but after Yahweh "revives" and "comforts" his people, he "creates praise on the lips" (prob. lit. "the fruit of lips," cf. Heb. 13:15) "of the mourners in Israel" (cf. Isa. 61:1–3; Ps. 147:1–3).

Additional Notes §51

51:7, 9 / **Hyssop:** Hyssop, a plant, was used in cleansing rituals (Lev. 14:4, 49; Num. 19:18). The image of sins becoming **whiter than snow** is also found in Isa. 1:18. The image of Yahweh's hiding his **face** is normally used in laments with a negative sense of disregarding the speaker of the psalm, but here **my sins** are the object.

51:8 / **The bones you have crushed:** While this phrase clearly refers to some kind of previous punishment that Yahweh himself has caused, it need not necessarily be physical. For example, the Hb. behind "my whole being" in 35:10 is "my bones." Here the term is obviously metaphoric for the individual as a whole because the "bones" rejoice and utter articulate praise.

§52 The Wicked Uprooted and the Righteous Flourishing in God's House (Ps. 52)

Commentators have found this psalm difficult to analyze according to the traditional form-critical categories and difficult to locate within a setting. This commentary argues that Psalm 52 shows greatest affinity to the liturgies of temple entry. We hear a prophetic indictment of the evil person (vv. 1–4) and his sentencing (v. 5); a liturgist's testimony to the congregation in the form of a taunt (vv. 6–7), and his testimony of the benefits of entering God's house and praising him (vv. 8–9). The opening four verses might sound like a lament over the wicked, but the psalm contains no petition. There is no hint the speaker is singled out for attack, and it is unlikely there is any mention of victims. (See below on v. 7 and the Additional Notes.) In fact, the speaker is already certain that God has taken the matter in hand (v. 5). The presence of mere description of evil character and actions followed by a pronouncement of judgment (v. 5) implies verses 1–4 are an indictment. More specifically, they may be a prophetic indictment. Within the Psalter, this psalm shares most in common with Psalm 36, a psalm of temple entry (see the Introduction) whose opening verses are designated as "an oracle." Some judgment speeches in the prophets also have literary forms similar to those in verses 1–7 (e.g., the Hb. interrogative *mh*, "what/why?," in Ps. 50:16–21; Isa. 22:16–19 and the taunt in Isa. 14:4–10; Hab. 2:6–20).

The psalm contains several unexpected shifts that are probably best explained by a liturgical setting. There are two shifts in addressee: the wicked are addressed directly in verses 1–5 and then referred to in the third person in verses 6–7. God is referred to in the third person throughout except in the closing verse. The former may reflect a development from direct address of the wicked (perhaps simply as a dramatic form—they need not be physically present) to a testimony about the wicked to the listening congregation. Then, the closing verse turns to God in direct praise. Another shift occurs between the group and the individual: from the righteous (vv. 6–7) to the speaking "I" (vv. 8–9), who may have been a representative of the righteous group. The confession in the closing verse makes explicit that this speaker performs the psalm in a public ceremony. There may also have been different speakers, who would signal a change in the thrust of each section.

The description of the evil person appears to derive from the character profiles of the righteous and the wicked developed in the psalms of temple entry. Most notable is the attention given to the speech of the evil person, as it is to the speech of "the worker of righteousness" in the entry instruction of Psalm 15:2–4. Both Psalms 52 and 36 appear to begin with prophetic oracles describing the character and speech of the wicked: "your tongue plots destruction, O you deceitful tongue" (52:2, 4 // 36:3–4, also 5:6, 9, and contrast 24:4, NIV "what is false"), and "you love evil rather than good, falsehood rather than speaking the truth" (52:3 // 36:3–4; contrast 15:2). Similarly, both psalms refer to Yahweh's worshipers receiving abundant nourishment in God's house: one in the image of an olive tree flourishing (52:8) and the other in the image of a rich banquet (36:8–9). Further parallels lie in the mention of evil (52:1 // 15:3, NIV "wrong") and the importance of trusting in God as one's stronghold (52:7–8 // 28:7–8, NIV "fortress"; 26:1).

These observed parallels may explain why the psalm contains no lament and no petition. The opening description of the evil person is not a report on a particular person at a particular historical moment, nor was the psalm occasioned by a specific crisis. Rather, the psalm belongs to these liturgies of temple entrance, where the separation of the ways occur: the righteous who may enter and so flourish (v. 8), and the wicked who may not and so are "torn away from the tent" (lit., v. 5). The intent of the psalm is thus not to respond to a specific event but to teach would-be worshipers of Yahweh as they seek entrance to his temple.

52:1–5 / In light of the above, we may elucidate the liturgical development of the psalm as follows. A temple prophet indicts the evil person (actually or dramatically present) with a description of his character that focuses on his boastful, deceptive, and destructive speech. **You mighty man** (or "hero") contains an obvious tone of sarcasm. The prophetic voice then announces the verdict and punishment.

52:6–7 / Next either the same speaker or another liturgist describes how **the righteous** endorse this judgment: they mock the evil person's misplaced trust and rejoice in God's judgment of reversing his fortunes. They are so designated because only the doer of righteousness may be admitted into the temple (15:2).

52:8–9 / In the closing verses, a liturgist speaks on behalf of the congregation, turning their attention to their vertical relationship to God. Here the welfare, character, and action of the worshiper are presented as an antitype to that of the evil person. The use of agricultural images links their respective fates: while the evil one will be "uprooted from the land of the living" and "torn" from the "tent" ("your" in the NIV is not present in the Hb. text), the speaker is **like an olive tree flourishing in the house of God** (cf. 92:12–15). This contrasting parallel may imply that the "tent" (Hb. ʾōhel) of verse 5 is God's (not the evil person's), as referred to in Psalm 15:1 (Hb. ʾōhel, NIV "sanctuary"). Another contrast lies in the object of one's trust: the evil person trusted in his great wealth (v. 7), but the speaker trusts **in God's unfailing love** (v. 8). Trust is the issue that determines the fate of each. A third contrast lies in the object of one's praising. The evil person boasts (lit. "to praise one's self," derived from the Hb. verb *hll*, "to praise," v. 1) of evil; the speaker praises (Hb. *hôdâ*, v. 9) God. Here we see that the descriptions of the righteous and the wicked, while perhaps based upon actual, particular social groups in ancient Israel, are nonetheless shaped by one another in the context of liturgy.

The closing vow of praise reads literally, "I give thanks to you forever, for you have done (it); and I await your name for it is good before your devoted ones" (the *ḥᵃsîdîm*, who trust in God's *ḥesed* or unfailing love in v. 8). The act of waiting for Yahweh's name before the congregation may refer to their waiting for his self-revealing judgment promised in verse 5. The psalm clearly encourages the community of the righteous to commit the punishment of the ungodly to God and to not take it into their own hands. Overall, therefore, within the entrance liturgy this psalm moves us from the judgment of evil to the celebration of God and the benefits of his house.

Additional Notes §52

52:1 / You who are a disgrace in the eyes of God: The MT as it stands does not make sense in the second half of this verse: "Why do you boast of evil, O hero, *the unfailing love of God* (Hb. *ḥesed ʾēl*) all the day." It is difficult to explain how the NIV arrived at its rendering. The Syriac suggests reading *ʾel-ḥāsîd*, "against the godly," which may help explain the taunting of the righteous (vv. 6–7) and the speaker's praising God for doing judgment (v. 9 with v. 5).

52:7 / Grew strong by destroying others: The NIV tries to make sense of a difficult Hb. text, which lit. reads, "he prevailed *in his ruin/destruction* (Hb. *bᵉhawwātô*)." The NIV's attempt is probably incorrect because "others" must be supplied, and the word for "destroying" is actually a noun that denotes a state of destruction, not the act of destroying. The Syriac and Targum suggest reading Hb. *bᵉhônô*, "in his wealth," which forms a better parallel to **his great wealth** in the preceding line.

§53 There Is No One Who Does Good (Version 2) (Ps. 53)

53:1–7 / Psalm 53 is virtually identical to Psalm 14. While Psalm 14 refers to "the LORD," Psalm 53 refers to **God**, as is customary in the Elohistic Psalter (Pss. 42–83). Psalm 14:5–6 is here collapsed into a single verse (53:5), which omits the mention of God's protection of "the righteous," and instead expands on God's judgment of the **evildoers**. For further discussion, see the comments on Psalm 14.

§54 Deliverance from Godless Opponents (Ps. 54)

The historical superscription includes a citation from 1 Samuel 23:19. The ancient interpreter who wrote the superscription and first associated this psalm with this event in David's life was probably prompted to do so by some similarities of situation and by the phrase, "to seek one's life," found in both Psalm 54:3 and 1 Samuel 23:15. As discussed in the Introduction, this is a very intriguing and helpful way of reading the psalm, once one understands "David" as the archetypal person of God. But as also discussed, psalms were first and foremost composed within and for a liturgical setting, not within a desert setting (1 Sam. 23:15), where prose prayers appear to have been the custom (e.g., vv. 2, 10–12).

In the quest for this psalm's original setting, some interpreters begin with what appear to be the clearest references to the circumstances troubling the speaker. The opening petition points to a situation of injustice ("vindicate me," or lit., "may you bring me justice"), the cause of which is clear by the references in the lament, the petition, and the anticipated praise, namely godless persons who threaten the speaker directly ("strangers" who "are attacking me" and "seek my life," "those who slander me," and "my foes"). Scholars such as W. Beyerlin (*Die Rettung der Bedrängten*, p. 23) and Kraus (*Psalms 1–59*, p. 514) have argued that the speaker has been falsely accused and now seeks Yahweh's acquittal at the "supreme court" of the temple (see further endnote 6 in the Introduction). We must be cautious, however, whenever we try to pin down the original circumstances for which a psalm was composed or to limit its application beyond these circumstances. What may appear to us to be a description of circumstances may instead be a poetic image depicting threat in general.

54:1–5 / Psalm 54 is a good example of the key motifs characterizing individual prayer psalms. Much of it is composed of formulaic language, that is, phrases and expressions that appear repeatedly in other psalms (53 percent by Culley's count; see his *Oral Formulaic Language,* p. 103). The introductory petitions (vv. 1–2), in addition to using standard formulas such as **Save me** put the focus on God's "bringing justice" (NIV **vindicate me**) by the agency of his **name** and **might.** The body of the psalm (vv. 3–5) contains the three key elements of a prayer psalm: a lament, a confession of trust, and a petition. The lament (v. 3) is virtually identical to 86:14, another psalm composed of formulaic language (49 percent by Culley's count). On the phrase, **seek my life,** see the Introduction. The confession of trust (v. 4) not only allows the worshiper to encourage himself; it also leads him to make confession of how he differs from **men without regard for God,** mentioned in the preceding verse. The petition in the body of the psalm (v. 5) seeks Yahweh's retributive justice of "like for like": **let evil recoil.** Modern readers may not think of the petition, **destroy them** (or better, "silence them," Hb. *haṣmîtēm;* see Holladay, *Hebrew Lexicon,* p. 307), as an expression of God's **faithfulness,** but in the context of threat that this action against the opponents is a reflection of God's protection of the worshiper. The phrase, **those who slander me** (Hb. *šōrᵉrāy*), is more accurately translated "those who watch/lurk for me" (see further on Ps. 5).

54:6–7 / Individual prayer psalms typically close with a vow of praise, but this one specifically promises sacrifice and not just verbal praise (vv. 6–7). The phrase **I will sacrifice a freewill offering to you** points to a temple ritual, and its parallel vow, **I will praise your name** (also note "your name" in v. 1), is not simply another general expression of praise but one that points to the "name" of God that dwells at the temple (see below). Following this promise is a quotation of what will be the substance of the anticipated praise (we should probably read, "I will praise your name: 'He has delivered me . . .' "). Since thanksgiving was to be performed publicly (see on Ps. 30), the anticipated confession, **my eyes have looked . . . on my foes,** envisages a public vindication as requested in the opening verse.

Additional Note §54

54:6 / I will praise your name: This "name theology" is esp.
characteristic of Deuteronomic literature (e.g., Deut. 12:5). The tensions
with which this theology of God's presence deals are perhaps best illustrated in Solomon's prayers at the dedication of the temple. On the one
hand, he refers to the temple as "a place for you to dwell forever"
(1 Kgs. 8:13), but on the other he mentions "heaven, your dwelling
place" (1 Kgs. 8:30, 39, 43, 49 and 32, 34, 36, 45). And neither "this
temple" nor "the heavens . . . [can] contain you" (1 Kgs. 8:27). The
temple is, strictly speaking, not where God himself dwells or localizes
himself; it is where he has chosen his name or self-revelation to dwell.
Solomon defines "this temple" as "this place of which you said, 'My
name shall be there' " (1 Kgs. 8:29). It is "a temple for the name of the
LORD, the God of Israel" (1 Kgs. 8:16–20, etc.). This understanding
within Deuteronomic literature is an attempt to allow for the freedom
of God: he is no longer tied to a particular place as his principal residence. Rather, the temple is merely the channel through which he
chooses to reveal himself to his people (note the emphasis on God's
choice in 1 Kgs. 8:16). We may further note from this prayer that "confessing your name" is spelled out as "praying and making supplication
to you in this temple" (1 Kgs. 8:33, 35).

§55 Betrayed by a Friend (Ps. 55)

This prayer psalm of the individual faces threat from each dimension: from social enemies engaged in oppression (vv. 9–11, 23) and from a personal enemy who was once "my companion" (vv. 12–14, 20–21). Betrayal is what makes this distress particularly wounding. The psalm also contains a singular expression of *inner* conflict (vv. 4–8) with which many could identify at one time or another. But the speaker does not appear to be alone. The exhortation of verse 22 (cf. 27:14; 31:23–24) and the testimony of verses 16–19 (where God is referred to) may reflect the presence of other people during the psalm's performance.

55:1–8 / Psalm 55 contains the motifs typical of prayer psalms, but it is longer than most and intersperses these motifs, rather than leaving them in discrete sections. It opens with the expected petitions for God to **hear** (vv. 1–2a) and with a lament (vv. 2b–8). This first lament focuses on personal anguish caused by **the wicked.** The speaker's inner turmoil **(My thoughts trouble me, my heart is in anguish within me,** and **fear and trembling have beset me)** and his temptation to escape **(Oh, that I had the wings of a dove!)** find a place in this prayer because the God to whom they are addressed can be moved to pity. Instead of fleeing **from the tempest and storm,** the speaker commits the matter to the Lord. The psalm has several parallels to Jeremiah's laments (e.g., Jer. 9:2–9), which also reflect personal betrayal (cf. also Mic. 7:5–6) and the temptation to escape, as well as a focus on the speech of the wicked.

55:9–15 / Next come petitions (v. 9) and other laments that reflect corporate threat **in the city** (vv. 10–11) and personal betrayal (vv. 12–14). As found in the descriptions of "the wicked" in most other psalms, attention is given to **their speech** (v. 9; "his speech," i.e. of the betrayer, is mentioned in v. 21). That **they prowl** (Hb. *sbb*) evokes the image of the wicked as a pack of dogs (cf. 22:16; 59:6, 14, where dogs "surround" or "prowl," Hb. *sbb*).

What gives this lament a sting beyond other laments over the wicked is that among the opponents is a one-time **close friend.** (The direct address of v. 13, **But it is you,** may imply the betrayer was physically present, though in vv. 20–21 this singular traitor is simply referred to.) Their intimacy was not merely social but spiritual as well, described as **sweet fellowship as we walked with the throng at the house of God.** Closing this section is a petition (v. 15) that the enemies would experience an untimely death because **evil** has made its home with them.

55:16–21 / The psalm now turns to a different tone and a different audience. God is referred to, not addressed directly. Verses 16–19a confess that God **hears my voice** when I **cry out in distress. Evening, morning, and noon** echoes the same beginning and ending of the "day" found in Genesis 1 ("there was evening, and there was morning"). God is depicted both as redeemer **(he ransoms me)** and king **(who is enthroned).** A lament follows somewhat awkwardly (as a lit. translation reveals: "God will hear and answer them, even [?] the one enthroned of old—*Selah*—with whom [pl.] there is no changing [?] and *they* do not fear God. *He* stretches out his hand . . ."), and it may have been displaced from the earlier lament of verses 10–14. The conflict, earlier portrayed as urban violence and personal betrayal, is now presented in the image of war **(battle** and **war,** both Hb. *qᵃrāb* in vv. 18, 21, and **drawn swords).**

55:22–23 / Closing the psalm is an exhortation and an assurance. The exhortation, **cast your** (sing.) **cares on the LORD,** may have been the petitioner's self-exhortation or an exhortation recited by a liturgist. If the latter, the voice of the petitioner returns in the closing line affirming he will indeed do as instructed: **But as for me, I trust in you** (the LXX adds, "O LORD"). The closing assurance is addressed to the Lord as praise, but as an echo of verse 15 it also serves to remind him of the earlier petition.

Psalm 56 is one of the many prayer psalms of the individual that laments enemies who are attacking. As is typical, no specifics are offered on the identity of the enemies or the speaker. The opponents are described as lurkers (NIV "slanderers," Hb. *šôrēr*) who hound (NIV "hotly pursue"), and press their attack (vv. 1–2). They conspire, hide (NIV "lurk," Hb. *ṣpn*) and watch the speaker's steps (vv. 5–6). While these enemies are depicted as social prowlers hiding in secret, mention is also made of peoples (Hb. *ʿammîm* without the definite article; NIV "the nations," v. 7). This could refer to foreign peoples who may have taken a direct part in the speaker's distress, but it is more characteristic for an individual prayer psalm to refer to the nations simply as part of the wider tradition of Yahweh's judgment (see on 7:6–9).

56:1–4 / A unique element of this psalm is how the repeated confession of trust (vv. 3–4, 10–11) encourages faith in the midst of distress. It first comes after the opening petition, **Be merciful to me,** and the lament describing the lurkers (vv. 1–2). We misread this confession if we assume it expresses the poet's current feelings of courage. A psalm is not an expression of the composer but a liturgy to lead worshipers in expressing themselves to God. We should not regard this absence of fear as part of the composer's psyche. Rather, the psalm puts words in the worshiper's mouth that he may hear himself utter, both a good reason for him not to fear **(in God I trust . . . What can mortal man do to me?)** and his own determination not to fear **(I will not be afraid).** He first utters these words to God (note **you** in v. 3) and then apparently to himself (note God is referred to in v. 4). The object of **praise** is uniquely God's **word.** It would be anachronistic, however, to think of written scriptures. In the context of the Psalms, it probably points to Yahweh's word commanding salvation (cf. 12:5–6; 35:3; 107:20; 130:5) and to the word revealing his ways (cf. 17:4; 18:30; 105:8; 147:19), as proclaimed during the temple worship.

56:5–8 / This confession of trust is not the end of the matter because the lament resumes with another description of the lurkers (vv. 5–6). In contrast to God's secure word, these conspirators **twist my words.** So that there be no **escape** for them, God is implored to respond in **anger** and **bring down** "peoples," that is, any groups who would stand independent of God. The NIV's "in their pride" in verse 2 is a paraphrase of "from a height." God is thus petitioned to "bring them down." A literal translation of the psalm's final petition (v. 8) makes clear that the confessed trust and the rejection of fear have not been without emotional cost: "You have recorded my wanderings; put my tears in your bottle (or perhaps, "in your presence"); are they not in your book?" Evidenced here is the belief that God does not stand aloof during distress—perhaps contrary to appearances—but takes personal note of his people's emotional suffering (metaphorically at least).

56:9–13 / Now after the second expressions of lament and petition (vv. 5–8), the psalm repeats the confession of trust (vv. 9–11), adding that **my enemies will turn back.** Closing the psalm is a vow of praise, in particular, a vow to **present my thank offerings.** This refers to the performance of thanksgiving sacrifice (Lev. 7:11–18; Deut. 12:5–7) and a thanksgiving psalm (e.g., Ps. 116, esp. vv. 17–19). Typical of such vows, thanksgiving is offered in anticipation of the deliverance (cf. 13:6; 54:6–7; 86:12–13): **for you have delivered my soul** (as noted in the NIV's margin) **from death.**

§57 God's Salvation for the Individual and the International Manifestation of His Glory (Ps. 57)

Psalm 57 is a prayer psalm of the individual, but one that presents the individual's need within the wider context of God's glory with its cosmic revelation (v. 5 = v. 11) and international proclamation (vv. 9–10). Initially, the psalm appears to have several internal inconsistencies. How do we explain the transition from lament motifs in the first half (vv. 1–4) to hymnic motifs in the second (vv. 5–11)? How do we explain that the concerns of an individual seeking protection become overshadowed by concerns for God's international and cosmic manifestation? How do we explain the spatial discrepancy that the speaker takes "refuge in the shadow of " God's "wings" (v. 1) and that God "sends from heaven and saves" the speaker (v. 3)? Could these inconsistencies be explained by an artificial splicing together of originally separate texts? This hypothesis gains some validity after we observe that verses 7–11 are virtually identical to 108:1–5, a psalm which is itself a composite (108:6–13 are identical to 60:5–12). But there are three considerations that point to integrity in Psalm 57. First, its halves do have linguistic ties. There is word repetition around the vocative "O God" in verses 1 and 7. The word pair "love" and "faithfulness" appears in verses 3 and 10. And God's position relative to the heavens is noted in verse 3 and the refrain of verses 5 and 11 (also v. 10). This last parallel indicates that the cosmic dimension of God's action is also present in the prayer section for the individual.

Second, there is a key symbol of temple that may help explain the broadening of horizons from the individual to the international and cosmic spheres. "The shadow of your wings," under which the individual worshiper seeks refuge, may allude to the cherubim-ark (in 36:7–8; 61:4 Yahweh's wings are closely associated with his house). Especially by means of this symbol, Israel perceived a unity between God's earthly and heavenly temples (see esp. the comments on Ps. 68:1, 4, 17–18, 24, 33–35, where—during the course of a ritual procession of the ark—God is depicted both "in his sanctuary" and as "he who rides the ancient skies/heavens above"). Hence, at one and the same time, the speaker may take refuge in "the shadow of your wings" at the temple, and God sends from heaven and saves him (cf. Ps. 11). This symbol also helps us to make sense of the petition in verses 5 and 11. As the cherubim-ark ascended into the temple (see on Pss. 47; 68), so God was envisaged as ascending above the heavens (cf. 18:10). Also associated with the cherubim-throne was Yahweh's royal glory, which was seen to fill the earth (Isa. 6:1–3). Moreover, the earthly audience for this ascent was not merely the residents of Jerusalem but also the nations (hence, v. 9 of our psalm; cf. 47:8–9; 99:1–2).

There is a third consideration that helps us see that the psalm's two halves are not as far apart as may first appear. Verse 4 in most translations, including the NIV, reads like a lament, but it may, in fact, be a confession of trust (see the Additional Note): "In the midst of lions I (can) lie down." Verse 6 then elaborates further on the worshiper's security in the midst of threat. Thus, verses 2–4, 6 may function largely as a confession of trust or a testimony, not as a lament.

We usually imagine the prayer psalms of the individual being used by individuals in special need of God's protection from enemies. In this case, verses 1–4, 6 seem appropriate to an occasion of false accusation. But if we attempt to read this psalm as a formulary for a petitioner falsely accused, we cannot account for verses 5, 9–11, which dwell on the international and cosmic revelation of God's glory. Because this topic surfaces primarily in corporate hymns, we should probably suppose the speaking "I" here is a representative liturgist speaking on behalf of the people of God, who regularly experience opposition from non-believers. Several factors point in this direction. First, these verses find their closest parallels in corporate psalms (for vv. 5 and 11, cf. 8:1; 21:13; 46:10; 99:2; 113:4; 148:13; for harp and lyre in v. 8, cf. 33:2; 81:2; 92:3; 150:3; for v. 9, cf. 9:11; 18:49; 96:3; for v. 10, cf. 36:5, a temple entry liturgy). Second, the psalm's only formal petition for the individual speaker is a general supplication in the opening line: "Have mercy on me." Third, the primary point of verses 2–4, 6 is not to lament or to petition for rescue out of distress but to testify how from heaven God shelters the individual *in the midst of* distress (note that in vv. 2–3 God is referred to). Fourth, if the symbol of the cherubim-throne is, in fact, operative here, this psalm's use at the temple and in temple liturgy is strengthened. In light of these considerations, the psalm as a whole presents a general petition for God's mercy, a testimony about God's heavenly love that saves in the midst of dire threat (in the first half), and an invocation that God publicly manifest his glory (in the second half). The individual's need is thus presented within the wider context of God's glory.

57:1–4 / The psalm opens with a petition for God's **mercy** and an affirmation that **I will take refuge in the shadow of your wings**. The **disaster** from which the speaker seeks protection is instigated by enemies who are depicted first as **ravenous beasts** (v. 4) and then as hunters (v. 6). (This dual comparison is also used in 10:9–10, a corporate prayer that laments social injustices.) Particular attention is given to their destructive speech (their **tongues are sharp swords**). The psalms of temple entry also give attention to the use of the tongue: its improper use is symptomatic of those who are to be excluded from temple privileges (5:9; 15:3; 52:2, 4; on these psalms see the Introduction). As noted above, verses 2–4 confess that in the midst of such abusive speech God sends help.

57:5–11 / Enveloping the speaker's own vow to spread God's praises worldwide (vv. 7–10) is his invocation (or doxology) that God make his **glory** manifest across **the heavens** and **all the earth** (vv. 5, 11). (The first five verses in Ps. 108, a composite psalm, draw from vv. 7–11, which include the vow of praise and the closing invocation. It thus selects the international components of Ps. 57 and omits all references to individual distress.) What is the meaning of this invocation? Is it an appeal strictly for the speaker's deliverance from distress (i.e., for a theophany) or for the sake of God and his praise? If it is a petition for God to intervene merely for the speaker's sake, it seems odd that God's action be described as his *exaltation* **above** the heavens, when his action on the speaker's behalf has just been described as the *descent* of his salvation from heaven (v. 3). The second invocation, following a proclamation of praise (vv. 7–9) and hymnic praise (v. 10), is clearly associated with the praise of God. For verse 5, falling between two confessions of trust (as argued above), the same may be true. Verses 2–4 affirm God's salvation for the speaker, and verse 6 the self-retribution that befalls any assailants. The only other instance of this petition in the OT points to a

request that Yahweh make manifest what he has just promised
(Ps. 21:13). In 46:10, Yahweh similarly announces, "I will be exalted in the earth." Like Psalm 57, this psalm earlier confesses the
security Yahweh provides in the midst of distress (note, e.g.,
"God is within her") but also anticipates a worldwide manifestation of his exaltation. According to the theology of the temple,
Yahweh's "glory" was revealed primarily at the temple (26:8;
63:2; cf. 24:7–10). Thus, this petition that it **be over** "all the earth"
means that Yahweh's manifest presence should now extend from
Jerusalem worldwide. The psalm thus shows a strong linkage between the individual, international, and cosmic realms. It may
initially seem odd that the first invocation should come before
verse 6 rather than after it. But the present location of verse 6
provides two key contrasts. The falling of the enemies in verse 6
contrasts both with God's exaltation in verse 5 and with the
speaker's **steadfast** (lit. "established") heart in verse 7.

Additional Note §57

57:4 / **I am in the midst of lions; I lie among ravenous beasts:**
The only other occurrence of "I lie (down)" (Hb. *ʾeškᵉbâ*) in the Psalter is
in 4:8, where it exhibits a peaceful trust in Yahweh. Psalm 3 uses the
same verb to express the same assurance (v. 5, Hb. perfect). Psalm 3
shares two other features in common with Psalm 57:4: (a) this "lying
down" occurs with myriads of attackers surrounding, and (b) attention
is given to the **teeth** of these attackers. Cf. Dan. 6.

§58 A God Who Judges Unjust Judges (Ps. 58)

Psalm 58 is a corporate prayer psalm, but who are the rulers addressed in the opening verse and censured in the rest of the psalm? This psalm shows some parallels with Psalm 82, which also complains of authorities or judges who practice unjust judgment. Although there the judges appear to be spiritual beings (who, unlike our psalm, are distinguished from "the wicked" in v. 4), here in Psalm 58 they appear to be human judges, who have a heart and hands (v. 2). The description of the wicked in the verses immediately following are clearly human (note "birth" and "the womb," v. 3).

58:1–5 / The opening verses lament that the judging of these **rulers** is characterized by **injustice**. It is not done **uprightly** (lit. "with equity"), a quality that characterizes Yahweh's judging in the psalms of Yahweh's kingship (96:10; 98:9; 99:4). And not only that, they promote **violence**. They are described as "venomous" and out of control.

58:6–9 / The central section consists of petitions (v. 6) and wishes (vv. 7–9, reading "may the wicked be" in v. 9) which pray for their destruction with graphic images of toothless **lions**, **water** dissipating in a dry wadi, blunted **arrows**, a melting **slug**, and a **stillborn child**. While these are a form of curses, they are not used directly on the wicked but expressed to God as wishes **(let, may)**. Prayer, not incantation, is the means prescribed by the psalm. The Israelites were to appeal for Yahweh's personal involvement, not to attempt to manipulate spiritual forces, as was customary in the surrounding cultures.

58:10–11 / A closing confession of trust signals how **the righteous** will **be glad** at God's justice. Certainly verse 10 employs an ancient cultural image of warfare that we cannot endorse (2 Sam. 11:1a illustrates this cultural assumption), but we must recall that God's judgment of the wicked marks the end of

the injustice, violence, and lies mentioned at the psalm's beginning. Moreover, these righteous are themselves the victims of the
injustices (**when they are avenged,** lit. "when he has seen vengeance"). As shocked as we modern readers may be, these biblical images should at least awaken us who live in the comfortable
West to the Bible's realism about injustice and how victims feel.
This is especially true because they are powerless to execute just
retribution themselves. Justice and peace are not mere ideals;
utopia is not a mere state of being. Injustice is practiced by "work-
ers of injustice," and so must be stopped by judgment that falls
on human beings. Justice and the **God who judges** become visible only when there is judgment on the unjust and liberation for
the victims. Zenger notes, "a true god (or rather, *the* true God)
must be judged by whether 'there is a reward for the righteous'
in that god's realm. Ultimately, this is the question of theodicy"
(*God of Vengeance?*, p. 37).

Additional Note §58

58:1 / **Rulers:** The Hb. text actually reads "silence" (Hb. ʾēlem),
thus "Do you indeed in silence speak righteousness?" This word probably reflects a scribal corruption of "gods" (Hb. ʾēlîm), a reference that
scribes would have found difficult. The variation between "gods" (Hb.
ʾēlîm) and "men of power" (Hb. ʾêlîm) in the Hb. manuscripts for 29:1;
89:6; Ezek. 32:21 (see *BHS*) reflects this tendency. The NIV paraphrases
Hb. ʾēlîm as "rulers" on the basis of Exod. 21:6; 22:8–9, 28, where Hb.
ʾᵉlohîm may mean "judges" (cf. Ps. 45:7). In Ps. 82:1, 6, however, the Hb.
ʾᵉlohîm in the "council of God/El" (as noted previously, Hb. ʾēl is a general Semitic name for the highest God) are probably divine beings (cf.
138:1). It is possible the term "gods" in our psalm is applied to the
human judges sarcastically.

§59 Threats from Personal Attackers, Urban Unrest, and Foreign Nations (Ps. 59)

Psalm 59 contains the motifs typical of prayer psalms, but it uniquely combines threats from personal enemies, urban unrest, and foreign nations—all within a structure whose development is more complex than what we find in most individual prayers.

Verses	Form-Critical Motif	Opponents
1–4	petition and lament	individual's enemies
5	petition	all the nations
6–7 (refrain A)	lament	urban/foreign prowlers
8	confession of trust	nations
9–10 (refrain B)	confession of trust	those who slander (lit. "lurk for") me
11–13	petition	enemies of my people, Jacob
14–15 (refrain A)	lament	urban/foreign prowlers
16–17 (refrain B)	vow of praise	individual

So what occasion does this psalm reflect: an individual beset with personal accusers, social conflict within Israel, or a military siege by foreign nations? A singular voice predominates, but in verse 11 he refers to "O Lord our shield," in parallel to "my people." Moreover, God's intervention will make "known to the ends of the earth that God rules over" Jacob (v. 13). The divine titles ("LORD God Almighty" and "the God of Israel") used in the petitions regarding all the nations (v. 5) are generally found elsewhere in corporate, liturgical psalms (e.g., 24:10; 46:7, 11; 48:8; 68:8, 35; 80:4; 89:8). The speaker may thus be a representative liturgist. Psalm 59 could suit a situation of military siege by foreign armies (esp. if we read, they prowl around the city in

vv. 6, 14), whose lies (vv. 12 and 7) allege that Jerusalem has violated an international treaty. A possible link for all three threats would be to see the king as speaker, but there is nothing especially royal about the psalm. Moreover, we should note that the weapons (swords) of the "prowlers" lie in their speech (v. 7). The enemies of "my people" use their mouths for curses and lies (vv. 11–13), perhaps referring to incantations invoked in the names of other gods.

Parallels with other psalms may point to social unrest within Israel. Psalm 55 also generally reads like a prayer psalm of an individual, but it also laments social unrest (vv. 9–11). Further, its structure is long and complex, interspersing the form-critical motifs. Thus, Psalm 55:10, "Day and night they prowl (Hb. *sbb*, Polel) about on its (i.e., the city's) walls," uses the same verb found in 59:6, 14. In our psalm we should perhaps read, they prowl through the city. (The ambiguity of the NIV's "about" actually suits the Hb. text.) Similarly, both psalms refer to the opponents' bloodthirsty nature (55: 23; 59:2) and to their speech (55:9, 21; 59:7, 12), which consists of lies (55:11, 23; 59:12) and is comparable to swords (55:21; 59:7). Other parallels appear in Psalm 9–10, which is also a composite drawn from various traditions and combines threats from personal enemies, foreign nations, and social violence. Its primary function appears to be to seek for social justice within Israel. It also contains several key linguistic ties with our psalm: God as fortress (59:9, 16, 17; 9:9, where NIV translates "stronghold," both Hb. *mśgb*), blood-violence (59:2; 9:12), enemies who lie in wait (59:3; 10:9), enemies whose mouths are full of curses (59:12; 10:7), and of course nations (59:5, 8; 9:5, 15, 17, 19, 20; 10:16). Both psalms also explicitly quote the enemies, who claim there is no God to take notice of their actions (59:7; 10:11, 13, also v. 4).

In the end, we cannot be conclusive about for what recurring setting this psalm was composed. It may have been reshaped in various stages for various needs. We may imagine the speaker being a king or liturgist praying about a social or international crisis. But we can also imagine the psalmic liturgy directing the common individual to see his or her distress as an occasion to pray about the wider threats that typically face the people of God (note, e.g., that vv. 1–4 lament they who lie in wait "for me," implying personal enemies, but v. 5 petitions the God of Israel to punish all the nations). It is this flexible quality that explains the psalms' preservation and popularity.

Psalm 59 appears to develop in three stages (as marked off by *Selah* in vv. 5, 13). Aside from the psalm's introductory petitions, each section opens with lament, which is countered with petitions in the first stage, with confessions of trust and petitions in the second, and with a vow of praise in the third.

59:1–5 / The psalm opens with petitions and laments that draw Yahweh's attention to **my enemies** who **conspire against me** without just cause. This section climaxes with petitions that **the God of Israel . . . punish all the nations.**

59:6–13 / The opponents are likened to a pack of **dogs,** and then their speech is likened to **swords.** These laments are countered with confessions of trust that Yahweh is both the God over the **nations** and **my** own **loving God.** As noted in the royal Psalm 2, verse 4, Yahweh is seen to **laugh . . . at all those** nations. Petitions follow for a judgment that will be both memorable for **my people** and definitive **to the ends of the earth.** The primary indictment against these foes concerns **the curses and lies they utter.**

59:14–17 / The psalm closes with a repetition of the lament depicting the opponents as prowling **dogs** (vv. 6, 14) and a repetition of the confession of Yahweh as **my loving God** (vv. 9, 17), but in each case there is not mere repetition. This confession is transformed into a vow of praise: "I watch for you" (v. 9) becomes **I sing praise to you** (v. 17). And the expanded lament sets up a contrast to this vow of praise: these dogs **howl if not satisfied, but I will sing of your strength,** and **they return at evening,** but **in the morning I will sing of your love.**

§60 Defeat in Battle with Edom (Ps. 60)

This psalm concerns an impending attack against Edom (v. 9) and comes out of the background of a recent, devastating battle defeat (vv. 1–4, 10). The divine oracle (vv. 6–8), which is either a citation of an earlier prophecy or a newly delivered one, presupposes a united monarchy, where Ephraim and Judah are part of the same kingdom. Though not apparent initially, the historical superscription can be fitted with the OT's historical narratives. David did defeat Philistia (v. 8; cf. 2 Sam. 8:1), Moab (v. 8; cf. 2 Sam. 8:2), and Edom (v. 8; cf. 2 Sam. 8:13–14). He also fought Aram Naharaim (i.e., "Arameans . . . from beyond the River" in Mesopotamia; cf. the psalm heading and 2 Sam. 10:16–19) and Aram Zobah (cf. the heading and 2 Sam. 8:3–6, 12; 10:6–15). But 2 Samuel records only David's victories over these peoples, and Psalm 60 clearly presupposes a defeat. Moreover, the superscription credits Joab with having "struck down twelve thousand Edomites in the Valley of Salt," but 2 Samuel 8:13 credits David with "striking down eighteen thousand Edomites in the Valley of Salt." This seeming impasse may be resolved by 1 Kings 11:15–16, which refers back to this period but also alludes to an Israelite defeat and credits Joab with having "struck down all the men in Edom." This superscription thus informs us of battles not recorded in 2 Samuel. (See further B. S. Childs, "Psalm Titles and Midrashic Exegesis," *JSS* 16 [1971], pp. 146–47; Broyles, *Conflict of Faith and Experience*, pp. 144–45). Verses 5–12 are identical to 108:6–13, where they appear to be reapplied in a prayer for Yahweh's final, eschatological "day of vengeance" when he establishes his lordship among the nations.

60:1–5 / The psalm opens, not with a description of a battle defeat, but with a conclusion reached because of it: **You have rejected us, O God.** God, not the enemies, is the problem addressed in the psalm. The remainder of this section focuses on how he has reversed the normal pattern of a Yahweh war.

He performs the expected actions but does so *against* his own people. He has **burst forth** against their battle lines (Hb. *prṣ*, contrast 2 Sam. 5:20). **You have shaken the land** echoes the older songs celebrating Yahweh's coming to save and the earth's shaking in response (Judg. 5:4; Ps. 18:7; cf. 1 Sam. 14:15)—except this time he appears and is **angry** with his people. **You have given us wine that makes us stagger** is a metaphor picturing how stunned or woozy Yahweh's reversal has left them (cf. Isa. 51:17–23). Verse 4 is somewhat problematic but probably contains a wordplay and should be rendered "You have given those who fear you a banner (Hb. *nēs*), to flee/escape (Hb. *hitnôsēs*) from before the bow." Thus, rather than raising a banner to rally the forces for victory, Yahweh has summoned the troops to retreat (cf. Jer. 4:6). The NIV's **But** is not in the Hb. text.

Included in the complaint against God are two petitions that Yahweh reverse the damage he has caused (**restore us** and **mend the land**). Closing this section are petitions that he take a more proactive role: **Save us and** "answer" (Hb. *ᶜanēnû, Kethib*, not **help**) **us with your right hand.** Adding motivation to these appeals is the reminder that the petitioners are **those you love,** a designation that matches the preceding phrase, **those who fear you.** The petition for God to "answer" is perhaps intentionally ambiguous, meaning both "answer" us with saving action and "answer" us with saving words. The latter sense is most prominent in what follows.

60:6–8 / In this divine oracle God "exults" (Hb. *ʾeᶜlōzâ,* "I exult," NIV **in triumph**) as a victorious warrior parceling out the territories and spoils of war. **Shechem** was a city between Mounts Ebal and Gerizim in northern Israel, inhabited before the conquest. **The Valley of Succoth** lies just to the east of the Jordan River. These locations Yahweh **will parcel out,** implying they have just been conquered. **Gilead** denoted the broader region in Transjordan where two and a half tribes eventually settled. **Manasseh** and **Ephraim** were the primary tribes of the north, and **Judah** lay in the south. These tribes Yahweh gives positions of status, as his peculiar possessions **(mine),** his impressive military armor **(helmet),** and his symbol of rule **(scepter).** **Moab** and **Edom** were neighboring nations to the southeast and **Philistia** to the southwest. These longtime enemies are given a humiliating status (v. 8).

When was this oracle first delivered? Was it Yahweh's immediate answer to the preceding petition, "answer us," or was this a citation of an earlier oracle? Two features imply the latter is correct. First, the scope of the oracle is much broader than the psalm's immediate concern, which is Edom (v. 9). Second, if it were Yahweh's immediate answer to the preceding petition, the subsequent lament and petition (vv. 9–11) make little sense, because Yahweh would have just made his position clear. Thus, **God has spoken** (or "God spoke," Hb. perfect) **from his sanctuary** probably introduces a quotation of an earlier divine promise, which the psalm now uses as a reminder to God.

60:9–12 / The reason for citing this oracle becomes clear here: **Who will lead me** (i.e., in a military attack) **to Edom?** Verse 10 presents the problem that God should lead his people as commander-in-chief **(Is it not you, O God)** but he is the very one who appears to **have rejected** his people (see v. 1; cf. v. 10b with 44:9b). The concluding petition of the psalm does not ask merely for God to restore damages (as in vv. 1–2), nor merely for him to "save us" from defeat and retreat (vv. 4–5), but asks for him to **give us aid against the enemy.** Supporting this petition is a motivation that plays on the words **man** (Hb. *ʾādām*) and Edom (Hb. *ʾedôm*). The closing confession of trust does not address God directly, and so may have served as an expression of confidence to the congregation: **With God** (probably "Yahweh" originally before the psalm's inclusion in the Elohistic Psalter) **we will gain the victory.**

§61 A Pilgrim's Prayer to Fulfill Vows at God's House (Ps. 61)

61:1–8 / The particular request of this prayer psalm appears to be for safe escort to the temple, so the speaker may fulfill his vows. Several indicators converge at this point. First, we may note the speaker's longing for passage to **your tent** and **the shelter of your wings** (v. 4). The wish for guidance to **the rock** (v. 2) could be associated with the rock of the temple mount. Psalm 27 also uses "tent," "shelter," and "rock" as parallel expressions for Yahweh's dwelling (27:5). It also contains several other connections with Psalm 61: the depiction of Yahweh as a refuge/tower/stronghold (61:3 // 27:1), the desire to worship at his dwelling forever (61:4–5, 8 // 27:4), and the request for guidance (61:2 // 27:11). Second, **the ends of the earth** (Hb. *hāʾāreṣ*, v. 2) should probably be rendered "the ends of the land." The mention of **you have given me the heritage** (v. 5) points to Yahweh's allotment of land elsewhere in the OT, especially in Deuteronomic material (Deut. 2:5, 9, 19; Josh. 12:6–7; cf. Deut. 2:12). Closely connected to Yahweh's land grant are the speaker's **vows**, mentioned in the parallel line. The attention given to previous vows (v. 5) and their fulfillment (v. 8) may point to prayers and vows made at the beginning of the agricultural year for bountiful harvests (see on Ps. 65, where the fulfillment of vows is connected with Yahweh's blessing the land). They could be fulfilled in the offering of firstfruits (described in Deut. 26:1–11, which refers to Yahweh's "giving an inheritance" and to Israel's "taking possession," an expression that uses the verb form of the word rendered "heritage" in our psalm).

Third, seeing this psalm as a prayer for safe pilgrimage to fulfill vows for Yahweh's grant of a bountiful harvest helps us to make sense of the intercession for the king (vv. 6–7). Like these verses, Psalm 72 consists of intercessory wishes for the king (i.e., "may he . . ."; see the NIV marginal note). It grants us insight into the common belief of the intimate connection between the king's reign and the fertility of his land (72:3, 6–7, 16). Both psalms also pray for the king's long life (72:5, 15, 17). In addition, Psalm 84, which is clearly a psalm of pilgrimage, includes an intercession for the king (84:9). Psalm 63, another pilgrim psalm, also speaks from a land removed from Yahweh's sanctuary (63:1–2) and expresses a concern for the king's welfare (63:11). Also characteristic of Psalms 61, 63, and 84 is an almost physical longing for God's dwelling place (61:2; 63:1; 84:2). Psalm 42–43 (probably a single psalm) is another psalm expressing physical longing for the house of God (42:1–4) from a distant land (42:6) and also prays for guidance to his dwelling (43:3). (Also cf. Ps. 121, which exhibits anxiety at the thought of the pilgrim journey.) In view of the above, Psalm 61 was sung probably not at the temple but in the pilgrims' home region before the journey began.

Reference to the king indicates the psalm originated in the monarchical period. "Your tent" need not be restricted to the tabernacle of the pre-temple period. In 27:4–5, it is used in connection with "house" and "temple." (Cf. 15:1; Isa. 33:20.) The use of "tent" after the temple's construction shows how the earlier tabernacle traditions were transferred to the temple. The mention of **refuge in** "the shelter of your wings" (v. 4) probably points to the symbolism of the cherubim (see on Ps. 57). The mention of "a foe" (there is no **the** in the Hb. text) may not point to an actual, personal enemy. The psalm contains no formal lament, so characteristic of other psalms describing direct enemy attack. The reference may simply derive from the temple symbolism of Yahweh as **my refuge** and **a strong tower.** Thus it may signify any form of threat.

Before we examine the psalm's structure and thematic development, we should note that the requests (Hb. imperfect) that the NIV renders as imperatives should be rendered as wishes: "may you lead me" (v. 2), "may I dwell" (v. 4), "may you increase" (v. 6), and "may your love and faithfulness protect him" (v. 7). Psalm 61 is thus composed of three sections (vv. 1–3, 4–5, 6–8), each containing a request expressed as a wish (vv. 2, 4, 6–7) and a supporting motivation (introduced by **for,** vv. 3, 5, or **then,** v. 8). The first two sections begin with a prayer for escort to the temple (vv. 1–2, 4) supported by an argument based on what God has done (v. 3) or heard (v. 5) on the speaker's behalf. The prayer that **your love and faithfulness** act as the **king's** bodyguards (vv. 6–7) is not a pious afterthought but a prayer essential to safe escort to the temple (v. 8). Note that the connective "then" closely ties the speaker's fulfilling his vows to the king's welfare. Supporting this petition and the whole psalm is a vow (v. 8), this one emphasizing that the speaker will fulfill the earlier vows that Yahweh heard (mentioned in v. 5).

Particularly noteworthy in the psalm's theology is the understanding or insight that God's gifts are both mediated through special channels and immediately accessible to the speaker from anywhere. God's special presence is at the temple (v. 4), but he hears the speaker's praying "from the ends of the land" (v. 2). God's provision that the speaker may fulfill his vows is in part worked out through the king's government (vv. 6–7), but God's sheltering of the speaker is both direct and intimate (v. 3). The psalm also emphasizes to God his twofold bond to the worshiper (both expressed in connective clauses, vv. 3, 5, 8). He is bound to him from the past when he proved himself to be a refuge. He is also bound to him in the future so the speaker may fulfill past vows. Underlying these beliefs is the conviction that God takes seriously his past relationships and his people's promises for the future.

Additional Notes §61

61:2 / The NIV translation follows the MT. "The rock that is too high for me" may be a more accurate rendering. This would coincide well with the preceding self-description of being faint and would underline the need for divine intervention. LXX and Syriac read "upon a rock may you exalt me," which is similar to 27:5.

61:4 / **I long to dwell:** The NIV's "long to" is a paraphrase of a Hb. cohortative, which should normally be translated, "may I dwell." This rendering is supported by the following verse, "for you have heard my vows," which appears to substantiate a request, not a confession of trust (as v. 3, **for** . . . , supports the requests of vv. 1–2).

61:6–7 / This may not be a hyperbolic wish for eternal life for the current monarch but simply a wish for the dynasty as a whole.

61:7 / **Appoint . . . to protect:** The verb for "protect" in v. 7 is not an infinitive but another imperfect, thus, "may they protect." The verb for "appoint" does not make syntactical sense in the Hb. text and does not appear in two manuscripts, nor in Jerome. It may reflect dittography; that is, a scribal error in which a part of the text is repeated.

§62 Rest in God (Ps. 62)

We admire the confidence and security reflected in this psalm, but we should not imagine they come easily or naturally. In fact, this psalm of trust admits that these qualities do not come without effort. This is not a personal testimony of one boasting in his confidence but a liturgy that leads worshipers to lay claim to the salvation that is in God.

The exhortations of verses 8 and 10 are plural and imply a congregation or assembly ("O people") is present. Verse 8 seeks to apply to the group ("God is our refuge") what the speaker or liturgist has just applied personally ("he is . . . my refuge," v. 7). Verses 1–7 may thus act as the liturgist's instructive testimony to the congregation (God is not addressed directly here). With this shift from "my refuge" to "our refuge," the remainder of the psalm consists of direct exhortations to the audience (vv. 8–10) and their supporting reasons, expressed in hymnic praise (vv. 11–12). In this light, the opponents of verses 3–4 may not be personal enemies or a specific group, and we should note that the man assaulted is not explicitly identified as the speaker. The hypocritical speech singled out in verse 4 is, in fact, a regular element in the character profile of the wicked person used in the temple entry liturgies (e.g., 5:6; 26:4; 28:3; 36:2–3; 52:1–4; cf. 15:2–4; 24:4; see further "Temple Entry Liturgies" in the Introduction; also cf. the warnings against trust in riches in 62:10 and 52:6–7). Given the character of the wicked as presented in these regular temple liturgies, the worshipers using the psalms, and this one in particular, should expect such typical hostilities from those who oppose the people of God.

62:1–4 / We should probably read the opening verse not as a statement of confidence (so the NIV) but, as translated in verse 5, as advice or an exhortation to one's self: "Toward God is rest, O my soul; from him is my salvation" (lit.). The liturgist instructs himself, and so by example encourages the worshiping participants to do the same. The Hebrew word order shows the emphasis lies not in the phenomenon of **rest** itself but in its source. **God,** or probably "Yahweh" originally (this psalm being part of the Elohistic Psalter), as distinct from other so-called gods, is where our eyes should be directed. This exhortation for the eyes is underscored further in the subsequent confession, **He alone is my rock.** While verse 3 addresses the opponents directly **(you;** v. 4 then refers to them: **they),** we need not assume they were physically present. Liturgical performance in ancient Israel included such dramatic devices (cf. 4:2; 6:8; 114:5–6).

62:5–10 / Verses 5–6 echo verses 1–2. Following the self-exhortation (v. 5) is a public exhortation (vv. 8–10). The emphasis of the imperative, **Pour out your hearts to him,** lies on where the "pouring out" is to take place: "pour out *before him* your heart" (lit.). Lament itself is not the key, but to whom the lament is committed is key (cf. the title to Ps. 102; 142:2; contrast 42:4).

62:11–12 / The closing verses, which may recall God's speech contained in an earlier oracle, serve to undergird the liturgist's exhortations found in verses 9–10. "Strength belongs to God" (lit.), not to the wealthy or "highborn." "Love" (lit., Hb. *ḥesed*) also belongs to him, so those who "trust in him" have reason to be assured. These two attributes signify that God is both able and willing, and so they are to determine the congregation's aspirations. Thus, riches themselves are not what you should "set your heart on" (v. 10); rather, "pour out your hearts" to God (v. 8) and he **will reward each person according to what he has done** (v. 12). Christian readers might be disinclined to take comfort in this last claim, but we must interpret this reference to behaviors and their rewards within the context of the OT psalms and especially of the temple entry liturgies, where one either "does what is righteous" (15:2) or "does evil" (see esp. 28:3–5). We should therefore not presume this verse points to an absolute standard of perfection (as in Christian theology); rather, it points to an attainable standard whereby one identifies with righteous conduct as opposed to evil conduct. After all, according to the parallelism of verse 12, the Lord's "rewarding a person" is presented as an expression of his **loving** nature. This closing verse is the only one that addresses God directly. The psalm thus finishes not with mere instruction but with praise.

§63 The Pilgrim's Thirst for God in a Dry and Weary Land (Ps. 63)

Psalm 63 promotes a special intimacy with God. It consists primarily of confessions of trust and vows of praise (vv. 3–4, 11) and so is most akin to the prayer psalms, but it has no formal petition (though conceivably some of the Hb. imperfects could be rendered as wishes). Its primary function apparently is confessing to God the worshiper's intentions of "seeking" and "staying close to" God, and affirming that God will in turn sustain and protect him. The psalm confesses what has drawn the worshiper to the sanctuary (vv. 1–2), the value and benefits of being there (vv. 3–8), and the consequences for fellow-worshipers and their opponents (vv. 9–11).

The psalm is not explicit about for what recurring occasion it was recited. The speaker could be the king, referring to himself in the third person (v. 11), who is engaged with military opponents (vv. 9–10). But the psalm lacks any appeal to royal/Davidic privileges, as is characteristic of psalms that are clearly royal (e.g., 2:7–9; 20:1–9; 89:19–51; 132:11–12, 17–18), so there are little grounds to suppose verse 11 is anything other than a simple reference to the king. Moreover, as the parallelism of verse 11 shows ("the king" // "all who swear"), the reference is not to the king in particular but to the king's people. The speaker could be one falsely accused. Mention is made of liars and those "who seek my life" (vv. 9, 11). Seeking refuge in the sanctuary may also be implied (vv. 2, 7–8). But there is no allusion to a legal case. And neither of these theories account for the longing for God himself in verses 1–5 and the general lack of petition.

These opening verses make best sense as an expression of anticipation of a pilgrimage festival. In 42:1–2 this same "thirsting for God" is envisaged to culminate in "appearing before God" at the sanctuary. The claim, "I have seen you" in the sanctuary, refers to a past event (Hb. perfect) and may point to the speaker's previous participation in the regular festivals. The expression, "My soul will be satisfied as with the richest of foods" (Hb. *dešen*), is probably not merely metaphoric for a banquet but may involve the symbolism associated with thanksgiving sacrifices, where half was burnt as an offering to God and the other half was shared as a communal meal eaten before the Lord (22:26; 65:4; Lev. 7:15–16; Deut. 12:5–7; 1 Sam. 1:3–4, 9). Similarly, 36:7–9 claims that those who "find refuge in the shadow of your wings . . . feast on the abundance (Hb. *dešen*) of your house; you give them drink from your river of delights" (cf. 46:4). Psalm 36 was probably part of a regular temple liturgy. We can thus see that it was characteristic of Yahweh's worshipers to consider themselves "refugees" at the temple and there to enjoy the temple feasts. We may be able to be more specific about which festival is in view, especially if the reference to a dry and weary land is more than metaphoric. From May to September Palestine annually experiences drought, and the fall festival of Tabernacles occurs on the eve of the seasonal rains. The reference to "the king" might seem out of place until we observe that other pilgrim psalms also show special interest in the king's welfare (61:6–7; 84:9). (For further elaboration on the king's key role in agricultural produce, see the comments on Pss. 61; 72.) The king was considered to be the principal human host at the pilgrimage festivals, which are characterized by "rejoicing" (Passover in 2 Chron. 30:1, 13, 25; Tabernacles in 1 Kgs. 8:2, 65–66; cf. Deut. 16:14–15; Lev. 23:40).

63:1–2 / The opening confession, **O God, you are my God,** is no trite confession. In the ancient Near East, "my God" (i.e., my personal, guardian deity) was simply one deity among many (see the Introduction, section on "My God"), but here the psalm claims "my personal God" is none other than "Yahweh" (whose personal name was probably part of the original text and later replaced with *ʾelōhîm* or "God" when the psalm was included in the Elohistic Psalter). The image of "thirsting" **in a dry and weary land** graphically portrays the soul's longing for God as a fundamental appetite of the worshiper.

We may wonder how a worshiper could claim, **I have seen you in the sanctuary.** First, we should note this expression is sometimes used in the OT for the pilgrim's encounter with God at the sanctuary (see the Additional Note on 42:2). Second, the terms found in the parallel phrase, **beheld your power and your glory,** point to the symbolism of the cherubim-ark (see esp. 78:61; 80:1–2; 132:8; cf. 96:6–7; note also "in the shadow of your wings" in 63:7). Hence, this "seeing God" was done via this symbol, probably during a procession led by the cherubim-ark at one of the major temple festivals (see esp. on Pss. 47 and 68).

63:3–8 / The confession, **your love is better than life,** is striking. Life and its preservation from threats (e.g., enemies, sickness) is a supreme value in the Psalms (see, e.g., 21:4; 34:11–12; 64:1; 103:4), but here God's love transcends it. The psalm, however, does not pit one against the other or necessarily imply an experience of God's love beyond life (Hb. *ḥyym*) because the next verse clearly foresees praising God in this life: **I will praise you as long as I live** (Hb. *ḥyym*). If we are correct in reading this psalm against the background of the Feast of Tabernacles, which occurs at the turning point of the agricultural year (note the "Gezer Calendar" in *ANET*, p. 320), then the point of this verse is to place greater value on Yahweh himself than on the physical trappings of agricultural produce and religious feasts. There are a few other psalms that betray a similar intimacy with God and that place such value on relationship with him (Pss. 16; 23; 27; 42–43; 73), some of which also reflect the notion of pilgrimage. The praise of God is not merely vocal; it also postures the body in adoration: **I will lift up my hands.** The feelings of longing and of dissatisfaction, as expressed in the opening verse, are not to be disdained, for they compel God's pilgrims to find ultimate satisfaction in worshiping in God's very presence.

The confession, **On my bed I remember you,** expresses the devotion the pilgrim feels even in his private moments. The desire to **sing in the shadow of your wings** (alluding to the symbolism of Yahweh's cherubim-throne) in connection with God's **help** or protection is echoed in another pilgrim psalm (61:3–4; also cf. 17:8; 36:7; 57:1). The expression, **My soul clings to you,** is literally "I pursue after you" (Hb. *dbq ʾḥr*; cf. Judg. 20:45; 1 Sam. 14:22; Jer. 42:16; 1 Chron. 10:2), thus reflecting the journey of the pilgrim. (On **your right hand upholds me,** cf. 73:23.)

63:9–11 / To this point the only parties mentioned in the psalm have been the speaker and his God. These final verses introduce **they who seek my life** and **liars,** and **the king** and **all who swear by** "him" (see below). We had noted above that Psalm 36 has certain parallels with our psalm. It too mentions personal opponents (v. 11) who are characterized by deceit (v. 3) and closes with an affirmation that they will be stopped (v. 12). Thus, we must not assume Psalm 63 was designed for special needs of individuals. Whatever were the particular circumstances of this psalm's performance, the speaker's participation in God's worship will have widespread effects. Verses 9–10 illustrate with a concrete image the protection God grants his own, as sung in verses 7–8. According to the imagery of the psalm, life and death are determined by the satisfying of one's thirst (v. 1) and hunger (v. 5) at the sanctuary. If this psalm is a set prayer to be sung by pilgrims or their representative, the confession of trust in verses 9–10 offers assurance that any opponents who would try to prevent their access to the temple will not succeed. The mention of "all who swear" and its opposite, **the mouths** (lit. "speakers," Hb. *dôberê*) **of** "liars," may be explained by the liturgies of temple entry, where only those who swear (15:4; 24:4) and speak (Hb. *dōbēr*, 15:2) truthfully may **rejoice** and **praise** at the temple (e.g., 5:11). "Liars" probably includes those who worship false gods (cf. 24:4; 26:4; 31:6; 40:4, and esp. 4:2, in which the context is the issue of which deity will provide agricultural goods), not merely those who are morally corrupt.

Additional Notes §63

63:9–10 / **They who seek my life ... will be given over to the sword and ... jackals:** While it is possible this could be a graphic portrayal of a horrible death for one's personal false accusers, the mention of sword and jackals (Ezek. 13:4; Lam. 5:18) points more naturally to a military defeat, not to an execution. It may apply to foreign invaders, who threatened Yahweh's farmer-pilgrims. In the later, postexilic passage of Zech. 14, it is interesting that after a dramatic military conflict "the survivors from all the nations that have attacked Jerusalem will go up year after year ... to celebrate the Feast of Tabernacles" (v. 16).

63:11 / **All who swear by God's name will praise him:** The words, "God's name" and "him," are not present in the text. We should instead read, "all who swear by him (i.e., the king; cf. 2 Sam. 15:21) will boast (Hb. *hll*, Hitpael)." The parallel phrase, **rejoice in God,** makes clear this boasting is in God.

§64 The Wicked with Tongues like Arrows and the Divine Archer (Ps. 64)

64:1–10 / Several features of this prayer psalm point towards its use as a liturgy concerned with the general issue of social injustices. First, while the psalm begins with the voice of an individual (**I, me,** and **my** in vv. 1–2), its attention is thereafter devoted to two groups, **the wicked** (vv. 2–8, called *the* **enemy** in v. 1, not "my enemy") and **the righteous** (vv. 4, 9–10). This shift is understandable if the opening "I" is a representative speaker. Second, the psalm's structure does not make clear sense if we attempt to read it as a unified prayer of a lone individual. It opens with the psalm's only petitions (vv. 1–2), that God **hear** and **hide** the speaker, and then laments (vv. 3–6) the conspiracies, verbal attacks, and traps of the wicked, who act without fear of divine judgment **(Who will see?).** But then from verse 7 onward God is no longer addressed directly, and a remarkably different tone of certainty breaks forth. Verses 7–8 announce that God has taken the matter in hand, and verses 9–10 describe and invoke the proper human response of praise. Because verses 7–10 appear to answer the prayer of verses 1–6, it is likely that the voice of a second liturgist or temple prophet is to be heard in the second half. We should note this announcement goes far beyond the petitions of the first half. Verses 1–2 simply request protection, but verses 7–8 promise the downfall of the wicked, and verse 9 envisions an international response. The second half is nevertheless connected to the first by echoing images that show God's retribution will be in like measure to the crimes. Since they **aim their words like deadly arrows,** which they **shoot . . . suddenly** (vv. 3–4), **God will shoot them with arrows; suddenly they will be struck down** (v. 7). Since they **sharpen their tongues like swords** (v. 3), God will **turn their own tongues against them** (v. 8).

Third, Psalm 64 contains phrases and motifs common to other psalms, some of which have clear liturgical settings: insolent quotations from the wicked (64:5 and 10:4, 11, 13; 12:4), the wicked shooting arrows at the innocent (64:3–4 and 11:2; cf. 52:2), God shooting arrows at the wicked (64:7 and 7:12–13), the wicked becoming their own victims (64:8 and 7:14–16), the suddenness of their downfall (64:7–8 and 73:18–20; 11:6; 36:12; 52:5), people's "fearful" response (64:8b–9 and 52:6–7) and their pondering Yahweh's works of judgment (64:9 and 28:5), and the righteous in refuge rejoicing (64:10 and 5:11–12). Fourth, the descriptions of the **evildoers** have the same focus as those in the psalms of temple entry (see the Introduction), namely their speech (vv. 3–6). This is their primary weapon: their tongues are likened to swords, and their words to arrows, which **they shoot from ambush** (lit. "hiding places"). Their words promote **conspiracy** (vv. 2, 5–6). In addition, such images leave the psalm open to a variety of social situations. Conceivable are those of gossip, slander, false accusation, mockery, temptation, and incantations.

At the psalm's opening we hear an individual voice petitioning God for protection **from the threat of** the enemy (vv. 1–2). A lament (vv. 3–6) then describes the wicked especially in terms of their speech, which is deadly, presumptuous, and **cunning.** Verses 7–8 respond with an announcement of God's impending, just judgment. The closing verses (vv. 9–10) prescribe the appropriate human responses: **all mankind will fear,** and the righteous in particular are invited embrace this judgment by "rejoicing" and "taking refuge" in God.

A number of psalms speak of the wicked threatening the righteous and of Yahweh's impending judgment. We should not regard them as mere pious confessions or as head-in-the-sand attempts to deal with present realities. These are not quiet songs. They are said in the face of circumstances that tempt one to the opposite conclusion, namely, that God does not see and human behavior does not matter. The liturgy is meant to instruct and encourage the believing community to look beyond mere circumstances, to have their eyes opened to Yahweh's hidden, yet inescapable work. The people of God are to govern their lives by transcendent values and ultimate ends. The liturgy does not avoid or deny reality; it challenges us to see the wider picture.

§65 Praise to the God of Zion as Creator and God of Agricultural Fertility (Ps. 65)

This corporate hymn has three sections, each focusing on a different locale and each placing Yahweh in a distinct role. He is the atoner at the temple (vv. 1–4), the warrior who establishes order in all creation (vv. 5–8), and the dispenser of water and fertility in the land (vv. 9–13). Several key phrases confirm this structuring of the psalm's contents. The respective locations form an inclusion for each strophe: Zion and temple (vv. 1, 4), "all the ends of the earth" and "where morning dawns and evening fades" (vv. 5, 8), and the land and grasslands and hills, and meadows and valleys (vv. 9, 12–13). Beginning strophes one and two are divine epithets that link them: "You who hear prayer" (v. 2) "answer us" as "O God our Savior" (v. 5). The second strophe is marked off by the mention of awesome deeds (derived from Hb. yr°, v. 5) and by noting that those living far away are in awe (Hb. yr°, NIV "fear," v. 8). As the second strophe ends with "you call forth songs of joy" from the dawn and sunset, so the final strophe ends by observing that the meadows and the valleys "shout for joy and sing." Some commentators believe verses 9–13 are a later addition because their meter and content appear distinct (Kraus, *Psalms 60–150*, p. 28), but the links noted in the interpretation below show an integrated development throughout the psalm.

The psalm is sung at the temple (v. 4) in Zion (v. 1). Rituals performed with the psalm are the fulfillment of vows (v. 1), made in connection with an earlier prayer that Yahweh has now heard (v. 2), and fellowship offerings, implied in the phrase, "we are filled with the good things of your house" (v. 4; cf. 22:26; 36:8–9). Portions of the fellowship offerings (Lev. 3; 7:11–36) that are "the result of a vow" were eaten by the worshipers themselves (7:16; cf. Deut. 12:5–7; 1 Sam. 1:3–4, 9). At the moment Psalm 65 was sung, it is apparent that Yahweh has "visited the land" (lit., v. 9), which is now "covered with flocks and . . . mantled with grain"

(v. 13). "You crown the year with your bounty" (lit. "goodness," v. 11) implies its fruitfulness is at its peak. These clues suggest the votive offerings are in response to Yahweh's blessing the agricultural year, and they are now to be offered at its climax in the spring. This points to the Feast of Unleavened Bread, which marks the beginning of the barley harvest (Deut. 16:9; see J. A. Thompson, *Deuteronomy*, TOTC [Leicester: Inter-Varsity, 1974], pp. 196–97). Much of the year's crop, however, would still cover the fields. Thus, seven weeks (hence Feast of Weeks) or fifty days (hence Pentecost) later a feast was celebrated to mark the end of the wheat harvest. The earlier prayer and its attendant vow, mentioned here in verses 1–2, may have been made at the beginning of the agricultural year in the fall, perhaps at the Feast of Tabernacles. The "Gezer Calendar," a tenth-century B.C. Hebrew inscription (see *ANET*, p. 320), begins the agricultural year in the month of the Feast of Tabernacles. This eight-day festival occurred five days before the Day of Atonement, which coincides with verse 3, "you forgave our transgressions." Thus, Psalm 65 appears to celebrate Yahweh's blessing the agricultural year, for which the people had prayed and confessed their sins at the year's beginning.

As with many praise psalms, this one begins with a recollection of the past, namely prayers, vows, and confessions of sin, probably offered the previous fall. Verse 4 thus brings us to the present liturgical moment: the invited congregation enjoys a sacrificial meal before their divine host at his house. The second strophe (vv. 5–8) celebrates the answer to these prayers, evidenced by Yahweh's establishing and maintaining creation order. While this is an act of the distant past, it also continues to the present (see below). The third strophe moves from God's universal act of creation ("all the ends of the earth" and "those living far away," vv. 5, 8) to his particular act of providing Israel's territory ("the land," v. 9) with rain and fertility. It is this good produce of the land that provides the good offerings "of your house."

Modern readers may wonder what links the psalm's various sections and topics have with one another. What connections are there between Yahweh's temple and atonement, his control over mountains and seas, and his care for the land with its crops and flocks? Here we moderns, who tend to compartmentalize life, can learn from the integrated world view of this psalm. Each strophe makes a distinct emphasis in connection with the psalm as a whole. In the first, we learn that the people's status before

God at the temple can influence the fertility of the land. In the second, we see that creation order is not to be taken for granted—its preservation is an answer to the congregation's prayer, an act of salvation, and an expression of Yahweh's righteousness. In the third, creation is not merely an object; it responds to God with song.

Yahweh's goodness is experienced both at the temple ("the good things [Hb. *tûb*] of your house," v. 4) and in the land (God cares for "the land . . . . You crown the year with your bounty" [Hb. *tôbâ*, lit. "goodness"], v. 11). The connection between sacrificial worship enjoyed at the temple and the land's fertility is also prominent in Joel. A consequence of drought (Joel 1:10, 12, 19–20) and locust plagues (1:4ff.) is that "grain offerings and drink offerings are cut off from the house of the LORD" (1:9, 13). "The food" being "cut off before our very eyes" means that "joy and gladness from the house of our God" are likewise cut off (1:16). On the other hand, Yahweh's bringing fertility to the land (Joel 2:19–27), which is his "blessing" (2:14a), results in the restoration of "grain offerings and drink offerings for the LORD your God" (2:14b). We see that the land's prosperity is in no way a consequence of self-indulgent satisfaction. Rather, it is a consequence of finding satisfaction through celebrating with the holy dispenser of fertility himself. In view of what nature may or may not offer, one's relationship with this personal Yahweh is fundamental.

65:1–4 / While two-thirds of this psalm focus on God as creator and dispenser of fertility, the opening strophe clearly establishes the personal dimension of the worshipers' relationship to Yahweh. He is the one to whom they have made promises (vows), the hearer of their prayers, the atoner of their transgressions, the one who has chosen and summoned them, and the host at whose house they are satisfied. The particularity of their relationship is established before the liturgy progresses to embrace Yahweh's activity toward all the ends of the earth (v. 5) and in the land (v. 9). A literal translation of verse 1, "To you silence is praise," reveals that the mere act of waiting exemplifies respect for and dependence on God. Verses 2–3 recognize that all who come to God do so "with confessions of iniquities" (see the Additional Notes). According to this psalm, a characteristic assumption of "coming to God" is that worshipers will confess their sins and seek God's atonement.

65:5–8 / The second strophe celebrates the wider context of Yahweh's role as creator. Here modern readers must adjust their categories to those of the ancients. For the Israelites, creation was an act not unlike salvation. In this strophe describing Yahweh's creative acts—including his stilling of the sea—he is addressed as **O God our Savior** (v. 5). Psalm 74:12–17 similarly addresses God as the "worker of salvations" (lit., v. 12), describes his victory over the sea and its monster, and establishes his creation order. (Further on this conception of creation and chaos, see "Tradition of Divine Kingship" in the Introduction.) When we think of God as creator, we tend to think of something he engineered "in the beginning," with the world in a static state maintained by his laws. But this psalm's depiction of the creator is a dynamic one: he is the heroic warrior who **armed** himself **with strength** and **formed the mountains by** his **power** and **stilled the roaring of the seas** (vv. 6–7). As creator, God did not merely create matter and put it in order; he established order by warring against chaos. Thus, natural law is not self-enforcing and the order of creation cannot be taken for granted—this order requires God to exert his strength regularly. Another adjustment modern readers must make to their world view is that creation is also an expression of God's **righteousness** (v. 5). This characteristic does not belong to the moral sphere alone, the sphere of *right* and wrong. Hence, God has put the cosmos *right* by establishing *right* order. We should also note his righteousness is presented as a saving answer, not as a threat to the worshipers' coming before God (v. 2).

The two main acts by which Yahweh established creation order are highlighted by the use of two Hebrew participles (each beginning with the Hb. letter *m*, vv. 6–7). First, Yahweh is the one "*who establishes* mountains by his power" (lit.). Mountains in the OT symbolize the earth's pillars that stabilize it over the chaotic waters (18:7; 104:5–6; Job 9:5–6). Second, Yahweh is the one "*who stills* the roaring of the seas" (lit.). Although we tend to think of creation as simply an act of the distant past, and even the Hebrew Bible speaks of creation "in the beginning," nonetheless the acts described in verses 5–8 continue to the present (the present tense is more appropriate to the Hb. participles than the NIV's past tense). They are described as **awesome deeds,** by which **you answer us** (i.e., the contemporary congregation, v. 5). It is this answer in creation that gives evidence God has heard their prayers made at the temple (v. 2). They are also described as **your**

wonders (v. 8, lit. "your signs," thus indicating Yahweh's current involvement in creation), which cause **those living far away to fear.**

65:9–13 / In the third strophe Yahweh's creative role is depicted as dispenser of fertility and water. Like Psalm 104, our psalm shows us that Yahweh not only subdues the roaring waters (v. 7), he also "channels" (Hb. *peleg*) water to fruitful purposes (v. 9). Thus, in contrast to roaring waves, Yahweh provides water that is gentle (v. 10). Perhaps implicit in this psalm, which connects "the good things" of God's temple (v. 4) with his "goodness" (v. 11) in the land, is the image of "the channel of God" (lit., v. 9) that flows from the temple and gladdens God's people at the temple (see on 46:4; cf. Ezek. 47:1–12; Isa. 33:20–21; Joel 3:18; Zech. 14:8). This psalm should act as a pair of glasses for us moderns to see the world neither as a scientific accident nor as a mere commodity to be used at our convenience. It is nurtured by God and here personified as responding to him with song. This psalm invites us to hear something we have perhaps never heard: creation "singing" (v. 13, cf. 96:12; 98:8; Isa. 55:12). Singing for joy is here characteristic of creation and can be characteristic of Yahweh's worshipers if they partake of this insight and sing this psalm (called "a song" in the superscription).

Additional Notes §65

65:2b–3a / **To you all men will come:** Perhaps, "To you all flesh comes with words (i.e., confessions) of iniquities" (cf. Hos. 14:2). This *BHS* emendation establishes a 3+2 meter through vv. 1–6.

65:4 / **Those you choose and bring near to live in your courts:** Parallel to this expression is the speaking we, who "are satisfied" (lit.) **with the good things of your house.** This would suggest that those chosen to live at the temple are not a special class of Levites but simply those who have been admitted to Yahweh's temple through the entrance procedure (described in Pss. 15 and 24 and by 5:7). The "living in your courts" is not Hb. *yšb*, "to dwell (permanently)," but *škn*, "to tent." "Tenting" at Yahweh's "tabernacle" is the privilege of all who are admitted through the entry liturgy (note *škn* is used in 15:1), not merely of the Levitical personnel.

65:7 / **And the turmoil of the nations:** This phrase lies outside the regular 3+2 metrical sequence of the preceding verses. This irregularity and the absence of political references elsewhere may imply that this political equivalent to **the roaring of the seas** may have been an interpretation added later.

65:8 / **Where morning dawns and evening fades:** The NIV obscures the meaning of the second half of this verse by making the verb intransitive. The object of the verb "you make shout for joy" is "the going forth of morning and evening" or "dawn and sunset." Creation itself, not merely its human inhabitants, responds with joy.

65:9 / **You care for** (lit. "visit") **the land and water it; you enrich it abundantly:** This verse balances—poetically and conceptually—Yahweh's direct intervention in the sustaining of creation. It also hints at the notion of natural law: "The divine stream is full of water; you prepare its grain, for thus you establish it (i.e., the land)" (lit.). The land yields grain because Yahweh established it to do so.

§66 Corporate and Individual Thanksgiving to the God Who Acts (Ps. 66)

This psalm contains both corporate hymnic praise (vv. 1–12) and individual thanksgiving (vv. 13–20). Some commentators (e.g., H.-J. Kraus, *Psalms 60–150*, vol. 2 of *Psalms, A Commentary* [trans. H. C. Oswald; Minneapolis: Augsburg, 1989], p. 36), thus believe it consists of two psalms (or their fragments) that were originally separate. But several linguistic features imply they were composed together:

Verses 1–12	*Verses 13–20*
"Come and see what God has done,	"Come and listen, all you who fear God;
how awesome his works in man's behalf!" (v. 5)	let me tell you what he has done for me" (v. 16).
"Praise our God, O peoples,	"Praise be to God,
and let the sound of his praise (Hb. *tᵉhillātô*) be heard" (v. 8).	who has not set aside my prayer (Hb. *tᵉpillātî*), or withheld his love from me" (v. 20).

We should perhaps not view this linkage of corporate praise and individual thanksgiving as unusual. Logically, the time we should expect people to offer thanksgiving at the Jerusalem temple is during the pilgrimage festivals. In this light, the festival liturgies were composed to give occasion for worshipers to offer their individual thanksgivings within this corporate setting. Psalms 107 and 118 also place individual thanksgiving in a corporate setting.

Problems with the unity of this psalm disappear once one recognizes the liturgical nature of the psalm's performance. Key indicators of the psalm's structure are the imperatives introducing most of its sections (vv. 1, 3, 5, 8, 16). These were presumably spoken by a liturgist addressing the congregation. The recognition of a liturgist in the psalm's performance helps us to make sense of the speaking "I" in verses 13–20. It represents not a lone individual but one who leads a congregation in worship and speaks on their behalf. As noted above, one of the parallels between the psalm's corporate and individual sections lies in these imperatives (vv. 5 and 16). The liturgical and ritual performance of the psalm is also clear from the liturgist's descriptions of offering sacrifice at the temple (vv. 13–15) and testimony to the congregation (vv. 16–20). Testimony is also evident in the corporate section (vv. 5–7 and 8–12).

A possible scenario for the psalm's performance is as follows. It opens with a liturgist calling for praise from all the earth (vv. 1–2). The choir answers, addressing God directly with assertions of his power and how his enemies and all the earth respond (vv. 3–4). A liturgist then testifies to the congregation—perhaps with the aid of dramatic performance—about a specific instance of God's power, namely, the exodus deliverance (vv. 5–7). After another call for praise from a liturgist (vv. 8–9), the choir confesses to God the gracious purpose that he has had for his people through their historical trials and deliverances (vv. 10–12). The liturgist then initiates the thanksgiving ceremony before and on behalf of the congregation with the presentation of sacrificial animals (vv. 13–15) and a generic testimony (vv. 16–20). Afterwards the actual thanksgiving meal would follow.

Overall, the psalm helps to contextualize human experience of God. Its scope moves from the universal (vv. 1–4) to the national (vv. 5–12) and finally to the individual experience of God (vv. 13–20). These three divisions are also evident in the three vocatives used with the psalm's key imperatives: "all the earth" (v. 1), "O peoples" (v. 8, the surrounding verses imply this points to Israel), and "all you who fear God" (v. 16). First, all the earth experiences "your power" (Hb. ʿōz) in general terms (vv. 3–4). Second, the nation experiences his power (Hb. gᵉbûrâ) through the exodus deliverance (vv. 5–7). And the nation also confesses that God's dealings with them, though at times arduous, are for their purification (vv. 10–12). Third, the individual worshiper celebrates God's hearing of prayer and bestowal of his love (vv. 19–20). Thus, we also see a shift in the attention to divine attributes: from power in the first half (vv. 1–7) to grace in the second (vv. 8–20). (We should note that this transition does not occur at the supposed form-critical division of the psalm at v. 13.)

The succession of Psalms 65 and 66 may not be accidental or merely literary (i.e., as part of the formation of the *book* of Psalms); they may have formed part of the same preexilic liturgy.

Psalm 65	*Psalm 66*
"In Zion . . . vows will be fulfilled" to "you who hear prayer" (vv. 1–2).	"I will come to your temple . . . and fulfill my vows to you" (v. 13) and God "has heard my voice in prayer" (vv. 19–20).
The psalm closes with meadows and valleys that "shout for joy" (v. 13).	The psalm opens with all the earth commanded, "Shout with joy!" (v. 1).
God's "awesome" saving acts in creation (v. 5).	God's "awesome" deeds towards all humanity (v. 3) and towards Israel in their history (v. 5).
In the context of creation God exercises his "strength" (v. 6), which transforms the "seas" (v. 7).	In the context of the exodus God exercises his "strength" (v. 7), which transforms the "sea" (v. 6).

Psalm 65 may have been sung at the Feast of Unleavened Bread. Since Psalm 66 focuses on the exodus, it may have been sung at Passover. Because these festivals had been joined into one, these psalms may be linked in the festival liturgy. If so, we see here God's awesome deeds in creating and blessing the land and in delivering his people linked into a praiseworthy whole. This is particularly evident in God's manipulation of the "sea": he stills its roaring, which threatens creation order (65:7) and he turns it into dry land, through which his people may escape oppression (66:6).

66:1–4 / The liturgist's opening summons is for the congregation to **shout,** which reveals their exuberant worship. The repeated reference to God's **name** (vv. 2, 4) with no explicit reference to "Yahweh" may be explained by the psalm's location in the Elohistic Psalter. Thus, the psalm in its original form probably read "Yahweh" where it now reads **God.** How can it be said that **all the earth bows down to you; . . . they sing praise to your name** (v. 4)? We must recognize that, as an expression of praise, this verse makes a statement primarily about God, not about humans. It thus points not to the virtue of human behavior but to the understanding that Yahweh is the one true God. Thus, all worship that humans offer reflects a measure of acknowledging Yahweh himself.

66:5–9 / The supreme demonstration of God's **awesome . . . works in man's behalf** (v. 5; cf. "awesome . . . deeds" in v. 3) lies in the exodus deliverance (v. 6), the foundational datum for Israel's existence. Here we have a clear example of how Israel's historical traditions were mentioned in liturgy. Attention is directed to the mere event of God's intervention. Historical and geographical details—present in the exodus narrative—are ignored (e.g., no antecedent is given for "they" in v. 6, but it is plain from the well-known story). Little is said about particulars of the event, but much is said of its theological value. It lies in its awe-inspiring display of God's rule, especially for the nations (vv. 5–7), and in its purifying results for the people of God (vv. 10–12, if these verses also refer to the events surrounding the exodus).

Verse 6 reveals an interesting aspect of Israel's use of historical traditions in their liturgies: **He turned the sea into dry land, they passed through the waters on foot**—"there" (lit., not **come**, as in NIV) **let us rejoice in him.** The worshipers are led to identify themselves with their ancestors in their experience of God's deliverance. (We may call this "contemporization" or "actualization.") Past history is made present in liturgy. Israel's reliving of key saving events is also evident in Deuteronomy 6:20–25; 26:5–10. The imperative introducing this section, **come and see what God has done** (v. 5), also implies that God's saving act at the exodus is virtually visible to the congregation (see also Ps. 46:8). Thus, the individual worshipers are instructed by this psalm to align their *present* experience of God not only with humanity in general and with corporate Israel in particular but also with *past* history. Individual worshipers are invited to see their own experience of deliverance in light of the nation's exodus, and vice versa.

66:10–12 / In verses 10–12 the choir or congregation confesses that suffering may act as a form of refinement (on **fire and water,** cf. Num. 31:23; Isa. 43:2). Within the context of the Psalter, this is a striking claim. Most psalms that mention suffering refer to it as something from which deliverance is either sought or celebrated. Here it is seen to have value in itself. Moreover, God's purposes for his people are seen to be ultimately beneficial, even though for a time they may be oppressive. It is not clear whether the statements **you . . . laid burdens on our backs . . . but you brought us to a place of abundance** (vv. 10–12) refer to the Egyptian oppression and subsequent exodus or to the Babylonian exile and subsequent restoration. The use of **us** is not determinative. **They** is used in connection with the exodus in v. 6, but the same verse also specifically commands, "there let us rejoice in him," and verses 10–12 may serve to fulfill that invitation.

66:13–20 / In verses 13–15, it would be better to read the verbs in the present tense. The liturgy here describes the ritual that accompanies it. This is not a promise to fulfill vows in the indefinite future. In light of the liturgical reading proposed above, the testimony of verses 16–20 need not refer to a particular deliverance of the individual speaker. Since he serves as the spokesperson for the congregation, these words may serve either as a model for the testimony of each individual worshiper's own personal experience or as a testimony on behalf of each worshiper for the national experience of deliverance. Thus, we do not have here an individual's thanksgiving but the thanksgiving of many individuals. Its essence reflects the essential tradition of individual prayer psalms, namely, **I cried out to him** and **God . . . heard my voice in prayer.**

Additional Note §66

66:12–13 / **A place of abundance:** The Hb. expression here (*rᵉwāyâ*, "overflow, saturation") is the same as found in 23:5, where the NIV translates it "overflows" referring to "my cup." There the "table" and "cup" at "the house of the LORD" probably point to the thanksgiving offering. In this light, the verse that closes off the hymnic praise of 66:10–12 acts as a suitable transition to the thanksgiving offering in vv. 13–20.

§67 The God Who Blesses Israel's Harvests and His International Praise (Ps. 67)

To know how to read this psalm aloud and what tone of voice to use, we need to recognize its function or genre. The Hebrew text (using imperfect verbs) leaves the question open: should we read each verse as a humble request ("May God be gracious," so NIV) or as confident assertions ("God is gracious to us")? The familiar echo of the Aaronic blessing (Num. 6:24–26) in the opening verse immediately implies that the NIV's rendering in verses 1, 3–5 is correct. The notion of the peoples praising God repeated in verses 3 and 5 is thus correctly translated as a wish or request. In the Psalms, this motif is usually expressed as a command or wish, rather than as a prophetic declaration. Reading Psalm 67 as a psalm of petition is confirmed by the LXX. In addition, verses 6–7 should also be translated as petitions: "The land yields its harvest; may God, our God, bless us. May God bless us, so all the ends of the earth may fear him."

What is perhaps most unique about this psalm is how it blends together the priestly blessing on the nation's harvests (vv. 1, 6–7) and the wish that Yahweh's praise extend to the nations (vv. 2–5), as expressed in the psalms of Yahweh's kingship (Pss. 47; 93; 96–99). Several features suggest that the composer was not attempting a distinctly original poem but combined traditional phrases, if not entire verses, into a new whole. The psalm is thus not an authored composition but an edited one. First, we may note the odd shift in mid-sentence from third-person reference to God in verse 1 to second-person address in verse 2: "May God be gracious to us, so that your way may be known on earth" (lit., v. 2 is a dependent Hb. clause, not a separate petition, as in the NIV). Second, we should note the similarities and differences between verses 2–5 and 6–7.

	Verses 2–5	*Verses 6–7*
Subject	peoples, nations	the ends of the earth
Action	praise, be glad, sing	fear
Reason	God judges and guides the nations	God blesses us with rich harvests

The differences between the respective actions of the nations and their supporting reasons are certainly not incompatible, but the next observation suggests they may be explained by different sources. Third, the verses referring to God in the third person (vv. 1, 6–7) show particular affinity to priestly material in the OT, and those addressing him directly (vv. 2–5) show affinity to the Yahweh Kingship psalms. We have already noted the echo of the Aaronic blessing in verse 1, and its request, "may God bless us," is repeated in the closing two verses. The formula, "the land will yield its harvest" (or "produce," v. 6) is found particularly in priestly material (Lev. 26:4, 20, i.e., the blessings and curses of the Holiness Code; Ezek. 34:27; Zech. 8:12). The verses in our psalm that address God directly (vv. 2–5) echo the Yahweh Kingship psalms, which also summon "the peoples" to praise God (esp. 47:1; 96:1–3, 7–9; 98:4–6; 99:1–3), be glad (or "rejoice," 97:1), and sing for joy (98:4) because his salvation will be known on earth (98:2–3; also 97:6) and he "will judge the peoples with equity" (96:10, 13; 98:9).

These two threads have been woven together to form a poetic whole. The opening two verses introduce the psalm's theme by combining the priestly blessing on Israel (v. 1) and the nations' recognition of Yahweh (v. 2), familiar from the psalms of Yahweh's kingship. Verses 3–5 develop verse 2, expressing the desire that "all the peoples praise you." Verses 6–7 develop verse 1, specifying that God's blessing be on our harvest. (For those fond of discovering such literary features, we may note this forms a chiastic structure.) The psalm thus invokes God's blessing on his people and especially on their agriculture with the hope that it results in international acclaim for God.

67:1–2 / Verse 1 is an echo, not a verbatim citation, of the Aaronic blessing. First, it uses key words and phrases but presents them in a different order. Second, it is not a blessing bestowed by the priesthood as in Numbers 6 ("Yahweh bless you") but a wish invoked on behalf of the congregation ("May God bless us"). Third, and perhaps most significant, is the change in the preposition: the Aaronic benediction has God's face shining "toward" or "upon" you, but Psalm 67 has it shining "with us" (lit.). This may imply that "we," the recipients of God's blessing, will ourselves shine. The rest of the psalm confirms this reading: Israel, by virtue of God's blessing, will become an attraction to the nations. Verse 2 should not be read as an independent request **(may)** but as a dependent purpose clause: "in order that your way may be known on the earth, your salvation among all nations." The worshipers' reason for seeking God's blessing is not to be self-centered; it is to serve a wider purpose of revealing internationally God's characteristic **ways** of doing things. As is often typical of Hebrew poetic parallelism, the second line specifies the first: Yahweh's way is a way of **salvation.** Similarly, in verse 7 "we" petition God to "bless us, so that all the ends of the earth may fear him."

67:3–5 / Marking off the beginning and end of the second strophe is the inclusio, **may the peoples praise you.** At the center of the psalm is its longest verse and a tricolon. We must be clear that the statement, **for you rule** (or "will rule") **the peoples justly,** is a claim about how God characteristically rules, not a claim about world affairs (i.e., that justice now prevails). According to the psalms of Yahweh's kingship, the international manifestation of Yahweh's judgment is future: Yahweh *"is about to* come to judge the earth; he *will* judge . . . peoples with equity"* (lit., 98:9; also 96:10, 13). As we have seen in other psalms, this judgment is not something negative (which is a common modern perception); it is a cause for joy because it ensures fair treatment for all.

67:6–7 / In verse 6, the NIV's **then** is not present in the Hebrew text. God's blessing Israel's **harvest** is not a consequence of the nations' praise of God but a prerequisite to it. As argued above, these verses should also be read as requests: "may God, our God, bless us." And the Hebrew grammar of verse 7 (the simple *waw* attached to the imperfect in a volitional sequence) underscores further the ultimate purpose of this blessing on "us": "so that all the ends of the earth may fear him." What draws the nations to **fear** (i.e., stand in awe, believe) God is not a military defeat or a legal judgment but a blessing on his own people. The precise nature of this blessing and the precise means used to attract the nations is thus not made apparent until these closing verses, namely an agricultural blessing.

Psalm 67 shows us that election does not mean that God has his favorites but simply that he has a chosen channel of blessing for all. Election has to do not with God's *goal* for humanity, that his blessing is restricted to some and denied to others. It has to do with his *means* of extending that blessing to all. The quest for God's blessing has obvious benefits for the seeker, but its ultimate aim is to publicize God's saving way for others. More specifically, the means of incorporating the nations is not military subjugation and their annexation into an Israelite empire but the attraction of agricultural blessing and their voluntary participation. The goal to be sought is not the extension of Israel's kingdom but the extension of God's praise. Finally, we may ask, what is the connection between a blessed harvest (vv. 6–7) and fair judgment and guidance (v. 4)? (Even if we see these verses as drawn from traditional material, the editor's choice to join these differing concepts needs explanation.) The answer may be found in the parallel psalms of Yahweh's kingship. Here creation order and international justice are two arenas of the same action of God, namely his ability to order things harmoniously (see esp. 96:10).

Additional Note §67

67:6 / **The land will yield:** The oddity of the Hb. perfect in a psalm dominated by jussives and imperfects has raised considerable debate among commentators. Its presence may be explained if the phrase is drawn from a text such as Lev. 26:4, which uses the perfect but attaches it to a *waw* thus throwing the action into the future.

§68 In Celebration of the Ritual Procession of the Cherubim-Ark (Ps. 68)

Psalm 68 is notoriously difficult to interpret, especially if one tries to explain its unity and development solely by literary means. The key to its interpretation lies in recognizing its original use as a liturgical text accompanying a ritual. Its composition, therefore, is governed primarily by ritual factors, not simply by literary and thematic considerations. There are at least four allusions to the cherubim-ark throughout the psalm. We should probably imagine Psalm 68 sung alongside a ritual procession with the ark and cherubim at its head. It represents some of the earliest poetry of the OT (cf. pre-monarchic passages such as Deut. 33:2; Judg. 5:4–5) and appears to stem from the period of the united monarchy (v. 27), though some verses may have been added during a later application of the psalm (e.g., cf. vv. 30–31 and Isa. 18:1–19:25; 30:4; 33:7).

68:1–6 / The first allusion to the cherubim-ark appears in the opening verse, which quotes the song of the ark as recorded in Numbers 10:35. There is a slight variation, however, in the shift from direct address ("Arise, O LORD") to a third-person wish **(May God arise).** According to Numbers 10:33–36, this song was sung "whenever the ark set out" to bid Yahweh to "rise up" and lead his people in victory during their wilderness journeys.

A second allusion appears in verse 4, which refers to God as **him who rides on the clouds**. We should also note later references to "him who rides the ancient skies above" (v. 33), and to "the chariots of God" mentioned with the many "hosts" who accompany him (v. 17; cf. Num. 10:36). These expressions may be clarified by other psalmic passages. In the context of a thunderstorm theophany we hear: "He parted the heavens and came down; dark clouds were under his feet. He mounted (Hb. *rkb*, lit. 'rode') the cherubim (Hb. *krwb*) and flew;

he soared on the wings of the wind" (18:9–10). And in Psalm 104 God, who "wraps himself in light" (v. 2) and "lays the beams of his upper chambers on their waters" (v. 3), "makes the clouds his chariot and rides on the wings of the wind. He makes winds his messengers, flames of fire his servants" (vv. 3b–4). From these verses it becomes apparent that the "rider of the clouds" (a title the Canaanites claimed for Baal; see Gibson, *Canaanite Myths*, p. 43) does so in his cherubim-chariot. Its tangible symbol would be the cherubim above the ark. Thus, the earthly symbol of the cherubim chariot corresponds to the heavenly symbol in the clouds and wind.

The procession thus begins with the song of the ark, imploring God to arise. The resulting fates of **the wicked** and **the righteous** are then petitioned, the one to **perish before God** and the other to **rejoice before God** (vv. 2–3). A second imperative summons the congregation to enact this rejoicing: **sing to God** and **extol him who rides on the** clouds (v. 4). A substantiating description of God then follows (vv. 5–6).

68:7–18 / There ensues a historical review that follows God's journey **from Sinai** and **through the wasteland** to the people's settlement in the land (identified as God's **inheritance**) and then climaxes in his ascent **into his sanctuary**, located on **the mountain where God chooses to reign** (vv. 7–18). Both the beginning and the end of this historical recital contain allusions to the cherubim-ark. Verse 7 specifically mentions God's guiding presence through the wilderness: **when you went out before your people, O God, when you marched** through the wasteland. As noted, the song of the ark commemorated Yahweh's guidance through the wilderness by means of the ark. The recital then reviews God's journey from the wilderness and **Sinai** through to the conquest and settlement of the land. This sequence climaxes in the claim, **the Lord has come** from Sinai into his sanctuary (clarified in v. 29 to be the one in Jerusalem; also cf. Deut. 33:2). As in 47:5, the movement, **you ascended**, was symbolized by the ascent of the cherubim-ark, where "God is seated on his holy throne" (47:8; see the commentary). And comparable to 47:3–4, this ascent was part of a procession celebrating the divine warrior's victory over the conquered Canaanites: **you led captives in your train; you received gifts** (i.e., victory tribute) **from men.** Psalm 24 also alludes to the ascent of Yahweh, "mighty in battle," and his victory procession, led by the cherubim-ark.

68:19–27 / The psalm then moves to a renewed call for praise, substantiated by another hymnic description of God and an oracle that promises rescue and retribution (vv. 19–23). There follows a description of the ritual **procession of my God and King into the sanctuary**, noting **the singers** and **musicians** and select tribes of Israel (vv. 24–27).

Although Psalm 68 makes several allusions to the ark and cherubim throughout, can we be certain that they are anything more than literary or historical? The explicit phrase **your procession has come into view, O God** (v. 24) implies that some of these allusions at least are ritual ones. The hearers do not merely call the cherubim-ark to their minds, they see it in the ritual procession. Moreover, verses 24–27 are not merely a reference to the existence of a procession but a description of its present enactment. And the title ascribed to God in the procession is that of King, which is the divine role symbolized by the cherubim as a throne and the ark as a footstool.

68:28–35 / A fourth allusion to this key symbol appears in the closing section, which appeals repeatedly to God's **strength** and **power** in particular (in vv. 28, 33–35 the NIV uses both terms to translate the one Hb. term ʿōz). It does so in close connection with God's dual presence above (**him who rides the ancient skies above**) and below (**you . . . , O God, in your sanctuary**). Elsewhere in the Psalms, God's "strength" was embodied by the ark (78:61; 132:8). This final section thus petitions the manifestation of **your** power to **the nations** (vv. 28–31). As a result, **kings will bring you gifts** or tribute (v. 29), as had been celebrated earlier in the historical recital of the ark's journey (v. 18). Closing the liturgy is a call for further praise in anticipation of victory (vv. 32–35).

This psalm gives us insight into the power of God. First, this power does not strut and flaunt; it saves and frees, as the reasons substantiating the psalm's calls to praise make clear. (He is "a father to the fatherless, a defender of widows; our God is a God who saves," vv. 5–6, 19–20.) Second, its existence is not questioned, but its exertion in the present is not taken for granted. It must be "summoned" (v. 28). Undergirding this summons is an appeal to historical precedents: **show us your** strength, **O God, as you have done before**, to which the historical review of verses 7–18 testifies. In addition, the actualizing of this power is encouraged through a ritual procession with the ark, the supreme symbol of God's strength. This ritual dramatizes earlier displays of God's power in connection with the ark. This is not an attempt at magical manipulation but an appeal that is expressed in both word and ritual action. Similarly in the New Testament, the ritual of the Lord's Supper brings the church into a special realization of God's presence and power. Christian readers may not feel comfortable with the notion of sacred space, but it is just as present in the New Testament, though reidentified. Paul in no uncertain terms identifies the people of the church as God's "sacred temple" (1 Cor. 3:16–17; Eph. 2:19–22).

§69 From the Miry Depths (Ps. 69)

If we attempt to reconstruct the situation for which the individual prayer (vv. 1–30) was appropriate, there emerges a complex web of circumstances. First, in verse 4 there are "my enemies without cause," by whom "I am forced to restore what I did not steal." (Are these false accusations of robbery for which he is forced to make restitution?) Second, in verses 7–12 he is alienated and endures scorn (v. 10) from family and neighbors "for your sake," which is defined further as "zeal for your house" and connected with the rites of fasting and sackcloth. He thus suffers religious persecution. (Does this zeal for Yahweh's house have to do with reforming the preexilic temple or with rebuilding the postexilic temple?) Third, in verses 19–29 he also endures scorn (v. 20), but here it takes the form of persecution for some kind of pain he suffers, apparently inflicted by Yahweh himself (vv. 26, 29). (Could this refer to physical illness?) Fourth, in verses 5–6 he admits personal guilt, which could bring shame to "those who seek you." (Is this to be connected with being overly zealous for Yahweh's house and/or with his affliction from Yahweh?) The speaker clearly feels near death (vv. 1–2, 14–15), but whether this is due to social accusations, religious persecution, or personal sickness, or any combination thereof, we cannot be certain.

The prayer psalms generally make it notoriously difficult to ascertain the precise circumstances for which they are appropriate. First, it is difficult to recognize when their descriptions are literal or metaphoric, especially for readers at a great historical and cultural distance. Second, because of this, the descriptions are very complex and sometimes appear to conflict. Third, these psalms by their very nature are open to multiple interpretations and uses. In the history of their transmission, therefore, verses were sometimes modified, added, and subtracted to suit new situations. Such appears to be the case for Psalm 69.

It is comparatively long, and its closing verses clearly promise Zion's restoration after Babylonian exile. Verses 35–36

speak from the perspective that Jerusalem and its cities are not
only in ruins but also that their inhabitants are in a foreign land.
Psalms 22 and 102 are also long prayer psalms with apparent additions alluding to the restoration from exile (see the Additional
Notes to Ps. 22). Like Psalm 22, this one appears to have served a
dual function. In the preexilic period verses 1–30 (or so) may
have functioned as a prayer for an individual. The zeal for *reforming* "your house" and the persecution that comes as a result is well
illustrated in Jeremiah's life (esp. 7:1–29 // 15:15–18; 26:1–24;
38:6). In the exilic period God's people may have used the prayer
as a vehicle to express their lament, where the people were personified as the speaking "I" (the reference to mourning and fasting in vv. 10–11 would have made Ps. 69 esp. suitable; cf. Zech.
7:3–5; 8:19; Isa. 58). In the late exilic or early postexilic periods
verses 34–36 may have been attached as a promise that responds
to this lament. In this new context the zeal for *rebuilding* "your
house" and its attendant persecution could refer to opposition
from among the Jews themselves (implied in Hag. 1:2–4) or from
outside the Jewish community (see Ezra 4–6).

Whether the work of an author or editor, several repetitions in the psalm and its form-critical motifs make its final structure clear. The terms and images related to drowning (vv. 1–2 and
14–15) and shame (vv. 6–12 and 19–20) are repeated, thus dealing
with the distress in two stages (vv. 1–12 and 13–29). The first
gives more attention to lamenting the distress, and the second to
petitions and wishes that seek to overcome it. Each stage contains two further subunits (vv. 1–5, 6–12 and 13–21, 22–29), as
described below. The whole psalm is marked off by God's "salvation." It opens with, "Save me, O God" (v. 1) and closes with,
"God will save Zion" (v. 35). The second prayer section is also
marked off by appeals to "your salvation" (vv. 13, 29). The psalm's
third section consists of praise and also falls into two smaller
units, the first celebrating God's hearing the speaker (vv. 30–33)
and the second God's saving of Zion (vv. 34–36).

69:1–5 / The psalm opens with the general petition,
Save me, O God. The rest of this section is devoted to lamenting
the distress from which salvation is sought. Its urgency is depicted through the image of drowning in a **miry** cistern. Lime-
plastered cisterns were used in the ancient world to catch and re-
tain rainwater. Being underground, they also evoked images of
the grave and the underworld (cf. 40:2; 88:3–7; see Keel, *Symbol-*

ism, pp. 62–73). Although **the waters have come up to my neck,**
the psalm also confesses, **my throat is parched,** because he is
worn out shouting aloud to God. This irony makes clear the
speaker is in a "no-win" situation. Although the speaker has **enemies,** it is twice emphasized they are so **without reason** or **cause.**

Following immediately this claim of innocence before humans, there comes an admission of **folly** and **guilt** before God.
This guilt, however, is not developed beyond the next verse, and
thus does not appear to be a key issue of the psalm. There is no
formal confession of sin or petition for forgiveness (as in 25:7,
18; 32:5; 38:1–5, 17–18; 41:4; 51:1–14; 79:9–10). Moreover, the
phrasing implies it is not a social or public issue: **You know** and
not hidden from you. The emphasis is on the extent of God's
knowledge.

69:6–12 / Like the preceding section, this one opens
with a petition and then laments the speaker's plight. This petition is a negative wish that there be no consequences of **shame** is-
suing from the speaker's situation and befalling the seekers of
Yahweh. The two divine titles in verse 6 are unusual among
psalms of the individual. Together in the same psalm they are
found in 46:7, 11 and 84:8, both of which sing of the city of Zion.
(It is possible that 69:6 was added when vv. 34–36 were added.)
Psalm 24, a liturgy of temple entry, also refers to the Lord Almighty (v. 10) and *"those who seek* the face of the *God of Jacob"* (lit.,
v. 6). Thus, 69:6 may be a prayer especially for those who seek entrance into Yahweh's **house** (v. 9).

Verses 7–9 emphasize that the speaker's suffers **for your
sake** (esp. evident in the Hb. with the opening "upon you" in v. 7
and the closing "upon me" in v. 9; cf. 44:22), not for his own. Implicit here is that Yahweh bears some obligation to intervene on
the speaker's behalf. What particularly incurs the **scorn** of family
(v. 8) and neighbors (v. 12) is the speaker's expressions of mourning **(I weep and fast, I put on sackcloth).** Whatever is meant by
zeal for your house, these verses together imply that the speaker
sees something gravely wrong about the temple, but the people
do not want to be bothered.

69:13–21 / Having expressed the bulk of the lament, the
psalm again reviews the distresses but now seeks to redress them
through petition. Thus, in contrast to **the drunkards** (v. 12), who
in effect **insult you** (v. 9); **I pray to you.** In the context of the
Psalms, **the time of your favor** may refer to the morning (5:3;

46:5; 143:8; cf. 32:6) and to the time of the morning sacrifice in particular (Num. 28:1–8). The image of drowning in a cistern is repeated, but here it is the subject of petitions: **Rescue me from the mire** (vv. 14–15). In addition, a parallel is drawn between **the deep waters** and **those who hate me.** Formulaic petitions follow that focus on turning God's **face** (vv. 16–18). The emphasis in this section lies in reminding God of the case that has been personally set before him: **You know how I am scorned** and **all my enemies are before you** (cf. v. 5). Particular attention is given to the speaker's social alienation (vv. 20–21).

69:22–29 / Although the imprecations of these verses sound severe to modern ears, these wishes and petitions do focus on judgment in kind. They seek a reversal. Moreover, as prayers, they commit this just retribution to God. Because "they put gall in my food" (v. 21), **may the table set before them become a snare** (v. 22). Because "my eyes fail" (v. 3), **may their eyes be darkened so they cannot see** (v. 23). Because "I am a stranger to my brothers" (v. 8), **may their place** (or **tents**) **. . . be deserted** (v. 25). Because "I sink in the miry depths" (vv. 2–3, 14–15), **may your salvation, O God,** "set me on high" (Hb. *teśaggebēnî,* NIV **protect me,** v. 29). (On **the book of life,** see on 87:6.)

69:30–33 / The vow of praise concluding this psalm is unusual and could be taken as a disclaimer regarding ritual sacrifice (vv. 30–31). Normally a thank offering (see 116:17, which is part of a thanksgiving psalm) accompanied the **song of thanksgiving.** But the references to the expensive sacrificial animals mentioned in verse 31 must be read in light of the following verse: **the poor will see and be glad.** In other words, this is not a polemic against sacrifice per se but a confession that Yahweh cherishes the thanksgiving of the economically disadvantaged (cf. 22:24–26). The Hebrew text contains a wordplay: Yahweh shows greater regard for a song (Hb. *šîr*) **than an ox** (Hb. *šôr*). Moreover, these "poor" are further identified as **his captive people** (cf. 79:11; 102:20), that is, those who are estranged from the sacrificial altar of the temple.

69:34–36 / Similar to Psalm 22, this one closes with hymnic praise that reaches cosmic proportions **(heaven and earth,** and **the seas).** The reason for this praise **(for)** is not the deliverance of the individual speaker but the promised restoration of **Zion** after the exile.

§70 Shame for My Persecutors and Joy for God's Worshipers (Ps. 70)

70:1–5 / Psalm 70 is virtually identical to Psalm 40:13–17. Psalm 40 appears to be a liturgy for worshipers to give thanks for past deliverances (vv. 1–3, 9–10) and to pray for future deliverances (vv. 11–17). It also testifies of the attitude and behavior that Yahweh seeks in his worshipers (vv. 4–8). In Psalm 70, however, a portion of the petition section has become an independent prayer psalm. For further discussion, see the introductory comments on Psalm 40 and those on 40:11–17.

§71 When I Am Old and Gray (Ps. 71)

Old age can be a fearful time, especially as one becomes more and more vulnerable to the manipulations of others. This psalm is a prayer of an old person ("when I am old," v. 9, and "when I am old and gray," v. 18) whose devotion to God has been lifelong ("since my youth," vv. 5, 17, "from birth," v. 6). The bond between the speaker and God is expressed in the characteristic phrase of the individual prayer psalms, "my God" (vv. 4, 12, 22), that is, "my personal God." The psalm also gives repeated attention to "your righteousness" (vv. 2, 15, 16, 19, 24; cf. 5:8; 31:1; 119:40; 143:1). We should not think of this as a static, moral description of being but a dynamic, characteristic action of putting things right. Its parallel expressions illustrate the point: "your salvation" (v. 15) and "your mighty acts" (v. 16). Thus, key to understanding the spirituality of this psalm is that while it makes reference to the speaker's lifelong devotion to God, its ultimate appeal is to "your righteousness."

It consists of familiar formulas. The general development of the psalm is as follows. After beginning with a litany of petitions for rescue (vv. 1–4), it rehearses the speaker's past life of praise (vv. 5–8), then turns to present threats and petitions (vv. 9–13), and climaxes in extended vows of future praise (vv. 14–24).

71:1–4 / The opening verses consist largely of a series of familiar petitions (**let me never be put to shame, rescue, deliver** (twice), **turn your ear, save**). The Hebrew text of verse 3 is problematic (the NIV's rendering is difficult to justify), but it was probably originally identical to 31:2b–3a: "Be my rock of refuge, a strong fortress to save me, for you are my rock and my fortress." The psalm thus implores Yahweh to actualize in experience what he is confessed to be in praise. Thus, the believer cannot simply assume that whatever one confesses of God will become an automatic reality ("You do not have, because you do not ask God,"

James 4:2). The opponents of this psalm are here described in moral terms: they are **the wicked,** who are **evil and cruel.**

71:5–8 / A distinction among the individual and corporate prayer psalms is that the former have confessions of trust and the latter have references to earlier saving deeds. In Psalm 71, however, the confessions of trust come close to functioning as references to earlier saving deeds in the life of the speaker. **Since my youth** Yahweh has proven himself to be a valid source of **hope** and **confidence** (lit. "trust"). The NIV's translation of verse 6 attributes more conscious action to the speaker than is justified **(I have relied on you** and **I will ever praise you).** Since these actions are **from birth** and **from my mother's womb,** it is more appropriate to translate "upon you I have been supported (Hb. *nismaktî*)" and "in you has been my praise continually"—in other words, "you have been the source of my praise." Verse 6 is thus more a statement of God's doing, than of the speaker's. (Cf. 139:13–16 and esp. 22:9–10, where the "my God" relationship is similarly traced back to birth.) Even verse 8 places God's **praise** and **splendor** in the foreground and the speaker's act of praising in the background. The only verb of the verse (**declaring** is simply supplied by the NIV translators) is passive, **My mouth is filled** (Hb. niphal) **with your praise.** Thus, while verses 5–8 are a testimony of the speaker's lifelong praise, their emphasis lies on the difference God has made to his life.

The Hebrew term behind **portent** *(môpēt)* is the same one used in the word pair familiar from the exodus story, "signs and *wonders.*" There is thus the sense that the speaker's life is an inexplicable wonder **to many.** Most often the term denotes a wonder or portent of judgment, like those against the Egyptians (78:43; 135:9; Exod. 7:3; 11:9–10; Deut. 6:22; 34:11). This negative connotation is implied by the parallel line of our psalm: because many perceive the speaker's life to be an omen of judgment, he contends, **but you are my strong refuge.**

71:9–13 / This section focuses attention on **my enemies** and the theological problem they raise. **They say, "God has forsaken him."** Presumably they reason that because the speaker is **old** and his **strength is gone,** he now lacks God's blessing and is thus Godforsaken and vulnerable. What precisely is their intention is left openended. The Hebrew phrase, which is literally, "those who watch my life," is much more ambiguous than the NIV's **those who wait to kill me.** As noted in the Introduction, psalms often speak in extremes so as to include any form of situation. Thus, while the opponents say, " . . . **pursue him and seize him**" and the psalm describes them as **my accusers** and as **those who want to harm me,** this could include anything from harming his reputation, to seizing his property, or to homicide. We should note that the fate invoked upon them focuses on their **shame** (vv. 13, 24), not their destruction (in v. 13 instead of Hb. *yiklû,* "let them come to an end," several MSS and the Syriac read *yikkāleʿmû,* "let them be humiliated").

To counter these presumptions, the lament concerning the foes is surrounded by petitions. The first petitions are negative: **Do not cast me away, do not forsake me** (using the same verb as the enemies), and **be not far from me.** The psalm thus allows the speaker to reckon with this fear as a possibility but then quickly asks God to exclude it as a reality. The positive petitions are first on the speaker's behalf, **come quickly, O my God, to help me** (reminding him of the "my God" relationship), and then against the foes. These are expressed as a wish (Hb. jussive), **may they perish** (or "be humiliated"; see *BHS*) **in** shame and **be covered with scorn and disgrace.**

71:14–19 / This section is an extended vow of praise. The phrase, **I will come** or "I will enter" (Hb. *ʾābôʾ;* cf. 5:7; 42:2; 66:13; 73:17; 118:19), may allude to entry into the sacred assembly to offer formal praise of a recent deliverance. While verses 5–8 focus on God as the source of praise and on the speaker's lifelong praise in the past, these verses focus on the speaker's act of lifelong praising in the future. (Note, e.g., that in v. 8 the verb is passive, "my mouth is filled," but in v. 15 it is active, **my mouth will tell.**) They also repeat the fundamental apprehension of verse 9, **Even when I am old and gray, do not forsake me,** but this time add the motivational clause, **till I declare your power to the next generation** (v. 18; on transmitting God's story to the next generation cf. Deut. 6:20–25). A more literal translation of verse 14 reveals part of the psalm's logic: "But I will wait/hope, and I will add to all your praise." In other words, he awaits a new act of salvation that will in turn further Yahweh's praise. As noted elsewhere in this psalm, Yahweh's praise is centered on **your righteousness** (i.e., "your putting things right"), which is explicated further as **your salvation** and **your mighty acts.** Verse 17 echoes and develops motifs found in verses 5–8 ("since my youth"), which relate the past history God and the speaker have shared. It illustrates the personal, mutual commitment each party has in the relationship: **you have taught me** and **I declare your marvelous deeds.** As a specific foretaste of the kind of praise he offers, he praises God's incomparable **righteousness** in hymnic terms.

71:20–21 / Verse 20 contains a confession of trust that is one of the most poignant of the Psalms: **Though you have made me see troubles, many and bitter, you will restore my life again.** There is no presumption here that Yahweh promises a life free from pain, but there is equally the certainty and hope of Yahweh's life-restoring intervention. This is not mere faith, but tested faith. (We are privileged here to hear the wisdom of an old person who has had a lifelong experience with Yahweh as "my God.") Troubles in themselves need not signal Godforsakenness—rather they are a time to seek refuge in him (v. 1) from troubles, even if they are troubles that "you have made me see." This is an irony that most of us do not recognize, that even if God has made us see hardship, that hardship should drive us not from him but to him. If we may expand on this further, God does not plan for his people a life of steady equilibrium but a life of trials and restorations.

Within the horizon of the NT, claims like **from the depths of the earth** (i.e., the underworld of Sheol) **you will bring me up** could denote resurrection, but, within the horizon of the Psalms and the OT, they probably denote rescue from near-death distress (cf. 30:1, 3; 40:2; 69:1–2, 14–15). The phrase, "from the depths of the earth," illustrates how the psalms use cosmic language to describe experiences of personal salvation.

71:22–24 / This section consists of another vow of praise, this time emphasizing its formal, public performance with musical instruments, **the harp** and **the lyre** (obviously both cannot be played by one individual at the same time!). In the Psalms, this word pair is found in contexts that indicate a public performance (33:2; 57:8–9 = 81:2; 92:3; 108:2–3; 150:3). The divine title, the **Holy One of Israel,** is found elsewhere in the Psalms only in 78:41 and 89:18, both corporate psalms, but is prominent throughout the book of Isaiah (e.g., 1:4; 41:14; 60:9). To this vow of praise is attached the normal thanksgiving—given in anticipation of deliverance—which is specific to the speaker's need: **for those who wanted to harm me have been put to shame.**

Additional Note §71

71:20 / **You have made me see:** The MT reveals an ambiguity. The NIV goes with the reading provided in the MT margin (called the *Qere* or the "to be read" reading), but the reading in the main text (called the *Kethib* or "written" reading) points to a corporate reference: "you have made *us* see" and "*our* lives" and "bring *us* up" (see *BHS*). In other words, this verse may also describe the destiny of God's people, perhaps through events such as the Babylonian exile. In addition, if the *Kethib* reading was the original, Ps. 71 may have been performed within a group setting and not by a lone individual.

§72 Intercession for the King to Bring Prosperity to the Land and Justice to the Needy (Ps. 72)

72:1–20 / Psalm 72 is a royal psalm, used on behalf of the preexilic Davidic kings of Israel/Judah. The opening parallelism of **the king** and **the royal son** particularly fits the official coronation of the crown-prince designate, but this may be pushing poetic parallelism too far. The elevated court language is consistent with what we see in other ancient Near Eastern texts. This should not surprise us. By its own admission, the OT is clear that kingship was a foreign import (1 Sam. 8:5). It was an expedient quickly introduced as a rallying point to counter the military threats of Ammon and Philistia. With the ancient Near Eastern institution of monarchy came the language of the court.

Psalm 72 consists of three sections (vv. 1–3, 4–11, 12–17). This outline is confirmed by the symmetry that it reveals in the Hebrew poetic lines. The entire psalm is 21 lines. The first section is three lines, and the second and third are 9 lines each. Verses 18–20 are not a constituent part of the psalm but a doxology and a colophon closing Book II of the Psalter (Pss. 42–72). To each of the five "Books" of the Psalter a doxology has been attached. The introductory section (vv. 1–3) establishes the key attributes that are to characterize the king's reign: **justice, righteousness,** and wellbeing (Hb. *shalom*, NIV **prosperity**). The whole psalm then cycles around four topics: **the needy,** agricultural fertility, the king's longevity, and his influence among the **nations.** The first two topics denote the spheres in which the king is obliged to exercise these key attributes, and these spheres are treated in all three sections: the poor (vv. 2, 4, 12–14) and agricultural fertility (vv. 3, 6–7, 16). The second two topics denote the benefits that should follow the king's performance of these obligations, and these benefits are treated in the second and third sections: longevity (vv. 5, 15, 17a) and international influence (vv. 8–11, 15, 17b). These benefits of longevity and international influence appear in clauses that are dependent on the main clauses, which outline the king's obligations toward the poor and agricultural fertility. In all three sections, the poor are the first of the topics mentioned. This structural and grammatical analysis establishes that the king's longevity and empire are contingent on his provision of fertility and prosperity and especially on his care for the poor, the first topic in each strophe. In other words, the actions to which the king is to give his attention have to do with the poor and the land's fertility. The long life of the king and his dynasty and the extent of his kingdom are results following from these actions.

The only petition in the imperative mode appears in the opening line: **Endow** the king **with your** justice. In keeping with this petition, the Hebrew imperfect verbs of the psalm should probably be read as jussives: thus not as **he will . . .** , but as "may he . . ." (see the NIV marginal note). The entire psalm, therefore, consists of petitions addressed to God, even though he is mentioned only in the first two verses.

In the opening section (vv. 1–3) the key abstract qualities that are to characterize the king's reign are presented with two word pairs. The first, justice and righteousness, appears twice chiastically (i.e., following an ABBA pattern) in the opening two verses. As a word pair, they define the *social* relationships under the king's reign. They are exercised on behalf of **your people, your afflicted ones,** and the needy (in v. 4 the verb form "administer justice" [Hb. *špṭ,* NIV **defend**] is used). The second word pair, **righteousness** and prosperity (Hb. *šālôm,* "peace" or "welfare") appears in verses 3 and 7. As a word pair, they define primarily the *ecological* relationships under the king's reign, though the social dimension is not excluded. They are produced by **the mountains** and **the hills** in verse 3, and they **flourish** in verse 7 as a result of the **rain** (v. 6). Both of these key terms carry a broader range of meaning than the English terms. "Righteousness" means "right order" and *shalom* means "wholeness," and each is applied in the OT to both society and the cosmos (see, e.g., 85:9–13). In Psalm 72, the king's righteous rule is to have direct ecological benefits. To this extent, ecology follows sociology: how the king manages the people has a direct impact on the land (cf. Hos. 4:1–3). Although these terms (justice, righteousness, prosperity/ well-being) could be taken as abstract, and therefore meaningless (a temptation common to Israelite monarchs and all persons in power), the rest of this psalm is devoted to spelling out how these moral qualities are to be manifested. The king is to give due attention to the right order and the well-being of his land. And closely related, he is to give due attention to right order and justice in his society, especially to its powerless.

That the king is to care for the poor is an obvious point to be drawn from this psalm. But what is most striking is that this exercise of justice is the standard by which Israelite monarchs were to be measured—not by their military campaigns or by their building projects, as in Egypt, Assyria, and Babylonia. The Israelite monarchy was to be judged by how it looked after its powerless. The powerful can take care of themselves in any society. Thus, what makes a king's government stand above others is how it cares for the unfortunate. Power is not to be exercised to attract more power. The king of Psalm 72 is to exercise it in a direction contrary to the politics of power. He acts on behalf of the power*less*, not so as to ingratiate the nobles and the power*ful*. By ignoring the politics of power, he—remarkably—in turn gains a powerful empire.

This caring for the poor, in the context of this psalm, is not compassion or mercy—it is justice and righteousness. It is putting things right, the way they should be. It is what is expected, not an action undertaken voluntarily. Moreover, the form of the king's justice is not merely to respond where legal counsel is called for; it is to actively **save** (vv. 4, 13). He is no mere judge—he is a savior. Particularly noteworthy among the verses describing the king's attention to the poor is verse 14 (lit.): "From oppression and violence may he *redeem* their lives." Contrary to popular OT usage, where the duties of redemption lie within the family, this psalm calls for the chief political figure of the land to exercise the duties of redeemer. In its original use, "to redeem" was primarily an economic term meaning "to buy back." According to Leviticus 25:24–25, if a person falls into poverty and must sell his property, the kinsman-redeemer was to "redeem" him from debt (cf. Jer. 32:7). According to verses 47–49 of the same chapter, if a person falls into poverty and must sell himself to a foreigner, the kinsman-redeemer was to redeem him from his debt. For those who either have no family or no family with means, God himself becomes their redeemer (Prov. 23:10–11; cf. 22:23; Jer. 50:33–34). But in Psalm 72 the king is to be redeemer for his people.

The success of his reign—in terms of its longevity and international influence—is determined by his exercise of saving justice for the needy and his attention to the fertility of the land. Thus, his kingdom would extend not by military takeover but by the sheer attraction of his just society and prosperous land (on the latter cf. Ps. 67). Only of **his enemies** (i.e., those who actively oppose him and his exercise of justice) is it said that they **will lick the dust.** According to the theology of this psalm, power is to be achieved not by grasping for the most but by caring for the least.

Verse 17b echoes the Abrahamic or patriarchal promise of blessing to the nations (Gen. 12:3, etc.), but Psalm 72 here departs from the rest of the OT and ties it directly to the monarchy. The structural outline described above shows a progression from the moral qualities of justice and righteousness to the fulfillment of the Abrahamic covenant. The path to international blessing begins with Yahweh's bestowal of justice and righteousness on the king. Key to remaining on this path is the king's treatment of the poor. Thus, the fulfillment of the Abrahamic promise (v. 17b) and offering of tribute by the nations follow from the king's care for the poor and the resulting prosperity.

Psalm 72 does not provide a comprehensive portrait of the king's/messiah's government. It does make clear, however, that militarism is not the defining characteristic of his government, an impression one might infer from other royal psalms, especially Psalms 2 and 110. It becomes clear that, when faced with violent opponents, he will exercise force. Psalm 72 itself makes brief mention of this in verse 9. But the reason his action is to be so decisive against enemies is not because his rule must be preserved for its own sake or even simply because it is divinely appointed (esp. evident in Ps. 2). It must be preserved because he is the agent of God's just and righteous rule, particularly on behalf of society's helpless. To this extent, Psalm 72 (and perhaps Psalm 132) comes the closest to presenting the program of the king's government. In the OT, the king is both judge (cf. 2 Sam. 15:1–6; 1 Kgs. 3:16–28) and warrior. The latter function surfaces in times of crisis (more frequent, however, than we experience today, cf. 2 Sam. 11:1), but the former defines his more day-to-day function on society's behalf.

§73 God's Goodness Redefined: The Nearness of God (Ps. 73)

This psalm is a favorite for many because it rings so true to our feelings and experience. Many of us have felt disappointed in God. When we feel life has treated us unfairly, we often betray our belief in the sovereignty of God by blaming and abandoning him! The psalm confesses what we are afraid to admit, and so helps us to be honest before God about life's temptations and our readiness to sell out. The psalm's first half is largely negative (vv. 1–14) and the second half largely positive (vv. 15–28). Marking this pivot is the beginning of direct address to God ("your children," v. 15). As noted below, key words (particularly evident in the Hb. text) help to mark the sections and development of the psalm. This psalm is particularly about the heart (vv. 1, 7, 13, 21, 26).

73:1–5 / The opening verse sounds like a common confession or proverb that any of Israel's pious would have happily affirmed: **Surely God is good . . . to those who are pure in heart.** But as the psalm develops, we discover the proverb has become fair game for the critical test of personal experience. In the very next verse we are surprised by the openness of a confession that sounds autobiographical: **But as for me, my feet had almost slipped.** His reason is equally frank: **For I envied . . . the prosperity** (Hb. *šālôm*, also "peace" or "welfare") **of the wicked.** Verses 4–5 explain what they enjoy in their prosperity, namely they are spared **the burdens common to man.**

73:6–12 / In verses 6–11, the speaker's description takes a decidedly different tone and engages in a moral evaluation. This is spelled out not so much in terms of their abuse of victims but in terms of the wicked themselves and of their attitudes toward God. Their tyrannical arrogance is illustrated with imagery concerning their clothing (v. 6), their **hearts** and **minds** (v. 7), and their **mouths** (vv. 8–9). Because the **conceits of their** minds **know no limits** (as illustrated in the spatial image of **heaven** and **the earth** in v. 9) they are cavalier about God: **They say, "how can God know?"** They do not deny his existence, simply his aware-ness of their activities. Verse 12 then rounds off the description with a summary statement.

73:13–14 / The moral valuation of the wicked in verses 6–11 may seem out of place. We may not have missed it if the psalm had moved straight from verse 5 to verse 12, and we may wonder, how could the conceitedness described here be an ob-ject of envy, as mentioned in verse 3? But its contribution be-comes evident from the personal admission that closes off the psalm's negative half: the feeling that his achievement of a **heart** that is **pure**—which should lead to God's goodness (v. 1)—and of **hands washed in innocence** has been **in vain** (v. 13). **All day long I have been plagued** (v. 14), he claims, in contrast to the wicked, who in spite of their moral depravity "are not plagued by human ills" (v. 5, in both cases alluding perhaps to physical illness). The psalm marks this admission with the same certainty that at-tended the opening proverb: both begin with **surely** and both comment on the rewards for a **pure heart.** This half thus ends with a contradiction that reflects on God himself: is God, in fact, "good . . . to those who are pure in heart" (v. 1)?

73:15–17 / Now with the beginning of direct address to God **(your children),** the psalm begins to pivot. The question im-plicit in verse 15 is, What shall I publicly confess? (or **speak;** this deliberation over what to say contrasts with the free speech of the wicked in v. 8). It is surprising that what restrains the speaker is not his loyalty to God but his loyalty to his children. By his own confession, private deliberation became an **oppressive** "burden" (Hb. *ʿāmāl*, v. 16). This is the same Hebrew word found in verse 5 and translated "burdens," which are common to (ordinary) man but not so for the prosperous wicked.

The turning point is identified as the speaker's entry into **the sanctuary of God** (v. 17). His own searching was futile until understanding came from this external source. But what did the speaker experience? And how does the revelation explained in the rest of the psalm emerge from the mere act of passing through the temple gates? The analysis of the temple entry psalms contained in this commentary helps to answer this ques-tion (see the Introduction). In this rite of passage the worshiper hears and perhaps sees dramatized the separation of "the two ways": the wicked are excluded from the temple and its rock of stability. Yahweh, thus, casts them down. The righteous, who receive Yahweh's righteousness, are admitted to the temple and are received into God's very presence. They, in turn, proclaim his deeds.

Psalm 73, in fact, contains numerous echoes of the psalms of temple entry: the importance of a "pure heart" and "innocent hands" (73:1, 13 // 24:4; 26:6); the description of the wicked as "arrogant" (73:3 // 5:5; cf. 52:1), with special attention to their "speaking evil" with their "mouth" (73:8–9 // 5:6; 28:3; 36:3; 52:3; contrast 15:2) and some attention to their "wealth" (73:12 // 52:7); the image of their instability and imminent "fall" (Hb. *npl*, 73:18 // 5:5, 10; 36:12; cf. 52:5; 24:3); Yahweh's hatred toward them and promise to "destroy" them (73:20, 27 // 5:4–6); the designation of Yahweh's group of worshipers as a "generation" (73:15 // 24:6); Yahweh's "guiding" his pilgrims (Hb. *nḥh*, 73:24 // 5:8); his "glory" (73:24 // 24:7–10; 26:8); the symbolism of Yahweh as "refuge" (73:28 // 5:11; 36:7); and the promised "telling" (Hb. *spr*) of Yahweh's deeds (73:28 // 26:7). In this light, Psalm 73 probably functioned as a testimony that reflects on the liturgy of entering Yahweh's temple. The speaker's new understanding, obtained when he **entered** the sanctuary of God, consists of the destruction of the wicked (vv. 18–20), the guidance and reception of the pilgrim (vv. 21–26), and a summarizing conclusion (vv. 27–28). (Cf. esp. Ps. 52, where the wicked are cast down and the righteous find abundant life through God's presence at the temple and promise to acclaim him publicly.)

73:18–20 / Thus, verse 18, the verse introducing this revelation, is marked by the third and final **Surely** of the psalm. (The second "Surely" had retracted what the first had claimed.) As noted above, the liturgies of temple entry make plain the instability and imminent fall of the wicked. The description of verses 19–20 implies there was a time when they were stable and then a clear moment, a sudden and dramatic one, when they fall. We may wonder what judgment the psalm is here describing (Is it death? Was it a particular catastrophe of the writer's lifetime?). But we must note that the psalm sets up a contrast between what the speaker "sees" (Hb. *rʾh*, v. 3) from his own observation and "understands" (Hb. *byn*, v. 17) from his entry into the temple. Verses 18–20 do not record what is immediately evident in human experience; they report what was revealed at the temple (v. 17a) concerning "their final destiny" (or lit. "their end," v. 17b). The clarity of their judgment, as described here, is probably due to the certainty of divine judgment, made plain in the temple entry liturgy.

73:21–28 / Also prominent in the psalms of temple entry and pilgrimage is the assurance that Yahweh **guide**[s] his pilgrims (Hb. *nḥh*, 5:8; 23:3; 43:3; 61:2; cf. 27:11; 31:3; 32:8; 139:24). If we are correct in reading Psalm 73 in light of the speaker's entry into the sanctuary of God (v. 17), then the following phrase, **and afterward you will take me into glory,** most probably refers to the pilgrim's reception into "the place where your glory dwells" (26:8). In other words, "after you have guided me along the pilgrim path, you take me into the glory of your temple." Thus, in language familiar elsewhere among the psalms, the speaker celebrates Yahweh as **my portion** (16:5, where we should read, "Yahweh is my portion"; 119:57; 142:5) and **my refuge,** symbolized by the temple itself, and promises to **tell of all your deeds** (v. 28). We should also note the enchanting image created by verses 2 and 23: the speaker is like a child (note the reference to "your children" in v. 15) whose feet slip from underneath him but whose parent holds him by the hand (cf. Isa. 41:13).

The new understanding related in the second half of this psalm, however, is not simply a repetition of the pilgrimage and temple entry psalms. It also contains some profound breakthroughs in OT faith. What is distinctive in the revelation of verses 18–26 (concluded in vv. 27–28) is not that Yahweh will bring the unjust **to ruin,** nor that God guides his people and can be their **strength** and portion. These claims are widely attested elsewhere. The breakthrough concerns two qualities of God marked by two conjunctions: **yet** in verse 23 and **but** in verse 26, both of which contrast divine and human qualities. First, we see *divine persistence* in that although one may be **embittered** and **a brute beast before you, yet . . . I am always with you; you hold me. . . . You** guide me. (Thus, contrary to initial appearances, vv. 21–22 are not displaced from the psalm's first half.) God's continuance with his people is not dependent on *their* unwavering loyalty (e.g., feet that do not slip, cf. 26:1); its tenacity stems from God himself. Second, we see *divine sufficiency* in that although **my flesh and my heart may fail** (i.e., my physical properties deteriorate and I lack the freedom from human ills, envied in vv. 4–5) **but God is the** strength **of my heart and** my portion **forever.** The confession, **earth has nothing I desire besides you,** shows that the speaker has found the antidote to his earlier envy (v. 3); now to have God is to have all. In much of the Psalms and OT, we see the expectation that the righteous will be blessed and the wicked will be judged, sometimes stated in material terms (e.g., the blessings and curses of Deut. 28, the "two ways" of Proverbs and Ps. 1; cf. Ps. 128). Now Psalm 73 shows us that God personally is the reward of faith and relationship with him is its chief value. While God, in fact, *may* give evidence of his goodness in material terms, the only guarantee we have as believers is that he will evidence that goodness in personal terms. Psalm 73 is extraordinary among the psalms in that a resolution is won, but it does not consist in a deliverance from troubling circumstances but a new understanding of God's ultimate design.

The closing pair of verses then summarize the speaker's discovery in the spatial image of **far** and **near.** In the end, we find the writer does not deny the proverb with which he began, but he does clarify its two key phrases as a result of his own experience and the revelation received during his entry into the temple. He who would strive to be pure in heart (also v. 13) will find that his own heart fails and that its strength must lie in God alone (v. 26). Ultimately *divine* agency must be invoked for one to achieve inner purity. Secondly, God is good to Israel (v. 1) in that **it is good to be** near **God** (v. 28). While the first "good" is ambiguous, and many have taken it to mean good in a material sense, the second "good" is specific, namely the nearness of God. With these discoveries the speaker is now ready to turn from confessing (Hb. *spr*, v. 15, NIV "speak") the vanity of keeping a pure heart (vv. 13–14) to confessing (*spr*, v. 28, NIV "tell of") Yahweh's deeds.

Psalm 73 represents an intriguing approach to reality. The whole problem underlying the psalm arises from a realistic and frank appraisal of a claim made for God (v. 1) in light of human experience that belies a contrary claim (vv. 2–14). But the psalm does not limit reality to human experience (vv. 2–14) and human rationality (v. 16); it opens us to an ultimate (reflected in expressions like "final destiny," v. 17) and divine reality that transcends the immediate reality around us. It also represents a bold faith: a willingness to test, and thus possibly relinquish, a promise of God, only to receive a deeper understanding of it and thus grasp it more tightly.

Many believers have treasured verses 23–26, and rightly so, but we must appreciate that they were not achieved by a deferential, docile, unquestioning faith but by a critical, reflective faith. What is revelatory in the psalm is not simply the goal of verses 18–28 but also the process of verses 1–17. Without the struggle and questioning of the first half, it is doubtful the second half would have ever been written. The first half helps us see why the Psalms place such high value on honesty with God, expressed especially in its many lament psalms. The Psalms thereby invite us to make a frank appraisal of how the promises of God are evidenced in reality and to bring our feelings of disappointment to God (the speaker in Ps. 73 at least goes to "the sanctuary of God"). We do so because he—after all—is the one who can resolve our dilemma, whether by changing circumstances or by changing our understanding and redirecting our expectations. As a result of this encounter, our relationship with God is enhanced, not diminished. Other OT characters, such as Habakkuk and Job, have taken similar pilgrimages.

Psalm 73 also attests to the value of liturgy and worshipers' need for constant participation. It sheds revelatory light into our own limited understanding and embittered confusion (vv. 16–17, 21–22).

Psalm 73 may have achieved another breakthrough, or we at least are invited to read it in a different light once we compare with two other biblical passages. It is possible that verse 24 does not refer merely to the speaker's reception into God's temple presence but also to his reception afterward, that is, after death (note v. 26). The verb in the expression, "you will take (Hb. *lqhh*) me into glory," is identical to that found in Psalm 49:15 ("But God will redeem my soul from the grave; he will surely take me to himself") and Genesis 5:24 ("Enoch walked with God; then he was no more, because God took him away"), both of which seem to point to a divine act that transcends death. (See also 2 Kgs. 2:3, 5, 9, 10.) The conception of most psalms (6:5; 30:9; 88:10–12) and most of the OT, however, is that the dead face a shadowy existence in Sheol and are believed to be cut off from Yahweh. Psalm 73 may be consistent with this majority view, but it may also share with Psalm 49 and Genesis 5 a belief that one's relationship with God is indissoluble.

If verse 24 does point to some kind of resurrection, it is interesting to note how the writer arrived at this conclusion. He did so not by virtue of a supposed immortality of the soul (a notion foreign to the OT, where life is ever contingent on God, not an inherent property of humans; note esp. the tree of life in Gen. 3) but by virtue of God himself and the kind of relationship he establishes. Because "God is the strength of my heart and my portion forever (v. 26), I shall therefore live on with God." (For further discussion see G. von Rad, " 'Righteousness' and 'Life' in the Cultic Language of the Psalms," pp. 253–66. The confession that "God is . . . my portion" [Hb. *ḥēleq*] may point to the Levites, who had no "portion" or real estate in the land, as the other tribes, but who had God as their "portion." See Num. 18:20, where the NIV uses "share" to translate *ḥēleq*.)

In sum, Psalm 73 functions as a testimony about the realization that only those who enter God's dwelling enjoy true security and what is good, and that the wicked, far from God's temple presence, will indeed fall to their ruin. The speaker, although he had nearly slipped with the wicked, discovers that those who enter the temple have God as the strength of their failed heart and his nearness as their good.

Additional Note §73

73:10 / **Drink up waters in abundance:** The MT is difficult to decipher and probably disturbed. Hence, the NIV has rightly followed a sound reconstruction of the Hb. consonants in the verse's first half. It has tried to stay with the MT in the second half, but here a minor reconstruction is probably also in order: "and their words they drink deeply" (see *BHS*). The entire verse thus refers to the many "converts" of the wicked.

§74 The Destruction of the Temple and the Eruption of Chaos (Ps. 74)

With the destruction of Jerusalem and the exile of Judah in 587 B.C., the people of God experienced not only a national crisis but also a religious one. They lost three tangible symbols that marked them as the people of God: the land, the Davidic king, and the temple. This psalm laments the temple's destruction, and it takes on the seemingly impossible task of appealing to the God who has apparently rejected the temple's "congregation" (Hb. *ʿēdâ*, not "people" as in the NIV, v. 2).

It is thus a psalm sung without the temple, either in Babylonian exile or in the land of Israel itself, as the book of Lamentations appears to have been. Other passages hint that there were regular services of mourning and fasting during the years of the ruined temple (Zech. 7:1–7; 8:19). In this psalm, we hear the voice of an individual liturgist ("my" in v. 12) interceding on behalf of "us" (v. 9), the "congregation" (v. 2). It has a simple three-fold structure: a lament (vv. 1–11), a hymn that serves as a reminder to God (vv. 12–17), and petitions (vv. 18–23).

74:1–2 / The opening verses question God about his apparent attitudes of rejection and **anger,** both of which appear self-defeating and contrary to his investment in his people. The question **Why?** throws the problem back to its source. As the image of **the sheep of your pasture** illustrates the illogic of a shepherd's anger consuming his own sheep, so the petition to **remember** reminds him of the long-term **(of old)** investment he has made in this "congregation," whom he **purchased** and **redeemed** (lit. "bought back"—an economic metaphor). This petition, though brief, also draws God's attention to the two fundamental election traditions whereby God formed a people for himself. The terms "purchased of old" and "redeemed" echo the exodus from Egypt (cf. the Song of Moses in Exod. 15:13, 16, and Pss. 77:15; 106:10), and **Mount Zion** refers to God's chosen "dwelling" (cf. 132:13–14).

74:3–11 / These verses walk God, as it were, through the **ruins of the sanctuary** (lit. "Pick up your feet through the ruins"). The invaders are depicted as wild animals "roaring" (v. 4, Hb. *š°g* is usually used of lions in the OT) and as those who regard the temple as a mere **thicket of trees** to be **cut through.** Their burning **your sanctuary** is presented as a premeditated act of defilement and an attack against God himself (vv. 7–8). (Cf. Ezek. 25:3, where Ammon's gloating over the defilement and destruction of the temple will result in Yahweh's judgment of extermination.)

The laments, **we are given no . . . signs; no prophets are left,** probably reflect the sentiments of the exilic period. Lamentations 2:6–9 similarly mourns the destruction of Yahweh's "meetingplace" (Hb. *môʿēd,* cf. Ps. 74:4, 8), the enemies' shouting in the sacred temple (cf. Ps. 74:4, 23), and the absence of prophetic visions, which Ezekiel had foreseen as a judgment of the exilic period (Ezek. 7:26). Thus, because **none of us knows how long,** the question is now asked of God directly.

The lament section of the psalm ends as it began with a question of "Why?" complaining directly to God. For verse 11 we should probably read, **Why do you hold back your hand,** why is **your right hand** "kept back in" **the folds of your garment?** The psalm does not depict God as actively hostile towards his people and temple; rather, he passively allows the invaders to ravage his temple. Active and deliberate hostility is reserved for **the foe** who **revile[s] your name.** The point the psalm makes to God is that, however he feels towards his people (v. 1), he should be enraged against these insolent aggressors.

74:12–17 / Now the psalm takes a surprising turn to praise and a seemingly irrelevant tangent about a conflict between God and a **monster** that took place **of old.** Although its connection with the temple escapes modern readers, it would have been apparent to the ancients. This confession of God as **king from** of old and of his victory over the monster **in the waters** points to the tradition of divine kingship familiar in the ancient Near East (see the Introduction). Thus, while these verses are phrased as praise, they function in the context of the psalm as a stirring reminder that the divine king must have a "palace/temple" (Hb. *hêkāl* denotes both). In addition, this

recitation of God's **salvation** when he vanquished **the sea** and
Leviathan draws an implicit parallel between them and the
temple invaders, who roar (v. 4) as wild beasts (v. 19), producing
clamor, an uproar (v. 23), and a chaotic destruction (vv. 5–8). This
parallel may also imply that with the temple's destruction primeval chaos once again threatens creation order. Thus, as God
brought salvation in the past, so he must do the same in the turmoil of the present.

It seems odd to us moderns that creation could be viewed
as an act of salvation. One might prefer to see Leviathan (see Additional Notes) as a derogatory term for Egypt, as "Rahab" is
used on occasion (87:4; Isa. 30:7; cf. also Ezek. 29:3; 32:2), and to
see God's "splitting open the sea" as a reference to the deliverance at the Reed Sea (Exod. 14). But the verses closing this
hymnic section clearly celebrate God's establishing creation order
(vv. 16–17). Other psalms are clear that creation was viewed as a
heroic act whereby God brought order out of chaos (e.g., "O God
our Savior, . . . who formed the mountains" and "who stilled the
roaring of the seas," 65:5–7).

74:18–23 / As the preceding hymn serves as a reminder
to God, so the dominant imperatives of this petition section are
remember (vv. 18, 22, also v. 2) and **do not forget/ignore** (vv. 19,
23). They call God's attention to **how fools mock you** and to **your
afflicted people.** Consistent with the passive role attributed to
God in verse 11, the other negative petitions plead, **do not hand
over the life of your dove to wild beasts** and **do not let the oppressed retreat in disgrace.** And the only positive petition calling for divine action is, **Rise up, O God, and defend your cause.**
To this point, he has been considered passive, but now the divine
king, who also acts as the supreme judge, is to arise from his
throne and "legally dispute his own legal dispute" (lit., Hb. *rîbâ
rîbekā, v. 22*). The psalm does not bother to specify the kind of action God should undertake because it is either obvious from the
case at hand or left to his discretion as judge.

The overall strategy of the psalm now becomes clear. God
is seen as the divine king and supreme judge. It begins by questioning his indignation against his own "congregation." On the
one hand, the speaker argues that Yahweh, the divine judge is, in
fact, the injured party and that these invaders are the offenders.
He appeals to God's reputation (vv. 22–23) and how these insolent aggressors have **reviled your name** (vv. 10, 18, and v. 7). On

the other hand, he argues that this "congregation" is also an injured party by appealing to the rights of the poor: **may the poor
and needy praise your name** (v. 21, a form of the vow of praise).
By portraying them as "your dove," "your afflicted people," and
"the oppressed" (vv. 19, 21), he also appeals to God's sense of
pity. Finally, the psalm also appeals to a legal document, namely
your covenant (Hb. *bᵉrît*, "treaty," v. 20), which probably points to
the Sinai covenant (cf. 50:5, 16; 78:10, 37; 103:18; 106:45; 111:5, 9).
In sum, the psalm endeavors to enrage God against the invaders
and so redirect his anger from his people (v. 1) to these revilers.
The nation's problem is really God's ("your cause").

Additional Notes §74

74:11 / **Take it from. . . and destroy them:** "Take it" is not in
the Hb. text and is simply supplied by the translators. The MT's petition,
"destroy" (Hb. *kallēh*), seems out of place in this section of the psalm. Instead we should probably read, "kept back" (Hb. *kᵉluʾâ*), which forms a
better parallel to **hold back.** With the LXX, **your right hand** should be
placed in the second line.

74:14 / **The heads of Leviathan:** Cf. Isa. 27:1. In the Ugaritic
Tablets Baal "smote Leviathan the slippery serpent (and) made an
end of the wriggling serpent, the tyrant with seven heads" (Gibson,
Canaanite Myths, p. 68).

§75 It Is God Who Brings Down and Exalts (Ps. 75)

Psalm 75 consists of both human praise and a divine oracle. Their combination may be explained by a liturgical framework. The voice of a representative liturgist is apparent in the alternation between the opening "we give thanks" and the closing "I will sing praise" (v. 9). At issue is Yahweh's judgment and who may "lift up one's horn" (vv. 4–5, 10, a metaphor of one's power and rank, illustrated esp. in 92:10).

75:1 / Instead of reading **we give thanks,** however, we should probably translate, "we have given thanks" (within the Psalms, only here does this verb appear as a Hb. perfect). A liturgical context helps to make sense of this reference to past praise. The opening verse refers to psalms used earlier in the wider liturgy. The telling of Yahweh's **wonderful deeds** is also prominent in the psalms of Yahweh's kingship (96:3; 98:1) and in the hymnic praises of his saving, historical acts (105:2, 5; 107:8, 15, 21, 24, 31).

75:2–5 / Without introduction (the NIV translators have simply supplied **You say**), Yahweh himself speaks (vv. 2–5). While the absence of a transition to the oracle is awkward when the psalm is read as literature, it would not have been so when another voice, a prophet, steps forward. Yahweh's speech rings with echoes from the psalms of Yahweh's kingship. The connection drawn between Yahweh's claim to judge with equity (NIV **uprightly**) and his claim to **hold** the **pillars** of **the earth firm** (both introduced by **it is I,** Hb. *ʾanî* and *ʾānōkî*) may seem strange, but these Hebrew terms and motifs are likewise juxtaposed in these psalms (96:10, 13; 98:9; 99:4; cf. 93:1). There we see that the divine king's ability to preserve order in nature gives evidence that he will ensure order in society. Also in these same contexts, the earth **and all its people** (98:7, both psalms use *yōšᵉbê*) **quake** (they "tremble" in 96:9 and "tremble" and "shake" in 99:1). In particular focus are Yahweh's judgments on **the wicked** (cf. 97:8, 10). The reason that they are told, **Do not lift your horns against**

heaven (lit. "on high") is simply because Yahweh dwells "on high" (93:4; cf. 68:18). This oracle thus states the character of his judging—it is fair—and the magnitude of its enforcing power—he steadies the earth itself. The oracle thus warns the wicked not to arrogate power that is God's.

75:6–8 / A liturgist then steps forward and confirms the same themes (vv. 6–8; note the connective phrase, **it is God who judges**) but in the language of praise psalms, not that of the psalms of Yahweh's kingship. In view of the farthest horizons (cf. v. 6 and 113:3), it is to be acknowledged that God, who dwells "on high," is the one who **exalts** (113:5–8; 138:6). Yahweh will **pour . . . out** judgment on **the wicked of the earth,** and they will drink from this **cup** (cf. 11:6, where the NIV translates the same term with "lot"). The Song of Hannah (1 Sam. 2) in particular echoes both Yahweh's earlier oracle (Yahweh's setting the earth on foundations in 1 Sam. 2:8, his warning against pride and arrogance among the wicked in vv. 3 and 9, and the reference to one's horn in v. 1) and the liturgist's affirmations (Yahweh "humbles and he exalts" in vv. 7–8).

75:9–10 / In the closing section the liturgist leads the congregation in a renewed vow of praise. With the words **as for me,** he distinguishes himself from **the wicked,** described in the previous verses. While they would "speak . . . against heaven" (v. 5), **I will sing praise to the God of Jacob.** In the closing verse, we could read, he **will cut off the horns of all the wicked,** thus understanding it as the substance of the liturgist's vowed praise, but we should probably read it as a resumption of the divine oracle, **I** (i.e., Yahweh) **will cut off the horns of all** the wicked. Yahweh is the one who hews off horns that would exalt themselves and exalts those who entrust—with praise—that prerogative to him.

Part of what makes this psalm work is the assumption that one wants one's "horn" exalted. This goal is not in dispute, but what separates the wicked from the righteous is the means they choose. The latter give thanks and tell of Yahweh's deeds. The former boast and exalt their own horns. Thus, they assume powers belonging solely to God. The principal characteristics of the human and divine roles are clearly drawn: God acts, humans are to respond with praise.

§76 The God of Zion Breaks the Weapons of War (Ps. 76)

This is another of the Songs of Zion (see the Introduction and the comments on Ps. 46), which celebrate Yahweh's dramatic protection of the temple and its sacred mountain from foreign invasion. Yahweh's deliverance of Jerusalem from Assyrian invasion in 701 B.C. may be a case in point (Isa. 36–37).

76:1–3 / The psalm begins with Judah's special knowledge of Yahweh. **His name,** or self-revelation, **is great in Israel.** The terms chosen to designate Yahweh's dwelling **in Zion** point to the antiquity of the tradition. The term for Jerusalem is **Salem,** its pre-Israelite name (Gen. 14:18). The term for **his tent** (Hb. *sōk*), meaning "hut," may allude to the ancient tabernacle (27:5; cf. 2 Sam. 11:11). **His dwelling place** (Hb. *me'ônâ*) is also used of "the Tent of Meeting" (1 Sam. 2:22) in Shiloh (vv. 29, 32). These well-chosen words may also convey other meanings. "Salem" (Hb. *šālēm*) also points to "peace" (Hb. *šālôm*), a notion exemplified in the next verse. The terms for "tent" (Ps. 10:9; esp. Jer. 25:38) and "dwelling place" (Ps. 104:21–22; Nah. 2:11–12) are also used in the OT for a lion's den. Implicit here is the image of Yahweh emerging from his den in Zion as a lion to destroy threats from attackers (cf. the same image in connection with Zion in Isa. 31:4–5).

Verse 3 states the evidence that Yahweh has chosen Zion as his special dwelling: **There he broke . . . the weapons of war** (cf. 46:9; Isa. 2:4). The importance of Zion in God's dealings is underscored by the frequent use of "there" in the Songs of Zion (48:6; 87:4, 6; 132:7; and perhaps 122:4, 5) and elsewhere (69:35; 133:3). The next section narrates this event of Yahweh's defense of Zion.

76:4–10 / This evidence is unpacked as praise addressed directly to Yahweh. With this turn to praise there is no subsequent mention of Zion or its distinctive privileges—attention is focused exclusively on God. The Hebrew text of verse 4 is somewhat problematic. We should perhaps read, "You are feared (cf. v. 7, *nôrā'* instead of *nā'ôr*), more majestic than the everlasting mountains" (see LXX and cf. Deut. 33:15; Hab. 3:6). In any case, it is clear that Yahweh is greater than any mountain and that there is nothing inherent or magical in Mount Zion itself.

As a divine warrior, the **God of Jacob** (used in the psalms of Zion as a parallel expression to "Yahweh of [military] hosts," a title of the divine warrior, 46:7, 11; 84:8; cf. 59:5; 69:6; 20:1), flattens all the opposing **warriors. Both horse and chariot lie still** echoes Yahweh's defeat of Pharaoh at the Reed Sea (Exod. 14–15, esp. 15:1, 4, 21). Yahweh, the divine warrior, is also the divine judge: **you, O God, rose up to judge.** Two features of this judgment indicate that Yahweh's actions are not inextricably tied to Zion. First, **from heaven**—not from Zion—**you pronounced judgment.** Implicit here may be the image of Yahweh as the God of the skies (Hb. *šāmayim* denotes both "skies" and "heaven"; if so, the NIV's rendering in v. 4a may be correct, cf. 104:1–2). Yahweh's **rebuke** in battle is elsewhere connected with the God of the thunderstorm (18:15; 104:7; cf. 68:30, 33). Second, God's reason for judging was not to defend his mountain but **to save all the afflicted of the land.** He acts on behalf of the oppressed, not on behalf of sacred space. Emotions play a central role in this narrative. Yahweh's emotion is anger (vv. 6–7, 10) and the human emotion in response is fear (vv. 7–8, 11–12).

76:11–12 / The psalm closes with imperatives addressed apparently to both Israel **(the LORD your God)** and to **all the neighboring lands.** Israel is enjoined to present a votive offering (Lev. 7:16), probably as an expression of thanksgiving. **The kings of the earth** are to bring **gifts** (Hb. *šay*), that is, tribute, to the victorious King. This term is used elsewhere only in 68:29 (cf. vv. 17–18) and Isaiah 18:7, both of which describe foreign peoples bringing gifts to the temple in Zion/Jerusalem.

Nothing like the silence of God in the face of distress brings the sinking feeling of despair. The Bible does not offer a prepackaged answer to this problem, but—remarkably—the divine word is a humane word, and so comes alongside to help. It offers not only God's words to us but also words that we may bring to God—even when he does not seem to be listening. Psalm 77 gives no hint as to what may have been its immediate occasion. It simply refers to distress (v. 2). It soon becomes evident that the overriding problem is not this distress, whatever it may be, but God's silence in the face of this distress. The immediate trouble has become simply a backdrop for a larger dilemma of faith.

Psalm 77 is a peculiar composite: it consists of lament typical of the prayer psalms of the individual, and it consists of praise of God's historic deeds typical of corporate hymns. It may simply be a variant of individual prayer psalms, thus befitting any worshiper who feels ignored by God. But the questions raised in verses 7–9 have a ring of ultimacy that extends beyond a lone person. Likewise, the praiseworthy acts recited in verses 14–20 are corporate ("your people"), public ("among the peoples"), and even cosmic ("the waters, the skies, the earth"). Since the speaker's memory of God (v. 3) and of "the years of long ago" (v. 5) gives him grief (vv. 5–6), it appears God no longer performs saving deeds as before. There are other psalms that combine motifs normally associated with discrete individual and corporate psalms and traditions (Pss. 22; 51; 69; 102). Each of these, in their final forms at least, shows affinity to the crisis of the exilic period (roughly 587–538 B.C. and beyond). In these psalms, it appears the people of the exile adopted prayer psalms of the individual to express corporate lament, where the nation is personified as the speaking "I." In addition, both halves of Psalm 77 contain literary echoes from the text of the book of Exodus (esp. 34:6), as do other psalms (Pss. 103, 111, and 145), each of which also has affinity to the exilic and early postexilic periods. Thus, Psalm 77, in its final form, may have been used by the people of the exile.

So what is this psalm about, with its unique combination of diverse motifs? For fear of getting lost in the details, we need first to make some general observations. The psalm contains no formal petition, and the lament in the first half does not address God (on v. 4 see Additional Notes). This takes place only in the hymnic praise of verses 11b–20. The lament reports on past prayers that have had no effect (vv. 1–2) and on memories and reflections (vv. 3–6) that have yielded despairing questions about God (vv. 7–9). Verse 10 is problematic and is discussed below. Many commentators have supposed the transition to praise in the second half signals a change of mood in the composer. But the psalm gives no hint that anything has prompted a mood swing, especially because both halves of the psalm result from the same act of remembering and musing on God (Hb. *zkr* and *śyḥ* in vv. 3, 6, and 11–12). We should note that other corporate laments contain hymnic praise or a recital of Yahweh's past saving events (Pss. 9–10; 44; 74; 80; 89). In these psalms, references to Yahweh's saving deeds function not as praise but as precedents that remind Yahweh of how he has revealed himself in the past—with the clear implication this is what he should do in the present. Thus, the second half of Psalm 77 does not signal a change in the speaker's supposed mood but a change in thepsalm's appeal to God. Instead of appealing through the speaker's cries (vv. 1–2), it appeals to God's past praiseworthy acts.

77:1–9 / Verses 1–2 report that there have been many past prayers but they have found no satisfying resolution (**my soul refused to be comforted**). Their fervency is underscored by references to voice (**I cried out,** lit. "with my voice") and body (**I stretched out untiring hands**). This description of the act of praying tells us something about God and offers advice to ourselves. Prayer need not be audible for God to hear it, but this psalm reflects a respect for God as a person. God is no mere mystical force that we can presume knows our minds automatically. Instead, the psalm describes the petitioner as engaging God with his whole person, both outward ("voice" and "hands") and inward ("soul"). Prayers said in the mind can quickly become daydreams, but those said with soul and body awaken us to the personal encounter that prayer is.

Verses 3–6 recount the speaker's attempts at finding comfort through private meditation. But the memory of **God** in **the
former days** presents a marked contrast to the God who is silent
"in the day of my distress" (lit.; NIV has only "distress"). These
lonely musings yield pain and longing, leaving the speaker sleepless, speechless, and lost in nostalgia. Verses 7–9 express questions that would otherwise be unthinkable. They are similar to
those found in other laments, but there they are addressed to
God and function rhetorically to move God to act. Here they are
presented as private musings and thus as real questions. What is
most haunting about them is that they probe the ultimate and
final cessation of all that is good in God **(forever, never . . . again,
forever, for all time).** The attributes mentioned are those confessed repeatedly in the OT to be central to Yahweh's character:
"the LORD, the compassionate and gracious (= **merciful** in Ps.
77:9) God, slow to anger, abounding in love and faithfulness"
(Exod. 34:6; cf. Num. 14:18; Neh. 9:17; Joel 2:13; Jonah 4:2; Pss.
86:15; 103:8; 111:4; 145:8).

77:10–20 / **Then I thought** (lit. "and I said") signals a response to the preceding, here proposing a change to the preceding course of events (cf. 55:6; 139:11). The psalm will now **appeal**
to salvation history. At first, we might wonder what prompts the
change from the lament of the first half: both halves engage in the
same acts of remembering (vv. 3, 6, and 11) and musing (vv. 3, 6,
and 12, where the same verb is rendered **consider**) on God. But
there are two decisive differences. First, God is now addressed directly. Second, the object of the memory is given clearer focus.
Formerly "I remembered God" and "the former days," now **I will
remember the deeds of the LORD** (four times in vv. 11–12 the
psalm emphasizes the object of memory). The speaker now not
only remembers God in his own heart and spirit (vv. 3, 6, i.e. privately); he reminds God of the saving precedent that he established himself by his own acts. When left to ourselves, memories
can lead to nostalgia and despair, but when presented to God
they can become a powerful appeal for renewal. And it is far more
difficult to comprehend what God might be like than it is to understand his specific, concrete acts of salvation.

The recital found in verses 13–15, 20 contains strong echoes of portions of the Song of Moses found in Exodus 15:1, 11, 13,
16. God is **holy** (lit. "in holiness"). **What god is so great . . . ,
who performs miracles** (lit. "working wonders")? References

are made to **your power,** and, **with your mighty arm you re-deemed your people, you led your people . . . by . . . Moses.**

Verses 16–19 appear to interrupt the natural narrative sequence of this recital, and they also have a very different meter (tricola [three poetic lines] instead of bicola [two poetic lines], evident in the NIV). And the perspective, characters, and their roles are very different. We see God not as redeemer and shepherd of his people, but as the God of the skies at whom the cosmos quakes. These variations may stem from different traditions: the exodus tradition in verses 13–15, 20 and the theophany tradition in verses 16–19 (cf. 18:7–15; 29:3–10; 68:8, 33–34; 97:4; though note their combination in 114:1–8). Why should these verses be inserted where they are? It may be that verses 19 and 20, though originally distinct, now share a realization that is critical for this psalm. God's appearance in verses 16–19 was heroic, dramatic, and decisive, and yet **your footprints were not seen** (lit. "known"). God's redemption of his people in verses 13–15 was public and powerful **(you display** your power **among the peoples),** nevertheless "you led your people . . . by" **the hand of Moses and Aaron,** that is, by human agents. In other words, even in this most magnificent of God's revelations, he remains profoundly hidden. His acts must be recognized by faith.

Why does the psalm end so suddenly? It concludes with the people of God still on a journey and dependent on their guide. It may be that this is precisely the situation out of which Psalm 77 was composed, namely with the exiles in need of God to lead them back to the promised land.

This psalm presents God with a forceful appeal for help and also guides the worshipers who use it to new paths. Although it contains no formal petition, its reminding praise takes up this function, and it gives God the freedom to act according to his own discretion. With blunt honesty, worshipers confess that they have failed to reach God in prayer and that their attempts to find consolation in the past and to fathom the ways of the Most High yield only despair. The psalm reshapes the worshipers' appeal from a quest for their own deliverance to a quest for God's renewed praise (a theocentric appeal). Doubt is not to be hidden from God, or from ourselves. For most of us, doubt is a part of life before the invisible God. In this psalm it is embraced as part of the overall appeal to God. The psalm shows that faith has more to do with God than with feelings. Within, the speaker senses no hope, yet he recounts to Yahweh what Yahweh has done and can therefore do again. What makes a difference is not how we feel but how we cry to our God.

Additional Notes §77

77:4 / Instead of reading **you kept** (Hb. *ʾāḥaztā*) we should probably read "I kept" (Hb. *ʾāḥaztî*). In the context of the psalm, direct address to God seems inappropriate to the lament of vv. 1–9. Moreover, this act of keeping the **eyes from closing** echoes the speaker's act of "stretching out untiring hands" (v. 2). In addition, we should note that the NIV's "you" in v. 3 is not present in the Hb. text.

77:10 / The Hb. form *ḥallôtî* (rendered **appeal** in the NIV) is problematic. In the seventeen other uses of the Piel of *ḥlh*, it appears with the Hb. term for "face" (with the exception of Deut. 29:22) and means to "appease/entreat the face of." Some of the ancient versions appear to have read this same Hb. verb form but derived it from *ḥll*, thus meaning "my wound." Other ancient versions read the qal form (Hb. *ḥᵃlôtî*) of *ḥlh*, thus "my sickness." Another Hb. word is also problematic: *šᵉnôt* can be translated **years** (as it must be understood in v. 5) or "changing" (from *šnh*). Thus, we have either "This is my wound/sickness: the changing of the right hand of the Most High" or "This is my entreaty: the years of the right hand of the Most High." In view of the striking turn that takes place in the psalm's appeal at this point, the latter rendering is more appropriate for this transitional verse.

Like most psalms, Psalm 78 is explicitly meant for public performance ("O my people, hear," and "things we have heard . . . we will tell," vv. 1–4), but unlike most, which are either prayers (Hb. $t^e pillâ$) or praises (Hb. $t^e hillâ$), this one is explicitly teaching (Hb. $tôrâ$; only here in the Pss. does this term not denote God's "teaching/law"). Like Psalm 49 (v. 4, cf. Prov. 1:6), it designates itself as a parable (or "comparison," Hb. $māšāl$) and as "riddles" (rendered "things hidden" in the NIV). Thus, we should expect to find in Psalm 78 explicit teaching and lessons but also something of a puzzle and mystery (as in 49:5–6, 15). The lessons are clear in virtually every verse (esp. in light of vv. 5–8), but the mysteries become apparent only after considering the psalm as a whole. To this we shall return.

The teaching of Psalm 78 takes place on two levels: one has to do with the *personal* decision the current generation of listeners faces, the other has to do with *corporate* tribes and God's elected program for Jacob-Israel. The first is explicitly set forth in the opening section: "we will tell the next generation the praiseworthy deeds of the LORD, . . . so the next generation . . . would put their trust in God and . . . not be like their forefathers" (vv. 4–8). Each generation must hear the story of salvation and so choose to trust God. In sum, God has revealed his deeds (vv. 4, 7, 11), wonders (vv. 4, 11, 12, 32, 43), power (v. 4), and signs (v. 43). He has established his law (vv. 5, 10), statutes (or "testimonies," vv. 5, 56), covenant (vv. 10, 37), and his commands (v. 7). He has guided (vv. 14, 53, 72) and redeemed (vv. 35, 42) his people; he has provided them with water and bread (vv. 15–16, 23–25), shepherded them (vv. 52, 70–72), and settled them in the land (vv. 54–55). He has plagued their enemies in Egypt (vv. 12, 43–51) and delivered them through the sea (vv. 13, 53). And he was merciful and atoned for their iniquities, even though their repentance was phony (vv. 34–39). In spite of this, the people responded by being stubborn and rebellious (vv. 8, 17, 40, 56); they forgot (v. 11) and did not remember God's deeds (v. 42); they did not believe or trust him (vv. 22, 32). They did not keep his covenant (vv. 10, 56). And so they continued to sin (vv. 17, 32) and put God to the test (vv. 18, 41, 56). They were not loyal (lit. "fixed" or "resolved") or faithful (vv. 8, 37). In response, God became very angry (vv. 21, 31, 58, 59, 62) and slew them (vv. 31, 34) and gave them over to destruction (v. 62, cf. vv. 61, 64). The anger (vv. 49–50), the slaying (Hb. *hrg*, v. 47), the giving over to destruction (vv. 48, 50), and the devouring (vv. 45, 63) that God had previously reserved for their Egyptian oppressors, he now turned on Israel. And so he rejected them and abandoned the sanctuary (vv. 59–60). The psalm's solution to this dilemma for "the next generation" lies in retelling this story, so they, unlike their forefathers, would not forget but know, put their trust in God and keep his commands (vv. 4–8). A living memory of God and his acts is the crucial factor.

The second level of the psalm's teaching has to do with the fact that God's saving activity was first centered in the northern tribes and expressed in the traditions concerning the exodus, wilderness journeys, and the conquest. But now it has shifted to Judah and the traditions concerning David and Zion (vv. 68–72). For ancient Israel, this was a striking development that demanded explanation. The OT refers to this northern region not by the designation "northern Israel" but often by its most prominent tribe, Ephraim (Ps. 78:9, 67; cf. Isa. 7:2; Jer. 7:15; Hos. 4:17). The patriarch Ephraim was the first-blessed son of Joseph, Jacob's own favorite. National leaders such as Joshua (Num. 13:8) and Samuel were from Ephraim. King Saul was from the northern tribe of Benjamin. The fundamental traditions of salvation history especially beloved in northern Israel were the exodus, wilderness, and conquest stories (evidenced, e.g., by 1 Kgs. 12:28 and by the prophets sent to northern Israel: Hos. 2:14–15; 11:1–5; 12:9, 13; 13:4; Amos 2:9–10; 4:10; 5:25; 9:7). Amos 3:1–2 especially makes clear that northern Israel identified their election as the people of God with their exodus out of Egypt. Understandably, the stories of Israel's sojourn in Egypt were especially beloved by the descendants of the patriarch Joseph (Ps. 78:67). But now God rejected the tent (singular not plural as in the NIV) of Joseph (perhaps alluding not merely to the people but also to the tent or tabernacle of v. 60) and "did not choose the tribe of Ephraim; but he chose the tribe of Judah," Mount Zion, which he loved and at which he built his sanctuary. In particular, he chose David (vv. 67–70). Now the fundamental traditions of election are the David and Zion traditions centered in the tribe of Judah. (The parallelism of tribe and sanctuary in v. 68 implies the same parallelism applies in v. 67.) Remarkably, we find that while God had rejected Israel (v. 59), Jacob-Israel has been reconstituted under God's new economy (v. 71). In this light, we can now see that the shift lies not so much in a rejection of northerners and a choice of southerners as it does in a transfer of the political government and the religious sanctuary from the north to the south.

The structure of Psalm 78 unfolds in three parts, the last two paralleling each other in theme and terminology.

1–8 *Introduction*

9–11 Ephraim *turned* because *they forgot his wonders.*	40–43 In the wilderness they *turned* because *they did not remember his wonders.*
12–16 He *guided* his people from Egypt and in the wilderness.	44–55 He *guided* his people from Egypt and in the conquest.
17–20 *They rebelled against the Most High* and *put God to the test* in the wilderness because of their appetites.	56–58 *They rebelled against the Most High* and *put God to the test* in the land because of their idolatry.
21–31 Yahweh *was very angry* and brought *fire* in the wilderness, sending quail and a plague.	59–64 God *was very angry* and brought *fire* during the Judges period, rejecting Israel and abandoning the tabernacle and ark.
32–39 They continued to sin in the wilderness and in the land with the judges, but he restrained his anger.	65–72 The Lord suddenly defeated foes, rejected Ephraim, and chose Judah, Zion, and David.

Both of these reviews of Israel's history begin with the memory of the events of the Egyptian exodus. The first simply makes a general reference to the miracles done in the land of Egypt (v. 12); the second provides a detailed description of the plagues in Egypt (vv. 43–51). Both make brief mention of the Reed Sea deliverance, the first focusing on its miraculous nature (v. 13) and the second on its protective nature (v. 53). The first then gives extended attention to the wilderness period (vv. 14–33), but the second omits this entirely and moves straight from the exodus itself (vv. 52–53) to the settlement (vv. 54–55). Both then appear to move into the Judges period, the first emphasizing God's mercy in spite of their merely circumstantial repentance (vv. 34–39) and the second emphasizing his rejection and abandonment of them (vv. 56–64).

78:1–8 / Much of this section has been elucidated above. The purpose of this history lesson is clear: so the next generation will not repeat the mistakes of their forebears. Memory is the critical factor, and it should result in the attitude of **trust in God** and in the behavior of keeping **his commands.**

78:9–11 / It is not certain to what **battle** these verses refer, if in fact a particular one is in view. Three possibilities emerge from the Bible. One is Israel's defeat by the Philistines when the tabernacle of Shiloh (v. 60), in the tribal territory of **Ephraim,** and the ark were taken captive (1 Sam. 4–6). A second is when Israel was defeated again by the Philistines, and Saul, the king from the north, was killed (1 Sam. 31). A third is the utter fall of the northern kingdom of Israel and its capital Samaria at the hand of the Assyrians (2 Kgs. 17). The reason for Ephraim's retreat, however, is clear: **they forgot** his **wonders** and **did not keep God's covenant.**

78:12–16 / This section recounts briefly the events of the **miracles** (i.e., plagues) done **in the land of Egypt,** the dividing of the Reed Sea, and Yahweh's guidance in the wilderness by pillars of **cloud by day** and of **fire all night.** The two incidents of his providing **water** from **rocks** (Exod. 17:1–7; Num. 20:1–13) are combined into one account that emphasizes God's miraculous provision and says nothing of Israel's failure (as does its parallel section, vv. 44–55). Both pentateuchal counterparts record the Israelites' prior murmuring, including their testing God (Exod. 17:2, 7) and rebelling (Num. 20:10), but in Psalm 78 this is postponed until its next section recounting the quail incident: but they continued to sin by rebelling and putting God to the test (vv. 17–18).

78:17–31 / Verses 17–20 recount how the people provoked God by "testing" (i.e., pushing and virtually daring) him, and verses 21–31 recount God's angry response (the phrase, God's **anger/wrath** (Hb. *'ap*) **rose against** them, acts as an inclusio in vv. 21, 31). Israel's action here is characterized as **rebelling.** It is perhaps significant that it is not connected with "forgetting" God's deeds. In fact, their rebellion is predicated on these deeds: they say, **"When he struck the rock, water gushed out, . . . but can he also give us food?"** Their motives are clarified further: **for they did not believe in God or trust in his deliverance.** In other words, they did not trust in the person of God, nor did they believe he intended to bring his deliverance to the full. In each of the pentateuchal accounts of provisions of water, manna, and quail, the Israelites confess they think God may have delivered them out of Egypt with the malicious intent of allowing them to die in the wilderness (Exod. 16:3; 17:2–3, 7; Num. 20:3–4; cf. 11:4–5, 20). As in the incidents of water coming from rocks, verses 17–31 combine two separate incidents: the provision of **food** (lit. "bread")/**manna** (vv. 20, 23–25, Exod. 16), and the judgments with **meat/birds** (i.e., "quail, vv. 20, 26–31, Num. 11:4–34) and **fire** (v. 21, Num. 11:1–3).

78:32–39 / This section notes that **in spite of** these divine judgments, **they kept on sinning** and offered only superficial repentance. **Yet,** in spite of these human behaviors, God **was merciful.** Neither response follows as a logical consequence of the other party's behavior, but the human one is destructive (v. 33) and the divine one restorative (v. 38).

That "they kept on sinning" is directly attached to the fact that **they did not believe**—their lack of trust led to wayward behavior. As a result, the first generation liberated from Egypt **ended their days in futility** (cf. Num. 14:20–35). The repeated cycle (implied by **whenever** and **time after time**) of God's judgment, the people's temporary repentance, and God's relenting (vv. 35–39) are reminiscent of the cycle repeated in the book of Judges (see esp. Judg. 2:11–19). In this period, there were occasions when the people **would seek** God as a result of his "slaying" them. In fact, **they remembered**—the very action this psalm endeavors to elicit (cf. vv. 7, 11, 42). But as it turns out, this repentance reached only **their mouths,** and not **their hearts** (vv. 36–37, cf. v. 8). Nonetheless, God repeatedly **restrained his anger,** though justified, and **forgave their iniquities.** We should note that in the OT God is rarely the subject of the verb "atone." In most cases a priest performs the atoning sacrificial rites, but here God takes it upon himself (see BDB, p. 497). In addition, here it is God who remembers—in this case, human frailty.

78:40–43 / Verse 40 begins the second review of Israel's history. It returns us to **the desert** period and even earlier with a

retrospective look at the Egyptian period. The wilderness generations **rebelled** and **put God to the test** (terminology repeated
several times), and they also **grieved** and **vexed** him (terminology revealing God's emotional response). Israel's behavior
clearly brought emotional pain to the person of God. In this case,
their rebellion stems from their forgetting (contrast vv. 17–20
above): **They did not remember . . . the day he displayed his miraculous signs in Egypt.** Thus, like the introduction to the first
historical review (vv. 9–11), this one begins with Israel's failed
memory of God's **wonders.**

78:44–55 / Also like the first recital, there now follows a
thoroughly positive review of God's saving acts and how **he
guided them** (vv. 14, 53). It begins in **Egypt** as well but then extends all the way to the conquest: **he drove out nations . . . and allotted their lands** and **settled the tribes of Israel** (v. 55). Extended
attention is given to the plagues against Egypt. A comparison
with the Exodus account (Exod. 7–12) reveals that some of the
plagues are lacking (#3 gnats, #5 livestock, #6 boils, #9 darkness) and the rest appear in a different order (#1 blood, #4 flies,
#2 frogs, #8 locusts, #7 hail, #10 firstborn). Psalm 105, the other
psalm that details the Egyptian plagues also omits certain plagues
and reorders the remainder (105:27–36). Particularly striking here
in Psalm 78 is the omission of Mt. Sinai, of the establishment of the
covenant, and of the giving of the law from the narrative sequence. Once **he brought his people out** of Egypt, **led them . . .
through the desert,** and **the sea engulfed their enemies,** then **he
brought them to the border of his holy land.** This omission is all
the more surprising because the psalm elsewhere makes explicit
mention of his law (vv. 5, 10), statutes (vv. 5, 56), covenant (vv. 10,
37), and commands (v. 7). Sinai is similarly left out of the narrative
sequence of other historical psalms (see on Pss. 105; 135; 136).

78:56–58 / The generations of the settlement period are
here described in the same terms as the generation that came out
of Egypt (vv. 17–18) and the second generation in the wilderness
(vv. 40–41): **they put God to the test and rebelled against the
Most High.** Here their rebellion is not connected with their ap-
petites (vv. 17–20) or their failed memories (vv. 40–43); it is connected with **their high places** and **idols** (recurring themes in
1–2 Kgs.). These symbols **angered** God because they, in effect, reflect attempts to liken God to created images (unlike the cherubim and ark that symbolized his throne and footstool) and thus

restrict and demean him. They also reflect attempts to manipulate him. And, as implied by the phrase, **they aroused his jealousy,** they also reflect the worship of other gods. Thus, postsettlement Israel is described **as unreliable** (Hb. *nehpᵉkû,* in the sense of being twisted) **as a faulty bow.** This phrase echoes the earlier reference to "the men of Ephraim, though armed with bows," who turned back (Hb. *hāpᵉkû,* v. 9).

78:59–64 / Like its parallel (vv. 21–31), this section delivers God's response: **he was very angry** and brought **fire** against his people. Because of their high places (v. 58), **he abandoned ... the tent he had set up among men.** The phrase, **he rejected Israel completely** (better: "exceedingly," Hb. *mᵉʾōd*), needs to be interpreted in light of the events narrated in verses 60–64. The rejection is not ultimate, as evidenced by verse 71. These events are described in more detail in 1 Samuel 4–6 (see esp. 4:10–11), where the Philistines overran **Shiloh,** took the ark **into captivity,** and slaughtered the people with **the sword,** including the **priests** Hophni and Phinehas. The **widow** of Phinehas did **not weep** but died in childbirth.

78:65–72 / As noted in the outline above, the sections concluding each half of the psalm (here and vv. 32–39) do not contain verbal parallels like the other matching sections. But they do contain a striking thematic parallel: in both Yahweh acts unilaterally—for no prior reason he acts graciously. Although Israel's repentance amounted to lying to him, yet he was merciful (vv. 34–39). Now **the Lord** acts suddenly, and the abruptness is underscored by two graphic similes (sleep and intoxication) one would normally think inappropriate for God (v. 65). He chooses **Judah, Mount Zion,** and **David.** No reasons are given for these choices. Nothing is said that they possess the qualities that **Ephraim** lacked, such as remembering God's saving acts, believing God, or keeping his covenant. Focus is given to God's free choice.

God **beat back his enemies** probably refers to David's defeat of the Philistines, among other opponents (2 Sam. 5:6–25; 8:1–14). The phrase, **he rejected** and **did not choose the tribe of** Ephraim, could refer to a variety of events narrated in Samuel–Kings, including the final destruction of the northern kingdom with the fall of Samaria to the Assyrians (2 Kgs. 17). However, since its counterpart is **but he chose the tribe of** Judah and **he chose** David, we should probably assume that God's refusal of Ephraim refers to the demise of Saul's dynasty under Ish-Bosheth, who was made king over "Ephraim, Benjamin (Saul's tribe) and all Israel" (i.e., the northern kingdom, 2 Sam. 2:9). God's choice of David is shown to be particularly apt because he could **be the shepherd of his people,** just as God had shepherded "his people . . . like a flock" (v. 52). As God led them like sheep, so **David shepherded them . . . ; with skillful hands he led them.**

Not only did God chose a new king, he also chose a new place for **his sanctuary,** namely Mount Zion, **which he loved.** Earlier he had abandoned the tabernacle of Shiloh (v. 60). (The parallelism of tribe and sanctuary in v. 68 implies the same parallelism may apply in v. 67: "the tribe of Ephraim" and "the tent [not **tents**] of Joseph.") This time, however, **he built** his sanctuary . . . **like the earth that he established forever.** Southern Israel has now been entrusted with oversight of Israel's government and religion.

We can now return to the "riddle" implicitly raised at the beginning of this psalm. Like its "teaching," this psalm's mystery is twofold. On the personal level it contains a lesson that each generation must remember God's saving acts and so trust him. But there is also the mystery of why—in view of God's "wonders" whereby he has "redeemed" and "shepherded" his people—do they (we?) treat him with such contempt? On the corporate level, Psalm 78 explains why God's program of salvation has shifted from northern Israel and the exodus, wilderness, and conquest traditions to Judah and the David and Zion traditions. But there is also the mystery of the freedom of God and the grace of God. Both sections closing the respective halves of the psalm present initiatives from God that are the opposite of what we should expect. Without prior cause he acts graciously. We thus have two mysteries: that of human ingratitude and perversion and that of divine freedom and grace.

Additional Note §78

78:41 / **Again and again:** This is a paraphrase of Hb. *wayyāšûbû,* which is lit., "and they turned." Though not the same word, it echoes "the men of Ephraim . . . turned back" (Hb. *hāpᵉkû*), in the parallel section noted in the table above.

§79 God's Reputation and the Destruction of Jerusalem (Ps. 79)

No event in ancient Israel's history was more devastating than the fall of Jerusalem in 587 B.C. and the subsequent exile. It marked not just a national crisis but a religious one as well. As we read in Psalm 74, the people had thereby lost three principal symbols from their God: the land, the king, and the temple. When we readers of the Bible consider the exile, we usually do so from the clear perspective of the Former (e.g., 1–2 Kgs.) and Latter Prophets (e.g., Isa.; Jer.). We may wonder how there could be any legitimate view other than to see it as deserved divine judgment. But the Bible itself also embraces the human response, even one that expresses complaint and frustration to God (v. 5, cf. esp. Ps. 74), though without presuming the people stand in the right (vv. 8–9). Psalm 79 has two main parts: the laments (vv. 1–5) and the petitions (vv. 6–13).

79:1–5 / Although the psalm acknowledges that Jerusalem's devastation is the result of Yahweh's **jealousy** (v. 5), it begins and ends with the agents of that devastation—**the nations.** The psalm centers its appeal to God not by challenging the validity of his judgment but by reporting human atrocities. The first relates to their violation of Yahweh's own property—**your inheritance** (i.e., the land, cf. 68:9) and **Jerusalem**—an act depicted as a sacrilege: **they have defiled your holy temple** (or "palace," Hb. *hêkāl*). The second relates to their butchering of God's people, **your servants** and **your saints** (vv. 2–3). Corpses are left to **birds** and **beasts,** and **blood** is **poured out.** The description of the nations "pouring out blood" may be more than a report; it may also be a cruel irony and a further indication of their acts of sacrilege. At the holy temple, which "they have defiled," they now usurp the role of God's appointed priests, who were to "pour out the blood" of *animal* sacrifices (see esp. Lev. 4). In light of this slaughter, the psalm does raise a complaint against God himself, not for

his anger per se but for its prolonged duration **(How long? . . .
forever?)** and intensity (it burns **like fire**).

79:6–13 / The transition from the laments to the petitions hinges on God's **wrath:** he should now redirect it from his
people (v. 5) to **the nations** (v. 6). Verse 6 provides another link to
the opening laments: as the nations "have poured out blood like
water all around Jerusalem" (v. 3, cf. v. 10), so God should now
pour out his wrath **on** the nations. (Verses 6–7 are echoed in Jer.
10:25. The preceding verse echoes Ps. 6:1.)
     The petitions and the motives (i.e., arguments) supporting
them move around the relational triangle of God, his people, and
the nations. First, the nations are characterized as those who **do
not acknowledge** (lit. "know") you. But, by referring to **the reproach they have hurled at you, O Lord** (v. 12), the psalm makes
clear that this is not mere ignorance but contempt. Second, the
nations' atrocities against the people are mentioned, echoing the
twofold reference to people (**Jacob**, v. 7) and property **(his homeland)** as found in the opening laments. Third, most attention is
devoted to the God-Israel side of the triangle (vv. 8–9, 11, 13).
Here the issue of God's forgiveness of **sins** comes center stage.
(Admissions of sin—25:7, 18; 32:5; 38:3, 18; 41:4; 51:2–3, 9;
103:10—and references to atonement—65:3; 78:38—are comparatively rare in the Psalms.) First, reference is made to **the** sins **of
the fathers** (Hb. *ᶜᵃwōnōt riʾšōnîm*, lit. either "former iniquities" or
"iniquities of the ancestors") and then to **our sins.** This distinction may reflect the situation of the generation born in exile, who
were not directly responsible for the divine judgment of deportation. The psalm claims no merit for the people; it appeals
merely to God's **mercy** and **name** and to the people's pitiful condition **(for we are in desperate need).** The image of the exiles as
groaning **prisoners** who are **condemned to die** (v. 11) expands
further on their lamentable condition.
     Verse 10 makes clear that the preceding appeal to **the glory
of your** name is an appeal to his reputation: **Why should the nations say, "Where is their God?"** By making himself their God,
Yahweh has in some measure tied his reputation to Israel's welfare. To this extent Yahweh—remarkably—has jeopardized his
public image for the sake of this special relationship with his
people. The psalm mounts an argument on the basis of public
perception. (As noted above, it never challenges the justness of
God's anger, known to Israel.) Because the nations will assume

incorrectly that Yahweh's status is equated with Israel's, Yahweh should change his present course of action (cf. Exod. 32:11–12).

But we must not equate God's "name" merely with his reputation, as though it reflected mere self-interest. In the OT and the Psalms in particular, God's "name" functions as the identifying label associated with the revelation of his character and actions (e.g., Pss. 8:1, 9; 9:10; 48:10; 74:7; 75:1; 76:1; 83:16). Thus, his self-revelation to humanity is also at stake here. Psalm 79:9–10 unfolds the significance of God's name or self-revelation by imploring him to manifest three character qualities: mercy, loyalty, and justice. First, **for your name's sake** God is to **help** and **deliver us and forgive** "our sins." Above all, God has associated his name with compassion toward sinners (cf. esp. Exod. 33:18–19; 34:5–7). Second, God is implored to act on behalf of his **servants** (Hb. *ᶜabādîm*). Their relationship with God is twofold: they are servants of the king, who resides in his "palace," and they "serve," that is, worship (Hb. *ᶜbd* denotes both notions), him as their God (cf. Exod. 7:16, etc.). Third, God is petitioned to **make known among the nations** (i.e., to reveal publicly) **that you avenge . . . outpoured blood** (cf. v. 3). Old Testament law was clear that "avenging blood" (i.e., murder) was to be an act of justice, not mere retaliation (Num. 35:19, 21; Deut. 19:12; cf. Ps. 9:7–12, where God as judge "avenges blood"). Thus, much more than self-interest is at stake when it comes to God's name, especially over against these nations who do not yet **call** on that **name** (v. 6).

In effect, the psalm's appeal to God's name pits his judgment on his people against his self-revelation among the nations. God is petitioned to act in accordance with his revealed person and plan, rather than to treat his people as they deserve. In the historical review of Ezekiel 20 (an exilic prophet), Yahweh himself says repeatedly, "But for the sake of my name I did what would keep it from being profaned in the eyes of the nations . . . in whose sight I had brought them out" (i.e., out of Egypt, vv. 9, 14, 22, 44; cf. Ps. 106:8). Because of his interest in maintaining his reputation and a saving relationship to which he has publicly committed himself, God may not punish his people as they deserve.

Closing the psalm is a vow of praise, wherein God's relationship to his people is now likened to that of a shepherd and sheep (as above, echoing both God's people, i.e., **sheep,** and property, i.e., **pasture**). Instead of God's being angry forever (v. 5), there should be heard his **praise forever.**

§80 The Vinedresser and the Plundered Vine of Israel (Ps. 80)

The occasion underlying this corporate prayer psalm appears to be one of extreme national distress: passers-by ravage as they please, burning and destroying (vv. 12–13, 16). The people experience sorrow and strife (vv. 5–6). The question "How long?" implies that this tragedy has persisted for some time. As with most psalms, historical details are omitted so the psalm can be used for any similar national emergency (see the Additional Note).

This psalm, besides exhibiting the normal structure of the prayer psalm, also displays a matching structure of imagery (as in Ps. 44). God is depicted as a shepherd-king and the people as his flock (vv. 1–3, 5). He also appears as a gardener, the people as his vine, and the enemies as cleared weeds and stones (v. 9) and as beasts (vv. 12–13). The final conception is that of God and his divinely appointed king, "the man at your right hand" (v. 17). Each image places God in a role of responsibility for his people. This imagery enables the speaker to present clearly to Yahweh the ironies of the present distress.

80:1–3 / The introductory petitions pick up hymnic language which, by its very utterance, serves as praise of God but also functions to remind God of the roles he assumed in past deeds of salvation, here the exodus and conquest. Yahweh's leading **Joseph** refers to his guidance during the wilderness and conquest periods (cf. v. 8). The motif tying verses 1 and 2 together is the cherubim-ark and its role in Yahweh war (see the Introduction). As this symbolic throne-chariot of Yahweh led the people (hence the shepherd image) to victory over their enemies in Canaan (Num. 10:35; 14:44; Josh. 6:4, etc.), so Yahweh is implored to reenact this tradition by a dramatic appearance in their present distress. The psalm employs the divine name closely associated with the cherubim-ark, namely "Yahweh of hosts" (NIV "LORD God Almighty," vv. 4, 7, 14, 19; cf. 1 Sam. 4:4; 2 Sam. 6:2). In the language of the old tribal alliance, he is called upon to renew his warrior strength to bring about salvation. The psalm continues in petition with a refrain (v. 3) that is repeated with slight variation in verses 7, 19 (cf. v. 14). This refrain establishes the psalm's structure. The imperative, **restore us,** contains what may be an intentional ambiguity. It can mean "cause us to (re)turn," in the sense of repentance (Jer. 31:18; 23:22; Lam. 5:21), and also "restore us," in the sense of a renovation of fortunes. The latter of course has special reference to a reestablishment of the past glories just intimated. The petition of the parallel line echoes the Aaronic blessing (Num. 6.25): **Make your face shine.**

80:4–7 / The lament bemoans the present distress with the assertion that God is its cause. These verses touch upon each sphere of the people's life: religious (v. 4), personal (v. 5) and social (v. 6). Verse 5 in particular presents the irony of God's actions: he who has been the "Shepherd of Israel" has **made them drink tears by the bowlful.** This draws the contrast with past glory all the more graphically and infuses the repeated—though not simply repeated—cry for restoration with heightened urgency.

80:8–19 / The sudden turn in verse 8 presents a striking contrast. As in verses 1–6, the past splendor is that of the exodus-settlement period, and the present crisis is described in a lament. By "transplanting" the nation from Egypt to Palestine God assumed responsibilities like those of a gardener. As a recitation of God's saving history and the splendor that he bestowed on the **vine** (its height and breadth, vv. 10–11), these verses remind God of the historical precedent he himself set in saving his people. The petition of verse 14 offers a twist on the refrain. It pleads for Yahweh to turn not the people but himself. It displays an anthropomorphic progression of Yahweh's turning, looking, seeing, and finally nurturing his vine. The psalm then employs another image that points to a relationship that Yahweh has established, one that carries with it continuing obligations, namely that of **the son you have raised up for yourself.** Israel's king is also described as **the man at your right hand.** Yahweh is invoked to reaffirm his loyalty to the king by placing his **hand** upon the man of his "right hand." The vows of loyalty and of praise (v. 18) tacitly suggest an awareness of the people's past failure. The people still desire to cling to the one who has afflicted them (vv. 4–6).

Overall, the focus of the psalm's argument against God's intense, persisting anger lies in its impressing upon God the investment he has made in the people. This is noted by the imagery, by references to their past history together, and by the mere fact that in the clear majority of cases Yahweh is the subject of the verbs. Even where he is not the grammatical subject, the action follows as a result of divine initiative. The people's dependence on God is made prominent by imagery: they are helpless sheep of the shepherd, a defenseless vine, and even their kingship is a vassalage. The psalm remains fixed upon Yahweh who has bound himself to his people.

Additional Note §80

80:2 / **Before Ephraim, Benjamin and Manasseh:** Because of the tribes listed here (also Joseph, v. 1) and the omission of Judah, one might be inclined to read this as a psalm of the northern kingdom of Israel (922–722 B.C.). But several features tie it to Judah as well, either during the period of the united monarchy or even later. Benjamin was, in fact, part of the southern kingdom with Judah (1 Kgs. 12:21, 23; cf. Jer. 20:2). The allusions to the cherubim-ark point to the Jerusalem temple, and the expression, "the man at your right hand," suits the Davidic king (Ps. 110:1). It may be no coincidence that the choice of these three tribes in particular aligns with the three tribes encamped to the west of the tabernacle during the wilderness period (Num. 2:18–24, 34). Although they were not the first to set out (2:9, 24; 10:14, 22), it was in their direction that Yahweh arose to take Canaan from Transjordan.

§81 Listening to the Liberator (Ps. 81)

Psalm 81 begins like a hymnic praise psalm (vv. 1–5) but the bulk of it is a prophetic oracle (vv. 6–16; cf. Pss. 50; 95). While the divine oracle warns the congregation of their obligation to listen and obey, the psalm opens with a clear call for celebration (so also Ps. 95, another prophetic psalm). Joy is to characterize their relationship because Yahweh has liberated them from servitude and has promised protection and provision. Moreover, the kind of commitment that Yahweh demands is not arduous; it is thoroughly reasonable in view of the gracious relationship he has established.

81:1–5 / The opening imperatives call for corporate praise expressed through singing, shouting, and musical instruments (vv. 1–3). They specify the setting for this psalm as **the day of our Feast,** which points to one of the three major pilgrimage feasts (Exod. 23:15–16; 34:18, 22; Lev. 23:6, 34; Deut. 16:16). In particular, **the ram's horn at the New Moon** points to the trumpet blasts "on the first day of the seventh month" (Lev. 23:23; Num. 29:1), and **when the moon is full** points to "the fifteenth day of the seventh month" when the Feast of Tabernacles begins (Lev. 23:33; Num. 29:12). This festival commemorates when "I had the Israelites live in booths when I brought them out of Egypt" (Lev. 23:43). This festival setting is confirmed by later references to the liberating exodus from **Egypt** (vv. 5–6, 10), Yahweh's answering "out of a thundercloud" (v. 7, pointing either to the Reed Sea deliverance, as in Ps. 77:18, or to the Sinai theophany, as in Exod. 19:16), "the waters of Meribah" (v. 7, Exod. 17:7; Num. 20:13; Pss. 95:8; 106:32), the first commandment given on Mount Sinai (vv. 9–10 and Exod. 20:2–3), and the provision of food (v. 16; Tabernacles was celebrated "when you gather in your crops from the field"; Exod. 23:16; cf. Lev. 23:39; Deut. 16:13, 15).

81:6–10 / This portion of the oracle focuses on Yahweh's liberation from Egyptian slavery and his answering his people's

calls from **distress** (vv. 6–7), and on his consequent demand for
exclusive loyalty (vv. 8–10). The pivot determining Israel's destiny is their act of listening. As Yahweh had **answered** his people
when they **called,** so **my people** are implored to **listen to me**
(vv. 7–8), "but my people would not listen to me" (v. 11). In contrast, "if my people would but listen to me" (v. 13), they would
enjoy Yahweh's favor.

Verses 9–10 echo the first of Sinai's ten "words" and their
opening preface (Exod. 20:2–3). Yahweh bases his command, **you
shall have no foreign god among you,** not on territorial or metaphysical grounds (as in doctrinal monotheism) but on historical
and relational grounds: **I am the Lord your God, who brought
you up out of Egypt.** Israel's loyalty is to follow from Yahweh's
liberation. Yahweh's demand is thoroughly reasonable: since he
liberated them, he is the deity to whom Israel is obliged. Some
scholars believe the phrase **Open wide your mouth and I will fill
it** may have been displaced from its original position at the end
of verse 5. On the other hand, it may belong here as a promise of
food, as implied by the parallel structures of verses 8–10 and
13–16: the repeated phrase, "if my people would but listen to
me" (vv. 8, 13a), Yahweh's demand for obedience (vv. 9, 13b), and
a promise of food (vv. 10c, 16).

81:11–16 / The second portion of the oracle focuses on
Israel's past refusal and punishment (vv. 11–12), and on Yahweh's
renewed promise of protection and provision (vv. 13–16). In
spite of Yahweh's liberation (and promise of provision if v. 10c
belongs here), **my people would not listen to me.** As his demand
of loyalty was reasonable, his judgment is likewise reasonable:
he repays their disloyalty with abandonment—simply allowing
them **to follow their own devices** (cf. Rom. 1:24, 26, 28). Israel, in
effect, brings their own judgment on themselves. The only other
aspect of judgment presented in this psalm is that Israel, by for-
feiting their loyalty to Yahweh, forfeit his promises of subduing
enemies and of providing rich foods (vv. 14–16). The conclusion
of the psalm is open-ended. While their forebears forfeited their
opportunity with Yahweh, the congregation now hearing this
psalm can still make the right choice (vv. 13–16 are comparable to
Isa. 1:19–20).

§82 God Judges the Gods (Ps. 82)

This psalm is unusual because, except for in the opening and closing verses, God is the speaker, not the addressee. The movement from a prophetic oracle (with the opening verse describing the envisaged setting) to a petition makes best sense as a liturgy performed at the temple. The close parallels with the psalms of Yahweh's kingship imply a liturgical setting similar to theirs.

The crux of this psalm lies in determining the identity of the gods (Hb. ʾelōhîm) and addressees of verses 2–7. Are they human judges (cf. Exod. 21:6; 22:8–9, 28) or spiritual beings? Translation must always involve interpretation, and this is evident in the NIV's rendering of this psalm. In verse 1 the literal phrase "the assembly of El/God" is translated as "the great assembly," and "gods" is placed in quotation marks (likewise v. 6), though not indicated in the Hebrew text (Classical Hebrew does not have such punctuation marks). In verse 7 the words "mere" and "other" are not present in the Hebrew text.

The most obvious reading of this psalm, especially from the Hebrew, is to understand the ʾelōhîm and "sons of the Most High" (vv. 1, 6) as "gods" or "heavenly beings/angels." The Hebrew ʾelōhîm has a wider range of meaning than the English terms "God" and "gods." Elsewhere, the OT refers to God's "assembly" or "council" in heaven (Ps. 89:5–8; 1 Kgs. 22:19–23; cf. Isa. 6:1–8; 40:1–11; also Jer. 23:18; Job 15:8). Psalm 89:6 refers to its members as "sons of god(s)" (Hb. beonê ʾēlîm, NIV "heavenly beings"). The same phrase appears in 29:1 (which the NIV renders as "mighty ones"), in which they are to ascribe "glory" (29:1–2, 9) to Yahweh as the divine king enthroned in his heavenly palace/temple (Hb. hêkāl, 29:9–10). In Job 1:6; 2:1 the "sons of God" (NIV, "angels") "came to present themselves before the LORD," presumably as servants of the king. A phrase characteristic of Yahweh's praise is that he is incomparable among the "gods" (Exod. 15:11; Pss. 86:8; 95:3; 96:4; 97:9; 135:5).

Deuteronomy 32:8 (in the Dead Sea Scrolls and the LXX, see NIV margin) tells us, "When the Most High gave the nations their inheritance, when he divided all mankind, he set up boundaries for the peoples according to the number of the sons of God" (reading Hb. *b^enê ʾēl[îm]*). This implies that each people was assigned to a patron heavenly being. Similarly in Psalm 82 we see *ʾelohîm* committed with the administration of justice (vv. 2–4), apparently with respect to "the nations" (v. 8). Daniel 10:13, 20–21 refers to the "prince of Persia" and "the prince of Greece," both of whom are angelic figures presiding over nations. (One may also consider Paul's mention of "principalities and powers" in the NT.) Together these passages imply that Yahweh had assigned spiritual beings or angels to oversee justice for each nation.

Another parallel to Psalm 82, where the gods are on trial, lies in the trial speeches against the nations in Isaiah, especially 41:21–29. Here, in a courtroom setting, Yahweh challenges the gods of the nations to present evidence that they are gods, and in view of their apparent silence he declares, "See, they are all false!" Another indication that the *ʾelohîm* of Psalm 82 are not Israelite judges is that verses 5b and 8b give it an international, and even cosmic perspective, not one confined to the land of Israel.

82:1 / In the opening verse a liturgist or prophetic voice provides the congregation with the psalm's visionary setting in God's heavenly royal council chambers. Here, we enter a world very foreign to us.

82:2–4 / In the oracle of verses 2–7, we hear God's speech to the gods (note esp. v. 6). Verses 2–4 imply the task of administering justice had been committed to these *ʾelohîm*. Judgment is a leitmotif (recurring motif) throughout: the phrases **he gives judgment** (v. 1), **defend** (vv. 2, 3), and **judge** (v. 8) all translate the same Hebrew verb (*špṭ*, "to judge"). We now detect the irony that the judges have now become the judged: the *ʾelohîm*, who have been judges, are now on trial. More specifically, the administration of justice—in God's view—includes rescuing and delivering **the weak** and **the poor**. Judgment in the OT is not merely a legal term confined to the courtroom (cf. the prophets, esp. Amos). Because the powerful can ensure their own fair treatment, it is the particular task of God's appointed authorities to protect the powerless. The Hebrew idiom for **show partiality to the wicked** is literally "lift the face of the wicked" (as in a legal acquittal). (Note these *ᵓelohîm* are not identified with **the wicked** in vv. 2, 4.)

82:5 / The shift from addressing the *ᵓelohîm* directly ("you," vv. 2–4) to referring to them in the third person **(they)** in v. 5 should probably be understood as the impartial verdict on the accused *ᵓelohîm:* they are ignorant, presumably of the ways of justice. (This same shift from direct address to a third-person verdict occurs in the trial speech against the nations' gods in Isa. 41:21–29, esp. v. 29.) In the view of this divine oracle, their failure to judge justly results in nothing less than the collapse of world order: **all the foundations of the earth are shaken.**

82:6–7 / The phrase, **I said** or perhaps "I had said" (v. 6), probably reports an earlier decree: "You are *ᵓelohîm*." Verse 7 then contains the sentencing: "Therefore like man you will die, and like one of the officials you will fall" (lit.; neither **mere** or **other** is present in the Hb. text). The NIV's translation makes it sound like the addressees have been members of those classes of humans and rulers, but the Hebrew text implies that they are to *become* so.

82:8 / Once God has decreed these gods will fall, a liturgist then petitions that God himself **rise up** to **judge the earth.** (In v. 1 he "took his stand" "to judge" the heavenly council.) Since the gods have been deposed as judges, God is summoned to perform their former responsibilities himself. A more literal translation of verse 8b reveals a thought different than that implied in the NIV: "that you may inherit among all the nations" (the Hb. term behind the NIV's **inheritance** is a verb, not a noun). Thus, verse 8b offers not merely a legitimation for the petition that God judge the earth but also a motivation and a positive consequence.

Does Psalm 82 refer to a historical or an imaginary (perhaps mythical) event? If historical, is the event past (perhaps primeval) or future (i.e., eschatological)? These questions are best answered in connection with other psalms employing the motif of divine kingship (esp. the psalms of Yahweh's kingship). They also combine references to the "Most High" (47:2; 97:9), to the gods in the context of the nations (29:1; 96:4–5; 97:7, 9), and to international justice and world order (93:1b; 96:10–13; 98:7–9). They express the realization of Yahweh's kingship in dramatic terms, most notably by virtue of his victory over the chaotic seas (24:1–2, 7–10; 29:3, 9–10; 74:13–17; 93:1–5), but the possibility of a

time when he was not king is never given mention. The worshiping community is called to live now according to this divine
reality revealed to them, but it will not be realized fully and internationally until some time in the future. Israel is privy to
Yahweh's judgments because they currently experience his deliverance from the wicked (97:8, 10–12), but his judging the
nations is yet to be realized (96:10–13; 98:9). Psalm 82 should
probably be read in a similar light. Like Yahweh's victory over
the sea, his decree about the mortality of the gods is portrayed
without a specific time frame. Yet the congregation hearing the
psalm's performance are privy to this decree made in the heavenly council and thus should now regard him as the one God and
supreme judge. Its closing petition anticipates a time in the future when his judgment will be known internationally. Both
Psalm 82 and the psalms of Yahweh's kingship exhibit the tension of living between promise and fulfillment, as is also echoed
in the Lord's prayer: "Your will be done on earth as it is in
heaven" (Matt. 6:10).

The psalms of Yahweh's kingship also reflect a similar depiction of the gods. These psalms praise Yahweh as one who is
"feared" and "exalted above all gods," but at the same time they
claim these gods are mere "idols" (96:4–5; 97:7, 9). The gods are
given mention to show Yahweh's incomparability, but their effectiveness in reality is nullified.

Both Psalm 82 and the psalms of Yahweh's kingship share
close parallels with the Canaanite literature concerning El and
Baal. Psalm 82 reflects the imagery of El (note v. 1, lit. "the assembly of El"), who was the Most High and presider in the divine assembly. The psalms of Yahweh's kingship reflect the imagery of
Baal, who overcame "Prince Sea" and thus became the effectual
king. By using imagery so familiar to residents of the land of Ca-
naan/Israel, whether Canaanite or Israelite, these psalms dramatically presented Yahweh as the sole God in the world of the
gods and the world of nature.

Unlike other corporate prayer psalms, this one actually names the national enemies (vv. 5–8), and so it would seem we have one psalm we can date precisely to a particular crisis. But we cannot correlate the nations listed in this alliance with any event narrated in the OT. This list of ten nations appears simply to summarize those who have been national enemies of the people of God, thus making this psalm appropriate for any instance where national security is threatened. Unlike most other corporate laments where distress is already upon the people, here the distress is imminent. It is at the stage of conspiracy ("they conspire, they plot, they say, they plot, they form an alliance," vv. 3–5) not of actual attack.

83:1–8 / With a strong sense of urgency the introductory petitions try to stir God to action by drawing his attention to how his enemies **are astir** (v. 2). The lament portrays the conflict as one between these foes and God himself: **your foes . . . conspire against your people** and **against those you cherish** (vv. 2–3), and **they form an alliance against you** (v. 5). The poet does not endeavor to draw God into a conflict between human opponents—this dilemma is presented as God's business already. As evidence supporting the claim of conspiracy, a quotation from these foes is included in the prayer to God: **"come," they say, "let us destroy them as a nation"** (v. 4). At stake is the very existence of the nation.

83:9–15 / The next two sections are petitionary and both make comparisons, the first to enemies destroyed in history (vv. 9–12) and the second to elements destroyed in nature (vv. 13–15). The historical comparisons are drawn from the Judges' period, in particular from Deborah's and Barak's defeat of the Canaanite king, **Jabin,** and his commander, **Sisera** (Judg. 4–5) and from Gideon's defeat of **Midian** (Judg. 7) and its leaders, **Oreb and Zeeb** (7:25), and its kings, **Zebah and Zalmunna**

(8:1–21). Included here is another quotation (v. 12) similar to the one from Israel's current enemies. Thus, we see that earlier plotters were destroyed in their own schemes.

This psalm may draw a distinction between the fates desired for the leaders of this conspiracy and their armies. **Their nobles** and **their princes** are to suffer the same fate of Oreb and Zeeb, and of Zebah and Zalmunna. The conspirators are to be destroyed as Sisera and Jabin, both leaders of the Canaanite alliance. The actions to be taken against the enemies in the rest of the petitions (vv. 13–18), however, are not so final. Although the apparent intent of the enemies is Israel's destruction ("let us destroy them as a nation," v. 4), the intent of these concluding petitions does not go that far. **Wind** does not destroy **tumbleweed** and **chaff;** it drives them along. And although **fire consumes** a **forest,** the point is that it sets the human inhabitants on the run: **so pursue them with your tempest and terrify them with your storm.** These images may point to the eventual and hasty retreat of Israel's aggressors in battle.

83:16–18 / The final petitions (vv. 16–18) appear to show the same restraint. While a request is made that **they perish in disgrace,** this does not denote their deaths but simply their defeat, because the petitions both before and after seek to bring them to shame with the ultimate purpose of bringing them to the knowledge that **the LORD . . . alone** is **the Most High.** One of these petitions also echoes an earlier lament: they who plotted to destroy the memory of the name of Israel (v. 4) must **seek your name, O LORD** (v. 16).

§84 The Pilgrim's Longing to "See" the God of Zion (Ps. 84)

Psalm 84 was probably sung on behalf of pilgrims, either at the beginning of their journey or upon their arrival at the temple. It explicitly confesses the blessed state of "those . . . who have set their hearts on pilgrimage" (v. 5, the Hb. text here is somewhat unclear, but the NIV presents a reasonable interpretation). As they pass through various regions "till each appears before God in Zion," they require strength to make the pilgrim journey (vv. 6–7). Although this blessing seems to encourage hope for the anticipated journey, the opening descriptions of the temple (vv. 1–4) imply the temple is now in sight. The reference to "appearing before God" may help us to be more specific about the location of this psalm in Israel's liturgical calendar. This phrase is used repeatedly in connection with the three annual pilgrimage festivals (Exod. 23:15, 17; 34:23–24; Deut. 16:16; cf. Isa. 1:12). (Further on the history of this phrase, see on 42:2.) "The autumn rains" (v. 6) may connect it particularly to the Feast of Tabernacles, which was closely connected with Yahweh's bestowal of rain (Zech. 14:16–19).

This psalm bears connections with other psalms of the temple. Psalm 42–43, another pilgrim psalm, also uses this phrase "appearing before God" (v. 2, NIV "meet with God"). Like our psalm (v. 2), it describes the pilgrim's physical yearning (cf. 63:1, another pilgrim psalm) for the living God (42:2, a divine title found only in these two psalms within the Psalter). Both also draw an analogy with animal creatures to express the sense of attachment to God's house (birds and their nest in 84:3, and the deer and streams of water in 42:1). Psalm 65 is a hymn probably sung at one of the pilgrimage festivals (esp. the Feast of Unleavened Bread) and it too celebrates the blessed state of "those who dwell in your house" (84:4; 65:4) and the good things that Yahweh dispenses from the temple (84:11; 65:4). Both psalms also refer to the blessing of rains (84:6; 65:9–10). Other pilgrim psalms (61:6–7; 63:11) also make special intercession for the king (84:9). Like the liturgies of temple entry (15:2; 26:1, 11; see the Introduction), the pilgrims who may enter the temple and receive its blessings are "those whose walk is blameless" (or more accurately, "those who walk with integrity," v. 11). (Note also the combination of the two divine titles, "my King and my God," in 84:3 and 5:2.)

We can discern the psalm's structure by making the following observations. It alternates between addressing God directly in the second person (vv. 1, 3–5, 8–10, 12) and referring to him in the third person (vv. 2, 6–7, 11). Each of the verses introducing the four "you" sections contains the name "Yahweh of hosts" (NIV "LORD Almighty," vv. 1, 3, 8, 12). Thus, the psalm has four parts (vv. 1–2, 3–7, 8–11, 12). The first "you" section is comprised of hymnic praise (vv. 1, 3), the second of blessing (vv. 4–5), the third of an intercession for the king (vv. 8–9), and the fourth of another blessing (v. 12). In the three "he" sections we probably hear the supporting testimony of a liturgist speaking on behalf of individual pilgrims. It is possible that matching the change in address to God is a change of speakers: a priest recites the "you" sections and a representative pilgrim the "he" sections. The psalm's liturgical function is also implied by the alternation between individual ("my prayer" in v. 8) and corporate references ("our shield" in v. 9).

84:1–7 / The psalm opens with an exclamation of praise for **your dwelling place.** A speaker then confesses that he **yearns . . . for the living God.** In the context of the liturgical psalms, this longing will be fulfilled specifically at **the courts of the LORD,** as the parallel expression shows. In the image of nesting birds, verse 3 expands on this attachment to Yahweh's temple, though now praising him directly. The titles, **my king and my God** (i.e., my personal guardian Deity), bring together the corporate and individual roles that Yahweh fulfills for his people. The confessions, **Blessed are . . . ,** are not formal blessings pronounced over the pilgrims because they are addressed to Yahweh as expressions of praise. (Moreover, the Hb. word for **blessed** in vv. 4, 5, 12 is *ʾašrê,* which may also be rendered "happy" or "fortunate," not *bārûk.*) The fortunate estate of Yahweh's pilgrims, who journey through a transformed oasis, exemplify his virtues. **Those who dwell in your house** may refer to the

Levitical personnel, though in 27:4 and possibly 23:6 the same Hebrew verb for "dwell" *(yšb)* applies to pilgrims generally. We should not imagine that the promise then made to the worshipers, **they go from strength to strength,** guarantees an unbroken increase of strength. Implied in this journey are obstacles and opposition, but Yahweh will ensure that **each appears before God in Zion** (cf. Isa. 35).

84:8–12 / Yahweh is addressed again, this time with a general petition that Yahweh **look with favor** on the king, the **anointed one.** The psalm places the king in a role of significance that reflects his importance for Israelite pilgrims. First, he is Yahweh's "anointed one." Second, the psalm earlier acknowledges Yahweh as "king" (v. 3). Third, while the king is **our shield,** Yahweh is the ultimate **sun and shield** (v. 11). So the psalm immediately confesses, **better is one day in your courts**— that is, at Yahweh's temple-palace, not the king's palace (1 Kgs. 7:9, 12)— **than a thousand elsewhere.** As is prominent in the temple entry psalms (see the Introduction), this psalm explicitly rejects the company of **the wicked** (cf. esp. 15:4; 26:4–5) and promotes "walking with integrity." These moral choices appear to be addressed to the pilgrims directly (God is referred to in vv. 10b–11). Rounding off the psalm is summative praise extolling the fortunes of **the man who trusts in you.**

§85 A Forgiven People Seeking Forgiveness and God's Promise of **Shalom** *(Ps. 85)*

This psalm reflects the tension of living between promise and fulfillment. When the people of God had experienced the beginnings of his grace in the return from exile (vv. 1–3), they still suffered hardships in the early postexilic period (vv. 4–7). At the same time, they were still hearing future blessings promised to them (vv. 8–13). It reflects the tension of having been forgiven and still being in need of forgiveness. This psalm also shows us that OT worship consisted of more than a mere monologue; Yahweh was expected to answer. The first half consists of prayer addressed to him (vv. 1–7) and the second half of an anticipation of his answer (vv. 8–13). The enveloping concern of the psalm is that of the land and its harvest (vv. 1, 12).

85:1–7 / **You restored the fortunes** (or, "you turned the captivity," *šabtā šᵉbût [Kethib]* or *šᵉbît [Qere]*) is a phrase that appears in other passages referring to restoration from exile (e.g., 14:7 = 56:6; 126:4; Jer. 29:14; Ezek. 29:14). (See further the Additional Note on 126:1, 4.) The end of the Babylonian captivity marked the time when **you forgave** (lit. "lifted up" or "carried") **the iniquity of your people** (cf. Ps. 79:8; Isa. 40:2) and when **you . . . turned from your fierce** (lit. "burning") **anger** (cf. 74:1; 79:5). This dramatic turning point is described first in terms of the material changes for **your land** and for **Jacob,** then in terms of "your people's" religious status, and finally in terms of God's disposition **(your wrath).** While these about-faces are phrased similarly to hymnic praise ("you have done thus and such"), these verses do not serve as praise. They establish the precedent of God's mercy, which forms the basis for the subsequent petitions and rhetorical questions (vv. 4–7).

At first reading, verses 4–6 sound redundant in light of what has just been claimed. Why should we continue to hear of God's **anger** (vv. 3, 5) and the need for "restoration" (vv. 1, 4) if God had, in fact, **set aside all** his wrath at the decisive pivotal point of the return from exile? The Hebrew petition translated, **Restore us** (Hb. *šwb*, a key verb used in vv. 1, 3, 4, 6, 8), can also mean "turn us." Its ambiguity thus reflects both the people's need for physical restoration in the land and their need for personal conversion to Yahweh (cf. 80:3, 7, 19). This twofold need in the early postexilic period is confirmed by other OT passages. First, although God had opened the door for the exiles to return to their homeland, since the early postexilic period was marked by agricultural hardships (Hag. 1:6, 9–11; 2:15–17; Joel 1:4, 12) there was still the need for physical restoration in the land. Second, in Isaiah 40–55 God had promised he would return to redeem Zion (Isa. 52:8–9), but the people appear to have assumed God would do this automatically regardless of the people's heart. Hence, in the third section of Isaiah (56–66), God repeats the same promise and makes explicit the condition: "to those in Jacob who repent of (or 'turn from' [Hb. *šwb*]) their sins" (59:20). Psalm 85 thus fits this period of postexilic restoration that marked the end of God's wrath on Judah's iniquity (vv. 1–3), but because Judah continues to be in need of "turning" (i.e., repentance), God's anger is prolonged (vv. 4–5). Verse 8 will reiterate this same theme: "let them not return (Hb. *šwb*) to folly" (or as it reads in the LXX, which is a plausible reading of the Hb. consonants, "to those who turn their heart to him").

The more negative petitions and rhetorical questions of verses 4–5 are matched by the more positive rhetorical questions and petitions of verses 6–7. Instead of prolonging **your** anger, the psalm asks, would you not rather **revive us again, that your people may rejoice in you?** It also petitions God for his **love** and **salvation.** Regrettably the NIV translation overlooks a key wordplay (Hb. *šwb*) in verse 6a: "Will you not *turn* (and) revive us?" The restoration of the relationship requires both God's "turning us" (v. 4) and God's "turning" towards us (as BDB notes, this Hb. idiom in v. 6 means to "*reverse* one's action," p. 998).

85:8–13 / The appeal having been spoken to God, a liturgist now steps forward and turns the congregation to "listening": **I will listen to what God the LORD will say.** God's answer comes not in first-person speech but in hymnic language that echoes the announcements of **salvation** heard in Isaiah. **His** salvation **is near** (Isa. 51:5; 56:1), **that his glory may dwell in our**

land (Isa. 40:5; 46:13; 58:8; 60:1–2; cf. 6:3). In highly poetic language, the attributes of **love, faithfulness, righteousness,** and **peace** are personified as joyfully greeting each other (v. 10), and **faithfulness** and **righteousness** are portrayed as the earthly and heavenly (**Heaven** can also be rendered "the skies") partners in the agricultural cycle (v. 11). **Righteousness** is mentioned a third time as Yahweh's herald (v. 13). Other passages in the Psalms and Isaiah portray these attributes as heralds/escorts (Pss. 43:3; 89:14; Isa. 58:8) and as agricultural produce (Ps. 72:3, 7; Isa. 32:15–17; cf. also Ps. 36:5–6; Hos. 2:19–23). These relational attributes are mentioned in explicit connection with agricultural production: **The LORD will indeed give what is good, and our land will yield its harvest** (cf. Ps. 67:6). For worshipers of Yahweh the religious-social world and the natural world are not distinct, because one God superintends both. How humans act has direct bearing on the natural ecosystem. But the psalm climaxes not with a fruitful harvest but with nothing less than Yahweh's own advent: Righteousness **goes before him and prepares the way for his steps** (cf. the herald in Isa. 40:3–5, 9–11; 52:7–10; 62:11). (Cf. also Ps. 96:10–13, a psalm of Yahweh's kingship, where the heavens, the earth, and the fields respond with joy at Yahweh's coming to "judge the world in righteousness.") While agricultural productivity is an immediate concern, the ultimate concern is the people's relationship with God and his presence among them.

§86 A Servant Appeals to His Lord for Protection (Ps. 86)

This prayer of the individual consists of three sections of petition and hymnic praise. In each section the hymnic praise grants assurance to the worshiper and motivation to Yahweh to make good on his praise. An odd feature that strikes readers familiar with psalms is that, *after* verses 12–13 have nicely rounded off the preceding prayer with a vow of praise, verse 14 resumes the lament and introduces for the first time the issue of personal enemies. If Psalm 86 had closed at verse 13, no one would have suspected any verses were missing. But closer examination reveals several linguistic links that tie the psalm together, as noted in the discussion below. Furthermore, the problems of making sense of the psalm's development and discerning a train of thought do not end here. Why, for example, does verse 6 repeat the cry for Yahweh to hear after the opening petition, "Hear," and after the interjected hymnic praise of verse 5? Readers may also be disappointed by the frequent use of stock phrases. Psalm 86 adds nothing to the Psalms in terms of its individual phrases— most of them are paralleled elsewhere. But it is unique in the way it combines these phrases, using them to link verses and create a network of meaning. If we use an analogy of a deck of cards, the uniqueness of Psalm 86 lies not in what is on the face of the cards but in its particular hand of cards.

86:1–5 / In the first section, the psalm bases the plea, **have mercy on me,** on the claim, "for to you I call" (v. 3, note the original word order). In support, the hymnic praise then promises, **You are... abounding in love to all who call to you.** Another link and support is found in the term "(devoted) love" (Hb. *ḥesed*): the prayer claims, **for I am devoted** (Hb. *ḥāsîd*, v. 2), and the hymn claims Yahweh is abounding in (devoted) love (Hb. *ḥesed*, v. 5). Here we discover that the familiar or stock phrases are not a weakness of the psalm but a strength. Moreover, the

assuring hymnic praise of verse 5 is not an ad hoc attempt to pac-
ify the fears of a worshiper, but is a famous confession tested
through generations of believers (Exod. 34:6; Num. 14:18; Neh.
9:17; Jonah 4:2; Joel 2:13; Pss. 103:8; 145:8).

86:6–13 / The repeated invocation, **Hear my prayer**
(v. 6), begins a new strophe and links it with the opening petitions by the terms "hear" (lit., "[give] ear") and **mercy.** The subsequent confession of trust appears to build on the assurance
provided by the hymnic praise of the first strophe: because "you
are . . . abounding in love to all who call to you" (v. 5), **I will call to
you** (v. 7). Thus, while the first strophe pleads, "answer me" (v. 1),
the second expresses confidence that God **will answer me** (v. 7).
The hymnic praise of this strophe is also composed of time-tested
affirmations (e.g., Exod. 15:11; Deut. 3:24; Ps. 66:4; 89:6). At its
center is the incomparability of Yahweh himself (**you** in vv. 8, 10)
and of his **deeds** (in vv. 8, 10) **among the gods.** It thus follows logically from this theological affirmation that **all the nations you
have made . . . will bring glory to your name.** We should not
quickly assume this refers merely to a future reality at the end of
time, because other psalms describe foreign nations offering tribute to Yahweh at the preexilic temple (see Ps. 47, esp. v. 9, and Ps.
68, esp. vv. 18, 29; cf. 66:4). In response to this affirmation of nations' bringing "glory to your name," the worshiper petitions
that I may fear your name, and then vows, **I will glorify your
name forever.** This petition seeks for Yahweh's influence not
only in the worshiper's actions but also in his inner attitudes:
give me an undivided heart, that is, a single heart to will one
thing. As a result, he can promise, **I will praise you . . . with all
my heart.** The psalm thus seeks a single heart to worship the one
God (v. 10). This may be an echo of the Shema: because "the LORD
is one" Israel is called to "love the LORD your God with all your
heart" (Deut. 6:4–5; cf. also Jer. 32:39; Ezek. 11:19). The worshiper
thus demonstrates that he *wants* to do what all nations *must* do
because of who Yahweh is. Similarly, as Yahweh is hymned to be
great (v. 10) and abounding in love (v. 5), so the worshiper will
claim, **for great is your love toward me** (v. 13).

86:14–17 / As already noted, the lament opening the
third strophe seems out of place, but now that we have discov-
ered how the poet links his material by key terms we can see how
verse 14 appropriately follows verse 13. While Yahweh will have
"delivered me," now **a band of ruthless men seeks my** soul (NIV

life). (Note that in v. 4 the speaker had committed his soul to Yahweh.) And as "your love is great *upon me*" (lit., v. 13), so now "the arrogant have arisen *upon me*" (lit.). The psalm thus presents the full nature of the distress in stages. The hymnic praise of this strophe (v. 15) contains the fuller formula of praise abbreviated earlier in verse 5. The motifs of Yahweh's being merciful (NIV **gracious**) and **abounding in love** are thus repeated again. This is one instance where the worshiper in prayer anticipates Yahweh's hymnic praise; he had earlier expressed the desire to "walk in your truth" (Hb. *ʾemet*, v. 11) and now we hear that God is abounding in "*truth*" (*ʾemet*, NIV **faithfulness**). The petitions of this section thus ask him to actualize his praiseworthy **mercy on me** (thus echoing vv. 3, 6, 15) and to "make with me a sign for good" (lit.), **that my enemies may see it and be put to shame** (v. 17). Here the speaker once again identifies himself as **your servant,** thus tying the psalm's closing (v. 16) with its opening (v. 2).

The psalm bases the worshiper's appeal to God and his grounds of assurance on five motifs. First, the self-description of poor and needy (v. 1) appeals to the special interest Yahweh has in those who have no societal resources (see, e.g., 9:18; 40:17). Second, three times in the opening and closing strophes the self-description, "your servant," is used, and seven times Yahweh is addressed as "Lord" (Hb. *ʾadōnāy*). The psalm thus presupposes all the mutual responsibilities that a servant-lord relationship entails. Third, the speaker is described as "devoted" or "loyal" (Hb. *ḥāsîd*, v. 2), and Yahweh is described as "abounding in loyal love" (Hb. *ḥesed*, vv. 5, 13, 15). Similarly, the psalm presupposes all that a covenant relationship entails. We must keep in mind here that these self-descriptions do not follow from the character of the actual composer; they are to be adopted by worshipers if they wish the psalm to have its desired effect.

The fourth motif on which the psalm is founded is that of historical precedents. As noted above, the psalm quotes confessions well rooted in Israel's historical experience of Yahweh, especially from the exodus period. As Yahweh has been **compassionate and** gracious and abounding in love in the past, so he should do in the present. The fifth motif is related to the fourth. The psalm incorporates individual experience with corporate experience. As the nation has received God's mercy, so should its individuals. And as all the nations will bring tribute to Yahweh, so individual worshipers can do now from the heart.

Among the psalms of Zion, Psalm 87 makes the most positive, explicit statement about the nations. In the preceding songs, "kingdoms fall" (46:6), "kings" and their "forces" are "destroyed" (48:4–7), and "the neighboring lands" and "kings of the earth" bring tribute after a stunning defeat (76:11–12), but here they are "born in Zion"! The placement of this psalm after 86:9 is probably no accident: "all the nations you have made will come and worship before you."

87:1–2 / The opening verses express Yahweh's claim to **Zion,** a claim characteristic of the Zion psalms though expressed in various forms (48:1–3; cf. 46:4; 76:2; 122:3–4; 132:13–14). The opening verse is one line instead of the normal two. It is possible verse 5c was originally its second line (transposed in scribal error), with which it would form a better parallel than in its present location (**set his foundation** and "establish"; the latter Hb. verb is also used of Zion in 48:8, where it is rendered "make secure").

87:3–7 / Verse 3 addresses the **city of God** directly (cf. 122:2). Within the horizons of the Psalms and the OT, verse 4 catches us by surprise, but we must also note that it comes by way of a prophetic oracle. Among the psalms of Zion, however, we may compare the oracle: "I will be exalted among the nations" (46:10; another oracle is found in 132:14–18). What is surprising in 87:4 is that the longtime enemies of Zion are listed as **those who acknowledge me.** Egypt, signified by **Rahab,** and **Babylon** were the great empires on opposite sides of Israel. **Philistia** and **Tyre** were their immediate neighbors.

The commentary on Psalms 46 and 48 has noted several connections these psalms of Zion have with Yahweh's kingship. In a similar vein, the psalms of Yahweh's kingship not only command the "families of nations" to "worship the LORD" and "bring an offering . . . into his courts" (96:7–9; cf. 98:4–6), they actually describe them as being present at Jerusalem festivals and included with Israel: "The nobles of the nations assemble as (or 'with') the people of the God of Abraham" (47:9). The nations listed in our psalm show some affinity to the book of Isaiah, in which Zion theology is prominent. Only Isaiah's collection of oracles against nations includes each of them (Isa. 13–23). Outside Psalm 87, Rahab is used as a reference to Egypt only in Isaiah 30:7 and 51:9. **Cush,** in Upper Egypt or Ethiopia, is prominent in Isaiah (18:1; 20:3–5; 37:9). The twenty-fifth Dynasty of Egypt was Cushite. Also comparable is Isaiah's vision of "many peoples" making a pilgrimage to "the mountain of the LORD's temple" (Isa. 2:1–4; cf. Mic. 4:1–3). Later, because Yahweh's "house will be called a house of prayer for all nations," "foreigners who bind themselves to the LORD" are among those to whom he gives "an everlasting name" (Isa. 56:3–8; cf. 19:25). This action is perhaps comparable to his recording of these foreigners **in the register of the peoples** in our psalm. This seems to allude to the adopting of foreigners as citizens of Zion. In addition, Zion is depicted as a mother who is surprised by the number of children she has "borne" (Hb. *yld,* Isa. 49:20–21; 54:1; 66:7–8; cf. 60:4–5, 9). This image is comparable to the birth image in our psalm (Hb. *yld* in vv. 4–6). Zechariah also refers to "nations" who "will be joined with the LORD" and so become his "people" (2:11; 8:22–23; 14:16–19).

"The register of the peoples" may allude to a "book of life" that records the names of "the righteous" (Exod. 32:32–33; Isa. 4:3; Mal. 3:16–18; cf. Pss. 40:7; 56:8; 69:27–28; 109:13–15; Isa. 56:5; Ezek. 13:9). This image may stem from the temple entry procedures of the gate, where the "righteous" were identified and permitted to enter and worship (see the Introduction). In Malachi 3:16 this book is called "a scroll of remembrance" (Hb. *sēper zikkārôn*), which is "written in his presence." In the register found in our psalm, Yahweh promises to **record** (lit. "cause to be remembered," Hb. *ʾazkîr*) these nations.

§88 From the Darkness of the Grave (Ps. 88)

88:1–18 / Premature death is the subject of this prayer psalm of the individual. Like other psalms of sickness (Pss. 38; 41), it complains of social alienation (vv. 8, 18). As a psalm of the individual, the primary tradition on which it is based is that Yahweh should answer with deliverance when called upon, as summarized in the opening address, **the God who saves me.** Though the distress is extreme and prolonged—**all day long** the **terrors** of death **surround me** (vv. 16–17)—it has not muted the speaker's prayers. In fact, the psalm's tripartite structure (vv. 1–9a, 9b–12, 13–18) is determined by the three references to persistent prayer: **day and night I cry out before you** (vv. 1–2), **I call to you, O LORD, every day** (v. 9b), and **in the morning my prayer comes before you** (v. 13).

What is most striking about this psalm, however, is that in spite of the opening address, which claims God as the speaker's only hope, God is also his primary adversary. The psalm consistently attributes the cause of the affliction to Yahweh himself, as demonstrated by the many verses that begin with **you** and **your** (vv. 5–8, 14, 16–18). The principal reason for this lies in God's apparent lack of response to earlier prayers, which does not fit with the tradition fundamental to the individual prayer psalms. The speaker has cried day and night, yet Yahweh has evidently given no answer (v. 1). Because of this silence the speaker is compared with the dead since they too are not "remembered" by Yahweh and are **cut off** from his hand (vv. 4–5). The psalm then pushes this to its logical conclusion: **You have put me in the lowest pit** (v. 6). The conviction that Yahweh should answer and preserve his worshipers from premature death (vv. 10–12) provides further grounds for complaint. Hence, the speaker again asserts that he has cried to Yahweh for help (v. 13), but, since no help is forthcoming, the psalm asserts Yahweh has rejected him and hidden his face (v. 14). Thus, behind this hostile treatment lies an adverse disposition. The terrors of sickness and death he suffers result

from Yahweh's wrath (vv. 15–17; cf. v. 7). Even social relationships are determined by God (vv. 8, 18).

In view of this divine hostility the central concern of the
psalm's appeal is God himself. Thus, like most individual laments it describes the affliction in pitiful terms that would
move Yahweh, but unlike most it asserts that he is the problem.
In sum, the psalm appeals to God by addressing God as the
only source of help, by referring to persistent but unanswered
prayers, by depicting the extreme hardship as a divine act, by
posing questions that argue for God's best interest, and by appealing to the rights of the afflicted. The only formal petition is
in verse 2, where Yahweh is requested to give this **prayer** and **cry**
a proper hearing. The absence of any petition for intervention
suggests the form of deliverance required is self-evident from
the lament itself.

The diversity of images to depict the nearness to death
combine to convey the horror that presses in upon the speaker.
He approaches **the grave** (vv. 5, 11), and is likened to one going
down to the "pit," which suggests the image of a cistern, a place
dark and mucky, with no means of escape. Related to the cistern
image is the figure of drowning: Your terrors "surround me" **like
a flood** (v. 17), and **you have overwhelmed me with all your
waves** (v. 7). Other terms describing the realm of the dead inten-
sify the sense of horror: "the lowest pit," **the darkest depths**
(v. 6), **destruction** (v. 11) and **the land of oblivion** (v. 12). Those
inhabiting this region are **like a man without strength** (v. 4) and
like "shadows" (lit., NIV **those who are dead,** v. 10). Reference is
also made to emotional exhaustion: **my eyes are dim with grief**
(v. 9) and **I am in despair** (v. 15). The speaker refers to himself as
being "silenced" (NIV **destroyed,** v. 16), which is also characteristic of the dead, particularly because they are disqualified from
singing the praise of God (vv. 10–12). This last aspect becomes
the most horrifying of all: the dead are cut off from Yahweh (v. 5)
and from the worship of Yahweh (vv. 10–12) because he ceases to
perform saving wonders beyond the boundaries of death (v. 10).
The enigmatic phrase **I am confined and cannot escape** (v. 8b)
probably continues to describe the speaker's condition as one
confined to the grave. As one considered dead, he cannot join
his companions in the land of the living. Each reference to his
alienation thus appears to climax in his confinement to the place
of the dead. Verse 8 speaks of his inability to associate with the
living, and verse 18 of his only companion, **darkness.**

An additional element of the appeal is the rhetorical questions that argue that "the dead do not praise Yahweh" (vv. 10–12; see further on Ps. 30). Here the psalm points to Yahweh's praiseworthy attributes and deeds—his **wonders,** his **love,** his **faithfulness,** his **righteous deeds**—and asks, If you permit your worshipers to die, who then will you save and who will extol your kindness? These questions are phrased in general terms but the psalm then applies them to the speaker's own case: **But I cry to you for help.** Evidently the speaker has received no such wonders. Hence another rhetorical question follows: **Why, O LORD, do you reject me?** This is the enigma that permeates the texture of this psalm: why should the God who desires to save and receive praise deny deliverance to the speaker?

§89 A Hymn of Yahweh's Kingship, an Oracle of David's Kingship, and a Lament over David's Defeat (Ps. 89)

Psalm 89, in its final form, is a royal prayer psalm. It has three distinct sections: a hymn celebrating Yahweh's right to cosmic kingship (vv. 1–18); a prophetic oracle outlining the Davidic covenant (vv. 19–37); and a lament over the king's battle defeat (vv. 38–51). The last verse is a doxology for Book III of the Psalter (note that each Book closes with a doxology) and not, therefore, a constituent part. The lament appears to have been written in light of the oracle. It shares much of its key terminology, and the actions attributed to Yahweh in the lament are the reverse of those attributed to him in the oracle. Since the lament section does not pick up terms or motifs found in the hymn, we can account for its inclusion only by assuming that it was integrally joined to the oracle. Most probably the hymn, in which Yahweh's kingship is established, and the oracle, in which the Davidic kingship is established, were written earlier for the enthronement of a new Davidic king. The lament, occasioned by a battle defeat, was then written following the pattern of these already established promises. The lament thus builds on an earlier psalm so as to establish the basis for the appeal to Yahweh.

89:1–4 / In the hymn's introductory summary the liturgist proclaims his intention to acclaim Yahweh's **love** and **faithfulness,** the two key terms of the psalm. Verses 3–4 are inserted into the hymn of Yahweh's kingship to give a foretaste of the subsequent oracle concerning **David** and his **covenant,** the essence of which is the promise of a stable dynasty (v. 4).

89:5–18 / The basis for Yahweh's kingship is first established in **the heavens** and especially by his incomparable **faithfulness** and awesomeness in **the council of the holy ones** (vv. 5–8). The next arena in which Yahweh's kingship is established is the **sea** and the **earth** (i.e., the dry land, vv. 9–12). As is frequently mentioned in connection with divine kingship, Yahweh is declared superior to **the surging sea. Rahab,** in this context, denotes the sea monster of chaos (Job 9:13; 26:12; cf. the alternative name "Leviathan" in Pss. 74:14; 104:26; Isa. 27:1; Job 3:8). In verse 12a, we should probably read, **You created** "Zaphon and the seas." (Hb. *ṣāpôn* can denote either **north** or Mount Zaphon; see on 48:2. Instead of *yāmîn*, **the south,** we should read *yāmîm*, "the seas," following the LXX.) Thus, Psalm 89 goes beyond Genesis 1:2, where "the deep" or "the waters" are simply there as preexisting matter. "Zaphon" was considered by the Canaanites to be the dwelling of Baal. Also in focus are the mountains, considered the "pillars of the earth" (Pss. 18:7; 104:5–6; Job 9:5–6).

Verses 13–18 focus on the visible symbol of Yahweh's kingship—the cherubim-throne: **Righteousness and justice are the foundation of your throne** (cf. 97:2). Verses 15 is literally, "Blessed is the people who know shouting." This alludes to the shouting that accompanies the ascent of the ark into the sanctuary (see on 47:1, 5, 8, which also refers to "his holy throne"). In this context, the reference to **those . . . who walk in the light of your presence** probably alludes to the ritual procession that accompanied the ark's ascent (see commentary on 68:1, 17–18, 24–27, 32–35). An attribute frequently associated with the cherubim-ark is Yahweh's **strength** (vv. 13, 17; cf. 68:33–35; 78:61; 132:8), which here exhibits itself in the exaltation of the king (vv. 17–18).

89:19–37 / The hymn thus makes a smooth transition to the oracle concerning Yahweh's covenant with David and his dynasty. Instead of the normal messenger formula ("thus says the LORD" to his people) the verse introducing the oracle continues in direct address to God **(you spoke** and **you said),** thus incorporating the divine speech into the people's praise. Yahweh bestows on the Davidic king the same elements that are inherent to his own kingship: exaltation (vv. 16–18 and 19b–21), the crushing of foes (vv. 9–10 and 22–23), and supremacy (vv. 5–8 and 24–27). These promises give particular attention to how the Davidic monarch will stand relative to enemies and other peoples. In battle, he will subdue them and he will establish an empire. Focus is then drawn to the special relationship that will prevail between Yahweh and David, and then to his **line** (vv. 26–29). This promise does contain an **if** clause; the consequence is punishment but not annulment (vv. 30–33). The next quatrain (four line stanza) expands on the eternal stability of this covenant (vv. 34–37). Yahweh attaches it to his very **holiness.**

We should note this version of the Davidic covenant escalates the promises found in 2 Samuel 7. The Davidic king is not merely "my son" (2 Sam. 7:14) but **my firstborn.** His name will not merely be "great, like the names of the greatest men of the earth" (2 Sam. 7:9), he will be **the most exalted of the kings of the earth.** He will have not only rest from enemies (2 Sam. 7:10–11) but an empire (Ps. 89:25). He will have not only a successor ("he" in 2 Sam. 7:12–15) but a dynasty ("they" in Ps. 89: 30–32). And the "forever" of 2 Sam. 7:16 expands into nearly 5 verses in Psalm 89 (vv. 33b–37).

89:38–52 / Without transition the divine oracle is "interrupted" with a voice charging Yahweh with having **renounced the covenant** that he just swore would be established forever. A battle defeat is described in language that is the reversal of the preceding oracle. As the success of the Davidic dynasty was presented as a result of Yahweh's action, so now its demise is traced back to his action. The anointed one (v. 20) who was able to call God "my Father" (v. 26) is now rejected as an object of wrath (v. 38). The divinely initiated covenant (v. 3), which even in view of human violation (v. 31) would not be violated by God (v. 34), is now spurned and violated (NIV **defiled,** v. 39). Thus, the **servant,** once the recipient of the promised covenant (vv. 3, 20), is now the disappointed covenant-partner (v. 39). Yahweh had promised to exalt the people (vv. 16–17), and especially the king (vv. 19, 24) over his foes (v. 23), but instead Yahweh has **exalted** the king's **foes** (v. 42). Rejoicing, by virtue of Yahweh's name, was to characterize the people of God (vv. 15–16), but instead Yahweh gives the foe cause for rejoicing (v. 42). In sum, Yahweh's indestructible love (vv. 1–2, 14, 24, 28, 33) and faithfulness (vv. 1–2, 5, 8, 24, 33), which were once the sworn guarantors of the Davidic covenant (vv. 3, 35), are now lost from sight (v. 49).

Within the stipulations of the covenant, this reversal could not be explained from the human side. Transgression would be chastised, but it was not grounds for dissolving the treaty (vv. 30–33). Moreover, the closing lines of the hymnic section (vv. 33–37) make clear that God had vowed to stand by his word unconditionally. Human transgression could not break it

(vv. 30–33); divine holiness would not break it (vv. 34–37). Thus, because the resolution of this dilemma is not possible from the human side, it is instead committed to God. The final section thus calls on Yahweh to remember speedily his **great love** and **faithfulness**, the key terms of the psalm, which he **swore to David.**

§90 *Human Frailty and Sin, Divine Eternality and Anger, and a Prayer for Mercy (Ps. 90)*

Psalm 90 is a corporate prayer psalm bemoaning the brevity and travail of life. Although verses 2–6 speak of life's transience as a general condition of humankind, verses 13–17 intimate that a more particular dilemma has occasioned these reflections. The petitions, "Relent, O LORD! How long will it be?" (v. 13a) and "Make us glad for as many days as you have afflicted us" (v. 15), imply the people's current condition is considered harsher than usual. The work of their hands, for all their toil (v. 10), appears to decay right before them (v. 17). The people themselves feel destined to a life that is futile (vv. 9–10). The psalm does not point to any particular event or time period, but it does fit well with the hardships of the postexilic period (cf. Ps. 85 and esp. the references to God's anger). It may have served originally as a public prayer of penance, influenced by the wisdom tradition.

Several observations should make clear the psalm's structure. Verses 7–11 cohere as a lament, and verses 12–17 consist of petitions. Verses 1–6 have some hymnic features, though they initially sound similar to the subsequent lament (esp. "you turn men back to dust" and "you sweep men away"). But we should notice that while the lament of verses 7–11 is staged between "you" and "we" in particular, verses 2–6 are staged between "you" and "men" generally. Moreover, the subjects of these sections are different. Verses 2–6 concentrate on God's permanence over against the shortness of human life, and verses 7–11 focus on God's anger and the decay and poverty it brings the people within that short life. Thus, at verse 7 the psalm shifts its attention from God's eternity to God's anger and from humanity's transience to the travail of the speaker's own generation. Verses 2–6 should thus be read as a coherent piece praising God's permanence by contrasting it with human transience. Like other corporate prayers, Psalm 90 uses the praise of God as a platform from which it can express a persuasive appeal. It appeals to the eternal God to show pity to his perishing people.

90:1–6 / Verse 1 is like verses 2–6 in that it is hymnic, but it is like verses 7–11 in that it is staged between **you** and "us": **Lord, you have been our dwelling place throughout all generations.** It therefore ties these two sections together. Verses 2–6 give attention to the temporal aspect of this opening verse by showing how quickly the generations pass. Their imagery enhances the contrast between God's permanence, which exceeds that of **the mountains,** and the transience of humans, who are likened to **dust** and **grass.** What to humans is **a thousand years** to God is **like a day.**

90:7–11 / This section resumes the particular relationship between God and his people, noted in the opening verse, and shift the portrayal of God from creator to consuming fire (**indignation,** Hb. *ḥēmâ* denotes heat, rage, or burning anger). Verse 8 even seems to imply God preoccupies himself with **our iniquities.**

90:12–17 / The closing petitions seek to restore the relationship of God as "our dwelling place" (v. 1) by asking him to **relent,** or more literally "return" (Hb. *šûbâ*) and **have compassion.** They also request that he **teach us** how to use **our days** wisely (v. 12) and that his **love** may **satisfy us . . . all our days, for as many days as you have afflicted us** (vv. 14–15). Because of the people's solidarity with the preceding generations who knew Yahweh as their safe dwelling (v. 1), verse 16 summons him to renew his saving deeds: **May your deeds be shown to your servants, your splendor to their children.** Since it is characteristic of Israel's faith that it be founded upon God's saving, historical acts, their only relief from the futility can be found in a renewal of God's favoring work in their own history. The closing petition asks God to give permanence to **the work of our hands.**

In sum, the opening praise of God (vv. 2–6) refers to the temporal distinction between God and humanity. The lament (vv. 7–11) heightens this distinction further by introducing the moral distance between God and this particular generation. By themselves, verses 1–6 could be read as coherent praise of God, but juxtaposed with the following lament these opening verses simply bring to the fore the wide gap that the Creator has put between himself and his creation. Thus, by drawing upon this praise of God and by intensifying the separation to which it refers, the psalm makes clear to Yahweh that the people's only hope is a new revelation of his saving work in their own experience (vv. 12–17).

§91 The Protection of My God in the Midst of Threat (Ps. 91)

91:1–16 / A key to understanding this psalm in its original context lies in interpreting its imagery. The dominant image describing the obligation of the believer is that of taking "refuge" (vv. 1–2, 9, cf. v. 4). This seems to be not an abstract metaphor but a concrete symbol for trust in God that derives from the temple and the cherubim wings outstretched over the ark of the covenant. God's protection is further spelled out by images of a hiding place, a shadow from the burning sun, a military fortress (all in vv. 1–2), a bird protecting her young (v. 4a), military defenses (v. 4b), and **angels** (vv. 11–12). The images depicting threat derive from a hunt (**the fowler's snare,** v. 3a), disease (**the deadly pestilence,** v. 3b; **the pestilence** and **the plague,** v. 6), battle (**your shield and rampart,** which protect against **the arrow that flies by day,** vv. 4–5), and deadly animals (**the lion and the cobra, the great lion and the serpent,** v. 13). The variety of images allows this psalm to be used for any situation of threat.

The psalm exhibits the following structure, consisting of three main sections: verses 1–8, 9–13, and 14–16. The first two sections have the same three parts: a description of the believer who confesses Yahweh as refuge, Yahweh's promise of protective action, and promises of the believer's security. The obligation laid upon believers is presented as a description ("He who. . . . He says . . ."), not as an imperative. In this sense, the psalm issues an invitation, not a command. Thus, the liturgist seeks to elicit from the hearers a confession: "He says" (following the LXX in v. 2, not the MT, as in the NIV) **of the LORD, "He is my refuge."** These descriptions in verses 1–2 and in verse 9 are parallel: both use the divine names **Most High** and **Yahweh,** and both use the term "refuge." The third section (vv. 14–16) stands apart as a prophetic oracle (cf. Ps. 62, another psalm of trust closing

with a reference to God's speech, which forms the basis of the
preceding personal confessions).

For certain believers this psalm provides some of the most
comforting promises of the Bible. For others these promises are
some of its most unrealistic. For the faithful who have experienced tragedy, these promises smack of being cruel. How should
we respond to this psalm when calamity strikes us or those we
love? How can this psalm (esp. vv. 8, 10) be reconciled with the
many prayer psalms in which disaster has befallen the believer?
When read in isolation this psalm appears to provide believers
with blanket guarantees against harm. But what does this psalm,
in fact, claim?

Four features of this psalm and its context must be noted.
First, the closing oracle, in which Yahweh himself states his
promises, seems to promise less than the preceding verses. In
verse 15 Yahweh admits the believer may yet be in trouble.
Hence, verses 14–16 speak of Yahweh's promise to "rescue," "deliver," and "show . . . salvation." Here the believer is not assured
of being a detached observer, as verses 8 and 10 by themselves
appear to indicate. Second, verse 8 may also provide an interpretive key. The various threats listed in this psalm are seen as
"the retribution of the wicked" (NIV **the punishment of the
wicked**). In other words, these are not general disasters but
divine judgments aimed at the wicked. If this is the case, this
psalm promises not that believers are exempt from any calamity—
simply that they are free from divine retribution. Third, the
psalms of temple entry promise refuge and security to "the righteous" and pronounce judgment and disaster for "the wicked,"
who may not enter the realm of Yahweh's refuge (see the Introduction). If Psalm 91 was used in connection with these liturgies,
then its function may be to spell out further the refugees' protection against the afflictions that will befall the wicked (cf. the petitions of 26:9; 28:3). In addition, it may be that these promises
apply especially to protection during pilgrimage. Verse 1 alludes
to pilgrims to Yahweh's temple. It is here that conceptions such
as "refuge" (vv. 2, 9) and "under his wings" (v. 4) obtain meaning.
The expressions, "all your ways" and "you will tread"
(vv. 11–13), befit the pilgrim journey. (Perhaps the use of "your
tent" (v. 10) applies to those tents used during pilgrimage.)
Fourth, presupposed here are the fears common to ancient Near
Eastern peoples, especially plagues and military invasion. Psalm
91 describes the fearlessness that one who trusts in Yahweh may

have, in contrast to those who trust in magical amulets (see Keel, *Symbolism*, p. 82, fig. 93). In this respect, one of the primary purposes of Psalm 91 is not to issue guarantees against misfortune but to promote faith in Yahweh as opposed to other ancient Near Eastern religions.

§92 The Withering of the Wicked and the Flourishing of the Righteous (Ps. 92)

Initially Psalm 92 sounds like a psalm of the individual (esp. vv. 4, 10–11), but several features point to its liturgical use in a corporate setting. The speaker refers to "our God" (v. 13), implying he does not sing alone. The psalm contains several hymnic features typical of corporate worship (noted below) and several parallels with Psalms 52 and 75, both of which reflect corporate, liturgical worship. The speaking "I" may thus be a representative liturgist. The opening section calls for praise, the middle section states God's judgment on the wicked as the reason for the praise, and the final section celebrates the contrasting destiny of God's people at the temple and calls for further praise.

92:1–3 / The opening three verses are unique for a praise psalm in that they are neither a proclamation of praise ("I will give thanks"), typical of individual thanksgivings, nor an imperative call to praise ("Praise!"), typical of corporate hymns. The phrase, **It is good to praise the LORD,** finds parallels in hymnic verses (147:1; and 106:1; 107:1; 118:1; 136:1, where we could equally translate, "Give thanks to the LORD, for it is good"), in an individual prayer (54:6), and in an entry liturgy (52:9). Similarly, the mention of the **lyre** and **harp** together appears both in hymnic verses (33:2; 81:2; 150:3) and in individual prayers (71:22; cf. 57:8, which is part of a larger liturgy). The mention of praise **in the morning** and **at night** echoes the regular morning and evening offerings to be made at the temple (Num. 28:4, 8).

92:4–11 / The reason (note **for** in v. 4) given for this praise is Yahweh's joy-evoking **deeds** and **works** (cf. 145:4–7), which are unfolded as his judgments on **the wicked**. His **profound . . . thoughts,** which **fools do not understand** (cf. 94:8–11), relate in particular to the insight that "when the wicked sprout like plants . . . , it is so they may be destroyed forever" (lit.; the Hb. text lacks the concessive **though**). This literal translation shows that God, as both Judge and Creator, has designed the wicked specifically so that their flourishing is brief and final. In other words, their blossoming is no indication of their blessing; rather, this kind of blossoming is an indication of their judgment.

When we read of **my adversaries** we normally think the speaker has personal enemies, but we should note the parallel that the psalm draws between the opponents of Yahweh and the liturgist. As it refers to **your enemies, O LORD** (v. 9), so it refers to "my adversaries" (v. 11). As **you, O LORD, are exalted** (cf. 68:18; 93:4), so **you have exalted my horn.** (On **fine oils . . . poured upon me,** cf. 23:5.) Thus, we should not presume the speaker refers to his own private experience of personal enemies; rather he speaks of God's enemies as his own (see further on 139:19–22). A corporate and liturgical interpretation of this psalm is confirmed by certain parallels with Psalm 75. It too alternates between "I" (v. 9) and "we" (v. 1), and celebrates God's judgment of "the wicked" (vv. 2–8) and God's exaltation of "the horns of the righteous" (v. 10).

It may offend our modern sensibilities that such destruction should be seen as an expression of God's love and faithfulness (v. 2) and as a cause for **joy** (v. 4) for God's people. But it must be seen within the wider context of God's judgment in the Psalms. The "flourishing" of the wicked comes as rebellion against God and at the expense of others. In our psalm they are "those who rise against me" (lit., v. 11). In Psalm 75, they challenge God's own rule and exalt themselves over others (vv. 4–5), and presumably abuse them. As noted in our psalm, **your enemies will perish** because, as noted in Psalm 5 (a psalm of temple entry), "you destroy (lit. 'cause to perish') those who tell lies, bloodthirsty and deceitful men" (v. 6). Also similar to our psalm, "my enemies" are also God's, "for they have rebelled against you" (5:8, 10).

92:12–15 / While a singular voice is heard in verses 4–11, the liturgy closes with reference to a group (**the righteous** and **our God**). Like Psalm 52, a psalm of temple entry rehearsing God's indictment and judgment of the wicked, our psalm closes with a celebration of "the righteous flourishing" like a **tree** specifically **in the house of the LORD** and with a promise of continued praise (52:6, 8–9; also cf. 36:8–9). Both psalms also use a contrasting image to portray the fate of the wicked: in 52:5 they are "uprooted," and in our psalm they are likened to perishing **grass** (v. 7). Psalm 92 closes with an implicit call for further praise that summarizes the result of Yahweh's respective judgments on the wicked and the righteous: **"The LORD is upright"** and without **wickedness.** This psalm is thus a celebration of his saving justice (a form of the doxology of judgment; see 51:3–6).

§93 The Divine King Is Mightier than the Chaotic Waters (Ps. 93)

This psalm of Yahweh's kingship (see the Introduction) speaks in a foreign language. What the "lifting up" of the seas and their pounding waves have to do with Yahweh's reign is not self-evident to the modern reader. Nor is it clear how we get from the seas to Yahweh's house by the psalm's close. Here we must enter the thought world of the ancient Near East and of temple symbolism. Present in this psalm are the three motifs characteristic of divine kingship in the ancient Near East (see the Introduction): (a) "the LORD on high" (i.e., the God of the skies) demonstrates himself to be "mightier than the breakers of the sea" (vv. 3–4), and (b) the congregation thus acclaims, "the LORD reigns" (vv. 1–2). The psalm closes with admiration of (c) "your house," that is, the king's palace (v. 5). The change of address with respect to Yahweh may provide hints regarding the psalm's liturgical use. There are the third-person verses (vv. 1, 4), to which a choir responds with hymnic praise addressed directly to Yahweh (vv. 2–3, 5).

93:1–2 / This celebration of divine kingship begins with the acclamation, **the LORD reigns,** rather than with the scene of conflict with "the great waters," as is characteristic of ancient Near Eastern literature. The reasons for this reversal may be thematic or liturgical but they are certainly theological. As presented in this psalm, Yahweh's superiority to "the seas" demonstrates his kingship; it does not establish it. To interpret the claim, **Your throne was established long ago; you are from all eternity,** in its preexilic context we must understand that the expressions "long ago" (lit. "from then") and "eternity" (Hb. *ôlām*) do not denote infinite time but simply remote time. Nevertheless, while these temporal expressions describe Yahweh's established throne, they are noticeably absent in the parallel claim, **the world is firmly established** (a confession at home with other testimonies of Yahweh's kingship, 96:10; cf. 24:2; 89:11; 104:5).

The world's stability stands as a visible monument to Yahweh's rule, but that rule does not stand or fall with the world's stability. The psalm does not entertain the possibility there ever was a time before Yahweh became king.

After the opening acclamation there is admiration of his royal clothing: **the LORD is robed in majesty and is armed** (lit. "girded") **with strength** (cf. 104:1–2; 45:3, 8). The clothing is not merely the pomp that goes with the authority but additionally the power to execute it (cf. esp. 45:3–7, which speaks of the earthly monarch). Psalm 65 similarly sings of Yahweh "armed . . . with strength" and stilling "the roaring of the seas" (vv. 6–7), and of his "house" or "holy temple" (vv. 1–4).

93:3–4 / Although "your throne" is "from remotest time," Yahweh's kingship is here exhibited dramatically by his superiority to **the sea** (Hb. *yām*, v. 4). Contrary to the static views of divine kingship that many of us imagine (God merely sitting on his throne), this psalm presents King Yahweh exerting his warrior strength and waging battle against chaos and evil. The term for **the seas** (v. 3) is actually "rivers" (Hb. *nᵉhārôt*), which makes little sense without reference to Canaanite mythology (see the Introduction). In the story of Baal's kingship, the full name of his opponent is Prince Sea *(Yam)*–Judge River *(Nahar)* (see Gibson, *Canaanite Myths*, p. 37). The ocean was apparently conceived as a river enclosing the land. Such echoes of ancient Near Eastern mythology invite us to make a close comparison, which reveals striking contrasts. First, in the Mesopotamian "Enuma Elish" and especially in the Canaanite Baal epic, the storm god and the sea god are near-equal opponents. Second, in these ancient Near Eastern stories this conflict is presented as a pivotal event. Psalm 93 in no way tries to diminish the imposing threat of the "rivers" (**their pounding waves, the thunder** [lit. "sounds"] **of the great waters, the breakers of** the sea), but it simply sings that **the LORD on high** is **mightier.** In other words, whenever the seas look threatening, we must call to mind that Yahweh is greater.

93:5 / The closing verse refers to the third element of divine kingship, namely the deity's palace, here denoted by **your house** (also used in the Baal epic for a god's palace, Gibson, p. 54). The previous mention of "the LORD on high" reminds us to look for Yahweh in the skies. We must think of his earthly temple as a symbol of his heavenly palace in the skies (the Hb. term *šāmayim* denotes both "skies" and "heavens"). In this context, describing Yahweh's house as "holy" does not point to moral attributes primarily (though this was a later association, esp. in the postexilic period) but to its being set apart for its awe-inspiring resident (the Baal epic also describes his residence on Mount Zaphon as "holy," Gibson, *Canaanite Myths*, p. 49).

There are a number of possibilities for what is meant by the Hebrew term behind the NIV's **your statutes** (Hb. *ʿēdōtêkā*). It could mean "your testimonies" or "your assemblies" (though the plural form of this word is not attested in the OT). "Your testimonies" can denote decrees (see Ps. 99:7, where it is used with Hb. *ḥoq*, and Pss. 25:10; 132:12, where it is used with "covenant"). In this context, we should not think primarily of the pentateuchal laws but of royal decrees given by King Yahweh at his house or palace. (We should probably translate lit., "your testimonies are very firm/reliable at your house, a holy abode, Yahweh, for the length of days.") The verbal form for "testimonies" Yahweh uses in prophetic psalms when from his temple he "testifies" to his people of his judgments (50:7; 81:8; cf. Mic. 1:2–4). We should thus think not of codified legislation but of the dynamic encounter between Yahweh and his people at the temple. In sum, this psalm presents two things that are established (v. 2) or **firm** (v. 5) by virtue of Yahweh's established throne (v. 2): the world and his "testimonies." Verses 1–4 look especially toward the past, "long ago," and verse 5 toward the future, **for endless days.** His creation and his word exhibit his stable rule.

Additional Note §93

93:5 / **Holiness adorns your house:** The MT's *naʾawâ* is an odd form possibly meaning "befits" or "adorns." We should perhaps go with the DSS and read Hb. *nwh* and thus "at your house, a holy *abode*" (cf. Exod. 15:13, 17–18).

§94 Impending Judgment on the Oppressive Wicked and Interim Promises for the Righteous (Ps. 94)

This corporate prayer psalm reflects life between promise and fulfillment. Here, God's people live in the midst of, not away from, danger. Although there are no explicit liturgical references, the movement of the psalm makes best sense as a liturgy. Some scholars consider this psalm a mixed type because it combines a corporate prayer (vv. 1–7), wisdom traditions (vv. 8–13), and individual testimony, which appears to derive from a thanksgiving ceremony (vv. 17–19, 22). But the speaking "I" who confesses the Lord as "my God" (v. 22) refers to "the LORD our God" in the very next verse. He thus serves as a spokesperson for a participating group (perhaps a liturgist representing the congregation). As explained below, his testimony in verses 17–19 is integral to the surrounding context. It supports the claims and challenge made in verses 12–16 and the confession of Yahweh as "my fortress" in verse 22. Moreover, the entire psalm forms a unity around the theme of Yahweh as the divine judge: "the wicked" who oppress the innocent will receive their due and "the righteous" will find some protection in the meantime. Within this overarching theme are the opening seven verses that form a corporate prayer to God for judgment. Here, the actual prayer concludes. The rest of the psalm functions as an exhortation and testimony to the congregation so they may persevere until that judgment is realized. The subsequent verses that are addressed to God are praises: verses 12–13 in the form of a blessing and verses 18–19 in the form of thanksgiving. The content of these literary forms, however, supports the claims made in the surrounding exhortation (vv. 8–11) and confessions of trust (vv. 14–16, 22–23). Both the blessing and the thanksgiving offer assurances to *individuals* that God can protect them in the midst of turmoil. Implicit in this liturgy are the conviction that God will judge and the understanding that there is a "meantime" in which conflict and threat will continue. In sum, the liturgy unfolds as a corporate prayer to God (vv. 1–7), an exhortation to the congregation (vv. 8–11), a blessing on certain individuals that is addressed to God as praise (vv. 12–13), a confession of trust and challenge for the congregation (vv. 14–16) undergirded by a testimony of thanksgiving addressed to God (vv. 17–19), and finally a confession of trust that combines the liturgist's own testimony and further assurances for the congregation (vv. 20–23).

94:1–7 / The psalm opens with an appeal for a theophanic appearance (**shine forth;** see further on 50:2; 80:1). Although there is a clear call for vengeance in the opening verse, we must not presume it is a personal, emotional reaction. The next verse and the whole psalm make clear that it is characterized by just judgment **(O Judge of the earth),** that is, repayment for wrongs committed (vv. 2, 23). The rhetorical question introducing the lament section, which is addressed to Yahweh, implies the duration of the evildoers' jubilance is within his control and responsibility. The lament brings three characteristics of the wicked center stage: their arrogant speech (v. 4, cf. the psalms of temple entry), their oppression of **your people** in particular (v. 5) and the helpless in general (v. 6), and their denial of Yahweh's effectiveness (v. 7). The last item does not point to their atheism because their assertion is explicitly directed against **the LORD, the God of Jacob.**

94:8–13 / Their claim, "The LORD does not see" and "pays no heed," which is part of the opening prayer addressed to God, leads to an exhortation (vv. 8–11) addressed to **you senseless ones among the people,** who must **take heed.** This admonition aims to show the obvious logic that the one who creates an entity to do something can certainly do that something himself (v. 9), and that the one who exercises a given action certainly possesses the quality that produces the action (v. 10). This exhortation climaxes in the claim that Yahweh knows both human actions and human **thoughts** (v. 11). Implicit here is that God knows about the current oppression even though no action from him is immediately evident.

With the blessing in verses 12–13, the liturgy turns to address God as a form of praise. The claim that Yahweh **disciplines nations** and **teaches man** (Hb. *ʾādām*, corporate humankind, v. 10) leads to the mention of his blessing on **the man** (Hb. *geber*, i.e. the individual) **you discipline** and whom **you teach from your law** (v. 12). (Note that although the liturgy shifts from a corporate lament to an exhortation and then to a blessing, there are linguistic links for each transition: Yahweh's "seeing" in vv. 7 and 9, and his "disciplining" and "teaching" in vv. 10 and 12.) The specific blessing on this individual is that Yahweh "provides him with quiet" (lit.) **from days of trouble** (or "evil") **till a pit is dug for the wicked.** The promise is not for complete relief from evil, which is still future ("till"), but for some peace in the midst of evil.

94:14–16 / In agreement with this blessing, the subsequent confession of trust contains a promise stated in a negative form: **the LORD will not reject his people.** This form of promise, in fact, points to a hope that is spelled out in verse 15 in a positive form: **judgment will again be founded on righteousness.** In view of such assurances the liturgist calls for social action from his congregation: **Who will rise up for me against the wicked?** Implicit here is that courage is needed to withstand these opponents.

94:17–23 / Verse 17 is transitional. With the preceding confession of trust, it continues to refer to God in the third person and offers encouragement to those who would take up the challenge laid down in verse 16. It does so by introducing the speaker's own testimony of praise, which is addressed to Yahweh directly (vv. 18–19). Yahweh met his **slipping** with support and his **anxiety** with **consolation.**

The wicked (on v. 20, cf. 122:5) continue to oppress **the righteous,** but the liturgist confesses Yahweh as his refuge and reaffirms that **the LORD our God will destroy them.** These closing verses summarize God's action in the psalm, namely protection in the midst of oppressors (vv. 21–22) and ultimate punishment of oppressors (v. 23).

§95 Today, If You Hear His Voice (Ps. 95)

Like Psalm 81, Psalm 95 begins with a hymnic call for praise (vv. 1–7a) and then moves into a prophetic oracle warning the congregation with lessons from the exodus-wilderness period (vv. 7b–11).

95:1–7a / The hymnic praise contains two calls to praise, consisting of imperatives addressed to a congregation (vv. 1–2 and v. 6) and two reasons substantiating these imperatives (**for** in vv. 3–5 and v. 7a). The first imperatives call for "singing," "shouting" (a ritual action also prominent in the psalms of Yahweh's kingship, 47:1, 5; 98:4, 6; cf. 89:15), and **thanksgiving** (which may include thanksgiving sacrifices; see on 116:17). The second imperatives call for prostration (**let us bow down** and **kneel**). The reason for the shouting and singing concerns **the great King above all gods.** The psalms of Yahweh's kingship (Pss. 47; 93; 96–99) also celebrate Yahweh's superiority to the gods (96:4; 97:7, 9). The emphasis here is on the broad extent of this king's territories (from **the depths of the earth** to **the mountain peaks**), which he possesses because he created them (**the sea is his, for he made it, and his hands formed the dry land;** cf. 24:1–2). The reason for the ritual prostration concerns Israel's peculiar relationship with this cosmic King: **for he is our God and we are the people of his pasture.** The title, **our Maker,** which is formally part of the imperative clause, is ambiguous and may serve as a transition between these two reasons for praise. It can refer to Yahweh's act in creation (as biological creator) and to his act in history (as the one who constituted them as a people). The hymnic section of this psalm bears a striking resemblance to Psalm 100 (**shout, come before him,** "with thanksgiving," "the people" and **flock** "of his pasture").

95:7b–11 / The introduction to the prophetic oracle (cf. Ps. 50) is brief and comprises an "if " clause: **if you hear his voice.** The oracle implicitly forms the "then" clause. The **today** denotes

the festival day on which this hymn was sung (cf. 81:3) and
should provide a contrast with **that day at Massah in the desert.**
"Massah" (lit. "testing") refers to the first incident of Israel's
fearing that they would die in the wilderness for lack of water
(Exod. 17:1–7). **Meribah** (lit. "strife") refers both to this incident (Exod. 20:7) and to that of the second generation (Num.
20:1–13; cf. Pss. 81:7; 106:32). In both cases, the problem is not
merely one of thirst but of *dis*belief that Yahweh would continue to provide for the people he liberated. This is not mere *un*-
belief because, as our psalm points out, **they had seen what I did**
in Egypt. The reference to **forty years** and to **that generation**
points in particular to the first generation, judged by God because of their disbelief that he would fight for them in the conquest of Canaan (Num. 14, esp. vv. 33–34). In each of these three
incidents, the people complain, "Why did you bring us up out of
Egypt to make us . . . die?" (Exod. 17:3; Num. 14:2–3; 20:3–5). In
the oracle of Psalm 95, Yahweh's diagnosis in each judgment concerns the people's **hearts:** they are "hardened" (v. 8) and they
go astray (v. 10). Their fundamental error is **they have not known**
my ways. If they had, they would not have **tested and tried**
me (v. 9). As a result, Yahweh **declared on oath** (see Num. 14:21,
28), **"They shall never enter my rest,"** that is, the land (Deut.
12:9–10). We must be clear here that the reason for this judgment
(**so,** v. 11) stems not from Israel's refusal to live by a moral code
but from their fundamental misunderstanding of Yahweh himself (v. 10), exhibited in distrust that Yahweh would remain true
to "the people of his pasture" and provide water for "the flock
under his care" (v. 7).

   This prophetic oracle is no mere history lesson. While it
does concern **your fathers** (v. 9), it is clearly to be applied to the
you of the worshiping congregation (v. 7b). In fact, verse 8 speaks
of **you** as though the congregation were present at Meribah and
at Massah. It tacitly admits this corporate solidarity with generations past (note the same alternation of pronouns in Deut.
26:5–10 and Ps. 81:6–7), but phrased as a prophetic admonition
(today, if you hear his voice, **do not . . . as you did** that day), it
also indicates the present generation is free to choose another
destiny.

§96 The Divine King Comes to Judge the Earth (Ps. 96)

The liturgy of this psalm celebrating Yahweh's kingship opens with calls to praise stated in general terms (vv. 1–3). Reasons for the praise are then stated in terms of Yahweh's incomparability among those claiming divine status, his past act of making the heavens, and his royal attributes (vv. 4–6). The liturgy then moves to another section calling for praise but this time specifying how and where (vv. 7–9). The final section specifies the content of this praise, which looks especially to his future act of judging. In response, the whole cosmos is to reverberate with praise (vv. 10–13).

96:1–3 / The opening imperatives of praise are universal in scope: it is to be performed by **all the earth** and **among the nations.** The Hebrew word for **proclaim** *(bāśar),* meaning "to proclaim good news," is similarly used in Isaiah 52:7, where the content of the good news is spelled out as, "Your God reigns!" (cf. 40:9; 61:1). In particular, God's reign is to be evidenced by the restoration of Jerusalem after the exile, so that "all the ends of the earth will see the salvation of our God" (Isa. 52:10, which cites another psalm of Yahweh's kingship, Ps. 98:3).

In the context of these psalms of Yahweh's kingship, what is decidedly **new** in this **song** (also 98:1) is not necessarily its contents. The song is clearly new to the singers of the psalm, that is, "all the earth" (so in 98:1, 4.) They are to take up Yahweh's song—not those of "the gods of the nations" (96:5)—and sing of **his salvation, his glory,** and **his marvelous deeds.**

96:4–6 / Now the reasons for the opening imperatives (note **for** in vv. 4, 5) are expressed. The first is identical to the praise given in a Song of Zion (48:1): **Great is the LORD and most worthy of praise.** To our ears verses 4 and 5 may sound contradictory: on the one hand admitting **all gods** are real entities, and on the other calling **all the gods of the nations . . . idols** or "non-entities" (Hb. *ᵉlîlîm*). It is possible that verse 4 means to say that Yahweh is to be revered above all would-be "gods" or whatever humans trust in, strive for, and worship. But it is also possible "the gods of the nations" are those fabricated by the nations, and the "gods" of verse 4 are the divine beings of Yahweh's heavenly council (89:5–8 also refers to them to express Yahweh's incomparability; cf. 29:1; 148:1–2; 1 Kgs. 22:19). The next psalm of Yahweh's kingship also admits the same tension (97:7, 9). The chief evidence given for Yahweh's superiority and worthiness lies in his works: **the LORD made the heavens.** Yahweh has done something significant; these "nonentities" have not. The OT consistently argues for monotheism not on metaphysical grounds but on the grounds of a deity's words and acts (see, e.g., Isa. 41:21–29). Heavenly bodies were particularly favorite objects of worship in the ancient Near East (Deut. 4:19; 17:3).

Yahweh thus has legitimate claim to the royal attributes listed in verse 6. **Splendor and majesty** are applied to Israelite kings in the royal psalms (21:5; 45:3) and to Yahweh in 104:1, where he is depicted in a role of divine kingship. **Strength and glory** (Hb. *ᶜōz wᵉtipᵓeret*) have particular associations with the cherubim-ark, Yahweh's symbolic throne and footstool (see the Introduction). Psalm 132:8 refers to "the ark of your strength (Hb. *ᶜōz*)" and 78:61 simply refers to the cherubim-ark by the terms "his strength" (Hb. *ᶜōz*) and "his splendor" (Hb. *tipᵓeret*). It is therefore likely the cherubim-ark was actually present during the performance of this psalm to symbolize Yahweh's throne.

96:7–9 / This imperative section is virtually identical to 29:1–2, another psalm focused on Yahweh's divine kingship, except that here the **families of the earth,** not "heavenly beings," are the ones to do the praising. In addition, temple rituals are prescribed: **bring an offering and come into his courts.** We must recognize that the courts of the sacred temple were also regarded by the ancients as those of the divine, royal "palace." And the offering (Hb. *minḥâ*) was not only a religious sacrifice but also a political tribute to the king (e.g., 72:10; 2 Sam. 8:2, 6; 2 Kgs. 17:3–4). The qualities that the **nations** are to **ascribe to the LORD** are simply those that are inherently his, especially **glory** (Hb. *kābôd*, cf. v. 3; the Hb. word translated "glory" in v. 6 is *tipᵓeret*, which is usually rendered "splendor") and **strength** (cf. 6). The repetition simply acknowledges what is already an existing state. As is appropriate before royalty, especially divine royalty, the nations are to "bow down" (NIV **worship**). Commands for this posture also appear elsewhere in connection with the cherubim-ark (97:2, 7; 99:1, 5; 132:7–8).

96:10–13 / The substance of the message the congregation is commanded to **say among the nations** (cf. v. 3) is the cry of acclamation, **"The LORD reigns."** This confession of Yahweh's rule leads to a look backward at his "establishing" **the world** and to a look forward to his "judging" **the peoples with equity** (cf. 93:1–2, 5). Already mentioned in the psalm is the present proclamation of Yahweh's salvation, glory, and marvelous deeds (vv. 2–3), known in present human experience. Psalm 96 thus helps us to see that faith must live in all three tenses: Yahweh established creation order from the beginning, he intervenes with salvation in the present, and he will restore order by "judging" **the world in righteousness** in the future. The fact that Yahweh's present action is defined as "saving" and that he promises a future action of "judging" implies that present adversities do not deny the reality of Yahweh's reigning. Believers must reckon with the tension of living between the times.

Also striking is that verse 10 places in parallel Yahweh's work in creation and his moral government of human affairs, implying that both spheres reveal his divine kingship and that the same order underlies both nature and society. It might seem strange that impending divine judgment should be a cause for rejoicing, but that is because Christian theology gives prominence to judgment as a criminal trial of each person as a sinner before the perfect God. But in the context of the Psalms, Yahweh's "judging the world in righteousness" means "putting things right" and restoring order and harmony. Judgment thus calls for joy.

Also revealing are the agents called to express this joy. In this section, praise extends from the families of nations (v. 7) to all creation: **the heavens, the earth, the sea, the fields,** and **the forest.** Here, the OT anticipated by millennia the modern discovery of the ecological connectedness of the natural and human worlds. Yahweh's "setting things right" among **the peoples** has its effects among all God's creatures (this notion underlies Rom. 8:19–23). Social order and creation order are inevitably intertwined.

§97 The God of the Thunderstorm and the Proclamation of His Righteousness (Ps. 97)

This psalm of Yahweh's kingship picks up where Psalm 96 leaves off: "let the earth be glad" (cf. 96:11). After this opening invitation, we hear of a thunderstorm demonstrating Yahweh's supremacy and righteousness (vv. 2–6). We hear of the responses of idol worshipers and of Zion, along with a summary statement of Yahweh's supremacy (vv. 7–9). The closing section spells out the implications of the above: Yahweh's people must shun evil and then they will be granted protection, light, and joy (vv. 10–12).

97:1 / In response to the opening acclamation, **The LORD reigns,** there is to be worldwide praise.

97:2–6 / Yahweh's kingship is here exhibited, not by a static deity sitting on a throne, but by the dynamic appearance (i.e., a theophany) of the God of the storm (cf. Pss. 18:7–15; 29:3–10; 68:1–4, 32–34; 104:32; Exod. 19:16–19; 20:21; Deut. 4:11; Judg. 5:4–5; Hab. 3:3–15). He is not seen directly, however, for **clouds and thick darkness surround him.** What is visible is **fire** or **lightning,** located **before him,** and the earth's response of "trembling" and "melting mountains" (as in erosion from heavy rains, cf. Mic. 1:3–4).

Readers might wonder what possible connection there might be between "clouds and thick darkness" (Hb. *ʿᵃrāpel*) and **his throne.** Yahweh's throne and footstool were symbolized in Israelite worship by the cherubim and the ark (see the Introduction). Because of their winged character, the cherubim could symbolize both a chariot and a throne, in which the outer wings provided mobility and the inner wings formed the throne. At the temple's dedication after the ark entered the darkness of the Most Holy Place (1 Kgs. 8:12), Solomon said, "The LORD has said that he would dwell in a dark cloud (Hb. *ʿᵃrāpel*)." This earthly representation had a counterpart in the **heavens** (also "skies," Hb. *šāmayim* signifies both). In another thunderstorm theophany, we read, "dark clouds (Hb. *ʿarāpel*) were under his feet. He mounted the cherubim and flew" (Ps. 18:9–10). An allusion to the cherubim-ark is confirmed by the title, **the Lord of all the earth,** which has particular associations with it (Josh. 3:11, 13). (On **righteousness and justice** as **the foundation of** his throne, cf. 89:14, which alludes to a ritual procession of the cherubim-ark.)

It is understandable how the heavens **proclaim** Yahweh's **glory,** but modern readers might be puzzled how they proclaim **his righteousness.** This expression is certainly problematic if we insist on understanding God's righteousness strictly as a moral term. But if we consider the usage of the Hebrew term *ṣedeq* in the Psalms, we discover its moral sense derives from its broader, basic meaning of "rightness/right order" (a state) or "putting things right" (an action). In the ancient Near East, divine kingship and superiority (an issue that surfaces in v. 9) were established when the god of the storm with his arrows of lightning overcame the chaotic and life-threatening god of the seas (see "Tradition of Divine Kingship" in the Introduction). In this sense, the thunderstorm was an expression of establishing "right order." For Yahweh in particular, "right order" comes center stage and is expressed in nature, as seen here in verse 6, and in human affairs, as seen in verses 10–12 (cf. esp. the thunderstorm theophany in 50:2–6). Yahweh's **foes** could thus be cosmic, chaotic forces (cf. 93:3–4) or the wicked (v. 10, cf. 68:1–4, possibilities that join together the song of the ark and appearance of "the rider of the clouds" against "the wicked").

97:7–9 / As already noted in connection with 96:4–5, these verses reveal the same tension regarding other so-called divine beings. On the one hand, there are **idols** (Hb. *ᵉlîlîm*), which are more literally "nonentities." On the other, there are **gods,** who are commanded to **worship** Yahweh and above whom Yahweh is **exalted.** Yahweh is depicted as **the Most High . . . above all gods,** that is, above the divine council (cf. 29:1; 82:1–7; 89:5–8; 1 Kgs. 22:19). The Hebrew term translated "exalted" is more literally "ascended" (Hb. *naʿalêtā*) and echoes Yahweh's "ascent" in Psalm 47. This psalm appears to reflect a ritual where the cherubim-ark, symbolizing his throne (47:8), ascends into his temple-palace with great celebration (47:5). This ritual dramatized to the congregation that Yahweh is, in fact, "the LORD Most High" (47:2).

In the only section addressed directly to Yahweh, verses 8–9 celebrate the privileged position **Zion** has enjoyed. In contrast to idol-worshipers, who **are put to shame, the villages of Judah are glad because of your judgments** (v. 8 is identical to 48:11, found in a Song of Zion). Yet we should recall that the opening verse has invited the earth also to be glad. What judgments are in view is not specified and may vary according to the particular place Psalm 97 had in the larger liturgy at the temple. They may relate to Yahweh's righteousness revealed in the thunderstorm theophany against his foes ("justice" in v. 2 and "judgments" in v. 8 translate the same Hb. word), to the judgment announced in the previous psalm (96:10–13), or to the kind of judgment pronounced in the assembly of "gods" (Ps. 82), among others.

97:10–12 / Among the psalms of Yahweh's kingship, these verses make the clearest moral comment, contrasting **the righteous** and **the wicked.** The moral imperative to **hate evil** is clearly not doctrinaire but set within a warm relationship. It applies to **those who love the LORD** and in turn promises them protection, **light,** and **joy.** It is worth noting that while God's people are promised joy (Hb. *śimḥâ*), they are commanded to **rejoice** (Hb. *śimḥû*) **in the LORD.** Joy is a gift of God, but it still requires an act of will to express that joy and to direct it back to God.

Psalm 97 presents us with a perceptive insight on the nature of Yahweh's presence. This one presence may at times be shrouded in clouds and thick darkness (v. 2) and at others it may shed light (v. 11). This psalm speaks clearly of God's presence without compromising its mystery.

§98 The Saving Righteousness of the Divine King and the Cheers of Nature and the Nations (Ps. 98)

Most of this psalm of Yahweh's kingship is comprised of calls to praise (vv. 1a, 4–8), along with substantiating reasons that look to Yahweh's past (vv. 1b–3) and future (v. 9) actions. Like Psalm 96, it opens with a general call for all the earth (v. 4; 96:1) to sing a new song (v. 1; 96:1) about Yahweh's marvelous things/deeds (Hb. *niplāʾôt*, v. 1; 96:3) and salvation (v. 2; 96:2). It similarly contains three verses of commands to the human world to join in a ritual celebration of "the LORD, the King" (vv. 4–6; 96:7–9), and a closing section inviting the natural world to join in applauding his coming to judge the earth (vv. 7–9; 96:10–13).

98:1–3 / Much in this psalm is paralleled in other psalms of Yahweh's kingship, but these verses in particular raise the intriguing question: to what event(s) does this **salvation,** which **all the ends of the earth have seen,** refer? His "making known" **his salvation** is also described as "revealing" **his righteousness** and as "remembering" **his love.** Because several phrases are closely paralleled in Isaiah 40–55 (e.g., cf. vv. 1–4 and Isa. 40: 5, 10; 52:9–10; and vv. 7–8 and Isa. 42:10; 55:12), it seems likely that Psalm 98 had special relevance to Jerusalem's restoration after the Babylonian exile. But these exilic prophecies probably represent a later application of these preexilic psalms.

If we look among the psalms of Yahweh's kingship we discover a variety of revelational events that are to be recognized internationally. Thus, these opening verses probably refer not to specific **marvelous things,** but to all the many instances within Israel's salvation history in a summative fashion. As verse 2 claims, he **revealed** his righteousness **to the nations,** so 97:6 makes a similar claim, and this revelation occurs via a thunderstorm visible to "all the peoples." Similarly, Psalm 93 speaks of the superiority of "the LORD on high" to "the great waters" (vv. 3–4). Psalm 99 commands "the nations" to "tremble" (v. 1) because of Yahweh's special revelation to "Zion" and "Jacob" (vv. 2, 4), as exemplified through "Moses and Aaron" and "Samuel" (vv. 6–8). Psalm 47:1–4 commands "all you nations" to acknowledge Yahweh as "King over all the earth" because he "subdued nations under us" and "chose our inheritance for us," thus referring to the conquests under David (2 Sam. 5; 8) or Joshua. Finally, perhaps the closest parallel to 98:1 is 44:3. Although Psalm 44 is a corporate prayer, it confesses Yahweh as "my King" (44:4). Both 98:1 and 44:3 confess that Yahweh's "right hand" and "arm" "worked salvation" ("to work salvation for," which particular Hb. construction is found only here in the Psalms). Psalm 44 appears to refer to the conquest of the land (v. 2, like 47:3, refers to Yahweh's subduing "nations"). Thus, in view of the psalms of Yahweh's kingship as a group, 98:1–3 probably refers in summary fashion to all of Yahweh's public saving deeds.

98:4–6 / These verses consist solely of imperatives calling for a festival celebration with shouting, singing, and musical instruments **before the LORD, the King.** In particular, the commands to **shout** and **make music** (lit. "sing a psalm," Hb. *zammērû*) and the use of the **ram's horn** or "trumpet" (Hb. *šôpār*) echo Yahweh's ascent in 47:1, 5–7. This psalm appears to reflect a ritual in which the cherubim-ark, symbolizing Yahweh's throne, ascends into his temple-palace with great celebration, thus dramatizing the fact of his kingship.

98:7–9 / This closing invites creation (using Hb. jussives) to reverberate with applause at Yahweh's "coming" **to judge the earth** and is closely parallel to 96:11–13. There are, however, a few variations, especially among the creatures invited. Instead of the heavens and the earth, this psalm has **the world, and all who live in it** (a phrase found elsewhere only in 24:1, a psalm of temple entry that also celebrates Yahweh as the King). Instead of the fields and the forest, this psalm has **the rivers** and **the mountains.** Instead of Yahweh's judging "the peoples in his truth" (lit. "his faithfulness"), he does so here **with equity.**

§99 Holy, Holy, Holy Is the Responsive Divine King (Ps. 99)

The uniqueness of this psalm of Yahweh's kingship lies in its attention to Israel's historical traditions and specifically to Yahweh's execution of justice. Accompanying this liturgy was the congregation's ritual prostration toward the cherubim-ark at the temple (vv. 1, 5, 9). It is likely the psalm was performed by more than one voice. One possible scenario is that one liturgist or choir proclaimed the declarative statements and imperatives (e.g., "The LORD reigns," "he sits enthroned between the cherubim," "Great is the LORD . . . , he is holy," "The king is mighty . . . ," and vv. 5–7, 9) and another sang out the appropriate responses of worship and praise addressed directly to Yahweh ("let the nations tremble," "let the earth shake," "Let them praise . . . ," "you have established equity . . . ," and v. 8).

99:1–3 / Like Psalms 93 and 97, this psalm of Yahweh's kingship opens with the acclamation, **The LORD reigns.** The phrase, **he sits enthroned between the cherubim,** is actually a continuation of the full name that was invoked over the cherubim-ark: *"the LORD of hosts who is enthroned between the cherubim"* (lit., 2 Sam. 6:2; cf. 1 Sam. 4:4). Thus, this title and perhaps the symbol of the cherubim-ark itself face the congregation with the enthroned King Yahweh. In response, **the nations** are to **tremble.** The reason is made clear by the prepositions of the next verse: **Great is the LORD *in* Zion; he is exalted *over* all the nations.** The notion of Israel's privileged position in Yahweh's self-revelation is the focus of later verses. But the nations are not excluded from enjoying the benefits of his revelation channeled through this one nation—they are invited to participate. Specifically they are to **praise your great and awesome name.** Prescribing the name as the object of worship does not imply there is anything inherently magical about it. Rather, it is the personal label that identifies the body of God's self-revelation to Zion.

Other psalms celebrating Yahweh's kingship similarly place importance on identifying Yahweh's name in worship (29:2; 68:4; 96:2, 8).

At the close of each of the psalm's three sections, the congregation hears pronounced, **he is holy.** In Isaiah's vision, the seraphs' "Holy, holy, holy is Yahweh of hosts" is an echo of this worship of the divine name (Isa. 6:3).

99:4–5 / This section brings center stage what particularly makes Yahweh "great . . . in Zion" (v. 2), namely his **justice: in Jacob you have done what is just and right** (the emphasis in the Hb. lies on "you"). How he "does justice" is further expounded in verses 6–9. In the world of the nations (vv. 1–2), and in the ancient Near East in particular, the singling out of this feature is striking. Other deities tended to boast of empires, military victories, and building projects (see further the Additional Note).

His footstool is an allusion to the ark of the covenant (132:7–8; 1 Chron. 28:2), his throne, which is symbolized by the cherubim (v. 1) standing over it. Thus, at the moment of the liturgist's directions, **Exalt the LORD our God and worship** (lit. "bow down") **at** his footstool/holy mountain (vv. 5, 9), we should imagine the congregation prostrating themselves toward the temple and ark, and a priest then pronouncing, **he is holy.** Yahweh, invisibly and symbolically seated at the cherubim-ark, is thus exalted by the congregation's bowing down before him. (This "exaltation," Hb. *rwm*, before the cherubim-ark is therefore ritually distinct from its processional ascent, Hb. *ʿlh*, into the inner temple, as celebrated in 47:5, 9 and mentioned in 68:17–18; 97:9.) In view of verse 2, we see the congregation enacting ritually what is already true spiritually, namely that "he is exalted."

99:6–9 / The emphasis of the praising narrative of this section lies on the dialogical relationship between Yahweh and his people, as exhibited through historical figures. These verses also continue to highlight the name: **Moses, Aaron,** and **Samuel . . . called on his name; they called on the LORD.** What is especially central is Yahweh's responsiveness: **and he answered them. He spoke . . . ,** and as expressed in direct praise, **O LORD our God, you answered them.**

The reference to Yahweh's **statutes** and **decrees** does not point us to a religion of mere law, that is, behavioral conformity to a lawcode. Because they are given in direct response to human calls, we should probably translate these Hebrew terms as "testimonies/counsels" (Hb. *ʿēdôt*) and "prescriptions" (Hb. *ḥōq*). (In both Exod. 19–20 and Deut. 5 the Ten Commandments are clearly presented as divinely initiated.) The inclusion of Samuel supports this emphasis, because he did not receive laws as such, though he did receive specific instructions. Moreover, the kind of answering that Yahweh provides in verse 8 is to show himself to be **a forgiving God** (cf. Exod. 34:7, where he responds to Moses' intercession). Psalm 99 here portrays Yahweh not merely as Lawgiver but as a God who listens. His justice is not executed coldly or legalistically; it is responsive to human intercession and needs. (Instead of **they kept** [Hb. *šāmᵉrû*] **his** statutes, we should perhaps read, "they *heard*" [Hb. *šāmᵉû*] them, which better suits the dialogical context of these verses.)

Verse 9 repeats verse 5, except reading **his holy mountain** (Zion), instead of "his footstool" (the ark), and supplying the fuller name, **the LORD our God.** With the threefold cry of **holy** now complete, the psalm closes.

Additional Note §99

99:4 / The King is mighty, he loves justice: How we should translate this line is uncertain because "mighty" in the MT is a noun and "King" has no definite article ("the"). Moreover, it is somewhat odd that this line does not address Yahweh directly like the rest of the verse. It is possible it states a general principle, "And a king's strength is the judgment/justice he loves," and the rest of the verse praises Yahweh directly for fulfilling the condition of being a strong king.

§100 An Invitatory to Enter the Temple's Gates with Praise (Ps. 100)

An unusual feature of this hymn is that the first four verses are mostly imperative calls to praise (seven of them in vv. 1–4) and only the closing fifth verse provides the formal basis for this praise (with "for," which normally begins a hymn's introductory summary). This may imply we have only a fragment of a psalm or that Psalm 100 is complete but merely a portion of a larger liturgy. The congregation is summoned to worship and specifically to come before him and enter his temple (the Hb. verb *bōʾû* is used in both vv. 2 and 4) for the purpose of offering thanksgiving and praise (v. 4). We should perhaps imagine a liturgist or Levitical choir calling the congregation, who are outside the temple gates, to enter by a procession.

100:1–2 / Particularly noteworthy for this psalm is the universal summons: **all the earth**—not merely the covenant people—is invited to join in a joyful relationship with Yahweh. The first imperative, **shout,** indicates that Israelite worship was not to be characterized by civilized restraint. Biblical Hebrew does not have a word comparable to the generic English word **worship,** but the Hebrew word translated "serve" (NKJV; Hb. *ʿbd*) may be the closest equivalent. The third imperative shows this service is not an impersonal duty but is to be performed **before him** (lit. "to his face," Hb. *lᵉpānāyw*). And it is to be characterized by **gladness** and **joyful songs** (lit. "joyful shouts"). The liturgy thus creates a sense of anticipation in the worshipers by making them aware that they are about to encounter Yahweh's "face."

100:3 / In the context of public worship, the Hebrew verb for **know** (Hb. *ydʿ*) denotes both internal recognition and external acknowledgment. Knowledge was a key component in Yahwistic faith. The congregation is commanded both to understand its rationale and to make it known. The primary datum is

that **the** LORD, as opposed to other claimants to deity, **is God.**
The rest of the verse unpacks the significance of this. The claim,
it is he who made us, can refer to God's roles as creator of humankind and as creator of a covenant people (cf. Isa. 43:1, 15;
44:2). The designations, **his people** and **the sheep of his pasture**
(cf. 23:1), point particularly to the latter role. These phrases,
among others, are closely paralleled in Psalm 95, where both divine roles are in view: he is both cosmic Creator and "our God"
in particular (vv. 3–7). Thus, in Psalm 100 Yahweh has a right to
this confession of him as God because he is our maker, possessor,
and provider. Our dependence on him is clearly implied in the
sheep-shepherd image—we belong to him and we need him.

To assume this psalm teaches that all the earth (v. 1) are his
people, the sheep of his pasture (v. 3) would be to misread the
psalm. While the psalm summons "all the earth" in the opening
imperative, only the worshiping congregation that actually makes
the acknowledgment of verse 3 and brings the offerings of verse
4 can lay claim to being his people.

100:4 / In Israelite religion "entering [Hb. *bōʾû*] the temple
gates and courts" was tantamount to "coming [Hb. *bōʾû*] before
him" (v. 2). The temple was not a building conveniently constructed for congregational worship—it was Yahweh's dwelling.
We should not attempt to see a progression in entering **his gates
with thanksgiving** (Hb. *tôdâ*) and then into **his courts with
praise** (Hb. *tᵉhillâ*), as though praise were a higher form of worship. Following and balancing this imperative to **enter** are two
more imperatives, the first of which is **give thanks** (from Hb.
hôdâ). This offering of thanksgiving (Hb. *tôdâ*), noted both in this
verse and the superscription, could refer either to a thanksgiving
sacrifice (116:17; Lev. 7:12–15) or to a thanksgiving psalm.

100:5 / The closing verse provides the formal rationale
for the above commands (though v. 3 has already provided some
reasons). Their basis lies on Yahweh's beneficent attributes: his
goodness, **love,** and **faithfulness.** This psalm contains two statements, "the LORD is God" and **the LORD is** "good," that encapsu-
late two fundamentals of theology: God is all-powerful and God
is good.

§101 Vows About Acceptable and Unacceptable Associates (Ps. 101)

The genre and function of this psalm are difficult to determine because it is unique. It begins with phrases familiar from individual thanksgivings ("to you, O LORD, I will sing praise"), but what follows are not confessions of what God has done but vows of how the speaker will live. Their closest parallel in the Psalms appears in the liturgies of temple entry (e.g., 26:1–8, 11; see the Introduction).

101:1–2a / While the whole psalm is probably recited to Yahweh, only these opening verses are explicitly addressed to him. The interchange between **I** and **you** exemplifies the reciprocal relationship. In the opening line the speaker confesses, "I" **will sing of . . . love and justice.** We need to note that the NIV's **your** is not reflected in the Hebrew text because the subsequent confession concerns the speaker's practice of justice, not Yahweh's. Nevertheless, as the parallel line indicates, this confession is an expression of singing praise to Yahweh. Were the question **when will you come to me?** included in a prayer psalm, we would read it as a lament, but no distress is mentioned here, nor is there any petition. As part of the reciprocal relationship between God and worshiper, it probably expresses a humble anticipation of Yahweh's "coming to" his people during worship at the altar (Hb. *bōʾû,* Exod. 20:24; perhaps cf. Isa. 38:22). There is also tacit acknowledgment that when it takes place is up to Yahweh's discretion (cf. "let everyone who is godly pray to you while you may be found," 32:6; and "I pray . . . in the time of your favor," 69:13).

101:2b–8 / Most commentators believe this psalm was written for the Davidic king, for whom the references in verses 6 and 8 seem most appropriate: he who **will minister to me** may be a royal servant; 1 Chronicles 27:1; 28:1; and **I will cut off every evildoer from the city of the LORD.** For him, Yahweh's justice should be of prime interest (72:1). A priestly leader, however, could also be appropriate (the Levites "minister to" the Aaronic priests in Num. 18:2, where the NIV renders the same verb as "assist"). In this light, what is striking about this psalm is that the leader is subject to the same "torah" (or "instruction") that is applied to every worshiper of Yahweh, as expressed in the liturgies of temple entry, which use the same terminology (5:3–6; 15:2–4; 24:4; 26:1, 3, 5, 11; 28:3–4; 36:1–4, 11–12; 52:2–4; 73:3, 8, 12, 27). For example, the speaker is to aspire to "integrity" (101:2, 6; Hb. *tāmîm* and *tōm*, for which the NIV's **blameless** is a misleading translation; see further on 15:2; 26:1, 11) and is to avoid deceitful speech (101:5, 7). Our whole psalm exemplifies the maxim of 15:4a, that Yahweh's worshiper is he "who despises a vile man but honors those who fear the LORD."

As a psalm of temple entry, Psalm 101 presents Yahweh's pilgrims with "instruction" about what the God who inhabits the temple desires of his worshipers. For the purpose of clear instruction Yahweh's expectations are embodied in two character profiles, "the righteous" and "the wicked." One's loyalty to Yahweh is measured, in part, by the company with which one aligns oneself. These psalms, including Psalm 101, do not advocate a separate community (a ghetto, if you will), but they do advocate avoiding any participation with evil company in the deeds they practice.

§102 A Prayer for the Afflicted and for the Ruins of Zion (Ps. 102)

A distinctive feature of this psalm is its blending of prayer and praise. Its structure makes clear the central issue. Juxtaposed are "my days," which are cut short (vv. 23–24), and Yahweh's years, which go on through all generations (v. 24). The speaker's days are a leitmotif appearing at key turning points: twice in the introductory petitions ("in the day of my distress" and "in the day I call," v. 2, though not evident in the NIV), in the verses opening and closing the main lament (vv. 3, 11, and in v. 8), and toward the end of the psalm where the lament is resumed (vv. 23, 24). Yahweh's permanence is the subject at the opening of the hymnic praise (v. 12) and at its closing (vv. 24b–28). In each case it surfaces as a direct contrast to the impermanence of the speaker's days. The point is to motivate the eternal Yahweh to grant the speaker to live out the full days of his generation.

Another distinctive feature is the blending of concerns for the individual and for the people of Zion. The point here is also to motivate Yahweh: as he promises to respond to the prayer of the destitute (v. 17), so he should "hear my prayer" (v. 1). The destitute here are clearly God's people of the exilic period, while Jerusalem lies in ruins (v.14) and is in need of rebuilding (v. 16). (The psalm exhibits the same blending of individual and corporate traditions in the exilic period as seen in Pss. 22, 69, and Lam., with which it shares some significant parallels. See the Additional Notes to Ps. 22.)

102:1–2 / Psalm 102 contains a superscription that is somewhat unique, but it makes explicit what is implicit for the prayer psalms of the individual. They are composed not for the special use of their composers but for the general use of anyone who is **afflicted** and wants to "pour out" **his lament before the LORD.** The psalm opens with familiar petitions that seek a face-to-face encounter with God **(Hear, come to you, your face, turn**

your ear). This is noteworthy especially considering that the Jerusalem temple is apparently in ruins—its restoration is yet to come (vv. 13–17). At present Yahweh is in "his sanctuary on high," that is, in heaven (v. 19). In contrast to other deities, Yahweh is not tied to a place; he transcends earthly institutions.

102:3–11 / This section is a lament, mostly devoted to the personal affliction, which is described in physical terms **(my bones burn, my heart is . . . withered, I forget to eat my food so I am reduced to skin and bones).** The speaker is sleepless and his loneliness is compared to lonely birds (vv. 6–7). His emotions are made explicit by expressions of mourning (**ashes** and **tears,** which are also his **food** and **drink,** thus underlining his destitute and emaciated condition). Enveloping this whole section are references to **my days,** which are about to pass into the night of death. As in most individual laments, there are **my enemies** who **taunt me,** but they are not this psalm's chief concern. They simply exacerbate an existing condition (note the logical connective **for** in v. 9), one that may ultimately be traced back to God: **because of your great wrath.** A literal translation brings out the notion that God's treatment has a note of cruelty: "you have picked me up and cast me away/down."

102:12–22 / This section consists of hymnic praise blended with promises and assurances for the future. But in this lament psalm this is not praise in its own right, as the contrast with the preceding lament makes clear: "My days are like the evening shadow" . . . **But you, O LORD, sit enthroned forever.** Psalm 22:2–3 makes a similar contrast between the speaker's condition and Yahweh's and also depicts him as sitting enthroned as king. In Psalm 102, however, the contrast does not have the same sting because the primary function of this praise is to move Yahweh to pity.

The actions of God described here are in the future, but they are not in the first-person speech that is characteristic of the prophetic psalms (Pss. 50; 81; 95) and the prophets, but are in second- and third-person speech, which is characteristic of praise (note esp. v. 18). It is first addressed to Yahweh directly (vv. 12–15), and then after the reference to **the name of the LORD** (v. 15) it shifts to using the name, **the LORD,** in third-person praise (vv. 16, 18–19, 22). Shortly after the second reference to **the name of the LORD** (v. 21), the psalm returns to praising him in direct address (vv. 24–28).

Hymnic praise of Yahweh's permanence (vv. 12, 24b–28) surrounds praise of Yahweh's liberating compassion (vv. 13–22). The king who sits enthroned soon **will arise and have compassion on Zion.** Yahweh's mercy is interjected three times, first toward the city (v. 13), then toward **the destitute** (v. 17) and **the prisoners** (v. 20). Highlighted in each case is the gracious condescension of his mercy: Yahweh's **glory** is manifested not as royal pomp but as attending to the destitute (vv. 16–17). From his heavenly perspective, he views all **the earth,** but he "hears" specifically **the groans of** the prisoners (vv. 19–20). The actions that he will perform on their behalf are to **rebuild Zion and appear in his** glory (v. 16), where **his praise** will in turn **be declared** (v. 21). In turn, the news and praise of this divine act will reverberate to **the nations,** who **will fear** the name of the LORD (v. 15) and **assemble to worship the LORD** (v. 22).

This praise serves as praise to Yahweh and his name in its own right, and as a promise that assures the speaker and the people. In addition, it serves as a motivation supporting the prayer. The connective **for** (Hb. *kî*) supplies reasons why Yahweh should act. Yahweh will have compassion on Zion, for **it is time to show favor to her** (v. 13). Why? **For her stones are dear to your servants** (not to Yahweh, as we might have expected). Yahweh is assured that reverence of his **glory** will extend to the nations, **for** he will appear in his glory (vv. 15–16). He is also assured that his praise will extend to **a future generation,** "for" he released the prisoners (vv. 18–20, this time the NIV neglected to translate the Hb. *kî*). In other words, Yahweh must restore Jerusalem for his praise to continue and spread. The praise of this section also has direct bearing on the individual speaker. As Yahweh will hear **the prayer of** the destitute (v. 17), so he should "hear my prayer" (v. 1). As he will **release those condemned to death** (v. 20, lit. "the sons of death"), so he should heed the near-death lament (vv. 3–11) and "not take me away . . . in the midst of my days" (v. 24).

102:23–24a / Although the praise of God's permanence continues in verses 24b–28, a lament and a petition that resume the earlier theme of **my days** are interjected here. Their effect is to create a striking contrast. While the lament is brief, it focuses entirely on God's role in the distress: he—that is, the praised Yahweh of verses 12–22—**cut short my days.** The petition then returns the psalm to direct address: **Do not take me away . . . in the midst of** my days; your years go on through all generations.

Thus, although verses 24b–28 are formally praise, there is also a note of complaint: "I am not permitted to live a full generation, but you continue through all generations."

102:24b–28 / God's permanence is demonstrated by first looking back to the past when **the earth** and **the heavens** were created and then by looking to the distant future. Here God's permanence transcends even that of creation, as illustrated by the analogy of **clothing.** The closing reference that **the children of your servants will live** (lit. "tent") **in your presence** probably alludes to God's people "tenting" before the temple during pilgrimage festivals (see on 15:1; 65:4). This image depicts them as God's congregation "serving" (see on 100:2) him in worship. Thus, the closing verse is said not merely for the benefit of God's people but also for the benefit of God's continued praise (see esp. vv. 12, 18).

§103 The Lord Compassionate and Slow to Anger (Ps. 103)

Because this psalm combines individual thanksgiving (vv. 2–5) and corporate hymnody (vv. 6–18), commentators have debated which is indicative of its function (see Allen, *Psalms 101–150*, [WBC 21; Waco: Word, 1983], pp. 19–20). As I have argued, this separation between individual and corporate settings has been overstressed. Whether the concerns were individual or corporate, Israel's worship was primarily public. In this public setting, a liturgist would lead the singing of psalms and speak on behalf of both the corporate body and its individual members. A postexilic date is implied by the Hebrew grammar (e.g., the irregular forms of the feminine pronouns in vv. 3–5) and by the possible influence from Aramaic (see GKC, p. 256). The psalm's apparent use of written sources, as noted below, may also point in this direction.

The scope of this psalm broadens enormously: it opens with a command to the self and closes with a command to all his works. (In contrast, Ps. 19 moves from the heavens to the individual speaker.) It progressively moves from the individual sphere ("my" in vv. 1–5), to the social, national, and broadly human spheres ("the people," "us," "those who fear him" in vv. 6–18), and then to the heavenly spheres ("you" in vv. 19–22). Its development can be elucidated further by its dovetailing of key terms:

God's "love and compassion" (vv. 4, 8, 11, 13)
Response (attitude): "those who fear him" (vv. 11, 13, 17)
God "remembers" (v. 14), humans "remember" (v. 18)
Response (behavior): creatures "obey" (vv. 18–22)

The psalm makes a gradual shift in attention from God's mercy to the proper human response to his mercy. The hinge of this shift lies in remembering: as God remembers us, so we are to remember his covenant. And the human response is explained first in terms of attitude and then in terms of behavior. Echoing this shift is a change in God's role from giver of mercy to king (vv. 19–22). Key terms also serve to unite the three main sections. For example, "Bless Yahweh" (a more accurate rendering than the NIV's "praise the LORD") unites the first and third. Helping to unite the first and second are love and compassion and the forgiving of both the speaker's "iniquities" (Hb. ʿāwen, not **sins,** as in NIV, v. 3) and the people's iniquities (v. 10b).

103:1–5 / From the expression, **Praise the LORD, O my soul,** we hear the speaker in conversation with himself (cf. 42:5, 11; 43:5; 104:1; 146:1). We often falsely assume that praise, to be genuine, must be spontaneous. But here we learn that the self can be commanded to exercise itself to confess God's mercy. Praise, it appears, need not come naturally to God's creatures. Even Yahweh's "heavenly . . . servants who do his will" are likewise commanded (vv. 20–22).

The conversation actually continues through verse 5 because the speaker is still addressing his soul (see NIV margin). The **benefits** listed in verses 3–5 are those commonly mentioned in the prayer and thanksgiving psalms of the individual, especially healing and deliverance from death. But unlike the thanksgiving psalms of the individual, the emphasis lies on repeated—not singular—action (the Hb. participle, not the finite verb). The speaker's praise is summative, not focusing on a single, recent deliverance. An expression striking among these benefits is that God **crowns you with love and compassion** (v. 4), thus extending royal benefits to each believer (cf. Ps. 8:5). The parallelism between God's forgiving of **sins** (lit., "iniquities") and healing of **diseases** (v. 3) suggests there may be a connection, but it would be fallacious to infer that the connection is inevitable. The simile of the **eagle's** renewal (v. 5) is echoed in Isaiah 40:31.

103:6–18 / The next section offers a prime example of what the terms **righteousness** (vv. 6, 17) and **justice** (v. 6) mean in the Psalms, especially when they are qualities of Yahweh. In Christian theology, they tend to have negative connotations, related to condemnation. But here we see these attributes spelled out as liberation—as exhibited in the exodus from Egyptian oppression—and compassion—as exhibited in the rebellion centered on the golden calf (Exod. 32–34). These verses, and verses 7–8 in particular, contain echoes from Exodus 33–34. Most prominent here is the confession, **The LORD is compassionate and gracious, slow to anger, abounding in love** (Exod. 34:6; cf. also

verse 7 of our psalm and Exod. 33:13). It is cited frequently in the
OT, several times in liturgical contexts (Pss. 86:15; 145:8; Neh.
9:17). This confession forms the basis for the use of the key word
pair—**love** and **compassion**—in our psalm, but it also introduces
the subject of God's anger toward **sins, iniquities** (v. 10), and
transgressions (v. 12), the same three terms used in Exodus 34:7.
While celebrating God's mercy, the psalm does not ignore the reality of his wrath, though it does focus on its delay (v. 8), tempo-
rality (v. 9), and sparing application (v. 10).

To emphasize the extent of Yahweh's mercy the psalm
passes through three similes (using **as**). The first two are spatial:
vertical in verse 11, horizontal in verse 12. The third is relational
(v. 13). Somewhat surprisingly the explicit basis for this love
(v. 11) and compassion (v. 13) is traced not to the narrative of the
golden calf incident but to the creation narrative (Gen. 2:7): **for
he knows how we are formed, he remembers that we are dust.**
The motif of human frailty continues in the simile of humans **like
grass** and **like a flower of the field** (vv. 15–16), which also appears in 90:5–6 (cf. also Isa. 40:6–8). Other parallels with Psalm 90
are God's being **from everlasting to everlasting** (103:17 and 90:2)
and humans compared to dust (103:14 and 90:3). Rather striking,
however, is their contrasting perspective on human transitori-
ness. In Psalm 103, it is grounds for divine mercy; in Psalm 90, it is
evidence of divine wrath (vv. 7–11).

Verse 18 introduces the notion of obedience, triggered perhaps by the key term **remember.** The human mind is to follow
the pattern of the divine (v. 14). The object of people's memory is
God's **covenant,** whose mention may be explained as an echo
from Exodus 34:10, 27–28. In addition, verses 17–18 appear to repeat Exodus 20:6 (Yahweh's **love** to generations and **those who
keep his** covenant or commandments).

103:19–22 / This motif of obedience continues in the final
strophe, which names heavenly "heroes" (suggested by several
Hb. terms) who **do . . . his word** and **will** (vv. 20–21). Also consistent
with the notion of obedience, Yahweh is depicted as King (v. 19).

To cover the praise of God, we can see the psalm blends
together a variety of Israelite traditions: those related to the individual (vv. 3–5, as echoed in the prayer psalms of the individual), to Israel's history and covenant (esp. 6–10, 17–18), to
creation (vv. 14–16), and to Yahweh's kingship and heavenly
hosts (vv. 19–22).

The psalm contains several creative tensions. Yahweh's forgiveness and compassion dominate verses 3–18, and—perhaps ironically—they are most available to those who keep his covenant and remember to obey his precepts (v. 18). He is slow to anger, but he may harbor his anger for a time (vv. 8–9). Yahweh "heals all my diseases" (v. 3), yet humans' days are like grass—they flourish and wither like a flower of the field (vv. 15–16). In cases such as these, we would be wrong to take such psalmic statements as absolute claims. It is understandable that psalmic praise, in order to be musically metrical and liturgically forceful, will not be laden with qualifications covering every possible ramification. Thus, when we consider both sides of each claim in the balance, we can see that the obedience described in verse 18 is not flawless, though it is intended. And the point of verse 3 is not to claim that Yahweh will heal each disease in every case but to attribute all such healings to Yahweh.

Additional Note §103

103:6 / **Righteousness:** The Hb. term is in the plural, meaning "acts that put things right."

§104 The Creator and His Providential Ordering of Creation (Ps. 104)

Psalm 104 hymns Yahweh as Creator. Every four or five verses (or lines of Hb. poetry) appear to be marked off by repeated terms and to treat a distinct realm of creation (vv. 1–4, 5–9, 10–13, 14–18, 19–23, 24–26, 27–30, 31–35; see further Allen, *Psalms 101–150*, pp. 31–32). The psalm is very cosmopolitan, echoing motifs from Israelite creation traditions (e.g., Gen. 1, showing both parallels and contrasts), wisdom traditions, Canaanite Baal imagery, and the Egyptian "Hymn to Aton" (written in the mid-fourteenth century; see *ANET*, pp. 369–71). It therefore demonstrates in the language of the ancient culture that Yahweh is the true divine King over creation.

104:1–4 / The opening section introduces the LORD as the divine King (esp. **clothed with splendor and majesty**), who appears as God of the skies (on this language of theophany, i.e., a divine appearance, see under "Tradition of Divine Kingship" in the Introduction). Like the sun, **he wraps himself in light.** He unfolds "the skies" (Hb. *šāmayim* denotes "skies" and **heavens**) as though they were a mere **tent.** He **makes the clouds his chariot,** which has **wings** (thus echoing the image of the cherubim-chariot; see 18:9–14). The **upper chambers** of his palace lie on the **waters** of the skies (i.e., clouds). His attendants are **winds** and **flames of fire** (i.e., lightning). These images echo those applied to the Canaanite god Baal, the "rider on the clouds" (see, e.g., Gibson, *Canaanite Myths*, pp. 48, 60–61, 65) and to other ancient Near Eastern deities (e.g., Marduk in "Enuma Elish," *ANET*, esp. pp. 66–72). Where we moderns may see merely a front of clouds crossing the sky, this psalm opens our eyes to see a manifestation of God's power.

104:5–9 / He made **the earth** immovable **on its foundations** (cf. 24:1–2; 93:1; 96:10, all psalms celebrating Yahweh as the cosmic King). Whereas Genesis 1 begins with "the deep" covering the earth (vv. 2, 9), our psalm goes back further and attributes this phenomenon to God: **you covered it with the deep.** As the God of the skies, he "rebuked" **the waters,** which **fled at the sound of** his **thunder,** and he "bounded" them. This imagery portrays the waters as God's opponent, and thus stems not from Genesis 1 but from the tradition of the divine king and God of the skies.

104:10–13 / Not only has Yahweh bounded the waters, whose chaotic forces traditionally threaten to extinguish life, he has also channeled them to promote life. Once rebuked, they went down into the valleys (v. 8), so **water . . . flows between the mountains** and gives **water to all the beasts** and **the birds** that **nest by the waters.** And not only does he provide these waters below, he also **waters the mountains from his upper chambers** in the skies.

104:14–18 / Yahweh provides **grass, plants,** and **trees** for **cattle, man,** and **birds** (mentioned a second time, also in v. 12). The psalm expands on his provisions for humans: **wine** and **oil** that "gladden" them and **bread that sustains** them. Also in focus is God's provision of place for his creatures: the trees for the birds and even **the high mountains** for **the wild goats.** The point of these verses lies in God's providence for these creatures, not on their creation as such (unlike Gen. 1). Particularly striking is the image of Yahweh as gardener **(the cedars of Lebanon that he planted),** which indicates his regular intervention in creation. The OT doctrine of creation is not merely about the distant past (the "beginning"); it is also about the Creator, who personally oversees the promotion of life and order.

104:19–23 / This section concerns **the moon** and **the sun,** and **night** and day, with a particular emphasis on the former of each pair. The phrase, **you bring darkness,** lays explicit claim to Yahweh's creation of darkness (cf. Isa. 45:7; contrast Gen. 1:2). Even in this realm and even with creatures as fearsome as **the lions,** his providence still governs, for they **seek their food from God. Man** too is listed within this daily cycle, as he **goes out to his work** when **the sun rises.** This section contrasts sharply with the Egyptian "Hymn to Aton," who is the god of the solar disk. When night falls in this text, "the land is in darkness, in the manner of death," thieves prowl, and "every lion is come forth from his den; all creeping things, they sting"—all because "he who made them rests in his horizon."

104:24–26 / Verse 24 breaks into a summative doxology—**How many are your works, O LORD!**—with particular focus on creation as an expression of Yahweh's **wisdom**. The multitude of his **creatures** is exemplified in **the sea, teeming with creatures beyond number.** While we moderns may simply see **leviathan** as another creature, the ancients would have heard this reference as a radical departure from the common cultural understanding (see esp. the Baal epic in Gibson, *Canaanite Myths*, pp. 50, 68). He was the "monster of the sea" and embodied the primeval chaos that the God of the skies had to vanquish to establish creation order. The OT uses this imagery in poetic passages (74:14; Isa. 27:1). But in our psalm he is demythologized as a mere creature who "frolics" in the sea. Indeed, the sea itself, rather than symbolizing chaos, is presented as a realm under God's blessing.

104:27–30 / With the survey of the various realms of creation now ended, the psalm turns to speak of these creatures' daily dependence on their provider: **These all look to you to give them their food at the proper time.** Again, Yahweh's personal oversight is center stage: he may **open** his **hand** or **hide** his **face.** And he may **take away their breath** or **send** his "breath"/ **Spirit** (Hb. *rûaḥ* can signify both).

104:31–35 / Unlike the preceding verses that hymn the praise of God (where he is the predominant grammatical subject), the closing section is comprised of grammatical forms typical of prayer psalms, though still with the intent of furthering his praise. There is first the wish that God's **works** of creation, also designated as **the glory of the LORD, may . . . endure forever,** and especially that he **rejoice** in them. We often egocentrically assume the earth is at our disposal for our enhancement, but here we learn that it gives God pleasure. God is not a detached divine clockmaker who winds up his handiwork and lets it go on its own. The next verse, phrased as hymnic praise, seems incongruous with God's taking delight in his works, but it certainly makes clear that creation is at his disposal and not ours. Moreover, the "trembling" of **the earth** and the "smoking" of **the mountains** at his presence (note again his personal engagement: **he looks** and **touches**) continues the theophanic language of the God of the skies begun in verses 1–4. There, attention was given to his activity in the skies; here, it is given to the earth's quaking response (cf. 18:7; 68:8; 77:18; 97:4; 144:5).

Although modern readers may enjoy the notions of singing and **meditation** in verses 33–34, the wish expressed in next verse seems to spoil an otherwise pleasant psalm: **may sinners vanish from the earth.** But a distinctive and constituent part of the OT theophany tradition of the God of the skies is that his appearance is specifically to judge the wicked and to save his people (18:16; 68:4–6, 33–35; 77:15, 20; 97:8–12; 144:5–8). In addition, a key theme of the psalm is that each creation (waters, sun, and moon) and creature have their place. This psalm reflects an awareness of ecology and extends this principle of nature to the religious and moral realms as well. Sinners, who corrupt the religious order, and **the wicked,** who corrupt the moral and social order, should vanish from God's ordered creation. Our place as humans and our proper response to the God of the skies and **his** works is to vow our praise: **I will sing to the LORD all my life.** As **the LORD** is to "rejoice in his works," so **I rejoice in the LORD.** It is significant that while the psalm takes considerable delight in Yahweh's creation, it prescribes the primary object of our rejoicing to be **the LORD** himself.

§105 In Praise of the Lord of History: From Abraham to the Settlement in the Land (Ps. 105)

105:1–45 / The opening calls for congregational praise (vv. 1–6; v. 7 being an introductory summary) clearly signal that this is a hymnic praise psalm. It recites God's praise not in general terms (e.g., referring simply to his "mercy" and "mighty acts") but in the specific terms of historical acts, namely those of Israel's early history also narrated in Genesis–Joshua. Verses 1–15 are contained in 1 Chronicles 16:8–22, where they are included in the psalm of thanks sung during the ark's first ascent into Jerusalem (see further "David and the Psalms" in the Introduction). The connection between this psalm and the ark may seem strange, but there might be a link in the imperative, **Look to the LORD and his strength; seek his face always** (v. 4). Initially we might think "his strength" simply denotes a divine attribute, but in 132:8 the ark is specifically designated as "the ark of your strength" (NIV "might") and in 78:61 it is designated as "his strength" (NIV "might"). (For more on the connection between the ark and Yahweh's "face" see commentary on 89:14–15.)

The psalm's framework is established by **the covenant he made with Abraham,** whose goal is **the land** of promise (vv. 8–11, 42–44). The body of this psalm thus traces Israel's history from the ancestors to the settlement: the ancestors (vv. 12–15), Joseph (vv. 16–22), the Egyptian period (vv. 23–36), and the exodus and wilderness (vv. 37–41). As hymnic praise, this psalm not merely narrates the events but also attributes these events to Yahweh's initiative. In this respect it goes beyond some of the claims of the Pentateuch. In Genesis, the reasons given for Joseph's harsh treatment are traced to his brothers' jealousy (Gen. 37) and to the sexual frustration and embarrassment of Potiphar's wife (Gen. 39). But in Psalm 105 Joseph's imprisonment is explicitly placed within God's refining process (vv. 18–19). In Exodus the reasons given for the Egyptians' oppression of the Hebrews are political and social (1:8–14), but in this psalm they are theological: **The LORD . . . made them too numerous for their foes, whose hearts he turned to hate his people** (vv. 24b–25a). Moreover, the events of this period are told in such a way as to show the unlikelihood of the Abrahamic promise ever finding fulfillment aside from divine intervention. We begin with the patriarchs **few in number** and "wandering" (vv. 12–13). At first, Yahweh **allowed no one to oppress them** (vv. 14–15) but he then providentially **sent . . . Joseph,** who is **sold as a slave** and taken as a prisoner (vv. 17–18). His suffering is not considered a wrinkle in God's plan; it is, in fact, instigated by **the word of the LORD,** which "refines him" (lit., NIV **proved him true**). Jacob left the land of Canaan and **entered Egypt . . . as an alien.** When his descendants become sizable enough to be a threat, the Egyptians **conspire against** them. Nevertheless, though Israel's entry was ignoble, Yahweh **brought out Israel, laden with silver and gold** (v. 37) and eventually **gave them the lands of the nations** (v. 44). Thus we see that Yahweh can fulfill a promise that his people have no power in themselves to accomplish, and that suffering in itself does not necessarily lie outside God's purpose.

It is interesting to compare the treatment of the Abrahamic covenant, the Joseph story, and the plagues in Genesis–Joshua with that in Psalm 105. The substance of the Abrahamic covenant is abridged to the promise of the land **of Canaan** (v. 11). In Genesis, Abraham is called a "prophet" (20:7) and a "prince" (23:6), but not one of Yahweh's **anointed ones** (v. 15). More attention is given to Joseph than to the other individual patriarchs, even Abraham (note also the wisdom emphasis in v. 22). In the sequence of the plagues, **darkness** (the ninth in Exod.) is made first, and the plagues of **flies** (the fourth) and **gnats** (the third) are reversed in the parallel lines of verse 31. The plague on livestock (the fifth) and the plague of boils (the sixth) are omitted. Psalm 105 deviates somewhat from Exodus and Numbers in its telling of the wilderness tradition. Instead of the **cloud** being a "pillar" to guide them by day, it is **a covering** (v. 39), presumably to protect the people from the desert sun. The **quail** incident is related as an example of Yahweh's providential response to the people's request, not as a means of Yahweh's angry judgment on the people's murmuring (Num. 11:4–6, 10, 33; cf. Ps. 78:17–31; 106:14–15). Although the land is made the key element in the Abrahamic covenant, only one verse is given to the conquest-settlement period (v. 44). Here no active, military role is attributed to Israel; the land is presented solely as a gift from God. Interestingly, the giving of the Law on Mount Sinai is not part of the narrative sequence. Its only reference is found in the closing verse, where the stated purpose for Yahweh's giving the land is **that they might keep his precepts and observe his laws.** The only **covenant** (vv. 8, 10) mentioned is that "made with Abraham."

§106 A Confession of Sin from Israel's History: Mercy for the Generations of the Exodus and the Exile (Ps. 106)

106:1–47 / Like Psalm 105, this psalm rehearses Israel's early history, but the differences between the two psalms could not be more striking—they are so divergent, in fact, that one might call them contradictory. This is particularly evident in their accounts of God's provision of quail in the wilderness (105:40; 106:14–15). Also like Psalm 105, this psalm begins with the hymnic call to praise **(Give thanks to the LORD)**, but then in verse 3 a "blessing" takes us in a very different direction. Our focus changes from that of God's saving acts to human obligation: **Blessed are they who maintain justice, who constantly do what is right.** The petition of verse 4 then brings us entirely out of the realm of praise to that of the prayer psalm: **Remember me, O LORD, when you show favor to your people. Giving praise,** from the perspective of this psalm, is thus future (v. 5). The words introducing this psalm's historical review, in fact, signal a confession: **We have sinned, even as our fathers did** (v. 6). Closing this review and this psalm is another petition—**Save us, O LORD our God, and gather us from the nations**—along with the tacit admission that praising God is a future act (**that we may give thanks,** v. 47). Thus, although Psalms 105 and 106 share a similar content, a form-critical analysis of each reveals they are designed for very different purposes. Psalm 105 is hymnic praise throughout, and so God and his praiseworthy acts are the grammatical subject. Psalm 106 is a corporate prayer psalm that confesses and laments the people's failure, and so they are the grammatical subject. Thus, both psalms cover the same historical period, but their selectivity from that narrative is directly opposite. Psalm 105 reads the story of Israel's beginnings as an occasion for praise; Psalm 106 reads it as an occasion for confession of sin and of hope in the midst of crisis.

A congregational setting for the psalm is implied by the opening call to corporate praise ("Give thanks" is plural) and the alternation between I/"me" (vv. 4–5) and **we** (vv. 6–7). Thus, a liturgist appears to speak as a representative of the congregation. The petitions are all addressed explicitly to Yahweh (vv. 4–5, 47). The closing petition ("gather us from the nations") and its preceding verse **(all who held them captive)** suggest an exilic setting for the psalm. As confirmation of this dating, we should note that included in the account of the rebellion at Kadesh (cf. Num. 13–14) are the threats that not only would God **make them fall in the desert** but he would also **make their descendants fall among the nations and scatter them throughout the lands** (vv. 26–27). Rebellion at the entrance to the land thus points toward eventual exile from the land. In addition, Psalm 106 shows some peculiar similarities to the historical review in Ezekiel 20, namely that Israel was sinful even **in Egypt** (Ps. 106:7; Ezek. 20:8), and that Yahweh acted **for his name's sake** (Ps. 106:8; Ezek. 20:9, 14, 17, 22). (Also note the reference to **Glory** in v. 20, a favorite expression for God's self-manifestation in Ezek.)

Closer inspection reveals further the function of this historical review. Judah's situation in the exile is seen to be analogous to these events of Israel's early history. The psalm bases its appeal to God on these historical precedents of divine mercy in the face of human rebellion. The review begins with a confession of sin for both the present generation and for past generations: "we have sinned, even as our fathers did." In Egypt and by **the Red Sea, they rebelled.** But the review is then followed by brief praise of God's saving mercy: **he saved them** and **redeemed them** (vv. 8–12). There then follows a series of seven incidents of Israelite rebellion and divine judgment (vv. 13–43), which are presented in a different sequence than that found in Exodus–Judges. (1) **They soon forgot what he had done and . . . in the desert they gave in to their craving. So he . . . sent a wasting disease upon them** (vv. 13–15; cf. Num. 11). (2) **They grew envious of Moses and of Aaron** and **the earth . . . swallowed Dathan** (vv. 16–18; cf. Num. 16). (3) **At Horeb they . . . worshiped an idol,** and God **would destroy them—had not Moses . . . stood in the breach** (vv. 19–23; cf. Exod. 32–34). (4) **They did not believe his promise** regarding **the pleasant land, so he swore . . . he would** make them fall in the desert (vv. 24–27; cf. Num. 13–14). (5) **They yoked themselves to the Baal of Peor, and a plague broke out among them** until **Phinehas . . . intervened** (vv. 28–31; cf. Num. 25). (6) **By the waters of Meribah they angered the LORD, and trouble came to Moses because of them** (vv. 32–33; cf. Num. 20).

(7) **They mingled with the nations** and **worshiped their idols,** and so God **handed them over to the nations** (vv. 34–43; cf. Judges). Yet in spite of their persistence in rebellion, the climax to this sequence is further praise of another divine act of mercy (vv. 44–46): **out of his great love he relented.** Then without any explicit transition the psalm launches itself forward to the present moment of the exile and pleads to God, "Save us"—a petition that echoes God's first act of mercy: "he saved them" (vv. 8, 10). It seeks a reversal of God's earlier judgments (cf. esp. "gather us from the nations" and vv. 27, 41).

Psalm 106 exemplifies the impact that the exile had upon the people of God. For example, the psalm is a lesson in memory, of Israel's regularly forgetting Yahweh's saving acts (vv. 7, 13, 21, etc.) on the one hand, and Yahweh's gracious remembering of his covenant (v. 45) on the other. The prophetic and Deuteronomistic preaching (cf. vv. 40–46; see further Allen, *Psalms 101–150*, pp. 51–52) had impressed upon the people that sin and wickedness prevailed *among* the people of God, not just beyond. Then, with the judgment of the exile, the people of God gained a heightened awareness of the problem of sin in the human heart. It is thus not surprising that a psalm like Psalm 51 appears to have emerged precisely in this historical period (see the commentary).

106:48 / Verse 48 is not a constituent part of the psalm but a doxology closing Book IV of the Psalter.

§107 *The Lord of Reversals: Thanksgiving of Desert Wanderers, Prisoners, the Sick, and Sailors (Ps. 107)*

Psalm 107 is unique in the Psalter. It opens with an imperative call to praise, familiar to the corporate hymnic praise psalms (note esp. the two preceding psalms), but it does not celebrate Israel's corporate experience as a people or refer to any particular historical events or traditions. Rather, it rehearses the deliverances of various unspecified groups of individuals. In this respect, it shares similarities to the thanksgiving psalms, but these generally celebrate an individual's recent deliverance. The repeated summons for these groups to give thanks (vv. 1, 8, 15, 21, 31) and the attendant call to sacrifice thank offerings, while telling "of his works with songs of joy" (v. 22) probably indicate that this psalm is a festival summons for the formal performance of thanksgiving, in both thanksgiving psalms and thanksgiving sacrifices. Whether these would occur individually or en masse, we cannot be sure.

Verses 33–43 do not fit with the patterns followed in verses 4–32, which narrate the experiences of various groups (note "some" in vv. 4, 10, 17, and "others" in v. 23). For example, they make no mention of people's crying for help. Instead, this section is closer to a hymn (note "he" in v. 33, etc.) than a thanksgiving. It may have been a later addition. Verses 2–3 appear to refer to Judah's restoration from Babylonian exile. The verses in these two sections strongly echo passages in Isaiah addressed to exilic or postexilic audiences. The designation, "the redeemed" (Hb. *gᵊʾl*, as a qal passive participle) appears only here in verse 2 and in Isaiah 35:9; 51:10; 62:12. Verse 3 is closely paralleled in Isaiah 43:5–6, and verses 33–35 in Isaiah 42:15 and 41:18–19. (The sequence of developments in vv. 33–41 may reflect those of the Canaanite conquest, the Israelite settlement, the exile, and the restoration.) Thus, while the psalm's final form appears to be postexilic, the rest of the psalm, especially verses 1, 4–31, may have been sung at the first temple in the preexilic period.

107:1–32 / After the opening invitations to praise (vv. 1–3), there follow four narratives of different groups (vv. 4–32). **Thirsty** travelers in the **desert** had **cried** to Yahweh, and **he led them . . . to a city** and "satisfied" them (vv. 4–9). Rebellious **prisoners,** whom Yahweh had punished, **cried** to him, and **he brought them out** (vv. 10–16). Next, the sick, ailing **because of their iniquities, cried,** and he **healed them** (vv. 17–22). Finally, sailors who experienced Yahweh's **tempest** at sea **cried, and he stilled the storm** and **guided them to their desired haven** (vv. 23–32).

The four narratives about desert travelers, prisoners, the sick, and sailors (vv. 4–32) follow a regular pattern. **Some** encountered distress, and **then they** cried **to the LORD in their trouble,** and **he** saved them. Each group is enjoined, **Let them give thanks to the LORD for his unfailing love and his wonderful deeds for men.** The first two narratives close with **for he,** followed by a generalized, hymnic description of his saving action. The last two narratives close with further invitations for praise **(Let them).** These observations make clear that a pattern may be observed in human experience: this pattern is what **whoever is wise** should **heed** (v. 43). The verses describing this pattern make explicit mention of interventions of God that caused distress for the prisoners (v. 12) and for the sailors (vv. 24–25). The section concerning the sailors adds several other expansions. In the two middle narratives, the prisoners (v. 11) and the sick (v. 17) are called rebels.

The variations in the causes of distress in these four narratives are striking. For the sailors, the distress is caused by Yahweh without any mention of the sailors' moral state. For the sick, the distress is merely described, with no explicit mention of its cause, though they are described as committing iniquities. For the prisoners, the distress is Yahweh's punishment on their sin. For the desert wanderers, the distress is simply described with no mention of Yahweh's involvement or their moral state. In view of the repeated patterns among these four strophes, these variations are probably significant. There exists no single form of interpretation for life's distresses. Sometimes they are Yahweh's judgment on sin; sometimes they are attributed to Yahweh; sometimes they are just there. The consistency among these verses is that Yahweh delivers when called upon.

107:33–43 / Verses 33–41 break from the pattern of crying to Yahweh and his saving response by showing a series of reversals.

They recount how Yahweh **turned . . . a fruitful land into a salt waste, because of** the inhabitants' **wickedness,** and how **he turned the desert into pools of water** for **the hungry,** whom **he blessed** and **increased.** Then they **decreased by . . . oppression,** and he made **nobles . . . wander in a trackless waste,** but **the needy** he rescued and **increased** their numbers. In view of these recitations, the contrary, verbal responses of **the upright** and **the wicked** are noted in the closing verses: the former **rejoice** and the latter **shut their mouths.** Finally, the wise person is enjoined (v. 43) to ponder Yahweh's **love**—the very attribute highlighted at the psalm's opening.

As in verses 4–32, some events are connected with a clear cause and others are not. Wicked inhabitants caused God to change fertile land to salt wastes, but the only "virtue" of those who later enjoy **a fruitful harvest** is that they are "the hungry." **Then**—without explanation—**they were** "bowed down" (NIV's **humbled** incorrectly implies a moral consequence) by oppression, **calamity and sorrow,** each of which is circumstantial, not theological (i.e., not attributable to Yahweh's action or people's sin). The next events are attributed to Yahweh, but they are contingent simply on one's position in society: **he . . . pours contempt on** nobles, **but he lifted the** needy **out of their affliction.**

In this psalm that calls for celebration of Yahweh's goodness (v. 1) and love (vv. 1, 8, 15, 21, 31, 43), special attention is given to his act of delivering from distress. Yahweh's action is that of reversal. In verses 4–32, he does so when called upon for help; in verses 33–41, he does so largely at his own initiative. This psalm is profoundly realistic. It presents Yahweh as sovereign deliverer, not as one who promises a steady state of blessing and not as one who is predictable. Change is the one constant element of human experience in this psalm.

§108 Prayer for God's Exaltation and for His Victory over "Edom" (Ps. 108)

108:1–13 / Verses 1–5 were drawn from Psalm 57:7–11, an individual prayer. They consist of a vow to praise God internationally and an invocation for the universal manifestation of his **glory**. By excluding 57:1–6 our psalm omits all references to individual distress. Verses 6–13 of our psalm were drawn from Psalm 60:5–12, a corporate prayer lamenting a battle defeat. These verses consist primarily of an oracle promising military victory and of petitions for victory, both of which concern **Edom**. By excluding 60:1–4 our psalm omits the lament over a battle defeat. The significance that lies in the combination of these disparate psalm segments is difficult to ascertain. The references to **the nations** and **the peoples** (v. 3) in the first segment and to **Edom** in the second are linked in Isaiah 34:1–11; 63:1–6. These prophetic passages depict Edom as the quintessence of the nations who are hostile to Yahweh, and they foretell his final (perhaps eschatological) "day of vengeance." Thus, the oracle (108:7–9), drawn from Psalm 60, probably foreshadows Yahweh's establishment of his lordship among the nations. And the petition of verse 5, drawn from Psalm 57, probably seeks this final and universal manifestation of Yahweh's glory. For further discussion see the comments on 57:5–11 and on 60:1–5, 6–8, 9–12.

§109 A Prayer Against Those Who Curse and Accuse (Ps. 109)

109:1–31 / This prayer psalm of the individual troubles us. It utters curses on enemies with unnerving relish. It even seeks to obstruct the possibility of the enemies' finding divine forgiveness (vv. 14–15). While it may sound initially like an interpretive dodge, there are several indications that verses 6–19 are a quotation of the speaker's enemies, as noted in the NIV margin. They are thus not endorsed by the psalm but rather upheld as reprehensible. (For further discussion see L. C. Allen, *Psalms 101–150*, pp. 72–73; Kraus, *Psalms 60–150*, p. 338.) First, in verses 2–5 and 20–29 the opponents are always in the plural, but in verses 6–19 the object of the curses is always singular. There is no clear explanation for this shift unless the singular object is the speaker of the psalm. Second, both before and after these curses, the speaker refers to their **words of hatred** that **surround** and **attack** (v. 3), and about his foes he states explicitly, **they . . . curse** (v. 28). As for the allegations made in verses 16–18, we should note, **they have spoken against me with lying tongues** (v. 2). Third, the explicit wishes that the speaker addresses to Yahweh are for his opponents' **shame** (vv. 28–29), but the curses of verses 6–15 go far beyond this. They include his legal "condemnation" (vv. 6–7), his premature death (vv. 8–9), the suffering and extermination of his descendants (vv. 10–13), and the sins of previous generations never being forgiven (vv. 14–15). Moreover, the prayer of verses 21–31 is focused on the speaker's deliverance (esp. vv. 21, 26, 31), not on their retribution. In fact, what the opponents are to realize is that Yahweh "saves" and that, while they "curse," he "blesses" (vv. 26–28). Fourth, the petitions and wishes (i.e., "let" or "may," Hb. jussive) of verses 1, 21, 26–29 are clearly addressed to Yahweh as prayers. The curses of verses 6–19, however, are not. They are curses in the formal sense of the term. Elsewhere in the Psalms, such wishes are addressed to God as prayers (as made clear by vocatives and imperative petitions, 35:1–8, 19–27; 58:6–9;

69:22–28; 83:14–18; cf. 71:9–14). Fifth, verse 20 is not a curse or a wish but a statement (see below), summarizing the "work" or "repayment" of **my accusers.** (Note that vv. 4–5 refer to how **they repay me evil for good.**) The **this** of verse 20 probably denotes the preceding quotation. The **But you** introducing verse 21 thus marks off a new section, where the speaker turns to petition Yahweh. Sixth, these two voices in the psalm help us make sense of key repetitions. In his prayer of verses 21–31 the speaker makes claims contrary to verses 6–19. While his opponents claim, **he . . . hounded to death the poor and the needy** (v. 16), so he claims, **I am poor and needy** (v. 22). As they cursed, **let an accuser stand at his right hand** (v. 6), so he claims, **the LORD . . . stands at the right hand of the needy one** (vv. 30–31).

We are now in a position to analyze the psalm's structural development. Its opening petition that God **not remain silent** is supported by a lament over **wicked and deceitful men** who "repay me evil for good" and who attack and **accuse** the speaker **with** words of hatred (vv. 1–5). These words are spelled out in the lengthy quotation of their curses (vv. 6–15, 19) and false accusations (vv. 16–18). Thus, in contrast to their curses (v. 20), the speaker is to petition Yahweh to **deliver** and **save** him (vv. 21, 26) because of his lamentable condition (vv. 22–25). Other requests follow that **my accusers** may **know . . . that you, O LORD, have done it,** so they **will be clothed with disgrace** (vv. 27–29). In closing, the speaker vows to publish this praise himself (vv. 30–31).

Additional Notes §109

109:14 / **Before the LORD:** This phrase (Hb. *ʾel-Yhwh*) is lacking in the Peshitta and disturbs the verse's metrical balance. It may be a later insertion.

109:20 / **May this be the LORD's payment to my accusers:** "May . . . be" is not a translation supported by the Hb. text, which lacks the verb *hyh*. The verse should be rendered as a declaration, "This is the work/reward of my accusers" (Hb. *pᵉˁullat śōṭᵉnay*, a construct chain). All of the "may . . . be" curses of vv. 7–9, 12–13, 15, 19 use a jussive form of the verb *hyh*. Similar to v. 14, the phrase, "the LORD's" (Hb. *mēʾēt Yhwh*, lit. "from Yahweh," not "of Yahweh"), disturbs the verse's metrical balance, and may also be a later addition. If it is to be retained, we should probably read this pregnant phrase to mean, "These preceding curses from Yahweh are my accusers' repayment to me."

§110 The Davidic King Promised Dominion over Enemies (Ps. 110)

Psalm 110 is a royal psalm composed originally for the pre-exilic Davidic kings and was later applied to the Messiah, as the many NT citations make evident (the NT cites this psalm more than any other OT passage). Like Psalm 2, it refers to Yahweh's installation of the king on Zion and to his promise of military dominion over enemies. Both of these psalms may have been sung at the king's enthronement (implied by "sit at my right hand") or annually "in the spring, at the time when kings go off to war" (2 Sam. 11:1). Also like Psalm 2, it includes prophetic oracles. These provide the structure of our psalm: verses 1–3 and 4–7 each consist of a brief introduction, an oracle (in quotations), and its expansion.

110:1–3 / In the phrase **the LORD says to my Lord,** "the LORD" (Hb. *Yhwh*) is obviously Yahweh, the second "Lord" (Hb. *ʾdōnî* not *ʾdōnāy*, which denotes God) is the king, and the "my" points to the prophetic speaker as one of the king's subjects. The divine oracle contains both promise and limitations. It does promise the most exalted position imaginable, **at my right hand,** and victory over **your enemies.** But it also makes clear that the king's authority is a grant derived from God and that it is subservient to the greater King at whose right hand he sits. That the Davidic king serves simply as vice-regent to Yahweh is made clear in all the royal psalms. Verses 2–3 expand on this oracle, referring to Yahweh in the third person. The importance of **troops** being **willing** for **battle** is echoed in the victory song of Deborah (Judg. 5:2, where the NIV's "people" translates the same Hb. word rendered "troops"). The Hebrew text of verse 3b is problematic. We should probably read, "On the holy mountains, from the womb of the dawn, like the dew I have begotten you" (a reading that has textual support, as noted in *BHS*). If this reading is correct, Yahweh's "begetting" the king provides another parallel with Psalm 2 (see further on 2:7). The figurative comparison with the dew of the dawn implies the life-giving hope (in a land noted for summer's dryness) at the king's coronation.

110:4–7 / When read as a literary text, we generally assume this second oracle is also addressed to the king. It is possible, however, that when performed liturgically another figure may have been addressed, notably the high "priest" (perhaps the spokesman who delivered the first oracle, thus implying a dialogue within the psalm, whereby the priest addresses the king in vv. 1–3 and the king responds to the priest in vv. 4–7). This possibility obtains some support from the priestly **order of Melchizedek,** which may point to David's appointment of the line of "Zadok," a name that derives from the same Hebrew root. It is perhaps significant that "the priests who have charge of the altar" are designated as "the sons of Zadok" in Ezekiel 40:46, etc. It names the order of Zadok, not the order of Aaron, as the priestly line.

If, however, the Davidic king is addressed, the Davidic dynasty is here granted the more ancient, royal prerogatives of the dynasty of Melchizedek, who was both "king of Salem" (i.e., Jerusalem) and "priest of God Most High" (Gen. 14:18). Verse 2 of our psalm specifies that the king will rule "from Zion," that is, Jerusalem. We should not make too much of the king's being granted the title priest because elsewhere the OT does not bestow distinctively priestly functions upon him. As he sits at Yahweh's right hand (v. 1), so **the Lord** is at the king's **right hand** (v. 5). The first image points to Yahweh's appointing the king to royal office, and the second to Yahweh's support of the king in battle. Although the psalm employs militaristic and triumphalistic language, we should note this is to be an expression of divine, just judgment: the Lord . . . **will judge the nations.** The puzzling reference in verse 7 may possibly be explained in light of 1 Kings 1:38–39. Here "Zadok the priest" "anointed Solomon" as king "and escorted him to Gihon," where was the spring that served as the water source for the city of Jerusalem. Thus, verse 7 may allude to a ritual that was part of the Davidic king's coronation.

Additional Note §110

110:1 / **The Lord says to my Lord:** In Matt. 22:41–46; Mark 12:34–37; Luke 20:40–44, Jesus challenges the scribes and the Pharisees to rethink their assumption that "the Christ" is "the son of David," a relationship that to them implied subordination. In the fashion of "haggadic" debate he uses this OT text. The "my Lord" is resignified as "the Christ" or "messiah" and the speaker as David. Thus, David addresses the Christ as "Lord," implying a relationship of David's subordination to the Christ. Although Jesus' use of Ps. 110 is not consistent with its *original* use as a liturgy addressed to the Davidic kings, his reinterpretation is endorsed by the book of Psalms itself. The historical superscriptions invite readers to re-read the "psalms of David" as those authored by David (see the Introduction). Jesus, in his debate with the scribes, adopts this secondary setting for Ps. 110. There are other cases where an OT passage is reinterpreted in the NT with divergent meanings, esp. when a key term is resignified. For example, the promise of Abraham's "seed" (Gen. 12:7; 13:15; 17:7–8; 24:7) is generally interpreted as a collective singular, meaning "descendants," (Luke 1:55; Acts 7:5–6; cf. Rom. 4:16, 18), but on one occasion Paul interprets it as a singular individual, meaning Jesus (Gal. 3:16).

§111 Pondering the Lord's Great Works of the Exodus and Conquest (Ps. 111)

Psalm 111 forms a unique blend of Israel's historical traditions (vv. 4–7a, 9a), legal traditions (vv. 7–8, 9b), and wisdom traditions (v. 10). Throughout this psalm God and his people are referred to in the third person. In verse 1, and in this verse alone, a speaking "I" addresses the council of the upright and the assembly. But is this a liturgist addressing a congregation or a teacher addressing the school of the wise? The parallel phrase, "the assembly of the righteous," appears in Psalm 1:5, a psalm reflecting the wisdom tradition. Wisdom influence may also be suggested by the "motto" of Proverbs in verse 10 ("The fear of the LORD is the beginning of wisdom," Prov. 9:10; 1:7), the acrostic or alphabetical form (note esp. Pss. 37; 112; 119), and the use of Yahweh's law or "precepts" (v. 7) as the source of wisdom (note esp. Pss. 1; 19; 119). On the other hand, wisdom influence need not rule out liturgical use (see W. M. Soll, "Babylonian and Biblical Acrostics," *Bib* 69 [1988], pp. 305–23). Such a setting may be suggested by several parallels with Psalm 103 (esp. vv. 17–18), which has liturgical features. Key to both psalms is the allusion to Exodus 34:6 in the phrase, "the LORD is gracious and compassionate." Both psalms also appear to make several other allusions to the book of Exodus. In addition, the stated intention of Psalm 111 is, "I give thanks" (lit., NIV "I will extol"). Elsewhere this verb is used for "praising" in a liturgical setting, not merely "confessing" in a teaching setting. Verse 4 could suggest the particular setting was Passover (see the parallel with Exod. 12:14 noted below). Several features point to a postexilic date. The brief and stereotypical references to particular traditions (see below) imply that these traditions are well established. The term used for food (Hb. *ṭerep*, v. 5) in its early usage meant "prey" but later came to denote food generally (Mal. 3:10; Prov. 31:15).

111:1–3 / The opening words, **Praise the LORD** (lit. "hal-lelujah"), lie outside the alphabetical pattern of the rest of the psalm. In the first verse we hear a speaking "**I**," perhaps a litur-gist, announcing his intention to fulfill this command whole-heartedly before a public assembly. Verses 2–3 extol Yahweh's **works** in general terms, describing them as **great**. Their great-ness is exemplified by the human response they produce: **they are pondered** (Hb. *drš*) **by all who delight in them.** They elicit not a sense of duty or obligation but of discovery and delight. **His righteousness,** being in parallel with **his deeds,** points to his characteristic actions that "put things right," not merely to his moral character.

111:4–9 / The next section alludes to those works spe-cifically in the exodus-conquest period. Verses 4–6 pass through this review more or less chronologically: exodus, Sinai **cove-nant,** and conquest. Here the verbs carry the descriptive flow, thus focusing on action. The one exception is, **the LORD is gra-cious and compassionate,** a key confession drawn from Exodus 34:6. Verse 7a serves both as a summary of **the works** just men-tioned and as an introduction to the **precepts** of the covenant, given special attention in verses 7b–8. Here the descriptive phrases focus on their relational aspects, especially as expres-sions of God's **faithfulness.** Verse 9 closes off the section that rehearses Yahweh's deeds and thus echoes key terms and mo-tifs used in verses 4–6 (the exodus **redemption for his people** and **his covenant**); it likewise directs our attention to his ac-tions **(he provided, he ordained).** Climaxing this account of Yahweh's acts is, **holy and awesome is his name** (v. 9c), a phrase that points to God's self-revelation. The Hebrew term for "awe-some" serves as the link to the closing verse: as Yahweh's name is awesome/fearful, so it evokes **fear**/awe (both terms derive from the Hb. root *yrʾ*) from humans. Throughout verses 2–9 Yahweh or his works have been the grammatical subjects, but attention now shifts to the proper human responses of fear and obedience.

A casual reading of the psalm may lead one to think it merely refers to Yahweh's works in general. But closer in-spection (following a more literal translation than the NIV) re-veals several echoes of earlier tellings of specific works of Yahweh:

Psalm 111	Early Salvation History	Exodus 34:10–11
"A memorial he made (Hb. ʿśh) for his wonders" (v. 4a).	"This day (i.e. Passover) shall be for you a memorial" (Exod. 12:14).	"I will do (Hb. ʿśh) wonders."
"Yahweh is gracious and compassionate" (v. 4b, terms reversed for the sake of the acrostic).	"Yahweh is a God compassionate and gracious" (Exod. 34:6).	
"He provides food for those who fear him" (v. 5a).	Yahweh provided manna and quail in the wilderness (Exod. 16; cf. Num. 11).	
"His covenant" (vv. 5b, 9b).	Sinai covenant (Exod. 20–24).	"I will make a covenant."
"The power of his works (also vv. 2, 7) he declared to his people, to give them the inheritance of nations" (v. 6).	Conquest (Josh.).	"And he said, '. . . before all your people I will do wonders that have not been created in all the land and among all the nations. And all the people in whose midst you will be will see Yahweh's work. . . . I am about to drive out from before you' [nations]."
"Redemption he sent for his people" (v. 9a).	Exodus deliverance (cf. perhaps Exod. 8:23).	
"He commanded forever his covenant" (v. 9b).	Sinai covenant.	"Keep what I am commanding today."
Covenant "precepts" (vv. 7b–8).		
"Holy and awesome is his name" (v. 9c).		"For that which I will do with you will be awesome."

In verses 9–10 the transition from Yahweh's awesome self-revelation to his people's response of reverential obedience may also be echoed in a passage from Exodus. After Yahweh's thundering appearance on Mt. Sinai, "Moses said to the people, 'Do not be afraid (Hb. *yr*ʾ). God has come to test you, so that the fear (Hb. *yr*ʾ*h*) of God will be with you (lit. "upon your faces") to keep you from sinning' " (Exod. 20:20).

111:10 / Yahweh's "fearful" self-revelation elicits **the fear of the LORD** from the people to whom he has bound himself in covenant. But lest there be misunderstanding that this response is enough, the psalm continues: "good understanding have all who do it" (lit., i.e., "the fear of the LORD"; NIV **all who follow his precepts**). This recital of Yahweh's saving deeds should evoke the mental engagement of "pondering" (v. 2), the attitude of "fearing," and the behavior of "doing." And each of these responses is to be done within the framework of the praise of God, which opens ("Praise the LORD") and closes the psalm ("his praise stands forever"). Each response is to be an act of celebration. Finally, as the phrase, "and his righteousness stands forever" (lit., v. 3b), closed off the general remarks on Yahweh's works (vv. 2–3), so the phrase, his **praise** "stands forever" (lit., v. 10c) closes the psalm.

Additional Note §111

111:10 / **His precepts** is not in the Hb. text, which reads, "who do *them*." The only plural antecedent that fits is "precepts," but it is strangely distant (v. 7) with several other divine properties mentioned in between (vv. 9–10a). The LXX, Syriac, and Jerome read, "who do *it* (feminine)," whose antecedent is **fear** (feminine) in the preceding colon (poetic line).

§112 Blessings of Those Who Fear the Lord (Ps. 112)

W. Brueggemann classifies this psalm as one of the "psalms of orientation" (*The Message of the Psalms* [Augsburg Old Testament Studies; Minneapolis: Augsburg, 1984], p. 45), which he believes reflect "a satisfied and assured assertion of orderliness" that "probably comes from the well-off, from the economically secure and the politically significant" (p. 26). But a closer reading of such a psalm reveals the reverse. Order needs to be affirmed most strongly in times of disorder, and there are indications of current disorder in this psalm and of a tension between what the world should and will be and what the world is now. We are unfair to this psalm if we assume the writer believes he is actually describing the visible reality of his own world (so cf. Ps. 1, whose opening verses closely parallel 112:1). Other psalms, some reflecting the same wisdom tradition, do not shrink from lamenting reversals of such promises (e.g., Pss. 49; 73). In this light, Psalm 112 prescribes what should be and describes what will ultimately be (e.g., "in the end," v. 8). Its chief aim is to encourage right behavior.

112:1 / Like the preceding psalm, this one is an acrostic, where each line begins with the successive letters of the Hebrew alphabet. The opening **Praise the LORD,** however, lies outside the acrostic (which begins with **Blessed is**) and was probably added when the psalm was collected with Psalms 111 and 113, both of which also begin with "Praise the LORD." Since it is now a part of the final form of the psalm, the whole psalm must be seen in a new light. It is not only a blessing for the benefit of the Yahweh-fearer; it also becomes a call to worship Yahweh himself.

The acrostic opens with the pronouncement of a blessing, and the rest of the psalm unpacks the nature of that blessing. The chief characteristic of its recipient is that he is one **who fears the LORD.** As is typical of Hebrew parallelism, the second line is more specific. It provides a concrete example of such character:

he **finds great delight in his commands.** "Fearing" and "delight-ing" may strike us as incongruous—even ambivalent—attitudes and emotions, but according to biblical psychology they define a healthy person. This "fear" is not trepidation or dread; it is awe and reverence. And this "delight" is not self-indulgence or amuse-ment; it is joy. The parallelism of "the LORD" and "his com-mands" does not reduce relationship with Yahweh to legalism. "His commands" relate to all of his instruction, not merely to for-mal commandments or laws. The one who truly reveres and re-spects Yahweh himself is one who gladly follows his counsel about living.

112:2–9 / The body of the psalm lists various promises for such people, along with further descriptions of their charac-ter. Foremost among these promises are those concerning **his children,** who will themselves **be blessed. His house,** being asso-ciated with children, should not be understood merely as a physi-cal structure but also as a "household" (cf. the wordplay on "house" in 2 Sam. 7:1–16). Similarly, while **wealth and riches** are usually understood in a material sense, the equivalent term in the parallel line, namely **his righteousness,** qualifies these "riches" as a quality, not as something to be quantified like ma-terial possessions. This same word pair appears twice in Prov-erbs, where each time "wealth" and "riches" are qualified in a non-material sense (8:18–19; 13:7). We should also note that **righ-teousness** does not point merely to a subjective, moral attribute, but also to an objective, state of being—namely "a right order." The inclusion of **forever** does not promise eternal life within the horizons of the OT, rather it points to his family line.

The words **even in darkness** admit that circumstances will not always be favorable for the Yahweh-fearer, but the words **light dawns for the upright** promise a sense of hope in the midst of adversity. It may strike us as unusual that the psalm should juxtapose generosity with **justice** and righteousness (vv. 5, 9). We might expect generosity to be paralleled by "mercy." But, as seen elsewhere in the OT (see on Ps. 72), caring for the unfortunate is "right" and is considered an act of "justice."

Verses 6 through 8 describe the security of Yahweh-fearer. While they may be taken to mean that he never experiences any-thing **bad,** closer examination reveals a significant ambiguity. Does his "unshakeability" (v. 6) refer to his material well-being or to his inner well-being? By whom will he **be remembered for-**

ever, by people or simply by God? Does the claim, **he will have no fear of** bad **news,** mean that he will never receive bad news, or that when he does he need not fear? The parallel line and the next verse, in fact, imply the latter. His security and freedom from **fear** rest not in circumstances but in heartfelt trust: **his heart is steadfast, trusting in the LORD. His heart is secure** (lit. "supported"). The repeated insistence that **he will have no** fear implies that he may, in fact, face circumstances that could give cause for fear. Likewise, the assurance that **in the end he will look in triumph on his foes** implies that "in the meantime" he may not. The promise here is not for a cushy life but for one upheld by God.

112:10 / The final verse drives home the fact that righteousness is the only means for obtaining ultimate satisfaction. **The wicked** will see their **longings . . . come to nothing.** We may infer from this psalm that one can argue for righteous conduct not only on the grounds that it is right but also on "selfish" grounds. The wicked, despite their complete freedom to choose whatever means to obtain their longings, will find those longings "come to nothing." The wicked **man will see** the ultimate success of the righteous, described in the preceding verses, **and be vexed.**

§113 The Incomparable God of Condescension and Exaltation (Ps. 113)

This is not a psalm for elitists. The chief symbols of power—all the nations in the earth and the heavens in the cosmos—do not impress King Yahweh (vv. 4–6). He, in fact, seems to delight in raising up society's helpless to positions of social status (vv. 7–9). This psalm is a hymn, and more specifically it is one that uses both imperatives and participles, along with a rhetorical question concerning Yahweh's incomparability (a form usually found in hymns, e.g., Exod. 15:11). The characteristic commands to praise at the beginning imply an audience of some kind is present. It is unclear whether the servants of the Lord (v. 1) are the general congregation or Levitical singers in particular. The opening verse of Psalm 135 calls on the same group, and its closing verses call on Yahweh-fearers and the houses of Israel, of Aaron, and of Levi, thus implying all Israel are considered his servants. Perhaps we should envisage a Levitical choir singing the prescribed words of the psalm on behalf of a congregation. In Jewish tradition, Psalms 113–118 form "the Hallel" to be sung at Passover (cf. Mark 14:26; Matt. 26:30). The psalm yields no conclusive signs of being either pre- or postexilic.

113:1–3 / The psalm's structure consists of three strophes with three Hebrew lines each. The psalm opens and closes with "hallelujah," "Yah" being a shortened form of the divine name. The object of the praise commanded in the opening three verses is Yahweh's **name**, which in terms of time and space is to be celebrated **forevermore** and over the entire planet.

113:4–6 / The rest of the psalm forms the basis of that praise. First, there is the declaration that Yahweh is **exalted** over all earthly and cosmic powers. Israel/Judah may be greatly overshadowed by empires with political and military might, but for this hymn that fact is beside the point. Second, it dares worshipers to name someone comparable to Yahweh, pointing particularly to the height of his throne. He is so high that he **stoops down to look** not only on **the earth** but also **on the heavens** (vv. 4, 6). In other psalms Yahweh looks down from heaven to examine humanity (11:4; 14:2), but here he does so to care for the helpless in society.

113:7–9 / By using terms that echo those in verses 4–6, verses 7–9 show that the qualities inherent in Yahweh's kingship are the ones that he exercises towards humanity. As Yahweh is exalted (v. 4), so he "exalts" (lit., NIV **lifts**) **the needy from the ash heap** (v. 7b). As Yahweh "makes high his sitting enthroned" (lit., infinitive of Hb. *yšb,* v. 5b), so he **seats** (Hiphil of *yšb*) the needy **with princes** (v. 8a) and **settles** or "seats" (Hiphil of *yšb*) **the barren woman in her home** (v. 9a, cf. "God makes the lonely dwell in a home," lit., 68:6). The one sitting on high stoops down to raise up the lowly to sit with the exalted of the earth. This is the kind of kingship that Yahweh exercises. His exaltedness over earth and heaven does not make him aloof from human affairs; on the contrary, it makes him involved. What is also noteworthy is that Yahweh's care is here extended not to corporate Israel but to individuals, and particularly to society's helpless and rejected—**the poor** and the barren woman. Having present a solid basis for praise, the psalm closes as it began, with another call for praise.

Psalm 113 shows some remarkable parallels with the Song of Hannah. Compare especially verses 7–8 with 1 Samuel 2:8, and verse 9 with 1 Samuel 2:5. Verse 7 of our psalm also closely parallels Mary's Magnificat in Luke 1:52, though it interestingly omits the motif of negative reversal. While Psalm 113 speaks only of the poor lifted up, Luke 1:52 adds, "He has brought down rulers from their thrones."

§114 Trembling at the Appearance of the God of the Exodus (Ps. 114)

114:1–8 / This is a hymn, but a unique one. It contains no imperative call for worship. The only mention of human figures are **Israel, Jacob,** and **Judah** of the distant past. The psalm's only imperative verb is addressed to the **earth** or "land." The listeners/readers are dramatically transported back to the historical moments of the exodus, wilderness wanderings, and the entry into the promised land. This reliving of Israel's sacred past is featured in other festival psalms (e.g., Pss. 46; 48; 66; 95). The prominence given to the exodus from Egypt may point to the Passover festival in particular, for which this event was central. Moreover, the OT narrative notes that immediately after the crossing of **the Jordan,** Passover was celebrated (Josh. 5:10). Finally, according to Jewish tradition, this psalm is the second of "the Hallel" psalms to be sung at Passover (see on Ps. 113). The date of the psalm is difficult to determine, though it was probably preexilic (see further Additional Note on v. 2).

This psalm has dramatic effects. To appreciate this, we must first recognize that the NIV translators have inserted **God's** into verse 2, which literally reads, "Judah became his sanctuary." Listeners are left wondering who it is that has appropriated **Israel** as **his dominion.** And what did **the sea** "see"? Moreover, geographical features are animated like living creatures: the sea **looked and fled,** the Jordan **turned back** (i.e., retreated); **the mountains skipped like rams.** (In the book of Exodus the Reed Sea was "driven back" and "divided" [14:21] and its waters "piled up" [15:8; on the Jordan cf. Josh. 3:16]. Mount Sinai "trembled" [19:18], as did the inhabitants of Canaan [15:14–16].) Verses 5–6 of our psalm are not a mere repetition; they are phrased as questions posed to the now fully personified waters and mountains. (These two verses, using the Hb. imperfect verb, should probably be translated in the present tense, thus making us—the audience—dramatically present.) In effect, they are asked to testify to the "land" (NIV "earth," v. 7) that there is good reason to respond to God's appearing as they have. These stylistic features reflect poetic license to impress generations far removed from the original events with the impact of God's interventions into history and nature. Thus, the key dramatic function of verses 1–6 is to create suspense in the listeners as to the identity of "his" in verse 2 and as to the cause of these reverberations in nature. The climax of the psalm appears in verses 7–8, where the answer is revealed. Here is proclaimed the name, **the God of Jacob.** Attention is drawn to God's mere **presence** (lit. "face"). The remarkable story of this psalm is that this awesome Presence has identified himself with a people, as the title "God of Jacob" in verse 7 recalls **the house of** Jacob liberated from **Egypt** in verse 1.

By virtue of God's appearing, each natural feature does what is contrary to its nature. The sea, massive and immovable, "fled," and the Jordan "turned back." The mountains, the firm pillars of the earth, "skipped." **The hard rock,** impenetrable and dry, produces **springs of water.** These contrary-to-nature transformations form the focus. No mention is made of the benefit they had for Israel: the sea provided escape from their Egyptian pursuers, the Jordan became their avenue into the promised land, and **the rock** in the wilderness gave drink to a thirsty people. The emphasis of verses 3–8 is thus on the sheer awesomeness of God's presence. They form a hymn, not a thanksgiving. (Cf. the theophany in Ps. 29, which also mentions reverberations in nature and mountains "skipping" in v. 6.)

In view of the psalm's historical progression, we should understand the imperative, **Tremble, O** earth, to be addressed first to the "land" of Canaan. (Cf. the response of Jericho's inhabitants, Josh. 2:9–11.) The Hebrew word for "earth" (Hb. ʾereṣ) also means "land." We can imagine this psalm's place in festival worship as it dramatically brings the congregation to the awesome Presence it worships. In addition, we can imagine that it may have been used before military campaigns (which, like Passover, occurred in the spring; cf. 2 Sam. 11:1), thus invoking the God of the exodus and conquest once again to reveal his awe-inspiring Presence. Finally, the ambiguity of the term "land/earth" may have been intentional, whereby the psalm warns the whole earth to tremble at Yahweh's ultimate appearing to judge it in the future (cf. 96:9–13).

Additional Note §114

114:2 / **Judah ... Israel:** Identifying precisely to what national bodies these terms refer is key to determining the psalm's date. There are no fewer than four possibilities (see further Allen, *Psalms 101–150,* p. 103). (a) "Judah" could refer to the southern kingdom, "Israel" to the northern. This would locate the psalm between 922 B.C. (the division of the kingdom) and 722 B.C. (the fall of the northern kingdom). (b) If the psalm were composed/used after 722 B.C., then "Judah" may be identified as the sole heir of the title "Israel." (c) "Israel" may refer to the whole kingdom, and "Judah" is simply singled out because of the temple in Jerusalem. In this view the meaning of "Israel" in v. 2 is identical to its meaning in v. 1. The period of the united monarchy thus becomes a possible time for the psalm's origin. Since the psalm makes no marked distinctions for these names, this is the most natural reading. (d) The parallelism may imply that "Judah" and "Israel" together became his **sanctuary** and **dominion.**

§115 The Maker of Heaven and Earth Praised and Invoked to Bless Israel (Ps. 115)

For Psalm 115 the major categories of form criticism, namely prayer and praise (or lament and hymn) do not exactly fit. It does have features of laments. Verse 1 is formally a petition, although it is explicitly not for the petitioners' sake but for Yahweh's. Verse 2 forms part of a complaint in 79:10, even though it also introduces a satirical contrast between "our God" and "their idols." Additionally, the psalm does have hymnic features. It predicates of God praiseworthy characteristics and actions (vv. 3, 16), but it also seeks his blessing in verses 12–15. We should also note the psalm is largely composed of formulas found in other psalms, one a lament (cf. v. 2 and 79:10) and the other a hymn (cf. v. 3 with 135:6; vv. 4–6, 8 with 135:15–18; vv. 9–11 with 135:19–20, also note 118:2–4). Whatever its form-critical genre, it does bear the marks of a liturgy. The variations in addressee and in the references to Yahweh (direct address "your" in v. 1, and third-person reference "the LORD," "he," etc., elsewhere) and to the congregation (e.g., "us/we" in vv. 1, 12, 18, and "you" in vv. 14–15) imply Psalm 115 was performed liturgically, not simply read as a literary piece. It is very likely that different voices sang different sections. Verses 9–11 may have been sung antiphonally (cf. Ps. 136).

The particular historical setting of this psalm is not made explicit. The dominant factors presented for the congregation's and Yahweh's consideration are theological, not historical. The psalm does offer hints, however, that it was postexilic, and if it was, some interesting theological observations emerge and are discussed below. The question the nations raise in verse 2 implies there is little tangible evidence of Yahweh's effectiveness. Of course we must recognize the kind of evidence that would impress ancient Near Eastern peoples; for them the status of a nation's god was measured by the political and military success of that nation. But what the psalm says and does not say is also telling: Our God "is in heaven," not "in Jerusalem" or "with our armies." The absence of any stated ties between Yahweh and Israel's welfare, aside from protection in the past (vv. 9–11, see below) and the anticipation of blessing in the near future (vv. 12–15), suggest that Israel has little political evidence to point to. This lack of self-determination fits the postexilic era, when Judah lived as a province under the Persian empire. The concern for "blessing" and "increasing" (v. 14) also reflects the situation of the exilic and early postexilic periods (Jer. 29:6; Isa. 49:14–23; 54:1–3).

115:1–8 / The psalm opens with a petition, "give glory" (lit., NIV **be the glory**), but the object of this honor is to be Yahweh's **name,** not the praying community. The reason this request is so phrased becomes evident as the psalm unfolds. While the function of verse 2 is debated (see Additional Notes), it is clear **the nations** claim to see no evidence that Israel's **God** has acted on their behalf. The point of verse 3, therefore, is to assert that Yahweh's welfare is not tied to Israel's; "our God" in heaven transcends the affairs of nations. The claim, **he does whatever pleases him,** is a statement of Yahweh's freedom, not that his actions are all predetermined or that he cannot be influenced (otherwise the petition of v. 1 becomes obsolete). The attack on "our God" leads to an attack on **their idols.** In stark contrast, they are ineffective and idle (vv. 4–7), as are their worshipers (v. 8).

115:9–11 / To support the validity of the claim that Yahweh—as distinct from the idols of the nations—makes a difference in human history, verses 9–11 offer historical testimony, in very general terms. These verses should probably be read as statements in the past, rather than as present imperatives (see below): "The house of Israel trusted in the LORD; he was their help and shield," etc. The ancestors of the houses of **Israel** and **Aaron** and of those **who fear** Yahweh "trusted" and proved him to be **their help and shield.** Thus, while those who trust in idols (v. 8) obtain nothing from them and become lifeless like them, those who "trusted in Yahweh" (vv. 9–11) received help and protection.

115:12–15 / On the basis of the witness of Israel's history, verse 12a announces on behalf of the present congregation (here speaking in first person, **us**) that they now stand at a turning point: "Yahweh has remembered (Hb. perfect) us and will bless (Hb. imperfect)." At key moments in their history, especially during a period of distress, Yahweh had "remembered" his people (Exod. 2:24; Pss. 9:12; 98:3; 105:8, 42; 106:45; 111:5; 136:23; also 74:2; 106:4). The three groups found within verses 9–11 are then assured in verses 12b–13 that Yahweh **will bless** them. The form of divine action sought here lies not in the momentous, historic deliverances of the nation but in the daily blessing of individuals and their families—both **small and great alike.** Verses 14–15 formally seek that blessing for the congregation (here addressed as **you**), also acknowledging the bestower of blessing as **the Maker of heaven and earth** (cf. Gen. 14:19).

115:16–18 / Closing the psalm, the liturgist leads the congregation (here speaking on their behalf in the **we** form) in what should be their response to Yahweh's "blessing," namely "praising" (v. 17) and "blessing" him (v. 18, lit. "we bless Yah," not NIV, **extol**). Yahweh blesses his people and they, in turn, bless him. Linking the last two strophes is a key word pair: the LORD retains the **heavens** (not to be shared with other deities as the nations and their idols of vv. 2, 4 would claim), but **the earth** he has entrusted to humans, whose primary symptom of being alive is to praise Yahweh. The reference to **the dead . . . who go down to silence** (v. 17) echoes the description of idolaters who become like their dumb and deaf idols (vv. 4–8). Overall, therefore, the psalm presents a marked contrast between the nations and their idols and Israel and **the LORD.** The former are inactive and lifeless; the latter are characterized by action and life.

This psalm appears virtually to equate the gods of the nations with their idols. This may be a case of reductio ad absurdum, where the psalm pushes the religion of "the nations" to its logical conclusion, namely, that any god that would be represented by a piece of lifeless metal of human manufacture must itself be lifeless. Yahweh, by contrast, is not experienced through icons but through historical help and protection (vv. 9–11; see further G. von Rad, "Some Aspects of the Old Testament World-View," in *The Problem of the Hexateuch and Other Essays* [London: SCM, 1966], pp. 144–65). In addition, it would not be fair to expect a liturgical song to nuance its statements and detail each logical inference as though it were a theological treatise. The psalm nowhere actually equates the gods with their idols. But it does claim that "trust" directed toward idols yields no observable or sensory effects. This approach is consistent with that of other OT passages. In the contest between Yahweh and the gods, the issue is not metaphysical but practical; it focuses on a deity's effectiveness, not its existence per se. "Trusting" or calling on such gods produces no salvation—it simply doesn't work (Deut. 32:37–38; Judg. 10:14; Isa. 44:9–20, esp. v. 17; 45:20; 46:1–2, 6–7; Jer. 11:12; also Deut. 4:28; Jer. 10:1–16; Hab. 2:18–19). In light of the above, Psalm 115 is not against symbolism as such but against direct representations of Yahweh. Thus, Yahweh's presence is located *in* the temple and *over* the ark of the covenant, but the presence itself always remains invisible.

We are now in a better position to understand verse 1, the only one addressed explicitly to God. The psalm as a whole makes us profoundly aware that the kind of deity people worship is a direct reflection on themselves. The nations worship their own handiwork and so become lifeless. We worship a God who is free and acts, and so we live. It is thus better that glory (or "honor" or "credit") go to God than to us, lest we become preoccupied with our own self-importance, trust in our own handiwork, and fail to be counted among those truly alive. In this connection, verse 3 is also a key statement on the kind of deity Israel worships. It reflects deep wonder at God but also contains a tacit resignation. It admits that we have no legal claim to demand that God, even if he be called "our God," act in a certain way on our behalf. "He does whatever pleases him." Yahweh is declared independent, even from Israel's wishes.

In this psalm Israel learns a valuable lesson, and it becomes particularly striking if we are correct in assigning the psalm to the postexilic period. In the eyes of the nations, there was no evidence of Yahweh's effectiveness. Israel had been subjugated and deported by Babylon and then restored to their homeland by the achievements of Persia. But this psalm does not give in to the assumption that a nation's political and military might are proof of God's power and blessing. Yahweh in heaven, on the one hand, transcends all human ties, but on the other, his eye is on "those who fear the LORD—small and great alike." Humans should aspire to virtues such as "trust" and "fear," not to power and might. Under such an economy, families, not nations, become central. This is a lesson for us all, especially in the West, where we Christians sometimes give in to the temptation of assuming that the status of God's work in the church can be measured by the "success" or "failure" of its institutions and programs.

Additional Notes §115

115:2 / This verse could be read as a motivation or argument supporting the petition of the preceding verse. In other words, "give glory to your reputation, because the nations mock your existence." (The Hb. verb could equally be translated, "Why *should* the nations say . . . ?") On the other hand, v. 2 could simply introduce the following verses: "For what possible reason do the nations say, 'Where is their God?', because our sovereign God does whatever he pleases without interference!" The psalm, in effect, mocks their mockery. Which alternative is correct may have been evident in the psalm's original liturgical performance, esp. if different speakers were involved. The bare text we have, however, allows it to function in either or both ways.

115:9–12 / **Trust:** The MT (and so the NIV) reads the verbs for "trust" in the first line of vv. 9–11 as imperatives. But the **their** of the second line seems strange; we should expect "your." The versions—the LXX, Syriac, and Jerome—read these verbs as Hb. perfects: "the house of Israel *trusted* in Yahweh; he was their help and shield" etc. In this reading, vv. 9–11 offer historical testimony. While engaging with the gods of the nations, the OT characteristically appeals to Yahweh's historical acts as evidence that his existence makes a difference (esp. 135:8–12, a psalm with many close parallels to Ps. 115, as detailed above; cf. Isa. 41:21–29). In addition, reading the verbs of vv. 9–11 as Hb. perfects (referring to the past) helps us to make sense of the Hb. perfect in v. 12a: "Yahweh *has remembered* us" (lit., the NIV, without good reason, renders this verb in the present). Otherwise, this pronouncement seems to come out of a vacuum.

115:14 / **Increase** is connected with blessing (also Gen. 1:22, 28) not because the Bible is merely interested in numbers but because it is symptomatic of health. The creatures themselves are healthy, and their environment is healthy enough to sustain them.

§116 A Thank Offering for Deliverance from Death (Ps. 116)

Psalm 116 is a thanksgiving psalm that celebrates deliverance from near-death distress (cf. esp. Ps. 30). It consists of a proclamation of praise and an introductory summary (vv. 1–2), as well as recollections of the distress (v. 3), of the cry to God (v. 4), and of Yahweh's deliverance (vv. 8–11). Contained in this report is hymnic praise (vv. 5–6; so cf. 30:4–5, which also "interrupts" a report of deliverance) that confesses a general principle of praise exemplified in this testimony. The closing section narrates the thanksgiving rituals and ceremony that accompany the singing of this thanksgiving psalm (vv. 12–14, 17–19), along with more embedded hymnic praise and personal testimony (vv. 15–16).

116:1–11 / The confession, **I love the LORD**, is not as common in the Psalms as we might imagine (31:23; 97:10; 145:20; cf. 18:1; loving God's name, 5:11; 69:36; 119:32; his house, 26:8; his salvation, 40:16 = 70:4). The chief reason for this bond is evidenced in the confession, **He heard my cry for mercy.** This reflects the fundamental tradition of the prayer psalms of the individual, namely that my God answers when I call (see the Introduction). The personal nature of this encounter is underscored by **my voice** and **his ear.** The hymnic praise exemplified in this individual's deliverance from the imprisoning **cords of death** (cf. 18:4–5) echoes a confession beloved in the OT: **The LORD is gracious and . . . full of compassion** (e.g., 86:15; 103:8; 145:8; Exod. 34:6; Neh. 9:17). A unique feature of this thanksgiving psalm is the turn to encourage one's own self: **Be at rest once more, O my soul** (cf. 42:5, 11; 43:5; 103:1–2). The report of salvation resumes in verse 8 with Yahweh's deliverance of **my soul** (thus linking with the previous address to "my soul"), **my eyes,** and **my feet.** The significance of the feet becomes clear in the following expression: **that I may walk before the LORD in the**

land of the living. Thus, the purpose of the rescue is not mere survival but a life lived before Yahweh.

116:12–19 / The closing verses elaborate on this "walking before the LORD" by raising the question, **How can I repay the LORD for all his goodness to me?** The verses that follow should probably be rendered in the present tense, not in the past as found in the NIV (the Hb. imperfect verb does not denote a tense as such): "I lift up the cup of salvation and call on the name of the LORD. I fulfill my vows to the LORD" (vv. 13–14), and "I sacrifice a thank offering to you," etc. (vv. 17–18). Thus, thanksgiving psalms are not private compositions *referring* to ritual worship; they are the liturgical words that actually *accompany* the thanksgiving sacrifice. Half of the **thank offering** was burnt as an offering to God and the other half was shared as a communal meal eaten before the Lord (22:26; 65:1–4; Lev. 7:15–16; Deut. 12:5–7; 1 Sam. 1:3–4, 9). **The cup of salvation** (cf. 23:5) may refer to a drink offering (cf. Exod. 29:40–41; Num. 15:5; 28:7). We should note that when OT worshipers **call on the name of the LORD,** this expression can denote praise (vv. 13, 17; cf. v. 2), and not merely a call for help (v. 4). The public setting for the singing of such thanksgiving psalms is evident in the expressions, **in the presence of all his people, in the courts of the house of the LORD—in your midst, O Jerusalem.**

§117 Nations to Praise the Lord for His Faithfulness (Ps. 117)

This is the shortest and simplest of the psalms. Its structure is typical of hymns, in that it consists of a call for praise, which is repeated at the conclusion, and the grounds for that praise, which is expressed in a "for" statement. Its liturgical use is plain from the repeated call to worship. Its brevity may lead us to suppose we have but a fragment of a larger psalm or that it forms either the conclusion of Psalm 116 (as some Hb. manuscripts have it) or the introduction of Psalm 118 (as other Hb. manuscripts have it). But change is unnecessary because Psalm 117, as with most hymns of the Psalter, probably formed only part of a larger liturgy and was thus sung in combination with other psalms.

117:1 / As typical as this hymn is, it is somewhat unusual in that it contains a summons to **all you nations** and **all you peoples.** In attempting to trace the source of this universalism we need not appeal to supposed recent military victories of Israel, to prophetic innovations (e.g., Isa. 40–66), or to developments in eschatological (i.e., end-time) beliefs. In the hymns that share this feature, for example the psalms of Yahweh's kingship and Psalms 68:32; 100:1; 113:3, the universal summons stems from their distinctive theological position that Yahweh, as universal King and Creator, merits universal praise (see esp. on Ps. 47, which implies foreigners were present at major Israelite festivals).

117:2 / The basis for this call to praise lies in Yahweh's attributes (not specifically his deeds) of **love** and **faithfulness.** While these terms are prominent in the confession of Exodus 34:6, the frequency of this word pair in psalms of all kinds implies it was simply a favorite liturgical expression. A more literal translation reveals the striking word choice in verse 2: "for his love has prevailed (Hb. *gābar*) over us" (cf. the noun "warrior,"

Hb. *gibbôr;* and also a literal translation of 23:6: "surely goodness and love shall *pursue* me").

The psalm almost appears to tease its listeners with the question of who the **us** is in verse 2. Is it Israel alone, thus making "all you nations" praise Yahweh as mere witnesses of his goodness to Israel? Or does it include them, thus making them praise Yahweh as fellow-participants of his goodness (e.g., 65:5–8)? The answer may be the same as we saw for Psalm 100. Should foreigners choose to become worshipers of Yahweh, they may claim to be counted among the **us** of verse 2.

§118 A Festival Procession for Giving Thanks (Ps. 118)

This psalm uniquely combines corporate hymnic praise (vv. 1–4, 22–24, 29), individual thanksgiving (vv. 5–18, 21, 28; which includes a victory song [vv. 14–16]), a petition (v. 25), and a processional liturgy of entering the temple gates and processing to the altar (vv. 19–20, 26– 27). It alternates between referring to Yahweh in the third person and addressing him in the second person, and between hymnic sections, spoken by "we," and thanksgiving sections, spoken by "I." The "gate liturgy" (vv. 19–20, 26) illustrates that we cannot distinguish sharply between the individual and the group. A speaker commands, "Open for me" and "I will enter," but the psalm then points to a group: "This is the gate of the LORD through which the righteous may enter." Later, a speaker says, "Blessed is he who comes," and then says, "we bless you" (pl. "you all"). The "he" is simply any individual among the "you" group. The best explanation for this combination lies in the liturgical origins of the psalm, where a liturgist speaks on behalf of the congregation.

The identity or the social circle of this liturgist has been a matter of debate. Because he appears to represent the people and because of the allusions to military engagement and victory in verses 8–16, the king has been suggested as the liturgist. While this is certainly possible, several factors indicate otherwise. First, although the king was the commander-in-chief, these verses would be appropriate to any warrior who would testify publicly. There are no claims to exclusively royal prerogatives, as seen in the psalms that are clearly royal. Second, it seems incongruous to propose the king speaks verses 10–12 when the preceding verses disclaim any value to royal position. Third, "the nations" may refer not to a political entity but simply to outsiders (cf. 43:1, and see on 59:5, 8). The image of opponents (17:9, 11; 22:12, 16; 109:3), even an "army" (27:3), "surrounding" an individual is common in the prayer psalms of the individual. Fourth, portions of this psalm are found in psalms that appear to stem from the postexilic period, when Judah had no king (cf. vv. 2–4 and 115:9–12; 135:19–20; the antiphon in Ps. 136; cf. vv. 7–8 and 146:3–4; 147:10–11; Isa. 40:30–31; and perhaps Ps. 33:16–19). Our psalm also appears to cite the book of Exodus (vv. 14, 28 and Exod. 15:2), and other psalms that do the same appear to be postexilic (see on 103:7–8, 17–18; 111:4–9; 145:8). Thus, it seems more likely we should simply see the speaker as a liturgist representing the worshipers. The event mentioned here could refer to an actual, recent deliverance or to a liturgically remembered battle of corporate Israel's salvation history (see on Ps. 9). As noted, our psalm does echo the Song of Moses (Exod. 15), originally sung after the deliverance at the Reed Sea.

118:1–18 / In light of this liturgical setting before the **gates** of the temple precincts, we should probably understand the psalm's development as follows. Outside the temple a priest issues the hymnic, imperative call for the respective parties to engage in an antiphon (**His love endures forever**) and to **give thanks** (vv. 1–4). This points to a verbal "thank you" and to thanksgiving psalms and thanksgiving offerings (see Pss. 30; 116, esp. v. 17), which are also implied by the later reference to the altar (v. 27). In response, a representative liturgist (or liturgists) testifies to the congregation (vv. 5–18). Typical of thanksgiving psalms, he recites a brief report of distress, of his "crying to the LORD," and of Yahweh's "answering" (vv. 5–7). (In v. 5 the NIV misses a play on words: "From a narrow place I called Yah; Yah answered me with a broad place.") He next confesses that **refuge in the LORD** is **better . . . than . . . trust in man,** even in the noblest of them, **princes** (vv. 8–9). These verses underscore a key issue, already noted in his summary report, **What can man do to me?** The threat posed by human forces he graphically portrays in another thanksgiving (vv. 10–13): **All the nations surrounded me.** The sole means he uses to "confront" (see the Additional Note) "the nations" is **the name of the LORD.** The liturgist next leads the congregation in a victory song (vv. 14–16) that echoes the Song of Moses. It draws to their attention that Yahweh's **strength** and **right hand** have acted on **my** behalf and on behalf of **the righteous** together. Rounding off his thanksgiving, the liturgist renews his vow to praise Yahweh (vv. 17–18; cf. 30:12; 63:4; 146:2), and again summarizes his rescue. If the psalm is postexilic, this "chastening" may refer to the judgment of the exile (perhaps cf. 66:8–12, a psalm that also alludes to the exodus, vv. 5–7, and accompanies the performance of a thanksgiving ritual, vv. 13–20).

118:19–29 / The thanksgiving liturgy continues with the entry liturgy of the gate (**I will enter and give thanks,** vv. 19–21). This portion begins with the liturgist commanding **the gates of righteousness** to **open** (cf. Isa. 26:2). Next the congregation, and possibly the liturgist himself, are reminded, **this is the gate of the LORD through which the righteous may enter,** thus echoing the preexilic liturgies of temple entry in Psalms 15 and 24 (note that the NIV's "vindication" should be rendered "righteousness" in 24:5). This reminder may be a response from the gatekeepers (cf. 24:7–10). The liturgist's thanksgiving in verse 21 sounds repetitious until we understand that this is the first verse addressed directly to Yahweh, while its phrases were sung earlier as testimony to the congregation (vv. 5b, 14b, 19b). Then, the liturgist or the responding choir turns to address the congregation (**our** and **let us**) with praise to the God of reversal (vv. 22–24). With an image drawn from building construction, the psalm confesses that what humans "reject" Yahweh makes pivotal (to this extent we should avoid pressing the military imagery of vv. 10–16 too far). **The day** in which "we" **rejoice** is probably this festival day that celebrates Yahweh's reversal. Once again the liturgy turns to address Yahweh, this time with petitions for the congregation. The pleas, **save us** (Hb. *hôšî'â nā'*; cf. "Hosanna" and "Blessed is he who comes in the name of the Lord" in Matt. 21:9) and **grant us success,** might seem out of place during the course of a hymn and thanksgiving (though note 33:22), but they need not indicate a special need or circumstance. Rather, they may simply signal the worshipers' continued dependence on the Lord. The blessing on the entrants (**Blessed is he who comes** [or "enters"], and **we bless you** [pl.]) and the echo of the Aaronic blessing in the phrase, **he has made his light shine upon us** (Num. 6:25), indicate verses 26–27 are sung by a priest. (Cf. 24:5, where the entrants "receive blessing . . . and righteousness," lit.) Verse 27 is unusually long and the meaning of its second half is uncertain (see NIV margin). Rather than being part of the spoken liturgy, it may be a ritual instruction to the priests that crept into the main text. Now in proximity to **the altar** the voice of the liturgist returns in verse 28, once again addressing God directly with thanksgiving. Rounding off the psalm but not closing off the larger liturgy of thanksgiving, the psalm concludes as it began with a priest calling the congregation to **give thanks.**

Additional Note §118

118:10–12 / **I cut them off:** The Hb. verb here is elsewhere translated "I circumcised them"! But we should perhaps relate this verb to another Hb. root that surfaces in the word, *mûl/môl,* which means "front," thus reading "I confronted them" in these verses. The LXX, using *amynō,* appears to confirm this derivation ("I warded them off"). In addition, we should note that a more literal translation of **they died out** is "they were extinguished."

§119 Meditating on the Lord's Instruction: From A to Z (Ps. 119)

119:1–176 / Psalm 119 is an extended meditation on "walking" **according to the law of the LORD,** as stated in its opening verse. Other such torah psalms are Psalms 1 (cf. esp. 119:15, 47, 77, 97, 174) and 19 (cf. 119:103, 127). Eight synonyms are used throughout: law (always sing., Hb. *tôrâ*), **word** (Hb. *dābār*), **laws** (always pl. in the NIV, Hb. *mišpāṭîm*), **statutes** (or better "testimonies," Hb. *ʿēdût*, usually pl.), **commands** (Hb. *miṣwâ*, usually pl.), **decrees** (Hb. *ḥuqqîm*), **precepts** (Hb. *pᵉqûdîm*), and **promise** (lit. "word," Hb. *ʾimrâ*). The psalm's structure is an acrostic, with eight verses (perhaps an echo of the eight synonyms) given to each of the twenty-two letters of the Hebrew alphabet. These terms point to Yahweh's written "torah." To modern ears this sounds like a preoccupation with laws and legalism, but we must first recognize that the term "torah" itself means "instruction" or "teaching," not "law" in a formal sense. The verb form of this same Hebrew root is rendered **teach** in verses 33, 102. The book of Deuteronomy, with which this psalm has connections, introduces the Mosaic speeches by saying, "Moses began to expound this law" (Hb. *tôrâ*, 1:5), and there follows immediately a narrative of Yahweh's saving story. Within the book of Psalms, Psalm 78 identifies the history narrated from Moses to David as "teaching" (Hb. *tôrâ*, v. 1) and as "a testimony" (Hb. *ʿēdût*, not "statutes" as in NIV, v. 5). In verse 7, keeping Yahweh's "commands" is paralleled with remembering his "deeds." In Psalm 105 Yahweh's "wonders" and "miracles" in history are called "judgments" (Hb. *mišpāṭîm*, vv. 5, 7). Thus, Psalm 119 does not reflect a preoccupation with legal material or a general change in Yahweh's revelation from his deeds to his words.

This psalm does, however, signal a shift from a temple-based religion to a torah-based religion. The primary locus of Yahweh's revelation here is written Scripture, not the temple with its festivals, sacrifices, and liturgies, which receive no mention. This shift is also illustrated in the synoptic accounts of the OT. First Kings 8:25 and 2 Chronicles 6:16 are identical, except that the former, preexilic passage enjoins the Davidic kings "to walk before me" and the latter, postexilic passage enjoins them "to walk according to my law" (the NIV simply inserts "before me" without any warrant from the Hb. text). The former expression refers to Yahweh's presence at the temple, which Solomon is here dedicating. Thus, the Chronicler, in the new situation of the postexilic period, chose to redefine "before me" at the temple as "according to my 'torah.' "

Psalm 119 reflects a variety of OT traditions. Generally it reflects the scribal tradition, where written scripture is primary. As in wisdom literature, there is interest in instructing the **young man** (v. 9; cf. Prov. 1:4, etc.). The whole psalm reads somewhat like a random anthology of proverbs. The book of Deuteronomy also reflects a concern for written "torah" as scripture (17:18–19; 27:1–8; 31:9–13, 24). Like Deuteronomy, our psalm promotes meditation on "torah" (vv. 15, 23, etc.; Deut. 6:6–8; cf. Josh. 1:8), which one is to put **in my heart** (v. 11; cf. Deut. 6:6; 11:18; 30:14) and which **preserves my life** (vv. 50, 93; cf. Deut. 32:46–47). Psalm 119 uses phrases that are elsewhere associated with priests (e.g., **you are my portion,** v. 57; cf. Deut. 10:9; Num. 18:20; and **make your face shine,** v. 135; cf. Num. 6:25), who also bore responsibility to teach the law (Lev. 10:11; Deut. 33:10; Hos. 4:6–9). But, as already noted, the psalm shows no interest in temple or sacrifice. Finally, we shall see that this psalm also shows full acquaintance with traditions of individual prayer psalms.

The torah piety reflected in this psalm is an expression of devotion to Yahweh himself, as the frequent possessive pronouns show (e.g., **your law**). From its beginning, "keeping" **his** statutes and "seeking" **him** go together (v. 2, also v. 58). The purpose of this pondering on Yahweh's teaching is to seek guidance, not about minutiae (e.g., the precise regulations of ritual sacrifice), but about matters of general lifestyle: **Your word is a lamp to my feet and a light for my path** (v. 105). The psalm is filled with expressions of **longing for your laws** (v. 20; cf. vv. 5, 20, 40, 131, 174). Through the **day** and the **night** (vv. 147–148, 164) the speaker is mindful of Yahweh's instruction. In order to obey it, the speaker does exercise willful determination (vv. 44, 57), but even this exercise of will is predicated on Yahweh's supervision, in which he acts as one's personal tutor: "Teach (the Hb. verb form of *tôrâ*) me," **O LORD, to follow your decrees; then I will keep them to the end** (v. 33, and see vv. 34, 102). Envisioned here is not mere cognitive instruction but also divine intervention: **Direct my footsteps according to your word; let no sin rule over me** (cf. 19:13). The closing verse is telling: **I have strayed like a lost sheep. Seek your servant, for I have not forgotten your commands** (v. 176). Yahweh is no mere Lawgiver, for **your compassion is great, O LORD** (v. 156).

As noted, the psalm echoes the individual prayer psalms, but it also diverges from this earlier temple psalmody. It laments affliction (vv. 25, 28, 107, 143, 153) and persecution (vv. 23, 42, 51, 86, 110, 157, 161) and even contains complaint (vv. 82, 84). Likewise, the speaker "calls" on Yahweh (vv. 145, 169) and petitions him frequently. (Also cf. v. 115 and 6:8.) But unlike most prayer psalms, it perceives a redemptive value in being **afflicted** (vv. 67, 71, 75). The vow of praise, rather than being predicated on Yahweh's saving action (as characteristic of prayer psalms), is motivated by the "torah": **I rise to give you thanks for your righteous laws** (v. 62; cf. vv. 7, 13, 164, 172). In this psalm, Yahweh's "wonders" (Hb. *niplāʾôt*) reside **in** "your law" (vv. 18, 27), not specifically in his historical acts (e.g., 78:4, 11, 32). And here the speaker has **zeal** for **your words** (v. 139), instead of "zeal for your house" (69:9). Like Psalm 15:4, a psalm of temple entry, it promotes association with **all who fear you** (v. 63) and **indignation** against **the wicked** (vv. 53, 158). But the notion of "walking with integrity" (Hb. *hlk tmym*, which the NIV renders, "to walk blamelessly"), instead of being defined by the rites of temple entry (15:2; 26:1, 11), is defined by "the law of the LORD" (vv. 1, 80).

§120 *Sojourning in a Foreign Land Among the Deceitful and Warlike (Ps. 120)*

Psalms 120–134 comprise the Psalms of Ascent, as noted in the superscription of each. The precise meaning of this title is debated, though it probably refers to the pilgrims' "ascent" to Jerusalem (cf. 24:3; 122:4; Isa. 2:3). In these psalms we see a concerted interest in Zion and its sacred temple, so much so that good and evil are virtually determined by one's attitude toward Zion. They stand apart from most other psalms because they are brief and do not follow the typical patterns of the psalmic genres (e.g., prayer psalms, hymnic praise). They reflect public usage, with a liturgist and some kind of assembly (marked by the alternation of "I" and "we" forms and by direct address of a group), but there are no ritual allusions (with the exception of Ps. 132), as found in other temple psalms. They reflect a postexilic, second-temple background. In this collection, we see a chastened Israel, evident in the many allusions to suffering and to Yahweh as the only source of hope. Utter reliance on divine aid and blessing, along with patient waiting, is a recurring motif. Yahweh is hailed as "the Maker of heaven and earth" (121:2; 124:8; 134:3; elsewhere in the OT only 115:15; 146:6). Each of these psalms (except Ps. 131) contains a key term echoing the Aaronic benediction found in Numbers 6:23–27.

120:1 / It is not clear from the Hebrew text whether this psalm is a prayer for a current distress or a thanksgiving for a past rescue. In the NIV, it reads as a coherent prayer, but in the MT the action of verse 1 is complete: "I called . . . , and he answered . . ." (see further below). In any case, the opening verse confesses the fundamental tradition of the psalms of the individual (see the Introduction). Yahweh is the one who *rescues* us from distress, not the one who *preserves* us from distress altogether. Implicit here is the assumption that hardships will befall us. Their mere presence, in and of themselves, provides no comment

on whether God oversees our lives. God promises rescue, not
tranquillity.

120:2 / The next verse addresses Yahweh directly with
the actual petition that he **save** (lit. "deliver") the speaker from
deceitful speakers.

120:3–4 / These verses turn to address these liars. The
question, **What will he do to you, and what more besides** (Hb.
yōsîp), **O deceitful tongue?**, echoes the curse formula common in
the OT, "Thus may God do to . . . , and more also (Hb. *yôsîp*), if . . ."
(e.g., 1 Sam. 25:22; 2 Kgs. 6:31; Ruth 1:17). The speaker of the
psalm in effect threatens the liars with a curse from God. Their
punishment, namely **a warrior's sharp arrows,** is to be in keeping with the nature of their crime: they are for war and hate
peace (vv. 6–7). We must not limit our expectations, however, to a
literal fulfillment. God may not use a warrior's sharp arrows any
more than he should be expected to use **burning coals of the
broom tree.**

120:5–7 / Because the preceding section has a ring of
confidence, we are surprised to hear, **Woe to me** (an expression
used at funerals). Thus, while the psalm expresses a certain confidence in God for the future, it also gives free vent to feelings of
despair in the midst of present circumstances. The geographical
references of **Meshech** and **Kedar** are somewhat problematic, especially because they are far apart; Meshech is far to the north of
Israel and Kedar lies to its east. The disparity, however, may be
intentional to indicate that these locations are figurative and denote foreign regions full of hostile barbarians noted for their militaristic terror (for detailed discussion see Allen, *Psalms 101–150,*
p. 146).

Although verses 6–7 state the problem in terms of **peace**
versus **war,** verses 2–3 state it in terms of "deceitful tongues." The
psalms, in fact, often use the imagery of warfare as a figure for
hostile speech (27:1–3, 12; 35; 57:4; 64:3).

The psalm surprisingly closes without resolution (unless
we adopt the second interpretation of v. 1 below), thus leaving
readers/listeners with a profound sense of dissatisfaction at living in a foreign land. It may be for this reason that Psalm 120 became the introductory psalm of ascent, in the collection that
appears to serve pilgrims journeying to the Jerusalem temple.
This note of hostile foreigners also helps us make sense of this

collection's repeated wish for a peaceable Zion (122:6–8; 125:5; 128:6). Instead of the NIV's **dwell** and **live** in verse 5, the Hebrew text reads, "sojourn" *(gwr)* and "lodge" *(škn)*. These verbs therefore served as a subtle reminder to the postexilic Jews living in the Diaspora that they should regard their dwelling there as temporary.

Additional Note §120

120:1 / **I call . . . and he answers me:** There are no fewer than four possible interpretations for the situation and use of this psalm. (a) The opening verse functions as a reminder that Yahweh has answered when called upon in the past, and the rest of the psalm is a prayer for another, current distress. (b) The opening verse serves as a testimony of thanksgiving, and the remainder is a recollection of a past prayer presented in the narrative present for the sake of vividness (so Kraus, *Psalms 60–150*, p. 423). The entire psalm is thus a thanksgiving. (c) The MT of v. 1 should be corrected (from *wayyaᶜᵃnēnî* to *wᵉyaᶜᵃnēnî*) to read, "I called . . . so he may answer . . ." (cf. NIV). The whole psalm would thus be a prayer. (d) Allen reads vv. 1–4 as "interim thanksgiving" for the assurance that God has heard an earlier prayer—an assurance made known through a priestly oracle of salvation. Verses 5–7 are an implicit prayer that God now act on that promise and actually change the circumstances (*Psalms 101–150*, pp. 147–49).

§121 The Maker of Heaven and Earth Watching Over His Pilgrims (Ps. 121)

Among the psalms of ascent, hints of pilgrimage are particularly evident in this psalm. Mention of one's "foot slipping" and "your coming and going" point to travel. The journeys to and from Jerusalem were made through hills and under "the sun . . . by day" and "the moon by night."

The "my" in verses 1–2 and "your" in verses 3–8 point to a liturgist (perhaps a priest) and an assembly of pilgrims. Verses 1–2 read as a testimony and verses 3–8 as a priestly assurance to the pilgrims (cf. Ps. 91). The question must remain open as to whether the psalm was used originally on the departure to or from Jerusalem. While the psalm is not a formal priestly blessing (e.g., "may the Lord bless you" or "the Lord bless you"), it does share similarities to the Aaronic benediction ("the LORD bless you and keep [Hb. *šmr*, the same term used for "watch" in our psalm] you," Num. 6:22–27). In this case it may have been sung prior to the pilgrims' departure from the Jerusalem temple. On the other hand, the preceding psalm in the Psalms of Ascent collection implies that the pilgrim resides far from Jerusalem and the following psalm implies that the pilgrim has just arrived there. As such, Psalm 121 would fit at the beginning of the journey to Jerusalem.

121:1–2 / The psalm begins with a testimony from a liturgist. What is the significance of **the hills**? Are they a threat or a potential source of **my help**? There are three possibilities. First, in keeping with the notion of pilgrimage, they may represent hiding places for dangers en route (cf. the parable of the Good Samaritan in Luke 10). Second, they may represent touchpoints of divine help, as symbolized by shrines on the "high places." Third, they may be symbolic of natural stability because they were considered the earth's pillars that stabilize it over the chaotic waters (18:7; 104:5–6; Job 9:5–6; cf. Ps. 125:1–2, where mountains symbolize security). Although their original symbolism escapes us, the text before us allows for all three: dangers of travel, sacred space, and powers or natural forces. What is clear, however, is the speaker's confessed source of help, namely **the LORD**. The reason for this choice lies in Yahweh's role as **the Maker of heaven and earth**, not as the savior of Israel in particular.

121:3–8 / The psalm as a whole appears to be structured according to verse pairs. The opening verse pair consists of the liturgist's testimony of Yahweh as "my help." The next three verse pairs offer promises to the pilgrims and specify the nature of this "help" as "watching," which is used no less than six times in the Hebrew text (the NIV's **will keep** in v. 7 also translates the same Hb. word *šmr*). The first verse of each pair offers assurances that Yahweh will **watch** over the pilgrim with respect to distinct aspects of his or her person: **your foot** (v. 3), **your right hand** (v. 5), and **your life** (lit. "your soul," Hb. *npš*, v. 7).

The second verse of each verse pair spells out actions that Yahweh will or will not undertake (vv. 4, 6, 8). First, **He who watches over you** and **over Israel** is no ordinary watchman. As the Maker of heaven and earth, he **will neither slumber nor sleep** (v. 4, contrast Baal in 1 Kgs. 18:27). Second, as Creator, he rules the "two great lights—the greater light to govern the day and the lesser light to govern the night" (Gen. 1:16). The parallel expressions of **the sun** and **the moon** do not signify distinct entities (as though we should strain to discover how the moon itself could **harm** us) but rather the totality of **day** and **night**. The image of Yahweh as **your shade** also clarifies the use of the terms sun and moon: Yahweh overshadows you, not any natural or supposed divine powers (often attributed to the sun and moon in the ancient Near East). Third, Yahweh is promised to watch **over** another totality: **your coming and going.** In sum, the verse pairs unfold for us that Yahweh is the pilgrim's vigilant watchman (he **will not slumber**) over the totalities of time (day and night) and space (your coming and going).

Additional Note §121

121:1–2 / **Where ... from?:** The NIV is correct to read this Hb. term as an interrogative, not as a relative: "the hills, from where my help comes" (so KJV).

§122 Peace for Jerusalem, the City of Pilgrims (Ps. 122)

Like other psalms of ascent, this one contains hints of pilgrimage. The call, "Let us go to the house of the LORD," signals their journey's departure, and the declaration, "our feet are standing in your gates, O Jerusalem," signals their arrival in the holy city. The description of the tribes "going up" (Hb. *ʿlh*, v. 4) uses a key term for the worshipers' ascent to Yahweh's mountain (cf. 24:3). The voice of a representative liturgist is evident. The speaking "I" in verse 1 shifts to "our" in verse 2. In verse 6, the speaker issues an imperative to a group of listeners. The psalm opens with joy expressed over the thought of making a pilgrimage to Jerusalem (vv. 1–2), then praises Jerusalem itself (vv. 3–5), and finally encourages pilgrims to bless the city (vv. 6–9).

The psalm should be read in conjunction with other Songs of Zion. Admiration over its situation (122:3; 48:1–2) and protective walls (122:7; 48:13, NIV "ramparts") and citadels (122:7; 48:3, 13) reveals its virtually sacramental significance, symbolizing God as protector (esp. 48:12–14). Key here, of course, is the house of the LORD in its midst (122:1, 4; 48:9). Zion is personified by direct address (122:2, 6–9; 87:3–7). Psalm 84 is especially similar; in it the pilgrim expresses deep longing for and admiration over Jerusalem. Psalms 122 (v. 5), 84 (v. 9), and 132 also show the inherent connection between the holy city and the institutions of the king.

122:1–5 / Joy marks both the initial invitation of the pilgrimage (given in a familiar form, cf. Isa. 2:3 // Mic. 4:2; Jer. 31:6) and the arrival in Jerusalem. While the pilgrimage may be a duty (a **statute**, though see below), there are some elements inherently joyful about the place. First, the speaker admires the city's structure (vv. 3, 7). Second, he experiences the joy found only in community. He rejoices with the company who invited him to go to Yahweh's temple. Jerusalem **is where the tribes go up,** whom he later calls, **my brothers and friends.** Third, Jerusalem is where the **house of the LORD** is located. At this sacred place, there is the special opportunity **to praise the name of the LORD.** Regrettably we Christians, who assume God is everywhere present, sometimes undervalue a moment of special encounter with God in corporate worship.

Fourth, **there . . . the thrones of the house of David** reside **for judgment** (cf. Isa. 16:5). Initially, the institutions of the monarchy and the lawcourt may seem out of place in a psalm such as this. But other Songs of Zion show the integral connection between the city and the king (84:9; 132:1–18, esp. vv. 11–12, which also mention the Davidic dynasty's "throne" and their need to keep legal statutes). According to Psalm 72, the Davidic king was to be the supreme human judge in the land. His exercise of judgment was to yield "peace" (Hb. *šālôm,* "prosperity" in the NIV of vv. 3, 7). This connection helps us to understand in Psalm 122 the transition from judgment to peace in verses 6–8.

122:6–9 / As the psalm makes this move, we can see there is no peace without justice. Isaiah 2:2–5 (// Mic. 4:1–5), which shares key terminology with our psalm ("let us go," "go up," and "judge"), expands on this idea. The nations make a pilgrimage to Jerusalem in order that Yahweh may teach them and arbitrate their disputes, so war may be no more. A subsequent oracle in Isaiah 11:1–5 speaks of a future Davidic king who will be the just judge of the earth. In verses 6–8 of our psalm, prayers are made that Jeru*salem* live up to its name: **Pray for the** peace (Hb. *shalom,* used three times here) **of Jerusalem.** The reason given is twofold: the people's welfare is determined both by their loyalty to the city (v. 6) and by the welfare of the city itself (v. 8).

Additional Note §122

122:4 / **Statute:** This may refer to the commandments regarding the three pilgrimage festivals (Exod. 23:17; Deut. 16:16). On the other hand, this Hb. term, *ʿēdût,* could also be rendered "testimony." Hence: "a testimony of Israel to praise Yahweh's name." The DSS (cf. Symmachus) read *ʿᵃdat* and thus "the congregation of Israel."

§123 Seeking Mercy with Eyes Lifted Heavenward (Ps. 123)

This psalm is a patient prayer for mercy. The voice of a liturgist is evident in the "I" who begins the psalm and speaks on behalf of the "we/our" throughout the remainder. The psalm is performed not only by singing but also by the "lifting of the eyes" heavenward, an action emphasized in the first two verses. It contains no explicit connection to the temple. Yahweh is sought above: "I lift up my eyes to you, to you whose throne is in heaven." (When viewed in sequence, this claim regarding Yahweh's throne qualifies the relative authority of David's throne mentioned in 122:5.)

123:1–2 / The psalm is prayed with eyes "looking" (vv. 1–2), that is, wide open toward the skies. (Closed eyes are not a mark of piety here.) The posture itself implies subservience. It is this ritual action that leads to the simile of the slaves and the maid. Their looking to their respective masters is not for orders or direction, for they look **to the hand of** their masters. They await some provision for their own benefit. The point of this image is to portray dependence, not obedience. In this case **our eyes** seek **mercy.**

123:3–4 / The sole petition makes the simple request that Yahweh **have mercy;** it does not specify any form of intervention. This reticence makes sense in view of the humble stance explicitly adopted by the petitioners, who are as "slaves." The distress is one of **contempt** and **ridicule.** The instigators are not specified any further than as **the proud** and **the arrogant,** the antithesis of the slave image defining the petitioners. This characterization points not only to their moral failure but also to their religious failure, for "the proud" do not lift their eyes to anyone but themselves.

§124 Providing Escape from the Malevolent (Ps. 124)

This psalm of ascent is a testimony of thanksgiving, perhaps in response to the preceding prayer psalm. It begins with a liturgist's call to the congregation to join in affirming this testimony (v. 1). A choir, perhaps, then recalls the distress in terms of what would have happened had not "the LORD . . . been on our side" (vv. 2–5). Praise for the deliverance is expressed in the form of "blessing" Yahweh (vv. 6–7). The psalm closes with a hymnic confession that echoes the psalm's opening lines: the source of "our help" (cf. 121:1–2) is "the name of the LORD." The mention of human attack and of the people's escape fits well with their Babylonian captivity and their restoration to the homeland.

124:1–5 / The phrase, **let Israel say** (cf. 118:2–4; 129:1), indicates that this psalm aims to encourage the congregation to give voice to their gratitude. The NIV's translation, **If the LORD had not been on our side** (cf. 118:6), should not lead us to endorse a mentality of "God is on our side." A more literal rendering is "unless Yahweh had been for us." The psalm does not claim that God is in the habit of taking sides; it does claim that God may affirm and help a particular group in a particular situation, especially when under attack by chaotic forces.

Had Yahweh not made a difference for the congregation, they would have experienced death by drowning. Although the attackers are **men, their** flaring **anger** elicits images of "chaos." Their rage is like **raging waters,** unpredictable and out of control. This imagery also has overtones of the underworld. In the Psalms, Sheol has its "torrents" and "snares" (cf. v. 7) that threaten to overwhelm (18:4–5). Death and the grave are likened to a cistern (69:2; 88:3–7, 16–17) whose waters may "swallow" their victim (69:15; cf. 5:9, where the grave is likened to a throat; note also Jonah 2:2, 5). In addition, these images of being **swallowed** and of raging waters are reminiscent of the chaos monster of Israel's neighbors. In the Mesopotamian "Enuma Elish" there was Tiamat, who is depicted as both the chaotic oceans and a devouring sea monster (see *ANET*, esp. pp. 61–62, 67). And less remote, there were the Canaanite monsters Mot, the god of the underworld whose throat devours the dead (Gibson, *Canaanite Myths*, pp. 68–69), and Yam, the god of the sea (pp. 37–45). This imagery may suggest that there is a fine line between human anger and superhuman chaos. Over against this imagery of dark powers, however, we hear the closing claim loud and clear: **the LORD, the Maker of heaven and earth.** No matter how threatening any power, whether human or otherwise, may appear, it is circumscribed by its Creator.

124:6–8 / The climax of the psalm occurs in the exclamation, "Blessed (Hb. *bārûk*) be Yahweh" (the NIV consistently mistranslates this word as **Praise be to**). In this strophe, the imagery applied to the attackers shifts from chaotic forces to hunters (though there is a link in the images of "swallowing" in v. 3 and "teeth" in v. 6). In verse 6 they are animal hunters (as a literal translation makes clear: "who has not given us as prey for their teeth"), and in verse 7 they are human hunters. (On the image of **a bird** and **the fowler's snare,** see Keel, *Symbolism*, pp. 89–94.)

Yahweh's intervention, though evidently decisive, is not described as dramatic and miraculous, like that of the exodus out of Egypt. His action is described as preventative **(who has not let . . .)** and as a **help** (v. 8). The claim that "Yahweh had been for us" (v. 1) clearly affirms his support, but it does leave the form of that support open-ended. The remainder of the testimony focuses not on Yahweh's rescue but on "our escape." (Note also the use of the passive voice in **the snare has been broken.**) This certainly does not diminish the fact of God's intervention but it reminds us that it need not necessarily be obvious and dramatic.

§125 Wicked Rule to be Removed from the Land of Zion (Ps. 125)

This is a corporate prayer psalm. A liturgical setting may be implied by the changing references to Yahweh. Only in the petition of verse 4 is he addressed directly. The confessions of trust (vv. 1–3) and the admonition (v. 5), where he is referred to in the third person, were probably addressed to a congregation. The prayer appears to stem from the postexilic period after the Hebrews returned to their homeland under the government of the Persian empire. The opening comparisons with Mount Zion and the mountains surrounding Jerusalem imply the people are present in "the land allotted to the righteous," but it is under "the scepter," or control, of the wicked.

125:1–2 / The opening verses employ two similes, both drawn from the mountainous geography of Jerusalem. The first draws a point of comparison between **those who trust** in Yahweh and the stability of **Mount Zion** in Jerusalem (cf. 78:68–69 and the Songs of Zion, 46:1–7; 87:5). The second compares **the LORD** himself and the **mountains** that **surround Jerusalem,** which are actually higher than Mount Zion itself. This image implies protection.

125:3 / Were we to quote the opening verses in isolation, we might be misled. By themselves they could be taken to promise unqualified stability and protection, but verse 3 points to two tensions or qualifications with these claims. First, God's people, here called **the righteous,** do not now have control of this **land allotted** to them surrounding Jerusalem. Second, this verse also admits that, although "those who trust in the LORD . . . cannot be shaken," they might be tempted to **use their hands to do evil.** This could include using evil means to regain the land (perhaps by violence), defecting to the evil ones who hold the power, or despairing that Yahweh and obedience to him make any real difference (cf. Mal. 2:17; 3:13–15). Moreover, if they do turn to crooked ways, the Lord will banish them with the evildoers (v. 5). Their security is obviously conditional.

125:4–5 / The problem as stated in the confession of trust of verse 3 is that of the rule of the wicked. The solution sought, as expressed in the following petition is simply, **Do good, O Lord.** It seems deliberately nonspecific and so leaves the particular means to Yahweh's discretion.

The categories used for God's people in this psalm are very telling. The opening verses stress the relationship: "those who trust in the Lord" and "his people." The rest of the psalm uses moral categories primarily: the righteous (as opposed to the wicked), **those who are good** and **upright in heart.** This final qualification of the heart shows that we should be looking for more than mere good deeds. Thus, the petition, "do good, O Lord, to those who are good," while explicitly addressed to Yahweh, also contains a warning to the congregation who overhears. God may limit his "doing good" to that particular group. What is implicit in the petition is made explicit in the following admonition: **those who turn to crooked ways the Lord will banish.** Nationality or ethnicity does not guarantee Yahweh's favor— one must maintain a relationship to Yahweh and a moral heart. (It is possible to read v. 5 as a wish or petition, "may the Lord banish.") Perhaps so as not to end on a negative note, the psalm closes with a priestly benediction of **peace . . . upon Israel.**

§126 *The Restored Exiles Sowing in Tears and Reaping with Joy (Ps. 126)*

"When the LORD brought back the captives to Zion" appears to refer to the restoration from Babylonian captivity. This event was obviously met with a response of laughter and songs of joy. The early postexilic period, however, was also marked by hardships, and so there was still the need to petition Yahweh to "restore our fortunes" (see further below). This historical setting accords well with the psalms of ascent in general and with the two preceding psalms in particular. As with most psalms, however, Psalm 126 is open to numerous, recurring situations. It can apply to any instance where God has restored believers, who, in turn, seek to ensure that the restoration be all that God has promised (see esp. the marginal readings in the NIV).

The psalm begins with a reminder—both for Yahweh and the congregation—that Yahweh had graciously surprised his people with a restoration to their homeland (vv. 1–3). There follows a petition that he bring that restoration to completion (v. 4), accompanied by a promise that the songs of joy that came with the first news of restoration (v. 2) will return (v. 6). Psalm 85, which suits the same historical setting, follows a similar pattern: a reminder of the restoration from exile (using the same phrase, "restored the fortunes," vv. 1–3), petitions for further restoration ("restore us," vv. 4–7), and promises of restoration containing agricultural analogies (though there they have a clear prophetic delivery, vv. 8–13).

126:1–3 / The restoration from Babylonian captivity seemed too good to be true: **we were like men who dreamed.** The event was so remarkable that not only did God's people rejoice **with songs of joy,** but **the nations** also had to admire it: **"The LORD has done great things for them."** The echo of this praise in the congregation's own mouth **(for us)** underscores its significance.

126:4–6 / In verse 4, we see a stubbornness that is born of faith. Verse 1 rejoices that Yahweh has "restored" his people and verse 4 petitions that he **restore** them yet more fully. This persistence is echoed in Isaiah 62:6–7, another passage addressed to the postexilic community: "You who call on the LORD, give yourselves no rest, and give him no rest till he establishes Jerusalem and makes her the praise of the earth." Two images follow, the first from nature and the second from farming. **Streams in the Negev** refer to the wadis, or seasonal streams, of the south, which flow with the winter rains but are dry in the summer. Implicit in the second image, **Those who sow in tears will reap with songs of joy,** is a call for both hope and patience. Hope is as certain as reaping follows sowing. But as one must wait for crops to germinate and grow, so one must recognize that sorrow may remain for a time. It follows that **weeping** in itself cannot be taken as an indication that God ignores our sorrow (cf. 30:5; Matt. 5:4).

Additional Note §126

126:1, 4 / **Brought back the captives** and **Restore our fortunes:** In v. 1 of the MT, the Hb. word *šîbat* is an odd form, though possibly paralleled by an eighth-century Aramaic inscription, which reads, "The gods restored the fortunes of [my father's house]" (see M. Dahood, *Psalms III* [AB 17A; Garden City, N. Y.: Doubleday, 1970], p. 218). One manuscript of the MT has *šᵉbît* (also found in the *Qere* reading of v. 4, noted below), which derives from the Hb. root *šbh* and thus means "captivity." This is the reading taken in the main text of the NIV, though the phrase is best translated, "turn our captivity." A few other MT manuscripts, supported by the LXX, read *šᵉbût* (also found in the *Kethib* reading of v. 4, noted below), which probably derives from *šûb*. Thus the Hb. phrase *šûb šᵉbût* in v. 1 would be rendered lit. as, "when the LORD *turned the turning* of Zion," and idiomatically as, "when the LORD restored the fortunes of Zion" (see NIV margin). The Hb. phrase *šûb šᵉbût* or *šᵉbît* is found particularly in the prophets, where it points specifically to Israel/Judah's restoration from captivity (Deut. 30:3; Jer. 29:14; 30:3, 18; 31:23; 32:44; 33:7, 11, 26; Lam. 2:14; Ezek. 16:53; 39:25; Joel 3:1; Amos 9:14; Zeph. 2:7, 30). Thus, to some extent the issue is moot, whether the phrase refers to the turning of fortunes in general or of the Babylonian captivity in particular. In the early postexilic period, in which the psalms of ascent appear to have been set originally, the phrase's association with the restoration from exile would have been inescapable.

The disputed term is somewhat different in the MT of v. 4 than in the MT of v. 1. The *Kethib* reading is *šᵉbût* (the reading followed in the main text of the NIV) and the *Qere* reading is *šᵉbît* (the NIV margin). This difference may be accidental or intentional, to distinguish the restoration of v. 1 from that of v. 4. The qualifying phrase, **like streams in the Negev,** implies the term should have a positive connotation, hence, "fortunes."

The verb tenses of vv. 1–3 are problematic. Because v. 1 announces a restoration and v. 4 petitions it, one might read them as future. But the perfect verbs most often denote action completed in the past, and the confession of v. 3 certainly appears to look back to a past event. Moreover, the OT's witness of the early postexilic period describes a historical situation that helps us clarify these ambiguities and anomalies. The restoration from Babylonian exile was preceded by many grand divine promises, which certainly raised the people's expectations (see esp. Isa. 40–55). The actual period of the restoration, however, was beset by hardships: only a relatively small number of Hebrews participated in the first return of 538 B.C. (Ezra-Nehemiah), and drought (Hag. 1:6–11; 2:16–19) and locust plagues (Joel 1:1–2:27) befell the struggling community living under foreign rule. Thus, what initially appears problematic in Ps. 126 makes perfect sense in light of this historical period. In addition, note its similarities with Ps. 85 above.

§127 The Lord, the Builder of the House(hold) (Ps. 127)

The psalm shows affinity to the OT wisdom tradition, as reflected in Proverbs. The unity of verses 1–2 with 3–5 is the major interpretive question. It is impossible to say whether or not these proverbs had a life of their own before their combination here. But whether the psalm is an act of authorship or editing, it has certainly become more than the sum of its parts. A unity is achieved—whether by an author or editor—by several threads. Both sections share the distinctive theme of Yahweh's hidden, though decisive, involvement in house and home. In the Hebrew text, there is a wordplay between the "builders" (Hb. *bônāyw*) in the first half and the "sons" (Hb. *bānîm*) in the second. We also need to recognize the ambiguity building a "house" has in Hebrew (as in English): it can denote the physical structure but also the household, that is, the family (see below). While we cannot be certain the latter meaning was originally part of this first proverb, it certainly steps forward when seen in light of the second proverb. Thus, the whole psalm is concerned with the building of one's family. Finally, the combination of the motifs found in both halves is attested in ancient Near Eastern literature. Kraus cites a Sumerian song to Nisaba, the goddess of grain (dating from before 2000 B.C.): "Nisaba, where you do not establish it, the human being builds no (house), builds no city. . . . You are the mistress who grants joy of the heart, good seed you introduce into the womb" (*Psalms 60–150*, p. 455).

127:1–2 / The point here is clear: divine sovereignty overshadows human plans and efforts (cf. Prov. 16:1, 9; 19:21; 21:31)—in the areas of "building" a **house,** "watching" a **city** (cf. Ps. 121), and **toiling for food to eat.** The point is not to discount human effort, but to emphasize that, apart from God's intervention, it is **vain.** This theme climaxes in the third **in vain,** this time addressed directly to **you.** Verse 2 must not be read in isolation from verse 1: toiling for food to eat is in vain—**unless the LORD** is in it. (It does not, therefore, contradict Prov. 24:30–34.)

The claim, **he grants sleep to those he loves**, has troubled interpreters. (The Hb. term for "sleep," *šēnāʾ*, occurs only here in the OT and so its meaning is uncertain, though it is probably a variant spelling of *šēnâ*.) It seems to go contrary to the emphasis placed on diligence in Proverbs. But OT Wisdom literature sometimes likes to tease its readers with statements that initially sound contradictory but are intended to cause them to think and recognize different facets of a complex issue (e.g., Prov. 26:4–5). It likes to show paradoxical aspects of the same reality. Moreover, another psalm of ascent encourages one to consider the relative value of human achievements and the ultimate value of divine achievement, thus inviting one to limit his ambition and to find contentment and rest (Ps. 131).

127:3–5 / Verse 3 throws another surprise at us: **Sons are a heritage** (or "inheritance," Hb. *naḥᵃlâ*) **from the LORD.** Instead of our children inheriting our land or estate from us, we inherit them from Yahweh. The point is to show that while they may be indebted to us, we are ultimately indebted to God for them. It may seem odd that **children** can be used as "weapons" or **arrows** to counter one's **enemies in the gate.** The gate served as the town's courtroom (Ruth 4:1, 10–11; Amos 5:12; Prov. 22:22). **Sons born in one's youth** could offer one legal support in the face of a lawsuit. But **the gate** was also simply a gathering place (Prov. 31:31) or marketplace (2 Kgs. 7:1). Thus, in any case of rivalry, children could be presented as evidence that one has, in fact, been blessed by God. This psalm may provide us with some insight on the nature of personal "enemies" in the Psalms. Since the "ammunition" that is effective against these enemies consists of the number of one's children, it becomes apparent that the opponents in the Psalms are not always mortal enemies. "My enemies" may simply be "those who do not respect me." Conflict in the Psalms, even if military language be used as it is here, need not point to physical confrontation. (Cf. the Song of Hannah, where "my enemies" in 1 Sam. 2:1 are simply the rival wife, not life-threatening militants.)

To us moderns the claim that children are a reward from God might seem particularly offensive to parents struggling with infertility. But we must recognize that many biblical verses do not pretend to be the first *and* the last word on any subject. In

several biblical passages, Yahweh exhibits his love and concern
for "the barren woman" by promising her joy and a family, that
is, a home—whether literal or not (113:9; 1 Sam. 2:5; Isa. 54:1).

Additional Note §127

127:1 / Builds the house, its builders: In Hb., these phrases
are ambiguous, denoting either or both the physical structure and the
household or family dwelling in it. In both Gen. 16:2 and 30:3, the NIV's
phrase "I can build a family" (*ʾibbānê*) is formed entirely from the Hb.
verb "to build." In Exod. 1:21, the term "families" is lit. "house(hold)s"
(*bāttim*) and, in Ps. 113:9, the term "home," which certainly includes the
family, is "house" (*bayit*). One of the most important chapters of the OT,
2 Sam. 7, hinges on a similar wordplay. Here David determines to build
a "house" or temple for Yahweh and Yahweh in turn promises to build a
"house" or dynasty (similar to a household) for David.

§128 A Blessing on the Family Who Fears the Lord (Ps. 128)

With its interest in the family blessed by Yahweh and in eating "the fruit of your labor," this psalm has obvious connections with the preceding one. Verses 1–4 sound wonderful; their claims are lofty ("blessings and prosperity will be yours") and universal (for "all who fear the LORD"). But for many believers they may not ring true to life. How can the Bible make such claims, we wonder, when genuine believers endure cancer, desertion, and worse within their families? In this psalm, the claims are qualified immediately by the rest of the passage, which consists of a prayer or invocation that these ideals become reality: "May the LORD bless you" (v. 5), just as he "who fears the LORD" is described as blessed (v. 4) in the preceding verses. In other words, the opening statements are *not* automatic for Yahweh's believers. As explained further below, there are several contingencies for the opening promises. As we discover, they prescribe the ideal; they do not pretend to describe tangible guarantees.

The psalm consists of two main parts. The first, which reflects the wisdom tradition, is a statement of the blessed state Yahweh prescribes for all who fear the Lord (vv. 1–4). The opening and closing verses do so with generic third-person declarations of the general state of blessedness for those who fear the Lord. (Two different words for "blessed" are used: ʾašrê in v. 1 and brk in v. 4.) The next verses (vv. 2–3) personalize the promise with direct address ("you") and specify how the blessed state can be manifest. The second part is an invocation (vv. 5–6; the helping verb is "may," not are/will as in vv. 1–4), probably delivered by a priest, that "you" may indeed experience this promised blessedness. The closing benediction, "Peace be upon Israel," was probably delivered by a priest (cf. Num. 6:22–27). Since the blessing is to issue specifically from Zion and since this psalm is among the Psalms of Ascent, Psalm 128 was probably recited at the temple, perhaps at (the conclusion of) one of the major festivals. An agricultural festival is likely, in view of the similes of "a fruitful vine" and "olive shoots" and in view of the wish for the prosperity of Jerusalem.

128:1–4 / While the first line defines the attitude of **fear,** the second defines the behavior of "walking" **in his ways.** As the poetic parallelism suggests, the one considered **blessed** by Yahweh is an integrated person. Presumably, this promise of blessing is also held out as a motivation that worshipers adopt such an attitude and behavior.

What we so often take for granted was not the case in the ancient world, namely that **you will eat the fruit of your labor.** Because of the uncertainties brought on by war, famine, and disease, this was not a given (cf. Eccl. 6:1–2). In ancient Israel, the futility of not enjoying the produce of one's labors was, in fact, intensified. It may not merely be a result of circumstances; it could be a covenant curse (Lev. 26:16) and a divine judgment (Jer. 5:7; Amos 5:11). The problem was so much a part of Israel throughout their tumultuous history that the abolition of this futility became part of their vision of a "new heavens and a new earth" (Isa. 65:17, 22–23).

This psalm obviously reflects the man's point of view: **your wife** and **your** "children" (NIV **sons,** Hb. *bānîm,* the same term translated **children's children** in v. 6) will be healthy and **fruitful,** like "the fruit of your labor" (though a different Hb. word is used here for "fruit"). Implicit in the image is that as the man puts work into his agricultural produce and is enabled to enjoy its benefits (v. 2), so he puts work into his family and is enabled to enjoy them (v. 3). The wife and children are thus in a favored position as the beneficiaries of the father's labor. The choice of agricultural similes implies they provide visual evidence of blessing to the **house** and **table.** (The "blessings" listed in Deut. 28:1–14 are evidenced in three areas of life: agricultural produce, the family, and national security.) As for the male perspective in this psalm of ascent, we must keep in mind that "three times a year all the men are to appear before the Sovereign LORD" (Exod. 23:17; cf. Deut. 16:16) at the major temple festivals. Nevertheless, the meaning of this psalm is easily extended to include both male and female.

128:5–6 / Now the psalm seeks to make this ideal a reality, not merely through one's labor (v. 2) but through prayer.

Blessedness is not viewed as an automatic consequence of one's actions—it is a divine gift. The realization of the blessing is conditional on one's asking, on Yahweh's free choice, and to some extent on the circumstances of time. For example, much depends on whether or not one happens to live while **Jerusalem** is enjoying **prosperity.** If Jerusalem is under Yahweh's judgment, then one would not see its prosperity, no matter how much one feared Yahweh and walked in his ways. According to Zephaniah 2:3, for example, seekers of Yahweh and his righteousness are promised shelter on the day of Jerusalem's fall to the Babylonians, not prosperity. (Lest readers be tempted to become materialistic, they should recognize that the root meaning of the Hb. term rendered as "prosperity" in vv. 2 and 5 of our psalm is "goodness" [*ṭwb*].)

As is characteristic of the Psalms, blessedness is not universally accessible—it is mediated **from Zion,** the temple mount. This is a point that the pilgrims using the psalms of ascent would readily understand, but one that we modern believers all too easily dismiss. The Psalms do not conceive of a state of blessedness that is merely personal and private. It is received and enjoyed as part of corporate, ritual worship. In this psalm's second half, two areas of life are singled out as subjects for visual enjoyment: **may you see the** prosperity **of** Jerusalem **and . . . your** children's children. Again, in the Psalms God's blessing is enjoyed in the context of one's immediate and larger social groups. For Christians, this points to family and church.

§129 Oppressed But Not Crushed (Ps. 129)

129:1–8 / As with the other psalms of ascent, this psalm reflects a postexilic date (e.g., the use of Hb. *še-* instead of *ʾašer* in vv. 6, 7). As explained below, it has a three-part structure: a testimony regarding **Israel** and its wicked oppressors (vv. 1–4), wishes or statements regarding **Zion** and **all who hate** it (vv. 5–8a), and a closing blessing (v. 8b). The first half focuses on the people's suffering and liberation, and the second on retribution.

Key to identifying the psalm's genre and function is determining whether the verbs of verses 5–8 are wishes (**may they . . .,** so NIV) or statements ("they will . . ."). If they are a kind of petition, then the psalm is close to the prayer genre, and verses 1–4 may be seen as a reference to past saving deeds, urging Yahweh to carry his work of deliverance to its conclusion. If they are statements of confidence, then verses 1–4 may be seen as a corporate testimony to God's protection. Whether this ambiguity was intentional or not, the psalm as it stands allows for both interpretations. Which interpretation one stresses would depend on the particular circumstances and worshipers singing or reading the psalm. The absence of direct address to Yahweh makes the function of petition less likely. The closing line, **we bless you in the name of the LORD,** is probably not to be included in the quotation of the passers-by (as in the NIV). Rather, it appears to be a priestly benediction bestowed on the worshipers (cf. the closing benedictions in other psalms of ascent: Pss. 125, 127, 128, 134). This blessing on the congregation thus stands in stark contrast to the denial of blessing on the haters of Zion in the first half of the verse.

In the invitation, **let** Israel **say,** we hear a liturgist encouraging fellow worshipers to testify in the "I" form. The sufferings of the individual and of the community are thus seen together. The oppression of the individual is seen in the context of the corporate body, and national suffering is understood on the level of the individual. The testimony (vv. 1–4) of Israel that we have been "struck down, but not destroyed" (cf. 2 Cor. 4:9) is one that has applied to them since their **youth** as a people: from their beginnings in Egypt and the exodus, through the exile and restoration, to their troubles and perseverance in the postexilic period. Their history is one of resilience.

The integrity of the psalm is established by its agricultural metaphors. In verse 3, the wicked oppressors are likened to **plowmen** and the speaker's back to plowed land. But in the next verse, Yahweh **has cut . . . the cords of the wicked** (the words **me free from** are added by the NIV), thus disabling them from plowing the speaker's back with the harnessed oxen (on "cords," Hb. *ʿăbôt*, as a harness for plowing, see Job 39:10; cf. Isa. 5:18). This act exhibits Yahweh's **righteous** character, thus exemplifying for us that "righteousness" is not a limiting quality (as popularly conceived) but is a liberating one. In verses 6–8, all who hate Zion are likened to **grass on the roof, which withers before it can grow.** This reversal is key to the psalm's development: the plowmen who control the land become its useless produce.

The meaning of verse 8 can be clarified by reference to Ruth 2:4. Here we see the custom of a passer-by (in this case Boaz, the owner) greeting "the harvesters" (the same Hb. term for **reaper** in 129:7) with a blessing. Thus, verse 8 expresses the desire that no one would wish a blessing on this harvest of withered grass. ("The reaper" and "those who pass by" are thus simply incidental third parties to this conflict between Zion and its haters.) Thus, the fate expressed for the wicked is that of **shame** (v. 5), a "withering" existence (vv. 6–7; this need not denote death any more than the speaker's self-description of having a "plowed back"), and alienation from society's well-wishers and from Yahweh's blessing (v. 8).

Part of the attraction of the Psalms is their embrace of pain. Pain's existence within the believing community is not denied, nor does the presence of suffering itself deny the presence of God. The faith reflected in this psalm is far from naïve and simplistic. It testifies to life's harsh realities and faith's own resilience. Hard times are not denied, and their presence does not provide a reason for doubt. If the composer's expectations had been for an untroubled life, there would be no psalm. Yet, in spite of what some may regard as evidence to the contrary, we see a confidence—or at least a hope—that God will bring his righteous judgment full circle: the plowmen who cut the land will themselves become the useless harvest.

§130 Out of the Depths (Ps. 130)

In this psalm of ascent, we see both the individual ("I" in vv. 1–2, 5–6) and the corporate body represented (Israel in vv. 7–8). This duality makes best sense if we imagine a liturgist leading a congregation in worship. Here we see illustrated the educative role of liturgy: in verses 1–6, the liturgist exemplifies a humble and expectant piety, first in prayer to God (vv. 1–4) and then in testimony to the congregation (vv. 5–6). Moreover, in verses 7–8, he exhorts them to follow this model. Verse 6 indicates that a night performance of the psalm is particularly appropriate, though it may simply employ an image to convey a sense of longing.

As with most psalms, this one does not tie itself down to a particular historical occasion. The clearest allusion to a particular occasion for the psalm lies not in its petition, which is simply for Yahweh to hear (v. 2), but in the closing confession of trust (v. 8): "He himself will redeem Israel from all their sins." The expectation of corporate redemption fits the restoration of Israel from exile. The Hebrew words translated as "attentive" (here and in 2 Chron. 6:40; 7:15) and "forgiveness" (here and in Neh. 9:17; Dan. 9:9) are found elsewhere only in postexilic literature. Thus, the early postexilic setting implied in several other ascent psalms may well be this psalm's point of *origin,* but the confession in verses 3–4 extends its *application* to all peoples at all times.

130:1–2 / The opening verse is not actually a petition but a description of the act of praying. Implicit in the mere description of the act of "calling" (Hb. qr^{γ}, NIV **cry**) to Yahweh **out of the depths** (cf. the image of drowning in 69:1–2, 14–15) is that he can be moved to pity. The psalm does not *presume* Yahweh knows all and makes a deliberate effort to draw his attention to the speaker's plight. Similarly, the petition of verse 2 makes repeated efforts to obtain God's hearing. This too is not taken for granted; it is explicitly requested. These acts are not a reflection of doubt but of an understanding that the relationship is personal, not robotic.

130:3–4 / These verses strip each of us of any presumption that we are inherently "all right." The phrasing of verse 3 particularly disarms us by asking a rhetorical question: **If you, O LORD, kept a record of sins, O Lord, who could stand?** (Cf. 90:8.) Thus, on the one hand, this verse strips us of pride, but on the other it relieves us of pressures, both religious and social, to try to be something we are not. We need not pretend to God or to ourselves that we have "loved him with all our heart, soul, and strength" and "loved our neighbor as ourselves" (so Deut. 6:5 and Lev. 19:18). Nonetheless, the next verse makes clear that we should not infer from this question that Yahweh simply overlooks sin. A deliberate act on his part is required: **But with you there is forgiveness.** The seriousness of this act is underlined in the result clause that follows: "so you may be feared" (lit., NIV **therefore you are feared**). We may expect the power of forgiveness to result solely in gratitude or joy rather than in fear, but this psalm leads us to believe that such forgiveness is not automatic. It lies solely in Yahweh's discretion. This psalm shows considerable respect for Yahweh as a person.

130:5–6 / The speaker's lack of presumption is evident in the confession **I wait for the LORD.** It follows from the admission that forgiveness lies with Yahweh, that the appropriate human response is a deliberate posture of inaction. No attempt is made to procure divine forgiveness by human effort. As is characteristic of much Hebrew poetic parallelism, the second line is more specific. The precise object of this waiting is **his word.** This may denote waiting for either a priestly oracle of salvation (so Kraus, *Psalms 60–150*, p. 467; Allen, *Psalms 101–150*, p. 194) or the fulfillment of the prophets' word of Israel's restoration.

130:7–8 / In the closing verses, the liturgist addresses the congregation, exhorting them likewise to wait for (NIV **put your hope in**) Yahweh. Their "action of inaction" is also based on the premise that **with the LORD is unfailing love and with him is full redemption** (note the word order). The emphasis of the closing confession of trust thus lies not on the action but on the subject of the action: **He himself will redeem Israel.**

§131 The Quieted Soul (Ps. 131)

131:1–3 / Though one of the shortest of psalms, Psalm 131 is one of the most profound. Its image of tranquillity we readily admire, but its advice we all too readily dismiss as impractical. When things go wrong, the temptation is to make ambitious plans and redouble our efforts. Such was clearly the case for Judah in the hardships of the early postexilic period. But this psalm of ascent counsels God's people to engage in contemplation before action.

It is composed of a personal confession to God (vv. 1–2) and an exhortation to the congregation, **Israel** (v. 3). To some readers, the attachment of a corporate exhortation to so personal a confession might sound artificial (esp. perhaps in view of the identical imperative in the preceding psalm, 130:7). But, as this commentary has emphasized, the so-called division between individual and corporate is of our own devising. The combination of personal confession and public admonishment is attested in other psalms (e.g., 62:1–2, 5–7 and 8, 10).

The psalm's overall purpose is to teach and encourage the people of God, by means of an exemplary confession, to give less attention to human efforts and more to God's ordering of affairs. The opening "I" verses, while personal confessions, encourage the listeners to curb ambition and to find contentment and rest. Ambition is a matter of one's **heart, eyes** (i.e., one's focus), and walk (i.e., one's field of endeavors; **concern myself** is lit. "walk around"). In the simile of verse 2, the speaker is likened to a **mother** and his soul to **a weaned child.** This describes an act of self-composure. But the following verse enjoins the audience, **put your hope in the LORD.** This juxtaposition leads one to think further of Yahweh as mother, with one's **soul** or self as the weaned child that is **quieted** upon her (cf. Isa. 46:3; 49:15).

§132 A Tale of Two Oaths: David's for the Lord's Dwelling and the Lord's for David's Dynasty in Zion (Ps. 132)

132:1–18 / Most commentators believe this psalm was a liturgical composition used at the preexilic Jerusalem temple. It appears to presuppose the existence of the Davidic dynasty (esp. v. 17), the Solomonic temple (vv. 13–14), and the ark of the covenant (vv. 7–9). On the other hand, the psalm's presence in the Psalms of Ascent, an otherwise postexilic collection, may imply that at least the final form of the psalm stems from the postexilic period. Its petitions may point to the same period, when David's dynasty was a memory (v. 1) and in need of restoration (v. 10), though they could also be simply general petitions. (The mention of **David** can apply to both David himself and to the Davidic dynasty, as in Jer. 30:9; Ezek. 34:23–24; 37:24–25; Hos. 3:5.) The psalm's structure is framed by these two petitions (vv. 1, 10) with each followed by two quotations, all of which have a narrative introduction. Verse 2 introduces the quotation of verses 3–5, and verse 6 the quotation of verses 7–9. Verse 11a introduces the oracle of verses 11b–12 and verse 13, the oracle of verses 14–18. Thus, even if the psalm's final form is postexilic, the quoted material most certainly contains preexilic tradition. It is possible that these preexilic traditions reflect a ritual reenactment of the events narrated in 2 Samuel 6–7, wherein David brings the ark into Jerusalem (vv. 6–9 of our psalm) and Yahweh then promises David a dynasty (vv. 11–12). Psalm 132 also shows the connection between the David and Zion traditions. As David . . . **swore an oath to the LORD** to **find** him **a dwelling** (v. 2) on **Zion** (v. 13), so **the LORD swore an oath to David** to found for him a dynasty (v. 11). We should note, however, that in this version of the dynastic oracle, the Davidic covenant is clearly conditional: **if your sons keep my covenant . . . , then their sons will sit . . .** (contrast 89:30–37).

This psalm contains the sole explicit reference to the ark in the Psalms. It is not identified with Yahweh himself but is closely associated with him, as the phrase **you and the ark of your might** implies. This particular designation probably reflects its associations with Yahweh war. The phrase is the object of the imperative **arise,** which is reminiscent of the ancient song of the ark: "Arise, Yahweh" (Num. 10:35) or "May God arise" (Ps. 68:1). In the procession implied in this quoted material this imperative would presumably be enacted by the Levites who carry the ark. The goal of the ark's journey is **your resting place,** which echoes the phrase following the song of the ark in Numbers 10:36: "whenever it came to rest." In the wilderness period, the ark "arose" at the beginning of the day's journey and "came to rest" at its close. But at its journey's end in the period of the Davidic monarchy, it "arises" directly to its resting place. Prior to the call for the ark to "arise" is the ritual of "bowing down" (lit., NIV **worship**) **at his footstool.** In verses 13–14, Yahweh designates his **resting place** to be Zion. He declares that at this resting place, **I will sit enthroned,** thus emphasizing his throne and royal role.

In two respects, the theology of this psalm may be offensive to Christians. First, we see a human feeling the need to find a resting place for God and God, in turn, accepting this resting place. Does God need a human to find him a place, especially one for rest? Second, we see God aligning himself with a particular place, a particular people, and a particular political figure. At the same time, God also aligns himself against this monarch's enemies. Should he show favoritism? Should he not be the God of all peoples? Perhaps what is key to unraveling this problem is to understand that Yahweh here shows loyalty to one who shows him loyalty (this may explain the actual citation of vv. 3–5). While David feels compelled to find Yahweh a permanent dwelling, neither the text nor Yahweh claim that he actually needs such a place (in 2 Sam. 7:6–7 Yahweh denies this emphatically). So we must recognize that Yahweh does not give his loyalty blindly: David and his sons must "keep my covenant" **and the statutes I teach them.** "If"—the covenant is explicitly conditional—they do so, Yahweh may then freely ally himself to David and his people and oppose those who attack his covenant-keeping vassals. In this psalm embodying the David and Zion traditions, which make promises for the monarchy and its capital, a promise is also made concerning **her poor,** whom Yahweh will **satisfy with food.** This text does not give free rein to these human powers; instead they are given responsibility to keep Yahweh's covenant and statutes and so ensure the welfare of the poor. There is here no blind support of the status quo. Moreover, the oracle of verse 14 makes clear who is the supreme King: **here** "I will sit enthroned."

In this psalm we see Yahweh acting in response to human initiative. In response to David's swearing an oath to the Lord about finding for him a resting place, Yahweh swears an oath to David. But Yahweh's oath far exceeds David's vow to Yahweh. He promises that David's sons will sit . . . **for ever and ever** and that Yahweh himself will sit at his resting place **for ever and ever.** In response to the people's petition, **may your priests be clothed with righteousness; may your saints sing for joy** (v. 9), Yahweh promises in an oracle to fulfill this very request (with "righteousness" exchanged with **salvation,** v. 16). Therefore, in response to the petition that Yahweh not reject **David,** his **anointed one** (v. 10), Yahweh promises, **Here I will make a horn grow for David and set up a lamp for my anointed one** (v. 17). This is similar to 2 Samuel 7, where David takes the initiative to give to Yahweh but soon finds himself out-given. Throughout the psalm, Yahweh shows remarkable devotion to those who esteem him.

Additional Note §132

132:1–18 / For the view that Ps. 132 was a liturgical composition used in the preexilic Jerusalem temple see Allen, *Psalms 101–150*, pp. 206–209; A. A. Anderson, *The Book of Psalms* (vol. 2; London: Oliphants, 1972), pp. 879–80; Mowinckel, *Psalms in Israel's Worship,* vol. 1, p. 175; Weiser, *Psalms,* p. 779.

§133 The Heavenly Blessing of Harmonious Fellowship (Ps. 133)

133:1–3 / This celebration of fellowship and unity, as the NIV's exclamation point rightly implies, is a joyful surprise and not to be taken for granted. In two similes, it is compared to things that "come down" (the NIV's **running down** and **falling** both translate the same Hb. participle, *yōrēd*), namely **oil** and **dew.** This thrice repeated Hebrew participle may be inviting us to look heavenward for its origin, especially in the image of dew. The same implication of divine origin also resides in the image of oil. This is no ordinary oil, it is that which is **on the head, running down on Aaron's beard.** This reference is reminiscent of Aaron's anointing—performed by pouring oil on his head—whereby he was consecrated as Israel's high priest (Exod. 29:7; 30:22–33; Lev. 8:12). Divine origin is finally made explicit for "the" **blessing,** which **the LORD bestows.**

For the oft-dry land of Israel dew was life-giving (cf. Hos. 14:5, where Yahweh likens himself to "dew" that gives life). **Hermon** is the highest mountain of the eastern Mediterranean and lies above the northern Jordan Valley. For some it had been considered a sacred mountain (Judg. 3:3). But here its dew is transferred to the much lower **Mount Zion,** which is made the center point of earth, not because of its geography but because of its divine choice (cf. 48:2, where Zion, not Zaphon, is the true sacred mountain, and 68:15–16, where the higher "mountains of Bashan . . . gaze in envy" at Zion). In verse 3 there is a key Hebrew wordplay that underscores this (lit.): " . . . the mountains of Zion (Hb. *ṣîyôn*). For there the LORD has commanded (Hb. *ṣiwwâ*) the blessing." Again we see in a psalm of ascent that Yahweh has localized his channel of blessing to Zion. In particular "the blessing" manifests itself as **life** in all its promised fullness bestowed by "the Maker of heaven and earth" (cf. 134:3).

§134 Nocturnal Praise (Ps. 134)

134:1–3 / This psalm may have been placed last among the Psalms of Ascent because of its reference to **you servants of the LORD who minister by night in the house of the LORD.** It may thus serve as a closing wish that the praise of God sung by pilgrims during the day may continue into the night. Perhaps echoed here is an earlier psalm of ascent that claims, "he who watches over Israel will neither slumber nor sleep" (121:4). Also Isaiah 30:29 illustrates that "a holy festival" was celebrated into "the night." Further, it is possible these "servants" who "minister by night" are priests or Levites. The closing benediction (v. 3) may support this suggestion because a priest pronounces it upon the (departing?) congregation. However, each of the seventeen occurrences of "servants" in the Psalms denotes God's people in general. Though it may not be possible to determine the referent for "servants," Psalm 135, the following psalm probably supports the latter suggestion. The opening call to praise in Psalms 134:1 and 135:1–2 have virtually identical terminology and the closing call to praise in Psalm 135:19–21 addresses Israel, Aaron, Levi, and "you who fear him."

Because the NIV consistently (mis-)translates the imperative "Bless (Hb. *bārûk*) the LORD" as **praise the LORD,** it misses a decisive wordplay. As worshipers are commanded to "bless the LORD" (vv. 1–2), so he is in turn invoked, **May the LORD . . . bless you** (v. 3). Relationship with Yahweh is a mutual one: we bless him; he blesses us. Verse 3 contains what is a consummate irony for all and a stumbling block for many, especially in a pluralistic age. Yahweh is **the Maker of heaven and earth**—he is universal. Yet his source of blessing is **from Zion**—it is particular and contingent (cf. 128:5). What makes this particular mountain significant is, of course, the house of the Lord, which resides on it. This reality is the *raison d'être* for pilgrimage to Jerusalem and the psalms of ascents. It is one of the fundamentals of OT theology: Yahweh is the creator of all, but he makes himself known in historical relationships that are marked by particular people and particular places.

§135 Dumb Idols and the Living God of the Exodus (Ps. 135)

This hymnic praise psalm celebrates "that our Lord is greater than all gods" (v. 5) and evidences this confession by his saving acts in the exodus-settlement period. Its opening and closing calls to worship imply a liturgical use. The voice of the liturgist is heard particularly in verse 5 ("I know"; cf. "our God" in v. 2). Many of its verses are closely paralleled elsewhere (vv. 1–2 = 113:1; 134:1; v. 4 = Deut. 7:6; 14:2; Exod. 19:5; for v. 5 cf. Exod. 18:11; v. 6 = 115:3; v. 7 = Jer. 10:13; 51:16; v. 13 = 102:12; cf. Exod. 3:15; v. 14 = Deut. 32:36a; vv. 15–18 = 115:4–8; vv. 19–20 = 115:12–13). Because it appears to be an anthological composition and because some of these parallels are found in postexilic psalms (Pss. 102, 115, 134), its origins probably stem from the postexilic period. Several linguistic features also point to a postexilic date (e.g., the use of the Hb. relative pronoun as a prefix, še-, not as a separate word, ʾašer, in vv. 2, 8, 10). Verse 14 may thus have particular application to the postexilic restoration. Both Psalms 135 and 136 show how standardized and important the hexateuchal history (Gen. through Josh.) became for Israel in the exilic and early postexilic periods.

The structure of this psalm is somewhat chiastic:

A   Commands to praise (vv. 1–4)
  B   Yahweh's superiority to all gods (vv. 5–7)
    C   Yahweh's past salvation for his people (vv. 8–12)
    C′   Yahweh's future salvation for his people (vv. 13–14)
  B′   Uselessness of the nations' idols (vv. 15–18)
A′   Commands to praise (vv. 19–21)

135:1–4, 19–21 / The opening call to praise is addressed to **you servants . . . who minister in the house of the LORD,** and the closing call to the priests and Levites and to the general groups of **Israel** and **you who fear him** (vv. 19–20). As the initial reason substantiating the opening call to praise is Yahweh's election or "choice" of **Israel to be his treasured possession** (v. 4), so the closing command to praise locates both Yahweh and his praise in **Zion,** that is, **Jerusalem** (v. 21).

135:5–7, 15–18 / The "B" sections of the psalm, which confess the inferiority of other **gods** (v. 5) and the senselessness of **the idols of the nations** (vv. 15–18), are closely paralleled in 115:3–8, as noted above. We cannot be certain whether one borrowed from the other or both drew from stock traditional phrases. Yahweh's superiority to **all** gods is demonstrated by his free will **(the LORD does whatever pleases him)** in creation, that is, **on the earth, in the seas,** and especially **in the heavens** (the Hb. term also denotes "the skies"). The **clouds, lightning,** and **wind** are presented simply as elements of creation that Yahweh commands. This contrasts with the earlier theophanies of Yahweh as the God of the storm, where they are symbols associated with Yahweh's presence: "he makes the clouds his chariot and rides on the wings of the wind. He makes winds his messengers, flames of fire his servants" (104:3–4), and "your arrows flashed back and forth. . . . Your lightning lit up the world" (77:17–18).

135:8–14 / As further evidence of Yahweh's superiority, especially on the earth, the psalm presents a brief historical review that focuses on the nations, that is, those who worship these idols (v. 15). So the events narrated concern Yahweh's defeats of **Egypt** and **many nations,** including **the Amorites** and those in **Bashan** and **Canaan,** whose **land** Yahweh **gave . . . as an inheritance to his people Israel.** At this point, the liturgy turns to address Yahweh with praise, **your name, O LORD, endures forever** (though this address may be explained in part as a citation from 102:12), the substantiating reason for which is his current or imminent **compassion on his people** (vv. 13–14). The liturgy thus establishes Yahweh's superiority to other so-called gods on very practical grounds (esp. for a restored postexilic community): only Yahweh can make a difference.

§136 The Enduring Love of the Creator and Saving God of the Exodus (Ps. 136)

136:1–26 / Like Psalm 135, this one is hymnic praise with a historical content. Verses 17–22 are, in fact, virtually identical to 135:10–12. But the point of Psalm 136 is decidedly different. While it does direct praise to **the God of gods** and **the Lord of lords** (vv. 2–3), its emphasis is not on Yahweh's defeat of the nations but on his saving acts and compassion to **Israel** (v. 11) and to **us** (vv. 23, 24). We should probably imagine this psalm sung with antiphonal choirs, one singing the first line of each verse and another singing the second line, **His love endures forever.** Like the liturgy of Psalm 135, it opens and closes with a call for congregational worship (vv. 1–3, 26). It progresses through Yahweh's work (generally described as **wonders,** v. 4) in creation (vv. 5–9; on v. 6 cf. 24:2; on vv. 7–9 cf. Gen. 1:14–18) and in the exodus and settlement (vv. 10–22), and climaxes in his work for the present generation (**us,** vv. 23–24), indeed for **every creature** (v. 25). The mention of "us" marks a striking turn from the third-person reference to **Israel, his people,** found throughout the historical recital. The "us" probably denotes the generation of the restoration from exile. (On the significance of the title, **the God of heaven,** see the comments on 115:3.)

§137 Remembering Jerusalem by the Rivers of Babylon (Ps. 137)

Most psalms are cherished by Christians; this one is not. Its closing verses strike us as unimaginable cruelty. This corporate prayer psalm is clearly set in the Babylonian exile. We must understand what was at stake here for the exiled people of Judah. Deportation by the Babylonians was cruel: Judah lost not only a homeland but also the temple where their God had revealed himself, the king through whom God exercised his rule, and the land through which God blessed his people. Both their existence as a people and their faith in God were jeopardized. Christians may have difficulty identifying with such a localized religion (see esp. v. 4), but at this point of Yahweh's progressive revelation, place was very much tied to people—God's people.

137:1–4 / While the psalm ends with Judah's cruel wish for the Babylonians, it opens with the Babylonians' cruel wish for Judah: **our tormentors demanded songs of joy; they said, "Sing us one of the songs of Zion!"** Yet this is the very **Zion** that Babylon destroyed and that **we remembered** and then **wept.** The melancholic state of God's people is graphically portrayed: **By the rivers of Babylon . . . there on the poplars we hung our harps.** Memory is a key motif in this psalm. It is "remembering" Zion that triggers this opening lament (vv. 1–4).

137:5–6 / Now the speaker engages in a self-curse: if he were to **forget** and **not remember . . . Jerusalem,** he would wish his **right hand forget its skill** of playing "our harps." He would also wish his **tongue** would **cling to the roof of** his **mouth,** thus disabling him from ever singing. We must not misunderstand this passionate attachment to Jerusalem as a mere reflection of cultural identity or nostalgia. In the context of the Songs of Zion (esp. Pss. 46; 48; 87) Jerusalem had been where Israel met with God.

137:7 / There thus follows the psalm's sole petition that Yahweh **remember** how **the Edomites** had **cried, "tear it down to its foundations!"** (The twofold quotation of Jerusalem's enemies in vv. 3, 7 accents their cruelty.) Considering the heritage God had granted his people, their memory of it was critical for their survival as a people. Further, considering the enemies' persecution, God's memory of their destructive actions was also critical for the people's survival and for his maintenance of justice (for the inhumanity of the Edomites during the Babylonian invasion, see Obadiah).

137:8–9 / Verse 8, phrased as a blessing, is not problematic in itself. It simply endorses the message of the prophets (**doomed to destruction;** see, e.g., Isa. 13–14; 47; Jer. 50–51) and just retribution (**he who repays you for what you have done to us).** The interpretive key to the troubling verse 9 is Isaiah 14:21, which also refers to Babylon: "Prepare a place to slaughter his sons for the sins of their forefathers; they are not to rise to inherit the land and cover the earth with their cities." Thus, these expressions referring to the slaughter of children are a way of depicting the end of an oppressive dynasty. By invoking the end of Babylon's succession of power, these texts ensure that Babylonian cruelty is brought to a halt.

This closing "blessing" and the earlier self-curse (vv. 5–6) strike us moderns as extremely foreign. Such passionate loyalty is something with which few of us can identify, though not necessarily because we are more noble. We too should passionately guard the heritage God has given us, and we must ensure that our passionate rage be committed to God in prayer, as this psalm endorses, and not taken into our own hands. Otherwise, we abuse the text by ignoring its context, namely that Psalm 137 is in the mouth of powerless victims, not powerful executioners. As we have seen elsewhere in the Psalms, especially the laments, these prayers allow God's people to vent their feelings, even when they may not have complete theological endorsement or legitimacy (see the Introduction). Although, for example, the lament, "My God, my God, why have you forsaken me?" (22:1), is not an accurate reflection of God's actual relationship to the speaker (note how the psalm later withdraws this claim in v. 24), such impassioned expressions of feelings are not expunged from the canonized psalms.

§138 *The Lord on High Preserves the Lowly in the Midst of Trouble (Ps. 138)*

Psalm 138 is most like the thanksgiving psalms (cf. Pss. 30; 116), and it presupposes a preceding prayer or lament: "When I called, you answered me." Such psalms are the fulfillment of the vow of praise made at the conclusion of most prayer psalms. Psalm 138 contains the usual opening proclamation of praise (v. 1) and introductory summary (v. 3), but it also has some unique elements, among which are its cosmic ("before the 'gods' ") and international scope ("all the kings of the earth") and its closing petition.

138:1–3 / It is possible the expression, **before the "gods,"** can refer to human "judges" (perhaps Exod. 21:6; 22:8–9, 28), but it is more likely we should understand this term in the same sense as it is used in Psalm 82 (see the commentary), namely as "heavenly beings" (i.e., angels). **Your holy temple** also denotes "your holy palace," wherein Yahweh as king presides over his "divine council" of "heavenly beings" (cf. 29:1–2; 89:5–8; 1 Kgs. 22:19–23; Isa. 6:1–8; 40:1–11; also Jer. 23:18; Job 15:8). At this location, the worshiper engages in ritual prostration (**I bow down,** cf. 5:7). As with the thanksgiving psalms, the essential basis for thanksgiving is the testimony that God answers when called (v. 3). This belief reflects the fundamental tradition of the prayer psalms of the individual (see the Introduction).

138:4–6 / This form of hymnic praise (cf. 47:9; 96:3–4, 7–8; 148:11) echoes the speaker's own opening proclamation of praise: **May all the kings of the earth praise you** (Hb. *yôdûkā*, or "they will praise you"), **O LORD,** as "I will praise you (Hb. *ʾôdᵉkā*, v. 1), O LORD." Verse 6 should be translated, "For" (not the NIV's concessive **though**) the **LORD is on high, he looks upon the lowly.** Contrary to most human conceptions of "glory," an essential element of Yahweh's **glory**, which is **great** (v. 5), is that he condescends to help the lowly (cf. 113:4–9).

138:7–8 / After celebrating the international scope of Yahweh's praise, the psalm returns to the worshiper's own situation, this time with a view towards the future. His recent deliverance (v. 3) gives confidence for future protection: **Though I walk in the midst of trouble, you preserve my life.** Yet the ultimate basis for this confidence lies not in this historical precedent, but in the character of Yahweh himself: **your love, O LORD, endures forever.** To confirm this future relationship, this thanksgiving psalm closes with a petition that Yahweh **not abandon the works of** his **hands.**

Surprisingly, Yahweh's exaltation above all does not entail his distance from us. He does not become a remote monarch. In fact, paradoxically his exaltation goes together with his commitment to a relationship with the "lowly." Yahweh's subjugation of all enemies signifies his "exaltation" above all. And his subjugation of enemies entails the preservation of his allies.

§139 Surrendering to God's Inescapable, All-Searching Presence (Ps. 139)

Psalm 139 is perhaps the most intimate of psalms. It displays a striking awareness of God's interest in individuals. Understanding this psalm as a whole is key to its interpretation. At first it appears to be a meditation on God's omniscience (vv. 1–6), omnipresence (vv. 7–12), and omnipotence (vv. 13–15). But the sudden shift from sublime wonder at God's determined interest in the speaker to a denunciation of "the wicked" (vv. 19–22) sounds like an impulsive change of subject. Why are the wicked brought up in a psalm that to this point has made pleasant reading? Some commentators believe that interpretation of the psalm must begin with these verses. Its occasion would thus lie in the speaker's conflict with the wicked: they have accused him falsely and he now seeks vindication from God. In this view, Psalm 139 is to be interpreted in light of others that are said to reflect more clearly a situation of false accusation (Pss. 7 and 17). Although nothing in the psalm rules out this interpretation categorically, Psalm 139 is distinctively different from these psalms.

It is to be granted that verses 19–24 are a key component of the psalm. A point of God's knowing the speaker (which is at the heart of vv. 1–18) is to confirm the rhetorical question and confession of verses 21–22. But we must first note that the wicked in these verses pose no direct threat. They are, in fact, God's enemies and *become* the speaker's enemies only by adoption (vv. 21–22). They do not accuse the speaker: "they speak of you with evil intent" (v. 20). Second, there is no plea for rescue or protection, which is seen so clearly in Psalms 7 and 17. Third, if from the beginning the psalm reflects a notion of asylum or a desire that God examine the speaker and so acquit him, then it seems odd that verses 7–12 speak of flight *from* God. Fourth, the closing petitions are for God to search and know the speaker, which actions God has already been in the process of doing (v. 1).

To that extent the speaker is not seeking to initiate a judgment procedure himself.

The speaker also requests God to "lead me in the way everlasting." Now it may be granted that certain social needs can be cloaked in religious language, especially in prayers and psalms addressed to God, but the psalm as it stands gives no hint of a direct connection between the wicked and the speaker, only between God and the wicked, and God and the speaker. Everything mentioned in the psalm, including the wicked, is done so entirely with reference to God. The interest reflected here is not to clear the speaker's name before accusers and society but to establish his willingness to live in relationship with God and thus participate in his worship. The psalm was probably designed not as a special prayer for particular accused persons but as a regular prayer for the general population of Yahweh's worshipers. (We should note that Ps. 104 focuses entirely on Yahweh's creative work until its closing verse, which likewise expresses a wish that "the wicked be no more.")

If we look for parallels elsewhere in the Psalter, we may note that a connection between God's scrutinizing presence and the wicked is also found in the psalms of temple entry (see the Introduction). A prerequisite to entering the temple was meeting the requirements and passing God's judgment. As in 26:2 God is invited to **test** (v. 23) the speaker, and as in 5:8 to lead (note also v. 10) him along Yahweh's way (v. 24), which is perhaps the pilgrim way into the temple. It is possible that "the ancient way" (NIV "the way everlasting," Hb. *derek ʿôlām*) is related to the "ancient doors" (*pithê ʿôlām*, 24:7, 9), through which Yahweh's procession enters at the temple. Thus, the closing petition may not be a prayer for guidance in general but may have special reference to Yahweh's protective escort along the pilgrim way into his temple.

139:1–6 / Verses 1–12 hymn the comprehensive nature of God's knowledge and presence: from sitting to rising (v. 2), from activity **(going out)** to inactivity **(lying down,** v. 3), from the heavens to the depths (i.e., vertical space, v. 8), from the east ("the wings of the dawn") to the west ("the far side of the sea," i.e., horizontal space, v. 9), and from darkness and night to light and day (vv. 11–12).

The opening section of the psalm begins with a general confession that **you know me.** But even this general statement about divine omniscience does not indicate an *automatic* comprehension: **you have searched me.** The Hebrew verb behind **you discern** (Hb. *zrh*) **my** going out **and my** lying down is normally used for "winnowing" or "sifting" wheat. God himself participates in the process of becoming acquainted with us. His knowledge is not static; it too goes through a dynamic process. Examples of what God knows then follow. The various postures one takes during the day point to the various activities one may engage in. God's knowledge goes beyond mere activity to **my thoughts** and **my ways.** One's speech is also singled out as an area of divine interest. God's comprehension is comprehensive, both around and over us (v. 5). And so our ability to comprehend is limited, **such knowledge** is beyond us (v. 6). It is difficult to know whether God's actions in verse 5 are comforting or oppressive (e.g., Hb. *ṣwr,* **hem . . . in,** is often used in the OT for "besieging," and God's hand upon a person can denote affliction, cf. 38:2). The verse may be intentionally ambiguous, though we should note from the next section that the speaker's immediate response is one of flight.

139:7–12 / This section concerning God's omnipresence is phrased in terms of actions that the speaker does, and they are those of flight from God: **Where can I flee from your presence?** Verse 8 does not merely say, "As for the heavens, you are there; as for the depths, you are there." It says, **If I . . .** The speaker considers fleeing to the farthest points of space, both vertical—**heavens** and **Sheol** (see NIV margin)—and horizontal—**the wings of the dawn** (i.e., in the east) and **the far side of the sea** (i.e., to the west of Israel). (Cf. Amos 9:2–4.) He then considers **darkness** and **night** as a hiding place. Here we see the same response to divine omniscience (vv. 1–6) as is evident in Job, namely the desire to be left alone (Job 7:17–21; 14:5–6). God's scrutiny evokes wonder (v. 6) but also fear. Thoughts of flight need not betray a profound sense of guilt or the fact that the speaker has committed or been accused of a crime. The recognition that we are so scrutinized by another intrinsically makes us want to retreat. We may feel our privacy has been violated or we may fear we will inevitably disappoint the one who takes such an interest in us.

Verse 10 contains a surprise. After we flee from God, we would expect a reprimand from God. Instead, he acts graciously: he **guide**[s] (Hb. *nḥh*) and **hold**[s] **fast** (Hb. *ʾḥz,* together implying providential guidance and protection). These actions evidence divine pursuit and loyalty. Similarly, in Psalm 73 although the speaker confesses to have "slipped" (v. 2) away from God and become "a brute beast before you" (v. 22), "yet . . . you hold me fast (Hb. ʾḥz) . . . ; you guide (Hb. nḥh) me" (vv. 23–24). Both speakers also confess to being "at an end" (139:18, see Additional Notes, and 73:26), yet "I am still/always with you" (139:18 and 73:23).

139:13–16 / These verses, with their introductory **for you created my inmost being,** explain and substantiate the reason for this divine loyalty. God is portrayed as a skilled weaver and the speaker as his handiwork. God's interest in the speaker from his life's beginning evidences God's personal and long-term investment in him. As in the first section, this one also draws attention to the extent of God's knowledge, spatially (v. 15) and temporally (v. 16). In addition, this section substantiates that God can see equally in light and darkness (as claimed in vv. 11–12). The evidence is that **your eyes saw my unformed body,** which was **in my mother's womb, in the secret place, in the depths of the earth.** Verse 16 does not point to a notion of divine predestination but foreknowledge. In verses 1–12, the speaker reflects a sense of freedom (e.g., "when I sit" and "when I rise," and "if I go up," vv. 2, 8). What is divinely determined is God's inevitable presence and knowledge.

139:17–18 / The psalm then bursts into doxology. Yahweh's **thoughts** are not only wonderful (so v. 6); they are now **precious** (v. 17). Their vastness is particularly overwhelming.

139:19–22 / The main intent of these verses is not to petition for the destruction of the wicked. Formally verse 19 is not a petition but a wish: **If only you would . . .** And verses 20–22 simply state the relation of the wicked to God (v. 20) and the speaker's relation to them: **do I not hate those who hate you, O LORD?** Throughout this psalm concern is focused on the relationship between God and the speaker. The concern is the same here: "I stand with God over against the wicked." **The wicked** are introduced as a foil to demonstrate the speaker's loyalty to God. Thus, in response to God's loyalty (vv. 1–18), the speaker now avers his loyalty. Verse 19 is the first mention of any kind of moral judgment. To this point, interest has been fixed solely on the relationship between the speaker and God. Only once this has been established does the moral question take on any significance. To this extent, the sudden wish that

God would slay the wicked may not be as abrupt as interpreters have imagined.

139:23–24 / We now realize that the speaker's invitation for God to search him at the psalm's close is not a spontaneous response of piety but a reasoned surrender to God's inescapable, all-searching presence. Earlier the speaker's initial response was to escape; now he chooses to draw near to the God who pursues him. But why does the speaker petition God to do the very things he would do or has done in any case (note **search** and **know** in vv. 23 and 1, **see** in vv. 24 and 16, and **lead** in vv. 24 and 10 [NIV "guide"])? (Note how these closing verses pick up a key verb from each of the first three strophes.) Apparently the goal is not merely to increase God's knowledge but also to further the relationship between the speaker and his God. God has the prerogative to search the speaker, and he is now welcomed to do so. Although the speaker clearly disavows association with the wicked, he does not thereby presume to be without fault: he knows he may have **anxious thoughts** and **offensive way**[s]. The Hebrew term for the latter (ʿōṣeb) is a noun meaning either "hardship" or "idol." The ambiguity may be intentional.

After a close reading of this psalm, we see that verses 1–6 concern not just divine omniscience but also divine searching (vv. 1–6). Verses 7–12 concern not just God's omnipresence but also his pursuit (esp. v. 10). And verses 13–16 concern not just his omnipotence but also his personal craftsmanship and investment (vv. 13–16). The psalm expresses divine attributes in themselves and also divine loyalty to the speaker. They embody relational theology. The psalm is not a tranquil meditation on God; rather, it reflects the temptation to flee from him and is resolved by a reasoned surrender to God's pursuit. It is an argument and confession for engaging in a relationship with God.

Additional Notes §139

139:14 / **I am fearfully and wonderfully made:** The MT reads lit., "I am awesomely wonderful" ("made," which the translators simply added, is difficult to justify). We should probably follow the ancient versions and read, "*You* are awesomely wonderful."

139:15 / **The depths of the earth** is probably not a metaphysical statement lit. describing a (mythical) belief about the formation of the soul there, but a metaphorical statement lit. drawing the analogy between a dark, hidden place and the mother's womb (v. 13).

139:18 / **When I awake** (derived from Hb. *qyṣ*) is awkward at this point of the psalm. We should perhaps read, "were I at an end" (derived perhaps from Hb. *qṣṣ*, a denominative of *qṣ*), with the support of a few MT manuscripts.

§140 Just Justice for the Violent and for the Needy (Ps. 140)

Psalm 140 is another prayer psalm about personal enemies. They are described in the familiar categories of "the righteous" (v. 13) and "the wicked" (vv. 4, 8). These "men of violence" (vv. 1, 4, 11) are further described by moral adjectives such as "evil" (v. 1, and so they "devise evil") and "proud" (v. 5) and by a variety of images. They are warlike (vv. 2, 7) and are compared to hunters (v. 5) and "their tongues" to "a serpent's" (v. 3). The Hebrew expression behind the NIV's "slanderers" (v. 11) is literally "a man of the tongue," thus echoing verse 3. The righteous are further described by the moral term "the upright" and by economic terms, "the poor" and "needy," which may or may not be metaphoric. The issue of the psalm is that of justice (v. 12).

The psalm displays both individual and corporate interests. The enemies' attack is aimed directly at the speaker (they "have set traps for me," vv. 4–5, 9). But the closing three verses shift the concern to a corporate level, specifically the poor and the righteous who live in the land. Psalm 140 could thus be used for situations of individual distress, in which the individual's appeal is based on what Yahweh has promised for the group. Thus, because the speaker knows "that the LORD secures" justice for the poor, he hopes he will do so for him. On the other hand, Psalm 140 could also be used as a prayer for God's people, in which the speaking individual (perhaps a liturgist) acts as representative for the group.

140:1–3 / The introductory petitions, **rescue me** and **protect me,** are common among the prayer psalms. The lament concerning the foes focuses on what their "minds" (in the language of the OT, thinking takes place in **hearts**) **devise** and what their speeches **(tongues** and **lips) stir up.** Images of **war** and **vipers** dramatize the threat.

140:4–5 / Verse 4 largely repeats the petition of verse 1 but this time draws attention to their actions: with their **hands** they **plan to trip my feet.** Supporting this petition with a note of urgency is a lament that portrays the opponents as hunters (v. 5, cf. the successive psalms, 141:9–10; 142:3).

140:6–8 / The Hebrew text behind the NIV's **O LORD, I say to you** is literally, "I have said to the LORD." It is reported speech that follows, not contemporary speech. But how far does the reported speech go? It could include all of verses 6–11, but the NIV quotation marks are probably correct. In other words, the speaker confesses, "I have been saying, and not just now in this moment of distress, '**You are my God**'" (cf. 142:5). This is the most characteristic claim of the individual prayer psalms: by calling Yahweh "my God" I am obliged to trust and praise him, and he is obliged to protect me.

The petition that follows is therefore present speech. It draws God's attention, and ours, to the fact that this **cry for mercy** (lit. "the *voice* of my supplications") is no mere silent prayer of the mind but is said aloud. There follows a confession of trust that expands on the significance of confessing Yahweh as "my God": he **shields my head in the day of battle.** This choice of battle imagery responds to the warlike intentions of the enemies (v. 2). It therefore follows, as expressed in a negative petition, that the **plans** of my opponents should **not . . . succeed.**

140:9–11 / The petitions of verses 9–11 are wishes (Hb. jussives), which focus on the consequences to befall these men of violence, not so much on divine intervention, which is the emphasis of the imperative petitions. While Yahweh "shields my head" (v. 7), **let the heads of those who surround me be covered with . . . trouble.** Because their lips have the poison of vipers (v. 3), **the** trouble **their lips have caused** is what should "cover their heads" (a judgment in kind). As their judgment, **burning coals** are to **fall upon them,** and they are to **be thrown . . . into miry pits.** The phrase, **never to rise,** underscores the completeness of their fall. In the petition of verse 11, the psalm shifts its focus from the individual petitioner to **the land,** which is a figure of speech (metonym) for the inhabitants of the land. The primary weapon of the men of violence is their "tongue" (**slanderers** is lit. "the man of the tongue"). The final consequence petitioned for them is that the hunters of verse 5 become the hunted: **may disaster hunt down men of violence.**

140:12–13 / The psalm closes with a familiar confession based the experience of generations of Yahweh's people: **I know** (cf. 20:6; 41:11; 56:9) **that the LORD secures justice for the poor.** This confession both gives support to the preceding petitions on the individual's behalf and introduces the substance of the praise vowed in the closing verse. In contrast to most vows of praise that close individual prayer psalms, this one speaks on behalf of a group, here **the righteous.** The expression paralleling they **will praise your name** makes plain that this is no mere ritual act: they **will live before you,** or more literally, "dwell with your presence" (cf. 17:15).

Additional Notes §140

140:8 / **Or they will become proud.** *Selah:* Here we should probably read, "Don't let them be exalted (over me)" (cf. LXX and see *BHS*).

140:12 / **I know:** This is the *Qere* reading of the Hb. text. The *Kethib* reading is, "You know." It seems an odd form of address until we observe that this is the only verse of the psalm where Yahweh is referred to in the third person. It is therefore possible the psalm here addresses individual members of a congregation (note the praising "righteous" of the following verse), as we have seen in other prayer psalms of the individual.

§141 A Prayer for the Heart in the Midst of Threat and Temptation (Ps. 141)

This is a prayer psalm of the individual. Its first half focuses on the speaker's relationship to God (vv. 1–2) and on God's restraining him from temptation (vv. 3–5a). Its second half turns to the retribution of evildoers (vv. 5b–7) and his preservation from their schemes (vv. 8–10). The spirituality reflected in this prayer psalm is decidedly more reflective and introspective than what is found in most. We see here the realization that "there but for the grace of God go I." The speaker admits the possibility that the line between himself and the wicked is not sharply drawn. They are not merely enemies; they are also a temptation (esp. v. 4). Moreover, God is called upon not only to ensure the wicked are entrapped (v. 10) but also to direct the speaker's heart (esp. vv. 3–4). God is to influence social circumstances as well as one's internal choices and will.

141:1–2 / While the opening petitions are typical and reflect the standard tradition of individual prayers (i.e., Yahweh should **hear my voice when I call**), those in verse 2 are unique: **May my prayer be set before you like incense; may the lifting up of my hands be like the evening sacrifice.** It is not clear whether this is a mere comparison or it intends to prescribe verbal prayers as a replacement of ritual offerings at the temple. Nevertheless, it is clear that Yahweh is to regard "my prayer," that is, this psalm, as a pleasing ritual rite. And this psalm largely concerns a request to avoid joining the wicked. This comparison helps us to see that religious ritual and moral lifestyle were to be integrally connected in ancient Israel.

141:3–5a / The prayer for the worshiper himself builds on bodily images: **set a guard over my mouth, Let not my heart be drawn to what is evil,** and **my head will not refuse it** (which includes the metaphoric **oil** and the "striking rebuke" on the face from **a righteous man**). Attention is given to one's speech and **deeds** and to one's inner heart. While the psalm as prayer looks to God as the source for personal discipline, it also clearly keeps the worshiper open to human agents for this discipline: **let** a righteous man **strike me—it is a kindness.** All too often God's people may be willing to receive rebuke from the Almighty, but unwilling to receive it from a fellow human.

141:5b–10 / Verses 5b–7 then focus on the retribution of **the wicked** (on **our bones have been scattered,** cf. 53:5). The closing verses (vv. 8–10) turn the worshiper's attention to his relationship with God: **But my eyes are fixed on you . . . ; in you I take refuge.** The image of the speaker's refuge is complemented by the image of his opponents' entrapment, which in turn illustrates the principle of retribution in kind: **Let the wicked fall into their own nets, while I pass by in safety.**

§142 *Alone and Persecuted (Ps. 142)*

This prayer psalm is for those who are alone: "no one is concerned for me" (v. 4; note also the superscription "When he was in the cave"). "The righteous will gather about me" (v. 7) is described as a future event, only after the psalm has been answered. This psalm, therefore, does not seem suited to public performance. Devoid of supportive social relationships, the speaker directs his "voice . . . before him," that is, to Yahweh. He is the special protector of those who are alone, the alien, the fatherless, and the widow (Pss. 10:14, 18; 68:5; 146:9). The depictions of threat and distress are varied—trappers (v. 3), pursuers (v. 6), and prison (v. 7)—thus indicating they are not describing actual circumstances but are portraying images that denote feelings of attack and confinement. This allows the psalm to be used for a variety of needs.

142:1–2 / The opening verses refer to Yahweh in the third person and describe the act of praying—they are not a formal part of the prayer itself. Why, we may wonder, bother with this? Why not just get on with praying? And to whom are these verses addressed, if not to Yahweh and not to a congregation? To answer these questions, several observations are in order. The emphasis of these verses is made clear by echoes in each of the parallel lines. Verse 1 literally reads, "With my voice to Yahweh I cry, with my voice to Yahweh I make supplication." The place of this vocal prayer is clear from the similar echo in verse 2: **before him; before him.** The "telling" of one's **trouble** is also described as a "pouring out." Each of these parallel expressions directs the worshiper to think of personal engagement with God. These descriptions thus act as a kind of instruction to the would-be petitioners themselves (cf. the instructive superscription to Ps. 102 esp. with 142:2–3). These observations confirm the conclusion that psalms are written not to express the recent experience of their composers but to help express the varied experiences of any worshiper who wishes to sing them.

142:3–4 / **My spirit grows faint** is an expression used elsewhere in the Psalms but always as part of a lament (77:3; 143:4; cf. the superscription to Ps. 102). Here it introduces a confession of trust: **it is you who know my way.** Yahweh's knowing his way is vital because in this way or **path, men have hidden a snare for me** (cf. the same hunting image as in the preceding psalms, 140:5; 141:9–10). Perhaps to our surprise the psalm continues with the petitions, **Look . . . and see,** in spite of the preceding confession that "you . . . know my way." Recognizing that God knows our affairs should not lead to a passive acceptance of circumstances or of God's so-called will, nor should it lead to a presumption that God must intervene on our behalf. According to the Psalms, there should always be a dynamic engagement in the relationship, in which we show initiative to cry aloud to the LORD (v. 1) and he is expected to respond and **rescue** (v. 6). The significance that **no one is concerned for me** at **my right** is explained elsewhere (16:8; 73:23; 109:31; 110:5; 121:5), where the place of the helper was at the right side.

142:5–7 / Similar to verses 1–2, verse 5 is also a description of the act of praying but this time it is a report of *past* confessions. The verbs (Hb. perfect) should be rendered, "I have cried to you, O LORD, I have said . . ." (cf. 140:6). In other words, the speaker claims that the confessions reported here are not insincere and manipulative, as though he had suddenly become religious in the face of an emergency. **"You are my refuge"** (Hb. *maḥsê*) is a familiar confession and becomes especially meaningful in view of the preceding lament of having no refuge (Hb. *mānôs*). Claiming Yahweh as **my portion in the land of the living** is particularly associated with the Levites (Num. 18:20). However, it is also found in psalms that do not appear to be the peculiar property of the Levites (16:5; 73:26; 119:57).

The subsequent petition again draws attention to the speaker's being seemingly "insignificant" (Hb. *dll;* **in desperate need** is a paraphrase) in society. The actual petitions for God's intervention are two. One or both of them must be metaphoric, for if taken literally their images are incompatible. The first reflects feelings of being chased **(Rescue me from those who pursue me),** and the second feelings of confinement **(Set me free from my prison,** cf. 143:11b in Hb.). Each has a supporting motivation.

The first points to the opponents **(for they are too strong for me)**, and the second to God **(that I may praise your name).** The latter doubles as a vow of praise. It is in the context of this future praising, not this present praying, that the psalm foresees that **the righteous will gather about me,** thus signaling the speaker's reincorporation into the believing community. Closing the psalm is thanksgiving given in anticipation of the deliverance: "because you have acted on my behalf" (lit., cf. 13:6; 116:7).

§143 No One Is Righteous before God (Ps. 143)

This individual prayer psalm is highly formulaic, that is, it consists of stock phrases repeated elsewhere in the Psalms (v. 3 // 7:5; Lam. 3:6; v. 4 // 77:3; 142:3; vv. 5–6 // 77:2, 5, 12; v. 6 // 63:1; v. 7 // 69:17; 88:4, 14; 102:2; v. 8 // 90:14; in general cf. Pss. 25; 86; further parallels listed in Culley, *Oral Formulaic Language,* p. 107). Yet it reflects an intimacy with God that is strikingly singular among the psalms.

143:1–2 / The opening and closing verses draw attention to **your righteousness** (vv. 1, 11) and for good reason: **Do not bring your servant into judgment, for no one living is righteous before you.** Although this admission may be obvious in Christian theology (e.g., Rom. 3:23), it is remarkably rare among the psalms. They contain a number of admissions of acts of sin (25:7, 18; 32:5; 38:3, 18; 41:4; 65:3; 79:9; 103:10), but only here and in 51:3–5, 130:3–4 is sin noted as part of the general human condition. In fact, such confessions seem to go contrary to claims of righteousness found elsewhere in the Psalter (see esp. 18:20, 24; 35:24; 112:3–9). How far we seem to have moved from the first psalm of the Psalter, which clearly divides humanity into two groups: "the righteous" and "the wicked" (1:5–6)! This verse also seems to go contrary to explicit petitions that invite divine judgment: "Judge me, O LORD, according to my righteousness" (7:8; cf. 26:1; 35:24; 43:1).

How are these discrepancies to be explained? First, we must allow for theological development (progressive revelation) among the psalms. The shocking event of the Babylonian exile, accompanied as it was by prophetic preaching, raised the people's consciousness of sin within the nation (see further the Introduction, and comments on Ps. 106). We cannot be certain that Psalm 143 is postexilic, but verse 2 may reflect this theological development (cf. 130:3). Second, the Hebrew term "righteousness" can be used in a variety of senses. The request for judgment

"according to my righteousness" in 7:8 lies in the context of false
accusers (also 35:24). Thus, *relative* to these wicked, the speaker
of the psalm is righteous. The Hebrew terms for "wicked" *(rāšāᶜ)*
and "righteous" *(ṣaddîq)* can also be rendered "guilty" and "innocent" respectively (cf. 1 Kgs. 8:31–32). The context of these
psalms may thus be likened to a civil court case between two
parties. In 143:2, however, judgment takes place "before you."
Here judgment and righteousness are relative to God alone,
and thus take on an *absolute* sense. There is no third party here,
so this may be likened to a criminal case (further on this analogy, see C. S. Lewis, *Reflections on the Psalms* [London: Geoffrey
Bles, 1958], pp. 15–22).

Third, we need to consider the chief function of the designations "the righteous" and "the wicked" in the liturgies of
temple entry (which include Ps. 26). Here worshipers were asked
to confess their loyalty to Yahweh's prescribed way of "the righteous." Otherwise, they must be counted among "the wicked"
who were not granted entry. While only the one who vows to
be a doer of righteousness (15:2) may enter the temple, "he will
receive . . . righteousness from God his *savior*" (24:5, lit.). Thus,
worshipers were expected to show *loyalty* to Yahweh's revealed
righteousness but not to show perfection in the sense of absolute
righteousness. Yahweh would thus impute righteousness to them.
In this light we can make sense of psalms such as Psalms 14 and
32. In Psalm 32 the "righteous" (v. 11) are not morally perfect. In
fact, the key difference between them and "the wicked" (v. 10) is
that the righteous are "forgiven" sinners (vv. 1–5). Similarly,
Psalm 14, in spite of its blanket condemnation of "all the sons of
men" ("there is no one who does good, not even one"), still refers
to a group of the righteous (v. 5), the opposite of which is the
group of evildoers (v. 4).

143:3–6 / It is common in the Psalms to describe **the
enemy** as "pursuing," but in verse 3 he does not merely threaten—
he has already put the speaker in a state of virtual death (cf.
69:1–4, 14–15; contrast 22:15; 88:6–8, 15–18, where the state of
death is attributed to Yahweh). This image implies a feeling of being
cut off or alienated entirely from human society and support. The
subsequent petition of verse 7 seeks to ensure that the speaker
not be alienated from Yahweh (implied by the "hidden face").
Not surprisingly the alienation caused by the foes makes for a
spirit that is **faint** and a **heart** that is "desolate" (NIV **dismayed**).

The psalm thus gives worshipers the opportunity to vent their despair, but it also directs their thoughts to God: **I meditate on all your works.** The phrase, **I remember the days of long ago,** could allow for feelings of mere nostalgia, but there is more here than longing for "the good old days." The psalm directs the worshiper's body and soul to long for something from God in the near future: **I spread out my hands to you; my soul thirsts for you like a parched land.** The object of the meditation, "all your works" and **what your hands have done,** is left open-ended. It could denote Yahweh's saving acts, perhaps just celebrated in a corporate festival, or his works in creation. In 44:1 and 77:5, 11, the phrase, "the days of long ago," has particular reference to the period of Moses and Joshua (cf. 74:2). "Of long ago" (Hb. *qedem*) can describe "the skies" (68:33) and Yahweh's original establishing of the sun, moon, and earth (74:12–17). Thus, Psalm 143 directs worshipers to engage their memory as a means for cultivating personal encouragement in the present and for establishing precedents for Yahweh to act now—even "quickly," as the following petition pleads.

143:7–12 / The rest of the psalm is composed of petitions, each supported by a motive clause (usually **for . . .**). They focus on Yahweh's personal response (suggested esp. by **your face,** vv. 7–8a), on his directions for living (vv. 8b, 10), and on his rescue from **enemies** (vv. 9, 11–12). The **answer** sought in verse 7 may take the form of an oracular **word** (v. 8) delivered by a temple prophet in **the morning** (on the "morning" as the special time of God's salvation, see commentary on 46:5). It is perhaps not accidental that Psalm 32 contains phrasing virtually identical to verse 8 of our psalm, except it is stated as a prophetic oracle: "I will instruct you and teach you in the way you should go" (v. 8). Both psalms share a profound awareness of human sinfulness before God (32:1–5; 143:2) and show the need for God's direction for the speaker's life and for his protection from hostilities (32:6–7, 10). In our psalm, guidance is sought for the doing of **your will** (lit. "favor" or "pleasure," cf. 25:4–5, 8–9, 12) in the context of "my enemies"—hence his preference for **level ground** (cf. 5:8; 27:11; 31:3). In effect, the psalm directs the worshiper to please God in spite of opposition. Only here (and possibly 139:7, 10) is mention made of God's **Spirit** as the agent of guidance. The petitions regarding the opponents are twofold: for **rescue** and for their destruction.

The motives to move God to act on these petitions draw attention to the speaker's plight and to what God has at stake. Reference is made to his spirit that faints (lit. "is finished," cf. v. 4), his near likeness to the dead (v. 7, cf. 3), his trust in and the entrusting of himself to Yahweh (v. 8–9), and his resultant claim, **I am your servant** (v. 12). Corresponding to this last claim, he confesses, **you are my God** (v. 10), which entails that Yahweh should protect him. Hence, Yahweh is to act **for your name's sake** and **in your righteousness**, that is, according to your character that puts things right (v. 11). The psalm also twice appeals to Yahweh's **unfailing love** (vv. 8, 12).

§144 The Davidic Mercies and Deliverance from Foreigners (Ps. 144)

Often when reading the psalms we discover that verses and phrases repeat themselves. We may wonder if anything new is really being said. In such cases, we need to probe not at the parts but at how those parts have been woven into a new whole. Here in Psalm 144 virtually the entirety of verses 1–11 are drawn from formulas found in earlier psalms, especially Psalm 18 ("Praise be to . . . my Rock" in v. 1 = 18:2, 46; v. 1b = 18:34a; v. 2 = 18:2, 47b; v. 3 = 8:4; v. 4a = 39:5b, 11b; v. 4b = 102:11a; v. 5a [though an imperative] = 18:9a; v. 5b [imperative] = 104:32b; v. 6 [imperative] = 18:14; v. 7 [imperative] = 18:16, 44; for v. 8 cf. 12:2a; 63:11b; 26:10; v. 9 = 33:3a, 2b; for v. 10 cf. 18:50; v. 11 = 144:7–8). And verses 12–15 share a great deal in common with 128:1–4 (also cf. v. 15b with 33:12a).

The mention of "who subdues peoples under me" (v. 2), of rescue from foreigners (vv. 7, 11), and of David (v. 10), as well as the many parallels to Psalm 18, a royal psalm, have inclined most interpreters to read Psalm 144 as a royal psalm. But we need to observe that each royal feature stems from the psalm's dependence on Psalm 18, which is only one among the several psalms incorporated here. The other psalms represent a variety of genres, including hymns and individual laments, thus giving the impression the psalm is an anthology (cf. Pss. 9–10; 119; 135).

While the psalm's royal elements fit the preexilic period, other segments, especially the blessing in verses 12–15, have an affinity to the postexilic period, when Judah had no Davidic king under the Persian Empire (see Additional Notes). In its final form, therefore, the psalm appears to have been applied to the postexilic community, where people pray for deliverance from foreigners after the style of the old royal psalms and for blessing on the troubled community of the restoration. (For a situation comparable to deceitful foreigners see Ezra 4 and Neh. 4–6.) In effect, they appeal to God on the basis of a historical precedent by referring to this chief figure of their past who confronted foreigners. This transfer of royal prerogatives to God's people at large is similar to the exilic prophecies of Isaiah 40–55, where Davidic privileges are bestowed on Zion (Isa. 55:3–5; 52:1–2).

144:1–11 / To determine what this psalm is about we need to observe what distinctive twists it makes on traditional formulas and how it combines them into a new whole. Verses 5–11 are clearly dominated by petitions and a vow of praise. The repeated petitions in verses 7–8 and 11 imply that primary interest is in deliverance from foreigners, particularly by virtue of Yahweh's dramatic intervention (vv. 5–6). To accomplish this, Psalm 144 changes the declarative praises of Psalms 18 and 104 into imperative petitions (see the parallels to vv. 5–7 above).

The rhetorical question of verse 3, while leading to praise in Psalm 8, here leads to a lament. It thus functions as a motif to motivate God to intervene by supporting the petitions of verses 5–7. Instead of man's apparent insignificance being depicted relative to the night sky as in Psalm 8, it is here depicted relative to a breath and a shadow. It is not immediately apparent how verses 3–4 fit into the sequence of verses drawn largely from Psalm 18. In context, this human powerlessness applies equally to **foreigners** as it does to Israel. On the one hand, these foreign powers pose no threat to Yahweh, and on the other, Israel cannot mount any significant power to save itself relative to God. The placement of these verses here appears to set the stage for the petitioned theophany, thus underscoring that help must come solely from the divine side. As for verses 1–2, their grammatical form of praise is unaltered from Psalm 18, but their new association with prayer (as distinct from thanksgiving) makes them function not as praise in its own right but as a confession of trust supporting the prayer as a whole.

144:12–15 / These verses are set apart from the preceding because of their literary form and their lack of clear borrowing of psalmic phrases, and because most of the psalm's postexilic features are located here. Nevertheless, their coherence with the petitionary function of verses 1–11 becomes apparent once we recognize that they are a blessing invoked upon God's people. Instead of the NIV's **then** (Hb. ʾᵃšer, normally translated "which") **our sons,** we should read, "Blessed (Hb. ʾašrê) be our sons." This opening formula then matches the closing, **Blessed are** (Hb. ʾašrê) in verse 15. Thus, in keeping with verses 1–11, the verbs of the blessing should probably be rendered as invocations or wishes, not as declarations: "Blessed be our sons . . . , and our daughters be like . . ." As the blessing progresses it moves through ever widening circles: first for the family, then for the agricultural produce of the land, and then for national security against foreign invasion. As such, the entire psalm opens and closes with the notion of blessing. At the first, Yahweh is "blessed" (the NIV's "Praise be to the LORD" is lit., "Blessed be [Hb. *bārûk*] Yahweh"), and at the end the people are blessed (Hb. *ʾašrê*).

This psalm's use of earlier scripture, including passages fit for a king, provides a contemporary lesson on how we may apply old passages to new situations. Particularly enlightening is how privileges once thought to be the exclusive prerogative of the elite are democratized to become the privileges of all God's people, even when in lowly circumstances (as was the postexilic community).

Additional Notes §144

The postexilic features of the psalm are several. (a) The use of the Hb. prefix *še-* (v. 15), instead of *ʾašer* (vv. 8, 11), is characteristic of postexilic Hebrew. Hebrew *zan* ("kind," v. 13) occurs elsewhere only in 2 Chron. 16:14 and appears to be a Persian loanword (Allen, *Psalms 101–150*, p. 288). (b) Some of the psalms upon which Ps. 144 drew probably come from the exilic (Ps. 102) and postexilic periods (Ps. 128, and perhaps Pss. 33 and 39). (c) The psalm uses traditional motifs in untraditional ways, implying that psalm composition had become more literary than liturgical. Old phrases are given new functions. For example, while Ps. 144 is largely a prayer, it begins with praise. Verses 1–2 are, in fact, virtually identical to the verses opening Ps. 18, which is a thanksgiving. In another example, v. 9 must be regarded as a vow of praise, but it does not close the psalm; instead other petitions follow. And it is followed immediately not with the customary description of future praise but with a reference back to past praiseworthy deliverances (v. 10). (d) Verse 14 fits well into the postexilic period. (e) Psalm 144 is placed late in Book V of the Psalter, which consists largely of postexilic psalms.

144:14 / Some interpreters of the Hb. text believe that the interest in agricultural produce continues through this verse (see esp. Allen, *Psalms 101–150*, p. 288). However, this interpretation seems a bit pressed. It is most consistent with OT usage to read the Hb. terms, *pereṣ* ("breach"), *yôṣēʾt* ("going out"), and *reḥôb* ("town square"), as referring to urban terminology (note esp. Amos 4:3, which threatens "going out" through "breaches" in city walls). The verse thus reflects a wish that there be no more **captivity**, as the NIV renders it.

§145 The Divine King and His Universal Kingdom (Ps. 145)

The praise of this psalm is hymnic in that it praises God's attributes and deeds in general, but the speaker is "I" throughout ("we/us" does not appear), and the opening verses are characteristic of individual thanksgiving. It begins, not with an imperative summons addressed to a congregation, but with a proclamation of praise: "I will exalt you." The verses form an acrostic (i.e., each verse begins with a successive letter of the Hb. alphabet), but this feature need not imply the psalm is a literary composition not intended for liturgical performance. For example, Psalm 111 is also an acrostic and was probably intended for liturgical performance. Like Psalm 145, its praise consists of general nouns and adjectives that are drawn from Exodus 34:6. Although clear liturgical allusions are lacking in Psalm 145, a literal translation of the final verse makes clear that the psalm is intended for public proclamation: "Yahweh's praise my mouth speaks, so all flesh may bless his holy name." If it were tied to any festival, verses 15–16 are particularly appropriate at a time of harvest.

While the psalm is overwhelmingly positive, we should not regard its author as naïve or as an elitist who is blind to the harsh realities that some face in life. The psalm praises God by celebrating *his* praiseworthy attributes and deeds. What hints it does offer of the human condition are not all sweetness and light: God's people may be bowed down and thus call and cry to him for salvation (vv. 14, 18–19). This realization helps us to appreciate further this remarkable praise.

The structure of Psalm 145 is intricate. It alternates between "you" sections, addressing Yahweh directly, and "he" sections, referring to him in the third person. For the most part, the "you" sections describe the act of praising (or may call for praise if the imperfects are rendered as jussives, "Let me exalt you,"

vv. 1–2, 4–7, 10–12). The "he" verses unpack the substance of that praising, describing Yahweh primarily by adjectives (vv. 3, 8–9, 13b, 17–18) or by verbs (vv. 14, 19–20).

There are three exceptions to these correspondences. Verses 15–16, which are in the "you" form, describe Yahweh's providence toward his creatures. There are four possible explanations for this. First, they closely parallel 104:27–28, which are also in the "you" form, and may thus be a literary citation (compositional explanation). Second, because they express the primary testimony of Yahweh's universal providence, they may be accented by their direct address to him (thematic explanation). Third, the action described in the phrase, "the eyes of all look" to God, implicitly calls for direct address to him (ritual explanation). Fourth, if this psalm was originally sung at a harvest festival, these verses are the expression closest to that occasion (situational explanation). Verse 13a is also a "you" verse and it describes Yahweh's kingdom. As will be argued below, this verse climaxes the central section of the psalm. Verse 21 is a "he" verse and calls for the act of praising. This time, however, at the psalm's close, Yahweh is not told how people will praise him, instead all humanity (lit. "all flesh," NIV "every creature") is summoned to join in the speaker's praise.

Also corresponding to this alternation between "you" and "he" sections is praise of God's name. In the two opening verses and in the closing verse, the speaker announces his intention to do so. Verse 3 then makes the first mention of the name "Yahweh" (NIV "the LORD"). Here, we observe a shift to the third person when referring to him. Each of the three subsequent shifts to third-person speech mention the name "Yahweh" twice in successive verses (vv. 8–9, 13b–14, 17–18). It thus appears that praise of God's name refers to him by name in the third person.

Also indicative of the psalm's structure is the repetition of key words ("bless," "praise," "works," "mighty acts," "king[dom]," "splendor," "great[ness]," "love," "good[ness]," "righteous[ness]," and "desires"), which tie its nine sections together. (The Hb. word translated in the NIV as "praise" in vv. 1, 2, 21 and as "extol" in v. 10 is lit. "bless.") The same Hebrew term (which lit. means "works") lies behind the expressions rendered in the NIV as "your works," "all he has made" or "all you have made." A progression can be seen in its use. In its first occurrence it is an object of praise and is a general designation, as the parallel term, "your mighty acts," implies (v. 4). Next, "all [the people] he has made" are the recipients of Yahweh's goodness and compassion (v. 9). As a result, "all you have made" becomes a subject praising God (v. 10). The final two instances are identical and emphasize his works as objects of his compassion: Yahweh is "loving toward all he has made."

In terms of motifs the structure of Psalm 145 may be analyzed this way:

Praising God	1–2	10	21
God's greatness	3–6	11–13a	
God's goodness	7–9	13b–20	

The verses that refer to the mere act of praising mark the two major sections of the psalm (vv. 1–9 and 10–21). In the first half, four verses are devoted to God's greatness and three to his goodness (4 + 3). In the second half, three verses are given to his greatness and eight to his goodness (3 + 4 + 4). Overall, the psalm moves from the general to the specific (e.g., cf. vv. 3 and 20).

The chief roles in which Yahweh is depicted are King and providential Creator. The latter is evident in the repeated expression referring to his "works" or "all he has made" and this role is the focus of verses 15–16. The former is evident in the opening address of Yahweh as the King. Here, "King" is aligned with "my God." Such identification of God is characteristic of the prayer psalms of the individual. Yahweh's depiction as king is especially evident in the psalm's central section (vv. 10–13a), which celebrates Yahweh's kingdom (vv. 10–13a). His royal role is also plain from the references to his glorious splendor (vv. 5, 12). Both of these roles are closely related in other psalms where divine kingship is achieved by establishing creation order (see e.g. Pss. 24; 29; 74; 93; 104). But noticeably absent in this postexilic psalm is any reference to conflict with chaotic powers.

145:1–3 / In the opening verses, the speaker announces his intention to **exalt** Yahweh as **King** and to "bless" (NIV **praise**) his **name**—**every day** (frequency) and **for ever** (duration). In verse 3, he does so with the first mention of the name "Yahweh" (NIV **the LORD**). In spite of the speaker's ever-flowing praise, it fails to come close to exhausting the **praise** of which he is **worthy** because **his greatness no one can fathom.**

145:4–9 / Even beyond his own lifetime—from **genera-tions** past to generations future—praise of Yahweh's **mighty acts**

will continue (vv. 4–7). Praise of his **great deeds** continues, as does attention to his royal role in the praise of **the glorious splendor of your majesty.** The final verse of this section turns to the beneficent aspects of Yahweh's reign: **your abundant goodness** and **your righteousness.** The motif that **the LORD is good** continues in the third-person praise of the name, "Yahweh," mentioned twice in verses 8–9. Verse 8 is a confession drawn from Exodus 34:6, part of the narrative of Yahweh's saving acts towards Israel. But in verse 9 this confession is universalized: **he has compassion on all he has made.**

145:10–14 / In verses 10–13a, these recipients of Yahweh's goodness are now described as praising him themselves. This central section focuses attention on his kingdom and climaxes in actual praise of its enduring nature (v. 13a). The next section returns to praise of the divine name Yahweh, where his **loving** nature is evident in that he **lifts up all who are bowed down** (vv. 13b–14).

145:15–21 / In the context of the Israelite Psalter, we might think that this refers to the people of God in particular, but the next section makes the universal horizon clear: **The eyes of all look to you** and you **satisfy the desires of every living thing.** With eyes directed to God, the words of the psalm are now directed to him ("you" praise). Verses 17–20 return to third-person praise of the name **the LORD** and expands further the nature of his goodness. But here it is not the timely goodness that he initiates **(at the proper time, you open your hand)** but his responsive goodness: **the LORD is near to all who call on him, fear,** and **love him.** The horizon narrows from **all he has made** to **all who call on him.** With this shift to the human sphere there is introduced the possibility of choice: one may be counted among **all who call on him in truth,** whom he **saves,** or among **the wicked,** whom **he will destroy.** In closing the speaker reiterates his intention to praise Yahweh and makes explicit its purpose: so "all flesh" (NIV **every creature**) will "bless" the **name.**

Those familiar with the Psalms must be struck by the universalism of this one (e.g., Hb. *kol-*, translated "all" or "every," appears no less than seventeen times). It does not give a favored position to Israel. Yahweh is portrayed as Creator and King, whose acts are toward all and whose kingdom is known by all. Even the famous confession of Exodus 34:6 (in v. 8) and the designation, "your saints" (lit. "your loved ones," Hb. *ḥᵃsîdêkā*, v. 10), both of which elsewhere apply to Israel, are applied to "all he has made" (in v. 9 his compassion and in v. 13b his loving [Hb. *ḥāsîd*] nature). The only stipulations for receiving Yahweh's salvation are to call on him in truth (cf. John 4:24), to fear him, and to love him (vv. 18–20). While this psalm opens the door of salvation to all, it may close it for some. Their favor with God rests not on their ethnicity but on their sincerity. The line is not drawn between Israel and the nations but between **all who** love him and **all** the wicked (v. 20). While Psalm 145 may sound general and repetitious (and therefore perhaps uninteresting), it has a specific and remarkable case to make. Yahweh's great and benevolent kingdom, to which Israel's experience is a testimony (as evident from the citation of Exod. 34:6), is open to all. His kingdom has no boundaries: "all flesh" is to "bless his holy name" (v. 21). This is a theme Jesus and the NT writers develop over and over.

Additional Note §145

145:8 / **Gracious and compassionate:** As in Ps. 111:4, these terms are reversed from their original order in Exod. 34:6 for the sake of the acrostic. And "great of love" appears instead of "abundant of love" to echo the terms "great" used in vv. 3 and 6.

§146 *The Helper of Those Who Cannot Help Themselves (Ps. 146)*

The liturgical nature of this hymn is apparent from the combination of commands addressed to a group (vv. 1a, 3, 10b), namely Zion personified (v. 10), and the testimony of a liturgist ("I" in v. 2). Thus the psalm opens with a call to praise (v. 1a), followed by the liturgist's proclamation of praise (vv. 1b–2) and his instruction to the congregation (vv. 3–9), particularly in the form of a blessing (v. 5) and praises to Yahweh (vv. 6–9). It then closes with a summary addressed to Zion and a concluding call to praise (v. 10).

146:1–2 / **Praise the LORD** is actually the familiar Hebrew phrase, *hallelujah*. After this call to praise to the congregation (which in Hb. is plural), a single voice steps forth to declare his intention to praise God. This is probably a liturgist acting as an exemplary worshiper. This proclamation of praise is similar to what we see in thanksgiving psalms, but instead of offering thanks for a singular, recent deliverance (cf. 30:1a), it expresses the intention of a lifetime of praise (cf. 30:12b), **as long as I live.** These opening verses are virtually identical to 104:33, 35b.

146:3–4 / The speaking "I" now addresses a group (**your** in v. 3 is plural), apparently to be identified with the congregation, referred to as Zion (v. 10). He issues another imperative but this time for the purpose of instruction. Here surfaces the chief issue of the psalm: whom will you trust, **mortal men** (vv. 3–4) or the God of Jacob (vv. 5–9)? (Cf. 33:16–17; 118:8–9.) The injunction **Do not put** your **trust in princes** may reflect the exilic disillusionment with the Davidic monarchy and the postexilic hopes of its revival. Human political power will fail because **their plans** die with them. This is a sober warning, that we should never put too much hope in human institutions, even if they be instituted originally by God.

146:5–9 / Formally, verse 5 is a pronouncement of blessing, but it also acts as instruction, for it identifies the human characteristic that makes one an object of divine blessing. But the only "virtue" named lies in the source of one's **help.** Thus, rather than focusing on human attributes (as in 1:1; 41:1; 106:3; 112:1, 5; 119:1–2; 128:1), this blessing transmutes into the praise of God (Hb. participles). The point is that rather than aspiring for a great faith, one should aspire for a little faith in a great God.

This praise contains two themes: the power of God (v. 6) and the condescension of God (vv. 7–9). The fall of Jerusalem in 587 B.C. precipitated the greatest theological crisis Israel experienced. There emerged two theological explanations among the general populus: either Yahweh was weaker than the gods of the Babylonians (or the Persians) or he did not care about his people. (Cf. how Isa. 40, the chapter opening the section addressed to the exiles, also counters these two presumptions. See esp. v. 27.) Yahweh's power is proclaimed by a title that is characteristic of the Psalms of Ascent (Pss. 120–134), **the Maker of heaven and earth** (121:2 and 124:8 also confess him to be the source of help; 134:3; cf. 115:15). **The sea** is likewise one of his creations (cf. 95:5), not an opponent as depicted in other psalms (65:7; 74:13–14; 89:9–10; 93:3–4). The issue of Yahweh's devotion to his people is then addressed in the words **the LORD, who remains faithful forever.** His condescension is asserted in phrases also found in passages of the Psalms and Isaiah that probably stem from the late exilic and early postexilic periods: he "does justice for" (NIV **upholds the cause of**) **the oppressed** (103:6), **gives food to the hungry** (Hb. $r^{e c}\bar{e}b\hat{\imath}m$, 107:9; note **prisoners** and princes are also of interest in vv. 10, 40), **sets** prisoners **free** (cf. Isa. 61:1), **gives sight to the blind** (Isa. 35:5; 42:7; cf. 29:18), **lifts up those who are bowed down** (Ps. 145:14), and cares for **the fatherless and the widow** (68:5, a preexilic psalm). The message is this: contrary to the popular adage, God helps those who can*not* help themselves. Yahweh turns the world system upside down: in his economy, princes are devalued and the marginal in society are given value.

The divine name chosen in verse 5 may aim to awaken the memory of how Yahweh proved to be **the God of Jacob,** the patriarch who similarly experienced "famine" or "hunger" (Hb. $r\bar{a}^c\bar{a}b$, Gen. 42:5; 43:1) and whose son Joseph was a "prisoner" (39:20; 40:3, 5). When Jacob blessed Joseph, he called Yahweh "your father's God, who helps you" (49:25).

146:10 / The closing verse addresses **Zion** directly with a summary statement: **The LORD reigns forever, your God... for all generations.** (Unlike the acclamation familiar from the psalms of Yahweh's kingship, "reigns" is a Hb. imperfect verb.) The character of his kingship is to care for the powerless in society, a responsibility that human authorities generally fail to deliver. The same issue of trusting in God or humans underlies 33:16–19. This psalm also acclaims Yahweh as one who is "faithful," who "loves righteousness and justice" (vv. 4–5), who made "the heavens" and formed "the sea" (vv. 6–7), and who "foils the plans of the nations" (v. 10; cf. 146:3–4, 9). It also pronounces a "blessing" on those who choose Yahweh (v. 12), who promises to "keep them alive in famine" (v. 19). He is also described as "our help" (v. 20).

§147 God of Creation and Restorer of Jerusalem (Ps. 147)

Psalm 147 is a hymn that celebrates in particular the restoration of the exiles (v. 2). The reference to "the bars of your gates" implies a date after the rebuilding of the walls of Jerusalem by Nehemiah. As noted below, many phrases in Psalm 147 are echoed elsewhere, especially in Isaiah 40–66, which addresses exilic and postexilic Judah. Its threefold structure is established by the three calls to praise in verses 1, 7, 12. It also contains three themes: the restoration of Jerusalem in the first and third sections (vv. 2–3, 12–14), Yahweh's providence over creation in all three sections (vv. 4–5, 8–9, 15–18), and three contrasts of whom Yahweh favors (vv. 6, 10–11, 19–20). While each verse, section, and topic is profound in its own right, the total meaning that results from their combination is even more profound. The hymn presents parallels between Yahweh's work in creation and his work in history on his people's behalf, especially in terms of his commanding providence. Yet, there are also implicit contrasts between the general regularities of Yahweh's work in creation and the (sometimes surprising) particularities of his favor in dispensing his providence among humans. This is a skillfully woven poem that brings together the diverse threads of God's ways in creation and with humans.

147:1–6 / The Hebrew psalms have little to say about beauty and pleasure in their own right, but they do claim that praise is **pleasant** (or "lovely," Hb. *nāʿîm;* cf. 81:2; 135:3) and **fitting** (or "beautiful," Hb. *nāʾwâ;* cf. 33:1). Yahweh is presented through the metaphoric roles of "builder" of **Jerusalem** and "the healer" of **the brokenhearted** (cf. Isa. 30:26; 61:1; Hos. 6:1). The Hebrew verbs praising God in this psalm are mostly participles, thus placing emphasis on the subject performing the action, rather than simply on the action itself. The two roles of builder and healer go hand-in-hand because the city's former inhabitants are **the exiles of Israel.**

Without transition the psalm moves to **the stars.** The connection with the preceding lies not in the object of Yahweh's actions, namely the exiles and the stars, but in the nature of Yahweh's action. As the counter of the stars **calls them each by name** (cf. Isa. 40:26), so the builder of Jerusalem **gathers** the exiles. Summative praise then follows concerning his **mighty . . . power** and his limitless **understanding** (cf. Isa. 40:28–29). The NIV unfortunately misses a key wordplay: he is "the counter of the *number* of stars" but "his understanding has no *number*."

The transition to the human world in verse 6 might seem somewhat strained, except, as noted above, each of the psalm's three sections describes Yahweh's regular providence over creation and closes with claims about his particular favor in bestowing his providence to humans. There is another connection between verses 4 and 6 that would be obvious to the ancients but is lost to most moderns. The stars were considered by many to be the abodes of gods or to be gods themselves (cf. Deut. 4:19; 17:3), and thus the determiner of humans fates. But here **the LORD . . . sustains** and **casts . . . to the ground,** and he does so on a moral basis, depending whether one is among **the humble** or **the wicked** (cf. 146:9). There is another implicit connection between these verses. Verse 4 casts the reader's/listener's eyes to the stars, but, in verse 6, "the LORD . . . casts the wicked to the ground" (lit. "earth").

147:7–11 / The second section opens with a renewed call to praise and with attention to its musical accompaniment **(on the harp). With thanksgiving** (Hb. *tôdâ*) could denote an attitude, thanksgiving psalms, or thanksgiving offerings (Lev. 7:12–15), or any combination thereof. Praise of Yahweh (Hb. participles) as creator continues, but this time we behold **the sky** during the daytime. How simply **he covers** the sky **with clouds, supplies . . . rain,** and so **makes grass grow . . . for the cattle and for the young ravens.** His mighty power and limitless understanding (v. 5) have thus established an ecological chain of providence (cf. 104:5–30).

Among Yahweh's creatures, his providence extends from the large (the cattle) to the helpless (the young ravens), but, perhaps, not self-evident from creation are the objects of Yahweh's particular **delight.** It lies not in the natural **strength** of his creatures, whether it be **of the horse** or of **the legs of a man**—it lies in a particular human quality. Here the Bible differs sharply from social Darwinism: contrary to what one may infer from nature, survival does not belong to the fittest or strongest but to **those who fear him, who put their hope in** (or wait for) **his unfailing love** (cf. 33:16–17; 118:8–9; 146:3–4; Isa. 40:30–31).

147:12–20 / The third call to praise focuses on those commanded to sing Yahweh's praises: **Jerusalem.** (**Zion** is addressed directly as in 146:10.) As the transitional word in verses 13–14, we can see illustrated here that the Hebrew term *šālôm* has a broader range of meaning than the English **peace.** It includes both security from military attack (v. 13a) and "well-being" (vv. 13b, 14b) or to some extent, "prosperity" (so translated in the NIV in 72: 3, 7). Yahweh's particular action of "satisfying" the city **with the finest of wheat** (cf. 81:16) is naturally an extension of his general providence over creation (vv. 8–9). Yahweh's supplying agricultural fertility was a prime concern for the fledgling post-exilic community.

At the center of verses 15–18 is **his** *transforming* **word** (vv. 15, 18), which, at one moment, produces **snow** and an intolerable **icy blast,** and, at another, melting snow and **waters** that **flow.** Although his word works **swiftly** and effectively throughout creation, **his word** (so *Kethib,* "his words" according to *Qere,* v. 19) **he has revealed** to one particular people, **to Israel,** and **no other nation** (cf. Isa. 40:8; 55:10–11). As hymned in the opening verses, this is a *transformed* Israel, who no longer feel **his** icy blast but **his breezes** (Hb. *rûḥô,* "his wind" or perhaps "his Spirit"). His word **to Jacob** is specified further in the parallel line as **his laws and decrees** (in the Psalms this Hb. word pair, *ḥoq* and *mišpāṭ,* also occurs in 81:4; cf. 18:22). We should not think here of static statutes of a lawcode but of the dynamic, transforming word, as paralleled in creation. Overall, therefore, we marvel at Yahweh's general providence over creation and his particular unfailing love (v. 11) to Zion.

§148 Praise from the Heavenly Hosts and Creatures Here Below (Ps. 148)

148:1–14 / This hymn of praise consists almost entirely of imperative calls to praise addressed to lists of heavenly creatures (vv. 1–6) and earthly creatures (vv. 7–14). The creatures of the heavenly realm that are named are the spiritual beings **(angels, his heavenly hosts)**, the lights **(sun, moon, shining stars)**, and the clouds **(waters above the skies;** the NIV's **heavens** and "skies" translate the one Hb. term, *šāmayim*). Among the creatures of the earthly realm, it might seem strange to see **lightning, clouds, winds,** etc., listed here and not with the waters above the skies in the heavenly list. Perhaps in view here are those elements of weather (esp. storms) that directly affect the earthly realm. In addition, verses 7–8 may reflect the cosmology also found in Genesis 1:6–8, 20, naming those creatures in the waters under the firmament **(great sea creatures, all ocean depths)** and those in the waters above the firmament (though **birds** are not listed here but with other animals in v. 10). Next are listed elements of the land **(mountains, hills)**, vegetation **(fruit trees, cedars)**, and animals **(wild animals, cattle,** etc.). Two verses are then devoted to humans, first by political designations **(kings, nations,** etc.) and then by age and gender **(young men and maidens, old men and children)**.

Both the heavenly and earthly lists are rounded off with the invitation, **let them praise the name of the LORD,** and with substantiating reasons **(for,** vv. 5–6, 13–14). The reasons given for heavenly praise center on Yahweh's ordering **decree,** thus depicting him as the king who "commands" and it is done, and who establishes order (as in Gen. 1). The reason given for the closing invitation is twofold: (a) **his** royal **splendor is above** both the earthly and heavenly realms, and (b) his special self-revelation to **Israel.** The NIV margin notes, "*Horn* here symbolizes strong one, that is, king," but while the term is associated with the king

(89:17; 132:17), it most often simply denotes anyone's strength (75:4–5, 10; 92:10; 112:9). Moreover, the parallel line appears to associate the **horn** of **his people** with **the praise of all his saints.** In other words, Israel's power is now embodied in their worship of God. The liturgy of this hymn thus draws the congregation to exercise power not in a political or militaristic fashion but by means of praise. As his saints (Hb. *ḥᵃsîdāyw*, i.e., those bound to him by *ḥesed* or "love"), they are connected to Yahweh, whose splendor is above **the earth and the heavens.** And this power is exhibited in the very language of the psalm itself, where Israel acts as the liturgist commanding the antiphonal choirs of **the heavens** and **the earth** to **praise the LORD.** Remarkably, the worshiping congregation of the politically insignificant people Israel is seen as the center of the praising universe. (This is all the more stunning if this psalm was composed in the postexilic period—which is probably the case—when they were but a vassal state under the Persian Empire.) As the familiar Doxology goes, "Praise him, all creatures here below; praise him above ye heavenly hosts!"

§149 Praise in the Mouth and a Sword in the Hand (Ps. 149)

149:1–5 / This hymnic praise psalm begins with an imperative call to **sing . . . a new song** specifically **in the assembly of the saints** (or "devout/faithful ones"). Then three verses follow which invite them (**Let . . .**, Hb. jussive or wish, vv. 2–3, 5) to perform **his praise** with joy (Let **Israel rejoice**) and **with dancing** and musical instruments **(tambourine and harp).** Yahweh is depicted as their **Maker** and **King.** Supporting these appeals is a twofold reason **(for,** v. 4), one is for God's benefit **(the LORD takes delight in his people)** and the other is for how he benefits his people **(he crowns the humble with salvation).**

149:6–9 / In an otherwise wonderful collection of hymnody (Pss. 145–150), these verses sound particularly unpleasant. The image of **a double-edged sword in their hands** draws readers of the Bible to think of Nehemiah, who ensured that "each of the builders [of Jerusalem's walls] wore his sword at his side as he worked" (Neh. 4:13, 18). But the sword in this psalm is to be wielded not only in defense but **to inflict vengeance . . . and punishment.** And it is directed not merely at Judah's immediate neighbors but at **the nations** and **their kings.** Isaiah 60–61 contains some terminology that parallels our psalm (see Allen, *Psalms 101–150,* pp. 319–20). While it does refer to the nations as subservient to God's people (Isa. 60:10, 14; 61:5) and to their punishment (60:12), it does not envisage God's people themselves participating in that vengeance (Isa. 63:3–5 comments that Yahweh will execute "vengeance" without human agents). Any kind of literal interpretation of such militaristic language is particularly problematic in the postexilic period, in which this psalm was composed, when Judah had no standing army under the Persian Empire. The best key for interpreting this enigmatic sword is to be found in its parallel poetic line and in its neighboring psalm. The meaning of "a double-edged sword in their hands" is qualified by **the praise of God in their mouths.** In other words, Judah's power for punishment **on the peoples** lies in their worship of God. This reading is supported by the same kind of parallelism found in the closing verse of the preceding psalm, where Israel's "horn," or strength, is embodied in their worship of God (148:14). This interpretation, in fact, is consistent with the larger reinterpretation of the exercise of power that takes place in Psalms 144–148 (see "Limits of Psalmic Spirituality" in the Introduction). Thus, rather than calling on God's people to take up the sword, our psalm calls on them to inflict vengeance via the realm of worship. Finally, we should note that this is not blind vengeance; it the execution of justice **to carry out the sentence written** (lit. "written judgment") **against them.** Thus, by singing of how Yahweh rescues from "deceitful foreigners" (144:6–11) and thwarts and destroys "the wicked" (145:20; 146:9; 147:6, to list only references in Pss. 144–148), God's people remind God to execute his justice and punishment on the peoples. Similarly, two psalms of Yahweh's kingship, both also designated "a new song" in 96:1 and 98:1, sing of his "coming to judge the earth."

§150 Doxology to the Book of Psalms (Ps. 150)

Psalm 150 is hymnic praise that acts as the doxology closing both Book V (other elements, 41:13; 72:18–19; 89:52; and 106:48, mark the end of Books I–IV) and the book of Psalms itself. Its verses consist entirely of imperative calls to praise.

150:1–2 / Verse 1 specifies the location of this praise: **his sanctuary** and **His mighty heavens** (lit. "his powerful firmament"). As seen in Psalm 148, the congregation of the people of God stands as the liturgist summoning both the earthly and heavenly congregations to worship. Verse 2 provides the subject of praise, **his acts of power** and **greatness**.

150:3–5 / The bulk of the remaining calls to praise list the musical instruments that are to accompany the singing. The praise of God is not simply contemplation, confession, and prostration—it is also music, and so engages the mind, voice, body, and heart. It captures the emotions and the brain, both left and right brain. And these observations on praise have implications not only for humans but also for our understanding of God. He too is pleased with, even enjoys, music. It is no accident that the book of Praises (Hb. *tehillîm*, the Hb. name for the book we call "Psalms"), which is shaped for the worship of God, consists of poetry set to music. The God whom we praise is no mere ground of being or dispassionate judge; he is a person.

150:6 / The psalm closing the book of Psalms concludes with a summons that extends to the farthest reaches beyond the chosen people of God: **Let everything that has breath praise the LORD.** No one is to be barred from the worship of God, though we must be mindful this verse is an invitation, not a statement. Yahweh in his greatness is worthy of a concert by an orchestra and choir that include every creature.

For Further Reading

Commentaries

Allen, L. C. *Psalms 101–150*. WBC 21. Waco: Word, 1983.
Anderson, A. A. *The Book of Psalms*. NCB. 2 volumes. London: Oliphants, 1972.
Briggs, C. A., and E. G. Briggs. *A Critical and Exegetical Commentary on the Book of Psalms*. ICC. 2 volumes. Edinburgh: T&T Clark, 1906–7.
Craigie, P. C. *Psalms 1–50*. WBC 19. Waco: Word, 1983.
Dahood, M. *Psalms I–III*. AB 16, 17, 17A. 3 volumes. Garden City, N.Y.: Doubleday, 1966–70.
Gunkel, H. *Die Psalmen*. Handkommentar zum Alten Testament. Göttingen: Vandenhoeck & Ruprecht, 1926.
Kidner, D. *Psalms 1–72, 73–150*. TOTC. 2 volumes. Leicester: InterVarsity, 1973–75.
Kirkpatrick, A. F. *The Book of Psalms*. The Cambridge Bible for Schools and Colleges. Cambridge: Cambridge University Press, 1902.
Kraus, H.-J. *Psalms, A Commentary*. 2 volumes. Trans. H. C. Oswald. Minneapolis: Augsburg, 1988–89.
Mays, J. L. *Psalms*. Interpretation. Louisville: John Knox, 1994.
Stuhlmueller, C. *The Psalms*. Old Testament Message 21–22. Wilmington, Del.: Michael Glazier, 1983.
Tate, M. E. *Psalms 51–100*. WBC 20. Dallas: Word, 1990.
Weiser, A. *The Psalms*. OTL. Philadelphia: Westminster, 1962.

General

Becker, J. *Israel deutet seine Psalmen: Urform und Neuinterpretation in den Psalmen*. SBS 18. Stuttgart: Katholisches Bibelwerk, 1966.

Beyerlin, W. *Die Rettung der Bedrängten in den Feindpsalmen der Einzelnen auf institutionelle Zusammenhänge untersucht.* FRLANT 99. Göttingen: Vandenhoeck & Ruprecht, 1970.

Brown, F., S. R. Driver, and C. A. Briggs. *Hebrew and English Lexicon of the Old Testament.* Oxford: Clarendon, 1907.

Broyles, C. *The Conflict of Faith and Experience: A Form-Critical and Theological Study of Selected Lament Psalms.* JSOTSup 52. Sheffield: JSOT Press, 1989.

Brueggemann, W. *The Message of the Psalms.* Augsburg Old Testament Studies. Minneapolis: Augsburg, 1984.

———. *The Psalms and the Life of Faith.* Ed. Patrick D. Miller. Minneapolis: Fortress, 1995.

Caird, G. B. *The Language and Imagery of the Bible.* Philadelphia: Westminster, 1980.

Childs, B. S. "Psalm Titles and Midrashic Exegesis." *JSS* 16 (1971), pp. 137–50.

Clines, D. J. A. "Psalm Research Since 1955." *TB* 18 (1967), pp. 103–26; 20 (1969), pp. 105–25.

Culley, R. C. *Oral Formulaic Language in the Biblical Psalms.* Toronto: University of Toronto Press, 1967.

Davies, G. H. "The Ark in the Psalms." Pages 51–61 in *Promise and Fulfillment: Essays Presented to Professor S. H. Hooke.* Ed. F. F. Bruce. Edinburgh: T&T Clark, 1963.

Eaton, J. H. *Kingship and the Psalms.* SBT. London: SCM, 1976.

———. "The Psalms and Israelite Worship." Pages 238–73 in *Tradition and Interpretation.* Ed. G. W. Anderson. Oxford: Clarendon, 1979.

———. *Vision in Worship: The Relation of Prophecy and Liturgy in the Old Testament.* London: SPCK, 1981.

Gerstenberger, E. S. *Psalms, Part 1: With an Introduction to Cultic Poetry.* FOTL 14. Grand Rapids: Eerdmans, 1988.

Gibson, J. C. L. *Canaanite Myths and Legends.* Edinburgh: T&T Clark, 1977.

Gunkel, H. *Einleitung in die Psalmen.* Completed by J. Begrich. Göttingen: Vandenhoeck & Ruprecht, 1933.

Guthrie, H. H., Jr. *Israel's Sacred Songs: A Study of Dominant Themes.* New York: Seabury, 1966.

Holladay, W. L. *A Concise Hebrew and Aramaic Lexicon of the Old Testament.* Grand Rapids: Eerdmans, 1971.

———. *The Psalms through Three Thousand Years: Prayerbook of a Cloud of Witnesses.* Minneapolis: Fortress, 1993.

Keel, O. *The Symbolism of the Biblical World: Ancient Near Eastern Iconography and the Book of Psalms*. New York: Seabury, 1978.

Kraus, H.-J. *Theology of the Psalms*. Trans. K. Crim. Minneapolis: Augsburg, 1986.

Lewis, C. S. *Reflections on the Psalms*. London: Geoffrey Bles, 1958.

McCann, J. C., Jr. *A Theological Introduction to the Book of Psalms: The Psalms as Torah* Nashville: Abingdon, 1993.

Miller, Patrick D., Jr. *Interpreting the Psalms*. Philadelphia: Fortress, 1986.

_____. *They Cried to the Lord: The Form and Theology of Biblical Prayer*. Minneapolis: Fortress, 1994.

Mowinckel, S. *The Psalms in Israel's Worship*. 2 volumes. Oxford: Blackwell, 1962.

Pritchard, J. B., ed. *Ancient Near Eastern Texts Relating to the Old Testament*. 3d ed. Princeton: Princeton University, 1969.

Rad, G. von. *Old Testament Theology* 2 vols. New York: Harper, 1962–1965.

_____. " 'Righteousness' and 'Life' in the Cultic Language of the Psalms." Pages 243–66 in *The Problem of the Hexateuch and Other Essays*. Edinburgh: Oliver & Boyd, 1965.

Ringgren, H. *The Faith of the Psalmists*. Philadelphia: Fortress, 1963.

Sabourin, L. *The Psalms: Their Origin and Meaning*. New York: Alba House, 1974.

Seybold, K. *Introducing the Psalms*. Trans. R. Graeme Dunphy. Edinburgh: T&T Clark, 1990.

Waltke, B. K., and M. O'Connor. *An Introduction to Biblical Hebrew Syntax*. Winona Lake: Eisenbrauns, 1990.

Watson, W. G. E. *Classical Hebrew Poetry: A Guide to its Techniques* JSOTSup 26. Sheffield: JSOT Press, 1985.

Westermann, C. *Praise and Lament in the Psalms*. Edinburgh: T&T Clark, 1981.

Williams, R. J. *Hebrew Syntax: An Outline*. Toronto: University of Toronto Press, 1976.

Wilson, G. H. *The Editing of the Hebrew Psalter*. SBLDS 76. Chico: Scholars, 1985.

Zenger, E. *A God of Vengeance? Understanding the Psalms of Divine Wrath*. Louisville: Westminster John Knox, 1996.

Subject Index

Aaronic blessing, 55, 87, 277–79, 331, 440, 445, 448
Acrostic, 6, 21, 74, 133, 135, 168, 169, 179, 183, 417, 419, 421, 442, 504, 508
Allen, L. C., 394, 398, 407, 412, 428, 446, 447, 469, 473, 503, 517
Anderson, A. A., 473
Anderson, G. W., 38
Angels, 73, 170, 335–36, 361, 481, 515
Ark. *See* Cherubim-ark.
Asaph, 5, 28, 29
Atonement, day of, 266–68, 319, 323, 329

Baal epic, 25–26, 53, 96, 104, 128, 151, 218, 282, 309, 338, 356, 368–69, 398–400, 406, 449
Bathsheba, 28, 226
Becker, J., 122
Beyerlin, W., 38, 236
Blessing, 42, 44, 193, 342, 463, 475, 502
Broyles, C., 40, 97, 252
Brueggemann, W., 421

Caird, G. B., 192
Change of mood, 87, 315
Cherubim-ark, 14–16, 23, 29–30, 50, 60, 67–68, 69, 80, 104, 125, 129, 131, 149, 175, 208, 213–16, 218, 243–45, 262, 281–84, 321, 322, 324, 325, 330, 332, 356, 361, 376–77, 378–79, 382, 383–84, 398, 402, 432, 471–72
Childs, B. S., 252
Christ, Jesus, 1, 6–7, 20–21, 32, 44, 47, 73, 92, 115, 116, 120, 128, 129, 207, 415–16, 508
Chronicler, the, 15–16, 29–31, 40, 443
Composite psalms, 30, 102, 103, 108, 156–58, 201, 226, 243, 250, 277, 280, 286, 314, 460, 476
Conquest, 75, 202, 214, 218, 320–24, 330, 403–4, 417–19, 426–27, 476–77
Covenant, 22, 134, 135, 201–4, 223–24, 229, 309, 319, 320, 322, 349, 396–

97, 407; Abrahamic, 22, 298, 402–4; Davidic, 22, 46, 107, 114, 355–58, 471–72; Sinai, 22, 309, 324, 418–19
Craigie, P. C., 48, 65, 88, 104, 124, 142, 173, 177
Creation, creator, 22, 25–26, 71–73, 76, 108–9, 128, 131–32, 151, 166, 209, 229, 266–71, 280, 307–8, 356, 360, 365, 367–69, 371, 373, 377, 382, 387, 393, 396, 398–401, 454, 477, 478, 486, 506, 510, 512–14, 515
Cross, F. M., 103
Culley, R.C., 142, 237, 497

Dahood, M., 458
David, 1–6, 15, 22, 23, 26–31, 131, 226, 236, 252, 320–26, 355–58, 382, 416, 451, 471–73, 501
de Vaux, R., 147
Death, 37, 43, 62, 62–65, 73, 86, 97, 103, 118–21, 147–48, 154–55, 165–67, 186, 222, 263, 286–87, 293, 304, 352–54, 392, 431, 434, 453, 498
Decalogue, 92, 144, 224, 334, 385
Doxologies to the book of Psalms, 5, 194, 295, 355, 407, 519

Eaton, J. H., 40
Edited psalms. *See* Composite psalms.
Edom, 252–54, 411, 480
Elohistic Psalter, 5, 88, 202, 207, 235, 254, 259, 261, 274
Enemies, 12–13, 17, 35–36, 50, 56, 61, 62, 67, 70, 75, 76, 98–100, 106, 114, 116, 125, 133, 154, 157, 158, 171, 186, 192, 193–94, 197, 203, 226, 239, 241, 245, 249–51, 258, 285, 287, 291, 298, 325, 339, 365, 391, 412, 414, 461, 479–80, 482, 483, 489, 498–99. *See also* Wicked.
Enuma Elish, 25–26, 218, 224, 368, 398, 454
Eschatology, 337, 411
Exile, exilic period, 5, 35, 89, 115, 121, 133, 201, 227, 230, 276, 285, 294,

306, 314, 317, 327, 344, 390, 405–7, 440, 479, 497

Exodus, the, 22, 223, 273, 275, 306, 314–17, 319–24, 330, 333, 373, 395, 402–3, 405–6, 417–19, 426–27, 476–77

Face of God, 6, 14, 33, 55, 81, 85, 87, 97, 101, 113, 130, 143, 155, 196, 197, 203, 230, 390, 402, 427, 499

False accusation, 66, 98, 136–37, 141, 236, 244, 260, 285, 412, 483

Fear of the Lord, fearing God, 94, 108, 133–35, 165–66, 168–69, 175, 214, 253, 273, 279, 313, 348, 392, 394, 417–20, 421, 430, 432, 444, 463, 469, 476, 507, 514

Feast of Tabernacles, 14, 15, 24, 261–63, 267, 333, 341

Feast of Unleavened Bread, Passover, 14, 261, 267, 274, 341, 417, 424, 426–27

Feast of Weeks, 267

Fertility, agricultural, 25–26, 54, 96, 255–56, 266–70, 277–79, 295–97, 346, 464, 503, 514

Forgiveness, 109, 134, 161, 226, 328, 344, 385, 395, 397, 469

Formulaic/Stock language, 21, 74, 142–44, 156, 237, 288, 290, 347, 429, 497, 501

Freedman, D. N., 103, 124

Gentiles. *See* Nations.
Gerstenberger, E. S., 38, 88, 108, 185
Gezer calendar, 262, 267
Gibson, J. C. L., 151, 152, 212, 220, 282, 309, 368, 369, 398, 400, 454
Gilgamesh Epic, 224
God Almighty. *See* Yahweh of hosts.
God of the storm/skies, theophany, 102–5, 223, 281, 317, 371, 378, 398–401. *See also* Kingship, divine.
Gods, foreign, 23, 25–26, 52, 96, 151, 191, 207, 217, 248, 263, 335–38, 375, 379, 429–32, 477, 481
Gunkel, H., 85, 198

Hannah, Song of, 13, 311, 425, 461
Heidel, A., 40
Hezekiah, 24, 194, 201
Holiness, holy, 24–25, 32, 46, 57–58, 93, 95, 111, 145–47, 152, 199, 209,
215, 217, 293, 327, 355, 357, 369, 384, 418, 481

Holladay, W. L., 112, 114, 237
Hymn to Aton, 398–400

Image, imagery, 1, 3, 13, 18, 26, 35, 36, 38, 66, 67, 72, 79, 87, 117, 118, 180, 195, 209, 222, 233, 239, 263, 286, 302, 331, 353, 361, 446, 453, 467, 489, 490, 495

Integrity, 68, 94, 102, 105–6, 129, 136–38, 184, 205, 342, 389, 444

Jerusalem. *See* Zion.
Jesus. *See* Christ.
Joy, rejoicing, 86, 109, 143, 157, 163, 199, 206, 261, 333, 377, 380, 400, 450

Judge, judgment, 43, 68, 75–76, 80, 98, 136, 138, 146, 172, 204, 231, 237, 279, 336, 374, 377, 451, 486, 490, 497

Judges (period), 214, 321–25, 339, 406–7

Justice, social justice, 296, 388, 395, 422, 489

Keel, O., 103, 117, 137, 147, 185, 286, 363, 454

King, monarchy, royal house, 20, 44, 102, 110, 113, 149, 206, 256, 295, 330, 343, 355–58, 388, 414, 438, 471–73, 501, 509

Kingdom of God, 36–37, 40, 119, 506–8

Kingship, divine. *See also* God of the storm/skies *and* Psalms of Yahweh's kingship, 22, 24, 25–26, 151–53, 211, 269, 307, 355–56, 367, 379, 381, 396, 398, 425, 506

Korah, 5, 28

Kraus, H.-J., 38, 88, 95, 173, 236, 266, 272, 412, 447, 460, 469

Levites, 1, 29, 91, 96, 214, 270, 305, 389, 472, 475, 476, 495

Lewis, C. S., 498

Liturgy, liturgist, 1–21, 45, 52, 58, 64, 71, 91, 110, 113, 145, 190, 213, 217, 231, 244, 258, 264, 272, 304, 310, 342, 361, 364, 370, 375, 383, 406, 429, 436, 438, 450, 452, 455, 468, 471, 476, 478, 509, 516

Love, lovingkindness, 63–64, 114, 175, 227, 233, 259, 347, 355, 365, 395, 410, 436, 439

Luther, M., 208

Mary's Magnificat, 425
Mays, J. L., 38
Meditation, 1, 5–6, 42, 210, 219, 316, 401, 442–43, 499
Memory, remember, 119, 134, 196–97, 262, 306, 308, 314–17, 319–26, 351, 352, 358, 381, 394, 396, 405, 407, 430–31, 442, 479–80, 499
Messiah, 6, 21, 44, 114, 298, 414–16
Mettinger, T. N. D., 104
Milne, P., 124
Moses, Song of, 306, 316, 439
Mowinckel, S., 20, 473
Murphy, R., 22, 40
"My God," 17, 22, 23, 50, 86, 117, 154, 158, 261, 290–92, 434, 490, 500

Name, God's, 238, 329, 391, 418, 453, 505
Nations, foreign, 243, 298, 327, 339, 350, 392, 436, 481

O'Connor, M., 47
Oracle. *See* Prophecy.

Passover. *See* Feast of Unleavened Bread.
Pilgrim, pilgrimage, 97, 123, 127, 138, 141, 195, 255, 260, 272, 302, 341, 362, 445, 448, 450
Postexilic (period), restoration, 285, 344, 359, 375, 394, 408, 430, 439, 453, 455, 457, 466, 468, 470, 476, 501–3, 512
Power, use and abuse of, 37, 72, 111, 114, 165, 283–84, 297–98, 424, 510, 518
Priests, 11, 38, 55, 58, 84, 91, 119, 129–30, 145, 149, 227, 278, 323, 327, 342, 384, 389, 439–41, 415, 443, 448, 463, 473, 474, 475, 476
Procession, 2, 127, 217, 219, 281–83, 386, 438–41
Progressive revelation, 24, 35, 64–65, 479, 497
Promise and fulfillment, 338, 344, 370
Prophecy, prophet, oracle, 45–46, 82–83, 91, 107, 111, 113, 121, 148, 161–62, 174, 177, 208, 210, 223, 231, 253, 307, 310, 333, 335–37, 350, 355–57, 361–62, 373, 414–15, 471
Provan, I. W., 121
Psalmist, 4

Psalms of Yahweh's Kingship, 15, 75, 119, 213, 223, 277, 310, 335, 337, 350, 367, 373, 375, 378, 381, 383, 436, 511

Redeem, redemption, 109, 135, 137, 139, 156, 204, 169, 222, 240, 297, 306, 317, 319, 406, 408, 418, 469
Remember. *See* Memory.
Retribution, 36, 60, 69, 76, 148, 169, 170, 194, 237, 245, 248, 264, 288, 362, 480, 493
Righteousness, the righteous, 11–13, 41, 59, 61, 67, 68, 79, 80, 89, 93–94, 99, 105, 129–30, 158, 164, 175, 192, 232, 269, 290, 296, 346, 377, 378, 381, 395, 418, 422, 455, 489, 496, 497
Royal psalms, 20–21, 23, 50, 102, 110, 113, 206, 295, 414, 501

Sacred space, 24, 148, 284, 313, 448
Sacrifice, offering, 2, 23, 54, 110, 119, 124, 191, 229, 237, 261, 266, 273, 276, 288, 408, 435, 492
Sickness, 62, 87, 116, 157, 185, 187, 193, 195
Sin, 31, 133, 161, 187, 226, 328, 345, 405–7, 469, 497
Sinai, Horeb, 22, 223, 282, 324, 333, 404, 420
Soll, W. M., 417
Speech, human, 11, 54, 56–57, 60, 82–84, 91–92, 98–99, 144, 174–75, 187, 232, 239, 245, 250, 258, 263, 265, 300, 371, 389, 446, 485, 489, 492–93
Spirit, Holy, 35, 37, 227–29, 400, 499
Superscription, 5, 6, 26–31, 38, 39, 41, 44, 74, 107, 177, 195, 206, 226, 236, 252, 387, 390, 416, 445, 494–95

Temple, 2, 6, 23, 28, 79, 111, 123, 138, 175, 199, 209, 237, 246, 266, 327, 432, 439, 471
Temple entry liturgies, 10–13, 31–32, 35, 57, 82, 91, 99, 105, 128–31, 137–38, 146–50, 174, 224, 231, 245, 258, 265, 287, 300–302, 351, 362, 365, 388, 440, 444, 484
Temptation, 176, 179–80, 265, 299, 492
Ten Commandments. *See* Decalogue.

Theophany (appearance of God). *See* God of the storm.
Thompson, J. A., 267
Torah, 6, 8, 12, 91, 129, 138, 442

Vengeance, 36, 170, 329, 480
von Rad, G., 53, 94, 305, 431

Waltke, B. K., 47
War, battle, 102, 106, 110, 113, 131, 164, 170, 201, 252, 414
Warrior, divine, 104, 127, 203, 253, 266, 313
Wealth, wealthy, 52, 98–99, 178, 181, 187–88, 221–22, 233–34, 259, 301, 422
Weiser, A., 87, 473
Westermann, C., 19, 39, 40
Wicked, the, 11–13, 41, 56, 59, 79, 100, 137–40, 146, 158, 232, 247, 264, 299, 364, 370, 423, 455, 483, 489

Wilderness, 22, 223, 320–24, 373, 402–3, 426–27, 476–77
Williams, R. J., 86
Williamson, H. G. M., 40
Wisdom (tradition), 7, 10, 21–22, 41, 133, 168, 179, 187, 221, 370, 398, 400, 417, 443, 460

Yahweh war, 18, 22, 166, 252, 331, 472
Yahweh/Lord of hosts ("God Almighty" in NIV), 14, 23–24, 60, 127–28, 131, 208, 210, 214, 218, 313, 330, 342, 383–84

Zaphon, 218, 220, 356, 369
Zenger, E., 36, 248
Zion, Jerusalem, 15, 23, 95, 110, 111, 208, 217, 223, 266, 285, 288, 307, 312, 320–26, 341, 350, 380, 382, 383, 390, 414, 435, 445, 455, 457, 466, 471–72, 474, 475, 477, 479, 509, 514

Scripture Index

OLD TESTAMENT

Genesis 1, 166, 515; **1:1**, 26; **1:2**, 356, 399; **1:6–8**, 515; **1:14–18**, 478; **1:16**, 449; **1:20**, 515; **1:22**, 433; **1:28**, 433; **2:7**, 166, 396; **5**, 304; **5:24**, 222, 304; **6:2**, 73, 152; **6:4**, 152; **12:3**, 214, 298; **12:7**, 416; **13:15**, 416; **14:18**, 312, 415; **14:18–22**, 215; **14:19**, 431; **16:2**, 462; **17:7–8**, 416; **24:7**, 416; **30:3**, 462; **37–39**, 402; **39:20**, 510; **40:3–5**, 510; **42:5**, 510; **43:1**, 510; **48:15**, 126; **49:24**, 126; **49:25**, 510

Exodus **1:8–14**, 403; **1:21**, 462; **2:24**, 431; **3:1–4:17**, 34; **3:15**, 476; **4:16**, 207; **4:22**, 46; **5:22–6:8**, 34; **7–12**, 324; **7:1**, 207; **7:3**, 291; **7:16**, 329; **8:23**, 419; **11:9–10**, 291; **12:14**, 417, 419; **14–16**, 426; **14–15**, 313; **14**, 308; **14:21**, 426; **15**, 439; **15:1**, 316; **15:2**, 439; **15:1–4**, 166; **15:1**, 313; **15:4**, 313; **15:8**, 426; **15:11**, 335, 348, 424; **15:13**, 123, 125; **15:13**, 369; **15:16**, 306; **15:17–18**, 369; **15:21**, 313; **15:36**, 306; **16**, 419; **16:3**, 323; **17:1–7**, 322, 323, 374; **17:3**, 374; **17:7**, 333; **18:11**, 476; **19**, 104; **19:16**, 333; **19:16–19**, 378; **19:18**, 426; **19:5**, 476; **19–20**, 385; **20:1**, 92; **20:2–3**, 333, 334; **20:3**, 97; **20:5**, 101; **20:6**, 396; **20:7**, 132, 374; **20:14–16**, 224; **20:16**, 92, 144; **20:20**, 420; **20:21**, 378; **20:24**, 388; **20–24**, 419; **21:6**, 248, 335, 481; **21:12–14**, 38; **22:6**, 207; **22:8–9**, 248, 207, 335, 481; **22:25**, 95; **22:28**, 248, 481; **23:15**, 197; **23:15**, 341; **23:15–16**, 333; **23:16**, 333; **23:17**, 197, 341, 451, 464; **24:3**, 92; **25:20**, 60; **25:22**, 30; **28:28–30**, 30; **29:7**, 149, 474; **29:40–41**, 435; **30:22–33**, 474; **32:1–34:35**, 34; **32:11–12**, 329; **32:32–33**, 227, 351; **32–34**, 395, 406; **33:13**, 396; **33:18–19**, 329; **33:20**, 101, 130, 197; **34:5–7**, 329; **34:6**, 314, 316, 348, 395, 417, 418, 419, 434, 436, 504, 507, 508; **34:7**, 385, 396; **34:10**, 396; **34:10–11**, 419; **34:18**, 333; **34:20**, 197; **34:22**, 333; **34:23–24**, 197, 341; **34:27–28**, 396; **37:9**, 60

Leviticus 1, 229; **1:3**, 137; **1:5**, 137; **1:8–9**, 61; **1:12**, 61; **3**, 175, 229, 266; **4**, 327; **4:3**, 149; **6:8–13**, 229; **7:11–12**, 229; **7:11–18**, 242; **7:11–36**, 175, 266; **7:12–15**, 387, 513; **7:15–16**, 119, 124, 261, 435; **7:16**, 266, 313; **8:7–8**, 30; **8:12**, 474; **10:3**, 93; **10:11**, 443; **14:4**, 230; **14:49**, 230; **19:18**, 469; **23:6**, 333; **23:34**, 333; **23:40**, 261; **25:23**, 189; **25:24–25**, 297; **25:27**, 161; **25:35–37**, 95; **25:52**, 161; **26:4**, 278, 280; **26:16**, 464; **26:20**, 278

Numbers **2:18–24**, 332; **2:34**, 332; **6:22–27**, 55, 445, 448, 463; **6:24–26**, 277; **6:25**, 87, 331, 440, 444; **7:89**, 30; **8:5**, 63; **10:33**, 125; **10:33–36**, 281; **10:35**, 50, 67, 131, 216, 281, 330; **10:35–36**, 69, 472; **10:36**, 281; **11**, 406, 419; **11:1–3**, 323; **11:4–6**, 403; **11:4–34**, 323; **11:10**, 403; **11:33**, 403; **13–14**, 406; **13:8**, 320; **13:26**, 151; **14**, 374; **14:2–3**, 374; **14:18**, 316, 348; **14:20–35**, 323; **14:44**, 330; **15:5**, 435; **16**, 406; **18:2**, 389; **18:20**, 97, 305, 443, 495; **19:18**, 230; **20**, 406; **20:1**, 151; **20:1–13**, 322, 374; **20:3–4**, 323; **20:10**, 322; **20:13**, 333; **23:21**, 216; **25**, 406; **26:56**, 96; **27:21**, 30; **28:1–8**, 288; **28:4**, 364; **28:7**, 435; **28:8**, 364; **29:1**, 348; **31:23**, 275; **33:54**, 96; **35:9–34**, 38; **35:19**, 329

Deuteronomy **1:5**, 442; **2:5**, 255; **2:7**, 124; **2:9**, 255; **2:12**, 255; **2:19**, 255; **3:24**, 348; **4:11**, 378; **4:19**, 376; **4:19**, 513; **4:28**, 432; **4:41–43**, 38; **5**, 385; **5:22**, 92; **6:5**, 92, 469; **6:6**, 443; **6:6–8**, 443; **6:20–25**, 275, 292; **6:22**, 291;

7:6, 476; **7:23,** 218; **10:9,** 97, 443; **11:18,** 443; **12:5,** 238; **12:5–7,** 119, 124, 242, 261, 266, 435; **12:9–10,** 374; **14:1,** 46; **14:2,** 476; **16:9,** 267; **16:10–17,** 119; **16:14–15,** 261; **16:16,** 333, 197, 341, 451, 464; **16:18,** 38; **17:3,** 376, 513; **17:8–13,** 38; **17:9,** 107; **17:16,** 112; **17:18–19,** 443; **18:1–2,** 97; **19:1–13,** 38; **19:6,** 69; **19:12,** 329; **20:1–4,** 112; **23:19–20,** 95; **26:1–11,** 255; **26:5–10,** 75, 275, 374; **27:1–8,** 443; **28,** 303; **28:1–14,** 464; **28:54,** 181; **28:56,** 181; **29:20,** 227; **29:22,** 318; **30:3,** 458; **30:14,** 443; **31:9–13,** 443; **31:11,** 181; **31:19–22,** 224; **31:24,** 443; **31:28,** 224; **32:1,** 224; **32:8,** 336; **32:36,** 476; **32:37–38,** 432; **32:46–47,** 443; **33:2,** 281, 282; **33:10,** 443; **33:15,** 313; **34:11,** 291

Joshua **1:8,** 43; **2:8–11,** 218; **2:9–11,** 427; **3:11,** 379; **3:13,** 379; **3:16,** 426; **5:1,** 218; **5:10,** 426; **6:10,** 216; **6:16,** 216; **6:20,** 216; **6:4,** 330; **6:4–13,** 131; **6:5,** 216; **7:19–21,** 228; **8:31–32,** 40; **12:6–7,** 255; **13:7,** 96; **14:2,** 96; **17:5,** 96; **20:1–9,** 38; **20:5,** 69; **23:6,** 40

Judges **2:11–19,** 323; **4–5,** 339; **5:2,** 414; **5:4,** 253; **5:4–5,** 281, 378; **5:12,** 70; **7,** 339; **7:25,** 339; **8:1–21,** 340; **8:28,** 50; **10:14,** 432; **15:18–22,** 166; **20:16,** 227; **20:45,** 262

Ruth **1:17,** 446; **2:4,** 467; **4:1,** 461; **4:10–11,** 461

1 Samuel **1:3–4,** 119, 124, 261, 266, 435; **1:9,** 28, 119, 261, 266, 435; **2,** 311; **2:1,** 311, 461; **2:1–10,** 13; **2:5,** 425, 462; **2:8,** 425; **2:25,** 207; **4–6,** 322, 325; **4:4,** 131, 218, 330, 383; **4:5–6,** 216; **4:10–11,** 325; **7:9–10,** 110; **8:5,** 295; **10:24,** 216; **13:9–12,** 110; **13:14,** 6; **14:15,** 253; **14:22,** 262; **15:22–23,** 191; **16:14–23,** 4; **17:45,** 110; **17:52,** 216; **18:10,** 4; **19:11,** 28; **23–26,** 28; **23:1–12,** 30; **23:2,** 107; **23:4,** 107; **23:9–12,** 107; **23:15,** 236; **23:19,** 236; **25:22,** 446; **27:12,** 114; **30:7–8,** 30; **30:8,** 107; **31,** 322, 325

2 Samuel **1:17–27,** 2, 29; **1:18,** 2; **2:8,** 53; **2:9,** 326; **2:22,** 312; **5,** 214, 382; **5–6,** 30; **5:6–25,** 325; **5:7,** 23; **5:8,** 215; **5:20,** 253; **5:23–24,** 107; **6,** 29, 215; **6–7,** 28, 471; **6:2,** 23, 131, 214, 330, 383; **6:12,** 214; **6:15,** 214, 215, 216; **7,** 107, 357, 462, 473; **7:1–16,** 422; **7:6–7,** 472; **7:10–11,** 215; **7:14,** 46, 357; **7:15,** 114; **7:16,** 40; **7:29,** 114; **8,** 214, 382; **8:1,** 252; **8:1–14,** 325; **8:2,** 252; **8:2,** 376; **8:3–6,** 252; **8:6,** 376; **8:12,** 252; **8:13,** 252; **8:13–14,** 252; **10:6–15,** 252; **10:16–19,** 252; **11–12,** 28, 226; **11:1,** 44, 110, 247, 298, 164, 414, 427; **12:13,** 226; **12:15–24,** 28; **13,** 114; **15:1–6,** 298; **15:21,** 263; **15:25,** 123; **16,** 114; **22,** 102, 103, 107; **22:16,** 106; **24,** 165

1 Kings **1:33,** 209; **1:38–39,** 415; **2:3,** 40; **3:16–28,** 298, 324, 327, 379; **6:19,** 149; **7:9,** 343; **7:12,** 343; **8:2,** 261; **8:6–8,** 149; **8:7,** 60; **8:12,** 105, 378; **8:13,** 238; **8:16,** 238; **8:16–20,** 238; **8:25,** 443; **8:27,** 238; **8:29,** 238; **8:30,** 238; **8:31,** 67; **8:31–32,** 38, 66, 68, 498; **8:32,** 238; **8:33,** 238; **8:33–40,** 19; **8:34,** 238; **8:35,** 238; **8:36,** 238; **8:39,** 238; **8:43,** 238; **8:45,** 238; **8:49,** 238; **8:65–66,** 261; **10:21,** 161; **11:15–16,** 252; **12:21,** 332; **12:23,** 332; **12:28,** 320; **18:27,** 449; **18:33,** 61; **19:10,** 178; **21:8–13,** 178; **22:19,** 152, 376; **22:19–23,** 481; **22:26–27,** 178

2 Kings **2:3,** 304; **6:31,** 446; **7:1,** 461; **12:15,** 161; **14:6,** 40; **17,** 322; **17:3–4,** 376; **18:13–19:37,** 201; **22–23,** 201; **22:7,** 161; **23:2,** 7; **23:25,** 40; **23:29–30,** 201, 324, 325, 327

1 Chronicles **8:33,** 53; **10:2,** 262; **13–14,** 30; **13–16,** 29; **14:10,** 30; **14:14–15,** 30; **15,** 15; **15:16–17,** 29; **16:7,** 29; **16:8–22,** 402; **16:23–33,** 15; **16:27,** 30; **16:29,** 152; **16:35,** 30; **17:14,** 40; **20:1,** 219; **27:1,** 388; **28:1,** 388; **28:2,** 384; **28:5,** 40; **28:18,** 60; **29:15,** 189

2 Chronicles **6:16,** 443; **6:40,** 468; **7:15,** 468; **13:8,** 40; **16:14,** 503; **20,** 201; **20:3–5,** 19; **20:21,** 152; **24:20–21,** 178; **25:4,** 31; **25:11,** 219; **30:1,** 261;

30:13, 261; **30:25**, 261; **32:30**, 209; **35:12**, 31

Ezra **4**, 501; **4–6**, 286; **6:16**, 30; **6:18**, 31; **7:10**, 6, 108

Nehemiah **4–6**, 501; **4:5**, 227; **4:13**, 517; **4:18**, 517; **8:1–3**, 6; **8:1–8**, 7, 8; **8:10**, 30; **9:3**, 108; **9:17**, 316, 348, 396, 434, 468; **10:29**, 6; **13:1**, 31

Job **1:6**, 73, 152, 335; **2:1**, 73, 152, 335; **3:8**, 356; **5:17**, 63; **7:17–21**, 485; **9:5–6**, 209, 269, 448; **14:5–6**, 485; **14:6**, 189; **15:8**, 335, 481; **16:8**, 101; **21:19**, 101; **26:12**, 356; **38:7**, 73, 152; **39:10**, 467; **42:7–8**, 34

Psalm **1**, 40, 41–43, 108, 303, 417, 421, 442; **1:1**, 510; **1:1–3**, 42–43; **1:2**, 5, 44, 92; **1:4–5**, 43; **1:5**, 417; **1:5–6**, 497; **1:6**, 43, 80; **2**, 20, 39, 44–48, 289, 414; **2:1–3**, 45; **2:4**, 251; **2:4–6**, 45–46; **2:6**, 24; **2:7**, 207; **2:7–9**, 46–47, 260; **2:8**, 215; **2:8–9**, 47–48; **2:10–12**, 47; **2:11–12**, 48; **3**, 29, 39, 49–51, 246, 305; **3:1–2**, 49; **3:3–6**, 49–50; **3:4**, 64; **3:5**, 63, 100; **3:7**, 67; **3:7–8**, 50–51; **4**, 39, 52–55; **4:1**, 53, 99; **4:2**, 64, 263; **4:2–5**, 53–54; **4:3**, 55, 64; **4:4**, 100; **4:5**, 230; **4:6–8**, 54–55; **4:8**, 63, 100; **5**, 11, 38, 39, 56–61, 137, 174, 365; **5:1–3**, 58–59; **5:3**, 61, 63, 287; **5:4–6**, 59, 146, 301; **5:5**, 174, 301; **5:6**, 61, 99, 162, 174, 199, 232, 258, 301; **5:7**, 28, 93, 270, 292, 174, 176, 197, 481; **5:7–8**, 59; **5:8**, 61, 141, 290, 301, 302, 484, 499; **5:9**, 232, 245, 453; **5:9–10**, 60, 174; **5:11**, 99, 263, 434; **5:11–12**, 60–61, 265; **6**, 29, 39, 62–65, 226; **6:1**, 185, 328; **6:1–3**, 63; **6:3**, 346; **6:4–5**, 63; **6:5**, 37, 119, 304; **6:6**, 100; **6:6–7**, 63–64; **6:8**, 52, 444; **6:8–10**, 64–65; **7**, 29, 38, 39, 66–70, 178, 483; **7:1**, 69; **7:1–2**, 66–67; **100**; **7:3–5**, 38, 67, 99, 203; **7:5**, 497; **7:6–9**, 67–68, 241; **7:7**, 69–70; **7:8**, 498; **7:9**, 204; **7:9–16**, 60; **7:10–16**, 68–69; **7:11**, 70; **7:12–13**, 70, 265; **7:14–16**, 265; **7:17**, 69; **8**, 39, 71–73, 108, 497, 502; **8:1**, 71, 244, 329; **8:2**, 71–72; **8:3–8**, 72–73; **8:4**, 6, 501; **8:5**, 73; **8:6**, 152; **8:9**, 73; **9**,

74–76; **9–10**, 39, 250, 315, 501; **9:1–12**, 75; **9:5**, 227, 250; **9:7–8**, 67; **9:7–12**, 24; **9:9**, 250; **9:11**, 244; **9:12**, 431; **9:13–20**, 76; **9:15**, 250; **9:15–16**, 60; **9:17**, 250; **9:18**, 349; **9:19**, 67; **9:20**, 250; **10**, 77–78, 301; **10:1–11**, 77; **10:4**, 265; **10:5**, 84; **10:9**, 250, 312; **10:9–10**, 245; **10:11**, 265; **10:12**, 67; **10:12–15**, 77–78; **10:13**, 265; **10:14**, 494; **10:16**, 250; **10:16–18**, 78; **11**, 39, 79–81, 141, 244; **11:1–3**, 79; **11:2**, 265; **11:4**, 89, 204, 425; **11:4–7**, 79–80; **11:6**, 265, 311; **11:7**, 81, 97, 101, 197; **12**, 29, 39, 82–84; **12:1–4**, 83; **12:2**, 501; **12:2–3**, 56; **12:4**, 265; **12:5**, 83–84; **12:5–6**, 241; **12:6–8**, 84; **13**, 16, 17, 39, 85–87; **13:1–2**, 85–86; **13:3**, 23; **13:3–4**, 86; **13:5–6**, 86–87; **13:6**, 50, 76, 242, 496; **14**, 39, 88–90, 190, 498; **14:1–3**, 88–89; **14:2**, 425; **14:4–5**, 498; **14:4–7**, 89–90; **14:5–6**, 235; **14:7**, 344; **15**, 10, 11, 12, 38, 57, 68, 82, 105, 129, 137, 148, 149, 164, 174, 191, 270; **15**, 91–95, 440; **15:1**, 91, 233, 256, 270, 393; **15:2**, 12, 105, 149, 174, 232, 259, 263, 301, 444; **15:2–3**, 83, 146, 232, 258; **15:2–5a**, 91–94; **15:3**, 67, 169, 174, 224, 232, 245; **15:4**, 13, 95, 263, 174, 444; **15:5**, 95; **15:5b**, 94–95; **16**, 39, 53, 96–97, 141, 262; **16:1–4**, 96; **16:5**, 302, 495; **16:5–6**, 96–97; **16:7**, 63, 100; **16:7–11**, 97; **16:8**, 495; **17**, 38, 39, 98–101, 178, 483; **17:1**, 39; **17:1–2**, 99; **17:3**, 204; **17:3–5**, 99–100, 203; **17:4**, 241; **17:5**, 491; **17:6**, 64; **17:6–12**, 100; **17:7**, 101; **17:8**, 15, 262; **17:9**, 438; **17:11**, 438; **17:13–15**, 100–101; **17:14**, 101; **17:15**, 81, 197; **18**, 20, 29, 36, 39, 102–7, 494, 501, 502, 503; **18:1**, 434; **18:1–3**, 103; **18:2**, 142, 501; **18:4–5**, 434, 453; **18:4–6**, 103; **18:6**, 50; **18:7**, 209, 253, 269, 401, 448; **18:7–15**, 26, 80, 103–5, 317; **18:9**, 501; **18:9–10**, 14, 282, 379; **18:9–14**, 398; **18:10**, 244; **18:10–11**, 210; **18:13**, 210; **18:14**, 501; **18:15**, 313; **18:16**, 162, 501; **18:16–19**, 105; **18:20**, 497; **18:20–27**, 105–6; **18:22**, 107, 514; **18:24**, 497; **18:28–45**, 106–7; **18:30**, 107, 241; **18:34**, 501; **18:44**, 501; **18:46–47**, 501; **18:46–50**, 107; **18:49**, 244; **18:50**, 501; **19**, 40, 108–9, 417, 442; **19:1–9**,

108–9; **19:7**, 41; **19:9**, 133; **20**, 20, 39, 110–12; **20:1**, 313; **20:1–5**, 110–11; **20:1–9**, 260; **20:2**, 24; **20:2**, 50, 80, 105; **20:6**, 50, 80, 105, 491; **20:6–7**, 46, 141; **20:6–8**, 111–12; **20:9**, 46, 112, 141; **21**, 20, 39, 113–14; **21:1**, 46; **21:1–6**, 113; **21:4**, 114, 262; **21:5**, 72; **21:6**, 114; **21:7**, 113–14; **21:8–12**, 114; **21:13**, 46, 114, 244, 246; **22**, 39, 115–22, 191, 286, 288, 314, 390; **22:1**, 6, 32, 122, 480; **22:1–2**, 116; **22:1–31**, 120–22; **22:2**, 23; **22:2–3**, 391; **22:3–5**, 116; **22:6–8**, 116–17; **22:8**, 49; **22:9–10**, 117, 143, 291; **22:11**, 186; **22:11–18**, 117–18; **22:12**, 438; **22:12–18**, 2; **22:15**, 498; **22:15**, 7; **22:16**, 122, 239, 435, 438; **22:18**, 7; **22:19**, 186; **22:19–21**, 118; **22:22**, 20; **22:22–26**, 118–19, 229; **22:24**, 32; **22:24–26**, 192, 288; **22:25**, 20; **22:26**, 124, 261, 266; **22:27–31**, 119–20; **22:29**, 36, 122; **22:31**, 119; **23**, 39, 91, 123–26, 141, 262; **23:1**, 125–26, 387; **23:1–6**, 123–25; **23:3**, 302; **23:5**, 276, 435; **23:5–6**, 176; **23:6**, 126, 437; **24**, 10, 11, 15, 38, 57, 68, 82, 89, 95, 105, 127–32, 137, 148, 149, 162, 164, 174, 176, 191, 209, 214, 270, 287, 440, 506; **24:1**, 218; **24:1–2**, 25, 127–28; **24:2**, 153, 209, 478; **24:3**, 25, 32, 43, 153, 301, 445, 450; **24:3–6**, 91, 93, 128–31, 164; **24:4**, 67, 83, 99, 105, 132, 146, 149, 162, 169, 174, 199, 224, 232, 258, 263, 301; **24:5**, 12, 59, 132; **24:6**, 132, 301; **24:7**, 484; **24:7–10**, 25, 131–32, 153, 246, 301, 440; **24:9**, 484; **24:10**, 249; **25**, 39, 133–35, 497; **25:1–7**, 133–34; **25:4–5**, 499; **25:7**, 287, 497; **25:8–9**, 499; **25:8–11**, 134; **25:12**, 499; **25:12–15**, 134–35; **25:16–21**, 135; **25:18**, 161, 287, 497; **25:22**, 135; **26**, 11, 38, 39, 68, 136–40, 498; **26:1**, 105, 199, 232, 444, 497, 498; 149; **26:1–2**, 138–39; **26:1–5**, 99; **26:1–8**, 203, 388; **26:2**, 204, 484; **26:3–8**, 139; **26:4**, 258, 263; **26:5**, 174; **26:6**, 301; **26:7**, 301; **26:8**, 246, 301, 302, 434; **26:8–9**, 146; **26:9**, 146, 174, 362; **26:9–10**, 199; **26:9–11**, 139–40, 148; **26:10**, 501; **26:11**, 444; **26:12**, 140; **27**, 39, 141–44, 255, 262; **27:1**, 255; **27:1–3**, 446; **27:1–6**, 142–43; **27:3**, 50, 438; **27:4**, 28, 97,

255, 343; **27:4–5**, 256; **27:4–6**, 91; **27:5**, 255, 257, 312; **27:7–12**, 143–44; **27:11**, 255, 302, 499; **27:12**, 101, 446; **27:13–14**, 144; **27:14**, 159, 239; **28**, 11, 38, 39, 50, 137, 145–50; **28:1**, 142; **28:1–2**, 147–48; **28:2**, 123; **28:3**, 174, 199, 301; **28:3–4**, 148; **28:3–5**, 259; **28:4**, 146; **28:5**, 148–49, 265; **28:6–7**, 149; **28:7–8**, 232; **28:8–9**, 141, 149–50; **28:9**, 126; **29**, 39, 108, 151–53, 209, 427, 506; **29:1**, 248; **29:1–2**, 152, 481; **29:1–11**, 26; **29:2**, 384; **29:3**, 25, 162, 210; **29:3–9**, 152–53; **29:3–10**, 211; **29:10–11**, 153; **30**, 19, 29, 39, 75, 103, 154–55, 159, 161, 168, 237, 354, 434, 481; **30:1**, 103, 293, 509; **30:1–3**, 154; **30:2**, 23; **30:3**, 293; **30:4**, 20, 63, 118; **30:4–5**, 154–55, 159, 434; **30:5**, 59, 100, **30:5**, 458; **30:6–12**, 155; **30:9**, 37, 119; **30:9**, 304; **30:11–12**, 23; **30:12**, 439, 509; **31**, 39, 144, 156–60; **31:1**, 290; **31:1–8**, 156–57; **31:2**, 142; **31:2–3**, 141, 290; **31:3**, 302, 499; **31:6**, 53, 160, 263; **31:9–10**, 162; **31:9–18**, 157–58; **31:10**, 160; **31:14**, 23; **31:18**, 144; **31:19–20**, 158–59; **31:21–22**, 159; **31:22**, 64; **31:23**, 434; **31:23–24**, 159–60, 239; **32**, 39, 65, 161–63, 226, 498, 499; **32:1–2**, 161–62; **32:1–5**, 62, 498; **32:1–8**, 499; **32:3–4**, 226; **32:3–7**, 162; **32:5**, 287, 497; **32:6**, 288; **32:8**, 302; **32:8–9**, 162–63; **32:10–11**, 163, 498; **33**, 39, 164–67, 503; **33:1**, 512; **33:1–5**, 164–65; **33:2**, 244, 293; **33:2–3**, 501; **33:4–7**, 511; **33:5**, 141; **33:6–19**, 165; **33:10**, 511; **33:12**, 150, 501, 511; **33:16–17**, 202, 509, 514; **33:16–19**, 169; **33:16–20**, 439, 511; **33:20–22**, 165–67; **33:22**, 440; **34**, 21, 29, 39, 133, 168–69; **34:1**, 103; **34:1–7**, 168; **34:7**, 133; **34:8–14**, 168–69; **34:10**, 54; **34:11–12**, 262; **34:12**, 54; **34:15–22**, 169; **34:18**, 227; **34:20**, 7; **35**, 39, 170–72, 446; **35:1–8**, 413; **35:1–10**, 170–71; **35:3**, 241; **35:10**, 230; **35:11–18**, 171; **35:19–27**, 413; **35:19–28**, 171–72; **35:24**, 497, 498; **35:27**, 99; **36**, 11, 38, 39, 137, 173–77, 232, 261; **36:1**, 149, 177; **36:1–2**, 174; **36:1–4**, 12, 138, 146, 175; **36:2**, 56, 174; **36:2–3**, 258; **36:3**, 99, 162, 169, 174, 301; **36:3–4**, 232;

36:4, 100, 174; **36:5**, 244; **36:5–9**, 175; **36:6**, 207; **36:7**, 15, 79, 99, 174, 177, 262; **36:7–8**, 243; **36:7–12**, 138, 146; **36:8**, 124, 196; **36:8–9**, 147, 232, 147; **36:8–12**, 43; **36:10–11**, 174; **36:10–12**, 175–76; **36:12**, 265, 301; **37**, 21, 40, 133, 169, 178–84, 187, 417; **37:1**, 179; **37:1–11**, 180–81; **37:5**, 179; **37:12–15**, 181; **37:16**, 179; **37:16–20**, 181; **37:21–24**, 181–82; **37:24**, 179; **37:25–26**, 179, 182; **37:26**, 183; **37:27–29**, 182; **37:28**, 183; **37:28a**, 179; **37:30**, 179; **37:30–31**, 182; **37:32–36**, 182; **37:35**, 183–84; **37:35–36**, 179; **37:36**, 184; **37:37**, 184; **37:37–38**, 179; **37:37–40**, 182–83; **37:38**, 179; **38**, 39, 62, 65, 116, 185–86, 193, 226, 352; **38:1**, 62; **38:1–5**, 287; **38:1–12**, 185–86; **38:2**, 485; **38:2–6**, 162; **38:3**, 195, 497; **38:5–8**, 195; **38:11**, 116; **38:12**, 13, 116; **38:13–22**, 186; **38:15**, 23; **38:17–18**, 287; **38:18**, 497; **39**, 39, 187–89, 503; **39:1**, 187; **39:1–3**, 187–88; **39:4–6**, 188; **39:5**, 501; **39:7**, 187; **39:7–11**, 188–89; **39:8–13**, 62; **39:9**, 187; **39:10**, 187; **39:11**, 187, 501; **39:12–13**, 189; **40**, 39, 190–92, 229, 289; **40:1–10**, 39, 191–92; **40:2**, 286, 293; **40:3**, 229; **40:4**, 263; **40:9**, 375; **40:11–17**, 192, 289; **40:13–17**, 289; **40:16**, 434; **41**, 39, 116, 161, 185, 193–94, 352; **41:1**, 510; **41:1–3**, 193; **41:3–10**, 62; **41:4**, 287, 497; **41:4–9**, 193; **41:5–9**, 116; **41:10–12**, 193–94; **41:11**, 491; **41:13**, 5, 194, 519; **42–83**, 202, 207, 235, 259, 261, 274; **42–43**, 39, 101, 256, 262, 341; **42**, 195–98, 209; **42:1–2**, 260; **42:1–4**, 256; **42:1–5**, 195–96; **42:2**, 6, 14, 197, 261, 292; **42:3**, 195; **42:4**, 259; **42:5**, 395, 434; **42:6**, 195, 256; **42:6–11**, 196–97; **42:8**, 197–98; **42:9**, 195, 199; **42:10**, 49, 195; **42:11**, 195, 434; **43**, 141, 195, 199–200; **43:1**, 438, 497; **43:1–5**, 199–200; **43:2**, 195; **43:3**, 195, 199, 256, 302; **43:4**, 195; **43:5**, 195, 434; **44**, 22, 39, 201–5, 330, 382; **44:1**, 499; **44:1–8**, 202; **44:5**, 110; **44:9**, 254, 440, 498; **44:9–16**, 202–3; **44:16**, 72; **44:17–22**, 203–4; **44:22**, 7, 287; **44:23–26**, 204–5; **44:24**, 33; **45**, 20, 39, 206–7; **45:1–5**, 206; **45:6**, 207; **45:6–9**, 206;

45:7, 248; **45:10–17**, 206–7; **46**, 24, 29, 39, 208–12, 312, 350, 426, 479; **46:1–3**, 208–9; **46:1–7**, 455; **46:4**, 24, 196, 212, 261, 270; **46:4–7**, 209–10; **46:5**, 59, 100, 288; **46:6**, 350; **46:7**, 24, 217, 218, 249, 287, 313; **46:8**, 208, 212, 218; **46:8–11**, 210–11; **46:9**, 312; **46:10**, 208, 244, 246; **46:11**, 24, 217, 218, 249, 287; **47**, 15, 39, 120, 213–16, 244, 277, 348, 373, 379; **47:1**, 278, 373, 382; **47:1–4**, 213–14; **47:2**, 215, 337, 380; **47:3–4**, 216, 282; **47:5**, 15, 129, 214, 215, 282; **47:6–7**, 214–15; **47:7**, 215; **47:8**, 14, 16, 282; **47:8–9**, 215, 244; **47:9**, 68, 215, 351, 481; **48**, 24, 39, 208, 211, 212, 217–20, 350, 426, 479; **48:1**, 24; **48:1–3**, 217–18, 450; **48:2**, 220, 223, 474; **48:4–8**, 218–19; **48:6**, 312; **48:8**, 24, 249; **48:9**, 450, 480; **48:9–11**, 219; **48:12–13**, 208; **48:12–14**, 219, 450; **49**, 21, 40, 221–22, 304, 319, 421; **49:1–4**, 221; **49:2**, 52; **49:5–6**, 221, 319; **49:7–12**, 222; **49:13–15**, 222; **49:15**, 304; **49:16–20**, 222; **50**, 7, 29, 39, 54, 223–25, 333, 373, 391; **50:1–6**, 24, 26, 223–24; **50:2**, 84, 371; **50:5**, 309; **50:5–6**, 204; **50:7**, 161; **50:7–15**, 224; **50:8–13**, 229; **50:8–15**, 191; **50:15**, 64; **50:16**, 309; **50:16–21**, 231; **50:16–22**, 224–25; **50:23**, 191, 225; **51**, 28, 29, 35, 39, 65, 121, 122, 133, 226–30, 314, 407; **51:1–2**, 227; **51:1–14**, 287; **51:3–5**, 497; **51:3–6**, 227–28, 366; **51:7**, 230; **51:7–12**, 228–29; **51:8**, 230; **51:9**, 230; **51:11**, 35; **51:13–17**, 229; **51:16–17**, 191; **51:18–19**, 230; **51:19**, 54; **52**, 11, 29, 38, 39, 137, 231–34, 301, 364, 365; **52:1**, 234, 301; **52:1–4**, 258; **52:1–5**, 232; **52:1–6**, 138, 146; **52:2**, 245, 265; **52:2–4**, 162, 169; **52:3**, 144, 301; **52:4**, 245; **52:5**, 99, 174, 265, 301; **52:6–7**, 233, 258, 265; **52:7**, 234, 301; **52:8**, 232; **52:8–9**, 233; **53**, 39, 88, 190, 235; **53:1–7**, 235; **53:5**, 89, 235, 493; **54**, 29, 39, 236–38; **54:1–5**, 236; **54:6**, 238; **54:6–7**, 50, 76, 237, 242; **55**, 39, 239–40; **55:1–8**, 239; **55:9**, 250; **55:9–15**, 239–40; **55:10**, 250; **55:11**, 250; **55:16–17**, 64; **55:16–21**, 240; **55:21**, 250; **55:22**, 144, 159; **55:22–23**, 240; **55:23**, 250; **56**, 29,

241–42; **56:1–4**, 241; **56:5–8**, 242; **56:9**, 64, 491; **56:9–13**, 242; **56:12–13**, 76; **57**, 29, 39, 243–46, 256, 411; **57:1**, 15, 79, 262; **57:1–4**, 245; **57:2–3**, 64; **57:4**, 246, 446; **57:5–11**, 245–46; **57:8–9**, 293; **58**, 39, 247–48; **58:1**, 248; **58:1–5**, 247; **58:6–9**, 247, 413; **58:10–11**, 247–48; **59**, 28, 29, 39, 249–51; **59:1–5**, 251; **59:3–4**, 203; **59:5**, 313; **59:6**, 239; **59:6–13**, 251; **59:14**, 239; **59:14–17**, 251; **60**, 7, 29, 39, 252–54, 411; **60:1–5**, 252–53; **60:5–12**, 243; **60:6–8**, 253–54; **60:9–12**, 254; **61**, 39, 91, 255–57, 261; **61:1**, 510; **61:1–8**, 255–57; **61:2**, 257, 302; **61:2–4**, 142; **61:3–4**, 262; **61:4**, 15, 79, 91, 156, 243, 257; **61:6–7**, 257, 261; **61:7**, 257; **62**, 39, 141, 258–59, 361; **62:1–2**, 470; **62:1–4**, 258–59; **62:3**, 52, 64; **62:5–8**, 470; **62:5–10**, 259; **62:8**, 196; **62:9**, 52; **62:10**, 470; **62:11–12**, 259; **63**, 28, 29, 39, 141, 256, 260–63; **63:1**, 256, 341, 497; **63:1–2**, 196, 256, 261–62; **63:2**, 15, 97, 246; **63:2–5**, 124; **63:3–8**, 262; **63:4**, 439; **63:9–10**, 263; **63:9–11**, 262–63; **63:11**, 144, 263, 501; **64**, 39, 264–65; **64:1**, 262; **64:1–10**, 264–65; **64:3**, 446; **64:5**, 49; **65**, 39, 54, 55, 123, 219, 255, 266–71, 274, 341, 368; **65:1–2**, 274; **65:1–4**, 25, 209, 268, 435; **65:1–5**, 59, 93; **65:2**, 177; **65:2b–3a**, 270; **65:3**, 497; **65:4**, 28, 261, 270; **65:5**, 274; **65:5–7**, 209, 308; **65:5–8**, 269–70, 437; **65:6**, 274; **65:7**, 210, 270–71, 274, 510; **65:8**, 271; **65:9**, 271; **65:9–10**, 342; **65:9–13**, 270; **65:13**, 274; **66**, 39, 272–76, 426; **66:1–4**, 274; **66:5–9**, 275; **66:8–12**, 440; **66:10–12**, 275–76; **66:12–13**, 276; **66:13**, 292; **66:13–20**, 39, 276; **67**, 39, 277–80, 298; **67:1–2**, 278–79; **67:3–5**, 279; **67:6**, 280; **67:6–7**, 279–80; **68**, 2, 15, 39, 175, 216, 244, 262, 281–84; **68:1**, 14, 244, 472; **68:1–6**, 281–82; **68:4**, 26, 244; **68:5**, 494, 510; **68:6**, 425; **68:7–10**, 26; **68:7–18**, 282; **68:8**, 249; **68:9**, 150, 327; **68:15–16**, 474; **68:17–18**, 214, 216, 244; **68:18**, 70, 129, 216, 311, 365; **68:19–27**, 283; **68:24**, 216, 244; **68:28–35**, 283–84; **68:29**, 28, 313; **68:30**, 313; **68:32**, 436; **68:33**, 210,

499; **68:33–35**, 26, 153, 244; **68:34**, 210; **68:35**, 249; **69**, 39, 121, 122, 285–88, 390; **69:1–2**, 191, 293; **69:1–4**, 498; **69:1–5**, 286–87; **69:2**, 453; **69:6**, 313; **69:6–12**, 287; **69:9**, 444; **69:13**, 162; **69:13–21**, 287–88; **69:14–15**, 191, 293, 498; **69:15**, 453; **69:17**, 497; **69:22–28**, 413; **69:22–29**, 288; **69:25**, 7; **69:28**, 227; **69:30–31**, 191; **69:30–33**, 288; **69:34–36**, 288; **69:35**, 312; **69:36**, 434; **70**, 39, 190, 192, 289; **70:1–5**, 289; **70:4**, 434; **71**, 39, 143, 290–94; **71:1–4**, 290–91; **71:3**, 141; **71:5–6**, 117, 143; **71:5–8**, 291; **71:9–13**, 291–92; **71:9–14**, 413; **71:11**, 49; **71:14–19**, 292–93; **71:20**, 294; **71:20–21**, 293; **71:22–24**, 76, 293; **72**, 20, 39, 47, 255, 261, 295–98, 451; **72:1**, 389; **72:1–20**, 295–98; **72:3**, 256; **72:3–7**, 514; **72:5**, 256; **72:6–7**, 256; **72:8**, 47; **72:8–11**, 215; **72:15**, 256; **72:16**, 256; **72:17**, 214, 256; **72:18–19**, 20, 5, 519; **73–83**, 29; **73**, 34, 38, 40, 98, 178, 187, 262, 299–305, 421, 485; **73:1–5**, 299; **73:2**, 182; **73:3**, 188; **73:3–5**, 187; **73:6–12**, 299–300; **73:10**, 305; **73:12**, 187; **73:13–14**, 187, 300; **73:13–15**, 188; **73:14**, 187; **73:15**, 187; **73:15–17**, 300–301; **73:16**, 187; **73:17**, 196, 292; **73:18–20**, 265, 301–2; **73:21–22**, 187; **73:21–28**, 302–5; **73:23**, 182, 262, 486, 495; **73:24**, 222; **73:25–26**, 187; **73:26**, 486, 495; **73:28**, 99; **74**, 39, 209, 306–9, 327, 506; **74:1**, 123, 126; **74:1–2**, 306–7; **74:2**, 43, 150, 431, 499; **74:2–11**, 25, 26; **74:3–11**, 307; **74:7**, 199; **74:11**, 309; **74:12–17**, 26, 211, 269, 307–8, 499; **74:13–14**, 510; **74:14**, 309, 356, 400; **74:18**, 81; **74:18–23**, 308–9; **74:21**, 199; **74:22**, 199; **75**, 39, 310–11, 364, 365; **75:1**, 310; **75:2**, 161; **75:2–5**, 39, 310–11; **75:4–5**, 516; **75:6–8**, 311; **75:9–10**, 311; **75:10**, 516; **76**, 24, 39, 208, 211, 212, 312–13; **76:1–3**, 312; **76:2**, 156; **76:4–10**, 312–13; **76:9**, 24; **76:11**, 208; **76:11–12**, 313; **77**, 39, 314–18; **77:1–9**, 315–16; **77:2**, 497; **77:3**, 494, 497; **77:4**, 318; **77:5**, 497, 499; **77:6**, 100; **77:10**, 318; **77:10–20**, 316–18; **77:11**, 499; **77:12**, 497; **77:15**, 307; **77:16–19**, 26; **77:17**, 210; **77:17–18**,

477; **77:18**, 333; **77:19**, 162; **77:20**, 126; **78**, 15, 22, 39, 319–26; 442; **78:1–8**, 322; **78:4**, 444; **78:9**, 320; **78:9–11**, 322; **78:10**, 309; **78:12–16**, 322; **78:17–31**, 322–23, 403; **78:19**, 125; **78:32**, 444; **78:32–39**, 323; **78:37**, 309; **78:40–43**, 323–24; **78:41**, 293, 326; **78:43**, 291; **78:44–55**, 324; **78:52**, 126; **78:55**, 96; **78:56–58**, 324–25; **78:59–64**, 325; **78:61**, 149, 262, 283, 402; **78:65–72**, 325–26; **78:67**, 320; **78:68–69**, 455; **78:68–72**, 24; **79**, 39, **327–29**; **79:1**, 150; **79:1–5**, 327–28; **79:6–13**, 328–29; **79:9**, 35, 133, 497; **79:9–10**, 287; **79:10**, 429; **79:11**, 288; **79:13**, 123, 126; **80**, 39, 330–32; **80:1**, 14, 84, 124, 126, 149; **80:1–2**, 262; **80:1–3**, 330–31; **80:2**, 332; **80:3**, 345; **80:4**, 249; **80:4–7**, 331; **80:8–11**, 18, 124; **80:8–19**, 331–32; **80:10**, 207; **81**, 7, 39, 223, 333–34, 373, 391; **81:1–5**, 333; **81:2**, 244, 293, 512; **81:3**, 374; **81:4**, 514; **81:6**, 161; **81:6–10**, 333–34; **81:6–16**, 39; **81:11–16**, 334; **81:16**, 514; **82**, 39, 247, 335–38, 380, 481; **82:1**, 67, 73, 248, 336; **82:1–7**, 152; **82:2–4**, 336–37; **82:5**, 79, 337; **82:6**, 248; **82:6–7**, 337; **82:8**, 337–38; **83**, 39, 339–40; **83:1–8**, 339; **83:2**, 50; **83:9–15**, 339–40; **83:12**, 123; **83:14–18**, 413; **83:16–18**, 340; **83:18**, 228; **84**, 39, 208, 341–43, 450; **84:1**, 24; **84:1–7**, 342–43; **84:2**, 256; **84:3**, 24, 59; **84:7**, 101, 197; **84:8**, 24, 287, 313; **84:8–12**, 343; **84:9**, 256, 261, 451; **84:10**, 152; **84:12**, 24; **85**, 39, 55, 88, 89, 344–46, 359, 457, 459; **85:1–7**, 344–45; **85:2**, 161; **85:8–13**, 345–46; **85:9–13**, 296; **85:11–13**, 54; **86**, 39, 347–49, 497; **86:1–5**, 347–48; **86:4**, 129; **86:6**, 39; **86:6–13**, 348; **86:7**, 64; **86:12–13**, 76, 242; **86:14**, 237; **86:14–17**, 348–49; **86:15**, 316, 396, 434; **87**, 39, 208, 350–51, 479; **87:1**, 24; **87:1–2**, 217, 350; **87:3–7**, 350–51, 450; **87:4**, 308, 312; **87:5**, 455; **87:6**, 191, 288; **88**, 29, 39, 116, 120, 352–54; **88:1–18**, 352–54; **88:3–7**, 286, 453; **88:4**, 497; **88:6–8**, 498; **88:8**, 116; **88:10**, 120; **88:10–12**, 37, 119, 304; **88:14**, 497; **88:15–18**, 498; **88:16–17**, 453; **89**, 15, 20, 21, 29, 39, 47, 107, 207, 355–58;

89:1–4, 355; **89:5–8**, 335, 376, 481; **89:5–13**, 26; **89:5–18**, 355–56; **89:6**, 248; **89:6–9**, 152; **89:8**, 249; **89:9–10**, 510; **89:9–12**, 25; **89:9–14**, 211; **89:11**, 209; **89:15**, 14; **89:17**, 516; **89:18**, 293; **89:18–37**, 20; **89:19–37**, 356–57; **89:19–51**, 260; **89:24**, 114; **89:25**, 215, 357; **89:30–31**, 107; **89:30–37**, 471; **89:38–52**, 357–58; **89:42**, 203; **89:52**, 5; **89:52**, 519; **90**, 39, 359–60, 396; **90:1–6**, 360; **90:7–9**, 187; **90:7–11**, 360; **90:8**, 469; **90:8–9**, 189; **90:9–12**, 187; **90:11**, 187; **90:12–17**, 360; **90:14**, 59, 100, 210, 497; **90:15**, 187; **91**, 39, 141, 361–63, 448; **91:1–16**, 361–63; **91:4**, 60, 79; **92**, 39, 364–66; **92:1–3**, 364; **92:3**, 244, 293; **92:4–11**, 364–65; **92:10**, 310, 516; **92:12–15**, 233, 365–66; **93**, 39, 120, 209, 277, 367–69, 373, 381, 383, 506; **93:1**, 209, 310; **93:1–2**, 26, 367–68; **93:1–5**, 26, 211; **93:2**, 75; **93:3–4**, 209, 368, 510; **93:4**, 162, 311; **93:5**, 123, 368–69; **94**, 39, 370–72; **94:1**, 84; **94:1–7**, 371; **94:8–13**, 371–72; **94:12**, 63; **94:14–16**, 372; **94:17–23**, 372; **94:22**, 142; **95**, 7, 39, 223, 333, 373–74, 387, 391, 426; **95:1–7a**, 373; **95:5**, 510; **95:7**, 123, 126; **95:7b–11**, 373–74; **95:8–11**, 39; **96–99**, 120, 277, 373; **96**, 15, 29, 39, 375–77, 379, 381; **96:1**, 381, 518; **96:1–3**, 278, 375; **96:3**, 244, 310; **96:3–4**, 481; **96:4**, 214; **96:4–6**, 375–76; **96:6**, 15, 30; **96:6–7**, 262; **96:7**, 119; **96:7–8**, 152, 481; **96:7–9**, 278, 376–77; **96:8**, 30, 132; **96:9–13**, 427; **96:9**, 119, 152, 310; **96:10**, 68, 75, 119, 368, 209, 247, 278, 310; **96:10–13**, 377; **96:11**, 121, 378; **96:12**, 270; **96:13**, 16, 68, 75, 223, 278; **97**, 39, 378–80, 383; **97:1**, 278, 378; **97:1–6**, 16; **97:2**, 14–15; **97:2–5**, 210; **97:2–6**, 14, 26, 223, 378–79; **97:6**, 15, 119, 223, 278; **97:7**, 152; **97:7–9**, 379–80; **97:8**, 219, 310, 338; **97:9**, 215; **97:10**, 434; **97:10–12**, 380; **98**, 15, 39, 381–82; **98:1**, 310, 518; **98:1–3**, 381–82; **98:1–4**, 119; **98:2**, 16; **98:2–3**, 278; **98:3**, 15, 119, 431; **98:4**, 278; **98:4–6**, 278, 382; **98:7**, 121, 310; **98:7–9**, 119, 382; **98:8**, 270; **98:9**, 16, 68, 75, 223, 247, 278, 310; **99**, 39, 382, 383–85; **99:1**,

14, 15, 68, 216, 310; **99:1–2**, 210, 244; **99:1–3**, 278, 383–84; **99:2**, 15, 244; **99:3**, 214; **99:4**, 247, 310, 385; **99:4–5**, 384; **99:5**, 14, 119, 210; **99:6–9**, 384–85; **99:7**, 369; **99:9**, 210; **100**, 38, 39, 373, 386–87, 437; **100:1**, 436; **100:1–2**, 386; **100:3**, 126, 386–87; **100:3–4**, 123; **100:4**, 387; **100:5**, 387; **101**, 38, 39, 388–89; **101:1–2a**, 388; **101:2**, 162; **101:2b–8**, 388–89; **101:7**, 144; **102**, 39, 65, 121, 122, 196, 259, 286, 390–93, 476, 503; **102:1**, 39; **102:1–2**, 390–91; **102:2**, 497; **102:3–5**, 162; **102:3–11**, 391; **102:11**, 501; **102:12**, 476, 477; **102:12–22**, 391–92; **102:13**, 230; **102:16**, 230; **102:20**, 288; **102:21**, 230; **102:23–24a**, 392–93; **102:24b–28**, 393; **103**, 39, 394–97, 417; **103:1**, 195; **103:1–2**, 434; **103:1–5**, 395; **103:4**, 262; **103:6**, 397, 510; **103:6–18**, 395–96; **103:7–8**, 439; **103:8**, 348, 434; **103:10**, 35, 133, 497; **103:17–18**, 439; **103:18**, 309; **103:19**, 36; **103:19–22**, 396–97; **103:20**, 152; **103:22**, 195; **104**, 39, 108, 270, 398–401, 484, 502, 506; **104:1**, 195; **104:1–2**, 313; **104:1–4**, 26, 398; **104:3–4**, 477; **104:3–16**, 25; **104:5**, 209; **104:5–6**, 209, 269, 448; **104:5–9**, 26, 398–99; **104:5–30**, 513; **104:6–9**, 209; **104:7**, 210, 313; **104:10–13**, 399; **104:10–16**, 209; **104:14–18**, 399; **104:19–23**, 399–400; **104:21–22**, 312; **104:24–26**, 400; **104:27–28**, 505; **104:27–30**, 400; **104:28**, 54; **104:31–35**, 400–401; **104:32**, 26, 501; **104:33**, 509; **104:35**, 509; **105**, 10, 15, 22, 39, 324, 402–4, 405, 442; **105:1–15**, 29; **105:1–45**, 402–4; **105:2**, 310; **105:8**, 241, 431; **105:40**, 405; **105:42**, 431; **106**, 10, 22, 35, 39, 405–7, 497; **106:1**, 29; **106:1–47**, 405–7; **106:3**, 510; **106:4**, 431; **106:8**, 125; **106:10**, 307; **106:14–15**, 403; **106:45**, 309, 431; **106:47**, 30; **106:47–48**, 29; **106:48**, 5, 407, 519; **107**, 39, 408–10; **107:1–32**, 409; **107:8**, 310; **107:9**, 54; **107:9–10**, 510; **107:20**, 241; **107:33–43**, 409–10; **107:40**, 510; **108**, 39, 245, 411; **108:1–5**, 243; **108:1–13**, 411; **108:2–3**, 293; **108:6–13**, 243, 252; **109**, 39, 412–13; **109:1–31**, 412–13; **109:3**,

438; **109:8**, 7; **109:13–14**, 227; **109:14**, 413; **109:20**, 413; **109:31**, 495; **110**, 20, 39, 44, 298, 414–16; **110:1**, 332, 415; **110:1–3**, 414–15; **110:2**, 24; **110:4–7**, 415; **110:5**, 495; **110:7**, 50; **111**, 22, 39, 40, 417–20, 421, 504; **111:1**, 43; **111:1–3**, 418; **111:4**, 508; **111:4–9**, 418–20, 439; **111:5**, 309, 431; **111:9**, 309; **111:10**, 420; **112**, 40, 133, 417, 421–23; **112:1**, 133, 421–22, 510; **112:2–9**, 422–23; **112:3–9**, 497; **112:5**, 510; **112:9**, 516; **112:10**, 423; **113–118**, 424; **113**, 39, 421, 424–25; **113:1**, 476; **113:1–3**, 424; **113:3**, 311, 436; **113:4**, 244; **113:4–5**, 210; **113:4–6**, 424–25; **113:4–9**, 482; **113:5–8**, 311; **113:7–9**, 425; **113:9**, 462; **114**, 39, 426–28; **114:1–8**, 426–27; **114:2**, 428; **114:3–7**, 26; **114:5**, 64; **114:5–6**, 52; **115**, 39, 429–333, 476; **115:1–8**, 430; **115:2**, 433; **115:3**, 476, 478; **115:3–8**, 477; **115:4–8**, 476; **115:5**, 445; **115:9–11**, 430; **115:9–12**, 433, 439; **115:12–13**, 476; **115:12–15**, 430–31; **115:14**, 433; **115:15**, 510; **115:16–18**, 431–32; **115:17**, 119; **115:17–18**, 37; **116**, 39, 75, 103, 124, 159, 161, 168, 242, 434–35, 436, 481; **116:1–11**, 434–35; **116:5–6**, 159; **116:7**, 496; **116:12–19**, 119, 435; **116:14**, 20; **116:15**, 159; **116:17**, 229, 288; **116:17–19**, 20, 242; **117**, 39, 436–37; **117:1**, 436; **117:2**, 436–37; **118**, 38, 39, 436, 438–41; **118:1–18**, 439–40; **118:2–4**, 429, 453; **118:5–18**, 39; **118:6**, 453; **118:8–9**, 509, 514; **118:10–12**, 110, 441; **118:17**, 37; **118:19**, 292; **118:19–29**, 440–41; **118:22**, 7; **119**, 6, 40, 108, 133, 417, 442–44, 501; **119:1**, 41; **119:1–2**, 510; **119:1–176**, 442–44; **119:32**, 434; **119:40**, 290; **119:55**, 100; **119:57**, 302, 495; **119:175**, 37; **120–134**, 39, 445, 510; **120**, 445–47; **120:1**, 445–46, 447; **120:2**, 144, 446; **120:3–4**, 446; **120:5**, 241; **120:5–7**, 446–47; **121**, 256, 448–49, 460; **121:1–2**, 448–49, 453; **121:2**, 445, 510; **121:3–8**, 449; **121:4**, 475; **121:5**, 495; **122**, 450–51; **122:1–4**, 450; **122:1–5**, 450–51; **122:2**, 450; **122:4**, 312, 445, 451; **122:5**, 372, 452; **122:6–8**, 447; **122:6–9**, 450, 451; **123**, 452; **123:1–2**, 452; **123:3–4**, 452; **124**,

453–54; **124:1–5**, 453–54; **124:6–8**, 454; **124:8**, 445, 450; **125**, 455–56, 466; **125:1–2**, 217, 448, 455; **125:3**, 455–56; **125:4–5**, 456; **125:5**, 447; **126**, 457–59; **126:1**, 458–59; **126:1–3**, 457; **126:4**, 458–59; **126:4–6**, 458; **127**, 460–62, 466; **127:1**, 462; **127:1–2**, 460–61; **127:3–5**, 461–62; **127:5**, 13; **128**, 303, 463–65, 466, 503; **128:1**, 510; **128:1–4**, 464, 501; **128:1–6**, 141; **128:5**, 475; **128:5–6**, 464–65; **129**, 466–67; **129:1**, 453; **129:1–8**, 466–67; **130**, 65, 226, 468–69; **130:1–2**, 468–69; **130:3–4**, 35, 469, 497; **130:5**, 59; **130:5–6**, 469; **130:6**, 59, 100, 210; **130:7**, 470; **130:7–8**, 469; **131**, 445, 461, 470; **131:1–3**, 470; **132**, 15, 20, 208, 298, 445, 448, 451, 471–73; **132:1–12**, 40; **132:1–18**, 471–73; **132:7**, 312; **132:7–8**, 14, 377; **132:8**, 67, 262, 283, 402; **132:11–12**, 20, 260; **132:13**, 24, 217; **132:13–14**, 307; **132:13–18**, 39; **132:14–15**, 75; **132:17**, 516; **132:17–18**, 260; **133**, 474; **133:1–3**, 474; **133:3**, 312; **134**, 466, 475, 476; **134:1**, 476; **134:1–3**, 475; **134:3**, 445, 474, 510; **135**, 22, 39, 324, 424, 476–77, 478, 501; **135:1–2**, 475; **135:1–4**, 476–77; **135:3**, 512; **135:5–7**, 477; **135:6**, 429; **135:8–12**, 433; **135:8–14**, 477; **135:9**, 291; **135:10–12**, 478; **135:13**, 63; **135:15–18**, 429, 477; **135:19–20**, 429, 439; **135:19–21**, 475, 476–77; **135:20**, 8; **136**, 14, 22, 39, 324, 429, 439, 476, 478; **136:1–26**, 478; **136:4**, 228; **136:23**, 431; **137**, 39, 479–80; **137:1–4**, 479; **137:5–6**, 479; **137:7**, 480; **137:8–9**, 114, 480; **138**, 39, 481–82; **138:1**, 103, 248; **138:1–3**, 481; **138:3**, 64; **138:4–6**, 481–82; **138:6**, 311; **138:7–8**, 482; **139**, 37, 38, 39, 140, 204, 483–88; **139:1**, 141; **139:1–6**, 484–85; **139:7**, 37; **139:7–10**, 499; **139:7–12**, 485–86; **139:13–16**, 117, 143, 291, 486; **139:14**, 487; **139:15**, 488; **139:17–18**, 486; **139:18**, 488; **139:19–22**, 486–87; **139:23–24**, 487; **139:24**, 302; **140**, 39, 489–91; **140:1–3**, 489; **140:4–5**, 490; **140:5–6**, 495; **140:6–8**, 490; **140:8**, 491; **140:9–11**, 490; **140:12**, 491; **140:12–13**, 491; **141**, 39, 492–93; **141:1–2**, 492; **141:2**, 54; **141:2–5**, 37;

141:3–5a, 492–93; **141:5b–10**, 493; **141:9–10**, 490, 495; **142**, 29, 39, 494–96; **142:1–2**, 494–95; **142:2**, 196, 259; **142:3**, 490, 497; **142:3–4**, 495; **142:5**, 302, 490; **142:5–7**, 495–96; **143**, 35, 37, 39, 65, 226, 497–500; **143:1**, 290; **143:1–2**, 497–98; **143:3–6**, 498–99; **143:4**, 495; **143:7–12**, 499–500; **143:8**, 129, 288; **143:10**, 35, 37; **143:11**, 495; **144–148**, 518; **144–150**, 36; **144**, 36, 39, 102, 501–3; **144:1–11**, 502; **144:5–7**, 26; **144:6–11**, 518; **144:7**, 162; **144:7–8**, 501; **144:8**, 144; **144:12–15**, 502–3; **144:14**, 503; **145–150**, 517; **145**, 13, 36, 39, 504–8; **145:1**, 210; **145:1–3**, 506; **145:4–9**, 506–7; **145:7**, 63; **145:8**, 434, 439, 508; **145:10–14**, 507; **145:14**, 510; **145:15–21**, 507–8; **145:19**, 133; **145:20**, 434, 518; **146**, 36, 39, 509–11; **146:1–2**, 509; **146:2**, 439; **146:3–4**, 439, 509, 514; **146:5–9**, 510; **146:6**, 445; **146:9**, 494, 513; **146:10**, 511, 514; **147**, 36, 39, 512–14; **147:1**, 364; **147:1–3**, 230; **147:1–6**, 512–13; **147:6**, 518; **147:7–11**, 513–14; **147:10–11**, 439; **147:12–20**, 514; **147:19**, 241; **148**, 36, 39, 515–16, 519; **148:1–2**, 152; **148:1–14**, 515–16; **148:11**, 481; **148:13**, 244; **148:14**, 518; **149**, 37, 39, 517–18; **149:1–5**, 517; **149:6–9**, 517–18; **150**, 5, 39, 519; **150:1**, 80; **150:1–2**, 519; **150:3**, 244, 293; **150:3–5**, 519; **150:6**, 519

Proverbs **1:1–7**, 179; **1:4**, 443; **1:6**, 319; **1:7**, 169, 417; **1:8**, 169, 179; **2:1–11**, 179; **2:5**, 169; **2:8**, 179; **2:12**, 169, 179; **2:20**, 179; **3:1**, 179; **3:2**, 169; **3:7**, 169; **3:11–12**, 63; **3:16**, 169; **3:27**, 207; **4:1**, 169; **4:10**, 169; **4:11**, 179; **4:14**, 179; **4:18**, 179; **5:4**, 179; **5:7**, 169; **5:11**, 179; **8:13**, 169; **8:18–19**, 422; **8:32**, 169; **9:10**, 169, 417; **9:11**, 169; **10:27**, 169; **10:31**, 179; **11:27**, 169; **12:13**, 169; **13:7**, 422; **13:21**, 169; **14:12–13**, 179; **15:9–10**, 179; **15:16**, 179; **15:19**, 179; **16:1**, 460; **16:3**, 179; **16:6**, 169; **16:9**, 460; **19:20**, 179; **19:21**, 460; **20:21**, 179; **21:31**, 460; **22:22**, 461; **22:23**, 297; **23:10–11**, 297; **23:18**, 179; **24:14**, 179; **24:16**, 179; **24:19**, 179; **24:20**, 179; **24:30–34**,

179, 461; **26:4–5**, 183, 461; **31:15**, 417; **31:31**, 461

Ecclesiastes **1:2**, 187; **6:1–2**, 464; **12:8**, 187, 189

Isaiah **1:2–3**, 224; **1:4**, 293; **1:10–17**, 224; **1:11–17**, 191; **1:12**, 101, 197, 341; **1:18**, 230; **1:19–20**, 334; **2:1–4**, 351; **2:2–5**, 210, 451; **2:3**, 445, 450; **4:3**, 351; **5:18**, 467; **6:1–3**, 244; **6:1–8**, 335, 481; **6:2–4**, 152; **6:3**, 384; **7:2**, 320; **8:10**, 166; **9:6–7**, 21; **11:1–5**, 21, 451; **13–14**, 480; **13–23**, 351; **14:4–10**, 231; **14:21**, 480; **14:24–26**, 166; **14:32**, 24; **16:5**, 451; **18:1–19:25**, 281; **18:1**, 351; **18:7**, 24, 313; **19:18**, 132; **20:3–5**, 351; **22:16–19**, 231; **22:24**, 152; **25:7–8**, 37; **26:2**, 440; **26:19**, 119; **27:1**, 309, 356, 400; **29:8**, 24; **29:18**, 510; **30:26**, 512; **30:29**, 475; **30:4**, 281; **30:7**, 308, 351; **31:4**, 24; **31:4–5**, 2:4, 312; **32:15–17**, 346; **33**, 82; **33:7**, 281; **33:14**, 93; **33:14b–16**, 10, 91; **33:20**, 123; **33:20–21**, 270; **33:30**, 256; **34:1–11**, 411; **35**, 343; **35:5**, 510; **35:9**, 408; **36–37**, 312; **36:1**, 211; **37:9**, 351; **37:22–35**, 24; **37:36**, 212; **37:38**, 211; **38:22**, 194, 388, 381; **40–55**, 15, 16, 345, 459, 502; **40–66**, 436, 512; **40**, 167, 510; **40:1–11**, 481; **40:2**, 344; **40:3–5**, 346; **40:5**, 15, 346; **40:6–8**, 396; **40:8**, 514; **40:9–11**, 346; **40:11**, 126; **40:26**, 513; **40:28–29**, 513; **40:30–31**, 439, 514; **40:31**, 395; **41:13**, 302; **41:14**, 293; **41:18–19**, 408; **41:21–29**, 336–37, 376, 433; **42:7**, 510; **42:15**, 408; **43:1**, 387; **43:2**, 275; **43:5–6**, 408; **43:25**, 227; **44:9–20**, 432; **44:22**, 227; **45:7**, 399; **45:20**, 432; **45:23**, 132; **46:1–2**, 432; **46:3**, 470; **46:6–7**, 432; **46:13**, 346; **47**, 480; **47:1**, 181; **49:14–23**, 430; **49:15**, 470; **49:20–21**, 351; **51:9**, 351; **51:10**, 408; **51:17–23**, 253; **52:1–2**, 502; **52:7–10**, 346; **52:7**, 375; **52:8–9**, 345; **52:9–10**, 381; **52:10**, 15; **54:1–3**, 430; **54:1**, 351, 462; **55:10–11**, 514; **55:12**, 15, 270; **55:2**, 181; **55:3–5**, 502; **56–66**, 345; **56:3–8**, 351; **56:5**, 351, 351; **57:7–8**, 54; **57:14–21**, 230; **57:15**, 227; **58**, 286; **58:8**, 346; **60:1–2**, 346; **60:9**, 293;

60:10, 517; **60:12**, 517; **60:14**, 517; **60–61**, 517; **61:1**, 510, 512; **61:1–3**, 230; **61:5**, 458; **62:11**, 346; **62:12**, 408; **63:1–6**, 411; **63:3–5**, 517; **63:7–64:12**, 35, 227; **63:10**, 227; **63:10–11**, 35; **63:11**, 227; **63:16–17**, 227; **64:5–9**, 227; **65:17**, 464; **65:22–23**, 464; **66:1–2**, 229; **66:1–3**, 229; **66:2**, 227; **66:3**, 227; **66:3b–4**, 229; **66:7–8**, 351

Jeremiah **2:6**, 125; **4:6**, 253; **5:1–2**, 82; **5:2**, 132; **5:7**, 464; **5:26**, 61; **7:1–29**, 286; **7:4**, 53; **7:15**, 320; **9:2–9**, 239; **9:23–24**, 80; **10:1–16**, 432; **10:13**, 476; **10:24**, 63; **10:25**, 328; **11:12**, 432; **15:15–18**, 286; **17:9–10**, 228; **20:2**, 178, 332; **23:3**, 126; **23:5–6**, 21; **23:18**, 335, 481; **23:22**, 331; **24:6**, 148; **24:7**, 35, 227, 229; **25:38**, 312; **26:1–24**, 286; **29:14**, 344, 458; **30:3**, 458; **30:9**, 27, 471; **30:18**, 458; **31:6**, 450; **31:23**, 123, 458; **31:31–34**, 227; **31:33**, 229; **31:35**, 227; **32:7**, 297; **32:39**, 348; **33:7**, 458; **33:11**, 458; **33:26**, 458; **37:15**, 178; **38:6**, 286; **42:10**, 148; **42:16**, 262; **45:4**, 148; **50–51**, 480; **50:33–34**, 297; **51:16**, 476

Lamentations **2:6–9**, 307; **2:14**, 458; **3:6**, 497; **3:23**, 100; **5:18**, 263; **5:21**, 331

Ezekiel **7:26**, 307; **11:19**, 348; **13:4**, 263; **13:9**, 351; **16:53**, 458; **20**, 329, 406; **20:8–9**, 406; **20:14**, 406; **20:17**, 406; **20:22**, 406; **25:3**, 307; **28:14**, 60; **28:16**, 60; **29:14**, 344; **29:3**, 308; **31:11**, 207; **32:2**, 308; **32:21**, 207, 248; **34:11–16**, 126; **34:23–24**, 21, 27, 471; **34:27**, 278; **36:24–32**, 35, 227; **36:25–27**, 229; **36:25**, 229; **36:26**, 229; **36:27**, 35, 229; **36:28**, 230; **37:24–25**, 27, 471; **37:24–28**, 21; **39:25**, 458; **40:46**, 415; **47:1–12**, 209, 270

Daniel **6**, 246; **9:9**, 468; **10:13**, 336; **12:2**, 37, 119, 122

Hosea **2:8**, 53; **2:14–15**, 320; **2:17**, 96; **2:19–23**, 346; **3:5**, 27, 471; **4:1–3**, 296; **4:6–9**, 443; **4:16**, 126; **4:17**, 320; **6:1**, 512; **7:14**, 53, 54; **11:1–5**, 320;

12:9, 320; **12:13**, 320; **13**, 320; **13:4**, 320; **13:7**, 61; **13:12**, 101; **14:2**, 270; **14:5**, 474

Joel **1:1–2:27**, 459; **1:4**, 268, 345; **1:9**, 268; **1:10**, 268; **1:12**, 268; **1:13**, 268; **1:16**, 268; **2:13**, 316, 348; **2:14**, 268; **2:19–27**, 268; **3:1**, 458; **3:18**, 270

Amos **1:2**, 223; **1:14**, 216; **2:2**, 216; **2:9–10**, 320; **4:3**, 503; **4:10**, 320; **4:13**, 70, 228; **5:5**, 196; **5:8–9**, 70; **5:11**, 464; **5:12**, 461; **5:25**, 320; **5:26**, 53; **9:2–4**, 485; **9:5–6**, 70; **9:7**, 320; **9:14**, 458

Jonah, **2:2**, 453; **2:5**, 453; **4:2**, 316, 348

Micah **1:2–4**, 223, 369; **1:3–4**, 378; **2:1**, 207; **2:2**, 175; **4:1–3**, 351; **4:1–5**, 210, 453; **4:2**, 450; **5:2–5a**, 21; **5:4–6**, 130; **6:1–8**, 224; **6:6–7**, 229; **6:6–8**, 191; **7:2**, 82; **7:5**, 82; **7:5–6**, 239; **7:6**, 101; **7:7**, 59; **7:14**, 124, 126

Nahum **2:11–12**, 312

Habakkuk **1**, 82; **2:1**, 59; **2:6–20**, 231; **2:18–19**, 432; **2:20**, 79; **3:3–15**, 378; **3:6**, 313; **3:19**, 29

Zephaniah **2:3**, 465; **2:7**, 458; **2:30**, 458; **3:2**, 53; **3:5**, 70

Haggai **1:2–4**, 286; **1:6**, 345; **1:6–11**, 459; **2:15–17**, 345; **2:16–19**, 459

Zechariah **2:4–5**, 219; **2:13**, 79; **7:1–7**, 306; **7:3–5**, 286; **7:3**, 5; **7:5**, 122; **8:12**, 278; **8:19**, 5, 286; **9:9–10**, 21; **9:16**, 126; **14**, 263; **14:8**, 270; **14:9–21**, 24; **14:16–17**, 15; **14:16–19**, 341

Malachi **2:17**, 456; **3:10**, 417; **3:13–15**, 456; **3:16**, 351; **3:16–18**, 351

NEW TESTAMENT

Matthew, **1:1**, 6, 21; **5:4**, 458; **5:23–24**, 32; **6:10**, 338; **12:33–37**, 92; **21:9**, 6; **21:15**, 6; **21:19**, 440; **21:42**, 7; **22:41–45**, 6; **22:41–46**, 415; **26:30**, 434; **27:35**, 120; **27:46**, 6, 120

Mark **1:1–3**, 27; **12:34–37**, 415; **14:26**, 424

Luke **1:52**, 425; **1:55**, 416; **10**, 448; **20:40–44**, 415; **21:25**, 211; **23:46**, 157; **24:44–47**, 7

John **4:23**, 129; **4:24**, 508; **19:24**, 7

Acts **1:16**, 7; **7:5–6**, 416; **13:22**, 6

Romans **1:24**, 334; **3:23**, 497; **4:16**, 416; **4:18**, 416; **5:1–5**, 167; **8:19–23**, 377; **8:23–25**, 167; **8:36**, 7, 204; **11:2**, 27

1 Corinthians **3:16**, 25; **3:16–17**, 284; **11:27–32**, 93; **11:28**, 9

2 Corinthians **4:9**, 467

Galatians **3:16**, 416

Ephesians **2:19–22**, 284; **2:20–22**, 25; **4:26**, 54

2Timothy **3:16**, 7, 27

Hebrews **1:8–9**, 207; **2:6–10**, 6; **2:8–10**, 73; **4:7**, 27; **11**, 167; **13:15**, 230

James **1:23–25**, 9; **4:2**, 291

Revelation **1:5**, 47; **2:26–27**, 47; **11:17**, 16; **11:18**, 47; **12:5**, 47; **19:4**, 16; **19:6**, 16; **19:11**, 16; **19:15**, 47